Dec. 91

Fc

Ma + Pa.

LAW, LIFE AND LAUGHTER
Legal Anecdotes and Portraits

Ellison Kahn

LAW, LIFE AND LAUGHTER

Legal Anecdotes and Portraits

ELLISON KAHN

Professor Emeritus of Law in the
University of the Witwatersrand, Johannesburg

Juta & Co, Ltd

CAPE TOWN   WETTON   JOHANNESBURG

First Published 1991

© Juta & Co, Ltd 1991

PO Box 14373, Kenwyn 7790

ISBN 0 7021 2693 4

SET, PRINTED AND BOUND IN THE REPUBLIC OF SOUTH AFRICA
BY THE RUSTICA PRESS (PTY) LTD, NDABENI, CAPE
D784

Foreword

By the Hon Mr Justice M M Corbett, Chief Justice of the Republic of South Africa

> 'All the world's a stage,
> And all the men and women merely players:
> They have their exits and their entrances; . . .'

So said the Bard. And reading through Professor Ellison Kahn's fascinating collection of writings, stories, anecdotes and jokes about lawyers under the title *Law, Life and Laughter* one has the sensation of sitting near the front of the stalls and seeing passing before one like players on the stage these men of the law. Each one enters, reveals himself or is revealed to a greater or lesser degree, and then makes his exit, to make way for the next; and for a brief period each comes alive.

The players were in their day prominent lawyers: judges, magistrates, advocates, attorneys, professors, some more eminent and famous than others. Some lived and died recently; others belong to a much earlier era. The spread is wide. It spans from St Yves (patron saint of lawyers) to Stratford; De Groot to De Wet; Pothier to Pollak; Kersteman to Krause.

The collection is culled from books, articles, press reports, stories told to Professor Kahn himself and recorded by him, unpublished memoirs and letters. It often gives new insights into the kind of men these lawyers were and provides new perspectives about events that have passed into history. Inevitably some of the stories appear to be apocryphal, as for example where the same story is told about more than one person. An instance of this is the story of the inexperienced young advocate acting pro deo in his first murder trial who nervously announces to the court that he appears on behalf of the deceased, thereby provoking from the judge the quip: 'Aren't you being a bit premature, Mr— ?' I also heard a former colleague tell this about himself at a Cape Bar dinner. He rounded off the story with the wry comment: 'We were both right!'

In two instances I am able to add to the record. The first relates to Louis Cohen's anecdote about my great-uncle Christoffel Joseph Brand (pages 12–13). I cannot confirm or deny his Falstaffian behaviour in the case which Louis Cohen recounts, but it is not correct to say that his services were dispensed with by the Transvaal Government. He actually resigned from the Bench in October 1886 over the action of the President and the Executive Council of the South African Republic in the well-known *Nellmapius* case. (Sir John Kotzé devotes a chapter in his *Memoirs and Reminiscences* to this case and Brand's resignation.) In 1887 Brand was admitted in the Transvaal as an advocate (see *Ex parte Brand* 2 SAR 183) and, as far as I know, he practised there until his early death, probably in 1889.

The second instance relates to Sir Etienne de Villiers's nickname 'Oofy' (see page 36). I have a letter written by Sir Etienne to my grandfather, A J McGregor, in 1934 explaining the origin of this nickname. The relevant portion of the letter reads:

> 'My soubriquet is spelt properly *Ovie*, being a contraction of Ovid, pronounced in Afrikaans. Thereby hangs a tale, of my supposedly wrong pronunciation of the word "metamorphōses" which I pronounced (quite properly) with a long O, in construing in the junior matric class at SACS in 1889. I remember that the class were much amused at this and for some days

called me "Ovid's metamorphōses" but as that was too long for a nickname it became Ovid (pronounced in Afrikaans) and the diminutive of that is naturally Ovie. QED.'

I much enjoyed reading this book. I am sure that the legal profession and others will enjoy it too.

Chambers
Bloemfontein
    October 1991

Introduction

This is the first part of what I should like to think is a pleasant collection of South African legal anecdotes and biographical vignettes. Most of the material appeared in eleven articles, entitled 'Only Yesterday: Piquant Legal Portraits from the Past', published in the *South African Law Journal* from May 1988 to November 1990. But there is a considerable amount of additional material. For those who are interested in statistics, I would mention that I spent most of a day in ascertaining some details. They have not been audited by a chartered accountant, but they are more or less correct. There are some 630 entries from 85 books and 180 additional sources (law journals, magazines, newspapers and other printed matter, and manuscripts). The entries have 156 specifically named protagonists, and about 50 further ones, identifiable or anonymous, under the rubric 'Waifs and Strays'. The named authors of material quoted number 170; the unnamed ones, 30. The 110 illustrations come from 59 sources.

Perhaps what is to be found in the text will not go to prove the correctness of the conclusion of Professor Glanville Williams, 'Collections of anecdotes are usually poor things' (*Learning the Law* 11 ed (1982) 234). 'Anecdote' is used in its primary sense as defined by *The Oxford English Dictionary*: 'The narrative of an interesting or striking incident or event.' This collection is a mixture of a small dictionary of legal biography and a book of anecdotes relating to many of our leading figures in the law. As far as I know, the two aims have never been pursued in any single work published abroad, let alone in South Africa; indeed, I am not even aware of any dictionary of legal biography of this nature.

All assemblages of anecdotes and biographical fragments must be looked at with charitable eyes. First of all, some prominent and distinguished men and women of the law make no appearance on the stage; I can find no worthwhile story or comment about them. (I confess, to my shame, that no woman has a part at all, in the sense of being the protagonist of an entry. Nor do I feel any the better that the same is true of Martin Gilbert's *The Oxford Book of Legal Anecdotes* (1986). While, as is to be expected, the great majority of the entries relate to our judges, for they are exposed to the press and biographers, some eminent judges are missing or have at best a cameo part. As for our advocates, of only a few are there memorable recorded anecdotes or revealing sketches that are readily accessible. Attorneys are so modest and so hidden from the public eye that almost all of them pass from life to death without even an obituary.) On the other hand, a number of judges and a few advocates, most but not all of whom can be considered as both prominent and distinguished, have large roles, because there are many worthwhile stories or comments or both about them. Thus, for example, Carter J, Sir Henry Connor, Sir Henry (Lord) de Villiers, W E Hollard, Malan JA, H H Morris QC, Schreiner JA, Van den Heever JA and Sir John Wessels. Several professors of law also play important parts.

Secondly, the entries give a lopsided picture of the protagonist. No attempt is made to convey the essence of his personality. Some aspects of his personality may emerge, but other aspects, often the more important ones, will not. There is no pen portrait, no affecting tribute. That is not the object of the exercise, and I ask for no pardon. After all, I am in good company. Take, for instance, the five stories related of William Blake, consummate poet and painter, and a mystic, in

The Oxford Book of Literary Anecdotes (1975), chosen and edited by James Sutherland. The first relates how a visitor found Blake and his wife sitting in the summer-house in their garden, innocent of clothing. '"*Come in!*" cried Blake; "*It's only Adam and Eve, you know!*"' The Blakes had been reciting passages from *Paradise Lost*, in character. The third tells how the archangel Gabriel visited Blake; the fourth how Blake saw the ghost of a flea and painted it. In the second anecdote Blake does an imprudent thing. Only the fifth, on his death, brings out the true character of this noble man.

Collections of fragments portraying persons of note are perhaps a little fairer overall, but they are not always fair to a particular person. I take from my bookshelf the *Penguin Concise Dictionary of Biographical Quotation*, edited by Justin Wintle and Richard Kenin, and open it at random, to find on the right-hand page 'HAGGARD, SIR HENRY RIDER', the novelist who in his early life had connections with South Africa. Four entries. In the first Rider Haggard says 'Only little people are vain. . . . I grow humbler year by year.' Beautiful. Next come W H Auden's lines 'Sir Rider Haggard/Was completely staggered/When his bride-to-be/Announced "I AM SHE!"' In the third Andrew Lang writes to Rider Haggard 'Even your imagination is out of the fifth form'. The last contains the well-known verse by J K Stephen which ends 'When the Rudyards cease from kipling/And the Haggards ride no more'.

Thirdly, this collection is open to criticism as containing too many chestnuts. All I can do to defend myself is to repeat what Sir Arthur Quiller-Couch wrote in his preface to *The Oxford Book of English Prose* (1927): ' . . . [S]ome things are here which all men have applauded, and (frankly) because they have been so applauded as well as because my own judgement applauds. . . . I have tried to choose the best, and the best is the best though a hundred judges have declared it so.'

Certain anecdotes appear in the same or modified form in a number of publications. In this collection I have chosen what I consider to be the best version; unfortunately, sometimes it is the version that flowed from my pen: after all, I had the benefit of seeing the other versions.

I have followed the works that I have cited exactly, except for correcting obvious printing errors.

Every person of whom an anecdote is related or a biographical piece is offered is named, if a name has been available. All are dead.

Very seldom is a living person referred to in an entry, and when he or she is, except in a handful of instances, he or she is not identified. Fear not.

The Illustrations

The text is liberally embellished with illustrations—artwork, in printers' terminology—the great majority being caricatures, the balance sketches, paintings or photographs. How privileged I am to be able to reproduce so many caricatures by D C Boonzaier (1865–1950), of whose work it has been said that it 'is that of a brilliant artist, sensitive, cultured and witty'; the refined line art of the famous Japanese woodcut artists is unmistakable (Professor J du P Scholtz in *Dictionary of South African Biography* I (1968) 94). Boonzaier's legal caricatures are marked by strong, clean lines and sharp contrasts (see Murray Schoonraad & Elzabé Schoonraad *Companion to South African Cartoonists* (1989) 66–7). I take special joy in those of Sir James Rose Innes, Ralph Close, Jacob de Villiers (loping along the seashore—magnificent!), Morris Alexander, Sir Henry Juta, Fritz Krause, Charles Stallard and M T Steyn (beard and bulk—how striking!). If in a small way I have made some of the work of D C Boonzaier more accessible to the general public, I am delighted.

The caricatures of William Howard Schröder (1852–92) are not in the same class, happy though I am to be able to reproduce some of them. Said, after his death, to have been 'South Africa's only artist' (A Cowen in *The Schröder Art Memento* (1894)), Schröder in his sad, short life produced paintings, cartoons and other artistic work of great merit, but caricature was not his forte.

One other artist of the past whose portraits are reproduced calls for mention: Arthur Wynell Lloyd (1883–1967). Born in England, Lloyd was a cartoonist for the *Rand Daily Mail* from 1905 and for our *Sunday Times* from 1906, both until 1910. Thereafter until 1914 he worked for other South African newspapers. Then he left for London to become the parliamentary artist of *Punch*, which he remained until his retirement in 1952, receiving wide recognition as a cartoonist and caricaturist. He displayed great technical skill in his drawings.

Of the South African caricaturists of today, I am honoured to be able to give examples of the work of one of the finest, the one internationally best known—Jock Leyden.

Finally, I have to confess that I could not resist the temptation to reproduce a number of the pungent paintings, drawings and lithographs on legal themes by the great French artist, Honoré Daumier (1808–79), expressing his hatred of the law and its operation and functionaries in his country, and his deep desire for reform. Daumier's two main series of lithographs on legal themes were *Les gens des justice* (Men of the Law)—38 plates executed from 1845 to 1848; and *Les avocats et les plaideurs* (Lawyers and Litigants)—four plates published in 1857. But many other lithographs, drawings and paintings illustrate the functionaries of the law. Daumier's works have a universal and timeless quality, with their wry humour; high comedy; searching truthfulness; cutting sarcasm and irony; withering criticism of 'justice' in the law courts—the sham drama there, the theatricality, the falseness, the shame, the moral emptiness of it all; deep sympathy for those subjected to this 'justice'; horrifying depiction of the cynicism, boredom and disdainfulness of judge and lawyer; and pervading sense of pathos. Small wonder that Daumier has been called the Michelangelo of caricature.

Acknowledgements

Among those who were kind enough to give me permission to include copyright material—literary or artistic work—I would like particularly to mention and thank the following: First of all, Mr Gregoire Boonzaier, the distinguished artist, for permission to reproduce whatever caricatures were published by his father, the eminent D C Boonzaier. Then (the names appear in no particular order) Mr Jock Leyden and the editor of the *The Daily News*; Mr Tertius Myburgh, former editor of the *Sunday Times*, alas now deceased; Mr Harvey Tyson, former editor of *The Star*; Butterworths (Professional Publishers (Pty) Ltd); the William Fehr Collection; Dr N J van der Merwe, Head of Justice Training; Dr Denis V Cowen; Professor Willy Hosten, Dean of the Faculty of Law, University of South Africa; Mr (now Mr Justice) William de Villiers SC, as Chairman of the Pretoria Bar Council. Finally, there are four names I want especially to single out. The first is that of the late Eric Morris SC, who gave me permission to publish anything written by his father, H H (Harry) Morris QC, the copyright of which vested in his heirs. It will be obvious how much use I made of the three books of reminiscences by Harry Morris, who was not only a wit but wrote wittily.

The second name is that of the late Dr George Randell of Grahamstown, who not only gave me permission to quote whatever I liked from his publications but also to quote from his delightful letters to me.

The third name is that of Mr W H R Schreiner SC. He generously gave me unrestricted access to a large batch of letters by his father, Oliver Deneys Schreiner, and by his mother, Edna Schreiner, each to the other, and letters from others they received; letters that were discovered by chance only recently in the house in which Oliver Schreiner lived for some forty-four years and to the end. The house is owned by Mr Denis Whittaker and his wife Joan. They were kind enough to tell me of their discovery of the cache, and arranged for me to take delivery of it for transmission to Bill Schreiner. Had I had access to these letters when I was producing *Fiat Iustitia: Essays in Memory of Oliver Deneys Schreiner* (1983), I would have expanded somewhat on and modified slightly what I wrote about Oliver Schreiner; though, fortunately, I do not believe that anything of significance would have changed as a result of my reading of the letters. They have yielded a fair number of anecdotes and biographical nuggets for this collection.

The fourth name is that of the Hon Ramon Nigel Leon, former judge of the Natal Provincial Division, who made available to me the typescript and subsequent manuscript of his fascinating, humorous and compassionate reminiscences, *Truth in Action*, which have still to be completed, and generously gave me permission to pick for publication whatever plums from it I chose.

If I have unwittingly trespassed on the copyright of anyone, I beg forgiveness, and plead my innocent purpose of simply providing some fun and a tribute to the memory of many who made their mark in the administration of the law. I also cross my fingers, hoping that I am generally covered by s 12(3) of the Copyright Act 98 of 1978. It provides that the copyright in a literary work which is lawfully available to the public is not infringed by a quotation from it that is compatible with fair practice if the extent does not exceed the extent justified by the purpose, the source is mentioned and the name of the author is mentioned if it appears on the work. I would add, however, that I have been very circumspect in raising this shield against overseas publications, particularly as the United States recently became a member of the Berne Convention for the Protection of Literary and Artistic Works. The generous and gratis permission given to me by holders of copyright in this country caused me to have a warm feeling of belonging to a large extended family. How different was my reaction to the response by the United States publishers of a book of memoirs by a former South African, now long dead, to my request for permission to reproduce from it four pages of text and a beautiful portrait. The author was in the direct line of descent of a South African judge (whose portrait it was) and also of the founder of the firm of publishers of this work. The United States publishers wanted 350 dollars for their permission. On our pointing out the relationship between the author and the publishers of this work (which would hardly be a money-spinner), the United States publishers magnanimously reduced the fee to 250 dollars. We rejected its offer. This sad story will explain an omission that a few readers may observe.

A number of persons were good enough to write or speak to me, offering further anecdotes and other material. I would like to place on record how generous the late Hon G A Coetzee, former Deputy Judge President of the Transvaal Provincial Division, was with his time. In particular I would like to thank Professor Clinton Bamberger, of the School of Law of the University of Maryland; Professor Jonathan M Burchell; the Hon Mr Justice Michael M Corbett, Chief Justice, who honoured me by writing the foreword; the Hon Mr Justice John Didcott; the Hon Denis G Fannin, formerly judge of the Natal Provincial Division; Mr L J Fisher; Mr Gerald Gordon QC; Mr Barry Jammy; Miss Ruth Kuper; the Hon Mr Justice Geoffrey Leveson; the Hon Cecil S Margo, formerly judge of the Transvaal Provincial Division; Mr A Mendelow QC; Mr Chris Niland; Mr David Pistorius; the Hon Mr Justice H G Squires; the Hon F L H Rumpff, formerly Chief Justice; the Hon Mr Justice W Peter Schutz; Mr Ronald Selvan SC; Dr Henry Stein; Mr D A van der Bank; Mr Louis Venter; Professor Roger Whiting; Mr Richard Wood; Mr Basil Wunsh; Dr Percy Yutar SC; Professor David T Zeffertt; and the Hon Mr Justice Ralph Zulman. I feel sure that there are other names that I should mention; perhaps some of them appear in the text; if not, I apologise and offer my thanks to the bearers of them.

Mrs Fanny Goldman, of the Secretariat of the School of Law of my university, with the extraordinary skill, patience and dedication with which she has spoilt me for so long, typed the difficult manuscript. I am deeply indebted to her.

My wife, as always, assisted me greatly with proofreading and advice. She knows how much I depend on her devotion to me.

I want to express my deep gratitude to the publishers, Juta & Co Ltd, and in particular Mr Richard Cooke, for their courage and generosity in undertaking the publication of this unusual work. I can only hope that it attracts sufficient purchasers to pay its way. My warm thanks go to Mrs Madeline Lass of Juta for all her help. The Editorial Board of the *Annual Survey of South African Law* will stand good for part of the cost of publication, for which I am indeed appreciative.

Finally, my thanks go to The Rustica Press (Pty) Ltd for producing this book.

Honours

The customary abbreviations are used, save that where I have said no more than 'Knighted' and then given the date, it means that the person was made a Knight Bachelor (usually indicated by KB or Kt Bach or Kt or Knt). A Knight Bachelor is not a member of a royal order—put crudely, he belongs to the lowest form of knighthood. The great majority of knighthoods conferred on our judges were of this nature. A few judges were appointed KCMG—thus Henry de Villiers (subsequent to KB), Innes, Laurence (subsequent to KB), Shippard, William Solomon (subsequent to KB) and Upington. KCMG stands for Knight Commander of the Order of St Michael and St George, the ordinary class of the fifth order of knighthoods. (The highest class of the order, that of Knight Grand Cross of the Order of St Michael and St George—GCMG—was never conferred on a judge, though it was conferred on a few politicians, such as Sprigg.) William Solomon, already a KCMG, was unique in being made a Knight Commander of the Order of the Star of India (KCSI), the sixth order of knighthoods. This was in 1914, a result of his chairmanship of the commission, appointed in 1913 to consider the grievances of the Indian community, whose recommendations led to the passing of the Indians Relief Act 22 of 1914. No judge was ever made a baronet, which conferred the hereditary title 'Sir', and gave precedence over all other knights. The few baronets appointed in South Africa were either politicians (such as Sir David Graaff) or businessmen. Henry de Villiers was the only South African to be made a peer; it was on his appointment as Chief Justice in 1910. As is pointed out in the text, Feetham refused a peerage.

Until the conferment of peerages and knighthoods on South Africans came to an end following the resolution of the House of Assembly on 26 February 1925 praying His Majesty not to confer titles on Union citizens, it was customary for a knighthood to be conferred on a judge, who was not already a knight, on his appointment as Judge President of a provincial division of the Supreme Court. Jacob de Villiers was an exception; it would seem that he declined the honour. C G Maasdorp appears to have been another exception; he was appointed Judge President of the Cape Provincial Division in 1910. In 1914 he became a judge of appeal, but still was not knighted. As will be seen, a knighthood was occasionally conferred on a judge who was not a Judge President; examples are William Solomon, Lange, and Wessels.

From 1897, when it became possible for a colonial judge to be appointed to the Judicial Committee of the Privy Council, almost as a matter of course a South African Chief Justice was appointed to that august body, which resulted in his becoming 'The Right Honourable' in place of 'The Honourable'. (An *alternative* to the appellation 'The Right Honourable' is the appearance of 'PC' behind the bearer's surname; but it is quite wrong to write 'The Right Honourable Lord De Villiers PC'.) Sir Henry de Villiers was appointed to the Judicial Committee in 1897, being the first colonial appointee. With Jacob de Villiers the appointment was delayed until 1931; and it appears that Curlewis and Stratford were not appointed. But De Wet, who followed Stratford as Chief Justice, and Watermeyer, who followed De Wet, each became a Privy Councillor. In 1949, during Watermeyer's term of office, appeals to the Privy Council were abolished, and the appointment of the Chief Justice as a Privy Councillor ended.

Some Legal Terms and Abbreviations

W S Gilbert paid the members of his audiences the compliment of assuming that they had some knowledge of the law even if they were not trained in it—how, otherwise, would they have followed the plots of *Trial by Jury* or *Iolanthe*? To those of the laity who read this book—and I hope there will be many of them—I would not dream of paying them any less a compliment. Nevertheless, a few legal terms and particularly abbreviations might be explained.

ABBREVIATIONS

Judges

'J' behind a surname signifies 'Judge': 'Mr Justice, Miss (Mrs, Ms) Justice.' So 'Jones J' stands for Mr (or Miss, Mrs, Ms) Justice Jones. Accordingly

AJ = Acting Judge
JP   = Judge President
AJP = Acting Judge President
CJ   = Chief Justice
ACJ = Acting Chief Justice

Counsel

SC   = Senior Counsel (Counsel = advocate), appointed when the state is a republic
QC   = Queen's Counsel (Senior Counsel appointed before South Africa became a republic), as long as the sovereign is a queen
KC   = King's Counsel (Senior Counsel appointed before South Africa became a republic), as long as the sovereign is a king

Criminal law

IDB = Illicit diamond buying
IGM = Illicit gold buying
R   = Rex (or Regina)—The King (or The Queen). Before South Africa became a republic, the nominal prosecutor of criminals was Rex (or Regina).
S   = The State—the nominal prosecutor of criminals in the Republic of South Africa

Law Reports

These are collections of important legal decisions. The more important ones referred to in this volume are the following:

AD   = Reports of the Appellate Division (often incorrectly called Appeal Court) of the Supreme Court of South Africa
Buch = Buchanan's Reports of the Cape Supreme Court 1868–9, 1873–9
CPD = Cape Provincial Division Reports 1910–46
Kotzé = Kotzé Reports of the High Court of the Transvaal 1877–91
NLR = Natal Law Reports 1879–1932
NPD = Natal Provincial Division Reports 1933–46

OPD   = Orange Free State Provincial Division Reports 1910–46
Searle = Searle's Reports of the Cape Supreme Court 1850–67
SA   = South African Law Reports 1947– . The reference to the court
         involved is in the letter or letters in the last parenthesis of the citation.
         Example: *S v Soci* 1986 (2) SA 14 (A)—'(A)' stands for 'Appellate
         Division', '(C)' for 'Cape Provincial Division', '(D)' for 'Durban and
         Coast Local Division', '(E)' for 'Eastern Cape Division', '(N)' for
         'Natal Provincial Division', '(NC)' for 'Northern Cape Division',
         '(O)' for 'Orange Free State Provincial Division', '(SE)' for
         'South-Eastern Cape Local Division', '(T)' for 'Transvaal Provincial
         Division', '(W)' for 'Witwatersrand Local Division', and so on—all
         divisions of the Supreme Court of South Africa.
SC   = Cape Supreme Court Reports 1880–1910
TPD   = Transvaal Provincial Division Reports 1910–46
TS   = Transvaal Supreme Court Reports 1902–9

Legal Periodicals

SALJ   = *South African Law Journal*
THRHR = *Tydskrif vir Hedendaagse Romeins-Hollandse Reg*

General

ab intestato = intestate—of a person dying without a valid will
court a quo = the court from whose decision the appeal is brought
obiter dictum = a statement by a judge in his judgment on a point of law not
necessary for his decision in the legal case
op cit = in the work quoted (from the Latin 'opere citato')
overrule = a higher court decides that a lower court in its hierarchy was wrong
in its decision on a point of law in another case, by overruling it
provisional sentence = a rapid provisional judgment by the Supreme Court in
favour of the creditor on a document in which the debtor acknowledges a
clearly ascertainable debt, such as a cheque
puisne judge = a term of English law, no longer used in South Africa, meaning
a judge who is not the chief judge of the court ('puisne' (pronounced
'pew-knee') comes from old French, meaning 'younger')
qv = which [word, item, etc] see (from the Latin 'quod vide')
ratio decidendi = the proposition of law made by a judge as the basis of his
decision in a legal case
reverse = a higher court sets aside the decision of a lower court by reversing it
sv = under the word (from the Latin 'sub voce' or 'sub verbo')

JOHANNES ANDREAE

1270–c 1348. Postglossator (Commentator) and 'the first of the Canonists'. Professor of Canon Law in the Universities of Bologna and Padua.

'. . . [S]y vernaamste werk, die *Novella in Decretales*, is vernoem ter ere van sy dogter Novella, wat soms, tydens Johannes se ongesteldheid, sy voorlesings moes waarneem, maar agter 'n gordyn sodat haar skoonheid nie die studente van stryk sou bring nie. . . .'

—D H van Zyl *Geskiedenis van die Romeins-Hollandse Reg* (1979) 136. (A A Roberts *A South African Legal Bibliography* (1942) 36 says that the story is 'probably apocryphal'.)

ELEMER BALOGH

1881–1955. Professor of Law, University of the Witwatersrand, Johannesburg, 1936–46.

'In 1935 the Department of Law secured a second chair. Dr L C Hofmann, a distinguished lawyer from Holland, was appointed to the post. He had been a pupil of the great Professor E M Meijers and had written a series of textbooks which reflected the views of Meijers to such a degree that in the Netherlands Hofmann was known popularly as HMV (His Master's Voice, after the gramophone record). After a year Hofmann resigned, officially for health reasons but in truth, he told friends, because he could not work with so inadequate a law library. Not long was to pass before he was to perish in a concentration camp in World War II. Hofmann was succeeded by Dr Elemer Balogh, Hungarian by birth, who had quit his academic post in Germany when the Nazis seized power, and was working in Paris. He was appointed without an interview, because he had an apparently outstanding list of publications and recommendations from eminent professors of law. It was a dreadful mistake. Unkempt, incoherent in nine languages, and ignorant of much of what he professed to teach, Balogh was soon shunted into a position of research professor, where he remained until he reached the maximum retirement age of 65 in 1946. The University treated him most generously. On his death in 1955 a leading legal journal abroad in an obituary said that we had treated him shamefully. I had to restrain myself, out of respect for the dead, from sending a reply to the obituary. Balogh was a pitiful creature. There were three theories about him: he was not the real Balogh, but an imposter; there never was a Balogh; he was Balogh, but was suffering from premature senility. I was one of the several students he singled out to write his letters for him in English—he had an enormous correspondence. In my mind's eye I can see him buttonholing me on the library lawn and saying '"Allo my friend. You write a letter for me, no?"'

—Ellison Kahn *The Tablets of Memory* (1986) 8.

SIR WILLIAM HENRY BEAUMONT

1851–1930. Soldier. Magistrate. Judge of the Natal Supreme Court 1902–10. Knighted 1910.

'In a book called *My Patients were Zulus* the author, James McCord, attributes a judgment given against him by the Natal Supreme Court to the fact that the judge was related by marriage to his opponent. He does not mention the name of the judge, but it is obvious to me, with my knowledge of the personnel of the Bench at that time, that it was Mr Justice (later Sir William) Beaumont. Such an imputation is quite ludicrous, and that a man of the author's standing should have made it is disgraceful. Another more serious incident was related to me by the late Charles Barry, a former Judge President of the Transvaal. In the middle nineteen-thirties a number of Johannesburg financiers were criminally charged with fraud in relation to a company of which they were directors. They were convicted, but on appeal the Appellate Division set their convictions aside. Soon after the Appellate Division had given judgment Barry happened to be lunching at the Rand Club in Johannesburg at a table with some Johannesburg business men whom he did not know. The subject of discussion between them was not whether the Appeal Court had been bribed (that was taken for granted), but as to the precise amount which each judge had received. No one who knew the upright men who then constituted that Court could think for a moment that any one of them would have allowed his decision to be affected by all the gold in the Witwatersrand. A judge's personal integrity is his soul, and "what shall it profit a man if he shall gain the whole world and lose his own soul?" Or, to adapt the next verse, what will a man take in exchange for his soul? That was true in the middle nineteen-thirties and it is true now; so long as judges continue to be appointed as in the past it will continue to be true.'

—F N Broome *Not the Whole Truth* (1962) 266–7. (The author was a former Judge President of the Natal Provincial Division. On him, see MACKEURTAN. The Rand Club is 'the' club of Johannesburg; only the 'best' people are accepted as members. James Bennett McCord (1870–1950) was an eminent American medical missionary who gave a lifetime of devoted service to the blacks of Natal: see *Dictionary of South African Biography* IV (1981) 354.)

BEN ZION BEINART

1914–79. Professor of Law, Rhodes University, 1945–9. Professor of Law, University of Cape Town, 1950–74. Professor of Law, University of Birmingham, 1975–9.

'In some ways B. was the archetypal professor. He tended to be rather absentminded, and his lecture notes were always in a state of confusion; yet his courses on the whole reached a high standard. Of enormous girth, a trencherman, a lover and connoisseur of wine and cigars, ever mirthful, his booming voice enriched by a Malmesbury bray, he was popularly known as Big Ben; but his nickname, so far as his conformity with the correct time went, was very inappropriate. In everyday and academic affairs he was imperturbable. As an administrator he fell short of compliance with the calls of punctuality and observance of fine detail; but his innate integrity, courage, sound judgement, and warm-heartedness shone through his every action. As a teacher he insisted that his students match his own high standards of scholarship.'

—Ellison Kahn in *Dictionary of South African Biography* V (1987) 43. (Beinart was born and went to school in Malmesbury.)

'He never ceased to poke fun at his own, apparently unsuccessful, career at the Bar, and I well remember him introducing a statement of the law on some

BEN ZION BEINART
From De Jure U.C.T. publication law faculty
society *September 1962*

particular subject with the following comment: "This is the argument I once put to the Eastern District Local Division (as it then was). Needless to say I lost the case, but you can take this as being the law on the subject. . . .''"

—From a letter of 26 July 1988 by Mr Justice H G Squires to Ellison Kahn.

'Your note on Professor Beinart brought back a memory of this lovable man who taught me at Cape Town in the late fifties.

'As you point out, he had a very vague sense of time, and often his lectures would overrun their allotted span. A fellow student, Jeff Jowell (now Professor of Public Law in the University of London), had, for those days, a modern wristwatch with an audible bell-sounding alarm. He set the alarm for the time that the lecture was meant to end, and Ben heard it in midstream and without comment closed his lecture notes and left the room.

'For the next few lectures Jowell progressively set his alarm earlier and earlier, and Ben would hear the sound, stop lecturing and leave the room. Bets were taken as to how short we could make the lecture, and some students were of the opinion that we could, by this method, reduce the lecture period to about five minutes. But we were anxious to hear him and pass his exam and so we never tried our luck beyond shortening the lecture period by about a quarter of an hour.'

—From a letter of 29 November 1988 by Mr Richard Wood to Ellison Kahn.

SIR SYDNEY SMITH BELL

1805–73. Judge of the Cape Supreme Court 1851–68. Chief Justice of the Cape of Good Hope 1868–73. Knighted 1869.

'The Acting Chief Justice, Mr. Bell, reminded me of a respectable London butler out of place. . . .

'. . . He was the most wonderful combination of learning and ignorance I ever knew. I have heard him give judgments of great learning and research, and I have known him show ignorance which would shame a lawyer's clerk of three or four months' standing: thus in Grahamstown I had to defend the indorser of a promissory note on the ground that he had received no proper notice of dishonour.

'"Did ye get ye notice?" said the judge, who was very Scotch in his accent when he got excited.

'"Yes, my lord, but only seven days instead of one after being dishonoured."

'"But ye got ye notice; so I think I must give notice against ye."

'"Will your Lordship allow this case to be referred to the Supreme Court?"

'The judge, contemptuously—"Certainly, if ye wish it!"

'To the Supreme Court, accordingly, the case went.

'I stated what my defence had been, and the other two judges looked with some astonishment at Mr. Bell. A little whispering took place between the three judges, when Mr. Bell said—

'"Was this the form in which the case came before me in Grahamstown?"

'"Yes, my lord; if not, the fault must be mine"—by way of soothing him.

'Needless to add, the judgment was at once given in my client's favour.

'On another occasion I rose to re-examine my own witness. The judge stopped me, saying—

'"If ye want to put any other questions ye must do it through the Court."

'"Surely, my lord, I have a right to re-examine my own witness after he has been cross-examined by the other side?"

'"Where's ye authority for that?"

'My answer was, "I never expected to be called upon for an authority upon so simple a matter."

'"Then ye accept my ruling?"

'"On the contrary, my lord, I protest against it."

'The judge twisted about, evidently irritated, and asked the Registrar to hand him up "Roscoe on Evidence" in criminal cases. Having dived his spectacles into the book, he said—

'"I see ye're right; but ye can't expect me to carry all the law in my head, and "protest" is a strong word to use to the Bench."'

—A W Cole (q v) *Reminiscences of My Life and of the Cape Bench and Bar* (1896) 7, 11–12.

WILLIAM HENRY SOMERSET BELL

1856–1939. Attorney. Editor of the *Cape Law Journal* and the *South African Law Journal* 1884–95 and 1900–12. Author of legal and other works.

'There was a pugnacious streak in Bell's character. This was reflected in the polemical ring of the *Journal*, with the editorial "we" ever present, until the end of 1912, when he retired as editor. Especially in the early years much parochial and miscellaneous matter appeared, laced with editorial vitriol. An illustration from volume 1 will show the critical attitude Bell took from the start to judges who, in his opinion, deserved censure. Dealing with a criminal trial before Mr Justice Dwyer, Bell referred to the forbearance of the Crown Prosecutor, Mr W H Solomon (later to become the eminent Chief Justice), at the reflections that had been cast on him by the judge. The note went on to say: "Notwithstanding that the trial was one for alleged murder, Mr Justice Dwyer seems to have maintained a cheerful exterior and to have imparted some hilarious influence to the jury." It ended: "A few repetitions of such proceedings as those under discussion would speedily alienate the respect of the public from at least one of the judges of the Supreme Court" ((1884) 1 *Cape Law Journal* 157). This is stuff of a strength I would not dare, let alone wish, to publish today. The biographer of Bell in the *Dictionary of South African Biography*—a historian, not a lawyer—had a point in calling Bell a "legal journalist".'

—Ellison Kahn 'The Birth and Life of the *South African Law Journal*' (1983) 100 *SALJ* 594 at 599.

ANDRIES (CALLED ANDREW) BRINK BEYERS

1903–75. Member of the Cape Bar 1936–55. KC 1946. Judge of the Cape Provincial Division 1955–8. Judge of Appeal 1959. Judge President of the Cape Provincial Division 1959–73.

'Van Andrew Beyers se optrede in hoofsake is 'n keer gesê: "Hy kom voor soos 'n rugbyspeler wat skeidsregter geword het. By geleentheid kan hy hom beswaarlik beheer om 'n skop nie te los as die bal te naby kom nie."'

—*Rapport* 7 September 1975.

In the case of S v Daniels and De Keller (*CPD 17 November 1964 unreported*), one *of the great sabotage cases, Beyers JP said of a witness who gave evidence against the accused, his former colleagues, in return for an indemnity*:

'"These are the people you chose to conspire with to do damage to your own country. I have not seen all of them. I have seen, and had to listen to, that hero of the campus———. Your counsel, in his address, referred to him as a rat. I did not object at the time to that appellation, but on reflection I am not sure that it is not a trifle hard on the genus [*Mus*] *rattus*."'

—Miles Brokensha and Robert Knowles *The Fourth of July Raids* (1965) 144. (See also PATON.)

DAVID OTTO KELLNER BEYERS

1909–74. Member of the Pretoria Bar. QC 1949. Judge of the Griqualand West Local Division 1951–5. Judge President of the Orange Free State Provincial Division 1955–6. Judge of Appeal 1956–67. Wit.

'The news that the Bar was to produce its own journal, to be named *Consultus*, was refreshing. It is hoped, however, that its arrival will not evoke the same response as did the SALR [South African Law Reports] on their birth, as described by the late Otto Beyers, later the Honourable Mr Justice D O K Beyers of the Appellate Division. He said, in words to that effect, that he had welcomed the news that *all* the Law Reports, from *all* the divisions of the Supreme Court, would now be collected in one single volume and had looked forward with keen anticipation to the arrival of the first volume—for, to him, this was to be the Book of Judges. Then came the first volume and he read it most carefully. To his consternation he found that it was not the Book of Judges at all—it was the Book of Revelations!'

—Aaron Mendelow QC in (1988) 1(1) *Consultus* 34. (Yes, it should be the Book of Revelation, but why spoil a good story?)

FREDRIK WILLIAM BEYERS

1867–1938. Member of the Johannesburg Bar 1905–11. Attorney-General of the Transvaal 1911–15. Member of the Cape Bar 1915–24. Cabinet Minister 1924–9. Judge of Appeal 1932–7.

The Hertzog Cabinet appointed Tielman Roos (qv), retiring Minister of Justice, directly to the Appellate Division in 1929. He resigned in 1932 to re-enter politics. Shortly before Roos's resignation Beyers was also appointed directly to the Appellate Division. He had been a Cabinet Minister from 1924 to 1929. For many years prior to his elevation to the Bench he had not been in active legal practice. The organized Bar protested against both appointments. (See also ROOS.)

James Stratford J A (qv) to Sir James Rose Innes (qv)

> 'Chambers
> Bloemfontein
> 24th Sept. '32

'Dear Sir James,

'Saul [Solomon] writes to me from Pretoria saying that he has certain information—the source he cannot disclose—that Beyers will be appointed to fill the vacancy in the A.D. unless the P.M. can be assured that his appointment would meet with the unanimous disapproval of the A.D. Judges. Pirow he says is strongly in favour of Ovie's [sic: 'Oefie' de Villiers's—qv] appointment, & Roos, in talks I have had with him, confirms this. Saul seems to think that only a threat on the part of all of us to resign if Beyers is appointed would have any effect upon Hertzog's headstrong attitude in the matter. Such a threat to be made must be seriously meant to be fulfilled, and there is no use discussing it, for we would not be unanimous. What can be done to secure Ovie's appointment? Wessels says he will "speak very strongly" to Hertzog "if consulted"; also he said he would "not remain on very long" if Beyers is appointed. Previously he told me he would resign! Surely Wessels should take a stronger line, and, if not approached, he should make a point of seeing Hertzog & of representing both our strong feelings in the matter and, more particularly, the vital necessity of a sound appointment in the public interest. The A.D. is simply going to pieces! Often Counsel are unable to get through the headings of typewritten arguments put before us. Curly is again ill, Wessels, Roos and I are the Appeal Court. If my own merits were superlative we would still be a really bad Court of Appeal. The position is tragic. Will you not move in the matter, if only to write to Wessels privately suggesting what steps he should take [?] He will pay much more attention to you than to me or Curly, and you, in your great experience, will know how the matter ought to be approached. Perhaps you may be moved to make a direct appeal yourself. If you could bring yourself to that, however irregular such interference may seem to you, I feel sure Hertzog could not fail to be influenced in the right direction. At least you can influence Wessels & perhaps others.

'Please forgive this jumble. I am writing a judgment and reserving my best phrases for it!

'It will break Ovie finally if they pass him over again. He says he doesn't want anything, but I *know* he would feel deeply this final affront.

> 'Yours sincerely
> 'J. Stratford'

—From the Rose Innes archives, South African Public Library, Cape Town. My thanks to Mr Louis Venter, Attorney-at-law, Carletonville, for a photocopy of the letter.

Sir James Rose Innes's notation on the letter reads:

'[Indecipherable] No *locus* either officially or personally to approach Hertzog—Wessels in difficult position—if approached[?] will be consulted—if not his advice will not carry weight—hope they will consider well before threatening a judicial strike.'

No judicial strike took place. It is not known whether a protest was lodged with Hertzog, the Prime Minister, who was determined to secure the appointment of Beyers. The appointment took place on 4 October 1932.

On the protests of the Bar, see Adrienne E van Blerk *Judge and be Judged* (1988) 116–18. Every appointment to the Appellate Division since then has been from the ranks of the judges of provincial divisions. All the Bar achieved was the prohibition on the appointment as an acting Chief Justice or acting judge of appeal of a person other than a judge or former judge (Judges' Act 41 of 1941 s 1; now Supreme Court Act 59 of 1959 s 10(5)). W P Schreiner KC (q v), a leading Cape silk and former Cape Prime Minister, declined an offer of appointment as a judge of appeal in 1914 (Eric A Walker *W. P. Schreiner* (1937) 363). Graham Mackeurtan KC (1884–1942) (q v), brilliant Natal silk, also declined, owing to his terminal illness (see (1969) 86 *SALJ* 499). D P de Villiers QC, a leading Cape silk, declined in 1971, preferring to become managing director of Nasionale Pers, an important newspaper publishing house (see *Sunday Tribune* 18 July 1971; also personal communication).

Sir Johannes Wessels CJ to Sir James Rose Innes

'CHIEF JUSTICE OF SOUTH AFRICA
CHAMBERS BLOEMFONTEIN
26.4.33

'My dear Innes

'A very strenuous term has at last come to an end. We have had some long cases & also some difficult ones. We managed to get through the work without any complete collapses. I had a bad attack of lumbago which hasn't quite left me. Curly is just recovering from a bronchial cold whilst Stratford & Oefie are according to their own views always crocks. Beyers who feeds on scraped carrots, lettuce & lemon juice has been quite chirpy all the time. Our new addition Beyers is a curious card. He is no fool but has some curious ways of interpreting statutes & has the attorney's mind rather than the barrister's. On one thing he is adamant. He writes his judgments in Afrikaans & as he always writes one the volume of Afrikaans judgments of the Appeal Court will become quite respectable. His Afrikaans is anything but clear, it has a tendency to cheap highfalute [sic]. If counsel has a Dutch name he never addresses him in English, even though the parties are English, the record English, the addresses of counsel in English & the case being conducted in English. It is all very disconcerting but there it is—a thorough "handhawing" even though vulgar & impolite of the Hertzog cum Malan interpretation of the South Africa Act. Now the absurd part of it all is that one can see from his language that he thinks in English & that his English is far better than his Afrikaans. I have not been drawn in the least. I stick religiously to English unless of course counsel addresses me in Afrikaans. Beyers came to me with the sweet request that we should alternate the messenger's shout

Letter by James Stratford JA to Sir James Rose Innes

of Silence in Court with Stilte in die Hof. I thought it ridiculous that the 20 years' Silence should be replaced by an alternate Stilte. However I have satisfied his "handhawing" spirit by agreeing to Silence in the morning & Stilte in the afternoon. Of such stuff are judges of appeal nowadays made. You know how jumpy Oefie is—well he is more jumpy than ever & continuous conversation with him is well nigh impossible. However he is as alert as ever & when once he puts pen to paper he is as good as ever; Curly of course is just the same he dots all our "i's" & crosses all our "t's". I don't know what I should do without him. He still thinks aloud in the same old way & protracts a consultation about the simplest point ad infinitum but in the end he is nearly always right. He is the best critic of the details of a judgment this court will ever see—not a wrong typed letter, not a wrong comma, ever escapes him & as for ratio he's a perfect demon. I wish I had that gift. I read over a typed copy and miss the most glaring errors. I always assume there are none: Curly always assumes there are many & he is nearly always right. . . . Curly is again talking of resigning. It is true it is a cry of wolf wolf but one never knows but that the wolf may come. Do me a favour & talk to him seriously not to do it. He is perfectly well, likes the work when he has to do it & is a great standby to me. If he resigns I shall have to follow suit and the lord only knows whom they may appoint in our places: if I knew that they would not perpetuate a Beyers appointment again I should not worry because I believe in Horace's "solve senescentem equum ne peccet" but I should not like to be alive and see the Court of Appeal packed with disgruntled politicians. It is quite enough to have to do with one man who has had no judicial experience & is conceited to a degree and to realize what may happen. If I am dead they can do what they please. . . .

'As you have probably heard we are leaving for Europe on the Arundel Castle leaving on 12th May. . . . The upset state of Germany may make it difficult to go there. . . . I must say I never thought that Germans would ever have submitted to being led by a house painter & an Austrian sergeant [sic]. . . . Are there still, I wonder, any people who believe that the last war was a war to end war? A stupid war & a stupid peace has made this stupid world much more stupid than it need to be though Heaven knows it was stupid enough even before the war. . . .

'With best wishes

'Yours as ever

J.W.W.'

—From the Rose Innes archives, South African Public Library, Cape Town. My thanks to Mr Louis Venter, Attorney of the Supreme Court, Carletonville, for a photocopy of the letter.

The passage from Horace comes from *Epistle* I i 8:

'Solve senescentem mature sanus equum, ne
Peccet ad extremum ridendus et ilia ducat.'

'Be wise in time, and turn your horse out to grass when he shows signs of age, lest he end in a ludicrous breakdown with straining flanks' (translation by E C Wickham).)

Sir John Wessels was indeed poor in checking the authorities he invoked. His judgments are peppered with errors in citation. Typical is his omission of a vital word in a passage from Melius de Villiers *The Roman and Roman-Dutch Law of Injuries* that he referred to in *Attorney-General v Crockett* 1911 TPD 893 at 911. Rabie J said in *S v Motloba*

1969 (3) SA 314 (T) at 316: '. . . [I]n later sake waarin na hierdie passasie verwys word, word die verkeerde aanhaling telkemaal herhaal. Eienaardig genoeg is die aanhaling o.m. verkeerd in dié opsig dat dit die woord "public" voor "judicial office" uitlaat: dit is juis dié punt wat die regter wou beklemtoon het toe hy sy aanhaling uit daardie werk gemaak het.'

F N Broome, former Judge President of the Natal Provincial Division, is discussing in his memoirs the case of Findlay v Knight *1935 AD 58, a defamation action in which he successfully led for the plaintiff, Dr Knight, who had been a well-known Durban medical practitioner but who had been struck off the register as a result of convictions for culpable homicide and abortion.*

'Beyers was giving nothing away. His claims to a judicial appointment had not been strong, but then and later I formed a high opinion of him. Nearly all his judgments were given in Afrikaans, an unusual thing in those days, and I do not think that he has ever received due credit for what he did to develop the language during its formative period. But he was also a master of English. During my argument in this case I said: "The appellant will be liable if he was reckless whether the allegations he made were true or false." Wessels interrupted me: "Mr Broome, the correct way to state that proposition is that the appellant will be liable if he was reckless, *not caring* whether the allegations he made were true or false." Beyers immediately interjected: "I think Mr Broome has stated the proposition correctly. In English 'to reck' means 'to care', so 'reckless' means the same as 'careless'."'

—F N Broome *Not the Whole Truth* (1962) 147–8.

'His sneer'

'Hoffie [Jan Hofmeyr, who was staying in Oliver Schreiner's house, Edna Schreiner being in England] was inclined to be amused at the scare Beyers has given Havenga at Kroonstad—he thinks there is a little poetic justice in it, for the old Nats gave Beyers undeserved prestige by appointing him to the A.D. But I can't think that the voters will put Beyers in—his age is against him and so is his sneer.'

—Oliver Deneys Schreiner (q v) in a letter to his wife Edna, 16 November 1938. Schreiner family papers. (Beyers, on retiring from the Bench on 15 October 1937 at the statutory age of 70, entered politics again as a member of the National Party, led by Dr D F Malan. In the general election of 1938 he stood against N C (Klasie) Havenga, the Minister of Finance, in Havenga's constituency of Fauresmith, in the Orange Free State, which Havenga had held since 1915. Though the governing United Party won an overwhelming victory in the election, Havenga just scraped home with only 331 votes more than Beyers.)

CORNELIS VAN BIJNKERSHOEK (BYNKERSHOEK)

1673–1743. Advocate. Judge of the Hooge Raad van Holland, Zeeland en Wes-Friesland 1704–24. President of the Court 1724–43. Great jurist.

'Bynkershoek was undoubtedly a man of rare intellectual attainments and great force of character, and his integrity and fearlessness were beyond question. The moral outlook of his age apparently saw no wrong in his determined canvassing and scheming over a considerable period of time in order to secure his own appointment as President of the Supreme Court in May 1724.'

—A A Roberts *A South African Legal Bibliography* (1942) 69. (This canvassing and scheming was apparently necessary because he was a Zeelander and the majority of the members of the Hooge Raad were Hollanders.)

LESLIE BLACKWELL

1885–1976. Member of the Johannesburg Bar 1908–43. KC 1927. Prominent politician. Judge of the Transvaal Supreme Court 1943–55. Member of the Salisbury (Southern Rhodesia) Bar 1955–8. Professor of Law in the University College of Fort Hare 1958–9. Author of legal and other works.

'Sir John Murray, Chief Justice of Southern Rhodesia [q v], when he heard that Blackwell, on retiring from the Transvaal Bench, would be practising at the Bar in Salisbury, remarked: "With his enormous energy, no doubt he will become a judge again, then Chief Justice, receive a knighthood, and then a peerage. What will his title be? After Cross & Blackwell—Lord Preserve-us."'

—Ellison Kahn's commonplace book. (See also MALAN.)

'There are lawyers and Judges to whom stories seem naturally to cling; I was not one of them. But still I remember a story told about me at a Bar dinner many years ago. A doctor, newly returned from "Up North", was being sued by his wife for a judicial separation on the ground of his cruelty. The cruelty alleged was that, falsely, he had said that she was of unsound mind, and had endeavoured to get her immured in an institution. Counsel for the doctor appeared in Court with a long row of law books. "These", he said, "represent all the authorities I can find on the subject of judicial separation, and in not one of them can I find any precedent for the proposition that for a husband to say that his wife is mentally afflicted amounts to legal cruelty". "Falsely", I reminded him. "Not even if it be falsely", he replied. "Then", said I, closing up my papers, "if there is not such a precedent to-day, there will be one tomorrow".'

—Leslie Blackwell *Are Judges Human?* (1962) 42.

SIR CHRISTOFFEL JOSEPH BRAND

1797–1875. Advocate. Member of the Cape House of Assembly 1854–74. First Speaker of the Cape House of Assembly 1854–74. Knighted 1860.

Voet in hand

'Sir Christopher, who became the first speaker of the Cape House of Assembly, a learned advocate and a master of Roman-Dutch law, was arguing a matter before the Court in which he quoted and relied on a passage or two in the *Commentaries* of Voet. Mr. Justice Bell questioned the law as laid down by *Voet* (pronounced "foot") and this led to a spirited argument between the learned counsel and the Judge, in the course of which the former observed, "My Lord, with my Voet (foot) in my hand I defy the whole world!"'

—Sir John Kotzé (q v) *Biographical Memoirs and Reminiscences* I (1934) 90.

'In the Master's Office in Capetown there is a nondescript article of furniture made of laurel wood and cane. It is something like five cane-backed and cane-seated chairs all joined together. It is as strong and serviceable as it was on the day on which it was made, though it must date from the commencement of this century. It is *the* bench of the old High Court of Justice of the Cape of Good Hope; the bench on which used to sit the five grave and reverend signors who were the Judges under the Batavian Government of this Colony. One can imagine them with their pointed beards, flowing robes, big ruffles, three cornered hats and long clay pipes. "Pipes on the Bench!" you will exclaim. Quite true, however, their Honours used to smoke diligently while listening with all gravity to counsel and witnesses. The late Sir CHRISTOFFEL BRAND used to say that he had seen them thus engaged, and he slyly added that it had one good effect—it prevented Judges from perpetually interrupting Advocates in their arguments which I fear is a propensity with which some of us are afflicted.'

—The Hon Mr Justice A W Cole (qv) 'Reminiscences of the Cape Bar and Cape Bench' (1888) 5 *Cape Law Journal* 1 at 2.

CHRISTOFFEL JOSEPH BRAND

1853–?1889. Member of the Cape Bar 1880–2. Judge of the High Court of the South African Republic (Transvaal) 1883–6. Son of Sir Johannes Hendricus Brand, President of the Orange Free State, and grandson of Sir Christoffel Brand (qv).

'In the early days there lived in Pretoria a certain Judge Brand, who administered justice according to his lights which, to say the least, were peculiar—and liverish.

'His father, Sir John Brand, President of the Orange Free State, was one of the most enlightened and estimable statesmen that South Africa has produced. The son—eugenics notwithstanding—hardly followed in the footsteps of his distinguished sire, but withal a merry soul, who loved the flowing bowl much better than the judicial bench, and regarded juries as somewhat of a nuisance.

'One fine morning, two solicitors of Pretoria, representing plaintiff and defendant, wanted to get an order for their respective clients, and for that purpose sought the erudite Judge in Chambers. Failing to find his Honour in the abode of learning, and knowing something of the erratic Justice's pleasant vices, they proceeded to the Fountain Hotel, and there discovered the luminary enjoying his favourite beverage in the bar parlour. The genial toper—*le plus beau des viveurs*—received his visitors like Falstaff, in merry mood, until they told him that they each wanted an order; then his sunny amiability relapsed into gloomy silence, and he saluted them with whiffs of smoke from his cigar, while the enterprising and eloquent solicitors pressed their claims vigorously.

'At last the meditative one, whose principles were to change, blurted out a good live proposition. "I have listened with great attention to your arguments," he said; "stand me a drink and I will talk to you." With alacrity and Pretorian politeness, the two practitioners, seeing contempt of court staring them in the face if they refused such a mandate, complied with the seasonable request, and his honour, quaffing deeply of the golden liquor, all at once exclaimed to his learned hosts, "Now fetch me a sheet of paper and a couple of pens." These useful articles duly appearing, the sagacious judge, with solemnity and dignity took the foolscap, and proceeded to draw a target on its surface. When the sketch was

finished, the artistic Brand rose and stuck the pictorial design upon the wall,
regarded it admiringly, then handled the pens, and producing a penknife, he
improvised darts, finally handing one to each of the gaping solicitors. "There you
are," his Honour said, pointing to the wall, "there's the target—three shots
each—the one that gets nearest the bull's eye receives the order." Brand's services
were ultimately dispensed with by the Transvaal Government, and he retired to
the Orange Free State, where he practised as a lawyer. He was killed, I believe,
in the last Boer War, fighting for the *Vierkleur*.'

—Louis Cohen *Reminiscences of Johannesburg and London* (1924) 117–19. The final
reflections are suspect. Indeed, the whole account, as with all Louis Cohen's yarns, has
to be taken—if the cliché be pardoned—cum grano salis. Cohen (Liverpool 1854–
? London 1945), a journalist, one-time diamond buyer, served a prison sentence in
England from 1913–15 for perjury in a libel action brought against him by Sir J B
Robinson. Of him, Dr F R Bradlow says: 'As a journalist he was a robust writer, given
to malicious gossip, with a sardonic and rather Victorian sense of humour, but
nevertheless a shrewd observer of people and events. His books, even though filled with
personal prejudice, are notwithstanding valuable social documents . . .' (*Dictionary of
South African Biography* V (1987) 143). (See also BURGERS.)

CASPARUS PHILIPPUS BRESLER

1895–1970. Member of the Pretoria Bar. KC. Judge of the Transvaal
Provincial Division 1954–65.

'Like the rest of the country the bar was sharply divided into two factions,
those who supported the war effort and those who were against it. To the best of
my recollection only two members of the bar went on active service. One was
Oscar Galgut who rose to the rank of colonel in the Air Force, and the other was
Geert Coetzee who became a lieutenant and died on active service in Italy. . . .

'Outwardly pro- and anti-war colleagues maintained a correct and friendly
attitude towards each other in accordance with the traditions of the bar and its
spirit of camaraderie.

'One anti-war member, however, Cassie Bresler, kept very much to himself,
never came to the common room and even, in the early days of the war, returned
a brief which had been handed to him by the Government Attorney on the
ground that he was not prepared to act on behalf of a government which was at
war with Germany. Cassie Bresler's practice dwindled to almost nothing and it
was only on the return of the National Party to power in 1948 that he was again
briefed by the Government Attorney. At one stage Cassie Bresler was charged in
the Magistrate's Court of Pretoria for failing to furnish the requisite income tax
forms. At that stage he was in default of rendering his returns for a period of
about four years. His "defence" was that he was against the war effort and that
he was not prepared to pay income tax which would be utilised in a war effort of
which he disapproved. The magistrate very properly rejected this and returned a
verdict of guilty.'

—M Bliss QC 'Random Reminiscences' in *1877–1977 The Pretoria Bar/Die Pretoriase
Balie* (1977) 57 at 62.

LEONARD SYER BRISTOWE

1857–1935. Judge of the Transvaal Supreme Court and Transvaal Provincial Division 1903–22.

'This Judge came to us from the Chancery Courts, where he had been successfully expounding the principles of Equity. He stipulated that on his retirement his pension should equal his salary. This was his idea of Equity and a very good one, too. No Judge in this country has ever received such favourable treatment.

'He was a fine English scholar. Some of his judgments make beautiful reading, particularly if they are in your favour.

'I don't think he ever noticed me until he heard me pronounce "chivalry" as if it were "tjvalri" and found me putting the accent on the second syllable in "vagaries" instead of on the first syllable. He certainly was a Purist.

'He and I had one weakness in common. We both disliked Receivers of Revenue. He more so than I. I extracted from a plaintiff who was suing for damages for loss of income the fact, that while his income for the last five years was taxable, he had never made a return. In my address I spoke with loathing and contempt of a man who could defraud the entire population of the Union and invited the Court to reject his evidence. I then discovered that the learned Judge also had something in common with Little Audrey.

'I have told elsewhere the story of counsel who shrieked for protection when the lady in the box suggested that he was a frequenter of her establishment. It was Mr. Justice Bristowe who imitated Little Audrey and laffed and laffed and laffed.

'On his retirement he went to live in the Channel Islands, where there was no income tax or hardly any. Later he repented and returned to England.'

—H H Morris KC *The First Forty Years* (1948) 58. (The pronunciation of 'vagary' with the stress on the second syllable is the only pronunciation according to the first edition of *The Oxford English Dictionary* and a few later dictionaries. Some dictionaries give alternative pronunciations, the stress either on the first syllable (preferred by *The Shorter Oxford English Dictionary* and *Chambers*, for example) or the second syllable (preferred by *The Concise Oxford Dictionary* and *Collins*, for example). Finally, a few smaller dictionaries allow only for the stress on the first syllable: thus, for example, the best-selling *Oxford Advanced Learner's Dictionary of Current English* by A S Hornby. Bristowe may have been wrong.)

'THE LINGUIST

'A Jewish gentleman was suing for damages for assault. He gave his evidence in Yiddish. Describing the assault, he said: "Er hat mir ein brick gegeben." (He kicked me.)

'Mr. Justice Bristowe did not wait for the interpreter. One word impressed him and he made a note of it. In giving judgment he said it was a most serious assault. Plaintiff had said that the Defendant had hit him with a brick. That evidence had not been contradicted and it was a case for heavy damages.

'Heavy damages accordingly.'

—H H Morris KC *In and Out of Court* (1950) 9.

WILLIAM BROOME

1852–1930. Civil servant, Natal, 1875–82. Advocate and attorney, Natal, 1882–5. Civil servant, Natal, 1885–8. Magistrate, Newcastle, 1888–9.

Master and Registrar of the Natal Supreme Court 1889–97. Chief Magistrate, Durban, 1897–1900, 1902–4. Member of the Special Treason Court 1900–2. Judge of the Natal Supreme Court 1904–17.

'The legal profession welcomed his appointment to the Bench, not because he was a brilliant lawyer, which he never pretended to be, but because he was firm, upright and a most conscientious hard worker. He was always stern, sometimes perhaps even grim, and in his dealings with the Court staff he expected the deference and formality to which his office entitled him. In about 1943 an East African judge, who was spending his leave in the Union because of the war-time difficulties of overseas travel, called on me in my chambers in Pietermaritzburg. Seeing the photographs on the wall, he asked me to show him Tatham's portrait, which I did. He was an Englishman who, so far as I knew, had never been in South Africa before, and I asked him why he was particularly interested in Tatham. He then told me that for a short time before Union he had been a trooper in the Natal Police, and as one of the prisoners' escort he had attended the trial of two prominent farmers from Northern Natal charged with the murder of a Native. He had been enormously impressed with Tatham who successfully defended them. My father had not presided at that trial, but I asked whether he had not met him during that period. He had no recollection of ever having seen him. Then, after studying my father's portrait, he said: "Wait a bit, I think I do remember something. One morning, before the Court assembled, I was standing outside chatting to the prisoners when a middle-aged military-looking gentleman approached wheeling a bicycle. When he had passed us he stopped and turned back, and said to me: 'Young man, if you don't know a judge when you see one it is time that you did'. Perhaps that was your father." It most certainly was. Not only is the incident in character, but the reference to the bicycle—my father's sole means of transport to and from the Court throughout his judicial life—removes all doubt.'

—F N Broome *Not the Whole Truth* (1962) 23–4.

SIR (EBENEZER) JOHN BUCHANAN

1844–1930. Member of the Cape Bar 1873–80. Member of the Cape House of Assembly 1877–9. Judge of the Eastern Districts Court 1881–7. Judge of the Cape Supreme Court and Cape Provincial Division 1887–1920. Knighted 1901.

A chestnut

'[I]n . . . 1908 I was called before a handsome bearded judge sitting in the library of the old Supreme Court. My call in the Transvaal followed a few weeks later.

'"I see", remarked a casually met acquaintance of the Cape Bar, "that you have been called before "Old Necessity!" I looked a bit mystified, and, he added, "we call him 'Old Necessity', for necessity knows no law".'

—Leslie Blackwell (q v) *Are Judges Human?* (1962) 4. (See also CARTER; JORISSEN; WAIFS AND STRAYS s v 'Magistrate'.)

'Sir John Buchanan.'
'THE ACTING CHIEF JUSTICE.'
['OLD NECESSITY.' See BLACKWELL.]
Caricature by D C Boonzaier (1865–1950), from his
Owlographs: A Collection of South African
Celebrities in Caricature *(1901) 19*

HARRY OSBORNE BUCKLE

1867–1933. Chief Magistrate of Johannesburg 1908–16, 1919–20. President of the Transvaal Chamber of Mines 1920–4. Author of legal works.

The same Buckle

'The presiding magistrate was Mr. Buckle and arguing before him was an attorney who, to give point to what he was saying, explained he was quoting from pages so-and-so of Buckle and Jones—the accepted authority on magistrate court work and procedure.

'From the Bench, Mr. Buckle said: "Mr. X, I can reliably inform you that since that was written Mr. Buckle has changed his mind on the point you have quoted."'

—*Sunday Express* 30 September 1973. (See also GABRIEL STEYN.)

EXTON MABBUTT BURCHELL

1917–82. Senior Lecturer in Law, University of the Witwatersrand, Johannesburg, 1947–8. Professor of Law 1948–54. Professor of Law, University of Natal, Pietermaritzburg, 1954–82.

'O memory, hold the door! Let my mind go back to those days, long ago but deeply cherished, of our six years together in the Department of Law at Wits. The head was Professor H R Hahlo. He demanded much of his staff, but no more than he demanded of himself. How the three of us worked! How many different courses we gave, Exton and I often in early days just one lecture ahead of the class in our preparation of them! At the start there were only the three of us, and we covered practically the whole spectrum of the law. It was exhausting, but it was exhilarating. Sheila tells me that Exton, after a heavy day's lecturing, used to return home, his shirt wringing wet from perspiration caused by the effort and the strain. . . .

'Exton, I always felt, was playing to perfection the hardest, the most demanding game of all: To be true to himself and to others. How magnificently he played it. He was always my model: I tried to aspire to his perfection, but always knowing I could not get near to it. . . .'

'MR. H. O. BUCKLE'
Caricature by D C Boonzaier (1865–1950), from his Rand Faces *(1915) 12*

—Ellison Kahn, extracts from his tribute at the memorial service at St Alphege's Church, Pietermaritzburg, on 23 July 1982 (see (1982) 99 *SALJ* 637 at 638–40).

FRANK BRUCE BURCHELL

1882–1960. Attorney and advocate, Natal, 1907–22. Part-time coach to aspirant attorneys and to public servants from 1910. Part-time Lecturer in Law, Natal University College, 1919–22. Lecturer in Law 1922–3. Professor of Law, Natal University College, Pietermaritzburg, 1923–49. Professor of Law, University of Natal, Pietermaritzburg, 1949–54. Temporary Lecturer 1954–60.

'If Thomas Carlyle was right in saying that "the history of the world is but the biography of great men", then I am right in saying that the history of a law school is but the biography of its great law teachers. Frank Burchell was such a person. It was my good fortune to meet him on several occasions, and to have fond recollections of a man of exquisite, old-fashioned politeness and immense charm.

'. . . Burchell began private law teaching for public servants in his house in 1910, and built up a considerable reputation. The Natal University College was delighted to be able to attract him as a lecturer in law in 1920. . . . He continued his private law teaching, now of public servants and of candidate attorneys through correspondence courses, with an intensive "brush-up" of lectures in Pietermaritzburg in November, starting at seven in the morning, to students who came from far and near. Many a story is told of his quasi-paternal strictness cum avuncular benevolence towards his pupils—how he would arrange accommodation for them, confiscate their motor-car keys for the time being, and finally partake joyously in the celebrations at the end of the course. Several thousand young men and a few young women received their legal training from him in this way. They loved him, for he loved them. A pupil of his who succeeded in passing the attorneys' admission examination wrote this letter to him many years later: "I was one of your 'headaches' from 1932 to 1934, and I am sure you will remember me for two reasons. Firstly, I was the first student whose motor-car keys you confiscated in an effort to make me do a little work (and also in the general interests of interests of public safety), and secondly, I provided you with your best advertising material: you were able to cite me as the finest example of the achievement of the impossible."

'Frank Burchell's university work was equally successful. Of his lecturing it has been said that it was sheer artistry, infused with inimitable urbanity, making a dull day feel like high summer. Frank Burchell was also known to be a very kind teacher. The second last lecture in any course that he gave was attended by every student, for at the end of it he would remark, in a mock very serious and confidential tone, "I think you really ought to pay particular attention to. . . . They are very important parts of the course." Everyone knew that the examination paper would contain questions on the topics he had singled out.'

> —From Ellison Kahn, speech at the dinner on 19 October 1990 to celebrate the eightieth anniversary of the founding of the School of Law of the University of Natal, Pietermaritzburg.

PETRUS BURGERS

1854–94. Member of the Pretoria Bar 1882. Judge of the High Court of the South African Republic (Transvaal) 1882–6. State Attorney 1893–4.

'At the end of 1882 Petrus Burgers, nephew of ex-President Burgers of the Transvaal, was appointed first puisne judge at the age of twenty-eight, seven months after call to the Bar. A few days later Christoffel J. Brand [q v], son of the President of the Free State and grandson of Sir Christoffel who had taken so great an interest in the affairs of the Republic in its earliest days, was appointed second puisne judge at the age of twenty-nine, two years after call. Neither appointment was a success. The new judges were intemperate and failed to give satisfaction. Burgers resigned in 1886, and Brand followed suit later in the year. . . .

'Manfred Nathan in his autobiography, *Not Heaven Itself*, p. 155, alludes to his saying "good morning to two down-and-out ex-judges, Burgers and Brand. . . . Two figures more unlike High Court judges one could not imagine." As Dr. Nathan came to the Transvaal and was admitted to the Transvaal Bar only in 1897, . . . it is difficult to follow how he could have greeted Burgers, who had died in 1894. Possibly he might have seen Brand, though the probabilities are that Brand had died in 1889. . . .'

> —Ellison Kahn 'The History of the Administration of Justice in the South African Republic' (1958) 75 *SALJ* 397 at 405–6.

'About the year 1883 while a Republican judge, named Burgers, was on circuit at Lydenburg, the proceedings of his court were continuously interrupted by the persistent crowing of a cock. Presently his lordship lost patience and, stopping the proceedings, sent the sheriff to bring the offending fowl before the court. Thereupon he solemnly sentenced it to death for contempt of court, ordered a policeman to wring its neck and went on with the case.'

> —Napier Devitt *Memories of a Magistrate* (1934) 1935 edition 33.

There is good Roman-Dutch legal authority for the imposition of punishment (even the death sentence) on animals for committing a crime (see CHASSENAEUS),

From (1972) 13(1) Codicillus 37

though the judges in those days, unlike Burgers, followed the rules of criminal procedure where an animal was the accused.

The following translation of the proceedings of such a trial was published in (1907) 24 SALJ 233–4:

'CLAIM AND CONCLUSION made and taken in the matter of Lot Huygens Gael, Schout of the Town of Leiden, against and in respect of the dog of Jan Jansse van der Poel, named Provetie, with moreover the sentence of the court.

'Lot Huygens Gael, Schout of the Town of Leiden, prosecutor on behalf of his lordship [the Count of Holland] in criminal matters, accuses in the open Court of the Schepenen of the Town of Leiden the dog of Jan Jansse van der Poel, named Provetie, or by whatever other name he may be called, now a prisoner, and says that he, the said Provetie, did not scruple on Sunday last, being the 5th day of May, 1595, to bite the child of Jan Jacobsz van der Poel, which child was then playing at his uncle's house and had a piece of meat in his hand, and the said Provetie snapping at it did bite the said child and thus inflicted a wound in the second finger of the right hand, going through the skin to the flesh in such manner that the blood flowed therefrom, and the child a few days after died in consequence of fright, for which cause the prosecutor apprehended the said Provetie, all of which appears from the prisoner's own confession, made by him without torture or being put in irons; and whereas the aforesaid matters are of evil consequence, which in a properly governed town may not be tolerated, but ought, as an example to others and more especially to evilly disposed dogs, to be severely punished, the aforesaid prosecutor, in his above-named capacity, therefore prays that the prisoner may by final sentence of schepenen be condemned to be taken on the plain of the Gravesteijn in this town, where evildoers customarily suffer punishment, and that he be there hanged by the executioner between heaven and earth, and punished with the cord, so that death thereon may ensue, and that further all his goods shall be declared confiscated to the benefit of the countship, or otherwise, &c., &c.   (Signed) L. H. GAEL.

'SENTENCE.—The Schepenen of Leiden, having seen the claim and conclusion made and taken by Lot Huygens Gael, Schout of this town, against and to the charge of the dog of Jan Jansse van der Poel, named Provetie, or by whatsoever other name or surname he may be known, the prisoner being present, having seen, moreover, the information obtained by the prosecutur for the purpose, besides the prisoner's own confession made without torture or being placed in irons, doing justice and in the name of, &c., &c., have condemned and hereby do condemn him to be led and taken to the plain of Gravesteijn in this town, where evildoers are customarily punished, and that he be there hanged by the executioner to the gallows with a rope until death ensues, that further his dead body be dragged on a hurdle to the gallows-field, and that he there remain hanging to the gallows, to the deterring of other dogs and to all as an example; moreover, they declare all his goods, should he have any, to be confiscated and forfeited for the benefit of the countship.

'Thus done in the open court, all the schepenen being present, the 15th May, 1595.'

A slightly different account of the trial is given by Professor C G van der Merwe 'Diere voor die gereg' (1972) 13 (1) Codicillus 35. He gives much other interesting information, including the following:

'Hoe ongelooflik hierdie gebeurtenis ook al mag klink, kan dit tog gestaaf word. Tussen die 13de en die 18de eeu was vervolgings van diere in Europa 'n bekende verskynsel. Sowel die staatsmag as die geestelike gesag het diere verhoor en formeel gevonnis. By die voltrekking van vonnisse is dieselfde prosedure as in die geval van menslike misdadigers gevolg. Sommige van hierdie vervolgings het tot 'n halfjaar geduur. Hierdie vervolgings het veral voorgekom in Frankryk waar ongeveer ses-en-dertig gevalle geboekstaaf is. Die bronne maak melding van slegs vyf gevalle in die Nederlande, vier in Duitsland en twee in Engeland. In die dorpie Abbeville in Noord-Frankryk is ses doodsvonnisse tussen 1323 en 1490 voltrek.

'In baie gevalle is die doodstraf oor diere nie slegs uitgespreek nie, maar is die manier waarop die doodstraf uitgevoer moes word ook voorgeskryf. Sommige diere is onthoof, ander is verwurg, ander is lewendig begrawe, ander gestenig en ander verbrand. Partykeer is die diere menseklere aangetrek voordat die vonnis voltrek is. In sommige gevalle is die doodstraf deur verminking voorafgegaan. In 1836 is 'n vark wat 'n kind se arm en gesig verskeur het, gevonnis om eers aan die kop en poot vermink te word en daarna opgehang te word.

'Interessant is die gevalle van hane wat op die brandstapel moes boet omdat hulle eiers gelê het. Die eerste sodanige vervolging het in 1474 te Basel plaasgevind. Na die doodsvonnis as straf vir hierdie "afskuwelike en onnatuur-like" misdaad uitgespreek is, is die haan na 'n heuwel buite die stad begelei en terwyl 'n groot menigte toekyk op die brandstapel verbrand. Na hierdie vonnis is talle hane wat sogenaamde slangeiers gelê het in Frankryk, Duitsland en Switserland verbrand. Sodanige vervolgings het tot in 1730 voortgeduur hoewel 'n Franse wetenskaplike La Peyronie reeds in 1710 bewys het dat 'n haan onmoontlik 'n eier kon lê en dat die sogenaamde hane-eiers voortgebring is deur siek henne. Nou verbonde aan hierdie geval was die volksgebruik om henne wat soos hane kraai as van die duiwel besete te beskou. So 'n hen moes onmiddellik geslag word om onheil van die gemeenskap af te weer. 'n Grusame geval het in 1457 te Savigny voorgekom. 'n Sog en haar ses kleintjies is aangekla van "moord en doodslag" op 'n vyfjarige kind. Die sog is ter dood veroordeel. Daarenteen is die medepligtigheid van die ses kleintjies, hoewel hulle met bloed bevlek was, as onbewese beskou.

'Alle verhore van diere het nie noodwendig die doodstraf tot gevolg gehad nie. Ons lees van 'n geval in Rusland tussen die jare 1650 tot 1700 waar 'n stoterige bok verban is na Siberië. Die hond van die trommelslaner van Neurenberg is weer veroordeel tot 'n jaar gevangenisstraf omdat hy 'n lid van die stadsbestuur in die been gebyt het. . . .

'Net soos mense het diere ook 'n reg op verdediging gehad. Gedurende 1550 [sc 1521] het die boere van Autun die hulp van hul plaaslike biskop teen 'n muisplaag ingeroep. Die muise is drie keer voor die hof gedaag maar sonder sukses. Die beroemde juris Chassenaeus is vervolgens aangestel om die muise in hul afwesigheid te verdedig. Ten eerste beweer hy dat die dagvaarding onvoldoende was. Aangesien die belang van alle muise op die spel was, moes die dagvaarding by elke muisgat bestel word. Die eis word toegestaan. Daarna kla hy dat die tydperk wat aan die muise toegestaan is om voor die hof te verskyn te kort was. Sy pleidooi is dat die muise onmoontlik in so 'n kort tydjie in hul hordes na die hof kon kom veral omdat katte in talle dorpe vir hulle op die loer lê. . . . [Sien ook CHASSENAEUS.]

'Die jongste vervolging waarvan kennis gedra word, het in 1906 op die Switserse plekkie Delémont plaasgevind. Die feite van die saak is die volgende: 'n Reisiger word deur 'n vader en seun oorval en beroof. Die twee rowers maak van hul groot hond gebruik wat die reisiger bestorm en doodbyt. Die drie moordenaars, vader, seun en hond, verskyn gelyktydig voor die hof. Albei manne kry lewenslange gevangenisstraf, maar die hond sonder wie se medewerking die misdaad nie volvoer sou kon word nie, word as hoofdader ter dood veroordeel.'

—Further on trials of animals see WAIFS AND STRAYS s v 'Accused'.

CHARLES FITZWILLIAM CADIZ

1832–1915. Judge of the Natal Supreme Court 1876–88.

'By this time, however, Natal had become encumbered with another unsuccessful English import. . . . [T]he choice fell upon the Attorney-General of Tobago, Charles Cadiz (1832–1915). He was recommended by virtue of being a BA graduate of Oxford, an English barrister, and having been highly spoken of by the Governor of Tobago. However, these credentials raised entirely false expectations. The most that could be said of him in Natal was that he was genial and generous in colonial circles and "a great man at shopping" (*Natal Witness* 2 April 1881). When sitting on the Bench with Connor CJ, he would almost invariably concur. This he would do "with nothing to add", or by "setting aside Law, and looking at the matter in a plain common sense way". When presiding alone in civil matters, he relied heavily on counsel's assistance and often postponed his decision so as to elicit Connor CJ's assistance. His performance on circuit was described as "bungling", and his judgments were repeatedly set aside on appeal because of their inaccuracies, strange reasoning or poor grasp of the law. Cadiz J's legal deficiencies made him susceptible, in criminal cases, to popular prejudices, and he was applauded by colonists for his severe treatment of Blacks who had criminally assaulted Whites. Cadiz J had the habit of punctuating his brief judicial statements with severe criticisms of litigants who had fallen prey to bad business practices, drunkenness, adultery and other evils. This was especially unfortunate coming from a man whose personal life made his presence "a disgrace to the Bench". In 1878, he was rebuked by the Natal Executive Council for diverting public money to his wife, while engaged in compiling the statutes of Natal. During the last years of Cadiz J's judgeship (1886–8), he succumbed to a "confirmed habit of intemperance", prompting a memorial from local residents and comments in the press. Cadiz J finally persuaded a medical board to recommend his retirement on the ground of "bodily infirmity", so that he might retire on pension. Notwithstanding his supposed infirmity, Cadiz enjoyed a retirement of twenty-seven years, before his death in 1915.'

—Peter Spiller *A History of the District and Supreme Courts of Natal 1846–1910* (1986) 44–5.

HENRY COOKE CAMPBELL

1843–1925. Civil servant 1861–99. Judge President of the Natal Native High Court 1899–1910.

'Campbell was a dignified, unassuming old gentleman, and an able judge. He had a counterpart in Mr. Justice Kenneth Hathorn. Neither spoke Zulu, but both were well versed in Native law and custom. Courts of law are noted for their sombre and solemn atmosphere, often broken, however, by some amusing incident. . . .

'One was an occasion when an old magistrate was on the bench as an acting judge. He had a tendency for entering into lengthy discussions with counsel, and to clear his throat, frequently sipped water from a glass on the bench.

'After one of those interminable arguments, Mr. Campbell, who appeared to be dozing, but was very much awake, handed the Registrar a note on which was written, "Does it not appear contrary to the laws of nature that a windmill should be driven by water?"

'In another case a Native was charged with attempted rape, having been discovered by a sleeping woman in her bed. "What did you do?" asked the Prosecutor, "when you found the man in your bed?" "I picked up the chamber pot and emptied its contents over his head." Without a moment's hesitation His Honour said: "Mr Prosecutor, I think we can assume that this was a 'Defence *cap a pee*'."'

—H C Lugg *A Natal Family Looks Back* (1970) 102. (The last three words are pronounced the same as cap a pie, from Old French, meaning 'armed or accoutred head to foot'.) (See also 'THE REFEREE', under WAIFS AND STRAYS s v 'Advocate'.)

THOMAS FORTESCUE CARTER

1856–1945. Advocate and attorney 1885–1910. KC 1908. Member of the Natal Cabinet 1906–10. Judge of the Natal Provincial Division 1910–31. Journalist.

The unqualified judge

'When I was a young man there was a story current that he had secured his appointment to the Natal Bench just before Union on 31 May 1910. It was said that at a meeting of the Natal Cabinet various members were allocated jobs which they would have after Union. It was said that Carter said "What about me?", and that when he was told that they had not been able to think of anything for him he said, "Well, what about an appointment to the Supreme Court Bench? William Beaumont is due to retire on the 31st of May 1910 and I want an appointment in his place." It was said that this was agreed to and that he was thereupon appointed on 31 May, which was the last day of Beaumont's term of office, but that in consequence there might be said to be some doubt as to the legality of his appointment to the Bench at that time. However, be that as it may, he was appointed and did not retire from the Natal Bench until the early 1930s. He was an irascible judge; he was short-sighted and if a record was not easily legible to him he was inclined to refuse to hear the case, and was known on one occasion to pick up the record, tear it up and stalk off the bench in a rage. He was not notable for his knowledge of law, he was a severe criminal judge and probably shrewd and penetrating in his examination of facts. Some irreverent articled clerks used to call him Mr Justice Necessity.'

—The Hon D G Fannin, formerly a judge of the Natal Provincial Division, in his dictated unpublished memoirs (1986) page 2. (Actually, Carter was appointed on 28 May 1910—see below. But se non è vero, è molto ben trovato.) (See also BUCHANAN; JORISSEN.)

'Hello, Jeffreys!'

'Mr Justice Rooney, who was admitted to the Bar of Ireland in 1948, recalls the day George Gavan Duffy died. "I remember", he writes, "it was the day before a change of Government was due. The outgoing Prime Minister, Mr J A Costello SC, sought an assurance from Mr de Valera, who was due to take over from him, that a vacancy on the Bench created by Gavan Duffy's demise would be filled by the retiring Attorney-General, Mr J Casey SC. As Mr de Valera refused to agree to this proposition, Mr Costello felt obliged to secure the appointment of Mr Casey a few hours before he surrendered his seal of office!"

'I should add that this goes one better than the elevation of Thomas Fortescue Carter (simultaneously with K H Hathorn) to the Natal Bench on 28 May 1910, three days before Union, when he would have lost his seat on the legislature and his position as a Minister of the Crown in the colony. Carter had no formal legal qualifications, having qualified in the old Natal way by merely sitting in court for a year. Mr Justice Broome in his memoirs (*Not the Whole Truth* (1962) 112) regards Carter as the worst Natal judge of the century, rude, overbearing and slapdash, without knowledge of the law; and can find in his favour only that his integrity was never questioned. My family, which has long Natal connections, recollect him for his heavy criminal sentences; which brings to mind the story of Dr Manfred Nathan, who in his reminiscences, *Not Heaven Itself* (1944) 287, told the tale of Dove Wilson JP greeting Carter coming out of the criminal court with "Hello, Jeffreys!" Nathan unfortunately had overlooked the longevity of judges, for Carter was still alive, in his eighty-eighth year. Defamation proceedings commenced and the book was immediately withdrawn from circulation. But Carter died three months later, so all turned out well for Nathan.'

—Ellison Kahn in (1975) 92 *SALJ* 218–19. (Nathan had told the same story, but simply of 'a fellow judge', in (1935) 4 *South African Law Times* 89. He got away with it then.

'Jeffreys', of course, is the 'infamous Jeffreys' (1648–89), the English Chief Justice and Lord Chancellor, notorious for his bullying, invective and coarse conduct, and for proving to be a willing tool of the Crown in every State trial. His name is branded with infamy, particularly for his conduct at the trials at the 'Bloody Assizes' of the followers of the Duke of Monmouth (natural son of Charles II) after his abortive insurrection. Some 320 were executed; hundreds more were sold into slavery in the West Indies. Many of the trials were a mockery of justice.

Carter's sole memorial is his *Narrative of the Boer War*, which first appeared in 1882, a third edition being published in 1900, and reprinted in 1985 in the Scripta Africana Series. It is a reputable work that is still consulted by historians.

'In course of time he entered local politics and became Attorney-General in the minute Natal Parliament. His last act on the very eve of Union, May 30, 1910, was to have himself appointed a judge of the Natal Supreme Court. There are not many alive today who remember Judge Carter of Natal, but he achieved considerable notoriety in his day by the severity of his sentences in criminal matters. I remember once in Parliament receiving a letter from a Natal lawyer drawing attention to the fact that in an unpleasant incest case—these cases are all, of course, unpleasant—Carter had passed a sentence of twenty years' hard labour. I took the papers to Tielman Roos, then Minister of Justice. "What has Carter been doing now?" he said, and I told him. "Take the papers away," said Roos to me, "and give me a note suggesting what you think might have been a proper sentence, and I will have it reduced accordingly." I think I suggested three years, and so it was done.'

—Leslie Blackwell (q v) *Are Judges Human?* (1962) 10–11. (See comment to first extract.)

'This Judge resuscitated retribution. When he sentenced you, you knew you had been sentenced. Periodically his efforts were revised by the Department of Justice. . . .

'The story got about that one of his colleagues greeted him with "Hullo, Jeffreys". That story found its way into a book. The Judge sued. Death acting impartially slew both parties and killed the case.

'I appeared before him once. My client was charged with receiving stolen property, well knowing it to have been stolen. It concerned a large quantity of sugar. His Lordship, sitting without a jury, had given the thieves seven years' hard labour each. Here was my client, the alleged receiver, appearing before the same Judge with a jury. To add to my troubles my client was an Indian. Now if the thief got seven years, what is the receiver going to get? You know the old story, "if there were no receivers there would be no thieves". Things did not look too good. I went into Court to hear him do a few "sentences", just to get his hand in. The first man blamed drink.

'"Yes", said His Lordship, "You . . . went . . . to Baviaanspoort . . . to get . . . away . . . from . . . drink. You . . . got . . . away . . . from . . . Baviaanspoort . . . instead. Four . . . years' . . . imprisonment . . . with . . . hard . . . labour."

'There was a gasp at the back of the Court which I am sure came from my client. The second man said that he could never earn a living. He said that whenever he got a job the police went to his employer and he got the sack.

'"Yes", said His Lordship, "You . . . appear . . . to . . . be . . . the unfortunate . . . victim . . . of . . . a . . . series . . . of . . . short . . . sentences. I shall . . . attend . . . to . . . your . . . case. Four . . . years' . . . imprisonment . . . with . . . hard . . . labour."

'A few more gasps from the back of the Court.

'His sentences were short but his periods were long. With this encouragement I started. We got on very well. He had a strong sense of my brand of humour which was all I wanted. He also had a brand of his own. At the end of the day's proceedings a spectator said:

'"Mr. Morris, I have known Mr. Justice Carter for many years. Today is the first time I have seen him smile."

'In the end he was helping me to get an acquittal. We succeeded, but he had to put in some overtime. The jury were steeped in sugar to a man. On the second day Mr. Lennox Ward, the Attorney-General, threw in his hand. His Lordship directed the jury to find the accused "not guilty". He explained that the Crown was not proceeding with this case. The whole jury slid forward in their seats, threw back their heads and studied the ceiling. His Lordship repeated the direction. No one moved. Then His Lordship waded into that jury. It seemed as if someone was going to get the seven years which no doubt had earlier been set aside for my client. Then the foreman arose ever so slightly whilst the others remained transfixed and uttered the magic words.

'I met him again on the day of his retirement. He asked me whether I still attended Sunday school. He died at a very advanced age and survived all those to whom he had awarded long terms of imprisonment.'

—H H Morris KC *The First Forty Years* (1948) 60–1.

ALBERT VAN DE SANDT CENTLIVRES

1887–1966. Member of the Cape Bar 1911–35. KC 1927. Judge of the Cape Provincial Division 1935–9. Judge of Appeal 1939–50. Chief Justice 1950–7.

'. . . [T]o Schreiner Centlivres lacked an ordinary sense of humour. Wit and quirks of life, he once told me, would leave Centlivres cold, yet he would burst into laughter at a feeble joke. He had a bad ear for languages; for instance, he pronounced "farcical" as "farsisal"; and Hoexter, whom Schreiner regarded as a very clever man and found an amusing companion, would take Centlivres off behind his back. But Schreiner was extremely fond of Centlivres: he had a very strong sense of duty, was very kind, was as devoid of vanity as it is possible for man to be, had an engaging shyness, and was quick to make friends and popular not only at home but also abroad, where after his retirement he attended conferences in the United States and Australia. Agreed, Schreiner told me, he was not out of the top drawer of intellectual quality, and he was no literary stylist, but his judgments were well organized, especially where legislation was involved: he would cite all the relevant provisions, so that the judgment was admirably self-sufficient, and Schreiner tried to follow his model.'

—Ellison Kahn in *Fiat Iustitia: Essays in Memory of Oliver Deneys Schreiner* (1983) 34. (See also JONES.)

BARTHOLOMAEUS CHASSENAEUS (BARTHOLE CHASSENEUX, CHASSENÉE)

1480–1541. French writer of legal works that were often cited by writers on Roman-Dutch law.

It is said of Chassenaeus that he made his reputation in 1521 when 'he was appointed by the court to defend rats which had destroyed the barley crop of the province of Autun. When the rats failed to appear in answer to the customary first summons, he successfully argued that the citation had been too local and that, since the case involved all the rats of the diocese, all of them should be summoned. Once more the rats paid no attention, whereupon Chassenée claimed that his clients were afraid to stir out of their holes because of "evilly disposed cats" belonging to the plaintiffs. Yet a citation, he argued, implied protection of the individual on his way to and from court. It was only fair, he added, that the plaintiffs put up a heavy bond, to be forfeited if his clients were molested. The court considered the plea valid but the plaintiffs failed to put up a bond and the case was dismissed.'

—From *Reader's Digest* February 1939 p 38 (no source given), cited by A A Roberts in *A South African Legal Bibliography* (1942) 77. (See also BURGERS; WAIFS AND STRAYS sv 'Accused'.)

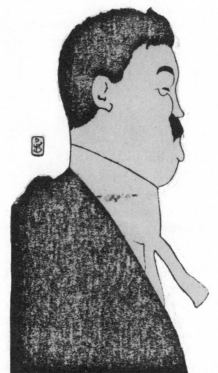

'ADVOCATE CLOSE'
Caricature by D C Boonzaier (1865–1950), from his My Caricatures *(1912)*

(For another caricature by Boonzaier of Close, see B UPINGTON)

RALPH WILLIAM CLOSE

1867–1946. Member of the Cape Bar 1894–1933. KC 1912. Minister at Washington 1933–43.

'Within a very short time after his admission, Fred Searle [later Mr Justice Searle] became Secretary of the Bar Council and became "Fred" throughout the legal world. "Father" Close was the president and that was the beginning of a peculiarly happy collaboration and one which had a profound effect upon the history of the Bar in South Africa. The period was one of transition from the exhaustive, laborious and conservative technique of the old school to the more selective and speedier methods of the new. The old school analysed every aspect of the case, the new school merely concentrated on what it considered the vital points; the new school used typewriters, the old school considered them inventions of the devil—and inventions in rather bad taste; the old school nursed a secret passion for formalism in pleading, the new school took considerable liberties in saying what it thought should be said; the new school used telephones freely, the old school, if they used them at all, concealed them in cupboards and kept their names out of the directory.

'There was, therefore, every chance of a sharp break between the two. And if that had happened many of the best traditions of the profession might well have perished in the process. Fate or good fortune threw Fred in to the breach. Between him and Father Close, two men so different in age, temperament and outlook, there grew a bond of friendship and understanding that bridged the transition period firmly and fully. Largely through Fred, the old school learned that the new, even if they did use telephones and typewriters, were not just hedonists. And it was largely through Fred that the new school accepted the professional standards of the old, not as a code but as part of a living tradition.'

—'H.H.B.' 'Mr Justice F. St. L. Searle' (1948) 65 *SALJ* 333 at 335–6.

GERRIT ('GERT') ABRAHAM COETZEE

1919–89. Member of the Johannesburg Bar 1946–72. QC 1959. Judge of the Transvaal Provincial Division 1972–85. Deputy Judge President 1985–7.

A photograph of Gert Coetzee in April 1961, sporting his then black Adolphe Menjou moustache

'Mr Justice Coetzee had two qualities that were outstanding—he was fiercely independent and an unrelenting perfectionist. If these two qualities were his strengths, they were also, possibly, his weaknesses. At a time when it became fashionable in certain quarters to attempt to place upon the shoulders of the judicial arm of government functions which rightly belonged to the legislative arm, he spoke out in defence of his judicial colleagues with a ferocity bordering almost on the aggressive. . . .

'His insistence upon perfection resulted in a measure of some unpopularity in the ranks of the junior Bar. What was often mistaken for abruptness on his part was, however, in essence nothing more than a desire for perfection. Counsel who had done his preparatory work properly and correctly had nothing to fear from Mr Justice Coetzee. He was impatient of shoddy work, and like many other great intellects, perhaps intolerant of fools. It was this feeling that led him to prepare the Practice Manual which became known, affectionately, as *Oom Gert Vertel*, after the poem by C Louis Leipoldt.'

—A Mendelow QC at the memorial ceremony for the Hon G A Coetzee in the Witwatersrand Local Division 23 December 1989. See (1990) 107 *SALJ* 324 at 326.

'Gert was a large man. In the old formulation, which I cannot get away from, he was at least 6′4″ tall; that is, 1.93 metres. Possibly he was taller—6′6″: about 2 metres. Whenever we stood side by side I would say to him "Gert, you are looking down on me and giving me an inferiority complex. Let's take a seat." But his height did not always serve him well. A colleague of his on the Bench has told me that when the two of them were at the Bar, he a junior and Gert a silk, they were briefed to appear in Swaziland. When they arrived at Mbabane they found that their attorney had forgotten to reserve accommodation for them in the only hotel that existed in those days. And it was booked out for a farmers' convention. After pleas by the two of them, the hotelier offered them a single room, which they accepted. No bed was available to fit Gert, so he put a mattress on the floor. He then collared his junior's pillows and used them as a resting place for his feet. And that is how he had to sleep for a week.

'Gert's personality was one of the strongest I have known. With it went an assurance of the correctness of his views. I mean no disrespect to his memory, which I treasure, when I say that at times he caused me to recall what Viscount Melbourne said of Thomas Babington Macaulay, "I wish I was as cocksure of anything as Tom Macaulay is of everything". Gert would probably not have liked to hear that remark, but he would have appreciated my telling him that he reminded me of Sir George Jessel MR in one respect. Jessel, when asked by Coleridge A-G whether he had any doubts on the decision in the *Alabama* case of 1871 between the United States and England, was alleged to have replied: "I may be wrong, and often am, but I never doubt." When asked if the allegation was correct, Jessel replied that most of it was, but "I could never have said I am often wrong". Well, the full bench of the Transvaal Provincial Division and the Appellate Division did occasionally say that Gert was wrong, but I fancy that he was not convinced that he ever was in his judicial pronouncements. . . .

'Gert had an enquiring mind, leading to convictions which he was not afraid to express, whatever embarrassment or possible hurdles to the advancement of his career it might cause him. He was not a member of any ordinary stable. One reads with a sense of astonishment, coupled with admiration, what he said, not in confidence, at the National Bar Conference of 7–8 April 1988, some nine months after his early retirement from the Bench at the age of 67, but when he was an acting judge in order to serve on the Rules Board. . . .

'At the time of the National Bar Conference Gert was an honorary Vice-President of the General Council of the Bar. No doubt he felt that he ought to say his say. He condemned the high cost of litigation, making it often impossible for a member of the middle class to afford to seek his rights. "There is something wrong somewhere if . . . the majority of us who sit here . . .—including judges—who have to get into any kind of litigation . . . face bankruptcy." Of appointments to the Bench, he said that over the past fifty years some had been of persons who were not the best material; "years ago there were appointments of persons who we thought at the time would be duds and who turned out to be duds". On the other hand, not all appointees from outside the Bar were disastrous. He had opposed the appointment of L C Steyn from the public service. But Steyn turned out to be an excellent trial judge, and "I for one had to eat my words about him". A remarkable confession of error by Gert. . . .

'The enquiring mind of Gert's was not confined to the law and the practice of law. The human comedy—all the multifarious aspects of life—was of never-ending interest to him. His friends and acquaintances came from all strata of society. There was not a vestige of racialism in him. Travel was a great attraction, enabling him to see the human comedy being enacted. In *The Star* of 27 April 1961 appears a photograph of Gert, showing the black Adolphe Menjou moustache he then sported, with its turned-up ends he loved to twirl, with the words: "He left the Union yesterday on tour which will take him to many Iron Curtain countries." Another tour was through Africa, Gert correctly sensing that the gates would soon shut to South Africans.

'There are other aspects of Gert's personality which struck me forcibly. One was his sense of humour. Jokes bubbled from his lips when he was in the mood, and his loud laughter was infectious. Another was his extraordinary forthrightness. Once he paid a friend—or was he an acquaintance?—this barbed compliment: "I have always been mystified how such an ugly fellow as you got married to so attractive a woman." I suppose he just could not help saying what sprung to his mind. The recipient of a remark of this type didn't often get upset.'

—Ellison Kahn 'Memories of Gert Coetzee' (1990) 107 *SALJ* 327 at 328–31.

'JUDGE COLE, Q.C.'
Caricature by William Howard Schröder (1852–92), from
The Schröder Art Memento *(Pretoria 1894)*

ALFRED WHALEY COLE

1823–1896. Member of the Cape Bar 1856–88. QC 1880. Judge of the Cape Supreme Court 1888–91.

'I was at the Capetown railway station preparing to start for Wynberg, when a respectably dressed man came sidling up to me. Touching his hat he said, "I beg pardon, Sir, but you don't seem to remember me?" "I really do not," I replied. "Where did I ever see you before?" "At Kimberley, Sir." "Indeed: What had I to do with you there?" "You sentenced me to prison, Sir." "What for?" In a deep whisper the answer was given "I.D.B.!" "How long did I give you?" "Three years, Sir." "*Only three years?*" I exclaimed. "Oh, Sir, that's just it. I expected to get seven, and you only gave me three. When I got back to prison I should have liked to drink your health, Sir." "I suppose I did not know what a scoundrel you were," was my ungracious reply. I believe this is the only man who was ever grateful to me for sending him to prison, and I am sure he is the only one who has ever claimed my friendship on that ground.'

—The Hon Mr Justice Cole 'Reminiscences of the Cape Bar and Cape Bench' (1888) 5 *Cape Law Journal* 1 at 12. (The sentence must have been imposed by Cole J when he was an acting judge, that is, in 1868 or 1885.) (See also GREENBERG, the two passages under the heading *No hard feelings*.)

SIR HENRY CONNOR

1817–90. Judge of the Natal Supreme Court 1857–65. Judge of the Cape Supreme Court 1865–8. Judge of the Natal Supreme Court 1868–74. Chief Justice of Natal 1874–90. Knighted 1880. Eminent jurist. Eccentric bachelor.

'[H]is whole life was given to study. He spoke of himself late in life as still a student. He never relaxed and his keen mind delighted in unravelling the subtleties of law and legal argument. His judgments, usually short and often excessively concise, showed his masterly power of getting at the heart of a case. But there was one serious defect, which perhaps does not show itself in the text of his decisions, but was well known to those who knew him or watched the course of cases coming before him; and it was due to his life as a recluse, as well perhaps as to a natural bent: he knew very little of the world of men and women and their ways. He lacked the give-and-take instinct, all that goes to make up a man of the world. He was, of course, a bachelor and did not go into society.

'His personality was strong and very picturesque: his presence could never be overlooked in any company. His bearing was simple and unconscious, and his habits most frugal. He lived alone in a cottage bare of everything but the most primitive and bare furnishings, a few tables and chairs and a couple of aged sofas, all covered with worn-out green "rep," plank shelves round the rooms full of books, and so forth. . . .

'. . . His character was that of a high-minded gentleman, without stain. With all his aloofness, he was soft-hearted and his manner, though shy and awkward, was in all circumstances courteous. Though far from good-looking, his eyes were keen and kindly: though rather ungainly in walk or gesture, he possessed to the full the dignity that attached to high character and perfect freedom from self-consciousness.

'Every now and then, he gave a dinner to four male guests, chosen from his official entourage. His caterer knew exactly what to do—always the same and always including a fine turkey. These dinners were looked forward to and remembered as a privilege. His conversation was animated and interesting, though constantly betraying a comical ignorance of life, while he would get completely lost if the talk turned on society. Sir Henry rarely went abroad. He was ill at ease in female company, and in fact knew nothing at all about women. It was said that he was a woman hater, which was a great mistake; and, more rightly, that a clever woman could turn him round her finger in giving evidence. I remember his saying in the course of a judgment (sadly modified in the *Reports*), in reference to the old exception in a mortgage bond: "The law throws the arm of its protection round a woman, and I am glad that it is so."

'His daily recreation was an afternoon ride on the gentlest of old steeds, which never stirred beyond a walk. Wholly unconscious of appearances, Sir Henry let his body sway to and fro and sideways to every movement of the horse.

'In court, his demeanour was silent; though, occasionally, he would lean suddenly forward and utter a strange, interrogative grunt, if counsel seemed to be making a mistake. In giving a long judgment, he would rise to animation, waving his hands for emphasis, and appearing about to thump the bench violently, but the arms relaxed and it passed quietly off into a grasp and tweak of his very large nose. . . .'

—Christopher Bird 'Some Recollections of Natal Judges' in *Later Annals of Natal* (1938) compiled and edited by Alan F Hattersley 203–5. (Also in (1936) 5 *South African Law Times* 213.) (Bird (1855–1922), a prominent Natal public servant, wrote from personal acquaintance.)

'Connor CJ had a number of eccentricities: for example, after the death of his mother, he never sat down to table without leaving a vacant place for her; and although for many years he rode out almost every afternoon on his horse he never replaced it when it died. Certain idiosyncracies were also apparent in his manner in court, such as the tugging of his nose when he wished to be impressive.'

—Peter Spiller *A History of the District and Supreme Courts of Natal 1846–1910* (1986) 35–6.

'Fervent in religious belief, it is said that when his medical attendant at his death-bed suggested that he should send for Dean Green, of Maritzburg, Sir Henry was able to reply, "I have tried so to live that I need not fear death".'

—(1919) 36 *SALJ* 224.

'. . . [W]hat is there in the shape of settled law or practice before the minds of the Judges? There are two folio volumes in Latin—*Voet ad Pandectas*. Mr Connor, I know, can read them. As to the other two Judges, this deponent sayeth not, and supposes he will not be asked for a certificate. But how do they treat this poor old Voet, or "Foot", read or un-read? At one time Mr Connor says from the bench, that unless the Court have recourse to Voet and similar text-writers, they cannot get on at all. At another time he says that whenever the opinions of Voet and such-like text-writers clash with his own ideas of what is just and equitable, he shall [not] feel bound to follow the former in preference to the latter. One would think it was "football" instead of "Foot". While Mr Phillips [Phillips J (q v)] is more cavalier still with the old Dutchman and his law; stating (from the Bench again, and with evident approbation of the advice) that he was advised by an eminent law authority in England, whose opinion he had asked on the subject, that with respect to the Roman Dutch Law—(which, I believe, he is sworn to administer)—excepting in matters of inheritance and such like—he was only to laugh at it; and again, that he was not going to follow the leading of a musty old law-book, the latest edition of which was nearly two hundred years old.

'In addition to Voet there are such books as Grotius, Van Leeuwen, Merula, Kerstemann &c., of which (so far as my "inadequate knowledge" goes) some are compends, some fragments, some on forms, some dictionaries, and the like; but as they are all (excepting Van Leeuwen's *Censura Forensis*, and Van der Keessel's *Theses*) in the Dutch language, Mr Harding [Harding CJ (q v)] gets the exclusive benefit of them and the puisne judges have nothing to do but to try to take the *ignotum pro magnifico*. . . . Truly (as Mr Walker has often said at the bar) the law (here at all events) is a wax nose capable of taking any shape you choose to give it; and a method much shorter, equally satisfactory, and more rational, would be, instead of chasing Roman-Dutch aphorisms and hunting up English common-law precedents, at the rate of five guineas an hour, for the two suitors to toss up a coin, which must come down head *or* tail. . . .'

> —Thomas Phipson in a letter published in the *Natal Witness* 31 July 1863, reprinted in R N Currey *Letters and Other Writings of a Natal Sheriff: Thomas Phipson 1815–76* (1968) 93–4.

'Mr Justice Vishnu [Connor] is of a different diathesis. Of mature years, and considerable experience, mild, patient, and painstaking; *suavis in modo, fortis in re*; many of the best attributes of divinity are to be found in him. His extreme scrupulosity, however, as to various minor matters, often of a merely technical kind, occasions so much inconvenience to his suppliants as to remind them of another deity, Eldon by name, whose dubitations, slowly evaporating into tardy justice, were sometimes as injurious as a speedy wrong.

'Nor is it always easy for the *profanum vulgus* clearly to foresee what variation of external appearance the inward essence of this deity may put on, or to ascertain what is the mystic standard of right and wrong set up in his godship's mind, or in what way the peculiarities of his idiosyncrasy are likely to impinge upon the law or the facts of a case. Yet, if alone, he might, perhaps, make a very tolerable sort of deity after all; but when his somewhat eccentric ideas have to be combined and amalgamated with the varying sentiments of his brethren, they frequently are the united cause of some very singular, unanticipated, and unpleasant results. If Vishnu, however, is ever met with in any of his personal avatars, he will be invariably recognized as the kindly recluse, the scholar, and the gentleman.'

> —Thomas Phipson (under the pseudonym of 'Clio') in the *Natal Witness* 14 August 1863, reprinted op cit at 97. (Lord Eldon, Lord Chancellor of England and Wales 1801–6, 1807–27, was a most learned judge, who contributed greatly to the settling of legal rules; but in his desire to do justice he was notorious for his delays in delivering a judgment; and he lacked literary grace. Both these defects appear from the opening sentence of his judgment in *Earl of Radnor v Shafto* (1805) 11 Ves Jun 448 at 453: 'Having had doubts upon this Will for twenty years, there can be no use in taking more time to consider it.')

Arthur Weir Mason (later Mason J) appeared before Sir Henry Connor and asked for rent 'to the day of judgment'. Connor replied that he was not sure that the court's jurisdiction extended for that period.

> —See (1925) 43 *SALJ* 247.

JACOBUS CUJACIUS (JACQUES CUJAX OR CUJAS OR DE CUJAS)

1522–90. Professor of law at French universities. Greatest of the Humanists. Frequently cited.

'"His lessons, which he never dictated, were continuous discourses, for which he made no other preparation than that of profound meditation on the subjects to be discussed. He was impatient of interruption, and upon the least noise he would instantly quit the chair and retire. He was strongly attached to his pupils, and Scaliger affirms that he lost more than 4,000 livres by lending money to such of them as were in want" (Encycl. Brit. s. v. Cujas). . . .

'"He was thick set, strong and well built" (we are told in the short sketch of his life prefixed to his opera omnia), "so much so that perspiration exuding from him had a not unpleasant odour (which benefaction of nature he had in common with Alexander of Macedo, as he sometimes boasted among his friends). He was short of stature with a beard long and white, but in youth very black, hair of the same colour, fresh complexioned and with a voice strong and clear."'

—A A Roberts *A South African Legal Bibliography* (1942) 99.

JOHN STEPHEN CURLEWIS

1863–1940. Member of the Pretoria Bar 1887–1902. Judge of the Transvaal Supreme Court and Transvaal Provincial Division 1903–24. Judge President 1924–7. Judge of Appeal 1927–36. Chief Justice 1936–8.

Cunctator

'We of the junior Bar regarded Curlewis as a veritable godsend. He always interrupted examination and cross-examination. This often put an advocate "off his stroke", and the examination began all over again. Not only did Curlewis cross-question the witness, but he cross-examined counsel as well. Often I felt as though I were a prisoner in the dock. He never accepted an assurance from counsel, but he wanted it all verified, and signed and sealed on the dotted line. He would give a tug to his short beard, and say: "Where do you get that from? How can I accept that?" He was very fond of deciding that the Witwatersrand Court had no jurisdiction in an application, and would refer the matter to Pretoria, or throw it out. Sometimes, when getting "worked up" in the course of a cross-examination, I would put a series of questions to the witness far too rapidly. "Watch my pen, watch my pen," he would say. This was all very well; but I could not watch his pen while watching the witness and watching my brief. All this sort of thing delayed the hearing of cases. An attorney said to me: "How long will this case last? A day, do you think?" "Who is on the bench?" I asked. "I hear Curlewis is sitting." "Then it will take a week," I replied. And it took a week. The benefit to counsel was the charging of refresher fees, for which one or other of the unfortunate litigants had to pay.

'One day Jim Leonard was leading me in a complicated insolvency case. I greatly admired the way he handled it. It was out of his usual line, consisting, as it did, mainly of figures, but he analysed them so lucidly that it was as interesting as though it had been a sensational criminal case. We began at ten o'clock, and the exposition of the case by Leonard lasted all morning. Curlewis carefully took down his opening statement. At about twelve o'clock he suddenly said: "Mr. Leonard, I never realised that this was the point in the case." He thereupon drew lines to obliterate all he had written in his notebook, and we started all over again.

'Once Innes asked Wessels: "What's Curlewis doing?" Wessels: "He's busy opposing *ex parte* applications." . . .

'Curlewis was just as garrulous off as on the bench. One day I heard him complain of Wessels as being long-winded!'

—Manfred Nathan *Not Heaven Itself: An Autobiography* (1944) 212–13.

'Off the Bench he was the most charming and genial of men. He had a genuine friendly feeling towards everybody. On the Bench, to say the least of it, he was difficult. He was never wrong, but he took all eternity being right. One Silk said, "I would sooner lose a case before anyone than win one before Curlewis." He took nothing for granted, and investigated everything with painstaking patience. Said Wessels to an inopportune visitor, "Go round and see what my brother Curlewis is doing." The visitor returned. "Your brother, Curlewis, is opposing all the unopposed applications."

'I once applied to him for an order to restrain a third party from paying out money to my debtor. He argued about this for two hours. I told him that by the time the order was granted the money would have been paid out. Then he came back to earth. We were only just in time. Those who knew him will always remember "Curly" with feelings of deep affection.'

—H H Morris KC *The First Forty Years* (1948) 53.

'Curlewis, to the disapproval of some of the extreme Uitlanders, had accepted an acting judgeship under the Kruger Government before the Boer War. After the War he practised for about a year at the Bar, and then became a judge, largely owing to the fact that Wessels, with whom he was on most intimate terms, strongly advocated his claims. His appointment was, however, fully justified. He was very plodding and painstaking, and he made thorough examination into the authorities so that it was seldom his judgments were reversed. On one occasion, however, he made a curious admission to me. He was the judge on circuit at Wakkerstroom, where I was prosecuting. Referring to a judgment in a recent case against an insurance company, which he had given against me, he said: "I really could not make up my mind; so, as your clients were a big company (the New York Mutual), I gave judgment against them, and they could take it on appeal if they liked." I made no comment; but we did take it on appeal and the judgment was reversed.'

—Manfred Nathan *Not Heaven Itself: An Autobiography* (1944) 211.

'Motion court today—Danie de Waal on the bench. Curly had two weeks there and the motion day lasted all the week. He's a real terror.'

—Oliver Deneys Schreiner (q v) in a letter to his wife Edna, 19 January 1926. Schreiner family papers.

'The slowest judge I ever sat under was John S. Curlewis. Fifty years ago the weekly Motion Roll in Johannesburg might run from twenty to thirty items. Believe it or not, this roll before Curlewis, J., would sometimes go to the second day, even for unopposed matters. Curlewis was sound, but unbelievably meticulous. It seemed to be a sort of game played between him and the Bar. If he, turning on his judicial microscope, could spot some irregularity, however petty, he would win. If he could not, then counsel was the winner. There is a story of a brother judge who was asked by one of his colleagues what he had been doing. He replied: "I have just been sitting in Curlie's Court watching him oppose unopposed motions." Yet, with it all, his decisions were extremely sound and, deservedly, he rose to be Chief Justice.'

—Leslie Blackwell (q v) *Blackwell Remembers* (1971) 162–3. (See also F W BEYERS; MURRAY; WESSELS.)

REGINALD PERCY BASIL DAVIS

1881–1948. Member of the Cape Bar 1908–35. KC 1924. Judge of the Cape Provincial Division 1935–48. Judge President 1948. Acting Judge of Appeal 1944–7.

'One other colleague was mentioned by him [Oliver Schreiner]: Davis, who sat so frequently as an acting judge of appeal from 1944 to 1947. Davis had told Schreiner that he had never disagreed with his great friend Watermeyer in the decision of a case, which Schreiner found an amazing statement.'

—Ellison Kahn in *Fiat Iustitia: Essays in Memory of Oliver Deneys Schreiner* (1983) 34.

'His great interest in rugby and, indeed, his impatient and at times irascible nature are reflected in an anecdote according to which he so forgot his judicial dignity as to tackle with an umbrella a man in his reserved seat.'

—M J Strydom in *Dictionary of South African Biography* II (1972) 161. (For photograph of Davis, see JONES.)

BENEDICTUS DE KORTE

1859–1922. Judge of the High Court of the South African Republic (Transvaal) 1888–96. Member of the Pretoria Bar 1902–22.

At the time De Korte, though only 37, had been on the Bench for eight years, and was first puisne judge.

'On 18th June, 1896, in the Eerste Raadzaal, Kotzé C.J. delivered the judgment of the judges and commissioners of the Special Court in the case of *State* v. *Judge Benedictus De Korte*, who was charged with misconduct (*wangedrag*). He said that the Court was limited to the charge in the indictment. The State Attorney *ex officio* had come into possession of Lionel Phillips's letter book, containing a letter to his partner Beit dated 26th March, 1894, of which the State Attorney had considered it his duty to inform the Government. De Korte was supplied with a copy of the communication to the Government. He was then suspended. "This is the first time that a judge has been suspended in this Republic, and we trust that it will be the last."

'The Court held that it was not misconduct for De Korte to have accepted the 100 Rand Mines shares from Phillips at par. On the allegation that he had drawn a draft of £250 on the firm Eckstein and Company, which Phillips testified to, De Korte was given the benefit of the doubt on his denying the transaction. De Korte did admit drawing a draft of £500 on the firm in March, 1894. He said he had owed the Transvaal Board of Executors £500 and had been threatened with legal proceedings for its repayment. In his dilemma he drew the draft on the firm of which Phillips was a partner. He then went to Johannesburg to see Phillips, leading to the interview of which the latter wrote in his letter to Beit. The Court found that De Korte was incorrect in saying that he had drawn the draft against the 100 Rand Mines shares, then worth between £8 and £10 apiece, which were still in the firm's possession. The firm had already bought the shares back and credited De Korte's account with £800. Phillips positively refused to accept the draft, but lent the Judge £500.

'The Court found that De Korte had borrowed money from the firm on several occasions without giving security. At the time he drew the draft he owed it

£1,500. Phillips's letter to Beit stated that when Phillips told De Korte that he must put a stop to his drawing on the firm, De Korte replied that he had done the firm a service. This was with reference to the *ex parte* application of L. Phillips and F. Eckstein on 18th January, 1893, heard and granted after office hours at the house of the Judge, instead of being made to stand over to the next day. But, said the Court, it was possible that Phillips misunderstood the words of De Korte. Nevertheless "we certainly cannot approve of the dealings of the Judge concerned, taking into consideration the dignity, the independence, and the importance of the judicial position". Kotzé C.J. spoke of De Korte's "reckless and careless dealings [which] serve to bring the judicial office in this Republic into disrespect among the people. . . . Although we cannot find him guilty of *wangedrag* in terms of the indictment, we are nevertheless of opinion that his actions in some ways are not compatible with the dignity of the Bench."

'Wessels, appearing for De Korte, asked the Court to cancel the suspension, but it proved disinclined to express an opinion on the matter. Mr. Wessels: But supposing the Government refuses to cancel that suspension? The Chief Justice: I can only say in reply that sufficient unto the day is the evil thereof.

'De Korte saved the situation by resigning.'

—Ellison Kahn & Brian R Bamford 'Last Spoonful of Sugar and Pinch of Salt: A Potpourri from Our Law Reports' (1968) *SALJ* 299 at 300–1.

'After the Anglo-Boer War he served as Librarian of the Supreme Court Library in Pretoria until his death in 1922. I have been told by one who used to practise at the Pretoria Bar that De Korte received a mere £5 a month—but then he did not do anything.'

—Ellison Kahn in (1977) 94 *SALJ* 99–100. (He must have had some sort of practice at the Pretoria Bar. His name is occasionally found in the law reports; for example, as junior counsel in *McLoughlin NO v Turner* 1921 AD 537.)

SIR (JEAN) ETIENNE (REENEN) DE VILLIERS

1875–1947. Member of the Cape Bar 1900–20. KC 1919. Judge President of the Orange Free State Provincial Division 1920–32. Knighted 1920. Judge of Appeal 1933–9.

'To those of us who knew him in his younger days, as a student, as a rising barrister, and as a Water Court judge, he figures somewhat unfamiliarly under the formal name of Sir Etienne de Villiers. We spoke to him and of him by the more affectionate nickname of "Oofy", and that is the name which recalls him to memory as we used to know him. Whether this nickname originated, as he maintained, in his pronunciation of the name of the Latin poet, Ovid, or whether it was an allusion, as some of his friends asserted, to the wealth which he derived from the winning of scholarships and prizes, I do not know for certain, but it was the name by which he was universally known even to strangers.

'He was a member of what is probably the best-known legal family in South Africa. For the past 74 years (except for an interval of 14 days) there has always been a de Villiers on the South African Bench, and at the present time there are three.

'When I went to Cambridge at the end of last century "Oofy" was just finishing an academic career of extraordinary brilliance. Cambridge had done well by her South African law students. General Smuts and Chief Justice de Wet had preceded him by a few years in their brilliant academic careers, but his success outshone even theirs. . . .

'In 1920, after having acted on several occasions as a Judge in the Cape Provincial Division of the Supreme Court, he was appointed Judge President of the Orange Free State Provincial Division. One of the main reasons was that he should act as a Judge of Appeal on the frequent occasions when a temporary appointment was necessary, and it was understood that he would very soon receive a permanent appointment to this Court.

'There followed several fruitful years in which he did splendid work as Judge President, and in which he gave many judgments of lasting value.

'But, alas, the brilliant future which seemed to lie before him was soon to be marred by tragedy, ill-health and disappointment, which profoundly affected his somewhat retiring and highly sensitive nature.

'In 1903 he was married to Minnie Drummond, who came from Somerset East and whom he had met as a student at Cambridge. Their marriage was a very happy one; she also was a scholar and qualified for admission to the Bar in 1915. But she was not possessed of the same retiring nature as "Oofy", and she kept him in contact with the social world. She was also a source to him of spiritual strength, and he was not merely attached to her but became dependent upon her judgment and advice in the matters of everyday life. Unfortunately she lost her life when he most needed her help and assistance, and this tragic occurrence brought about a change in his way of life and in his character which soon became evident to all.

'Apart from his grief at her loss, his health began to fail, and his preoccupation with his sorrow and his ill-health led to a gradual retirement into himself.

'About this time, too, in accordance with the hopes which had been held out to him, he was expecting to be appointed to a seat on the Appellate Division of the Supreme Court, but he had to suffer the mortification of seeing others, some of them lesser luminaries in the legal firmament, whatever might have been their standing in other walks of life, appointed to the place which was rightly his.

'The result of all this, particularly of his failing health, was that, in spite of efforts made by his friends to induce him to take an interest in life, he seemed to be unable to do so. I think that he feared responsibility and, unhappily, appeared to be incapable any longer of giving his best in his work during the last few years before he retired. . . .

'He finally retired from the Bench in 1939, and since then he has been rather a pathetic figure, living the life of a recluse in the house adjoining this building in which he lived for the last 26 years.

'I do not, however, wish to end these remarks by dwelling on the days of his decline. . . . [L]et us remember him in his prime, when Sir James Rose Innes, a former Chief Justice, described him as a legal genius possessed of the finest legal brain which he had ever known.'

—Mr Justice E F Watermeyer, Chief Justice, in a tribute paid to the memory of Sir Etienne de Villiers in the Appellate Division on 3 March 1947 (see (1947) 64 *SALJ* 137–40). The 'lesser luminaries in the legal firmament' were Roos JA (q v) and Beyers JA (q v). (See also F W BEYERS; WESSELS.)

'On various occasions De V. acted as an Appeal Judge, but was only appointed permanently to the Appeal Court on 1.1.1933. On 14.2.1939 he retired, six years before reaching the age limit, and spent the rest of his life in pathetic circumstances and utter loneliness. This was primarily brought about by bitter disappointment that he had not been appointed an Appeal Judge earlier. . . . Even more than this, however, the death of his wife in 1925 appeared to deprive him of all joy of living. He seemed to have lost an indispensable pillar of support.'

—Mr Justice V G Hiemstra in (1977) *Dictionary of South African Biography* III 220 at 221.

'Sir Etienne de Villiers, as a member of the Appellate Division, occasionally left the court during argument, and during one case was observed writing a letter, placing it in a stamped envelope and handing it to his clerk for mailing. There was no malice or churlishness in De Villiers JA, but merely an element of eccentricity which did not seem to impair his exceptional ability as a lawyer and a judge.'

—Mr Justice C S Margo 'Reflections on Some Aspects of the Judicial Function' in Ellison Kahn (ed) *Fiat Iustitia: Essays in Memory of Oliver Deneys Schreiner* (1983) 282 at 291.

'One of the most remarkable men who has ever sat on our bench was Sir J E R (Sir Etienne) de Villiers, also known as "Oefie". . . .

'His judgments were noted for their lucidity, brevity and scholarship. They were excellent. Yet this brilliant man was an eccentric. In earlier years I had the privilege of hearing first-hand stories about him from two men, both of whom had been his clerks. These men were A Fischer QC and Blen Franklin J. At times I am not always sure what I remember as coming from whom, but something of a composite recollection remains.

'The most devastating fact in Sir Etienne's life was the death of his wife in the 1919–1920 influenza epidemic, shortly after he had been appointed Judge President of the OPD. In a tribute to Sir Etienne published in (1932) 1 *SA Law Times* 55 on the occasion of his 57th birthday, the writer refers to her, formerly Miss M E Drummond, as ". . . a woman of unusual charm". Their house was the double-storeyed red brick house which still stands behind the parking area of the AD. (The present AD building was completed only in 1929.) For the rest of his judicial career Sir Etienne slept on a couch in the downstairs study. In a Miss Havisham gesture, his wife's bedroom was left as it had been at the moment of her death with the dresses in the wardrobe, a dress laid out for wear on the bed, the appointments on the dressing table and so on.

'When Sir Etienne had a meal at the [Bloemfontein] Club, he pocketed for his dog as much of the bread that had been provided for him as he had not eaten. But no consistency of character should be derived from such conduct. When his monthly cheque as a Judge of Appeal arrived (a large one in those days), he would indorse it alternately to one or the other of his two sons. He had enough income of his own to support his somewhat monastic life. Each Wednesday he and his clerk would go to see the latest film at the bioscope (taking turns to pay). It did not matter that an appeal had dragged on into the afternoon. On a signal from Sir Etienne, both would leave for the bioscope. If the appeal had not concluded upon their return, Sir Etienne would resume his seat on the bench. Apparently, none of the succession of Chief Justices could do anything about his unusual conduct. Some oblique confirmation in print may be found in the *Law Times* tribute, where the writer remarks, "it is said that he is also a cinema 'fan'". Sir Etienne was then still JP of the Free State, soon to be elevated to the Appellate Division.

'It did not end there. While giving every impression of listening to counsel's argument with appreciative nods, he would suddenly disconcert them by filling and licking an envelope and handing it to his clerk. Whilst listening attentively to the appeal he had also been conducting his private correspondence.

'I also remember a tale of this distinguished judge of appeal (I think from the late Philips AJ, also a Bloemfontein boy) of his trudging to and from home (sometimes no doubt with the bread in his pocket) with his walking stick stuck through the top of his briefcase, and the whole borne over his shoulder. Bloemfontein! . . .'

—W P Schutz SC (now Mr Justice Schutz) 'Sir Etienne De Villiers' (1988) 1 (2) *Consultus* 43. The author ends: 'A final warning on the good old days—these recollections are second hand, and suffer from a triple ravage of memory.' (As has been shown, Mr Justice Hiemstra puts the death of De Villiers's wife in 1925, which appears to be correct.)

Impressions of Oliver Schreiner in 1945

'Oofie de Villiers lunched at the [Bloemfontein] Club—he apparently always sits at a table by himself. He brings a little handbag in and according to Leopold [Greenberg] from time to time puts bits of bread etc into the bag to provide him with his other meals. He has a week's growth of beard on him—Leopold says he shaves once a week. After lunch he came and talked with us about all manner of trivialities. He is, as always, extremely thin but seems to be full of vitality. He moves about as actively as a man of 50 though he is over 70. But Leopold says that as soon as he steps out of the Club his whole body changes. He droops his otherwise square shoulders, bows his upright head and shuffles his feet about like an old beggar nearing the 100 mark.'

—Oliver Deneys Schreiner (q v) in a letter to his wife Edna from the Bloemfontein Club on 25 February 1945. Schreiner family papers.

'You would be amused to see our cronies (or 'eys?') at the [Bloemfontein] Club. There is the extraordinary Oofie who sleeps at home but spends most of the day at the Club where he moves restlessly about talking and generally behaving like a young man. Then he steps outside to go home and is transformed into an aged shuffler of, apparently, not less than ninety years.'

—Oliver Deneys Schreiner (q v) in a letter to his wife Edna from 'Judges' Chambers, Appeal Court, Bloemfontein, 27 May 1945'. Schreiner family papers.

'Oofie, who now sports a little Capt. Kettle beard, but who is otherwise normally abnormal, says . . . .'

—Oliver Deneys Schreiner (q v) in a letter to his wife Edna from the Bloemfontein Club on 24 September 1945. Schreiner family papers.

JACOB ABRAHAM JEREMY DE VILLIERS

1868–1932. Member of the Johannesburg Bar 1894–6, 1898–9, 1903–7. State Attorney of the Orange Free State 1896–8. Attorney-General in Botha's Cabinet in the Transvaal 1907–10. Judge President of the Transvaal Provincial Division 1910–20. Judge of Appeal 1920–9. Chief Justice 1929–32. Privy Counsellor 1931.

Caricature of Jacob de Villiers, then Attorney-General in Botha's Transvaal Cabinet, by Arthur Wynell Lloyd (1883–1967) 'Holiday Hobbies' in "Sunday Times" Book of Cartoons (1907) 61

'JUDGE PRESIDENT J. DE VILLIERS'
Caricature by D C Boonzaier (1865–1950), from his Rand Faces (1915) 11
(Loping along the seashore)

'Japie de Villiers was not so much a brilliant advocate as a dour fighter, who went on to the last ditch. A Free Stater, he began practice at Johannesburg. He was wounded on the Republican side and was sent to Bermuda as a prisoner of war. But he had already attracted attention as an advocate, receiving the coveted retainer of the Chamber of Mines. He was a thorough student of Roman and Roman-Dutch law. In manner he was stern, and he never allowed liberties in Court, being always mindful of the dignity of his office. In politics he favoured the extreme Nationalists, who had desired that he should lead their party. But he was somewhat indolent by nature, and wanted an easy passage in politics. He had been Louis Botha's Attorney-General in the one and only Transvaal Ministry, and on the formation of Union he wanted to continue in the Cabinet, instead of which he was appointed to the Bench. It was said that he actually asked Botha to take him into the Ministry, where he desired to be Botha's right-hand man, but Botha refused. In this Botha was justified, for he had to consider the claims of men from all the four Provinces of the Union to Cabinet rank. De Villiers made an excellent judge, but he cherished an animus against Botha on account of what had happened. In fact, Botha acted very generously by making him Judge President of the Transvaal. De Villiers was not a man of forgiving spirit. He practically "broke" with a brother judge who dissented from a judgment of his and declined to budge. A judge told me: "He was the most judicial looking man on the Bench, and if he had been as wise as he looked he would have been the greatest judge who ever lived." But he was criticised (though perhaps not too soundly) as being too fond of dragging in ancient authorities. He always said: "What does good old Ulpian say?" To me he once expressed himself cynically: "If you have been kind to a man he never forgives you." Taking him all round, he was a striking figure, and was a wide reader, if not a profound scholar, apart from law, in which he was thoroughly versed. His deficiencies may have been due to the fact that he was in continual ill-health—perhaps a relic of Bermuda.'

—Manfred Nathan *Not Heaven Itself: An Autobiography* (1944) 219–20. (De Villiers never took silk. Nor was he knighted, though at the time he was Judge President all the other judge presidents were knighted. There appears to be no comment in any publication on these singular missing honours. Possibly he refused offers of them on grounds of conscience.)

LORD DE VILLIERS (JOHAN HENDRIK (JOHN HENRY)), SIR HENRY DE VILLIERS (1877), FIRST BARON DE VILLIERS OF WYNBERG (1910)

1842–1914. Member of the Cape Bar 1866–73. Member of the Cape House of Assembly 1867–73. Attorney-General in Molteno's Cabinet 1872–3. Chief Justice of the Cape of Good Hope 1873–1910. Chief Justice of the Union of South Africa 1910–14. Knighted (KB) 1877; KCMG 1882. Privy Counsellor 1897. Created Baron De Villiers of Wynberg 1910.

'Regretful at quitting a political life, but proud at gaining at the age of thirty-one the most glittering prize open to an advocate, De Villiers . . . became, on 9.12.1873, the first colonial-born holder of the highest judicial office since the Charter of Justice of 1827.

'Public reaction was a mixture of approval and criticism based on his youth, alleged jobbery and alleged early milking by responsible government of its political talent. The aggrieved senior puisne judge, P. J. Denyssen (1811–1883), the story goes, refused to administer the oath of office to De Villiers, who, inwardly shaking but outwardly calm, swore himself in. . . .'

—Ellison Kahn in *Dictionary of South African Biography* I (1968) 224 at 225.

'When Sir Sydney Bell [q v] died, the Attorney General, de Villiers, was prevailed on, as it has since been shown, to accept the office of Chief Justice, but his appointment raised a storm of opposition in those days, and he was represented in the cartoon of that time as grabbing at the seat. Judge Denyssen refused to swear him in, and the new Chief Justice, never in his long life at a loss in a difficulty, promptly administered the oath to himself in open Court. Mr. William Porter [q v], then in England, was reported to have said on the other side, that in his opinion de Villiers would make an admirable judge! And so came into the glare of the footlights another of South Africa's great men, in some respects her greatest, certainly among her own sons the strongest and the wisest—a master not only of law, but of the most lucid and classic English, as his judgments will testify, which were and are models of complete expression.'

—Victor Sampson *My Reminiscences* (1926) 36–7.

'Of De Villiers as a jurist it may be said, as W. W. Buckland once said of John Austin, that if he "was a religion, today he seems to be regarded rather as a disease". As late as 1925 appeared in the *South African Law Journal* the patently exaggerated statement that there "can be no doubt that he saved Roman-Dutch

'CHIEF JUSTICE
SIR HENRY DE VILLIERS'

Caricature by William Howard Schröder (1852–92), from The Schröder Art Memento (Pretoria 1894)

law for South Africa". . . . The reaction became strident when . . . legal analysis took a more scientific turn, especially at the universities. But though one so steeped in our historical legal background as A. A. Roberts was justified in concluding that De Villiers "was not a profound scholar of Roman-Dutch law", it is only fair to remember Newton's words that, if successors can see further than precursors, it is sometimes because they stand on their shoulders.'

—Ellison Kahn in *Dictionary of South African Biography* I (1968) 224 at 227.

'De Villiers's reasons for judgment are occasionally marked by a lack of clarity . . ., a certain sponginess. As interpreters and developers of South African law other judges might have done better than he. De Villiers had an unparalleled opportunity, coming to the bench when, allowing for all the contributions of such Roman-Dutch scholars as William Menzies, Henry Cloete and E. B. Watermeyer, much remained to be done in assimilating the old law to modern conditions. . . . [H]is brethren of the Supreme Court over the years . . . were not his equals. With men like James Weston Leonard, James Rose Innes and W. P. Schreiner declining appointment, the Cape bench was a land of might-have-been.'

—Ellison Kahn op cit at 228.

'Wiry, square-shouldered, with a square-cut face, blunt features, firm jaw, long, thin, close-shut mouth and deep-sunk eyes, he had a mien severe if not forbidding. From his cheeks hung thin Dundreary weepers which later spread under his chin like a white crescent moon. Formal, aloof and reserved, in early years he tended to wear the dignity of his office as a mantle of protection. In the eighties the Chief Justice was a cold, austere man, much feared and little loved. Later he unbent a little, revealing at times his innate kindness. He was deficient in humour. An appreciation of social realities offset his lack of sophistication. He had the grace of simplicity, reflected in the spareness of his style in writing. It came out in odd ways; Rose Innes mentions his surprise in learning, when the Appellate Division first sat, that De Villiers never had any typing assistance, everything being written in his own hand.'

—Ellison Kahn op cit at 229.

'. . . [H]is very tendency to be dictatorial led to speedy justice. In his letters, reports and judgments he went to the point at once. He hated delay and, at times, showed impatience to get to the main issue. "No, no, Mr. X," he would say, "I want evidence led on this point." In later life he was apt to become restive if cross-examination were unduly prolonged, especially as the clock neared the hour of

'Sir J. H. de Villiers, Chief Justice.'
'JURE HUMANO'
'God works wonders now and then,
'Here's a lawyer—an honest man!'
*Caricature by D C Boonzaier (1865–1950),
from his* Owlographs: A collection of South
African Celebrities in Caricature *(1901) 17*

12.30, which marked the time of his departure to catch the lunch train home. Nor did he bear easily with verbosity. Once the most lovable, learned and long-winded barrister of the day was reading a declaration, which relentlessly followed each side-issue to its tortuous end. As the reading went on, page after page, de Villiers leaned back in his chair with closed eyes. At last counsel broke off to remark that, at this point, several letters should have been read but that, to avoid prolixity, they had been omitted. De Villiers leant forward and asked gently: "Did I understand you to say pro-lix-ity?" He practised what he preached. His judgments were sometimes long but never diffuse. He never overstated them; rather the reverse, for critics noted that he usually gave his reference to authorities in general terms and seldom declared within what limits or on what lines it was legitimate to apply the principles he invoked. Perhaps he did so because the less he said the less he might one day be called upon to unsay.'

—Eric A Walker *Lord De Villiers* (1925) 90.

'Three things especially moved him to wrath in Court—lying, sharp practice, and culpable ignorance. He knew what evidence was worth on its human side. The lying witness and the shifty counsel—if such there ever were at the Cape bar—fared ill before "the boy in ermine" with the eyes of an eagle set in the lean, grave face above the close-shut mouth and the square jaw. With increasing age and dignity, the effect of those deep-sunk eyes was still more paralyzing. Yet he rarely lost his temper and, on two of the few occasions on which this is recorded of him, the outburst was called forth not by the ape or the tiger in his fellow-man but by the donkey. Once, an advocate applied for the enrolment of another advocate at Grahamstown. The papers were all in order but the applicant gave the name of his client wrongly and was duly corrected. He then asked that his client be enrolled in the non-existent Court at Kingwilliamstown. "Try" cried de Villiers, "to read your papers before you come into Court," and jerked the papers down the long table with such force that they spilled off the far end. On the second occasion, he asked a young and somewhat bumptious advocate whether he had any authority on a given point. "No, my Lord," was the reply, "that never occurred to me." "Very well," said de Villiers, "the Court will adjourn till 2 o'clock, and perhaps by that time you will have something to tell it." In the afternoon he repeated his question. "No, my Lord," said the advocate, "I have nothing to add; but I expect your Lordship's

'LORD DE VILLIERS WELCOMES THE LATEST ADDITION (SIR SOTHERN HOLLAND) TO THE RANKS OF OUR ARISTOCRACY'

Caricature by D C Boonzaier (1865–1950), from his My Caricatures *(1912)*
(The caricature must have been drawn in 1912, for in June that year Reginald Sothern Holland (1876–1948), distinguished public servant, was knighted. Lord De Villiers was the only South African peer.)

judgment will prove both interesting and illuminating!" The judgment may have been all that counsel expected but the preliminary remarks were infused with such heat that he thereafter transferred his talents to a more equable atmosphere.'

—Walker op cit at 92.

'. . . [F]ew dared to take liberties with him. Few even ventured to laugh in his presence. Dignity clothed him as with a garment and spread its train over all the precincts of his Court. There were times when those present were hard put to it to contain themselves; and once it is recorded that he smiled, for the joke was against himself. An architect and a client were in dispute. The architect insisted that he had not advised the client to have an addition made to her house though he had suggested it. "Oh!" said de Villiers, "and what is the difference between suggestion and advice?" "Well," replied the unabashed Daedalus, "on a point of law I might suggest to your Lordship but I would never presume to advise." Usually de Villiers never relaxed a muscle. At a time when gramophones were less efficient than they have since become, a case came forward which included a question of audibility. De Villiers demanded that the court hear the instrument. Whether by chance or design it was set going to the strains of "We won't go home till morning." Tune and words were only too plain. "That will do," said the Chief; but all efforts to stop the machine proved fruitless. "Take it away," he commanded; and taken away it was triumphantly proclaiming its outrageous intentions diminuendo while de Villiers imperturbably gave his decision.'

—Walker op cit at 93. (See also JUTA; W H SOLOMON.)

'In the eighties the Chief Justice was a cold, austere man, much feared and little loved. I remember a lunch to which he was invited by the Bar at, I think, Prince Albert Road Station, on Circuit, where I, as junior, had secured the only accommodation. He sat with Upington and Leonard, who spoke to him in the most formal way, while the rest of us behaved as Dr. Johnson might have done in the presence of royalty. In later years, as Lord de Villiers, he unbent a great deal, and might even be said to have become quite genial.'

—Victor Sampson *My Reminiscences* (1926) 54–5.

'When the sitting of the court at Port Elizabeth was over, I returned to Grahamstown and joined the circuit again at Aliwal North, where I conducted the prosecution on behalf of the Crown. Of the cases on the calendar one was a charge of murder against a farmer who had beaten his young native servant-boy

LORD DE VILLIERS

From a sepia drawing in 1909 by J M Solomon, reproduced in (1921) 38 *SALJ* 247. A brilliant portrait. Solomon (1888–1920) was an architect by profession. An artist of ability, he left his mark on the cultural development of the country.

between the age of twelve and fourteen, and then tied him to one of the wheels of his wagon. It was winter, when there is a heavy frost at night in that part of the Colony. About nine p.m. the boy begged his master, who was inside the wagon, to let him have his blanket as a protection against the cold, but this request was refused. On getting out of his wagon the next morning the farmer found the boy dead. The body was unfastened from the wheel, weighted and thrown into a deep water hole in a river course, the river not running at the time of the year. Later the hole was dragged, but no body was found. The evidence in support of the Crown's case was clear. . . . [I]n summing up, the learned Chief Justice adopted the view urged on behalf of the Crown [that where the body of the alleged deceased cannot be found the court may be convinced beyond reasonable doubt that he was killed by the accused, as there was enough circumstantial evidence and a satisfactory explanation of the absence of the body]. . . . The jury retired and, after an absence of about half an hour, came back into court and returned a verdict of not guilty. Turning towards the jury, the Chief Justice thus addressed them: "Gentlemen, I hope you are able to reconcile your verdict with your consciences." The jury remained seated in their box, whereupon the Chief Justice discharged the accused, and said to me, "I think, Mr. Kotzé, we will have a fresh jury for the next case."'

—Sir John Kotzé *Biographical Memoirs and Reminiscences* I (1934) 206–7.

MELIUS DE VILLIERS

1849–1938. Member of the Cape Bar 1872–6, 1902–5. Judge of the High Court of the Orange Free State 1876–89. Chief Justice of the Orange Free State 1889–99. Professor of Zuid Afrikaansche Recht in the University of Leyden 1905–9. Author of legal and other works. Brother of Sir Henry (Lord) de Villiers.

'I was rather put out . . . by a witticism of Judge FitzPatrick at my expense. I was citing an authority in Latin about dogs worrying geese (*anseres*). Being in a somewhat nervous condition . . . I inadvertently translated *anseres* as "swans". "Well, Mr De Villiers," the judge remarked, "I trust that you are not one of those people whose geese are always swans."'

—Niconette du Toit 'Melius de Villiers' 1978 *De Rebus Procuratoriis* 417 at 418, citing a passage in Melius de Villiers's unpublished *Memories of Over Eighty Years*, lodged in the Orange Free State archives.

'In 1902 Milner offered him appointment as Chief Justice of the Orange River Colony; no other judge of the conquered republics was paid the compliment of an invitation to return to the judiciary. But De Villiers refused to accept it, for he had sworn to help regain the independence of the conquered republic.'

—Ellison Kahn 'The Birth and Life of the *South African Law Journal*' (1983) 100 *SALJ* 594 at 602. (Similarly M Wiechers in *Dictionary of South African Biography* II (1972) 185; Niconette du Toit 'Melius de Villiers' 1978 *De Rebus Procuratoriis* 417 at 420.)

An error

'Cowboys don't cry (and [Oliver] Schreiner did not cry). But is our history not full of this type of occurrence? Could any realist have expected the government to appoint Schreiner as Chief Justice? Worse befell the brilliant old Chief Justice of the Orange Free State, Melius de Villiers, at the hands of the jingoes after the Boer War. He was never appointed and in the end he was disgracefully compelled to petition the Union Parliament for a pension. C'mon.'

—Dirk du Toit 'Cowboys and Crooks; Judges and Legislative Intention' (1986) 11 *Tydskrif vir Regswetenskap* i at iv. (See also W P SCHREINER.)

JOHANNES CHRISTIAAN (J C) DE WET

". . . maar wat is die redelike man nou eintlik vir 'n ding?"

(Caricature of J C de Wet reproduced by kind permission of Butterworth & Co (SA) (Pty) Ltd)

1912–90. Senior Lecturer in Law, University of Stellenbosch, 1936–43. Professor of Law 1943–72. Professor of Law, University of Cape Town, 1973–8. SC 1989.

'J C de Wet was something of a legend even among his student contemporaries at Stellenbosch. He was the first-year in Dagbreek who was said to be able to speak Latin and Xhosa with the same facility as English and Afrikaans. He certainly made a deep impression on those who taught him, and in turn the generations he came to teach. His students today sit in the Appellate Division and in the provincial courts. Many are prominent in practice and in commerce; no less than six are currently deans of South African law faculties. But it was through his publications that for forty years he has come to cast such a long shadow over most fields of South African law. . . .

'In 1940 he joined the editorial board

of the *Tydskrif* and commenced to lay the foundation of his great lifework on
contract and criminal law. . . . [Two years] later followed his first publication on
agency, the subject to which he was to return thirty-five years later in his
definitive statement for the first volume of *The Law of South Africa*. Ellison Kahn
saw this as "a voyage of discovery, culminating in a brilliant piece of original
writing, based on a carefully considered systematic treatment and shot through
with new and penetrating ideas."

'In the 1940's in quick succession followed a series on contractual topics, water
law and historical subjects.

'In 1948 *Kontraktereg en Handelsreg* appeared, only the second legal textbook to
appear in Afrikaans. As C G Hall said with considerable understatement:

"It is written often in stately language and one can sometimes recognise the
voice of the professor laying down the precise terms of the common law in
measured tones which brook no contradiction."

'Others thought the tones less measured. In (1954) 71 *SALJ* 269 Leo van den
Heever wrote of "mentors . . . [who] without apology sneer, condescend and
scold" and cited De Wet's more caustic strictures, including

"Dit is amper amusant om te sien hoe Lord De Villiers met hierdie begrippe
geworstel het"

and

"Op een goeie punt in hierdie beslissing moet darem gewys word".

'If anything, the voice of the professor, raised against a phalanx of fumbling
scholars and errant judges, grew less forgiving. Thus in the third (1964) and
fourth (1976) editions he wrote of *SAR & H v National Bank of SA* 1924 AD 704:

"R WESSELS se ondeurdagte en wysgerige stukkie bespiegeling het egter
indruk gemaak op ander regters."

Many other decisions were "nie oortuigend" or even "net nie waar nie", while in
Hall v Milner 1959 2 SA 304 (O):

"redeneer die Hof in sirkels totdat hy uiteindelik die kluts heeltemal kwyt is".

'Against this background *Strafreg* received a rather wary reception. . . .

'In 1956 appeared De Wet's scathing critique of the Bill which was to become
Act 54 of 1956. He abhorred its prolixity:

"Is dit tegnies onmoontlik om 'n ordentlike waterwet met minder as vyftig
duisend woorde op te stel? Daar moet êrens 'n groot skroef los wees as 'n wet,
wat maar net die waterreg reël, die helfte van die woordruimte in beslag neem
wat die ganse Grieke Burgerlike Wetboek neem."

'In forty-five pages, he sets out an overview of the history of water law in
South Africa, a critique of principal decisions, and a remorseless exposé of
vagaries, fallacies and infelicities in the new Bill. His analysis was received in an
injured and frosty silence; the fifty thousand words passed into the statute books.
His memorandum on prescription to the Law Reform Commission and draft
prescription Bill in 1968 met a markedly better fate. . . .

'He also sought to bury *Hall v Milner, supra,* in his argument for the appellant
in *Phame (Pty) Ltd v Paizes* 1973 3 SA 397 (A). His heads of argument comprise
the most impressive array of authority: Holmes JA indeed went out of his way to
refer to him as "a learned opponent who reads Latin as facilely as Afrikaans and
English". To De Wet's chagrin, other counsels prevailed. The last word,
however, characteristically remains his. . . .

'. . . A look at the bibliography of publications by De Wet shows how much

South African law owes to him for the determination with which he has wielded that predatory pen for forty years. One may hope for more, but with little entitlement:

"(Why should the agèd eagle stretch its wings?)"

'Why indeed? He is, as Corbett JA described him in an address in 1975, "our own incomparable J C de Wet—pithy, pungent, sometimes remorseless". His endowment is unrivalled in our time.

'Si monumentum requiris, circumspice.'

—Jeremy Gauntlett 'The Predatory Pen: A Survey of Publications by J C de Wet 1939–1979' in *J C Noster: 'n Feesbundel* (1979) geredigeer deur J J Gauntlett 175 at 175–9. (See also INNES.)

'There was always something of a Delphic quality in mounting the steps to the imposing and yet unpretentious mansion at 44 Noordwal, ensconced behind high trees and just within earshot of the romance-evoking Eerste River at Stellenbosch. One's tread up the short incline to the house of J C de Wet could conjure up a combination of associations of pilgrims making their way to consult the oracle at Delphi and of visiting the grave of Gustav Radbruch in the *Bergfriedhof* of Heidelberg still ominously radiating its message of what lawyering in the West should be all about. For J C de Wet, more than any other academic lawyer who has ever spread his intellectual wings in our clime, has become something of a living monument to many values and contributions which, one can safely predict, will stand the test of time over generations yet to come, as well as to endeavours and achievements which will endure as impressive signs of their time. . . .

'. . . Mr Gauntlett's fleeting glimpses of JC's wit and verbal incisiveness and, let's say it, mischievous penmanship tell us so well why for so long and so profoundly the law faculty at Stellenbosch *was* JC, and JC *was* the Law Faculty. It says much, too much, of our present generation of legal scholarship that JC's attributes are so often lauded but so seldom emulated. . . .

'There was, of course, also JC "the man", whose memory will be treasured by those who knew him as their teacher and friend. Of this incredibly rich and almost mythical realm of the JC saga there is but the faintest echo in the *Feesbundel*. More's the pity, because those who knew him always found in him a depth of humanity quite unsuspected if one only knew him in print. Behind the sharp pen—alas, greatly mellowed over the last decade or so!—there is the humblest of all men, with a sense of humour that is legendary. Indeed, it was always said that the class attendance of JC was determined not by his rather dry lecturing style but by an unwillingness to miss a scintilla of his brilliant wit. But these are memories which those of us who knew him will prefer to treasure privately; too bad, once again, that this warm humanity finds so little reflection in the *Feesbundel*. . . .

'I can close my eyes now and see the puckish rotund man with the slight whistle in his soprano voice chain-smoking his way through lectures, with what seemed to be a perpetual smile engraved on his benign features and with slightly dreamy eyes wistfully focused on some distant and invisible horizon; I can hear him still hammering home principle after principle, sweeping his way impatiently and contemptuously through the thick nettle-infested overgrowth of curious curial learning; I can see again a bolt of mischievous delight flashing through those distant eyes when he cracked the whiplash of his acid wit on some (to him) incomprehensible bit of nonsense masquerading as the law; I remember him, as so many others also do, as the warm father of all of us who made our way through the Stellenbosch Faculty of Law, ever prepared to listen and counsel; even today as I mount the steps to the Delphic mansion along Noordwal my heart heaves with delayed embarrassment as I remember mounting the same steps as a second-year student about 2 am one lonely morning when, in an almost surrealistic attempt to unseat the Students' Representative Council, I urgently needed the services of an assessor for the arbitration court; when, instead of laying me low (quite deservedly) by the expected laser beam of caustic words, he laconically said: "Laat ek net my skoene kry, ek kom." I did not realize then, as I did much later, that ultimately the human dimension was the most important dimension in which JC placed his work and his life.'

—Barend van Niekerk '*J C Noster*: A Review and a Tribute to Professor J C de Wet' (1980) 97 *SALJ* 183 at 183, 184, 187, 188.

'Ander, soos James Yeats, was beter dosente as professor De Wet. JC het teks voorgedra, nie verduidelik nie. Sigaret in die hand, oë op die agterste plafon, heen en weer op die platform—tot op die presiese moment wanneer die klok lui, en dan stap hy uit. Eers die volgende lesing, as hy op sy stukke was, het hy die sin voltooi. Sonder 'n sin vir effek was hy nie, maar met genoeg van 'n vonkeling dat almal kon weet dis vir ons edifikasie, en nie uit eiewaan nie. Met 'n *Kontraktereg* of *Strafreg* voor jou kon jy die teks soms woordeliks met jou potlood volg, en in die proses uitvind watter voetnote vir doeleindes van die volgende mondeling belangrik was. En tog was JC se klasse nie vervelend nie. Vroeër of later kom 'n sweepslag teen die een of ander uitspraak wat die punt mis of, as die punt wel ingesien is, nie behoorlike erkenning aan die eintlike bron van insig gee nie. Ons het JC dit gegun om soms uit die hoogte te praat. Dit was sy goeie reg. En JC se goeie reg was die Romeins-Hollandse reg van Stellenbosch. Daardie reg, het hy verkondig, is eenvoudig. Dis nie nodig vir regters en die wetgewer om dit moeilik te maak nie. Moeilike reg is swak reg. Altans so onthou ek dit. JC het die skerpsinnigheid en deskundigheid gehad om deur die aanpaksels te breek, die patroon en simmetrie van die reg bloot te lê, en in enkele sinne glashelder te beskryf. Plek-plek het hy die reg tot 'n fyn kuns verhef.

'In ons oë, sy studente van die jare vyftigs, was JC nommer een. Nie uniek nie. Oubaas Mort [qv: MALHERBE] was uniek. Maar die fakulteit was JC. Wat weer eens toon dat dit by 'n dosent, soos by 'n goeie onderwyser, nie soseer gaan oor wat of hoe hy jou leer nie, maar oor wat hy is. Hoe skerper die stempel, hoe duideliker die afdruk.

'Ons het JC vereer en gerespekteer. Ons was trots om sy studente te wees. Ons beskou ons steeds as bevoorreg. Hy kon saam met ons koffie drink, met smaak oor sy kollegas stories vertel (hulle oor hom ook), skeidsregter speel by interklas-rugbywedstryde, saam partytjie hou by die jaarlikse afskeidsgeleentheid. Maar familiêr was ons nooit nie. Daarvoor was sy standaarde van integriteit en kwaliteit te onverbiddelik. Oor aansitterigheid en sentiment was hy genadeloos. "Mnr X," het hy in een getuigskrif geskryf, "is nie alleen dom nie. Hy is lui ook." Aldus die storie. JC sal jou vandag verseker dat die storie apokrief is, en bowendien was "X" nie dom nie.

'Hy kon dwars wees. Onmanipuleerbaar, en soms onvoorspelbaar in sy voorkeure en vooroordele. Maar dan: JC is geen gewone deursneemens nie en vir uitsonderlike mense geld die uitsondering.

'Volgens oorlewering het hy besonderhede gehou van elkeen van sy oud-studente. Ek weet dat hy meermale ver uit sy pad gegaan het om oud-studente te help, op veel meer as net akademiese gebied. Sommige van sy oud-studente het nou, onder aansporing en redakteurskap van Jeremy Gauntlett, 'n boek geproduseer onder die titel *J C NOSTER, 'n Feesbundel.* . . .

'Onder die name van die kontribuante is daar opvallende afwesiges, maar dit is nie die samesteller se skuld nie. Party was seker te besig. Ander was dalk skrikkerig dat JC sou lees wat hulle skryf. . . .

'JC het 'n grappie oor die drie betekenisvolle JC's in die geskiedenis. Professor JC van der Walt van RAU het 'n grappie oor die vier betekenisvolle JC's. Dit kwalifiseer hom reeds vir 'n plek in die bundel, al is hy nie 'n oud-student van professor De Wet nie.'

—P M Nienaber SC (now Mr Justice Nienaber, judge of appeal) in a review of *J C Noster: 'n Feesbundel* (1979) in (1980) 43 *THRHR* 333 at 333–6.

'*I was seven years and four months old when I first saw a school. It was the school of Maclear. I resented the very idea of going there and when I went, I was called "Uil". I suppose it was because I was small, even emaciated, with big eyes.*'

'An owl is *exactly* right: the measured, inexpressive stare. Johannes Christiaan de Wet sits behind his worn desk at 44 Noordwal, Stellenbosch, beneath the eclectic array of Wodehouse and Windscheid, and looks back over seventy-five years. It is all so familiar to any former student: the uncompromising house rising from the banks of the Eerste River, the sceptical voice inside, calling yet another generation of standard poodles (now William and Hadrian) to order, the welcome, and tea, in the little study upstairs, with pipes and page proofs on the desk and carpets on the chairs (whether for visitors or the dogs is never certain). It is difficult to imagine a Stellenbosch without his presence.'

—Jeremy Gauntlett 'J C de Wet at Seventy-five' 1987 *De Rebus* 581.

'JC de Wet sal egter veral voortleef in die herinneringe van sy studente. Hy was nie 'n besondere orator nie en die hedendaagse universitêre didaktici sou waarskynlik heelwat kritiek kan lewer op sy lesingstyl: sittend agter 'n tafel met 'n Westminster 85-sigaret tussen die vingers en met sy blik gerig op die punt waar die agterste klaskamermuur en die plafon bymekaar kom, het hy in 'n hoë monotoon sy voordrag gelewer. Vrae van studentekant is nie verwelkom nie. Maar die studente het aan sy lippe gehang, vasgevang deur die suiwer intellektuele krag van sy argumente en sy periodieke sardoniese tussenwerpsels. Die jaarlikse mondelinge eksamens vanaf die derde jaar was 'n verskrikking, maar van die soort waarvan jong mense hou: dit was 'n gevaar wat gesamentlik deur die klas oorleef is en waaroor nog jarelank gepraat kon word. Die styl by hierdie geleenthede was nooit dreigend of bars nie, maar wel een van totale akademiese afgetrokkenheid, afgewissel met droë opmerkings soos die legendariese: "Maar, mnr X, as u dan uit die Vrystaat kom, kan ek tog nie verwag dat u iets van die waterreg moet weet nie; daar prosedeer hulle mos nie oor water nie, hulle hou biddae vir reën."'

—A H van Wyk 'JC de Wet: Die Mens' (1991) 2 *Stell LR* 5 at 9.

SIR JOHN CARNEGIE DOVE WILSON

1865–1935. Judge of the Natal Supreme Court and Natal Provincial Division 1904–11. Judge President 1911–30. Knighted 1918.

'His ability to marshal the facts of a complicated case has, in my experience, never been equalled. He seldom reserved judgment, yet some of his extempore enunciations of legal principles are still cited as the last word. In another respect, too, I would put him at the top, namely in his ability to preside. His dignity was superb. No one ever dreamed of taking a liberty with him, but his touch was light. Never did he have to use the heavy hand. I suffered quite a few rebukes from him, which no doubt I deserved and from which I hope I profited, and he gave many judgments against me. But he would always have been my first choice of a judge before whom to appear. He was a keen golfer and fly-fisherman, and enjoyed all the good things. When news came of his untimely death after he had retired to his homeland it was my duty to represent the Bar in Court. I remember saying: "He warmed both hands before the fire of life, and the sinking of the fire found him ready to depart."

'I wish I could remember some of his *dicta* from the Bench which were current at the time. I can recall only one. He once presided at a jury trial of a man who had given evidence in his defence but who, in cross-examination, had been obliged to admit practically the whole of the Crown case against him. After the summing up a verdict of guilty seemed inevitable, but the jury acquitted him in the teeth of the evidence. Dove Wilson said to him: "You have given evidence substantially admitting your guilt. The jury have paid you the compliment of refusing to believe you. You are discharged."'

—F N Broome *Not the Whole Truth* (1962) 111.

'He was a good judge and a great judge in the making. If he had had the studious temperament he would have been a great judge.'

—Mr Justice A A R Hathorn in the *Natal Witness* 25 April 1935, cited by S D Girvin *An Evaluation of John Dove Wilson of Natal (1910–1930)* (unpublished LLM dissertation University of Natal, Durban 1987) 150.

WALFORD DOWLING

1897–1964. Member of the Pretoria Bar 1924–47. KC 1943. Judge of the Transvaal Provincial Division 1947–64. Known for insistence on the correct use of English.

'At a trial before Mr Justice Walford Dowling defence counsel—let his name be Mr Van der Merwe—had cross-examined the witnesses for the prosecution vigorously, but with scant success. Then the case for the defence began. Mr Van der Merwe: "I call the deceased." Mr Justice Dowling: "Aren't you being a little premature, Mr Van der Merwe?"'

—Ellison Kahn 'The Seven Lamps of Legal Humour Part 2' 1984 *De Rebus* 210 at 211.

'Always courteous and equable, he dealt gently with misconceived arguments by counsel that were sometimes put before him. His equanimity could be disturbed only by the mispronunciation of a word; even then, although he winced visibly, his correction was mildly administered.'

—Oscar Rathouse QC in a tribute at a special gathering of the Witwatersrand Local Division on 21 December 1965; see (1965) 82 *SALJ* 1 at 2.

GRAEME DUNCAN

1899–1979. Member of the Cape Bar 1922–70. KC 1942.

'G D was born in 1899 in Mowbray and went to Bishops. In 1916 he enrolled at the University of Cape Town but in June 1917 he went to the United Kingdom where, after an officers' training course at Berkhamstead, he was commissioned in the Dorset Regiment. September 1918 finds him in Palestine under Allenby with the Gurkha Rifles. In May 1919 he is back at UCT where, despite the break, he completed his LLB with distinction. He was admitted to the Cape Bar in January 1922 on the same day as Joseph Herbstein, Arthur Faure Williamson and Fred Silke, these four youths falling over themselves not to be Bar Junior, a position which then carried more onerous duties than today. They practised in an old building in Queen Victoria Street—without typists, tape-recorders, dictaphones or photostat machines and where the telephone was a status symbol and appearance on a sequestration earned them two guineas and they were glad to get it.

'Immediately G D showed himself an outstanding lawyer and he rapidly developed one of the finest legal brains this country has known. The law reports are studded with his appearances in matters calling for an incisive mind. Indeed, it may be said that the refinement of G D's mind is equalled only by the refinement of his character. Perhaps the cases in which his true mettle was revealed more than in any others were the constitutional conflicts of the early fifties. He then showed that, when it was necessary, he could be not only brilliant in legal argument but an indomitable fighter—and his particular force seems to have been in his reply to his opponents for which he reserved his most telling points.

'G D withdrew more and more from the stormy seas of the trial court and into motion and opinion work, and in due course he stubbornly refused all trial actions. To have G D as your opponent was an awesome experience. You knew here you had to deal not so much with the shrewd tactics of a Wally Mars or the cross-examining skill of a Bobby Bloch, but with one who, ruthlessly stripping the case of camouflage, would come cleanly and crisply to the essential weakness of your case and the essential strength of his. His argument would be backed, first, by authorities which his Bench knew from experience would never be strained to mean more than they could bear; and secondly, by his own, very individual, court manner—the slight, underplayed gesture, the dry humour, the gentle, but devastating, smile of dismissal. There is a classic purity about G's statements of the law which balances the frugality with which his facts are presented.

'His opinions have become part of the tradition of the Bar. One notices that, when a young advocate begins to lean towards chamber work on a high level, it is said of him: "So-and-So is building up a Graeme Duncan type of practice." So you see, Graeme, as Lord Sandwich gave his name to the language of the table, you have given yours to the language of the law. It is the deep regret of all that you chose not to take a permanent seat as a judge. You would have enriched the Bench as you did the Bar.'

—Gerald Gordon QC, Chairman of the Cape Bar Council, in a tribute to Graeme Duncan QC at a gathering in the Bar commonroom on 9 December 1970 (see (1971) 88 *SALJ* 9–10).

EWALD AUGUST(E) ESSELEN

1858–1918. Member of the Cape Bar 1885–6. Judge of the High Court of the South African Republic (Transvaal) 1886–90. Member of the Pretoria Bar 1890–4. State Attorney of the Transvaal 1894–5. Member of the Pretoria Bar 1895–1917. KC 1906.

He has been described as 'one of the greatest advocates South Africa has produced: he had a magnificent court presence, a charming personality, an alert and forceful mind, courage and a gift of eloquence. . . . He had the spark of genius without the solidity and dependability which would have made him a great man' (A A Roberts A South African Legal Bibliography *(1942) 359). While he was still in practice he was summed up in the* South African Law Journal *in 1906 (vol 23 p 231) as 'brilliant, versatile, impetuous, rugged, unconventional, fascinating, sympathetic, elusive'.*

'MR. EWALD ESSELEN, K.C.
'Impressing upon a doubting citizen the utter futility of endeavouring to discern even the slightest weakness in the general policy of the Botha Government'

Caricature by D C Boonzaier (1865–1950), from his Rand Faces *(1915) 27*

'George Angus Mulligan [qv] told me his favourite story of Esselen, who had a commanding presence and was the South African Lord Russell of Killowen. In a case concerned with mining claims Esselen and Jim Leonard KC [qv] were appearing before a Bench which included Wessels J in his most trying mood. At one stage Wessels leaned forward and, pointing his finger, said: "Tell me, Mr Leonard, have you considered what the Italian Commentators wrote on the subject of eminent domain?" Deathly silence, followed by Esselen's saying sotto voce, but intending to be heard by the Bench, "Jim, sê vir hom sy gat".'

—Ellison Kahn's commonplace book 28 August 1959. (Leslie Blackwell (qv) described Esselen as 'extremely Rabelaisian in his speech' (*Farewell to Parliament* (1946) 198).)

'Oswald Pirow [q v] met Ewald Esselen at the Pretoria Club at half-past nine in the morning. Esselen had already drunk three glasses of whisky and milk. When Pirow admonished him, he said "But I have to appear at ten before ——, —— and ——, and I have to bring myself down to their level!"'

—Ellison Kahn's commonplace book 11 November 1984, recounting an anecdote told him by an attorney, who was told it by an 'old friend', a judge of appeal. (See also WARD.)

BERNARD ARTHUR (SONNY) ETTLINGER

1899–1960. Member of the Johannesburg Bar 1924–60. KC 1943.

'An attorney briefed him to draft a will. Sonny Ettlinger returned the brief with these words: "My job is to taste cakes, not to bake them."'

—Ellison Kahn's commonplace book.

'Sonny Ettlinger's practice was enormous. Never one to charge high fees—his extreme moderation was at once the delight of the attorneys and the despair of his juniors—his annual income from the Bar gave no adequate reflection of the extent of his work.'

—Ellison Kahn in (1960) 77 *SALJ* 136.

The 'devil'

'There was once a junior at the Johannesburg Bar who undertook to "devil" an opinion for Jack Brink KC. But it was too much for him and so he decided—in his unorthodox way—to seek the advice of another leading silk—Sonny Ettlinger. Ettlinger gave him an hour of his valuable time and some advice. At the end of the meeting he said to him " ——, this seems to be a very complicated opinion to give to a man of your seniority". Unabashed, —— replied: "Oh no, Ettlinger, it's not my opinion: I'm devilling it for Jack Brink." And Jack Brink and Sonny Ettlinger (both racing men) were not the best of friends. Ettlinger was not amused.'

—The Hon Ramon Nigel Leon *Truth in Action* (the reminiscences of the former judge of the Natal Provincial Division, not yet completed or published).

H A FAGAN
From Q Fagan (ed) Henry Allan Fagan 1889–1963 *(1975) frontispiece*

HENRY ALLAN FAGAN

1889–1963. Professor of Law in the University of Stellenbosch 1919–20. Member of the Cape Bar 1920–38, 1939–43. KC 1927. Member of the House of Assembly 1933–43. Cabinet Minister 1938–9. Judge of the Cape Provincial Division 1943–50. Judge of Appeal 1950–7. Chief Justice 1957–9. Senator 1962–3. Playwright, novelist, short-story writer, poet, author of works on politics and other subjects.

'Chaucer said: "He is gentil that doth gentil dedis", and: "He was a verray parfit gentil knight." Henry Fagan was indeed a very perfect gentle knight.'

—Professor T J Haarhoff in *The Star* 10 December 1963.

'"Henry is such a kindhearted chap that if the devil himself dropped in for a friendly chat Henry would bring him a footrest for his cloven hooves and a peg to hang his tail on. It is instinctive with him."'

—Ellison Kahn in *Fiat Iustitia: Essays in Memory of Oliver Deneys Schreiner* (1983) 40, quoting from a letter by Oliver Schreiner to his wife, dated 24 October 1955.

'—— —— SC told me that on a car trip he said to Fagan that a certain person was evil. Fagan was shocked. "No one is evil" he protested.'

—Ellison Kahn's commonplace book 14 January 1983.

'My seun Cornelis [later regter], wat vroeër regter Fagan se registrateur was, het die volgende staaltjie van hom vertel toe hulle eenmaal op rondgang was. Dit was op Oudtshoorn, en Henry was vasbeslote om vir sy gesin as geskenk 'n volstruiseier in die hande te kry.

'Soos gebruiklik, was die koms van die rondgangregter en sy gevolg 'n gebeurtenis van groot belang en opgewondenheid vir die plaaslike magistraat, polisie, distriksgeneesheer, onderbalju, burgemeester, raadslede en algemene publiek.

'Om te verseker dat die regter sonder oponthoud die hofsaal sou bereik waar al die hoogwaardigheidsbekleërs hulle opwagting gemaak het om die verteenwoordiger van die gereg met gepaste eerbied te ontvang, is die betroubaarste verkeersbeampte op 'n groot blink motorfiets aangesê om die voorhoede te lei en te sorg dat die regter in die grootste en beste motor van die dag met spoed en sekerheid van die spoorwegstasie af die hofsaal sou bereik.

'Aanvanklik het alles met volmaakte doeltreffendheid verloop, en die stoet het groot opgang gemaak in die hoofstraat van Oudtshoorn. Maar toe gebeur die onverwagte, wat feitlik 'n ramp geword het.

'Skielik het die regter in die verbygaan in 'n winkeltjie volstruiseiers gewaar. In 'n oogwink het hy die bestuurder van die motor gevra om stil te hou. Die motor-

'ADV. H. A. FAGAN, L.V. VIR SWELLENDAM'—'PARLEMENTÊRE KOPPE DEUR RODI ROETERS' *From* Die Suiderstem *21 April 1937, reproduced in* Q. Fagan *(ed)* Henry Allan Fagan 1889–1963 *(1975) 63*

'Senator Fagan deur Bob Connolly.'
From Q Fagan (ed) Henry Allan Fagan
1889–1963 (1975) 72

fietsryer het in salige onkunde voortgery en met volmaakte stiptelikheid sy lewensbelangrike opdrag uitgevoer.

'Die gevolge was dat die groot motorfiets met gepaste rumoer by die wagtende groep van BBP's aangekom het, wat met groot vertwyfeling moes sien dat die voertuig van die rondgangregter om 'n onverklaarbare rede in die niet verdwyn het! Uiteindelik het die regter by die hofsaal opgedaag, salig onbewus van die ontsteltenis wat sy volstruiseierinkopie veroorsaak het.'

—A H Broeksma QC in Q Fagan (ed) *Henry Allan Fagan 1889–1963* (1975) 104.

CHARLES AKEN FAIRBRIDGE

1824–93. Notary, Cape Town, 1845–93; attorney, Cape Town, 1846–93. Member of the Cape House of Assembly 1854–8 and 1874–9. JP 1864. First President of the Law Society of the Cape of Good Hope 1884. Man of letters and celebrated collector of books, which are now housed in the South African Library.

'Charlie was admitted as a notary in 1845. His first Deed, dated 6 September 1845, was an Ante-nuptial Contract between John Barker, attorney, and Jane Silberbauer. His second was a Will, which includes a very useful clause which somehow has been dropped from our repertoire:

"And the Appearer having the most perfect trust and confidence in his wife the said Sarah Norton, did further declare to shut out and totally exclude from all interference with his Estate and affairs, the said Master and all other official or Magisterial or other persons who might or could otherwise by virtue of their office interfere therewith."

'What a pity this clause is no longer valid, particularly if it can be interpreted to exclude the Receiver of Revenue!

'. . . Charlie was in the habit of starting his Wills "In the name of God; Amen", possibly hoping that this would fortify his clause shutting out the Master and preventing him from interfering.'

—R M MacSymon *Fairbridge Arderne & Lawton: A History of a Cape Law Firm* (1990) 32–3.

'Mr Charles Aken Fairbridge, the senior partner of the firm, was a very able lawyer; he had been admitted as attorney so early as 1846. His failing was his

CHARLES AKEN FAIRBRIDGE

Caricature by William Howard Schröder (1852–92) from The Knobkerrie *1 September 1884*

neglect to make debits for the work he performed. To remedy this omission it was arranged that the costs clerk, a man named Duke, should keep a watchful eye on the work done by Mr Fairbridge and supply the debits. It was often said that Duke was the only man in the office who could read Mr Fairbridge's writing, which was almost illegible. On one occasion I had to brief some instructions for Counsel that had been drafted by Mr Fairbridge; I read the draft with great difficulty, but one passage I could not decipher at all; I went to Duke, who declared it was quite illegible; I then bearded the lion in his den and took it to Mr Fairbridge and desired him to read the passage; he promptly replied, "Ask Duke"; I explained that I had already submitted it to Duke, who was unable to read it; he said, "Well, if Duke can't make it out I am sure I can't"; and he left it at that; argument on such a point was undesirable and possibly unsafe, so I accepted this reply and omitted the illegible passage. He was a very popular man both in and out of the office. His hobby was his unique and large collection of South African books in his library at his Sea Point residence.'

—W H Somerset Bell *Bygone Days* (1933) 67.

RICHARD FEETHAM

1874–1965. Member of Milner's 'Kindergarten'. Deputy Town Clerk of Johannesburg 1902; Town Clerk 1903–5. Member of the Johannesburg Bar 1905–23. Member of the Transvaal Legislative Council 1907–10. MP 1915–23. KC 1919. Judge of the Transvaal Provincial Division 1923–30. Judge President of the Natal Provincial Division 1930–9. Judge of Appeal 1939–44. Chairman of a number of commissions abroad, including the Irish Boundary Commission 1924–5, the Kenya Local Government Commission 1926 and the Commission on the International Settlement of Shanghai 1929–31.

'Meanwhile peace had changed the atmosphere. We were no longer under a beneficent despot who could give us any powers we needed with a stroke of his pen. We were now under "the rule of law". It will shock readers to know that I, the Town Clerk, had not the faintest idea of what is implied by the rule of law. It began to dawn on me that a Town Clerk should know some law and though I had been called to the Bar at the Inner Temple, I had really no conception as to what the law was. So I told the Town Council that they ought to get a Town Clerk who was a trained lawyer. Their reply was that I must get a trained lawyer as Deputy Town Clerk, and left me to find one. Hichens and I then decided to send for Richard Feetham of New College, who lost no time in coming out from England.

'Roy, one of our best Councillors, afterwards told me the impression Feetham made when he first entered the Council Room dragging his feet as if his boots were made of lead. "Curtis has let us down this time," said Roy to his neighbour.

'The event was to prove otherwise. Sir William St. John Carr, the Mayor, sat alone, the Town Clerk, the Deputy Treasurer in front of him on a lower platform. When Carr had to give a ruling he leaned forward to ask me what he should say.

'This happened soon after Feetham's arrival and, with my usual light-heartedness, I suggested a ruling which the Mayor repeated to the Council. I saw a spasm pass over Feetham's learned face, and, like a frightened rabbit, asked him "What should I have said?" Feetham replied, "Well I think I should have told him something of this kind," and suggested a ruling so different from mine that I saw in a moment that he was right.

'This made me feel that the sooner I got out of the job and left it in Feetham's competent hands, the better for Johannesburg. A few days later Duncan told me that

'THE HON. RICHARD FEETHAM
JUDGE PRESIDENT, NATAL PROVIN-
CIAL DIVISION'

From (1933) 2 South African Law Times *24*

H. E. wanted me to come to Pretoria as Assistant Colonial Secretary to organise Municipal Government in Pretoria, Potchefstroom, Middleburg [sic] and the other towns of the Transvaal. I accepted at once and Feetham was appointed Town Clerk and ruled the Council with a rod of iron for several years. Sir William Anson, Warden of All Souls (who was then Minister of Education), sent him out John Dove, another New College man, as Deputy Town Clerk.'

—Lionel Curtis *With Milner in South Africa* (1951) 343–4.

'Wuthering Heights'

'Just as Graham Mackeurtan [q v] dominated the Bar when I joined it, so Richard Feetham, the Judge President, who had been promoted to this position in 1931 [actually on 1 May 1930] from being a puisne judge in the Transvaal, overshadowed his pleasant but comparatively undistinguished colleagues on the Natal Supreme Court Bench. Feetham was a man of parts. A member of Milner's Kindergarten, he had been Johannesburg's first Deputy Town Clerk under Lionel Curtis, and later served with distinction both in Parliament and at the Transvaal Bar before being elevated to the Bench. He was a sound lawyer, a brilliant classical scholar and, in his later years, a respected Chancellor of the University of the Witwatersrand, but an aloof, intolerant and cold personality. The devastating nickname of "Wuthering Heights", which Winston Churchill bestowed on the gaunt and austere Lord Reith, could with almost equal justification have been applied to Richard Feetham. We juniors appeared before him with no little trepidation, even on cast-iron undefended motion court briefs. Soon after his arrival in Natal Feetham applied himself to the task of dividing the Bar so as to bring Natal practice into conformity with that of the other provinces. . . .

'In June 1932 Feetham promulgated new Rules of Court making it obligatory for existing dual practitioners to elect within a period of five years within which branch of the profession, advocate or attorney, they would thereafter practise. Though there was general agreement (in which I shared) that an eventual division of the Bar was desirable, the dictatorial and tactless way in which Feetham handled the matter aroused bitter resentment amongst attorneys.

'The Natal Law Society decided to test the validity of Feetham's Rules of Court, and from them I now received my first big brief. In January 1936 I appeared, with P. Gordon (a Durban solicitor) as my junior, before Feetham J.P. and the full Court of the Natal Provincial Division seeking a declaration that the Rules of Court dividing the Bar were *ultra vires*. Against us were ranged Graham Mackeurtan K.C., Frank Broome K.C., and J. C. (later Mr. Justice) de Wet. The result of the case was a foregone conclusion, though I must in fairness gratefully record that both the formidable Feetham himself and my top-brass opponents treated me with heart-warming tolerance and patience as I battled for a day and a half to put my case. I had what Graham Mackeurtan once described as "a fighting case", namely one in which "you do all the fighting and the other fellow's got the case".

'When the appeal was heard in Bloemfontein, O. H. Hoexter K.C. led for the appellants, with myself this time in the silent and supporting rôle of junior counsel. From the very start of his argument, Hoexter was given a rough time, particularly by Sir John Wessels, the Chief Justice. By turns twisting his ample moustache and impatiently wagging his pencil, Sir John was most irascible. After Hoexter had battled for some twenty minutes to put over an argument which Stratford J.A., when later delivering the Court's judgment, praised for its lucidity, Wessels C.J. interrupted him, barked out two or three sentences and asked: "Is that what your argument amounts to?" On receiving an affirmative from Hoexter, the Chief Justice proceeded: "Then all I can say is that it is pretty poor stuff. Appeal dismissed. The Court will give its reasons later." Within minutes Hoexter and I sought to forget the case over a consoling game of golf.

'This was not the end of the story. O. R. Nel, the volatile, often irresponsible, but always likeable M.P. for Newcastle, who was a solicitor, sponsored a Bill in Parliament to entrench for life the rights of dual practitioners. He was seconded by myself, for though I was an advocate I did not approve a division of the Bar which operated retrospectively to deprive lawyers already in practice of their vested rights. The Government agreed to leave the Bill to the free vote of the House. . . . [H]is Bill eventually [received] the Governor-General's assent in 1939. In the same year the unpopular Feetham was promoted to the Appellate

Division, where he proved himself a better Judge of Appeal than he had been a
Judge of first instance or Judge President.'

—Leif Egeland *Bridges of Understanding* (1977) 64–6. (The Appellate Division decision
was *Ex parte Stuart; Ex parte Geerdts* 1936 AD 418. The Natal Advocates and Attorneys
Preservation of Rights Act 27 of 1939 preserved the rights to dual practice of
practitioners with those rights on 30 June 1937.)

'Sir John Dove Wilson was succeeded by Richard Feetham, who was a very
distinguished and able judge and who undoubtedly raised the standards of
judgments of his court. Later he went to the Appeal Court and I think that he is
too well known for me to add anything to that. He was the terror of the young
advocates and we all trembled when we knew we had to appear before him. I
remember on one occasion when he harried a young man on a point of law and
got him into such a state that he said "Well, my lord, that is my impression of the
law", and Feetham said "Your impression! Tell me someone else who has had
that impression and I might listen to you." I used to enjoy appearing before him
after I discovered quite early that if one stood up to him and insisted on making
one's point he would listen to one.'

—The Hon D G Fannin, former judge of the Natal Provincial Division, in his dictated
unpublished memoirs (1986) pages 2–3.

The rejected peerage

'At the memorial service for Feetham at St Mary's Cathedral, Johannesburg, on
10 November (he died in Pietermaritzburg on the 5th) I heard the Dean of
Johannesburg, the Very Rev Gonville ffrench Beytagh, say that Feetham had
been offered a peerage for his services as Chairman of the Irish Boundary
Commission, but that he had indignantly refused the offer, stating that all he had
done was his duty as a judge, and that he neither expected nor desired any reward.
I am assured by members of his family that what was said by the Dean was
perfectly correct, but that up to then it had been a closely guarded family secret.
Oddly enough, none of the newspaper reports of the memorial service mentioned
what the Dean had said. Feetham, however, did agree to become a Companion
of the Order of St Michael and St George (CMG).'

—Ellison Kahn's commonplace book. (The offer of a peerage must have been made
before 25 February 1925, for on that day the House of Assembly passed a resolution
praying the King not to confer titles on South African citizens. The only breach was the
conferring of a knighthood on Patrick Duncan in 1936 on his appointment as
Governor-General.)

GEORGE SCHREINER FINDLAY

1897–1978. Member of the Pretoria Bar 1932–71. KC 1945.

'George Schreiner Findlay, like Abou Ben Adhem, loved his fellowmen and
not only those who could reciprocate on the same social level. He thought it more
blessed to give than to receive. He was a notable humanitarian, a centre of
concern, sensitive to the inequalities and sufferings of the underprivileged, long
before the present-day awareness under the pressure of events. He had the
imagination to identify himself with deprivation, and the courage to expose
himself in doing so. Both complacency and bigotry, on whatever side they were

found, were abhorrent to him. As a social thinker and practical philosopher in the wider sense, he was on the side of *éclaircissement*, of enlightenment, and against any form of obscurantism and wishful thinking. This was perhaps a part of the Schreiner inheritance. He was sometimes formidable and could be caustic and satirical, but the root of his comments was not in a satirical nature, with an excess of salt and pepper, but in his compassion, his concern for the human condition, his large participation in *la vie humaine*.

'In less combative fields, to know him was to be aware of a singularly rich and generous nature. Even as a reformer there was a sort of Dickens-cum-Balzac in him. He was not an arid doctrinaire. His ancestry, as already suggested, no doubt played its part. On his father's side W P Schreiner, the Prime Minister of the Cape, was his great uncle and Olive Schreiner his great aunt, and on his mother's side Eugène Marais was his great uncle. Such antecedents may partly account for not only his humanitarianism, but his interest in the broad aspects of science, psychology and philosophy, archaeology and pre-history, as well as in poetry, literature and the arts, music, architecture and especially painting. A visitor to his and Molly's home was soon aware of their delightful and discriminating collection of pictures. George also gave much time and attention to the encouragement of drama. He was a great traveller and knew and loved every inch of this country, and saw much of other countries. He had an eye for place and scenery; with his open mind he was accessible to "daylight and champaign", in Shakepeare's lovely phrase. He found the world interesting and beautiful and wanted to enjoy it.

'Though he had a reputation as a radical, there was a powerful conservative element in his character. It found expression in personal and family history, the Findlay family having been established in South Africa for over 170 years. George treasured every letter and document about the family, and his greatest single hobby may be said to have been the family archive. He was a Pretorian of Pretorians. . . . Like W S Landor, he lived a long and distinguished life, and had a sort of Roman dignity; with all his concern for the underdog he had a certain patrician quality with his fine features and measured utterance. He had a Roman sturdiness along with his Greek clarity. Let me quote one of Landor's epigrams and see how far it fits George. "I strove with none, for none was worth my strife." No, this line does not describe George Findlay or Landor himself. They were both contention-tossed, and Landor was irascible enough to throw his cook out of the window, exclaiming afterwards, "Heavens! I forgot the violets!" I cannot imagine George treating a servant in this manner.'

—Tribute paid at the graveside by Professor R M Titlestad. See 'In Memoriam: George Schreiner Findlay QC' (1978) 95 *SALJ* 415 at 419–20.

JAMES COLEMAN FITZPATRICK

1816–80. Judge of British Kaffraria 1861–5. Judge of the Eastern Districts Court 1865–9. Judge of the Cape Supreme Court 1869–79. Wit. Devout Roman Catholic. Father of Sir Percy FitzPatrick, politician, author of the classic, *Jock of the Bushveld*. (When written or printed in lower case, the surname should have a capital 'P': FitzPatrick. See Dr Cicely Niven, daughter of Sir Percy and granddaughter of the judge, *Jock and Fitz* (1968) and in *Standard Encyclopaedia of Southern Africa* IV (1971) 561; Sir Percy FitzPatrick *South African Memories* (1932; revised edition 1979); J P R Wallis *Fitz: The Story of Sir Percy FitzPatrick* (1955); A P Cartwright *The First South African: The Life and Times of Sir Percy FitzPatrick* (1971); Andrew Duminy & Bill Grier *Interfering in Politics: A Biography of Sir Percy FitzPatrick* (1987). But in the law reports of the Cape Colony, in the *Dictionary of South African Biography* and commonly a small 'p' is used.)

'Funeral expenses in advance'

'It was somewhere about the year 1856 that he accepted the position of Chief Justice of the Gold Coast. The office was one which it was not easy to suitably fill, as the place had a most evil name for health and native troubles. There was no known remedy for the fever; almost every official sent out had died there; and many months elapsed before a successor could be found for the previous Chief Justice (the court was a one-judge court, and the judge was called Chief Justice). The Minister for the Colonies was so delighted when Fitzpatrick accepted the office, and so nervous lest the new Chief Justice might withdraw, that he lavished civilities and did not say more than he could help against the climate. He did not know that Fitzpatrick saw through the "little game," and was rather taken aback when, in reply to his last note asking if there was not *anything* else he could do, he received the request—"a not unreasonable request, in view of my predecessors' experiences, that you should allow me *my funeral expenses* in advance." After that they understood one another.

'He went to the Gold Coast in H.M.S. *Polyphemus.* It is a noteworthy fact that on this voyage was taken out the first consignment ever sent to Africa of a "new remedy" for fever, known then as "bark of Peru" or "Peruvian Bark"—our good friend "quinine." The ship took out a full complement of officials to replace, or relieve, or help those who had died or were expected to die. It is said there were thirteen all told. . . . Before the year was up Fitzpatrick was the *only one alive!*

'It is doubtful how many officials there were at the Gold Coast in those days, but the time came when Fitzpatrick was the only white one living or efficient. The Governor having died, he became Acting Governor, and it is remembered his saying—perhaps with slight joking exaggeration, or possibly referring to brief intervals—that he was Governor, Chief Justice, Colonial Secretary, Commander of the Forces, Marriage Officer and Postmaster, with only coloured staffs and a few white traders to help him.'

—Anon 'The Late Hon. James Coleman Fitzpatrick' (1904) 21 *SALJ* 89 at 90–1.

'He could be very witty on the Bench, and never lost an appropriate opportunity for displaying this faculty. Many anecdotes are told of the learned judge's propensity for fun and humour, at the display of which, when sitting in the Supreme Court, his colleague Denyssen always looked most solemn and austere. . . . Counsel having moved for provisional judgment with interest at the rate of 60 per cent., the judge said, "Call the defendant; I should like to see that man." While the name of the defendant was being called counsel informed the judge that he would withdraw the case, as he was just instructed to say that since the issue of summons the defendant had died; "And I don't wonder at it," was the ready reply from the Bench. Once on provisional day in the Supreme Court a certain case was called on for provisional judgment. Counsel, having several briefs to confess judgment, was not quite sure whether he appeared in the particular case called. He rose and in a halting manner said, "My lords, I appear to confess"; upon which Fitzpatrick, J., remarked, "I would advise you to be very careful. It is quite true that some confessions bring about absolution, but a confession of this kind brings down judgment absolute upon you at once." When Dwyer, J., [q v] was moved from the Eastern Districts' Court to Capetown he insisted on having the room till then occupied by Fitzpatrick, J., on the plea that this room was assigned to the Junior Puisne Judge, and as Fitzpatrick, J., had now become the Senior Puisne Judge on the retirement of Denyssen, he should move to the room till then occupied by the latter. This room was in a less convenient situation, and some distance away from the library. Fitzpatrick was not inclined to make any change, and finally disposed of Dwyer's request by jocosely saying, "Ah, I understand, brother Dwyer, you wish to be near the library, and I am sure you need it."'

—'The Late Hon. James Coleman Fitzpatrick' (1904) 21 *SALJ* 89 at 93–4.

FitzPatrick's behaviour on the Bench was the basis of a leading case on contempt of court, In re Neethling *(1874) 5 Buch 133. A letter had been published in the* Cape Argus, *written by a layman, M L Neethling, a member of the Cape Legislative Council, complaining of comments in that newspaper on his conduct in a legal action. The letter was held to constitute contempt of court. It ran: 'Had not Mr. Justice Fitzpatrick, with his wonted humour or abandon, given unrestrained license to his tongue, you would not have ventured to indulge in such intemperate language.' But often FitzPatrick would be amusing, as the following extract shows.*

'*Barkis is willin*''

'On another occasion an action was being tried as to the boundary between two farms. In the original grant the boundary was described as "a direct line" between two points: the diagram attached to the grant showed a meandering stream. It was near one o'clock when J., Attorney-General and Counsel for the plaintiff, bent down and from underneath the Bar table produced a whole armful of ponderous volumes.

'"And what are all those books for, Mr. Attorney?" asked Fitzpatrick in an inquisitive frame of mind.

'"Those, Me Lud," came in bland tones from Counsel, who was weak on principles but very strong on precedent, "are dictionaries."

'"But what for?" persisted the Judge in his inimitable brogue.

'"I am going to quote them on the question of what is a direct line."

'"Well, Mr. Attorney," said the Judge, "if it's the maning of a direct loine that ye want, just ye look at me, for I'm going in a direct loine to me lunch!"—and he went.

'In a suit involving the ownership of a cock ostrich which had strayed from his camp, the Judge was evidently puzzled at the constant references to the red legs of the bird.

'"What is the point," asked the Judge of a witness, "of your always talking of his red legs?"

'"It shows, My Lord," explained the expert in some surprise that all the knowledge in the world was not confined to an ostrich camp, "that it was the mating season."

'"Now, is that so," ejaculated Fitzpatrick, J., "I always thought that an ostrich was like Barkis."'

—Sir Henry Juta KC *Reminiscences of the Western Circuit* (1912) 74–5.

In 1878 a Select Committee of the Cape House of Assembly inquired into FitzPatrick's fitness and capacity to discharge the functions of a judge—the only inquiry of its kind in the history of South Africa. In 228 pages of evidence attached to the report of the Select Committee (A.6–'78) are to be found some splendid flights of oratory, replete with biting sarcasm and probing irony, by FitzPatrick in his defence. The Select Committee was a powerful one, including Thomas Upington A–G, Saul Solomon, J W Sauer and A F S Maasdorp (the future Chief Justice of the Orange Free State). Most of the charges (including all those alleging insobriety) were by unanimous vote found not to have been established. For FitzPatrick "twas a famous victory', but he did not celebrate it for long, as he died the next year just before the time he had decided to retire. The passages printed below come from Ellison Kahn 'The Trials and Tribulations of Mr Justice FitzPatrick' (1958) 75 SALJ 428–33.

'Colonel G. Dean Pitt: "I have never seen him in a state of drunkenness; in the army we have one term, 'drunk or not drunk'. I have never seen the judge drunk" (p. 145).'

'On the charge of insobriety, after dealing with the witnesses he [FitzPatrick] made the following comments on the behaviour of Maasdorp (pp. 212–13):

"What then prompted the prosecutor to make this unwarrantable assertion? Could it be that the honourable and learned member for Graaff-Reinet was, as a barrister on circuit, occasionally my guest, and that my unreserved bearing and unaffected enjoyment of social intercourse was too much for him? I plead guilty to the enjoyment of the society of my friends (or those whom, for the time, I believed to be my friends) after the labours of the day; and it may be that some guest, more straightlaced and abstemious than myself, has seen occasion to note in his diary that evening something like this: 'Dined with the judge this evening. A dozen or so to dinner; spent a pleasant evening; good dinner; good company; some music, &c., &c., but the judge enjoys himself too much. *This must be remembered. . . .*' I remember reading of a barrister who enjoyed the hospitality of a judge on circuit, and, when after long years he had occasion to allude in open court to those social reunions, he did not do so with the view of founding on them an unwarrantable charge against the judge, or supporting false accusations. No, he alluded to them to call up holy memories and ennobling reflections on scenes gone by. He alluded to those social evenings spent with the great judge, whom he then addressed, as his *noctes ambrosianae* for, said he,

We spent them not in toys or lust of wine;
　　But search of deep philosophy;
　　Wit, eloquence and poesy;
　Arts which I loved, for they, my friend, were thine.
But we live in a more practical age. . . ."

'And later (p. 217):

"The prosecutor extracted from one of the witnesses that some village gossip said, 'Maasdorp is a bold fellow to bring those charges'. I deny that emphatically. I say, on the contrary, that he and those who acted with him rather played the part of cowardly assassins. They have played with loaded dice. Their motto was 'get rid of him'; they said to themselves, 'we shall bring these charges against him; if we succeed in proving them he must go; but even if we do not, he is old and ailing, and the strain of his defence will kill him.' 'We shall have the vacancy all the same.''' '

—(On FitzPatrick, see also MELIUS DE VILLIERS.)

CHARLES JAMES GARDNER

1883–1963. Member of the Eastern Districts Bar 1907–44. KC 1927. Judge of the Eastern Districts Local Division 1944–9. Judge President 1949–53.

'Towards the end of his career on the Bench he became very deaf—almost certainly a legacy of his war service as an artillery man in World War I—but he found a hearing-aid irksome and of little use. An unkind critic when asked "Who's hearing the appeals today?" replied "I don't know, but Charlie Gardner's on the Bench." On one occasion when he was presiding in the Motion Court, Ken Graham appeared before him on behalf of the plaintiff in an action for divorce.

'"I am happy to inform your Lordship," said Graham, "that the parties have become reconciled. I therefore do not ask for a final order, and the matter may be struck off the roll."

'"You may take a final order of divorce, Mr Graham," said the Judge.

'"Your Lordship has misunderstood me. I am not asking for a final order," replied Graham.

'"I said you may *take* a final order," snapped the Judge. It took the combined efforts of Graham and the Registrar to explain the situation. "Well, why didn't you *say* so, Mr Graham?" demanded the Judge irritably.'

—George Randell *Bench and Bar of the Eastern Cape* (1985) 61. (See also HALL; KOTZÉ.)

ISRAEL GOLDBLATT

1897–1982. Member of the South West Africa Bar 1920–70. KC 1934.

Goldblatt is describing his earliest days in South West Africa.

'Prosecutions were under the control of a Crown Prosecutor, and it was as a clerk in his office that I was appointed—at £25 per month plus free quarters and rations (1s 6d per day)—in March 1918 from the Cape provincial administration.

'I replaced a sergeant of the military forces. In one of his files I came across a letter sent by him to the Director of Prisons, enclosing a death warrant "for favour of execution".'

—I Goldblatt 'Early South West Africa—Bench and Bar' (1977) 94 *SALJ* 490 at 492.

Goldblatt is on his way to South West Africa to join the Bar there, the judge of the territory being Gutsche J (qv).

'I left Cape Town by train at night in November 1919. No sooner had I got into bed than the door of my compartment opened and a liquored voice boomed, "Is there a fellow named Goldblatt in this compartment?" No reply.

'Then again, after a switching on of the lights, "Is there a fellow named Goldblatt in this compartment?"

'"Yes, I am Goldblatt."

'"You Goldblatt? You Goldblatt? Gold, jou ou bliksem, gee jou hand, I have been looking for you all over in Cape Town. Come and have a drink with me in the saloon."

'My youthful twenty-two years were overwhelmed. I got up and followed him to the saloon, where we had a couple of drinks for which I found I had to pay out of my very meagre resources—I only had a little cash and a letter to the Standard Bank by the famed C J Langenhoven guaranteeing an overdraft of £60.

'We were the first advocates to come to the Territory and Roché [Pohl] took me under his wing.

'We stayed at the best and the most expensive hotel, the Rheinischerhof Hotel, for three days, when we found it advisable to transfer to the cheapest hotel, the Stadt Windhoek Hotel.

'Roché spent the next few days enquiring as to the prospects of litigation, of deceased estates and of impending divorces etc.

'After he had satisfied himself, he told me that there would be a lot of work to be settled by our court, and what about the fees?

'I told him that I had brought with me a scale of fees arranged with [R P B] Davis [q v], based upon the Cape fees.

'"No, Gold, old chap", said Roché, "that will not do. We cannot allow these good people to fornicate at our expense."

'My scale of fees, however, remained. . . .

'The two of us were objects of curiosity to the German community.

'"Who are these two men?"

'The answer was given by a wit: "Der einer had noch keine Streitsache gefuehrt und der anderer hat alle seine verloren." (The one has not yet had any cases and the other one has lost all his.)

'At the suggestion of Gutsche I parted company with Pohl.'

—Goldblatt op cit at 494–5.

'Soon afterwards there arrived from the Transvaal Louis Oxley Pyemont— Pyemont of *Pyemont's Company Law* fame. He was about 70 years old, had practised in Ceylon, then gone to England, and came out to the Cape Attorney-General's Office, where he stayed for a short while. Then he migrated to the Transvaal Bar, where he did not make any mark, and now he came to join us here.

'A fine old gentleman looking a bit like an old Viking past his prime.

'He was not very elegantly dressed and went about dangling a "Springbok" brand tobacco bag from his hand.

'It was a matter of great curiosity to us to know when he would be able to light a pipe, because the front portion of the pipe had been burned away and when Pyemont assiduously tried to fill the pipe the tobacco would fall out. Oblivious of this fact, he would try to light the pipe, but it would not function. Then he saw the position and filled the pipe again, with the same results.

'A stickler for the proprieties and professional ethics, he also knew that a false quantity in a Latin quotation was a more heinous crime than rape.

'He was not without wit. On one occasion, as three of us were sitting in the Zoo Café opposite our chambers, drinking tea, Roché Pohl came up. He wanted to borrow one shilling and three pence for a telegram he wished to send off. It so happened that this was also the price of a whisky and soda. But he got it. Then he thought of indulging in a pleasantry, and said to Pyemont, who was a shortish man and took short rapid steps, "Pye, tell me, how many miles do you walk in a day?" "That depends", said Pyemont, "on how many poles make one rood."'

—Goldblatt op cit at 495–6. (A rood was a Dutch linear measure equal to 12.396 feet (3.78 metres), formerly used in South Africa; it also means 40 square poles (a quarter acre); a pole is a rod, a perch = $5\frac{1}{2}$ yards.)

'Soon afterwards R W R Toms came up from the Cape Bar to practise here. He was a genial Irishman, short and stocky. Because of his shock of black curly hair he was known, particularly among the Germans, as "Karakul" (the black karakul sheep, called "the black diamonds of South West Africa").

'Toms was regarded in his earlier days at the Bar in the Cape as a man of promise. Unfortunately, through his inability to withstand the charms of the fair sex he involved himself in financial difficulties.

'After he had arrived, he said to me in the robing-room: "Do you know, Goldblatt, there is a lot of money to be made here, but you have to work for it." Unfortunately, Toms did not work for it.

'Shortly before he arrived his wife sued him for divorce, the case being reported in the newspapers which arrived here. In that case the court had laid down a novel doctrine, namely that a spouse on divorce can claim maintenance from her husband (*Toms v Toms* 1920 CPD 455). Poor Toms! He had to pay this maintenance and that of his children from the divorced wife. Then soon after his arrival he was married to a divorcee who had children prior to her divorce, and he and his new wife had further children of their own.

'The sad thing was that Toms was engaged in a local divorce action in which his client was claiming maintenance from her husband, the defendant, and Toms had to rely upon *Toms v Toms* for his authority. To cap it all, *Toms v Toms* was later dissented from in the Union courts and ceased to be an authority.

'He, too, had a ready wit. In a case in which I opposed him he was making heavy weather with the judge. I passed him a note, "de minimis non curat lex", which I translated "the court takes no notice of little fellows". Instantly he wrote back to me, "You may have length but you have no breadth."'

—Goldblatt op cit at 496. ('Goldblatt' is German for 'gold leaf'.)

Goldblatt is discussing his pro deo defence of Jacobus Christian on a charge of treason arising out of the rebellion of the Bondelswart tribe in 1923. Christian was convicted; the Appellate Division upheld the conviction: R v Christian 1924 AD 101.

ISRAEL GOLDBLATT QC

Charcoal sketch by Fritz Krampe, dated 1958. Reproduced by kind permission of Mrs Naomi Jacobson, daughter of the late Israel Goldblatt

'After sentence had been pronounced a policeman informed me that Jacobus Christian's wife wished to speak to me. I went outside, and this dignified woman, unlettered and a member of a backward tribe, thanked me for undertaking the defence of her husband without a fee. She knew this because the judge had mentioned it when delivering his verdict.

'I mention this case because of the conduct of Jacobus Christian's wife, something that had never happened to me before and was never to happen to me since, although I appeared in numerous *pro deo* cases, for Blacks and some Whites.'

—I Goldblatt 'Early South West Africa—Bench and Bar' (1978) 95 *SALJ* 120 at 122–3.

Diamond cases

'An account of the development of the administration of justice could not omit a reference to diamond cases.

'South West Africa was known for its diamonds. The Consolidated Diamond Mines Company was world famous. The various German companies, Kolmanskop, Pomona and others, had been taken over by the Consolidated. A large area along the coast had been withdrawn from prospecting by the general public and reserved for the company. Lüderitzbucht (now Lüderitz) was the focal point of the diamond industry and the seat of the company until the discovery of new fields at the Orange River mouth, where, at Oranjemund, all activities passed to that region. Illicit diamond dealing flourished and the place where the deals took place was Keetmanshoop.

'The case of *R v Smith* possessed strange elements. The charge was one of robbery.

'A man in a Keetmanshoop hotel was approached by a native who said he had diamonds in his possession which he had acquired at the Orange River fields. As for obvious reasons no dealings took place in rooms, it was arranged that the diamonds would be handed over in the open veld at night and the money, some thousands of pounds, would be paid. The native was employed for the purpose by Bob Smith, an old and experienced illicit diamond dealer.

'At the time and place arranged and with the aid of an electric torch the deal was concluded. The diamonds were transferred and the money paid.

'There was a dramatic side to the affair.

'Feeling that the native might not carry out instructions or might double-cross him, Bob Smith, after warning him that he (Smith) would be hiding behind a nearby rock watching him, took up his stance behind the rock with his revolver trained on the native. In the final result Smith got the money.

'When the purchaser got to his hotel he tested the diamonds and found them all to be "schlenters" (paste diamonds).

'He was violently sick. His money was gone.

'He brought the police in, but dared not come out with the truth, that he had been defrauded in an illicit diamond transaction; so he trumped up a cock-and-bull story that he had been robbed.

'Bok J was on the Bench, on circuit at Keetmanshoop. L C Steyn [q v], then Attorney-General, and later Chief Justice of South Africa, prosecuted.

'It was not difficult to obtain an acquittal.

'During an adjournment of the proceedings in court I had tea with Bob Smith. I assured him that he would be acquitted, but in an avuncular manner—he was twenty years older than I—I asked him why he continued with this sort of thing: he would surely be found out sooner or later. His genial reply was: "Would you like me to get you a parcel?"'

—I Goldblatt 'Early South West Africa—Bench and Bar' (1978) 95 *SALJ* 260 at 265–6.

'Another case which aroused much interest was that of certain Cape Town owners of an aeroplane who employed two men to fly to a lonely part of the coast in the reserved area to pick up a bottle of diamonds that had been secreted at a certain place by an accomplice, who had previously been in the service of the Consolidated Diamond Mines. The plane landed successfully, but in somewhat soft sand, about fifty yards from the bottle. Fearing that they might have difficulty in taking off, they managed to ease the plane and made a trial run. This time one of the wings was buried in the sand, and it became impossible to take off again. So there they were within fifty yards of the treasure, able to acquire it but unable to take it away.

'Ultimately the police found them and they were prosecuted at Lüderitz in the circuit court. Junior counsel acting for the accused was J H Steyn, now a judge of the Cape Provincial Division.

'I was briefed by the Consolidated Diamond Mines to obtain a court order that the plane should be handed over to them or at least not be returned to the owners. Their object was to have every part of the plane examined and destroyed in case diamonds were secreted there.

'We got the order. The head of Consolidated Diamond Mines at Lüderitz made the comment: "What rotten luck to be so near success and yet so far."

'In sentencing the accused, the judge adopted, as he told me afterwards, a novel method. The value of the diamonds was known. So he decided upon a ratio of so many months to so many pounds.

'Now this question of a proper sentence had for years been a subject of interest to me. I had acted on the Bench and found that it was easier to decide upon the question of guilt than upon the sentence.

'What is there to go on? Does the judge appreciate the difference between a sentence of imprisonment for, say, five years and seven years? Does he know what solitary confinement means or suffering lashes? The unfortunate prisoner certainly does.

'I came to the conclusion that the only solution was that, for a judge to be able to appreciate the real nature of the punishment he was inflicting, he should previously have undergone it himself. And in discussing this matter with a judge, I went further and suggested that this principle should apply also when a sentence of death by hanging has to be passed.'

—Goldblatt op cit at 266. (On Goldblatt, see also VAN DEN HEEVER.)

SIR THOMAS LYNEDOCH GRAHAM

1860–1940. Member of the Cape Bar 1885–98. QC 1898. Member of the Cape Legislative Council 1898–1904. Member of the Cape Cabinet 1898, 1900–4. Judge of the Eastern Districts Court and Eastern Cape Local Division 1904–13. Judge President 1913–37. Knighted 1913.

'Gas lighting was installed in the new building [the Supreme Court in

'Hon. T. L. Graham, K.C.,
'Colonial Secretary.'
'OUR TOM'
SIR THOMAS GRAHAM WHEN HE
WAS A MEMBER OF THE CAPE
CABINET 1898–1904

*Caricature by D C Boonzaier (1865–1950),
from his* Owlographs: A Collection of South
African Celebrities in Caricature *(1902) 11
(For another caricature by Boonzaier, see*
B UPINGTON)

Grahamstown in 1912] and became such a part of the daily lives of the judges and court personnel that with the advent of electricity a change to electric lighting and heating was refused. The story goes, however, that during a trial presided over by Sir Thomas Graham, the Judge President, a peculiar, offensive smell pervaded the court, and grew worse as the proceedings went on. When the judge enquired as to the cause of the peculiar smell, counsel retorted, "Yes, my Lord, we noticed it even before your Lordship came in this morning". The Judge President then adjourned the court stood up to leave the bench, stumbled, and fell. It was then discovered that the unpleasant smell was caused by the sole of his shoe burning on the gas heater under the bench. Electric lighting and heating followed without delay. The magnificent bronze gas chandeliers, their gas-taps still intact today, were wired for electricity and are still in use.

'The electric heaters provided for the court are also in tube form and are situated under the bench at a convenient height to serve as a footrest. A certain judge, unaware that the heater was switched on, rested his feet on the tubes until the soles of his shoes began to char. As did his predecessor with the gas, he inquired into the source of the unpleasant smell, and counsel promptly replied, "My Lord, it must be your Lordship's feet".'

—N E Wiehahn 'The Eastern Cape Division of the Supreme Court of South Africa' (1968) 9(2) *Codicillus* 24 at 26.

LEOPOLD GREENBERG

1885–1964. Attorney 1909–11. Member of the Johannesburg Bar 1911–24. KC 1924. Judge of the Transvaal Provincial Division 1924–38. Judge President 1938–43. Judge of Appeal 1943–55. Known as Lippe (Lippy). Famed for his mordant wit.

Greenbergiana

'"We come to brother Lippo for all that,
Iste perfecit opus!"'
—Browning *Fra Lippo Lippi*.

'To be a really good judge demands many gifts, rarely combined in one person. It has been said that above all things a judge must be a gentleman, and this is doubtless true if the word "gentleman" be used in its proper sense and not taken to mean merely one who mistakes form for morals. And another requirement is a sense of humour, i.e. a power of analysis and the instinct to realize the incongruous. Both these gifts Mr. Justice Greenberg undoubtedly has. His whole judicial career shows the former: of the latter there are many stories current, of which I venture to tell one. In a jury trial in which he was the judge, the evidence of guilt was clear, and it contained no suggestion that the accused was *non compos mentis*; nevertheless the foreman announced the unanimous verdict of the jury to be "not guilty". Observing a look of surprise on the judge's face, he added hastily, "on account of insanity". "What, all nine of you?" asked the judge.'

—G A Mulligan (qv) 'Retirement of the Hon. Mr. Justice Greenberg' (1955) 72 *SALJ* 1 at 1–2.

'For the benefit of counsel in a case he once said: "An affidavit is a recital of facts, not an imaginative literary effort."'

—*The Star* 18 May 1953.

'Leaning forward ever so slightly as he speaks, his face more solemn than ever, Mr. Justice Greenberg periodically delivers these devastating ironies, and over the years there has now been amassed a whole collection of Greenbergiana.

'Let me quote just a few items from this rare and exciting collection.

'Counsel was arguing the amount of damages to which his client was entitled as a result of the loss of some cattle. Of a certain cow, counsel said its value should be assessed more highly "because it was in an interesting condition."

'Mr. Justice Greenberg leaned forward slightly, his voice soft and low. "Interesting to whom?" he said. I need hardly say that from then on counsel was more careful in his choice of clichés.

'In the trial of Mrs. Daisy de Melker, Mr. Harry Morris, K.C., was examining the accused who, it will be recalled, was charged with the murder of her son.

'"Was your son a member of the 'X' Cricket Club?" asked Mr Morris. On receiving the answer "Yes," he then put his next question, which contained an obvious slip. He said:

'"Before or after his death?"

'Whereupon Mr. Justice Greenberg interposed: "I thought this was a local club, Mr. Morris."

'Years ago in Johannesburg we had a rather woolly, moth-eaten barrister, who did not have much idea of what was going on. Let's call him Mr. X. On one occasion he appeared in the divorce court, on behalf of a Mrs. Smith. When the registrar called "Smith v. Smith," Mr. X assumed it must be his case. Peering shortsightedly through his glasses at the plaintiff, his examination went as follows:

'Is your name Muriel Johanna Smith?—No.

'Were you married at Johannesburg on December 15, 1923?—No.

'Is your husband permanently employed on the Railways?—No.

'At which stage Mr. Justice Greenberg intervened: "I'm going to suggest to you, Mr. X, that you take a short adjournment in order to become reconciled with your client."

'Fairly recently, in the Appeal Court, counsel was arguing the tricky question of how much (if anything) could be divulged of what went on in a jury room while the jury were deliberating. Legal authority was needed, and counsel said: "The first authority, I wish to quote to your lordships is an English case of 1423."

'Judge Greenberg leaned forward (ever so slightly). "A.D. or B.C.?" he asked.

'One more item—from the Transvaal Provincial Division. For four days a particularly tenacious counsel had argued his case. He wound up: "For these reasons I submit the appeal should be allowed."

'Greenberg, J.: What reasons?'

—Joel Mervis 'Wit and Humour of Mr. Justice Greenberg' *Rand Daily Mail* 25 June 1954. (See also L O MILLER; H H (HARRY) MORRIS; SAUL SOLOMON.)

'Many of the present judges and senior counsel appeared before him. Some of them suffered the gentle lash of his wit and irony.

'There was the occasion when the Motion Court was sitting and an advocate . . . instead of making a submission told Mr. Justice Greenberg that he "agreed".

'Taking off his glasses, Greenberg J. leaned forward and said quietly: "Mr. So-and-So, it is submission that interests me. Your agreement will interest me when you sit on the Bench with me."'

—David Rider in the obituary in *The Star* 15 September 1964.

'Judge C. S. Margo . . . recalled an incident when a certain witness, giving evidence at a trial presided over by Judge Greenberg, turned to the judge and said:

"May the Almighty strike me dead if I am telling a lie."

'Allowing a pause to pass, Judge Greenberg said: "Until there is a suitable response to this invitation, we have no choice but to proceed with the case."'

—*South African Jewish Times* 13 September 1978. (Maule J, Victorian English judge, responded similarly. So, too, Baron Alderson; see J R Lewis *The Victorian Bar* (1982) 14.)

'The old bugger'

'It was a boring case. It was afternoon. It was hot in court. Greenberg J sat, as usual, immobile. His hands were in front of his face, the tips of the fingers of each hand touching the tips of the fingers of the other hand.

'"Archie" Shacksnovis QC [q v] to his junior, in a whisper, his right hand in front of his lips: "The old bugger has fallen asleep.'

'Greenberg J: "No, he hasn't. Please carry on, Mr Shacksnovis."

—Ellison Kahn's commonplace book. A true story.

'The story is told of an exchange at the Bloemfontein Club between Greenberg and a Free State attorney who was a

'GREENBERG, J.'
From (1932) 1 South African Law Times *168*

Nationalist member of Parliament. As an MP, the attorney was a member of the High Court of Parliament, which in terms of the High Court of Parliament Act 1952 had to sit in review of any Appellate Division decision invalidating an instrument purporting to be and enrolled as an Act of Parliament. (The members of the High Court of Parliament were the members of the two Houses of Parliament.) When this body was about to sit in Pretoria, the attorney came up to the "old guard" of judges of appeal, who were having tea at the Club, and asked them whether he should wear his attorney's gown for the occasion or perhaps something else. To which Greenberg replied "What about a cap and bells?"'

    —Ellison Kahn's commonplace book 20 July 1983, from a letter sent to him by Mr Justice ——. (*Collins Dictionary of the English Language* 2 ed (1986) 233: '**Cap and bells** *n.* the traditional garb of a court jester, including a cap with bells attached to it.')

'Mr W P Schutz SC, of the Johannesburg Bar, has kindly given me a photocopy of a letter sent by Mr Justice Leopold Greenberg to Mr F B ("Fritz") Adler, who was then (as he was for many years) the reporter for the Witwatersrand Local Division reports. The letter was given to Mr Schutz by Mr Paul Adler, the son of Fritz Adler, who in later life was often referred to as Brigadier Adler (he had a distinguished career in the armed forces in both World Wars). The writing has been authenticated by Mr I A Maisels QC as being that of Mr Justice Greenberg. Mr Maisels says that it is a typical Greenberg letter. It reads:

"P.O. Box 442.   Judges' Chambers,
                               Supreme Court of South Africa
                               (Transvaal Provincial Division)
                               Pretoria.
                               2/9/29

"Dear Fritz,

    May I utter a small protest against the proofreading in the last issue of the Reports. In Schlesinger v. Donaldson (1929 W.L.D.) at p. 57 the report reads 'his length'—the original judgment filed in court says 'this length'. At p. 61 'patient' in the judgment has been reported as 'patent'; and at p. 62 (4th last line) the report would be slightly less nonsensical if after the word 'argument' the words 'to an extent' which appear in the judgment had not been omitted from the report.

    I am finding it increasingly difficult to support all the things I have actually said in the course of judgments, but if I am also called upon to justify what I have not said, the burden will be more than I can bear.

                               Yours sincerely,
                               Leo Greenberg."

'The passages involved are: Page 57: "I am not prepared, however, to go his [should be: this] length." Page 61: "With regard to the rights to the claims, there is also the point raised by Mr *Millin* that the deeds of sale by respondents of the various portions of the farm which respondents invoke as proving that they disposed of these claims are patent [should be: patient] of the construction that these claims . . . were not included in the deeds of sale." ("Patient . . . 2. . . . b. Of words, writings, etc.: Capable of bearing or admitting of (a particular interpretation)": the *Oxford English Dictionary*. As Mr Schutz writes, "an elegant and correct phrase has been garbled".) Page 62: "With regard to costs I do not think that the issues on which applicant has failed prolonged the argument [add: to an extent] which could be reflected on taxation. . . ."

'The case of *Schlesinger v Donaldson* ended Part I of the 1929 WLD reports. Part II contained a red slip headed "ERRATA", pointing out the mistakes.'

—Ellison Kahn in (1986) 103 *SALJ* 486.

Greenberg was a stickler for compliance with the Rules of Court. If the papers were not in order, counsel and the attorney were to rue the day.

'——, a retired SC, told me that he used to visit Greenberg after the judge had retired. Greenberg was very mellow and pleasant. He said that he was not really aware that he had been a terror to counsel, that he used to tear into them if the papers were not in order or if they deviated from the Rules of Court in the slightest. But once he had an inkling of his reputation. In the motion court in the Witwatersrand Local Division at the last moment he had to act as the substitute for a judge who had been taken ill. Counsel were not given notice of the replacement. Into court stepped Greenberg's registrar. Certain counsel blanched. One went up to the registrar and asked "Is your judge sitting?" "Yes." "Oh, God!" The registrar reported the reaction to Greenberg. Greenberg told ——, "Now I come to think of it, it seems that I was not very welcome".'

—Ellison Kahn's commonplace book 22 February 1979. (See also SUTTON.)

No hard feelings

'Greenberg told the guests at a dinner party that he once bumped into a man in Bree Street, when both were trying to avoid pedestrians. The man greeted Greenberg warmly and started conversing with him. Greenberg, puzzled, said to him: "You know, I have met you before, but I cannot quite place you." "Oh", came the reply, "I once appeared before you." Greenberg, rather surprised, said: "It was a civil case, I suppose." "Oh, no. It was a criminal case." "And what happened?" "You gave me three years." For once somewhat taken aback, Greenberg said: "Well, better luck next time."

'Greenberg also told the guests that far from people he had sentenced in criminal cases holding anything against him, on several occasions he had had to go to his front door at a persistent knocking, only to find someone he had sent to gaol who now wished to borrow money from him.'

—Ellison Kahn's commonplace book 10 May 1958. (See also COLE.)

The Schreiners on Greenberg

'This evening to the Haymans and afterwards with the Greenbergs to the Orpheum [theatre]. A really bad show. . . . But it did one's heart good to hear Leopold laughing at a couple of very ordinary variety patter artists. He fairly let himself go. It is strange, because to ordinary humans he is not very receptive—he gives a dry, self-contained smile. But a clown touches the spot every time. It must do him a lot of good.'

—Oliver Deneys Schreiner (q v) in a letter to his wife Edna, 20 January 1930. Schreiner family papers.

'How did the "horses" case proceed? It must have made matters more difficult for you to have Leopold's cold, unsympathetic eye fixed on your client's antics. Couldn't you tickle up his sense of humour a bit by reading out some of the choicier passages?'

—Edna Schreiner in a letter to her husband Oliver (q v), 2 May 1930. Schreiner family papers.

'When Rammy joins us things will go more easily. Leopold is of course a tower of strength. He is always ready for work and does it all with the smooth efficiency of an accurate machine.'

—Oliver Deneys Schreiner (q v) in a letter to his wife Edna, 14 August 1938. Schreiner family papers.

'I think Leopold is happy and enjoying himself. It is a great comfort to have him to go to for advice. . . . Leopold has just been talking over a point and now we are going to stroll [from the Club to court] together. You would be amused to see us with our little old men's ways—all very pleasant but funny too.'

—Oliver Deneys Schreiner (q v) in a letter to his wife Edna, 14 March 1945. Schreiner family papers.

Summing-up

'When Ludorf was elevated to the Bench some 17 years ago, Greenberg gave him some timely advice. The newly appointed Judge was advised to give his judgments immediately after he heard a case "if you can do so immediately, and if you wish to avoid having your judgments upset on appeal".

'On one occasion, Greenberg told Ludorf that when he was himself "a young Judge", he hardly ever reserved his judgments, with the result that his judgments were seldom upset on appeal to Bloemfontein.

'"But as I grew older," Greenberg told him, "I reserved my judgments more often, with the result that I found they were being upset now and again on appeal."'

—Isaac Goodman *Judges I have Known* (1969) 40–1. (See also GUTSCHE.)

'Greenberg's approach was "The result is Gilbertian, but it is the law"; Schreiner's approach "The result is Gilbertian; it cannot be the law".'

—Arthur Suzman (q v) in Ellison Kahn (ed) *Fiat Iustitia: Essays in Memory of Oliver Deneys Schreiner* (1983) 133.

REINHOLD GREGOROWSKI

1856–1922. Member of the Cape Bar 1878–81. Judge of the High Court of the Orange Free State 1881–92. State Attorney of the Orange Free State 1892–4. Member of the Orange Free State legal profession 1894–6. Judge of the High Court of the South African Republic (Transvaal) 1896–7. State Attorney of the South African Republic 1897–8. Chief Justice of the South African Republic 1898–1900. Member of the Pretoria Bar 1902–13. Judge of the Transvaal Provincial Division 1913–22.

He presided at the celebrated trial of the 'Reformers' in April 1896 after the Jameson Raid, at which four of the accused were sentenced to death for high treason. (Their sentences were commuted.) Today it is accepted that the criticism levelled at Gregorowski that he had made up his mind in advance to find the accused guilty was unfounded.

'[W H Somerset] Bell [editor of the *Cape Law Journal*; q v] believed that he and the others of the small fry in the Jameson Raid prosecution had been unjustly convicted and sentenced. In 1900 a scathing article appeared in the *Cape Law Journal* (not written by Bell, and actually toned down by him) ['Mr Justice Gregorowski and the Reform Trial' (1900) 17 *Cape LJ* 164], accusing the presiding judge, Mr Justice Gregorowski, of having decided in advance to find the accused guilty. The article was confessedly based on a book by Percy FitzPatrick [*The Transvaal from Within* (1899)], who had been one of the small fry. The anonymous writer made a cheap jibe at the judge's forbears having come from "Russian-Poland". (He could have gone further back, and pointed out that Gregorowski was the Polish version of the name of the distant founder of the family, a wandering Scot by the name of McGregor.) Gregorowski was challenged to reply. Gregorowski replied. He denied the allegations, going into extraordinarily personal details and saying that he had always had sympathy with the Reformers and their complaints. Of FitzPatrick, using a nice biblical allusion, Gregorowski said that "the truth is not in him".'

—Ellison Kahn 'The Birth and Life of the *South African Law Journal*' (1983) 100 *SALJ* 594 at 599–600.

'As soon as it was known that Sir William Smith had sent in his resignation two aspirants dashed off to interview J. B. M. Hertzog, the Minister of Justice, to represent their claims. They were Reinhold Gregorowski, the ex-Chief Justice, who had a leading practice at the Pretoria Bar (the juniors loudly and bitterly complained that he even took unopposed applications, and thus deprived them of their rightful perquisites), and F. W. Beyers, then Attorney-General of the Transvaal. Abraham Fischer, one of the Ministers, who hailed from the Free State, was strongly opposed to Gregorowski's appointment because Gregorowski had not treated his wife too kindly. However, Hertzog thought that Gregorowski's claims, by reason of his previous judicial experience, could not be passed over, and Gregorowski won. Gregorowski had very conservative ideas about the rights and position of women. One night he was dining at our house, and we opined that the law should be altered, so as to give a wife the right to succeed *ab intestato* to her husband (this has since been done). Gregorowski was entirely against this. A woman had no right to any of her husband's property. She must be wholly dependent on him; had no right to any separate property; and must take what, if anything, he was pleased to give her. He was even opposed to marriage settlements on the wife.'

—Manfred Nathan *Not Heaven Itself: An Autobiography* (1944) 210.

'We were always very friendly. I remember addressing a jury before him. My address was (to my mind) a masterpiece of invective, sarcasm and scorn. When the learned Judge summed up to the jury I heard my address come back to me like an echo. But what is a little plagiarism between friends? Between the two of us we got the accused off.'

—H H Morris KC *The First Forty Years* (1948) 59. (See also WESSELS.)

'MR. JUSTICE IVON GRINDLEY-FERRIS.'

From (1933) 2 South African Law Times *115*

IVON GRINDLEY-FERRIS

1876–1957. Member of the Pretoria Bar 1902–31. KC 1922. Judge President of the Natal Native High Court 1931–3. Judge of the Transvaal Provincial Division 1933–46.

'Gradually building up a substantial practice, he took silk in 1922. Two years later he began travelling the most protracted and circuitous route ever taken to reach the South African judiciary: acting judge in South West Africa for six months in 1924; acting judge in the Transvaal for a year from March 1927; acting judge in South West Africa from April to October 1928; acting judge in the Natal Native High Court (which only tried Blacks accused of crimes) for a few weeks towards the end of 1929; president of the Special Court for Income Tax Appeals in March and April 1930; acting judge in Natal from 1.5.1930 to 18.1.1931; and Judge President of the Native High Court from 19.1.1931 to 14.2.1933. Finally on 15.2.1933 he was appointed to a vacancy on the Transvaal judiciary, where he remained until he reached seventy, the age of retirement. After this he acted on occasion on the Transvaal Bench and the High Court of the High Commission Territories.

'G.-F. proved a competent trial judge; the pugnacious tilt of his jaw and his appearance of inscrutable reserve hid an innate courtesy and kindness to counsel. He was not one of those judges who insist that papers be absolutely in order, and, particularly in motion court, advocates were happy to appear before him. But he was not in love with the law. Its intricacies, its development, the solution of its vexed questions—these had little intellectual appeal for him and, especially towards the end of his judicial career, his judgments tended to be perfunctory. The most striking illustration is the case of *Davidson v. Plewman NO* 1946 WLD 196. Here, after full argument by counsel on the then very controversial question whether marriages by proxy were permissible (the law has since been changed to prohibit them), G.-F., without giving any reasons, ordered a magistrate to solemnize such a union. The basis of the law remained obscure, but the ruling had to be observed by his brethren on the Bench, for they could not find that it was clearly wrong.

'At one time G.-F. was a scratch golfer; in later years he tended to forget that that time had passed.'

—Ellison Kahn in *Dictionary of South African Biography* V (1987) 306. (See also H H (HARRY) MORRIS.)

HUGO GROTIUS (DE GROOT)

1583–1645. Advocaat-fiscaal of Holland, Zeeland and Friesland 1607–13. Pensionaris of Rotterdam 1613–18. Imprisoned 1619–21. Ambassador of Sweden to France 1635–45. One of the greatest jurists of all time.

'In 1613 Grotius was appointed pensionaris of Rotterdam, essentially the town clerk, who represented that city in the Staten of Holland; he became prominent in politics and in the Arminian cause. All his life he was a pious man of moderate views.

'The Arminians were in a minority in the country as a whole. The only provinces to have a majority in their favour were Holland and Utrecht. A dispute was raging on whether the Staten-Generaal was entitled to control religious belief, at the expense of the staten of the provinces. Civil war threatened, with the possible breakup of the Union. Maurits, who cared not a fig for either religious party, was concerned to achieve national unity before the end of the truce with Spain, and naturally lacked sympathy for the Arminians, so opposed to a hereditary sovereign with personal power. The upshot was the arrest of Oldenbarneveldt and Grotius in August 1618 through a dirty piece of deception. A special tribunal was convened, a type of kangaroo court. Conviction of the accused had been prearranged. The shameful consequence was the conviction of Oldenbarneveldt of treason and his execution on 13 May 1619. He was 71 years old. Probably it was felt that this had done the trick, for on 18 May Grotius was sentenced merely to life imprisonment with forfeiture of his estate, the formal verdict of guilty of treason and other crimes being pronounced only over a year later.

'On 6 June off went Grotius from detention in the Binnenhof to incarceration in the ancient castle of Loevestein (Loevenstein), almost two miles from Gorkum, South Holland. There he wrote a good deal, despite long bouts of illness, on religion and literature; but most important of all, he drafted his immortal *Inleidinge tot de Hollandsche Rechtsgeleertheyd*. His wife and children were allowed to stay with him. For exercise he spun a huge top every day. Books were permitted to be taken to him. They were brought and returned in a chest, not four feet long, which was also used to take laundry to and from Gorkum. After a while the guards stopped inspecting its contents. Maria then arranged with friends in Gorkum for her husband's historic escape, part of Dutch folklore. On 22 March 1621 Grotius, clad in his undergarments, wedged himself in the chest. Maria locked it, drew the curtain around Grotius's bed, and put his outer clothes on a chair. Soldiers, accompanied by the Grotius's brave maid, carried their burden, one remarking to Maria that it was so heavy that there must be an Arminian in it; to which came the reply "These are Arminian books". The chest reached Gorkum safely. Finally Grotius, clad as a mason, replete with hod, trowel and measuring-rod, escaped to friendly Antwerp.

'Maria Grotius confessed her complicity in the plan, but on 7 April she was released. There is a possibility that the authorities, if not actually silent parties to the escape, were deliberately careless in the custody of their prisoner. They did not give him an official exit permit, a one-way ticket, as is the modern practice; but then there are also illustrations today of deliberate laxity in supervision to allow a troublesome person to quit a country.'

—Ellison Kahn 'Hugo Grotius 10 April 1583–29 August 1645' (1983) 100 *SALJ* 192 at 195–6.

HUGO GROTIUS AT THE AGE OF 15

Engraving by Jacques de Gheyn 1599. Grotius is wearing the neck-chain with the medallion representing Henry IV of France, which was presented to him by the king when he accompanied Jan van Oldenbarneveldt in the virtually abortive mission in 1598 to persuade Henry IV to maintain support for the Dutch against the Spanish.

'From December 1631 to April 1632 Grotius was in Amsterdam, where he conducted a thriving opinion practice.

'But the Staten-General ordered his arrest, and in April Grotius left Amsterdam. Towards the end of the year he arrived in Hamburg. There a chance meeting led to his appointment in 1634 by Axel Oxenstierna, the eminent Chancellor of Sweden, as ambassador of the young Queen Christina to the Court of Louis XIII of France. For ten years Grotius held that post, becoming a Swedish national. He was in an awkward position, as Richelieu disliked him, but in any event was not disposed to be particularly friendly to Sweden. Grotius, honest man, devoid of guile, incorruptible, was no match for the wily Richelieu. "In politics he was neither a strategist nor a tactician", wrote R W Lee ("Hugo Grotius: 1583–1645" (1946) 62 *LQR* 53 at 56) in describing Grotius's character. "He did not look ahead, or weigh the consequences of his acts. It is said of him that he was born a man. It might be said that he remained a boy. He was not always happy in his contacts with individuals. Men of affairs were inclined to distrust him. He was too much of a talker." This evaluation seems unduly harsh. No doubt, he was not the same man after Loevestein, no more than was Sherlock Holmes after he, locked in the arms of Professor Moriarty, "the Napoleon of crime", had apparently fallen to his death down the Reichenbach Falls. Still, the qualities Lee saw in him in an earlier evaluation (*Hugo Grotius* (1930) 45) must have remained in large measure: serenity, energy, industriousness, cheerfulness, friendliness, accessibility and benevolence. The published letters of Grotius show throughout an admirable absence of bigotry, a desire for unity in Christendom, and candour, truthfulness and an absence of recrimination. His *De Jure Belli ac Pacis* is permeated by his personal horror of war, especially a religious war.'

—Kahn op cit at 197–8.

'In 1645, affronted by the appointment of a self-seeking tuft-hunter as virtually his equal as ambassador, Grotius requested his recall [as ambassador to France]. In Stockholm Queen Christina wished to appoint him Counsellor of State, but Grotius was determined to go, despite his poor state of health. What he had in mind to do remains a mystery. He set sail for Lübeck. A great storm forced the vessel, with a broken mast, to put in on the eastern coast of Pomerania. In an open wagon, en route for Lübeck, Grotius, very ill, could get no further than 60 miles, to reach Rostock in Mecklenburg, 80 miles from his destination. There, two days later, at midnight on 28–9 August 1645, he died. He was only 62. Though it is apocryphal, the popular belief is that his last words were the pathetic "By undertaking many things, I have accomplished nothing".'

—Kahn op cit at 198. (See also LEE.)

CLEMENS GUTSCHE

1876–1947. Member of the Cape Bar 1904–20. Judge of the High Court of South West Africa 1920–30. Judge of the Eastern Districts Local Division 1930–46.

'The judge was Clemens Gutsche, an advocate of the Cape Bar, who during the First World War was colonel in command of the Table Bay defences, and had been appointed as the first judge of the newly constituted High Court of South West Africa. . . .

'The High Court was opened on 6 January in the Hall of the Tintenpalast ("Ink Palace", as the Government buildings were known), which had previously housed the Landesrat. It was an impressive ceremony.

'The court-room was filled with intending practitioners and members of the public. The judge was sworn in by the Administrator, Sir Howard Gorges, who thereupon left, and first the advocates, and then the attorneys, were duly admitted to practise.

Mr Justice Gutsche sporting a wig and hiding his hairless pate—'he had a head as bald as a billiard ball'.

Photograph from (1980) 1(2) Codicillus 21

'To the surprise of all of us, Gutsche appeared in a wig, something that had been discarded long before by the Union judges. One theory was that he wished to impress the German community; another theory was that he wished to impress the natives. But the probability is that he wore the wig because he had a head as bald as a billiard ball.'

—I Goldblatt (qv) 'Early South West Africa—Bench and Bar' (1977) 94 *SALJ* 490 at 491, 493.

'Gutsche had an excellent sense of the aesthetic value of the English language. One felt one could die happy in the knowledge that he would on the following court-day pronounce the appropriate encomium.'

—Goldblatt op cit at 498.

'It was not necessary for him to give heed to the advice of Advocate L E Benjamin KC, leader of the Cape Bar, at the send-off given to Gutsche when he was appointed to the South West Bench. "Do not reserve judgment—you will probably be wrong. Give your judgment right away—you will probably be right."

'By sheer necessity Gutsche found himself delivering his judgments extempore—there was simply no time for reserving them. And the truth of Benjamin's advice is shown by the fact that only once was a decision of Gutsche's reversed by the Appellate Division. True, very few cases went on appeal, but this merely indicated the confidence that the public and practitioners had in his decisions.

'Mention should, however, be made of one instance where Gutsche did reserve judgment. The case involved German law and he was not sure that his tentative conclusion, which would have ruined one of the parties, was correct. So he reserved judgment, hoping that the divine afflatus would descend upon him. After nine months had elapsed the Registrar of the High Court received a letter from one of the attorneys in the case, who had previously come into conflict with the court and heartily disliked Gutsche, to the effect that the parties had got tired of waiting for his lordship to make up his mind and had settled the matter. "And a jolly good thing, too" was Gutsche's comment.'

—Goldblatt loc cit. (See also GREENBERG.)

'The commencement of criminal sessions was a bit of a show business. Gutsche's chambers were at the end of a large courtyard. In order to get to the court-room he had to walk along one side of the courtyard, thereafter along the side at right angles to it and finally into the building proper and into the court-room. Gutsche favoured the ceremonial side of justice. When the criminal sessions were on there was a procession from his chambers. First came a gentleman with a white staff, then came the senior member of the court, then Gutsche in his scarlet robes and full-bottomed wig, which made him look like "Judge Jeffreys" of the "Bloody Assizes", and at the rear the other members of the court. To the admiring gaze of the clerks in the Administration, who watched through the windows, the procession marched along in the open with great dignity, a distance of about fifty yards, until it disappeared into the interior.

'The courtyard also witnessed other events. On one occasion there was an offensive smell detectable in the court-room. Inspection into the source of the disturbance disclosed that the municipal lorry, which carried about twenty full sanitary buckets (a proper sanitation system was not yet in operation), had overturned. The court (Gutsche J) adjourned.

'In addition to the wig, Gutsche in criminal sessions invoked a practice which, if not already done away with in the Union, was destined to disappear soon thereafter—the wearing of the black cap when the death sentence was passed. When the court was about to reappear after considering the verdict and sentence in a murder case, the usher would come in and arrange the papers on the judge's desk. Counsel for the accused would look up to see whether he carried the judge's large note-book, for this was where the black cap was hidden. Then we knew what was going to happen. If the book was not carried you could hear a sigh of relief.

'I have already referred to his aloofness. When A J Werth became Administrator of the Territory in 1926 some wit adapted the old tag to the new situation:

"The people of Windhoek, South West
Have habits, peculiar and odd,
For the Werths only talk to the Gutsches,
And the Gutsches talk only to God."

'After some time, however, Gutsche allowed himself a relaxation. He was fond of racing, and indeed owned a very good horse which served him for ordinary riding purposes. He was persuaded to function as a judge at race meetings and he was as efficient in that capacity as he was a judge in court, being careful there, too, not to reserve his judgments. He entered his own horse for events, but in such cases he recused himself.

'This was the only bit of ease he permitted himself. But his aloofness did not prevent him from beating the prosecutor, defence counsel and the attorneys, by a short head, in acquiring a magnificent set of copper anklets worn by a female Herero accused in a criminal case.'

—I Goldblatt 'Early South West Africa—Bench and Bar (1978) 95 *SALJ* 120 at 120–1. (See also INNES.)

'About 1923 there was a ball in aid of some cause. The administrator, Gysbert Reitz Hofmeyr, and the judge, Clemens Gutsche, sat in different parts of the hall together with their wives. During the evening the Administrator sent his private secretary to the Gutsches' table to invite Mrs Gutsche to dance with the Administrator. Gutsche, in his iciest best, said: "Tell his honour that if he wants to dance with my wife he will have to come and ask her himself."

'They did not dance and a feud developed between the executive and judicial arms of the State.

'We were divided into Montagues and Capulets. The Bar sided with Gutsche. The breach persisted right until the termination of Hofmeyr's period of office at the end of March 1926.'

—I Goldblatt op cit at 262.

HERMAN ROBERT HAHLO

1905–85. Temporary Assistant Lecturer in Law, University of the Witwatersrand, Johannesburg, 1940–5; Senior Lecturer in Law 1945–6; Professor of Law 1946–68. Director of the Institute of Comparative and Foreign Law (later the Institute of International and Comparative Law), McGill University, Canada, 1968–77. (Called 'Bobby'.)

'In about 1937 he came one Sunday to tea at my parents' home. It so happened that a farmer friend had brought us four very young lion cubs, which were taking milk from babies' milk bottles held by my sister and me. This was an extraordinary experience for me, but my sister's nonchalance convinced Bobby that it was an everyday occurrence in our home. There are some photographs somewhere of Bobby cuddling a lion cub on our lawn.

'Years later, after World War II, I heard that Bobby, in the course of his lectures on the law of persons, told his classes of a certain minor, a student at Wits, who had lived with his parents in Johannesburg. The minor, without his father's consent, had contrived to acquire a camel from the South West Africa Police when they disbanded their camel patrol. The camel was railed to Johannesburg. The minor, regardless of the attendant risks, especially that of third-party liability, was determined to ride the beast to the University and tether it outside the Central Block while he attended lectures. Bobby explained to his classes the respective legal positions of the minor and of the father in these circumstances.

'This story, as it had reached Bobby, was an exaggeration and embellishment of the facts, but he was disposed to accept its authenticity, for had not he himself seen lion cubs in the said minor's home?

'A year or two ago I was having a drink with Professor Jim Gower, in London. Puffing at his pipe, Jim asked gently: "Was it not you who rode to lectures on an elephant or a dromedary or some such beast?" "Bobby again!" I thought, with a wave of affection.'

—Mr Justice Cecil S Margo 'Bobby Hahlo: Some Personal Reminiscences' (1984) 101 *SALJ* 419 at 420.

'Bobby's approach as a lecturer had always compelled attention by his students. I give one example. After the War, the Wits Law Faculty presented a refresher course for ex-servicemen who had returned to or who had commenced legal practice. Bobby lectured to us on the law of persons. Referring to *Benade v Benade* 1944 TPD 15, a case in which the plaintiff wife had sued for a restitution order on the ground of constructive malicious desertion, Bobby's comment, in his dry and precisely articulated speech, was something like this: "At one stage in the marital relationship the defendant attempted to murder his wife, and from this it was argued that there was a deliberate and settled intention to terminate further cohabitation between them. This argument, like the attempted murder, did not succeed, and so the plaintiff's endeavour to end the marriage was as much a failure as her earlier efforts to preserve it."'

—Mr Justice Cecil S Margo loc cit.

'I am afraid that so far I may have given an impression that Bobby's style of life was one of all work and no play. Actually, his superior ability left him with sufficient leisure to enjoy a pleasant social life. He is a most entertaining conversationalist and raconteur. He and his wife Hanna formed an accomplished host and hostess couple. Moreover, Bobby was a dedicated Rotarian.

'As to physical exercise ("mens sana in corpore sano" might have been written for him), horse-riding was his regular Sunday sport. A characteristic gesture of Bobby's may be mentioned in this context. When his horse Nelson reached the age of retirement Bobby provided him with a permanent home on a Free State farm. Until Nelson's death in 1976, Bobby, when visiting South Africa, always went to the farm to meet his beloved horse and friend.'

—J E Scholtens 'First Meeting and Lasting Impressions' (1984) 101 *SALJ* 421.

'Professor Hahlo did not deliver his lectures in a formal way. Without lecture notes he would pace up and down the room, bringing the law to life for his students. His lectures were dynamic and compelling, but most notable was the clarity with which he explained even the most complex of legal principles. He had the wonderful gift of keeping his students entertained and totally absorbed in the subject. Professor Hahlo cannot be described as a tall man, yet to his students he was a person of immense stature.

'In Professor Hahlo's classes students were regularly called upon to answer questions on reading that had been prescribed in the previous lecture. Students seldom came to lectures unprepared because somehow Professor Hahlo knew when a student had not done his work. Perhaps it was the way that these students tried to avoid the professor's sharp, formidable gaze that gave them away.

'A few years ago I was reminded of Professor Hahlo's lectures when I saw a film entitled *The Paper Chase*. The professor enacted by John Houseman bore not only a striking physical resemblance to Professor Hahlo but also shared with him many of his most endearing traits as a lecturer: his air of eminent authority, his humour, his intellectual power.

'The students loved and enjoyed Professor Hahlo's unique sense of humour. In impeccable English, with his distinctive accent, he could portray the most ordinary domestic scene with a touch of irony that would imprint the scene, and the legal principle that was being taught, in the minds of the students. I am sure that all who attended Professor Hahlo's Law of Persons course will recall the story of the husband and wife who were enjoying their breakfast together one morning when the messenger of the court arrived with a summons for the husband. Said the wife lovingly to her husband, "Darling, I am suing you for delictual damages".'

—Louise A Tager 'A Student's Memories' (1984) 101 *SALJ* 422.

'In its first phase our relationship was one of teacher and student. It began in 1953, when I enrolled for the LLB degree. I sat at his feet for three successive years (in those days the minimum period of study). My approach to law must have pleased him, for somehow I managed to persuade him that I was worth a first-class pass each time I presented myself for his examination—though others of the faculty were not always as perceptive. To call Hahlo a much-loved mentor would be mendacious. No Mr Chips he. Outside the classroom he presented a forbidding image, a voluntary visit to whose office was almost as unthinkable as a voluntary visit to the dentist. Perhaps this was just his way of ensuring that students did not waste his time. If so, it certainly worked. In the classroom, on the other hand, he revealed his participation in the human race. While his systematic expositions and crystal-clear explanations educated us, his wry humour—always in that inimitable (though much imitated) accent—amused us. Some students were misguided enough to think that Hahlo made law *too* simple, that he glossed over difficulties. I did not then agree; nor do I now. Those critics did not appreciate that Hahlo taught *principles*, letting the details take care of themselves. With him there was never the danger of missing the wood for the trees—a trap that other, less talented teachers are prey to. There is no virtue in making one's subject appear difficult; the art of teaching demands the reverse. . . .

'It was [after I joined the staff] that I learned many things. Though his academic and administrative commitments were heavy, Hahlo was unstinting with his time, help and advice. Whatever I wrote would disappear into his unpretentious cardboard suitcase (he needed no "executive-type" briefcase to seem erudite), to reappear without fail the next morning—no matter how many pages in length—complete with his pencilled comments. Then would come the summons to the big office. We would sit down together and go through my work, Hahlo criticizing (and sometimes praising), I defending and explaining my arguments. Interruptions might come—sometimes from very senior quarters of the university. Hahlo would give advice on matters of state, and then return to my fledgling attempts at legal writing. Usually it would end—an hour or more later—with my realizing that I had not expressed myself clearly enough. Hahlo tried to pass on to me some of his own remarkable talent for self-expression. I shall always be grateful for that.

'Time passed. We worked together. Sometimes we quarrelled a little, but never too much—Hahlo was far too clever for that. Once he said to me: "Paul, why are you so aggressive? It must be because your father was a policeman!"'

—P Q R Boberg 'Bobby Hahlo—Mentor, Preceptor, Leader' (1984) 101 *SALJ* 423 at 423–4. (Professor Paul Boberg's father was Colonel Ulf Boberg, who had been a retired member of the South African Police.)

'He tended to be the proverbial candid friend: a role that occasionally gives pain but in his case was meant for the best and almost always was valuable to the listener. Sometimes—unduly sensitive person that I am—I whispered to myself the words of George Canning, "Save me, oh, save me, from the candid friend". But his frankness in conveying not only his own views but the views of others on my many faults of character and performance I later saw helped me to become a better, though still far from ideal, person. . . .

'As I walk along the corridors of the Central Block of my university, where we spent so many years in a kind of partnership, he the senior member, I feel as though his shade were palpable. It was long ago, and yet it is as though it were yesterday: such was his presence, such was his personality. There I see him now, his hand darting forward in his characteristic way to shake my hand, his voice welcoming me warmly in its never-to-be-forgotten mid-Continental accent. . . .'

—Ellison Kahn 'In Memoriam: Herman Robert Hahlo' (1985) 102 *SALJ* 573 at 575, 578.

CYRIL GODFREY HALL

1886–1979. Civil servant. Attorney. Member of the Cape Bar 1922–49. KC 1944. Judge of the Cape Provincial Division 1949–55. Judge of Appeal 1955–6. Judge President of the High Court of South West Africa 1958–60. Editor of the *South African Law Journal* 1943–9. Legal writer.

'After his retirement from the Bench of South West Africa Hall acted as a judge in the Cape Provincial Division on various occasions in 1963, 1964, 1965 and 1966. By then he had become rather deaf. When counsel spoke in a normal voice Hall would frequently say querulously in his markedly un-South African accent: "What's that? What's that?" When counsel then raised his voice Hall was wont to say: "Don't shout at me!"'

—Ellison Kahn 'The Birth and Life of the *South African Law Journal* (1983) 100 *SALJ* 594 at 608. ('Foxy' Hall was born in Cumberland, and came to South Africa after completing his schooling in England.) (See also GARDNER.)

HAROLD JOSEPH HANSON

1904–73. Member of the Johannesburg Bar 1926–73. KC 1946.

'"Mr Hanson, you have put that question ten times already", remarked his Lordship with a petulant pout.

'"Yes, M'Lord," boomed Hanson in reply, "and I shall put it fifteen times if my case requires it."

'Perhaps you haven't the personality of the late Harold Hanson QC (and the incident occurred before he took silk) but you can profit by his example.

'He was probably right in his attitude towards the court, because the relevant consideration is not always how many times a question is put. What is relevant is how many different answers it elicits.'

—Eric Morris (qv) *Technique in Litigation* 3 ed (1985) 215.

'He . . . had a sense of humour. Once he told me ruefully that at the time when "Blackie" Swart was carrying out his policy of appointments to the Bench, he said ironically to a colleague at the Bar (I have changed the name) "Willy, they will soon choose you too!"—and they did.'

—Ellison Kahn 'The Jewish Contribution to the Law and Legal Practice in Johannesburg, 1886–1986' *Jewish Affairs* July 1986 p 32 at p 39.

WALTER HARDING

1813–74. Magistrate 'for all Natal' 1846–55. Acting Recorder, Natal, 1855–7. Recorder 1857–8. Chief Justice of Natal 1858–74.

'On 15 April 1858, the Lieutenant-Governor forwarded the appropriate Letters Patent of appointment to Harding. Thus emerged the highly anomalous situation that Natal's first Chief Justice was a man who had never attended a university, passed a legal examination or been admitted in his own right to the legal profession.'

—Peter Robert Spiller *The Natal Supreme Court: Its Origins (1846–1858) and Its Early Development (1858–1874)* (unpublished PhD thesis University of Natal 1982) 109.

'On one level, he tried to compensate for his limitations by assuming an air of pomposity. . . . He dressed in ostentatious robes of pink and blue silk (A Lady "Life at Natal" (1872) 5 *Cape Monthly Magazine* 113). . . . The Times of Natal described Harding, in his curious costume, as having "very much the appearance of a Chinese mandarin sitting in judgment" (*Times* 24/12/1873).'

—Spiller op cit at 119.

'An impression of the man can be gathered from the anonymous contribution "Life at Natal"—"By a Lady"—in (1872) 5 *Cape Monthly Magazine* 105 at 112–13, where, referring to the opening of the Legislative Council on 18 May, 1865, by the new Lieutenant-Governor, "dear" Colonel Maclean, "wretchedly ill" and "woefully shaky", the writer says: "Two of his attendant functionaries struck me with amazement and dismay. One was the Chief Justice, whose massive bulk was swathed in a marvellous garment made of pink and blue silk, like a huge pinafore." (The other, "a very small man", "a great man in his way", was Shepstone.)'

—Ellison Kahn in (1970) 87 *SALJ* 366. (See also CONNOR.)

In 1859 the Colonial Office raised the possibility of Harding CJ receiving a knighthood. Lieutenant-Governor Scott said he would canvass the views of Harding. Harding was very eager to receive the honour. Unfortunately for him, a change of government in Britain brought Newcastle to the Colonial Office. He was advised that Sir George Grey, Governor of the Cape, had expressed surprise 'that Mr Harding was ever appointed Chief Justice of Natal', and that he had been honoured enough. Harding pleaded in vain in 1860 and 1864 for reconsideration.

'Thus, the Chief Justice of Natal lived and died, plain "Mr Harding": a title more appropriate to his true abilities and character.'

—Spiller op cit at 129.

'Directing my glance last of all to the greatest of all gods, the divine Brahma himself, I was advised by some of my friends to use a glass smoked with the fumes of presumption, lest the great power and dazzling brilliancy of this resplendent *Numen* should totally overpower my weak nerves. Following this advice, and disregarding the perturbations caused by him in his celestial neighbours, and the effects produced by him on the tides of an adjacent pond, I perceived a personage whose gross and vulgar aspect, and rude and overbearing manners, bespoke a being of coarse material, cast in one of nature's roughest moulds. Contemplating him more narrowly, I found him possessed of large but casual experience, rather than of sound or systematic knowledge, to be clever rather than talented, cunning rather than wise, expert rather than judicious, ready rather than prepared, and cruelly severe rather than compassionately just. By a succession of adroit expedients he has succeeded (as he thinks) in keeping well both with the fates that rule the heavens and the simple mortals in whose public opinion appearances go far as substitutes for realities.

'So great a deity, dwelling in the tranquil ether of Nieban, is popularly supposed to be insensible to the human emotions of love or hatred, favour or dislike—an idea probably as correct as many other popular notions about religion; but it is possible that his passions never betrayed his prudence, and that he never openly attempted to repel an enemy or to crush a victim, till he had looked well around and ascertained that the sufferer was friendless, humble, helpless, and forlorn. In short, he has (to use Thersites' words) the "eye of dog, and heart of deer". In his earlier career his satellites were found among the lowest, not to say the most degraded dependants around him, nor could his subsequent association with some of the refined and polished of the upper regions ever assimilate his behaviour, even in appearance, to theirs.'

> —Thomas Phipson (under the pseudonym of 'Clio') in *The Natal Witness* 14 August 1863, reprinted in R N Currey *Letters and Other Writings of a Natal Sheriff: Thomas Phipson 1815–76* (1968) 98.

JAMES BARRY MUNNIK HERTZOG

1866–1943. Member of the Pretoria Bar 1893–5. Judge of the High Court of the Orange Free State 1895–9. Member of the Orange River Colony Bar 1910–12. Minister of Justice 1910–12. Member of the Orange Free State Bar 1912–24. Prime Minister of the Union of South Africa 1924–39.

'Advokaat Smuts was baie sterk filosofies aangelê, 'n man met 'n verbasend vlugge begrip—'n hongerige leser wat veel boeke deurgewerk en baie geassimileer het. Advokaat Hertzog was die stadige geleerde, wat noukeurig, met potloodstrepe en aantekeninge, 'n boek deurwerk, alles bepeins, om, as dit hom getref het, dit dan oor 'n rukkie weer na te gaan. So het hy, met tussenpose van jare soms, 'n beskouende werk oor die fisika agt keer sorgvuldig deurgelees.

'Die meer subtiele regsvrae het hom lewendig geboei. Ou, stewige regsboeke, met hulle harde, geel leer-buitebande, kon hy met 'n toewyding en vreugde sit en lees asof dit 'n roman is. Na ontspanningsleesstof het hy selde of ooit gekyk, maar naas sy studie van die reg het hy wysgerige werke ter hand geneem met dieselfde nougesette toewyding wat hy al sy studie aangepak het. Hy was die regte akademiese tipe, en sy begeerte was om hoogleraar in die regsgeleerdheid te word. . . . As hy 'n saak opsom, wou hy graag, met inagneming van die kleinste besonderhede, die geheel so duidelik as moontlik laat ontwikkel. Hy het nie dadelik op die kernpunt afgevlieg en daarop bly hamer nie. Stadig, soos iemand wat 'n trop skape na die kraal aanja en nou hierdie dan daardie klomp aandruk totdat almal by die hek in is, so het hy sy argumente byeengebring, op 'n wyse wat vir sy vlot kollegas soms vervelend was; hy kon nie sy toevlug neem tot geestelike ratsheid, woordspelinge, onverwagte knope en koddige buitelinge nie; sy aanleg was anders. As hy egter sy saak gestel het, baie omslagtig en breedvoerig uitgewerk, kon niemand twyfel aan wat hy presies wil nie. . . .

'Regter Hertzog het natuurlik 'n skraal ervaring as advokaat gehad toe hy op die regbank aangestel is, maar hy het hierdie tekort aan praktiese ervaring probeer vergoed deur studie, deur 'n regskennis wat 'n groot draagwydte het; as wetenskaplik opgeleide man het hy by vanself-sprekend sy gees in dié rigting van ewewigtige oordeel en strenge regverdigheid laat gaan. . . .

'Hierdie tydperk, vanaf 1895 tot die uitbreek van die Engelse oorlog, het van die gelukkigste jare in Barry Hertzog se lewe uitgemaak. Baie jare daarna sou hy met vreugde terugdink aan die gesellige dae saam met vriende deurgebring—jag, kampvure, grappe—en dan weer studie. . . .

'In politieke kringe het baie mense skaars van die jong regter notisie geneem; hy was weliswaar goed bevriend met die President en ander amptenare, maar almal wat sy boekeliefde opgemerk het, sy teruggetrokkenheid en voorkeur vir sy huislike kring geken het, het gemompel dat Barry 'n egte "boekwurm" is. . . .

'Op 20 Oktober 1904 het die Fakulteit van Regsgeleerdheid van die Universiteit Leiden . . . aan genl. Hertzog geskrywe om hom die leerstoel [in Het Zuid-Afrikaansche Recht] aan te bied, omdat hulle in hom volkome vertroue het. . . . Die aangewese man was vir hulle die studie-gretige regter van die Vrystaatse Republiek wat 'n gevierde Boeregeneraal geword het—wat dus denker en dader is.

'Genl. Hertzog se pad was egter vir hom duidelik. Die Vrystaat het hom nodig gehad; daarom moes hy hierdie aanbod van die hand wys.'

—C M van den Heever *Generaal J. B. M. Hertzog* (1943) 51, 56, 57, 59, 197. The professorship went to Melius de Villiers (q v). (See also ROOS; VAN DEN HEEVER.)

'In May 1910, when Gen. Louis Botha, about to assume the premiership of the Union to be established on the 31st of that month, had to constitute his cabinet, he apparently foresaw trouble with his English-speaking supporters if the fiery Free State champion of the Dutch language was included in it. He therefore got Gen. J. C. Smuts, and afterward also F. S. Malan, to sound Hertzog on his willingness to accept a seat on the Appeal Court. Hertzog, however, was not prepared to allow himself to be removed from the political arena in this way. Botha could not ignore him, and gave him the portfolio of Justice.'

—Mr Justice H A Fagan (q v) in *Standard Encyclopaedia of Southern Africa* V (1972) 505. (The biographical sketch *was* by H A Fagan, no matter that he died in 1963. See the list of contributors in *Standard Encyclopaedia of Southern Africa* I.)

SIR WILLIAM HODGES

1808–68. Chief Justice of the Cape of Good Hope 1858–68. Knighted 1858.

Hodges, who had been a member of the English Bar since 1833 and Recorder of Poole since 1846, and who had a practice at the Parliamentary Bar and, most important of all, had caught the eye of men of influence, was appointed Chief Justice of the Cape Colony on 2 February 1858. He set sail for Cape Town a month later. Meanwhile he had been knighted by Queen Victoria. He describes the occasion in the following letter, forwarded by Mr R L Selvan SC, to whom it was given by Hodges' great-granddaughter, Mrs Joan A Broster-Cremer (the author, Joan Broster), who authorized its publication in (1988) 105 SALJ 360.

'Bloomsbury Square,
Feb. 13–1858

'My dear Father,

'The first lines I write as "Sir William" I give to you who by your kind care of me when I was young, taught me the way which enabled me to kneel before a queen and receive that which I account a great honour.

'On Monday I had a note from the Colonial Office requesting me to attend Her Majesty at Buckingham Palace to-day at 3 o'clock—and accordingly and in good time I appeared there in full dress and waited with a lot of Corporation people in one of the Ante-rooms where Lord Ernest Bruce (who is Vice Chamberlain and knew me well at the Wiltshire quarter sessions) spied me at once and immediately took me under his wing and into a splendid apartment where all the Cabinet Ministers wearing their orders and in Full uniform, were waiting to attend a Council which Her Majesty was going to hold. I was there 3/4 of an hour and he introduced me to several of the Ministers—when bye and bye Sir George Grey came to me and said "Now come along, I'll take care of you" and looking over to old Lord Gough he said "Lend Her Majesty your sword, my Lord" so Lord Gough and Sir George Grey, preceded by pages in stage liveries, accompanied me through a long passage until we came to the Royal Closet, a small room where the Queen and Prince Albert were alone. Sir George Grey informed Her Majesty who and what I was. I knelt on one knee on the carpet and the Queen drew Lord Gough's sword from the scabbard, to his great horror for it was very sharp, and struck me smartly on each shoulder and said "Sir William arise". Of course I obeyed and she held out her hand that I might kiss it and then Lord Gough and I both backed out of the room and I assure you the Queen, and the Prince too, were most desirous of showing me that I was welcome to the Honor. They bowed to me with smiles at least 6 times and I with a tolerably jolly face under a long bottomed wig (often containing a sad and sorrowful countenance) went bowing my way backwards—but the whole thing went off decidedly well. As we returned along the passage, Lord Gough wished me joy but said the sword was too sharp for My Lady to touch. Then when I joined the Ministers again the Lord Chancellor came forward and in the kindest way wished me a long and successful career at the Cape and this being done and all the new acquaintances having in like manner congratulated me, I left the Palace after "Sir William Hodges'" carriage had been well called for. I thought that this short account might be interesting to you and I have just time to say that the children will be down on Saturday and we shall follow next week. John is in London and we all join in kindest love to you and all at home. We had a letter from Willie to-day. All well with him on the 1st. January.

> 'Your affectionate son,
> William.'

His only prejudice

'The presiding judge was the new Chief Justice, Sir William Hodges, then recently arrived from England. He was a pleasant, good-natured man, somewhat like a pork-butcher in appearance, but with no prejudices—except, as a friend wrote from England—except against the letter "h", and certainly that prejudice was very strong.'

—A W Cole (q v) *Reminiscences of My Life and of the Cape Bench and Bar* (1896) 14. (The splendid photograph by F York of Hodges in the *Cape Monthly Magazine* volume 6 (September 1859), portion of which is reproduced in (1934) 51 *SALJ* opposite page 303, bears out Cole's description.)

OSCAR HENDRIK HOEXTER

1893–1970. Member of the Orange Free State Bar 1918–38. KC 1929. Judge of the High Court of South West Africa 1938–44. Judge of the Eastern Districts Local Division 1944–8. Judge President 1948–9. Judge of Appeal 1949–63.

'Parliament then passed the High Court of Parliament Act 1952 by the ordinary bicameral procedure. It stated that any Appellate Division decision invalidating an instrument purporting to be and enrolled as an Act of Parliament had to be brought before the High Court of Parliament for review. The members of the High Court were the members of the two Houses of Parliament. When the Bill was before Parliament, Oscar Hoexter, in a letter of 30 April 1952, expressing the hope that Schreiner had fully recovered from the operation in the United States on his pharynx, could not resist giving vent to his Puckish sense of humour: "If I were an M.P., I would propose an amendment that no member of the [High] Court [of Parliament] having a law degree should be allowed to vote, provided that any Cabinet Minister having a law degree would be allowed to vote if he filed an affidavit that, in spite of his degree, he had no knowledge of law." He went on to remark that he had been told that "Hennie van Zyl, the ex J.P. of the C.P.D. [q v], is particularly bitter against me; he says that he never thought that I could associate myself with such a judgment. I am tickled because I do not know the old bird at all."'

—Ellison Kahn in *Fiat Iustitia: Essays in Memory of Oliver Deneys Schreiner* (1983) 36.

'"Oscar is quite a mad boy about playing things. After bowls he played bridge and since dinner he has been playing slosh—a form of billiards that old Bill [Oliver's brother] played a good deal of in his later years. If Oscar didn't have such an exceptionally quick mind he would never get through his work. As it is he dashes it off in half the time that I take."'

—Ellison Kahn op cit at 61, quoting from a letter by Oliver Schreiner to his wife Edna, dated 3 June 1959.

'He [Schreiner] was on good social terms with all [his colleagues on the Appellate Division] save those who had accepted appointment in 1955 when the court was enlarged. Hoexter was a special friend, and he found him amusing. Schreiner wrote about Oscar's "delving into the old authorities not because he thinks it necessary to do so but to satisfy Lucas [Steyn: q v] that the decision which the rest of us are agreed on is right. . . . Oscar quite enjoys himself hunting about in the dusty old tomes of various sizes and finding, every now and then, something to laugh at." On another occasion: "Oscar is chuckling because he has assigned to Hall [q v] the job of overruling Hein's [Heinrich de Villiers's] judgment. It is the sort of occasion for Schadenfreude that delights Oscar's heart.'"

—Ellison Kahn op cit at 62, quoting from letters by Oliver Schreiner to his wife Edna, dated 27 November 1956 and 6 March 1956.

WILLIAM EMIL HOLLARD

1836–1906. Soldier. Law agent, then attorney and advocate, in the Transvaal, 1871–99. A character who has left his name in the titles of several reported legal decisions.

In what follows reference is made to A A Roberts QC 'The Bar in Pretoria' in S P Engelbrecht et al (eds) Pretoria (1855–1955): A History of Pretoria (1955); Roberts's original manuscript for that article, which (understandably) did not include all the material in the manuscript; Manfred Nathan's account of Hollard in (1932) 1 South African Law Times 39 and in his autobiography Not Heaven Itself (1944); and a pamphlet, of doubtful accuracy in its content, Papers Relating to the W. E. Hollard Case (Pretoria 1878), issued by one William Leathern, a legal practitioner, which appeared shortly after Leathern had failed in an attempt to secure Hollard's disbarment.

'If we allow for the accuracy of the allegations in the pamphlet, it would appear that Hollard started off life as Emil Musik or Musick, about the year 1835, in Pomerania, near Danzig. He took up the trade of house painter and glazier, and then joined the German Legion. It is claimed that he deserted from it in 1859: but it is significant that in 1856 the Anglo-German Legion was disbanded on the conclusion of the Crimean War, and a large number of its members (some 2,351) settled in the Eastern Province in 1857. Manfred Nathan has it that he had originally been incarcerated in a German fortress for an offence, and had escaped to South Africa. The pamphlet goes on to say that, under the name of Emile Lemondowsky, he left Burghersdorp for the Free State, removing with him certain property belonging to the army and to an army captain. Then, writes Mr. Roberts (MS., p. 19), referring to the pamphlet, he "became a jailer at Smithfield, where he is alleged to have shared a wife with another jailer called Franz Hollard or J. Hollert. On 28th March, 1861, the Landdrost of Smithfield issued a warrant for his arrest, describing him as '5 foot 6 inches, forehead broad, nose straight, hair and eyebrows black, eyes blue, mouth middling, chin round, beard and moustache black, figure stout'. He was also said to be married (wife's name Catherine)."

'Probably it was around this time that he assumed his ultimate name of Hollard. It would appear that next he went to Basutoland. The story is not clear thereafter. Nathan (*Not Heaven Itself*, pp. 76–7) wrote that he had a period of freebooting on the Basutoland border. . . .

'Towards the end of the year [1877] William Leathern, appearing in person, obtained a rule nisi calling on Hollard to show cause why he should not again be removed from the roll. On 21st December, however, the rule was discharged with costs. Thereafter, it appears, Hollard was allowed to practise in peace. Leaving Wakkerstroom, he built up a large practice in Pretoria, where he ultimately became a prominent public figure, being influential with the Government and a property dealer in a large way of business. At the close of the Republican era he was, after De Vries, the advocate and attorney of the longest standing in the S.A.R. (*Staats Almanak voor de Zuid-Afrikaansche Republiek*, 1899, p. 131), though he no longer practised to any extent and his name had long since disappeared from the law reports as counsel engaged in the reported decisions.

'Unlettered but with great native shrewdness, intolerant of the conventions of behaviour, pugnacious and courageous, Hollard proved a dangerous opponent in a trial action, and he had the golden touch with juries. "He addressed the jury", says Nathan (*Not Heaven Itself*, p. 77), "in an extraordinary lingo, compounded of Dutch, English, German and Yiddish; but his winks, gestures and innuendos were so expressive that he carried great weight with the jury."'

—Ellison Kahn 'William Emil Hollard: Lawyer Extraordinary' (1959) 76 *SALJ* 97 at 98–9.

'Nathan gives two widely differing versions of a certain incident in his autobiography and in the *South African Law Times*. It is probably only our good friend Ben Trovato at work. Hollard was having a former partner of his, Sam Fox (after whom Fox Street in Johannesburg was named), prosecuted for perjury. Defence counsel had previously practised in the Dutch East Indies. Taking the better version in the *Law Times*:

WILLIAM EMIL HOLLARD
'Steely grey eyes, shaggy whiskers and shabby attire—a sly chap, the very Devil in Trousers'

"'Mr. Hollard', said the counsel, 'do you remember Landdrost X saying in a certain case that he thought you were overreaching the other party in a land transaction, and that he did not believe you?' 'Now I must think first', replied Hollard; 'was it when you were struck off the rolls in the Netherlands Indies, or was it when you did three months for fraud?" Counsel pursued the matter no further."'

—Kahn op cit at 101.

'Whenever in court he had as opponent "Jim" Leonard [qv], who had arrived from the Cape replete with silk, he would annoy him intensely and incidentally do no harm to his own case by referring to him as "mijn geleerde vriend, de advocaat voor de Koningin".'

—Kahn op cit at 101.

'"His aggressive and undisciplined character", writes Mr. Roberts (MS., p. 20), "is well illustrated by an anecdote told me by Mr. Sheppard who, as articled clerk, was personally concerned. In a certain matter feelings were running high when a document had to be conveyed to Hollard, who refused to pay any attention to it. At length the articled clerk was sent round with a copy to be handed personally to Hollard with instructions not to leave without a reply. The upshot was that Hollard flew into a temper, and telling the clerk to wait, strode off to the lavatory, returning shortly with the besmirched document, saying 'That's my answer'. I was assured that the document was subsequently produced in court with telling effect."'

—Kahn op cit at 102.

Son of a Gunn

'Hollard's tenacity and courage are illustrated in a passage from Kotzé's *Memoirs* (I, p. 513) wherein is told of the plausible adventurer who styled himself Captain Gunn of Gunn, and found himself cited as co-respondent in the famous Weatherley divorce suit (*Weatherley* v. *Weatherley* (1878) Kotzé 66). "In the course of his evidence in that case, he stated that he had seen active service and had been on the staff of Lord Napier of Magdala. The skilful cross-examination of Advocate Hollard, however, soon exposed the impudence of the witness, and brought out his admission that the position he had held on Lord Napier's staff was that of a common orderly! This cross-examination led to Gunn's challenging the advocate to duel with pistols. To his surprise the challenge was promptly accepted by Hollard, who had been a member of the German Legion and was accustomed to the smell of powder. The parties turned up at the appointed place with their seconds, but, as might have been expected, the valiant Gunn of Gunn offered Hollard an apology, and thus ended the fiasco. . . ."'

—Kahn op cit at 102.

'Before the Secucuni War was over there returned from Secucuni Land (but not actually from the front) that prince of adventure, the self-styled Charles Grant Murray Somerset Stuart David Gunn of Gunn.

'Gunn returned to Pretoria, and became in turn a martyr, was extolled as a hero, was arrested and tried for sedition by the British, figured as co-respondent in an unsavoury divorce suit and—was a principal of a duel.

'There are two versions of that duel. In Kotzé's "Memoirs and Reminiscences" the writer tells of how Gunn of Gunn was mercilessly flayed by Advocate Emile Hollard in the case quoted. Gunn of Gunn was so incensed that he challenged Hollard to a duel with pistols. Hollard, an ex-member of the German Legion, promptly accepted.

'The parties turned up at the appointed place but, so says Kotzé, Gunn of Gunn was the only absentee. Kotzé states that Gunn of Gunn offered Hollard an apology.

'The other version comes from the pioneer R. T. N. James who claimed to have been a witness at the duel which, so he said, took place on the Race Course in Pretoria West.

'According to James, everyone in Pretoria knew about the impending duel. All were determined that it should take place, but there should be no bloodshed. A merchant by the name of R. Winstanley, a man of many parts, had the key to it all. He was an amateur actor above the average. He happened to have two so-called "property" pistols, i.e. pistols used on the stage. Both of them were fitted with hammer and percussion caps. Both, on release of the trigger, made the noise requisite to a duel and released a spring.

'In collusion with a chemist, a phial containing a red fluid was prepared and one of the pistols was "loaded" with this harmless but, as was to transpire later, upsetting capsule. Both had percussion caps.

'At the given signal the two contestants turned and fired. Gunn of Gunn was the first to shoot. To his horror Hollard stood his ground, aimed carefully and pulled the trigger.

'Hollard was horror-stricken. His aim was true and he stood looking at an ever-increasing splash of scarlet on Gunn of Gunn's shirt front. He saw the gallows! He was himself dangling at the end of a rope! Transfixed, his eyes protruding, he stared at his adversary's shirt.

'Gunn of Gunn followed the flight of Hollard's eyes, glanced downwards, caught a glimpse of the spreading red—and fainted.

'To quote James again. "It was the perfect duel".'

—J C Vlok 'Glimpses of Early Pretoria' in S P Engelbrecht et al (eds) *Pretoria (1855–1955): History of the City of Pretoria* (1955) 31 at 40–1.

'These [mining] properties later on passed into the hands of the clever European adventurers, who soon became financial leaders, then magnates, and finally blossomed into arrogant Knights, of triple brass. But the golden gentry had not yet appeared to glorify the Rand, and, when they did, a trustful, generous fellow, such as Sam [Fox], had no chance with them. The only one of Fox's cluster capable of grappling with them was old Hollard—he of the steely grey eyes, shaggy whiskers and shabby attire—a sly chap, the very Devil in Trousers, who met any deep-set plans to lay him low with counter-manoeuvres of divine audacity.'

—Louis Cohen *Reminiscences of Johannesburg and London* (1924) 39–40.

'Hollard was one of the leading criminal men in that age. His eloquence was such that he could draw tears from himself. He helped to cut up Marshall Square and thus we got Hollard Street.'

—H H Morris KC *The First Forty Years* (1948) 41.

'Mr. W. E. Hollard was an astute lawyer and man of business and enjoyed a lucrative practice in Pretoria for many years prior to the Anglo–Boer war, acting in the dual capacity of advocate and attorney. . . . Shortly after the surrender of Pretoria to Lord Roberts it became necessary to provide house accommodation for many military persons of importance and with that object in view dwelling-houses in Pretoria were freely commandeered. Among these was Mr. Hollard's fine house in the suburbs. One morning an orderly called at his house and presented a letter addressed to the owner informing him that his house was required by the D.Q.M.G. [Deputy Quartermaster General] for military purposes. Hollard on reading the letter became infuriated and, turning to the orderly, said, "Tell the D.Q.M.G. that he can G.T.H." The soldier went off and reported faithfully to his superior officer. The D.Q.M.G. on hearing Hollard's message at once sent a platoon of soldiers to bring Hollard before him to answer for his sins, and this they did. When Hollard appeared the D.Q.M.G. was very angry and addressed Hollard at some length and with a warm flow of language and wound up saying, "And what the devil, sir, did you mean by saying the D.Q.M.G. can G.T.H.?" "Oh!" said Hollard in his most silken tones. "I merely meant that the Deputy Quarter Master General can Get The House"!'

—W H Somerset Bell *Bygone Days* (1933) 147. (Hollard was a secret agent for the Boers in the Anglo-Boer War. His house was *Friedesheim*, designed by the architect W J de Zwaan, 'an expensive and imposing residence . . . in the somewhat ostentatious style that suited the *nouveaux riches* in the Republic. The house, richly decorated with glass and wood-carving imported from Europe, was demolished in 1955, but three of the rooms were rebuilt in the Provincial Administration building in Pretoria. The mosaic floors, one of which bears the arms of the Transvaal Republic, were also relaid' (P van Warmelo in *Dictionary of South African Biography* IV (1981) 242).)

GEORGE NEVILLE HOLMES

1907–90. Member of the Natal Bar 1931–52. KC 1947. Judge of the Natal Provincial Division 1952–60. Judge of Appeal 1961–77.

'He was quick to see the essential points in a case and to work out how the law should be applied to the facts. When it was his turn to write a judgment he did so with great skill and pride in his craftsmanship and usually with electrifying speed—or so it seemed to some of his more ponderous colleagues.

'In the autobiographical note in [(1976) 9 *De Jure* 3] . . . Neville listed his recreation as "writing judgments". In this outwardly humorous remark (which, incidentally, gives an insight into the life of a judge of appeal) there lurked a great measure of truth. Neville loved writing; and most of his writing was devoted to judgments. He wrote with a raciness of style, a verve and a turn of phrase all of his own. He loved to introduce classical and literary allusions; he was fond of rich imagery and flights of rhetoric. Occasionally his more prosaic colleagues found Neville's imagery a little too rich for their taste and he was persuaded to use the blue pencil. He always did so with a good grace but, one felt, with a measure of sorrowful reluctance.

'Neville's judgments are always a pleasure to read, not only for the literary and other qualities which I have described but also for their limpid lucidity. He had a great facility for formulating legal principles in clear and simple terms—usually in numbered paragraphs and subparagraphs—and many of these formulations have become the classic statements of the law on the topic. A full catalogue of the branches of the law which Neville thus illumined would unduly protract this address, but I would like to mention just one.

'Neville took a great interest in, amongst other things, the criminal law and especially the problems relating to the sentencing of offenders. He was a very kindly man, with a keen appreciation of the often devastating effects of punishment upon the offender. His remarks about the death sentence, ". . . the incomparably utter extreme of punishment", have passed into the legal vernacular, as also has his graphic description, in the same judgment, of ". . . the slow tread of years when you are locked up". And, incidentally, one senses here the influence of his personal experience of incarceration while a prisoner-of-war. He was a firm supporter of the concept that the punishment of the criminal should always be blended with a measure of mercy, and he applied this in practice.'

—Mr Justice M M Corbett, Chief Justice, 'In Memoriam: George Neville Holmes' (1990) 107 *SALJ* 490 at 491–2.

'. . . [T]he Law Reports have afforded a host of . . . examples of his raciness of tone where appropriate, his dash of eloquence reminiscent of Gibbon, his classical and mythological allusions and his occasional touch of pathos, reminding us of Edmund Burke's haunting Homeric reflection in his speech at Bristol on declining the poll—"what shadows we are, and what shadows we pursue".'

—Ellison Kahn in (1975) 92 *SALJ* 219.

ULRIC (ULRICH) HUBER

1636–94. Professor of History and Oratory in the University of Franeker, Friesland, 1657–79 and Professor of Law 1660–79. Judge of the Hof van Friesland 1679–82. Honorary Professor in the University of Franeker 1682–91.

'Who goes now to Franeker will find few remains of the University of which Ulric Huber was in his day the brightest star. The University was suppressed by Napoleon. Such of the buildings as remain have been turned by one of fate's cruellest ironies into a *Krankzinnigengesticht* (mental hospital).'

—*The Jurisprudence of My Time (Heedendaegse Rechtsgeleertheyt) by Ulric Huber (1636–1694)*. Translated from the Fifth Edition by Percival Gane (1939) I 'Note on the Author' xx.

SIR JAMES ROSE INNES

1855–1942. Member of the Cape Bar 1878–90 and 1893–1900. Member of the Cape House of Assembly 1884–1902. QC 1890. Attorney-General in Rhodes's Cabinet 1890–3 and Sprigg's Cabinet 1900–2. Knighted (KCMG) 1901. Judge President of the Transvaal High Court April–October 1902. Chief Justice of the Transvaal (on the creation of the Supreme Court) October 1902–May 1910. Judge of Appeal May 1910–September 1914. Chief Justice of the Union of South Africa September 1914–February 1927. Privy Counsellor 1914. (His surname was Innes; 'Rose' was a family given name; his wife referred to herself as Lady Innes. Many writers spell his surname incorrectly as Rose-Innes.)

'But he has an essentially *honest mind*. The "lie in the soul" can effect no lodgment in his clear intellect and absolutely sincere nature.'

—Sir Alfred Milner, High Commissioner for South Africa, to Joseph Chamberlain, Colonial Secretary, 22 August 1900 (*The Milner Papers* edited by Cecil Headlam II (1933) 121). (See also LEONARD.)

'The apparent inconsistency in Innes's outlook from time to time [during his political career] can also be explained in terms of opposing forces in his make-up. His loyalty to and love for the Crown clashed with his respect and affection for his Afrikaner fellow citizens and urged him on, despite his liberal instincts, to support Milner in most matters. These pulls on conscience from different directions caused mental anguish to Innes throughout not only his political career, where they had to be resolved into decisions on action, but his entire adult life.

'Sir James Rose Innes'
'A ROSE INNES-CENT'
Caricature by D C Boonzaier (1865–1950), from his
Owlographs (1901) 9

Seen by most to be of a quiet, engaging personality, known as one who in his early days on circuit as an advocate entered fully into the corporate sense of fun, capable of good-natured repartee with a lightness of touch, he had running beneath his composed demeanour veins of pessimism that at times throbbed almost unbearably. How to get others to attain the level of integrity he demanded of himself?'

—Ellison Kahn 'James Rose Innes' in R M de Villiers (ed) *Better Than They Knew* II (1974) 57 at 70. (See also F W BEYERS.)

' . . . [T]he great Chief Justice had an acute feeling for the lines on which the Roman-Dutch law might properly be developed in South Africa. He of all our judges knew best how to prune the tree instead of uprooting it or letting it run wild.'

—A M Honoré *The South African Law of Trusts* 1 ed (1966) 62. (The last sentence does not appear in the latest edition, the third (1985), on page 44, where it would be expected to appear.)

'Occasionally a judge stands out, not because he actually is more determined than his colleagues to arrive at a just decision along rational lines, but because he gives a more vivid public impression of this endeavour. To this select band Innes belonged. Two dangers are inherent in the appointment to the judiciary of a person of unbending principle. First, he may be unable to appreciate the low scale of values to which so many men adhere, and thereby fail to arrive at the truth. Secondly, he may, for the same reason, be too severe in the punishment of transgressions. There have been one or two judges in our history in whom these dangers materialized; but there is no reason to think that they did with Innes.'

—Ellison Kahn 'James Rose Innes' in R M de Villiers (ed) *Better Than They Knew* II (1974) 57 at 76. (See also KRAUSE—the case of *Ex parte Krause* 1905 TS 221.)

' . . . possibly the finest judge the world has known.'

—R H Christie 'Plain Speaking in Law' (inaugural lecture as Professor of Law in the University of Rhodesia) 1967 *Rhodesian Law Journal* 134 at 137. (The Hon F N Broome, former Judge President of the Natal Provincial Division, wrote: 'I would rank him as the greatest judge South Africa has ever had': *Not the Whole Truth* (1962) 124.)

'With . . . conviction, he [Professor J C de Wet] believes that Sir James Rose Innes was the best judge South Africa has known. He, too, was a South African in his training. "*There is nobody near him.*"'

—Jeremy Gauntlett 'J C de Wet at Seventy-five' 1987 *De Rebus* 581 at 583.

'The official accommodation [of the judges] at Johannesburg [from 1902 to 1910] was not so satisfactory [as that in the Palace of Justice in Pretoria]. We occupied a ramshackle building in Marshall Street. It bore no outward sign of judicial tenure, though a neighbouring publican hinted at it by blazoning upon the wall of his licensed premises the words "HIS LORDSHIP'S LARDER". That the hint was not pointless was indicated by the reply of a dilatory juror to an inquiry from the Bench as to the cause of his tardy arrival: "I was in your larder, M'lud, and didn't notice the time." He evidently regarded that as a mitigating circumstance, but he found himself sadly mistaken. Not only were the premises externally shabby, but internally they were deficient in some of the essentials to civilized occupation. The lavatories, for instance, could only be approached by traversing a courtyard occupied by Natives awaiting trial, under the charge of Zulu police, fine stalwart men in smart uniforms. These sprang promptly to attention as soon as a judicial step was heard, thus as it were lining the road to the shrine of Cloacina. And the return journey had to be made under the same respectful but embarrassing regard. Judges engaged in administering justice in the present law courts on Von Brandis Square would be surprised at some of the inconveniences under which their pioneering predecessors laboured.'

—James Rose Innes *Autobiography* (edited by B A Tindall) (1949) 208.

'Sir James Rose-Innes, who succeeded Lord de Villiers in the Appellate Division, struck me as being somewhat hard and exacting. John X. Merriman is reported to have said of him, "He is so upright that he bends backwards."

'I had the pleasure of having a slight brush with him. It was a very cold day. The Motion Roll was being taken in a draughty courtroom. From the beginning to the end of that Roll Counsel had been getting into trouble. I was the last to get up. We had the Court to ourselves. I asked for a postponement of my matter, and, thinking that it had been granted, I began to pack up. His Lordship said, "You might wait until your application is granted."

'I replied that I thought it had been granted.

'He said, "The Junior Bar presumes far too much."

'I replied that the Junior Bar never presumed. We looked at each other for a few minutes and then the Court adjourned.

'I do not know whether he was waiting for me or not, but later on I appeared for the husband in an application brought against him by his wife. It was an application we had to win, but I warned the husband that I would not ask for costs against his wife. Sir James gave judgment in my favour and then said, "Do you ask for costs?"

'I said "No". He expected me to say "Yes", and before he could check himself he said, "You won't get them". The Bar fell into the same error as did His Lordship of thinking that I was going to say "Yes", whereas I said "No".

'After his retirement I met him in Cape Town. He was inclined to be friendly. We shook hands and he said: "Well, Ferris, how are you?" He was referring to Mr. Grindley Ferris (now a judge) [q v]. He had mixed up our noses. He was once kind enough to tell somebody that I always fought for my client. Perhaps he was again thinking of someone else.'

—H H Morris KC *The First Forty Years* (1948) 47–8. (Possibly Innes was somewhat rigorous in his demands on practitioners in his early years on the Bench. It is noteworthy, however, that in all the addresses delivered in the courts in his memory, emphasis was laid on his unfailing courtesy and charm of manner on the Bench.)

'I have mentioned meeting Innes when he was Attorney-General at the Cape (an office he filled under more than one Ministry). The knowing ones had already tipped him for the Transvaal appointment. The *Argus Annual* had described him as "distinguished for his ability and volubility". He certainly possessed both qualities. He often delivered an extempore judgment at the rate of 250 to 300 words a minute. With all due respect to his learning, which was considerable, though he was also noted for his careful examination of the authorities, he was sometimes (I say it with due respect to his memory) far too impetuous. Thus, in at least two reported cases he completely swallowed what he had said in previous decisions. He was, however, a completely dignified Chief Justice, though in little physical manifestations those who knew him could discern a touch of impatience. This may have been due to the fact that he was a confirmed dyspeptic. He was prematurely white-headed, with a sallow and somewhat pasty countenance, and a small dark moustache. The geniality I had first observed in him, before his elevation to the Bench, had vanished, and he was often "down" upon junior counsel. On one occasion, an appeal was argued by Sam Goch on behalf of the respondent party. The Court suggested to Goch that if he applied for an amendment of his plea he might succeed; but Goch said he was satisfied that the allegations in the plea were sufficient to cover the case. These are the actual words of the Chief Justice: "Now the Court went out of its way during the argument to suggest that an amendment should be made and indicated as plainly as it could that if an amendment were made the decision in the Court below would in substance be upheld. But counsel for the respondent notifies us that after consultation with his attorney they both think the Court is wrong, and they do not wish to apply for an amendment. Well, the Court cannot force a party to amend. . . . As the declaration does not disclose any ground for rescission, it is clear that the judgment cannot stand." These bitter words of the Chief Justice drove Goch away from practice at the Bar. Mr. Justice Solomon used an even stronger adjective. He said (I was in Court at the time) that "the attitude of counsel for the respondent is perverse". There is, however, no printed report of Mr. Justice Solomon's judgment. The attorney did not suffer. In due time he achieved a leading practice in Johannesburg.'

—Manfred Nathan *Not Heaven Itself: An Autobiography* (1944) 203–4. (Innes may have suffered from ill health, but he took pride in the fact that during his sixteen years of service on the Appellate Division he was absent only one day on account of illness (*Autobiography* 247).)

The case was *Weinberg v Aristo Egyptian Cigarette Co* 1905 TS 760. The passage cited is at 765–6. Professor H D J Bodenstein wrote in (1914) 31 *SALJ* 277: 'It is a pity that counsel for the respondent did not humour the Bench by amending his declaration as suggested from it, and so prevent a decision . . . which strikes the reader . . . as *summa injuria.*'

Another version

'While Innes was on the Bench in the Transvaal there was an extraordinary incident between him and counsel. Advocate S. F. Goch was arguing an appeal before a full court of three Judges from a single Judge in Johannesburg. During the course of argument Innes told Goch that he could not win the appeal on the pleadings as they stood, but that he could succeed if the pleadings were suitably amended. Goch, after taking some time to consider, told the Court that he thought that the pleadings were in order as they stood; and he declined to amend them. In the result the Chief Justice gave judgment dismissing the appeal, and blaming the dismissal on Goch. This at once finished Goch's career at the Bar, and he retired to the decent obscurity of a country town-clerkship. There are two points to this unhappy story. The first is that it does not pay to quarrel with the Bench, especially a full Bench, however much you may deem yourself to be right; the second, strangely enough, is that many sound lawyers, including Philip Millin, who have gone into the question, believed that Goch was right and Innes was wrong. But that does not excuse Goch; in the end his client was the loser.'

—Leslie Blackwell (q v) *Are Judges Human?* (1962) 20.

Yet another version

'I shall be very careful of what I say in criticism of any man and particularly a professional man. The attack will have to be necessary and 100 per cent. sound.

'I shall never forget the scathing judgment of a Transvaal Bench on counsel who ventured to differ from their Lordships on the form of a declaration. The judgment, as it appears in the Supreme Court Reports, is a well-watered version of what was said in open Court. The dramatic flinging down of his pen by the presiding judge and the undignified shout of "Sit down!" when the unfortunate man rose to ask for the amendment suggested by the Court are not reflected in the judgment. That judgment ruined that man's practice. He had to leave the Bar. He had a most unfortunate career thereafter.'

—H H Morris KC *The First Forty Years* (1948) 124.

Humility

'There are of course times when this privileged office [of judge's registrar] and the sense of power which is derived from proximity to the ante-chambers to the great have the tendency to produce a distinct enlargement of the ego, or at least, a weary disdain of somewhat lesser mortals. I well remember an incident involving a fellow-Registrar—then the handsomest of athletes and to-day a most successful professional man. We shared the same room. One morning after the dance of the night before, he answered the phone in what he no doubt took to be quite a tolerant tone. The enquirer apparently asked quite diffidently whether he might speak to Mr. Justice Bristowe [q v]. He was informed, however, by my companion that Mr. Justice Bristowe was already on the Bench and that this completely excluded any communication with, to, or from, the outer world. The diffident voice said that he quite understood that, but would it not be possible to send a message to the learned Judge? This he was equally coldly informed was quite out of the question too, as Judges once on the Bench remain quite inaccessible to members of the public. The enquirer appreciated this, but what he really wanted to convey, he said, was whether it was not possible to leave a message on the Judge's table asking him to ring him when convenient. This was reluctantly conceded, the enquirer being asked who he was, what his name was, and what his business was, whereupon the quite unassertive voice replied that he was Sir James Rose-Innes (the Acting Governor-General of the Union) and would Judge Bristowe please be good enough to ring him when he came out of Court?'

—C P Bresler (q v) *Lineage of Conflict* (1952) 159–60.

Chivalry

'Innes lived to a great age. He came of a long-lived family. He was eighty-seven when he died. He had retired from the office of Chief Justice of South Africa nearly fifteen years before. Under the conditions of his appointment he might have gone on as long as he lived, but he chivalrously retired in order to give Sir William Solomon the chance of holding the office for a year or two before his own retirement. It had come to be the custom to confer the office upon the next senior judge. . . . One day I remarked to another ex-Chief Justice: "I see both Sir James Rose-Innes and his wife are ill." "It's time they were," was the reply.'

—Manfred Nathan *Not Heaven Itself: An Autobiography* (1944) 204–5. (See also W H SOLOMON.)

WESLEY ERNEST JOHN

1885–1966. Patent agent.

'The incident during his apprenticeship which Mr John enjoyed recalling was when he was . . . sent to the Johannesburg Fort, which was by this time a civilian prison, to carry out some or other mechanical engineering maintenance job. He found that it was very much easier to get into the Fort than out of it. Upon arrival he duly explained his mission and was allowed inside. He did the job, but then found that the gates would not open on his explaining that he had completed the job. He had no pass. This led to a considerable delay and a great deal of difficulty before he was finally released. During that visit Mr John noted, again with amusement, that a certain band of convicts were being given special labour. It turned out that these men had been convicted for housebreaking, and the job given them was to repair Yale locks!

'Mr John had none of what we call the formal education necessary to be a member of our profession in this day and age. He had never received a matriculation through school, and all his qualifications were in fact obtained by night-time studies. He had the privilege of being awarded the first Mines Department Mechanical Engineers Certificate of Competency. . . .

'At about this time, Mr John joined our profession as a trainee with the firm D. M. Kisch & Co. He worked with such august people as the grandfather of the late Peter Kisch, and very closely with A. L. Spoor [q v], the founder of the firm which became Spoor & Fisher. Considering the times and conditions under which people worked in those days, some of the illustrative drawings for patent applications which Mr John did are absolutely outstanding. The firm was housed in offices somewhere near the old Johannesburg market, which was not paved, and the red dust from the soil permeated every nook and cranny of every office nearby. To draw a line with Indian ink, which incidentally had to be hand-crushed and mixed, required placing a ruler on the paper and then blowing the dust from the paper as the pen was traced across the paper. How many of us could produce work like that today, I wonder.

'A most interesting comment at that time was from Mr Spoor, who was somewhat of a mentor to Mr John, saying to him: "John, you have entered the wrong profession. Everything worth inventing has been invented."

'I believe Mr John was one of the first persons to qualify as a patent agent by examination under the provisions of the 1916 Act. . . .

'Mr John continued to practise as a consulting engineer and his patent agency was confined strictly to obtaining patents for local inventors. He never had, nor did he try to have, any "foreign" practice.

'So things went on until the outbreak of the Second World War. At that time Mr John was appointed the official examiner by the defence force to ensure that no patents were granted or published on inventions that could be used for war purposes. He closed his offices and referred all his clients during the period of the Second World War to his colleagues. . . .

'During Mr John's wartime occupation he refused to take a commission in the army, stating that "he did not want General Smuts or any other person interfering with how he conducted his work on behalf of the Government."'

—P D Fahrenheim 'The Late W. E. John, a Personality of our Profession' *The South African Institute of Patent Agents Newsletter* No 31–4/88 p 20 at pp 20–1.

'MR. JUSTICE P. S. T. JONES'
From (1934) 3 South African Law Times 54

PERCY SIDNEY TWENTYMAN JONES

1876–1954. Member of the Cape Bar 1902–26. KC 1920. Judge of the Cape Provincial Division 1926–46. Judge President 1946. Author of legal works.

'For the benefit of those who do not know him we may here mention that by vote of the Cape Bar taken about 1912 he was placed as its Most Handsome member, while at the less flattering end of the list, by (almost) unanimous decision, were to be found, bracketed equal and thoughtfully veiled, a certain member of Parliament and a certain (now) eminent K.C., for the identification of whom no prize is offered.

'Turning to things hardly less romantic we find that he is the only Judge who has represented South Africa in two branches of

'THE HONOURABLE MR JUSTICE
R. P. B. DAVIS'
Facing (1936) 53 SALJ *147 (See* JONES.)

'MORRIS ALEXANDER KC MP'
*(1877–1946). Caricature by D C Boonzaier (1865–
1950), from Enid Alexander* Morris Alexander: A
Biography *(1953) 145 (See* JONES.)

sport—cricket and Rugby football.
(Murray Bisset captained South Africa at
cricket.)'

—'Mr Justice Jones' (1928) 45 *SALJ* 1 at 2.
See his photograph. (The two who brought
up the rear in the Handsomeness Stakes
must have been respectively Morris Alexander KC MP (1877–1946) and R P B Davis
(later Davis J) (qv). Mention should have
been made by the writer of Vivian Herbert
(Boet) Neser (1894–1956), who captained
the South African cricket XI against Lord
Tennyson's XI and in all five test matches
against S B Joel's English XI in 1924–5. In
addition, he was the referee in all four of the
rugby test matches between the All Blacks
and the Springboks in 1928. He was a judge
of the Transvaal Provincial Division from
1943.)

' . . . Centlivres recounted a tale which
shows that Schreiner was exaggerating
in saying that Centlivres could not see
the ordinary comedy of human existence. "And this reminds me of a story
told me by Percy Jones yesterday. [He
would be Jones J of the Cape Bench.]
He was up in Bloemfontein in connection with an appeal in the spacious days
of Wessels J & was staying at an hotel
where the judges were also staying. He
had a room opposite the judges'
sitting-room & in those days the judges
held their conferences in this room at
night-time. Percy told me that Wessels' voice was heard all over the hotel:
there was apparently a heated argument going on about the merits of
Percy's appeal which was down for
hearing the next day. Percy bravely
decided to knock on the door of the
judges' sitting-room & tell them he did
not want to hear them discuss the
merits of his appeal!"'

—Ellison Kahn in *Fiat Iustitia: Essays in
Memory of Oliver Deneys Schreiner* (1983)
33–4, quoting from a letter by Centlivres
to Schreiner, dated 15 October 1953.

EDUARD JOHAN PIETER JORISSEN

1829–1912. Minister of religion in Holland 1854–75. Attorney and advocate of the South African Republic (Transvaal) 1876. State Attorney of the South African Republic 1876–8. Member of the Pretoria Bar 1878–81. State Attorney 1881–3. Member of the Pretoria Bar 1884–8. Special judicial commissioner in Johannesburg 1889–90. Judge of the High Court of the South African Republic 1890–9. Prominent politician. Author of theological and other works.

' . . . [T]he general legal standards were of necessity still very low when E. J. P. Jorissen arrived on the scene. A man of intelligence and determination, he was nevertheless so self-assertive, outspoken and uncompromising that the mass of anecdote attaching to him tends to obscure the important part he played in the legal life of the Transvaal from 1876 to the Anglo-Boer War.

'A minister of religion who had had a difference of opinion with his own church in Holland, he was asked by Pres. Burgers to come to the Transvaal for educational work. He sailed in November 1875, but on arrival at Cape Town it was suggested to him that he qualify for admission as a legal practitioner with a view to becoming Staatsprocureur in succession to James Buchanan. Before setting off for Pretoria via Durban, Jorissen bought the three books recognized by Volksraadsbesluit of September 19, 1859 as authoritative, viz: De Groot's *Inleiding*, Van der Linden's *Handboek* and Van Leeuwen's *Rooms-Hollandsch Recht*. He arrived in Pretoria by oxwagon on February 6, 1876, in a few months had satisfied the *Rechtsgeleerde Commissie*, was admitted to practise and on June 9, 1876 became Staatsprocureur.

'On the 10th March of the same year he wrote to his son, S. G. Jorissen: "De rechtbanken laag en hoog, bestaan uit onbedreven luiden die zich door de zoogenaamde slimheden der praktizijn in de luren laten leggen of werkelijk door omkooping en gunstebejag zich in hunne vonnissen laten leiden."

'So, too, on June 30, 1876 he wrote: "Ik wensch een bekwame rechtsgeleerde te zijn, omdat de lui met wie ik te doen heb sulke beunhazen zijn, rechtverknoeiers, uitgeslepen praktizijns, is het voor mij dubbel zwaar." . . .

'From February, 1884 to 1886 E. J. P. Jorissen was a member of the Volksraad and practised as an advocate and attorney, but, he says, merely as "consuleerend advokaat" without doing court work, because of the "constitution of the court" and because his son was in practice.

'This son was appointed to the bench on November 13, 1880 and Jorissen Snr., after his return from Europe in August 1887, practised in Pretoria until 1888 when he was asked by the Government to become judge in Johannesburg. The next year his son, S. G. Jorissen, died and in 1890 the Government offered Jorissen a seat on the bench of the High Court. He assumed duty on September 1, 1890.

'He was born on June 10, 1829 and was thus in his sixty-second year when he achieved this unique distinction of succeeding his own son on the bench. He remained in office until the Anglo-Boer War, but his eccentricities increased to such an extent that attempts were made to have him removed. Technical difficulties prevented such action from being taken until 1899, and soon afterwards his mental condition further deteriorated and he disappeared from public life until his death in The Hague on March 20, 1912. One cannot but be thankful that his long and faithful service to his adopted country was not marred by the attempted inquiry.'

—A A Roberts 'The Bar in Pretoria' in S P Engelbrecht et al (eds) *Pretoria (1855–1955): History of the City of Pretoria* (1955) 173 at 175, 177, 183–5.

'On circuit he became even more petulant and arbitrary. Court was to open in Barberton just before a weekend which Jorissen wanted to spend in Lourenço Marques. This annoyed him, but when, the evening before, he lost 5/- at 1d. nap, and then found Bishop Bousfield reading his paper, he was furious. He stormed into the hotel room of De Waal [later De Waal JP], who was prosecuting, and said "The Court will sit at six o'clock tomorrow morning". De Waal remonstrated but the Judge merely repeated his remark and left.

'De Waal rushed round informing counsel and such other interested parties as were on hand: he got a message to the gaoler, but witnesses and jurymen were not easy to locate. Promptly at six a.m. the Judge walked into Court and took his seat in the presence of all counsel, officials and accused, and ordered the first case to be called. De Waal explained that he had done his best but had been able to get only three jurymen.

'Jorissen forthwith adjourned the Court for two days, in time to catch the morning train to Delagoa Bay. De Waal telegraphed to Pretoria and Jorissen was back in Barberton within twenty four hours, and the Court resumed its sittings. The Judge, still furious, sat back, took no notes, and waved each witness out of the box without putting a question or allowing the jury to put any. At last a juryman got up and said that it had always been the custom to allow the jury to ask questions. Jorissen said nothing, but as soon as the next witness had given his evidence, the Judge pointed his finger at the juryman who had protested, saying: "What is your name?" "Jones, My Lord." "Mr. Jones, ask a question". "I have no questions, My Lord". "Ask a question!" shouted the Judge. "But, My Lord. . . ." "Mr. Jones, you shall ask a question". "But, My Lord, I have no question to ask this witness". "Gentlemen of the Jury, you are discharged!"

'Counsel for the accused contended that the jury having been sworn in and evidence heard, the accused had been in jeopardy and was entitled to his discharge.

'"Well, Mr. de Waal, he's correct, is he not?" said Jorissen. "The accused is discharged."'

—Roberts op cit at 185–6.

'Jorissen . . . was known as "old Necessity," because Necessity knows no

'E. P. J. JORISSEN'

Caricature by William Howard Schröder (1852–92), from A N Pelzer 'Pretoria in die Karikatuur' in S P Engelbrecht et al (eds) Pretoria (1855–1955): Geskiedenis van die Stad Pretoria *(1955)*

law. Afterwards I heard the same *soubriquet* applied to Mr. Justice Buchanan, at the Cape. In both cases it was rather unjust. Jorissen had plenty of common sense, but was most unjudicial in temperament. Sir John Buchanan was quite a good lawyer, but looked and spoke like a farmer. In Jorissen's case the real reason was that he had never been trained as a lawyer. He had been a parson in Holland without a benefice, and President Burgers selected him to be Superintendent General of Education in the Transvaal. On landing at Cape Town, however, Jorissen found a letter asking him to become State Attorney instead. He bought a couple of Dutch law books, which he read in train and coach on his way up north; and by the time he reached Pretoria he was fully qualified to become State Attorney.

'"Old Necessity" was not very dignified in his hearing of cases. . . . On occasion, however, Jorissen showed practical sense. A police sergeant named Smit was charged before him at the Barberton circuit with peculation (theft of Government funds). He was acquitted in the face of very strong evidence. In discharging him, the judge said: "When you say your prayers to-night—if you *do* say them—go down on your knees and thank God that you have been tried by a Barberton jury."'

—Manfred Nathan *Not Heaven Itself: An Autobiography* (1944) 134–5. (See also BUCHANAN; CARTER; WAIFS AND STRAYS sv 'Lawyers in general'; WESSELS.)

SIR HENRICUS HUBERTUS (HENRY HUBERT) JUTA

1857–1930. Member of the Cape Bar 1880–1914. QC 1893. Attorney-General in Rhodes's Cabinet 1894. Speaker of the Cape House of Assembly 1896–8. Knighted 1897. Judge President of the Cape Provincial Division 1914–20. Judge of Appeal 1920–3. Author of legal and other works.

'Literary gifts might have been expected of Sir Henry Juta. After all, he had an uncle who was a remarkable writer and a figure of historical renown—Karl Marx. This relationship was not something that was alluded to in the biographical sketch of the judge and former Speaker of the Cape House of Assembly in (1915) 32 *SALJ* 1, or in the belated obituaries in the South African press. (Sir Henry had gone with his family to England in 1923, after his retirement as a judge of appeal at the age of 65. He died in England on 16th May, 1930. Our newspapers picked up the news only five days later.) But it is well authenticated that Sir Henry's father, Jan Carel Juta, the bookseller and publisher, was married to Louisa (Louise), daughter of Herschel (Heinrich) Marx and Henriette Marx (born Pressburg) and sister of Karl Marx. The famous brother in his correspondence with Friedrich Engels spoke in cordial terms of this brother-in-law, J. C. Juta. A letter to Engels of 14th December, 1853, states that it was Juta who suggested that he contribute to *De Zuid-Afrikaan* to supplement his financial resources, and it appears that he did write for that paper.

'Sir Henry wrote an amusing little book, *Reminiscences of the Western Circuit* [see LANGENHOVEN], and a story of crime and detection, *Off the Track* (1925), that has been stigmatized, together with Mr. Justice Victor Sampson's *The Komani Mystery* (1930) and *The Murder of Paul Rougier* (1929), as an amateurish effort (J. P. L. Snyman, *The South African Novel in English (1880–1930)* (1952), p. 180). Juta J.A. and Victor Sampson J. will live on in the law reports, not in extra-curial writings.'

—Ellison Kahn & Brian R Bamford 'A Penultimate Spoonful of Sugar and Pinch of Salt' (1966) 83 *SALJ* 208 at 211–12. (The artist son of Sir Henry, Jan Juta, in his book *Background in Sunshine: Memories of South Africa* (1972) says of his father's mother simply that he had 'an excellent mother, who had been born in Germany' (p 36). The odd thing is that for the whole period during which Henry Juta read for the LLB degree of the University of London and studied for admission to the English Bar (he was called by the Inner Temple on 26 January 1880) he stayed with the Marxs in their house in London.)

'It would appear that Sir Henry Juta when he was at the bar would . . . occasionally make an odd remark. Mr Justice F G Gardiner recorded these "Jutarisms", as he called them, in his reminiscences, published long after his death: "They folded their arms, shut their mouths, and said. . . ." "The best way to make a man do a thing is to shoot him." (See (1963) 80 *South African Law Journal* 415. The second statement was made in the course of Juta's defence of the accused in the leading case of *R v Smith* (1900) 17 SC 561, on whether a soldier has a duty to obey an unlawful order of a superior.)'

—Ellison Kahn 'The Seven Lamps of Legal Humour Part 2' 1984 *De Rebus* 210 at 210.

'JUTA ON JUT–E.

This is Sir Henry,
Brimful of energy,
Pleading a cause at the Cape Town Bar.
Mark his gentility,
He has ability.
All give him best when it comes to l(j)aw.'

Caricature by D C Boonzaier (1865–1950), from his
Owlographs *(1901) 54*

(For another caricature by Boonzaier of Juta, see
B UPINGTON.)

'It sometimes becomes a question whether Counsel should argue for a position or on a point on which the Law *is clearly against him*. That depends first of all upon the words in italics. In the case of *Hunter's Trustees v. The Colonial Government* (4 J. 449) the Counsel for *Plaintiffs* declined to take up the time of the Court in argument as he stated that the Law was clearly *against* him: thereupon Counsel for the Defendant was called upon, and after hearing him the Court gave Judgment *for the Plaintiffs*.

'There can, however, be no doubt that it is bad advocacy to labour untenable points, or to treat all the questions of varying importance that arise in argument as if they were all equally important or matters of life and death. But even here it may be asked *when is a point untenable*?

'In the first appeal that fell to me, I took one point among others. The late Chief Justice [Sir Henry de Villiers] threw down his pen and asked me whether I was serious. I stuck to it, however, and eventually the Court held that that was *the only* point in the case.'

—Sir Henry Juta *The Conduct of Trial Cases* (1919) 152–3.

'SIR HENRY JUTA'

Caricature by D C Boonzaier (1865–1950), from his My Caricatures *(1912)*

W P Schreiner KC (qv), former Prime Minister of the Cape and leading silk, was inclined to lose his temper in court when he was suffering from overwork, strain, worry or ill health.

'Henry Juta, his old friend, whom he had found such a solace in England in his loneliness when he arrived at Cambridge, at times would trade on this weakness. Still, this baiting did not excuse an outburst in court on 22 August 1912, at a time when WP was weary, carrying—as so often—too much weight, suffering from a heart complaint and beginning to become deaf. The incident is vividly portrayed in a dignified letter to WP from Henry Juta:

"Chambers 22.8.12

"Sir,

"You stated in Court today with regard to a remark I made to the Judge as to the calling of Mr Bosman that it was imperfect. . . . You are entitled to your own recollection which differs from that of my junior and myself. But you proceeded to make the following public statement: 'It is not only incorrect but it is false—and my friend knows it.' This is so serious a matter that unless you are prepared to withdraw it—made I believe when you were very heated—as publicly as you made it it is obvious that our life-long friendship must be at an end.

"I cannot [? bring] myself to write any more. I can hardly write this: that is much too obvious.

"H Juta."

'Next morning the contrite Schreiner made *amende honorable*, explaining that the "statement was made in haste. . . . I wish to be permitted to express my regret to your lordship and to my friend and to withdraw the unjust remark, which but for the strain of protracted work and of this heavy case would never have been made."'

—Ellison Kahn 'Father and Son—W P Schreiner and Oliver' in *Fiat Iustitia: Essays in Memory of Oliver Deneys Schreiner* (1983) 100 at 108. (See also W P SCHREINER.)

ALEXANDER ANGUS KENNEDY

1907–76. Magistrate. Attorney. Member of the Natal Bar 1942–9. Judge of the Natal Native High Court 1949–55. QC 1955. Judge of the Natal Provincial Division 1955–72. Chief Justice of Swaziland 1974.

He presided at the complex trial in which Oshry's Stores sued the Durban City Council and Coronation Brick and Tile Company for damages arising out of the flooding of the plaintiff's property. After the fifteenth day of the hearing a settlement was reached.

'The presiding judge in that case was Mr Justice Alexander Angus (Sandy) Kennedy. He had an interesting and unusual background. He had been a magistrate in his twenties, then an attorney, then an advocate, and from the Bar he was appointed a Judge of the old Natal Native High Court. When the Native High Court was abolished he and Brokensha became members of the Supreme Court Bench. In appearance he resembled Debroy Summers, the band leader. He was a real character: very informal in manner, nevertheless he always wore a black jacket and striped trousers to chambers and a carnation in his button hole. At one time when he was practising as an attorney, he had been a partner with Gus Caminsky and Cecil Nathan. During the weekends the partners were members of the same poker school. Cecil Nathan (another great character), who was to become a close friend of mine, made an amazingly cynical comment about the fate of the partners after the partnership had dissolved: "The best lawyer (Caminsky) was struck off the roll; the worst lawyer (Kennedy) became a Supreme Court judge; and I just carried on." The comment, although very amusing, was by no means entirely accurate, for a person of Douglas Shaw's eminence regarded Sandy Kennedy as one of the best civil judges on the Natal Bench.'

—The Hon Ramon Nigel Leon *Truth in Action* (the reminiscences of the former judge of the Natal Provincial Division, not yet completed or published).

FRANCISCUS LIEVENS KERSTEMAN

1728–c 1792. Author of legal and other works.

'Born on 20/3/1728 in 's-Gravenhage into an unhappy Dutch household later broken up by divorce, he was educated at Voorburg, Leiden, Utrecht and Harderwyk with the help of an uncle. He died in poverty, probably about 1793. Unprincipled, improvident and somewhat of a Don Juan, he led a life full of adventures and vicissitudes which included the prison (he was arrested for crimen falsi on 17/3/1773, sentenced on 7/3/1775 and released on 19/4/1786), and the workhouse. He was in turn clerk, traveller, soldier, astrologist, law lecturer, advocate, preacher, editor of a libellous newspaper and author of a number of legal works (some being of an elementary or semipopular nature), memoirs, fiction and astrological works (under the name of Meester Franciscus, his nom-de-guerre as a necromancer): he published fully forty books and booklets. . . . His autobiography, published by his Good Samaritan, Elwe, in 1792 "om daar uit de kosten van myne begrafnis te vinden" is a fascinating document. Frequently omitting or concealing what we would like to know, but shamelessly frank on other occasions, it is at once instructive, amusing and pathetic. His chief claim to fame to-day is the Rechtsgeleerd Woordenboek, which he edited with the help of "een genootschap van rechtsgeleerden". The idea may have been his, and he probably had a good deal to do with the Woordenboek itself, but I am satisfied from internal evidence, the history and other works of the two men, that one of his collaborators, Lucas Willem Kramp, is really entitled to the fame which Kersteman has attained. Kramp was responsible for much of the Woordenboek and most of the more valuable

Aanhangzel. Who the other members of the "Genootschap" were, I have not
been able to discover. Kersteman had prepared the material for some of the 5th
(last) part of the Woordenboek but refused to continue when the 4th part was
only half ready for press.'

—A A Roberts *A South African Legal Bibliography* (1942) 174.

'Een van die dinge waaroor Schorer gekla het, was die gemak waarmee grade
aan die hoër skole en selfs erkende universiteite verkry kon word, en Schorer se
klagte skyn nie heeltemal ongegrond te gewees het nie. Die lewensverhaal van
F L Kersteman (1728 tot ongeveer 1792) bewys dit ook. Franciscus, wie se
familienaam eintlik Lievens was, het na die egskeiding van sy ouers sy moeder
se familienaam, Kersteman, aanvaar en is daarom aan ons bekend as Franciscus
Lievens Kersteman. Hy was 'n losbol wat 'n paar jaar aan die universiteit van
Leiden losbandig verslyt het, 'n ruk in die leër was, 'n doktorsgraad in
Harderwijk in ses weke verkry het, as advokaat gepraktiseer het, en selfs as
"lector juris" en "professor honorarius" te Heusden werksaam was. Kersteman
het blykbaar niks benede hom geag as hy maar geld daarmee kon maak nie. Hy
het sensasie-lektuur vervaardig en ook "regslektuur", selfs terwyl hy 'n paar
jaar in die tronk gesit het, gevonnis weens vervalsing. Kersteman se *Hollandsch
Rechtsgeleerd Woorden-Boek* was een van sy skemas om geld te maak. Die werk
is op inskrywing stuksgewyse uitgegee onder redaksie van Kersteman, wat hom
nog voor die voltooiing "onttrek" het. Die werk was so sleg gedoen dat die
uitgewer op aandrang van die intekenaars aanvullings moes maak, en dit is dan
ook gedoen in die "aanhangsel" tot die oorspronklike woordeboek. Die
"aanhangsel" beslaan twee bande, en die redakteur van die aanhangsel en
die slotgedeelte van die "woordeboek" was 'n "regsgeleerde" wat onder die
skuilnaam "Nisi utile est, quod facimus, stulta est gloria" geskryf het. Die
"regsgeleerde" met die mooiklinkende spreuk as skuilnaam, was die Amster-
damse notaris L W Kramp. Die woordeboek en die aanhangsel bestaan uit
artikels, kort en langerig, oor allerlei onderwerpe, alfabeties gerangskik. Op die
titelblad en in die voorrede van die "woordeboek" word vermeld dat dit die
werk is van 'n genootskap van regsgeleerdes, onder toesig van Kersteman, en
dat die inligting ontleen is aan die werke en toegestuurde geskrifte van
vermaarde regsgeleerdes. Wat van die "genootskap" geword het toe Kersteman
hom aan die onderneming "onttrek" het, is nie duidelik nie, want die arme
"boekverkoper" kon niemand kry om die werk te doen nie totdat Kramp in die
bresse getree het. Hoe dit ook al mag wees, die redakteurs Kersteman en Kramp
het veel ontleen aan die werke van voorgangers. Kersteman skyn 'n voorliefde
te gehad het vir Van Leeuwen, Van Zurck en Boel, terwyl Kramp weer die
oorgrote deel van die "aanhangsel" uit Voet oorgeskryf het en verder aan Van
Bijnkershoek heelwat ontleen het. Die "woordeboek" self is nie juis 'n
belangrike deel van ons regsliteratuur nie, maar die "aanhangsel" word nogal
dikwels gebruik weens die vertalings van stukke van Voet se Pandekte-
kommentaar, wat daarin voorkom.'

—J C de Wet *Die Ou Skrywers in Perspektief* (1988) 168–70 (footnotes omitted).

ANTONIE (ANTONIUS, ANTOINE) FRANÇOIS KOCK

1869–1948. Member of the Pretoria Bar 1895–8. Judge of the High Court of the South African Republic (Transvaal) 1898–9. Member of the Johannesburg Bar 1902–5.

'In 1896 the First Volksraad issued regulations for the appointment of government officials. These regulations provided, inter alia, that when appointments were considered, preference had to be given to fully-franchised inhabitants of the ZAR. This in effect meant that burghers were to be appointed to government posts in preference to uitlanders. Being a born and bred Afrikaner, and well-educated to boot, Antonie could benefit greatly from this patriotic generosity.

'And benefit he did. A year later, in September 1897, Reinhold Gregorowski retired from the Bench to accept an appointment as State Attorney, thus creating a vacancy on the Bench. Antonie recognised his golden opportunity, and on 18 September 1897 he addressed a letter to the State Secretary, making application "met alle bescheidenheid" for the vacancy on the Bench. In support of his application he cited the regulation described above, and the fact that he was properly legally qualified. He concluded his letter as follows:

"Hopende en derhalwe versekerd sijnde dat de Edel Achtbare Regeering met advies en consent van den Edel Achtb. Uitv. Raad, mij recht sal doen geschieden ter nakoming van hierboven aangehaalde V.R. Besluiten . . ."

'Antonie's application was supported by no fewer than four separate *memories* (petitions) from inhabitants of the Heidelberg and Mooiriver districts.

'They all urged the government to appoint Antonie on the grounds that he was "een zoon des landts" (a "son of the soil", as he later became known) and would, in the opinion of the petitionaries, be a fine judge and a credit to the country. In fact, the popular demand for his appointment was such that Antonie had to request the people, via a newspaper, to refrain from submitting further petitions. Two other applications were also received, but Antonie was the only one who was both properly and legally qualified and a son of the soil.

'Antonie's application did not, however, meet with universal approval. Eugène Marais wrote the following of Kock's application in *Land en Volk*:

"Het schryven van deze brief heeft veel amusement en tevens afkeuring verwekt onder de collega's van den heer Kock, want men achte zyn handelswyze niet precies in accoord met de tradities zyner professie."

'In contrast to the patriotic fervour of the burghers, the government showed some hesitancy and must have experienced difficulty in finding a suitable person to fill the vacancy, for it was not until June 1898 that Antonie Kock was appointed. As with his application, so with his appointment, approval was not universal. Antonie's youth and inexperience were the two big factors on which the criticism was founded. Somewhat laconically, Eugène Marais observed in *Land en Volk* that a person had to be over 30 years of age before he could be appointed a *landdrost*, but that this qualification did not apply to the exalted position of judge.

'Antonie François Kock was sworn in as fifth puisne judge of the High Court of the ZAR (together with JA Schagen van Leeuwen as fourth puisne judge) on 9 June 1898, three-and-a-half months before his twenty-ninth birthday. He was to remain a judge until the outbreak of the Anglo-Boer War in October of the following year.'

—Derek van der Merwe 'The Extraordinary Life of Judge Antonie François Kock' (1981) 22(1) *Codicillus* at 12–13 (footnotes omitted).

The Edgar case

'Apart from the controversy surrounding his appointment, Antonie's judicial career would have passed somewhat unobtrusively had it not been for the famous so-called Edgar case, over which he presided. The salient facts of this case are briefly the following: On the Saturday night before Christmas 1898 Tom Edgar, a member of the uitlander community in Johannesburg, was returning home round about midnight when he was stopped by four men not far from his home. An argument started, which resulted in Edgar, a big man, knocking one of the men unconscious with a blow to the head. He then proceeded home. The three remaining men thought their friend to be dead, and shouted for help. Four policemen arrived, amongst them Barend Stephanus Jones. They were also under the impression that the man was dead, and that a murder had been committed. They entered Edgar's house but he refused to open his bedroom door, whereupon the policemen forced it open. They entered the room with Jones in the lead brandishing a pistol. Edgar rushed at the men and hit Jones across the head with a stick to which a bolt had been attached. Jones fired his pistol and killed Edgar instantly. Jones was indicted for culpable homicide early in 1899 before Judge Kock. Ex-Chief Justice Kotzé was counsel for the defence. The jury, composed entirely of burghers, found him not guilty, being of the opinion that Jones had acted in self-defence. Judge Kock, in discharging Jones, said that he hoped the police under difficult circumstances would always know how to do their duty.

'Of course, the incident itself, the trial and Judge Kock's remarks served to further alienate the burghers and the uitlanders. It is probably no exaggeration to say that the Edgar case was a factor which contributed to the outbreak of the Anglo-Boer War some months later. This is evident, for example, from the feelings of the British High Commissioner, Sir Alfred Milner, who felt that "that verdict, and the attitude of the Judge throughout, indicated such bias as fully to justify . . . the widespread feeling among the Uitlanders that no justice was to be had in the Courts when their interests and sympathies clashed with those of the Burghers." On the other hand, many observers felt that no other verdict on the available evidence was possible, and that the decision was fully justified.'

—Van der Merwe op cit at 13–14 (footnotes omitted).

Blowing up the gold mines

'The Anglo-Boer War broke out on 11 October 1899. Martial law was proclaimed and the ordinary judicial functions ceased. Before the war, Antonie had gained a reputation for his fierce patriotism and antagonism towards the British. Antonie was appointed chief of staff of the commando led by his father. He was with his father when he was mortally wounded, but managed to escape capture, joining the commando of General Lucas Meyer (General Kock's successor) also as chief of staff. Apparently he was a confidante of many of the generals and even of President Kruger. At the Battle of Spionkop he was appointed to the rank of temporary general. After this battle, he continued to call himself "General" Kock.

'When Antonie returned to Pretoria on leave, he met F W Reitz, himself a former judge and State Secretary at the time. With the tide of the war turning against them, the ZAR government strongly entertained the idea of blowing up the gold mines of the Witwatersrand, to deny the British access to the means of a valuable revenue. Commandant-General Louis Botha, however, rejected such plans outright, and the idea was then officially dropped. Unofficially, however, some officials still clung to the idea. The arrival of the young and energetic Antonie Kock presented a first-class opportunity to carry out the plans. Reitz gave him a letter addressed to the Special Commandant of Johannesburg, Dr F E T Krause [qv], in which he was requested to supply Antonie with "karren, trollies, paarden of muilen en andere benodigdheden, om sekere instructies van de Regeering uit te voeren". Antonie presented this letter to Krause late in May 1900, but Krause refused him assistance, as he had received word from General Botha that he would be held personally responsible for the blowing-up of the gold mines. Krause also warned Antonie that if he persisted in his mission, he would do all he could to stop him, even if it meant shooting him.'

[Kock then went with an armed commando of a hundred men to the Robinson gold mine, where they found 120 000 ounces of gold lying unguarded in the open. It was intended that the gold be transported to the Government in Pretoria to prevent its falling into the hands of the British, but Kock was convinced that Krause had been treacherous.]

'In his anger at the supposed treachery, Antonie temporarily shelved his idea of destroying the mine, and returned to Johannesburg with his men, to confront Krause and demand an explanation. Upon arrival, Antonie left his men outside Krause's office and burst inside. With Dr Krause was Commandant van Diggelen, the police chief in Johannesburg. Krause denied all knowledge of the gold and in turn demanded to know from Kock what he was doing in the mine. Of course Kock then had to confess to his plans to destroy the mine. A heated argument developed, and before long Antonie whipped out his revolver and pointed it at Krause. Van Diggelen, however, was behind Antonie. He lunged at Antonie and pinned his arms to his side, thus rendering him powerless. Antonie was under arrest.

'The crisis was not yet over. Kock's armed and restless commando were still waiting outside for their "General". Dr Krause's quick thinking saved the day. He went outside, beckoned to the second-in-command, one Capt McCullum, an Irishman, and told him that their leader was involved in important negotiations, and that he had given orders for them to return to the mine and await his arrival. Fortunately they did not question Krause's statement and left for the mine. Antonie was taken to the Fort in Johannesburg and from there by armed escort to Pretoria, to face possible charges of attempted sabotage. [He was subsequently released.] Some historians hold that the legend of the missing Kruger millions has its origin in the discovery by Antonie Kock of the 120 000 ounces of gold on the site of the Robinson gold mine. This gold was apparently taken, upon the instructions of Dr Krause, under armed escort to the Fort, and from there to

Pretoria, from whence it was distributed to the Republican forces in the Lowveld. The legend, therefore, is destined to stay a legend, at least as far as this version is concerned.'

—Van der Merwe op cit at 14–15 (footnotes omitted).

Kock thereafter became President of the Military Court of the Boers. He sentenced many to imprisonment and even to death for crimes such as theft and sabotage (a crime which he had just avoided committing himself). Unpopular, he narrowly avoided being killed by the prisoners. In his De Geinspireede Gedichten *(Johannesburg 1903) in the* 'Biographie' *Kock says that he then left for Europe. There he met President Kruger and offered to introduce him to members of the royalty and aristocracy, to enable Kruger to plead his cause. The offer was declined. Kock then decided to return to the Transvaal, to fight for his country. He landed at Port Elizabeth on 21 September 1901, according to the* 'Biographie' *as a clean-shaven, blue-bespectacled individual clad in the garb of a Polish Jew and sporting the name of Polensky. Securing a position as a commercial traveller, he obtained military permits to travel to Cradock on behalf of the* 'Cordes Patent Friction Reducing Syndicate'. *What happened is now recounted by Mr Justice F G Gardiner, who, as a member of the Cape Bar, appeared for him at his trial before a military court at Graaff-Reinet in 1902.*

'The permits were in the name of Morees, but at Port Elizabeth Kock also passed under the name of Wilkinson. Some sapient military authority may have thought that a Patent Friction Reducing Syndicate was the very thing for a district like Cradock, where the Boers were roaming about.

'At Cradock he got permits to go to farms and went to the farm Roode Taaibosch, belonging to J. L. Botha. He took Botha's horse, after telling Miss Botha he was doing so, and joined a small body of rebels. The rebels first visited the farm, and took Kock with them. It was the following day that the horse was taken. . . .

'He was charged on four counts:

'1. *Being a spy*—in that landing at Port Elizabeth under the name of Polensky, in the disguise of a commercial traveller, for Constance of Paris, and being further engaged as a traveller for the Cordes Patent Friction Reducing Syndicate, he passed through the towns of Uitenhage, Grahamstown and Cradock under the assumed name of Morees, with a view to collecting information concerning His Majesty's Forces and conveying same to the enemy.

'2. By *fraudulent* means *obtaining a railway permit* from the military authorities.

'3. By *fraudulent* means *obtaining a road permit* from the military authorities.

'4. *Theft* (of Botha's horse) . . .

'When a military court convicts on any charge, it does not then announce its verdict. This is only done when there is a full acquittal. In case of a conviction, the verdict and sentence have first to be confirmed by the proper authority, and then are promulgated. Accordingly, when there was no announcement, I knew that Kock had been convicted of something. The Colonel who presided very kindly relieved my anxiety by telling me privately that on the charge of spying Kock had been acquitted. The fate of the other charges did not matter so much, for on them Kock could only be imprisoned, and in any case he was bound to be detained as a prisoner of war. I never heard what the actual verdict was.

'I have heard that Kock subsequently married a rich girl. Eventually he became insane and was sent to an asylum.

'I found him a very pleasant client to deal with. Though a member of the Bar, he always deferred to my views as to how the case should be conducted after we had fully discussed his ideas.

'This trial afforded an instance of how unreliable identification can sometimes be. When Kock joined the rebels, he was clean-shaven. By the time of his trial, he had grown a beard. An old Native was called to prove that Kock had asked him where the Boers were. At the trial the prisoner was allowed to sit next to me. The Native was asked, in a very fair way, whether he saw the man who spoke to him, in Court. No indication was given to him as to who the man was. He evidently noticed that there were two civilians playing a prominent part in the case, Kock and I. He looked at Kock, saw he was a bearded man, and then turned towards me; saying "Daarie baas", he identified me as having tried to join the Boers. Needless to say, this greatly amused the military court, with whom I was on the best of terms.'

—'Extracts from the Legal Reminiscences of Mr. Justice F. G. Gardiner' (1962) 79 *SALJ* 69 at 70–1. (Kock's 'Biographie' says that he was banished for life. En route to exile he escaped from the Umbilo Camp at Durban. In the mean time peace had been concluded. Kock arrived at Estcourt under the name of Marais; thereafter he went to Volksrust, Standerton, and finally to Pretoria, where he was arrested and given the choice between taking the oath of allegiance or exile. After some hesitation he decided to take the oath. Van der Merwe (op cit at 17; footnotes omitted) gives a moving picture of Kock's fate thereafter: 'The bold and adventurous life which Antonie had led tragically turned into a grey nothingness shortly after the war. Antonie became insane and was confined to a mental institution in Pretoria, where he died on 13 July 1948, more than forty long years later. The *Zuid-Afrikaansche Republiek* had blossomed and died, and remained but a fading memory. So, too, Antonie François Kock had blossomed with his beloved Republic, cramming a life-time of experiences into his youthful thirty-odd years, and then faded into obscurity.')

SIR JOHANNES GYSBERT (JOHN GILBERT) KOTZÉ

1849–1940. Member of the Cape Bar 1874–6. Member of the Eastern Districts Bar 1876–7. Judge of the High Court of the South African Republic (Transvaal) 1877–81. Chief Justice 1881–98. Member of the Pretoria Bar 1898–9. Attorney-General of Rhodesia 1900–3. KC 1902. Judge of the Eastern Districts Court 1903–4. Judge President 1904–13. Judge of the Cape Provincial Division 1913–20. Judge President 1920–2. Judge of Appeal 1922–7. Knighted 1917. Author of legal and other works.

The 'boy judge'

'At one corner of the square the Judge was holding the Court in a large room next to the Post-office which is kept for that and other public services. The Judge I had met at Pretoria, and had been much struck by his youth. One expects a judge to be reverend with years, but this was hardly more than a boy judge. He had been brought from the Cape Bar to act as Judge in the Transvaal before the annexation—when the payment even of a judge's salary must have been a matter of much doubt. But the annexation came speedily and the position of the newcomer was made sure by British authority. He at any rate must approve the great step taken by Sir Theophilus Shepstone. I was assured when at Pretoria that the colony generally had every reason to be satisfied with the choice made by the Republic. He will no doubt have assistant Judges and become a Chief Justice before long and may probably live to be the oldest legal pundit under the British Crown. I went into the Court to look at him while at work, but was not much edified as the case then before him was carried on in Dutch. Dutch and English have to be used in the Court as one or the other language may be needed. An interpreter is present, but as all the parties concerned in the case, including the Judge and the jury, were conversant with Dutch, no interpreter was wanted when I was there.'

—Anthony Trollope *South Africa* II (London 1878) 121–2.

The famous dismissal by President Kruger of Chief Justice Kotzé on 16 February 1898 arose out of the decision by the High Court in Brown v Leyds NO (1897) 4 Off Rep 17 *that besluiten (informal resolutions of the legislature (the Volksraad)) were invalid as to form, the Constitution (Grondwet) making fundamental law against which the judiciary could test legislation. The Volksraad then passed Law 1 of 1897, stating that the judges had no testing right, and that the President could require judges to state that they would not arrogate to themselves such right, on penalty of being dismissed by the President. Kotzé renounced his undertaking, for various reasons, whereupon Kruger dismissed him.*

'CHIEF JUSTICE KOTZÉ'

Caricature by William Howard Schröder 1852–92), from The Schröder Art Memento *(Pretoria 1894)*

'Legal opinion has been divided since the *tempus disputationis* whether the judgment in *Brown* v. *Leyds, N.O.* was correct, and whether the threats and actions of the legislature and the President were a dangerous intrusion on the independence of the judiciary. Hertzog in the Free State deprecated the activities of the Government. Esselen, on the other hand, supported the President. Lord Selborne, modestly disavowing any knowledge of the intricacies of the law, considered that Kotzé was wrong in his judgment, and that, in any event, he "has singularly mismanaged his case. He has been utterly beaten in the game of diamond cut diamond by Kruger." To which Milner replied: "The idea is, that he played his cards badly, but, as we can all see now, *he never had any cards to play.*"

But the unkindest cut of all was still to come. In his inaugural speech on 12th May, 1898, to the Eersten Volksraad on his election as President for the fourth time, Kruger addressed this homily to the Bench, using appropriate Biblical arguments:

"Honourable judges . . . only the Almighty, the Sovereign, God alone may set aside a statute, not the subjects. . . . The testing right is a principle of the Devil's."

Then Kruger dwelt long on the shock to the country, the uncertainty of the state of the law and the lack of confidence in the Republic consequent on the exercise by the court of the power to set aside statutes. He ended:

"Honourable gentlemen, I think so highly of the capacity of the former Chief Justice that, were I to know this would help, I would have him placed in a lunatic asylum, and wait until he is restored to health, in order to use his services again. His capacity was high, but he fell into error, in that he accepted the testing right, that principle of the Devil's.'''

—Ellison Kahn 'The History of the Administration of Justice in the South African Republic' (1958) 75 *SALJ* 397 at 415 (footnotes omitted).

'At the swearing-in ceremony that took place in Pretoria on 12th May, 1898, pursuant to his recent re-election for a fourth term of office, the President, in the course of his speech, availed himself of this public occasion to make some interesting references to the testing right. After addressing himself to the members of the *Volksraden* and certain other bodies represented at the gathering, he turned to the new Chief Justice, R. Gregorowski, and the other judges of the High Court and the State Attorney and delivered a lengthy homily which, if it was *fortiter in re*, could hardly be said to be *suaviter in modo*. In dealing with the question of the refusal by a court of law to give effect to statutes, he suggested looking back to the time of Moses. The latter made law but he was not entitled to depart from it. Only the Supreme Power, the Sovereign, God alone, not subordinates, could disapprove of laws. The Devil introduced the testing right into Paradise and tested God's word which said: Ye shall not eat of this tree lest ye die. But the Devil came and tested the word saying Ye shall not die, but God knows then you will be equal to God. So we see under Moses, the President said, that Korah, Dathan and Abiram arrogated to themselves the testing right and disorganised the country. Revolt and discord arose against Moses until God destroyed the three of them because they had acted contrary to the truth, contrary to God's law. Having cited the fate of Korah, Dathan and Abiram, the President proceeded:

"The testing right is a principle of the Devil. Listen with attention to what I say and do not regard it as too trifling. We will have to appear before God some day and I do not know whether I shall have the opportunity of addressing you again. This may be the last time. Also let the ministers (leeraars) hear what I say. Ye judges give the whole country a shock if you seize the testing right; for those who have acquired rights under whatever law or Volksraadbesluit will then be agitated because they do not know how things will go when the court has to decide, if the court is able to set aside a law. Then trust in our country will have collapsed and not only in the country but also in the court and the Volksraad."

'The President then proceeded to deal with ex-Chief Justice Kotzé, and after trouncing him for saying in a manifesto that, if the People would not assist him, he would apply to England, he remarked, *inter alia*, that the ex-Chief Justice's capabilities were good but that he went astray by accepting the principle of the

Devil, the testing right. None of the judges present has, so far as I am aware, left any record of the impression this speech made on his mind. If any of them did not remember the case of Korah, Dathan and Abiram, as is possible, it seems not improbable that that evening in his study he perused the report of it in the book of Numbers and meditated in sombre mood on the fate of those three misguided Israelites.'

—Introduction by B A Tindall, Judge of the Appellate Division (q v), to Sir John Gilbert Kotzé *Memoirs and Reminiscences II* (1949) xli–xlii.

Another extract from the inaugural speech of President Kruger on 12 May 1898

'"Our late Chief Justice (Kotzé), with some of his colleagues, assumed the right of criticism (of the laws) and became as wanton as a fish in the water that was free to swim about as it pleased. However, he jumped out of the water, that is to say, out of the law, on to dry land. The Volksraad then passed a resolution, with reference to the laws of the land, to the effect that, if a judge refuses to submit to them, I must dismiss him. I did my best, but the late Chief Justice was as slippery as a fish that has just jumped out of the water, so that I could not master him. Then his colleague, the Chief Justice of the Cape Colony, who knew the ability of our late Chief Justice, came, of his own accord, to my assistance, and we got him back into the water, that is to say, the law. Then I

was glad, because I knew the ability of the late Chief Justice and did not wish to lose him. After that, the late Chief Justice again became so wanton that he jumped so far out of the water that I saw no chance of getting him back and had to let him go, the more so as he then roundly declared that he did not wish to go back to it, because he refused to acknowledge the law as I understood it." The President went on to discuss the history of the controversy with Chief Justice Kotzé, and concluded his homely illustrations by adding: "Gentlemen, I appreciate the late Chief Justice's abilities so highly that, if I thought it would do any good, I would have him confined in a lunatic asylum (for I liked him greatly), and wait until he was cured to employ him again. His abilities were great, but he went astray when he accepted the Devil's principle, the right of criticism. Let me speak my mind to you, for the late Chief Justice has said that I dismissed him illegally. Now all the world can hear how the matter really happened."'

Caricature of Kotzé CJ of the Transvaal by William Howard Schröder (1852–92), from The Schröder Art Memento *(Pretoria 1894)*

—Manfred Nathan *Paul Kruger: His Life and Times* (1941) 415–16.

The 'boy judge' becomes too old

'There was Sir John Kotzé, who began almost as a boy-judge in the earlier days of the old Transvaal Republic, and had probably the longest judicial life of any lawyer in our history. He was Chief Justice of the Transvaal when, about 1897, he incurred the displeasure of President Kruger and his Government by pronouncing some of the laws or resolutions passed by the Volksraad to be invalid—much what the Court of Appeal did in our own time to two Acts of the Union Parliament. Kotzé was forced to resign, and there was much speculation as to who would succeed him as Chief Justice. One wag at the time, parodying Tennyson's poem, wrote of Kruger as saying:

"May there be no moaning at the Bar
When I put out Kotzé."

'Kotzé served for a time as Attorney-General in Rhodesia, then as Judge in the Cape, both in Grahamstown and Cape Town, and wound up as a Judge of Appeal. In those days there was no age limit for Judges, and Kotzé hung on to the end, although he had become extremely deaf. It was said that this limpet-like quality of his helped to lead the framers of the Union Constitution to put in an age-limit of seventy for judges.'

—Leslie Blackwell (qv) *Are Judges Human?* (1962) 192–3.

So they were

'One of those who read Kotzé's memoirs and found them "unutterably dull" was Sir John Wessels (letter to Innes of 2 June 1927).'

—Hugh Corder *Judges at Work: The Role and Attitudes of the South African Appellate Judiciary, 1910–1950* (1984) 37.

FREDERICK EDWARD TRAUGOTT (FRITZ) KRAUSE

1868–1959. Member of the Pretoria Bar 1893–6. First State Prosecutor in Johannesburg 1896–9. Member of the Cape Bar 1904–5. Member of the Johannesburg Bar 1905–23. KC 1912. Judge of the Transvaal Provincial Division 1923–33. Judge President of the Orange Free State Provincial Division 1933–8.

Krause goes to prison

'The humane attitude of Innes is well illustrated by his oft-cited judgment in the case of *Ex parte Krause* 1905 TS 221. Dr. F. E. T. ("Fritz") Krause, First State Prosecutor in Johannesburg in the old South African Republic and Special Commandant of the Witwatersrand during the Anglo-Boer War, had been convicted in England of an attempt to incite to the commission of the murder of J. Douglas Forster, one-time Kimberley advocate, a mysterious member of the British intelligence division, a man of very doubtful character, who in the British Press was advocating that all members of the Republican forces in the field should be summarily shot when captured, as being bandits and robbers. Krause responded by writing to Cornelius Broeksma, a former prosecutor on his staff who was then awaiting trial by court martial, that Broeksma's duty was to inform "our people" that Forster should be lawfully taken and shot or in some other way rendered harmless. These letters were intercepted. Broeksma was later sentenced by the military court to death for breaking his oath and inciting others to break their oaths of neutrality, of treachery and of high treason, and was executed. Subsequently came Krause's conviction in England. He was sentenced to two years' imprisonment, as a result of which he was removed from the roll of barristers by the Middle Temple, London, the Inn of Court that had admitted him. Before completion of his term of imprisonment Krause was released on probation and returned to South Africa in April 1904. As Milner would not permit him to enter the Transvaal, Krause commenced practising in the Cape. In terms of section 10 of the Administration of Justice Proclamation 14 of 1902 (T) all pre-war advocates had to apply for readmission. Krause's initial application to the Transvaal Supreme Court resulted in a reference by it to the Bar Council of that colony, which advised him to apply to the Benchers of the Middle Temple for reinstatement.

Unfortunately for him his petition there was rejected on 20 January 1905, despite his producing letters of recommendation from the Chief Justice of the Cape Colony, Sir Henry de Villiers, J. G. Kotzé, Judge President of the Eastern Districts Court and former Chief Justice of the South African Republic, J. C. Smuts and Victor Sampson, Attorney-General of the Cape. No hearing was afforded Krause. There was a close division, and there is cause to believe that political feelings ran high at the Benchers' meeting.

'That was the state of affairs when Krause applied once more to the full bench of the Transvaal Supreme Court, composed of the Chief Justice, Sir James Rose Innes, Mr Justice William H. Solomon and Mr Justice A. Weir Mason. The court held that a criminal conviction as such does not disqualify a person from admission as an advocate or an attorney—it will only do so if it shows that the culprit is of a character not worthy of admission to the honourable profession concerned; and further, that as Krause's offence was political in nature, not committed with any object of personal gain or revenge, the court would in the exercise of its discretion admit him as an advocate. To complete the story: Krause opened chambers in Johannesburg and built up what was probably the largest criminal practice ever known in this country. In 1912 he was appointed King's Counsel. Eleven years later he was elevated to the Transvaal Bench; 1933 saw his transfer to the Orange Free State Court as Judge President, where he remained until he attained the retirement age of 70 in 1938. Even thereafter the force of his personality, the agility of his mind and the interest he showed in the affairs of State and man, in particular penal reform, made him a public figure almost to the day of his death in 1959 at the age of 91.'

　　—Ellison Kahn 'James Rose Innes' in R E de Villiers (ed) *Better Than They Knew* II (1974) 57 at 88–9. (Krause was granted a free pardon by Edward VII in 1909. In 1921 the Middle Temple reinstated him. Cornelius Broeksma (1863–1901) had a son and grandson who achieved prominence in the law. They were A H Broeksma QC (1895–1977), one-time Attorney-General of the Cape and later a leading member of the Cape Bar, who split with the National Party on the 'Coloured vote' plan; and Cornelius Broeksma, judge of the Cape Provincial Division, who died in 1984.) (On Krause and the protection of the gold mines, see KOCK.)

　　' . . . Judge William Pittman [qv], who was with him the evening before histrial (Pittman was at that time enrolled as a student at Oxford and the Middle Temple), tells me that Krause was put to work in the prison laundry, where he kept the books, and that for the whole period of his imprisonment he was well treated in a manner which mitigated the rigours of ordinary prison life.

'Be that as it may, the conclusion seems inescapable that Krause's experience in

'DR F. E. T. KRAUSE'

Caricature by D C Boonzaier (1865–1950), from his Rand
Faces *(1915) 5*

gaol played an important part in equipping him for his remarkable career as a criminal lawyer, and what is much more important, his valuable services to the community in later life in the field of penal reform.'

—A A Roberts 'The Late F. E. T. Krause' (1959) 76 *SALJ* 364 at 368.

'Back in Johannesburg I was admitted to the Bar on the 21st March, 1906. Dr. F. E. T. Krause had been admitted the year before. He was looking for someone to share Chambers with him. He had approached some of his old friends of the Republican days. He had told them what he told me, namely, that there were certain firms in this town who would not brief him because of the part he had played in the Reform Trial. He said that if they did not brief him they would not brief anyone who shared Chambers with him. His friends declined the honour. I accepted the offer. He was right. They never briefed either of us. And so, under these unpromising circumstances, began what was for me a most pleasant and profitable association which lasted for seventeen years. It was terminated by his promotion to the Bench.'

—H H Morris KC *The First Forty Years* (1948) 39.

Krause held the degree of Doctor Juris of the University of Amsterdam, which he obtained in 1893, and sported the title of 'Doctor'.

'WHEN IS A DOCTOR NOT A DOCTOR?

'In the days when Doctor Krause and I shared Chambers, a Lady walked into my room. I immediately got the impression that she would be needing the attentions of a medical man very shortly.

'She asked if I was Dr. Krause.

'I was not.

'"Is he in?"

'"No."

'"Where is he?"

'I did not know.

'When would he be in?

'That also I did not know.

'"Does he still take cases?"

'This sounded like business, so I sat up.

'"He does."

'She gave her name and address. I must please tell Doctor Krause to be ready to attend her confinement at the end of the month. He was not to send any understudy. She wanted only the best.

'I told her he was a Doctor of Laws, and not a Doctor of Medicine. She seemed somewhat surprised. I was about to explain the difference. She interrupted me. She said she had never heard of a Doctor of Laws. She said it was a disgrace that a man of Doctor Krause's standing should go about telling people that he was a doctor when he was nothing of the sort. She said she had come all the way from Vrededorp to see him, and this is what she got for her trouble.

'In her condition she could hardly flounce out of the room. She made a very brave effort.

'The answer to the question is: "When he is Doctor Krause."'

—H H Morris KC *In and Out of Court* (1950) 20–1.

'The story is told that shortly after he was appointed a judge in 1923 Krause spoke with deep sympathy to a man who had pleaded with him to realise the tragedy of his appearance in the dock.

'"I can appreciate the tragic position in which you find yourself, perhaps better than you realise," Krause said. "But", he added, probably remembering the time when he, too, stood in the dock and listened to the judge's admonitions, "I have to do my duty and punish you for the crime you have committed."

'In the cells the prisoner asked a warder what the judge had implied by his remarks.

'"Don't you know," the warder said, "he was a gaolbird himself once and he served much longer than you will. He got two years. He's only given you six months."'

—Benjamin Bennett *The Noose Tightens* (1974) 204.

The anonymous letter in contempt of court

'The courts are extremely vigilant as to their reputation. In 1933 *The Friend* [a newspaper published in Bloemfontein] published an anonymous letter which started *inter alia*:

"Sir,—As an old Bloemfonteiner I wish to register my protest, with so many others of my townsmen, against the extraordinary and absurd decision of the Appeal Court to change the venue of a trial to Cape Town on the ground of the climatic conditions alleged to prevail here during the summer months. . . . If there are judges who do not like to reside or sojourn here, well, let them hand in their resignations. There are as many good fish in the sea as come out of it. . . . Do our other courts in the various provinces also wish to become peripatetic . . .? . . . [T]he health reasons relied upon by the Court are, in my opinion, as flimsy as a curtain of gossamer."

'The Appellate Division found that there could be "no justification before us of the opprobrious terms used and opinions expressed", that "the letter says that this Court gave an absurd judgment based upon no reasons whatsoever. That in itself is a clear contempt. And in addition there is the further insinuation of ulterior and personal motives. . . . The writer of the letter, who modestly disguises his identity under anonymity, . . . traduces the personnel of this Court." (Stratford

CJ in *In re Mackenzie* 1933 AD 367 at 370. [The judges almost certainly knew that the letter-writer was Mr Justice Krause, Judge President of the Orange Free State Provincial Division.]) The Appellate Division was prepared to give the editor "the benefit of any doubt it may have and assume that the penitence he now expresses is sincere". Its order was that he publish an apology in the terms accepted by the Court, and pay a fine of £50.'

> —Ellison Kahn & Brian R Bamford 'Sugar and Salt' (1965) 82 *SALJ* 53 at 58–9. (The cause of the writing and publication of the letter, which were preceded by almost as strong leaders of condemnation in *The Friend* and protests by the City Council, the Chamber of Commerce and the local Bar Council, was the decision of the Appellate Division in September 1933 in *Rhodesian Corporation Ltd v Globe and Phoenix Gold Mining Co Ltd* 1933 AD 357 to grant leave for the appeal to be heard in Cape Town during the vacation.
>
> Stratford ACJ, Beyers JA and J E R de Villiers JA held that the appeal was of unprecedented magnitude, intricacy and importance, likely to last over four weeks; that it was desirable that it be heard by the full court of five permanent judges of appeal, which would not be possible until mid-December; that the expense and inconvenience to the parties that would be caused by a postponement to a date in term-time—the end of March–April term—were not justified. But a hearing in Bloemfontein in the vacation during the hot summer months of December, January and February, it had been stated, would have deleterious effects on the health of leading counsel for the appellants (Graham Mackeurtan KC (q v)) and would affect the health and efficiency of others concerned in the case. Thus there were the exceptional circumstances justifying a change of venue in terms of s 16 of the Administration of Justice Act 27 of 1912. The appeal was heard on 18–22 December 1933 and 2 January to 2 February 1934; 1934 AD 293, 313.)

Another account of the famous letter

'A classical example of T. W. M's [Mackenzie's] devotion to Bloemfontein, against the background of what he felt was the national interest, occurred when *The Friend* took up the cudgels in an attempt to get the Appeal Court judges to make their headquarters and take up residence in the country's officially-recognized judicial capital. The paper published a scathing letter from an anonymous correspondent (years afterwards identified as none other than the Judge President of the Orange Free State, Mr Justice F. E. T. Krause) which criticized the members of the Appeal Court for giving all sorts of tenuous ("gossamer") reasons against such a move. There was an immediate reaction. T. W. M. [as editor] was charged to appear before the court—on a Saturday morning, when it did not usually sit—to answer a charge of contempt. It was a unique event in South African legal history. There was a full Bench, presided over by the Chief Justice (Mr Justice Stratford) and T. W. M. was found guilty. He was sentenced to pay a fine [of £50] and to publish an apology in the first available issue of *The Friend*. T. W. M. toiled during that week-end over a long, skilfully worded leader, suitably vetted by a senior advocate, and it appeared on the Monday.'

> —Louis Hotz 'Thomas William Mackenzie' in R M de Villiers (ed) *Better than They Knew* II (1974) 32 at 41–2. (*The Friend* on the Monday had the last word in a leader: 'If any of these changes or reforms [in the law relating to the sitting of the Appellate

'KRAUSE J.'
From (1932) 1 South African Law Times *128*

Division] are furthered by the present publicity, the £50 fine paid on Saturday may be regarded as another contribution by *The Friend* to a worthy public cause.' See René de Villiers in *The Star* 11 June 1982.)

Payment of income tax

'Judges have had to sit in judgment on themselves collectively as well as individually. They have faced the situation manfully. No one has suggested for a moment that they should have recused themselves *en bloc*. On the two best known occasions they found against themselves. The one was where they held that rules of court they had framed were *ultra vires (Ex parte Christodolides* 1953 (2) SA 192 (T)). The other was where Mr. Justice Krause unsuccessfully contended that the Income Tax Act of 1925 was not applicable to him because section 100 of the South Africa Act provided that the remuneration of judges should not be diminished during their continuance in office (*Krause v CIR* 1928 TPD 656, confirmed by the Appellate Division: 1929 AD 286). This case is also of interest because of the delicate question of costs it raised. Tindall J. found that the attitude of Mr. Oswald Pirow, K.C., counsel for the Commissioner for Inland Revenue, "was somewhat obscure" and Greenberg J. that it was "somewhat ambiguous" (1928 TPD 656 at 663, 667). Mr. Pirow's attitude was that while he had no authority to abandon a claim for costs, he did not ask for them. The court *a quo*, finding that it was its duty to award costs only when they were requested, made no order as to them. Of the four Judges of Appeal who sat in the court that upheld the judgment of the Transvaal Provincial Division, two simply dismissed the appeal, and two dismissed it with costs. Whether Krause J. paid anything is not known. (The story goes that Mr. Pirow was not keen on an order of costs in his favour, as he could not ask Krause J. to pay; whereas if there was no order the State would pay. It is also said that Krause J. paid only the travelling expenses of his counsel to Bloemfontein—they had to provide for their own subsistence, and, of course, they did not charge him a fee.)'

—'Ellison Kahn & Brian R Bamford 'Yet Another Spoonful of Sugar and Pinch of Salt' (1965) 82 *SALJ* 507 at 513–14. (The last sentence is based on a remark made to me by Walter Pollak, who was junior counsel for Krause. Pollak had given an opinion that the appeal was hopeless. So it was.)

Remarks

'He disliked the jury system intensely, and regarded it as an anachronism in this multi-racial country. The following story well illustrates his hatred of juries.

'An accused appeared before him on an I.D.B. (illicit diamond buying) charge.

Every effort had been made by the defence at the outset of the case to get certain of the empanelled jurymen removed, and Mr Justice Krause was quick to realise during the course of the trial that the verdict was most likely to favour the accused regardless of the evidence.

'When all the evidence had been presented, and the jurymen had been addressed by both the prosecution and the defence, Krause delivered what is, perhaps, the briefest address of its kind ever given in the history of our courts.

'"Gentlemen of the jury," he said, "you have heard the evidence for the Crown, and you have heard the evidence for the defence. If you believe the evidence for the defence you will believe anything. Please consider your verdict, gentlemen."

'The Judge was not far wrong in his belief. The jury, without retiring, brought in a unanimous verdict of not guilty.

'"I regret to say that the jury have found you not guilty," he told the smiling accused. "You can go."'

—Isaac Goodman *Judges I Have Known* (1969) 88–9.

'While he was on the Bench Krause showed that he had a great knowledge of all shades of humanity and in addition he displayed considerable understanding of criminals and their ways which was, of course, perhaps only to be expected. What impressed me was the fact that he never raised his voice, gaining all the effect he wanted by means of quiet intervention, frequently accompanied by a grim humour. . . . He was once presiding in the case of a woman said to have been loitering. Harry Morris was appearing for her but Krause was too occupied to look her way when she entered the witness box but the moment she mentioned her name he looked up and said with a broad smile, "Mr Morris, why didn't you tell me that it was Kitty?" This knowledge had of course been acquired officially because the lady in question apparently had been quite an habituée of the boulevards of Von Brandis.'

—The Hon C P Bresler *Tilt the Sack* (1965) 116.

'Krause's great sense of humour was well known, but at least on one occasion he gave vent to a remark which was not altogether to the liking of some of those present—more especially Mr Justice Ramsbottom.

'It happened on the occasion of a dinner which was given by the Johannesburg Bar in honour of Lord Chief Justice Goddard of England, who was on a brief visit to South Africa.

'During the course of the evening, the chairman called on Dr Krause to say "a few words".

'Krause, who had already retired from the Bench, said:

'"Mr Chairman, looking around this banqueting hall, I see many members of the junior Bar. Well, I want to give them a toast."

'Raising his glass, Krause said:

'"May crime flourish in our midst".'

—Isaac Goodman *Judges I Have Known* (1969) 80.

SIR JOHANNES HENRICUS LANGE

1852–1923. Member of the Kimberley Bar 1877–92. Member of the Cape House of Assembly 1888–92. Crown Prosecutor at Kimberley 1892–6. QC 1893. Judge of the High Court of Griqualand and Griqualand West Local Division 1896–1923. Knighted 1917.

'In 1917 he was created a Knight Bachelor. It was a signal honour for a judge in his modest position, a tribute to his public service, and to his continual display in extrajudicial duties of impartiality, sound judgment, and clemency.'

—Ellison Kahn in *Dictionary of South African Biography* V (1987) 435 at 436.

Another view

'Apart from the trial by the Special Courts [of the leaders of the 1922 mineworkers' strike] the Government appointed a Commission of Inquiry into the causes of the strike; Judge Lange, of the Eastern Districts Court [sic], being appointed Commissioner. He was so biased and one-sided that he automatically regarded most of our evidence as lies. I was urged to appear to give evidence before him, but I refused to do so as I did not wish to be told by a Supreme Court Judge that I was giving false evidence. Part of the "cooked" evidence to prove that the revolt was Red, was a red robe found in the New Trades Hall. We were able to show that it was a Father Christmas costume.'

—Morris Kentridge *I Recall: Memoirs of Morris Kentridge* (1959) 122–3. (Morris Kentridge was a prominent politician, who retired from the House of Assembly in 1958 after many years as a front-bencher. Earlier in his career he had played a leading role in Labour politics, and had been arrested and detained in gaol for his participation in the 1922 strike.)

CORNELIUS JACOB (C J) LANGENHOVEN

1873–1932. Attorney, Oudtshoorn, 1899–1901. Member of the Cape Bar 1901–2. Attorney, Oudtshoorn, 1902–12. Champion of Afrikaans. Journalist. Politician. Distinguished author. Wit.

The tolk

'An experienced Tolk once dealt with certain Greek quotations from the Bench as follows:—

'He addressed the jury in the usual low voice, and said: "Hij praat nou van die ou kêrels wat al honderde jare dood is en niks met die zaak te doen het nie. Als hij weer op die punt kom zal ik tolk." ("He is talking now of the old fellows who have been dead for hundreds of years, and have nothing to do with the case. When he comes to the point again I shall interpret.")

'Instead of trying to interpret such eloquence into equally good Dutch, which would be far beyond many interpreters and quite unintelligible to the jury, the experienced Tolk has a facility, generally gained by long experience, of putting the addresses of Bench and Bar into a few words of the simplest patois, in degrees of corruption suited to the prisoner. But it must be confessed that he sometimes goes beyond the necessities of the occasion.

'The following clever skit, which, by permission, I take over because it is better than a similar one which I had written, has much more than a substratum of truth in it,[1] exaggerated as it may appear:

'Scene:

'Circuit Court in the old days.

'The Judge does not understand a word of Dutch, but is very fond of delivering eloquent and impressive addresses.

'The Interpreter has long been thoroughly bored with the proceedings, and regards Judge, advocates, jury and witnesses with an eye of disdainful contempt.

Cover of 1877–1977 The Pretoria Bar/Die Pretoriase Balie *(1977)*

'The prisoner Piet Dragoender[2] has been found guilty of the crime of murder.

'*Chief Constable:* "Hear ye! Hear ye! All persons are strictly charged, upon pain of punishment, to keep silence while the sentence of death is passed upon the prisoner."

'*Tolk:* "Kijk hier, al julle spul loafers, wat net die lug hier van die Hof kom verpes, als zij Lordskap soveul als 'n ooglied zien beef zolank als hij hier de schepsel galg toe dons, zal hij julle laat slaan met die kats dat daar nie 'n nerf op julle bas blij sit nie."

'("Look here, all you lot of loafers, who only come here to poison the air of the Court, if his Lordship sees so much as the quiver of an eyelid while he sends this

---

[1] It is written by Mr. Langenhoven of Oudtshoorn.

[2] This is my nomenclature. Pi-ate Dra-go-en-der is exactly as it was pronounced on one of our Circuits by an English Barrister.

creature here to the gallows, he will have you flogged with the cat till there is not a nerve left in your hides.'')[3]

'*Judge:* "Prisoner at the Bar, Pi-ate Dra-go-en-der.''

'*Tolk:* "Heer jou, ou swart jong Piet Dragoender.'' ("Here, you old black boy.'')

'*Judge:* "You have been found guilty of the most serious charge which it can ever be the painful duty of a Court of Justice to investigate.''

'*Tolk:* "Jij zien nou dat dit julle swart schepsels niks help om julle poote uittestiek om allerhande gruwels aan te rig, en daan hier julle bek te kom oop maak en te lieg daar'oer nie.''

'("You see now, that it does not help you black creatures in the least to lift your paws to commit all kinds of atrocities, and then to come here and open your mouths to lie about it.'')

'*Judge:* "But you have been afforded all those opportunities of a fair, patient and impartial trial which constitutes the splendour and renown of the administration of justice in the dominions of Her Majesty, the Queen.''

'*Tolk:* "In plaats dat jij net sommer dadelijk gezeg het jij's schuldig, kom jij nog hier met jou infame leu'ens om die Hof hier te kom ophou, nes ons almaal rondloopers is soo's jij, wat niks te doen het nie als om te steel en te moor.''

'("Instead of your at once saying that you were guilty, you come here with your infamous lies to take up the time of the Court, just as if we were all tramps like yourself with nothing to do but to steal and murder.'')

'*Judge:* "Your Counsel, Mr. White, who was good enough upon the request of the Court to undertake your defence *pro deo*, has conducted it with a skill and ability which would undoubtedly have secured your acquittal had there been any flaw in the overwhelming proofs of your guilt, which Counsel for the prosecution, Mr. Black, has with equal skill and ability laid before the gentlemen of the jury.''

'*Tolk:* "Jou advokaatje, wat zij Lordskap onnoodig aangestel het om tijd te vermos, het jou net so veul gehelp als die vijfde wiel van die wa'e met al zij onnosele vra'e aan die getui'e en die kinderagtige bog stories wat hij aan die jurie vertel het. En die ander meneertje,[4] die advokaat v'r die Kroon, sou jou seker laat vrij spring als ik nie hier was nie.''

'("Your little advocate, whom his Lordship appointed quite unnecessarily to waste time, has helped you about as much as the fifth wheel of a wagon with his idiotic questions to the witnesses and the childish, silly stories he told the jury. And the other little gentleman, the advocate for the Crown, he would certainly have got you off if I had not been here.'')

'*The Judge* (after some harrowing details of the murder proceeds): "His eyes were closed in death; yes, not the death which is our common heritage, the dread of the wicked and the boon of the upright, to whom it brings a rest well-earned after a life well-spent; no! but the death inflicted by his brother-man, who may give or be made to give his own unworthy life in futile payment of that which he

---

[3] I have tried to translate the Dutch into English, but I am very conscious of its shortcomings. It is just that impossibility of rendering the Taal into English or any other language that makes the original stories so very unique.

[4] It is impossible to convey in English the contempt expressed by the diminutives "advokaatje" and "meneertje": *lit.*, "little advocate" and "little Mr."

hath destroyed, yet cannot restore one quiver to those stark eyes nor one breath of speech to those ghastly lips."

'*Tolk:* "Zij Lordskap zê daar die jong wat jij vermoor het sou tog maar op die end die moord gesteek het en jij ook. Als julle julle nie dood gedrink het nie dan sou julle op 'n andere miserabele manier uit die pad uit geraak het. Maar nou was jij nie tevrede om daarnaar te wag nie, en al wat jij daarmee uitgevoer het is, dat jij die dank van de publiek verdien dat 'n mens nou van jul al twee sal ontsla'e wees."

'("His Lordship says that the fellow you murdered would after all have committed murder himself and you too. If you had not drunk yourselves to death you would have been cleared out of this world in some other miserable manner. But you were not content to wait for that, and all that you have succeeded in doing is to deserve the thanks of the public that we shall now be rid of both of you.")

'*Judge:* "By that very silence of the speechless dead to which you consigned him, you vainly thought to escape retribution."

'*Tolk:* "Jij het gereken die dooi man sal nie hier teun jou kan kom getui'e nie en jij kan kom lieg soo's jij wil."

'("You relied on the dead man not being able to come here and give evidence against you, and that you could come here and lie as you pleased.")

'*Judge:* "Yet, oh! foolish, misguided man—"

'*Tolk:* "Jou slegte, swarte vuilis—" ("You bad, black dirt.")

'*Judge:* "Learn now that it is, alas! too late for you to profit by the lesson; but time for others to profit by the example. The arm of justice—wielded it may be in all human frailty by one who feels his own unworthiness for the solemn and awful task it is his duty to perform. Learn that the arm of justice is long as its voice is final."

'*Tolk:* "Die Regter sê dis nou te laat v'r jou om voordeel te trek uit die vervelige les wat hij v'r jou sit en opsê als was jij ook vatbaar v'r 'n goeie vermaning, wat ik nie gloo nie. Maar terwijl dit te laat is, mag sij Lordskap zelf weet, want ik weet dit wragtig nie, waarom hij nie op die end kan kom van sij storie nie."

'("His Lordship says it's now too late for you to derive any benefit from the wearisome lesson he sits saying to you, even if you were fit for an admonition, which I don't believe. But as it is too late, his Lordship may know, for I certainly don't, why he can't put an end to all his talk.")

'*Judge:* "Its voice, I say, is final, and for you, Pi-ate Dra-go-en-der, will be most certainly final. For though justice be ever tempered with mercy where the voice of mercy has the least claim to be heard, for you there can be no hope of mercy with justice, who showed no mercy in your injustice. You shall have the time for reflection, for preparation, for repentance which was denied the object of your hatred."

'*Tolk:* "Die ou sê jij sal nie veul tijd hê om jou te bekeer nie, want die galg staat klaar; en als dit mij sin was zou hulle jou sommer op die oo'enblik soo'en toe neem en klaar maak met jou."

'("The old man says you won't have much time for repentance because the gallows are ready; and if I had my way, they would take you there at once and have done with you.")

'*Judge:* "Prepare, therefore, Pi-ate Dra-go-en-der, for that fearsome and lonesome journey to the undiscovered country from whose bourne no traveller returns."

'*Tolk:* "Die Juds sê jij gaat nou peil reg uit verderf toe als jij jou nie bekeer nie en daarvoor het ek maar min hoop, of jij mag dit doen van bangigheid."

'("The Judge says you are going now in a straight line to perdition if you don't repent, and of that I have but little hope unless you do it out of funk.")

'*Judge:* "Have you anything to urge now, Pi-ate Dra-go-en-der, why sentence of death shall not be passed on you?"

'*Tolk:* "Die Juds vrâ of jij nog meer leu'ens het om te vertel, Piet."

'("The Judge asks if you have any more lies to tell, Piet.")

'*Piet:* "Asse ekke nog iets magge sê, baas, dan wil ekke vrâ dat die meneer vir Piet lievers erste moette ophang, en dan slegge maak."

'("If I may say something more, Baas, then I would ask that the gentleman would rather first hang Piet and then slang him.")

'*(Curtain.)*'

—Sir Henry Juta *Reminiscences of The Western Circuit* (1912) 114–21. (The skit was rendered into Afrikaans by Langenhoven, apparently in 1922, and was published sv 'Die Tweetalige Vonnis' in his *Versamelde Werke* Deel nege, the first edition of which appeared in 1933.) (On the tolk, see also McGREGOR; WAIFS AND STRAYS sv 'Tolk'; E B WATERMEYER; WESSELS; WYLDE.)

'In Afrikaans is C J Langenhoven se "Die Kys abaut die Forro" baie amusant. Die toneel is 'n stadsraadvergadering, waar in die begin raadslid Ryners aan die woord was. Hy het 'n voorstel ingedien dat die raad geregtelike stappe moet instel teen raadslid Aalryt om hom te belet om 'n sloot water uit die rivier te neem. Aalryt verag sy moedertaal, Afrikaans, en glo dat die taal wat hy praat Engels is. Sy antwoord op die voorstel is vol beledeginge, byvoorbeeld: ". . . hef aai neffer ien maai liewieng belief sots 'n tomfoel stoepet as dis bieutifoel jintelman, dies Mister Piet Ryners, dies bottomles piet; dies Pest, dies Rinderpest—". Die burgemeester doen sy bes om Aalryt te keer, maar tevergeefs; uiteindelik sê hy dat hy die polisie moet vra om Aalryt uit die vergadering te verwyder. Aalryt antwoord soos volg: "Joe ken kol ien 'n poliesman, joe ken kol ien die meijistreit, joe ken kol ien die houl boksemdaais of 'n volunteer kadet korps. . . . Bot aai wiel walk out of joor bieslie konsel keimer en aai wiel not kom bek wiedout 'n aafteroks horswiep. . . ."'

—Ellison Kahn 'The Seven Lamps of Legal Humour Part 4' 1984 *De Rebus* 306. ('Die Kys' can also be found in *Versamelde Werke* Deel nege.)

'Die lewenswysheid en humor van sy spreuke bevat menige les vir die regspraktisyn en sy kliënt. Lees maar wat hy te sê het oor die volgende:

'Testamente

'Verbind jou kinders se erfenis onder fideikommis en die vreemde wat jy wil daaruit hou sal dit des te goedkoper kry ter wille van die las wat daarop is.

'(Want 'n mens kan nie 'n erfenis hou en hom darem gee ook nie, net so min as wat jou erfgename hom kan weggee en darem hou ook.)

'Sorg meer vir jou erfgename as vir jou nalatenskap. Die plaas sal nie onder hulle uit loop nie maar hulle kan van hom af loop.

'(Die mens wik, God beskik; die erflater beskik, die erfgename swik.)

Lawyer: 'The case is moving along, moving along.'
Client: 'You have been telling me that for four years. If it continues at this pace, I will no longer have boots to follow it.'

Honoré Daumier (1808–79). Lithograph.
('Prosedeer oor 'n baadjie en hou jou broek klaar vir die onkoste': Langenhoven.)

'**Litigasie**
'Prosedeer oor 'n baadjie en hou jou broek klaar vir die onkoste.
'(En hou jou verder klaar om hom te was vir die nuwe besitter.)
'Jy sal vir 'n man stem om die sake van jou land te bestuur wat jy nooit sou droom om jou eie sake aan toe te vertrou nie.
'(In hierdie dae van korrupsie is dit al goed om iemand te kry wat nie bekwaam genoeg is om alte veel kwaad te doen nie.)
'Die man wat sy saak gewin het, beskuldig nie die regter van partydigheid nie.
'(Selfs wanneer hy weet dat die regter verkeerd was.)
'Die valse getuie het te min respek vir sy geheue, die eerlike dikwels te veel.
'(Min luister, min laster.)
'**Die Kontraktant**
'Moenie my so goed vertrou om my dokument te teken vóórdat jy dit gelees het nie. Ek het jou nie so goed vertrou om met jou belofte tevrede te wees sonder jou handtekening nie.
'(Vertroue is al wat bedrog op vertrou.)

'**Die Prokureur**
'Soek vir jou 'n dokter wat jou goeie moed inpraat en 'n prokureur wat jou slegte inpraat.
'(As jy hulle dan nou eenmaal móét soek.)
'Die onbekwaamste skatmeester is dié wat sy eie skade takseer; die onbekwaamste regter dié wat in sy eie saak oordeel; en die onbekwaamste prokureur dié wat sy eie kliënt is.
'(Maar die bekwaamste gids is die wysbordjie aan die stilstaande paal, en die bekwaamste sedeleraar dié wat nie sy eie leerling is nie.)
''n Man het nog nie klaar vir jou raad gevra nie of jy sien al watter raad hy graag van jou wil hê.
'(Raad? Hy soek geen raad nie. Hy soek bevestiging.)
'Dooie vriendskap is die aas van wetsgeleerde kraaie.
'(Aas van selfmoord.)
'**Skuld**
'Gee 'n man wat jy hom skuld voordat hy dit vra, en jou raad nadat hy dit gevra het.
'(Anders raai jy hom straks om jou verder uitstel te gee.)

'Borgskap

'Trek liewer vir jou vriend jou broek uit as om vir hom 'n baadjie borg te staan. Anders loop julle naderhand albei nakend.

'(Dat hy 'n borg nodig het, is die enigste rede om vir hom borg te staan. En die beste rede om dit nie te doen nie.)

'Borgskap is 'n kind van vriendskap, maar hy vermoor graag sy ouer.

'(Uit *Ons weg deur die wêreld* Deel II, *Versamelde Werke Deel* 9 *sesde* uitgawe, Tafelberguitgewers, 1974.)'

   —H F Mellet 'C J Langenhoven die regsgeleerde' (1973) 14(2) *Codicillus* 27.

Nog meer

Tronkstraf

'Die man wat onskuldig in die tronk kom, moet bitter voel maar nie so bitter nie, verbeel ek my, as die man wat die straf verdien het.

'(Die wat die minste voel, verbeel ek my, is dié wat die straf verdien het en dit vryspring.)

'Die dom dief steel die goed en kom in die tronk. Die slim dief steel eers die toestemming van die baas en bly ongestraf.'

   —C J Langenhoven 'Ons Weg deur die Wêreld' II 261, 276.

Eccentric genius

'. . . [Y]our presence here is a tribute to a sentimental man who wrote a great deal—some people say he did so more with his heart than with his head. This annual lecture is a tribute to an eccentric genius. A former colleague of mine tells me that his father, who at one time was Langenhoven's doctor at Oudtshoorn, had the strange task of cutting the veins in his wrists: Langenhoven had a horror of being buried alive! The cutting of the wrists took place *post mortem!*'

   —Mr Justice G P C Kotzé 'Regbank en Wetgewende Owerheid' Annual C J Langenhoven Memorial Lecture at the University of Port Elizabeth delivered in 1985.

'My dear sir, it is absolutely impossible for me to take your case. You are missing the most important evidence.'
(Aside) 'Evidence of money.'
   Honoré Daumier (1808–79). Lithograph.

SIR PERCEVAL MAITLAND LAURENCE

1854–1930. Member of the Kimberley Bar 1881–2. Judge of the High Court of Griqualand 1882–8. Judge President 1888–1910. Judge of the Cape Provincial Division 1910. Acting Judge of Appeal 1911. Acting Judge President of the Natal Provincial Division 1912. Knighted (KB) 1908, KCMG 1911. Author of legal and other works. Classical scholar. Educationist and pioneer of public libraries. (The 'Perceval' is usually incorrectly rendered 'Percival', and the 'Laurence' 'Lawrence', as in the first two extracts.)

'TAKING A CHANCE

'The late Arthur Upington was, like his brother Beau [q v], an orator and a classical scholar. He was defending a native girl on Circuit before Sir Percival Lawrence [sic] and a jury. Sir Percival was himself a fine classical scholar.

'Arthur was treating the countryside to a first-class oration. "And, gentlemen, as the Greek poet said"—here he quoted in Greek. "Yes, Mr. Upington," said His Lordship, "you will no doubt remember the succeeding lines." His Lordship quoted. "Yes, My Lord," said Upington, "followed by those beautiful lines in which the poet says. . . ." "Ah, yes," said Sir Percival, and he promptly followed Arthur's lead. Arthur was replying with another quotation, when His Lordship suddenly woke up and said: "But, Mr. Upington, where were we?" "Ah, My Lord," said Arthur, "Your Lordship was on the point of directing the jury to acquit the accused."

'History does not record what happened.'

—H H Morris KC *In and Out of Court* (1950) 30. (Further on Arthur Upington, see VAN DER RIET.)

Caricature of Sir Perceval Laurence by William Howard Schröder (1852–92), from The Schröder Art Memento *(Pretoria 1894)*

'During the hearing of a civil case before Sir Percival Maitland-Lawrence [sic] and a special jury, and after a lengthy trial and prolonged addresses by counsel for the parties concerned, the learned Judge remarked: "Gentlemen of the Jury, much sand has been thrown into your eyes and it is now up to me to supply some boracic acid in order to clear your vision."'

—F W Ahrens *From Bench to Bench* (1948) 51.

'In charging a country jury any literary allusion, however trite, would fall very flat; but a scriptural illustration is always quickly seized. The Circuit Court sometimes falls at the season of the quarterly *nachtmaal*, or communion, when half the countryside come to town for the special services. On one occasion, when we happened to be staying over Sunday, and attended the Dutch church, the Minister, on entering the pulpit, observed that, in view of the presence of the Judge and

SIR PERCEVAL LAURENCE

Caricature by D C Boonzaier (1865–1950), from his My Caricatures *(1912)*

jury, he should select a topical subject for his discourse, and proceeded to preach on Pontius Pilate on the judgment-seat!'

—Perceval M Laurence *Collectanea: Essays, Addresses and Reviews* (1899) 296.

Laurence is speaking of accused who are coloured or black persons.

'The prisoner of course has the right of challenge, and this sometimes requires a little explanation. When asked whether he has any objections to the jury, he some-times asserts that he "objects to the lot." On one occasion an old woman chal-lenged a highly-respected farmer and, on being afterwards asked whether she had had any special reason for her selection, explained that she thought she was bound to object to some one and had therefore picked out the ugliest. Another prisoner expressed himself as perfectly satisfied with the jury; *his* objection was to the "*ou baas in die rooi rok*" (the old master in the red robe [more accurately translated as "dress"]) on the bench.'

—Laurence op cit at 297.

ROBERT WARDEN LEE

1868–1958. Magistrate in Ceylon 1891–4. Lecturer in Law, University of Oxford, 1899–1914, and Fellow of Worcester College, Oxford, 1903–14. Professor of Roman-Dutch Law, University College, University of London, 1906–14. Dean of the Faculty of Law and Professor of Roman Law, McGill University, Canada, 1914–21. KC Quebec 1920. Professor of Roman-Dutch Law, University of Oxford, and Fellow of All Souls College, 1921–56. FBA 1933.

In 1926 Lee published his translation of Grotius's Inleidinge tot de Hollandsche Rechtsgeleerdheid, *under the title* The Jurisprudence of Holland. *It received a most favourable review from the very learned judge and jurist, Sir John G Kotzé.*

'How did Lee do it? He was very skilled in Latin, which a one-time student of his tells me he read almost as easily as English, and in which he wrote inscriptions in books that he presented; and he was a Romanist of some repute. These attributes must have been of help when he compiled his remarkably detailed volume II on the *Inleiding*, called *Commentary*, which was published in 1936. It contains translations of certain notes by Groenewegen, Voet, Coster, Scheltinga and Schorer, and from Van der Keessel's then unpublished *Dictata*. But whence came Lee's command of written Dutch, especially that of the seventeenth century? Assuredly he did not study the language at school or as a student at

Oxford, though very likely he picked up some reading knowledge of it in Ceylon, where he was a magistrate for four years after leaving university, from 1891 to 1894. Lee's knowledge of Dutch must have been of a passive variety. Shortly before his lamented early death, Professor H F W D Fischer told me, with a laugh, how he and his colleagues were once listening to a lecture in English being delivered by Lee at the University of Leiden, when suddenly Lee started quoting a long passage in a language of which no one could understand a single word. It turned out that the lecturer thought he was speaking in Dutch. Lee's Dutch seems to have been on a level below even that of the English of the Japanese professor of English described by Francis King in his tribute to the memory of Sir Maurice Bowra, the incomparable Warden of Wadham College, Oxford. The professor, head of the Department of English of a leading Japanese university, who, though he could write English impeccably, could hardly speak a word of it, insisted on King's giving him a letter of introduction to "Sir Bowra". King succumbed. Some weeks later Bowra wrote to him: "Thank you so much for sending me your Professor X. We had a long and interesting silence together." (See *Maurice Bowra: A Celebration* edited by Hugh Lloyd-Jones (1974) 150–1.)'

—Ellison Kahn 'Hugo Grotius 10 April 1583–29 August 1645' (1983) 100 *SALJ* 192 at 209 (certain footnotes omitted).

'It is sad to realize that the legendary Professor Lee is no longer with us, that his views, coming far from the day-to-day *disputatio fori*, but often keener for that, will no longer be heard. Up to the last few years advanced age had not been unkind to him, but then it turned away from him. I suppose that I was the last South African law teacher to see Lee. It was on a mild afternoon in late October last that I walked past Lincoln's Inn and its field to Gray's Inn Square. At flat No. 11 on the third floor I called on Lee. Some years before he had had a leg amputated. And now he had given up his artifical limb and taken to a wheel-chair. It was distressing to see this distinguished-looking man, lying propped up with cushions, hardly able to move his hands; with his hearing greatly impaired; and who found it difficult and exhausting to speak. There were flashes of his old humour, as, when I spoke of a well-known academic personage I had recently met, who was over sixty and, full of honours, was contemplating the not-too-distant packing of his bags, Lee said: "How is that ambitious young man nowadays?" Towards the end he said with a smile: "Twenty years ago my friends told me I was disgracefully old. What must I be today?"

'"Come next time you are here" I was asked as I took my leave. But the veil of death was falling over his eyes, and I knew, as I walked in the fading light towards the Chancery Lane Underground, that I would not see him again.'

—Ellison Kahn 'In Memoriam: Robert Warden Lee' (1958) 75 *SALJ* 1 at 4.

'A story is told of a distinguished ex-student of Lee who occupied rooms immediately below him when he was a don at Worcester. One morning the undergraduate found water leaking through his ceiling and dripping on his head. He sent his scout up post-haste to report what was happening, and in a few moments the messenger was back with Mr. Lee's compliments and an umbrella!'

—A A Roberts 'The Late Professor R. W. Lee' (1958) 21 *THRHR* 79 at 83.

'Lee was a debonair man who enjoyed life and company, with some detachment from both. His poker face and dry humour, at times verging on cynicism, made him a formidable legpuller. Even his friends never knew quite where they had got him. An exact scholar himself, he could on occasion make devastating remarks about what he regarded as arid scholarship. A happy worker, he had the farsightedness and sense of proportion which prevented him from ploughing the sands. He had an exceptionally long working life and never seemed to grow old.'

—F H Lawson 'In Memoriam: Robert Warden Lee' (1958) 7 *American Journal of Comparative Law* 659 at 661. (Professor Lawson was Lee's colleague at the University of Oxford.)

'Although Lee devoted a good part of his life to the study of Roman-Dutch law, he looked upon it with detachment. Himself a classical scholar who delighted in composing Latin verses . . . he was impatient of the historical bent of some South African lawyers and was apt to say, with a twinkle, that the old authorities should be burned. This has not happened, but the modern legal systems of South Africa and Ceylon have now come to be regarded as distinct from the Roman-Dutch law of renaissance Holland, and it has been said with some truth that this sturdy Victorian individualist was the last Roman-Dutch lawyer.'

—A M Honoré in *Dictionary of National Biography 1951–1960* (reprinted in *The Compact Edition of the Dictionary of National Biography* II (1975) 1747).

'I told him [an eminent academic] that Lee hadn't left our university the copyright in his *Introduction to Roman-Dutch Law*, as he had promised in a letter in his own hand that he had sent to Hahlo. But, came the reply, Lee had promised many people such things—he had promised him a number of old authorities which, of course, were not left to him. It was Lee's big bargaining counter in old age.'

—Ellison Kahn's commonplace book 5 March 1959.

JAMES WESTON LEONARD

1853–1909. Member of the Cape Bar 1876–88. Member of the Cape Legislative Assembly 1879–88. QC 1883. Attorney-General in Sprigg's Cabinet 1881 and Scanlen's Cabinet 1882–4. Member of the Johannesburg Bar 1888–99 and 1902–9. Member of the London Bar 1899–1902.

The examiner

'I sat for the LL.B. in 1877. The Cape University was a mere examining body, and the candidate for a law degree prepared for the ordeal as best he could. The task is easier now, but then the standard is higher. It was difficult, in those days, to find examiners. The little band who undertook the work, though sometimes likened by disgruntled candidates to recurring decimals, deserved the grateful recognition of those who profited by their labours and their indulgence. The duties of an examiner were sometimes found to be irksome, as the following incident will show. Soon after my admission to practice, the examiner in statute law, with whose questions I had but lately wrestled, asked me if I was busy. The reply, naturally, was in the negative. "Perhaps you would like to set the paper for this year", he remarked. "As you are last from school, the work might interest you." Amazed and disillusioned, I declined the honour. J. W. Leonard had passed the year before me, and to him I confided the story. "Well, what did you say?" he asked. I told him with some vehemence. "My dear fellow", was his reply, "it's all right; I set yours."'

JAMES WESTON LEONARD
*Caricature by William Howard Schröder (1852–92),
from* The Schröder Art Memento *(Pretoria 1894)*

—James Rose Innes *Autobiography* (edited by B A Tindall) (1949) 30.

'In 1888 he left Cape Colony and settled in the Transvaal, for which he foresaw a great future. The loss to the Capetown Bar is expressed in an anecdote related by Mr. Esselen, K.C., in replying on behalf of the Bar to the reference by the Chief Justice of the Transvaal to the deceased advocate on the news of his death having been received: "I remember after he left Capetown I visited the place about 1899, and went to see the old Registrar, who for many years occupied that position in the Supreme Court, and asking him how things were, he said to me, 'Well, as you see, I am getting old, but there is one thing—the charm of this Bar has gone: Mr. Leonard has gone to the Transvaal.'"'

—'The Late James W. Leonard, K.C.' (1910) 27 *SALJ* 1 at 5. (Leonard, known as 'Peerless Jim', became a Cabinet Minister at 28 and (what must be a world record) a silk at 30.) (See also ESSELEN; HOLLARD; T UPINGTON.)

'In his day, James Weston Leonard, K.C., was a giant, forensically, politically and physically. To-day he is a faint memory, and a bronze bust in the vestibule of the Law Courts, Von Brandis Square. Of the hundreds who daily swirl round that bust, few trouble to pause and read the inscription which tells us where and when he was born and where and when he died. The modern generation knows nothing of this giant.

'Mentally and physically he towered above his surroundings. This "silver-tongued orator" was a fine classical scholar with a prodigious memory. He was a man of infinite charm. In spite of the great mental qualities which he possessed, he had no forensic wit, or at all events nothing has survived. He seems to have preferred the broadsword to the rapier.

'The attorney who had drawn the agreement was in the box trying to explain it. '"Have you drawn any more agreements like this one?"

'"Oh, yes," said the attorney proudly, "I have drawn several of them."

'"And when are the actions coming on?"'

—H H Morris KC *In and Out of Court* (1950) 19.

'Richard Henderson Heffer, Editor of the "Critic", published a disparaging article about W. P. Struben, Chairman of the Pony and Galloway Club. Struben met Heffer at the Globe Theatre and, it is said, attacked him. Heffer, a consumptive, died a year later. Dunn, who succeeded Heffer, accused Struben of murdering Heffer. Struben sued both Dunn and the paper for defamation. Leonard appeared for Struben. In the course of his address, while dealing with the question of inferences, Leonard quoted the lines from Henry VI, Part 2:—

'"Who finds the heifer dead and bleeding fresh,/And sees fast by butcher with an axe,/But will suspect 'twas he that made the slaughter."

'The Court found that Heffer died from natural causes.'

—H H Morris KC *The First Forty Years* (1948) 30.

Mahatma Gandhi, practising as an attorney in South Africa, approaches Leonard for help.

'I recalled the late Mr. Pincutt's advice—facts are three-fourths of the law. At a later date it was amply borne out by that famous barrister of South Africa, the late Mr. Leonard. In a certain case in my charge I saw that, though justice was on the side of my client, the law seemed to be against him. In despair I approached Mr. Leonard for help. He also felt that the facts of the case were very strong. He exclaimed, "Gandhi, I have learnt one thing, and it is this, that if we take care of the facts of a case, the law will take care of itself. Let us dive deeper into the facts of this case." With these words he asked me to study the case further and then see him again. On a re-examination of the facts I saw them in an entirely new light, and I also hit upon an old South African case bearing on the point. I was delighted and went to Mr. Leonard and told him everything. "Right," he said, "we shall win the case. Only we must bear in mind which of the judges takes it."'

—Mohandas K. [Mahatma] Gandhi *Autobiography: The Story of My Experiments with Truth* (translated by Mahadev Desai) (1948) ch XIV.

ALEXANDER JOHN McGREGOR

1864–1946. Member of the Cape Bar 1889. State Attorney of the Orange Free State 1889–92. Judge of the High Court of the Orange Free State 1892–5. Member of the Cape Bar 1895–1913. KC 1907. Judge of the Eastern Districts Local Division 1913–15 and of the Orange Free State Provincial Division 1915–29. Writer of legal and other works.

'He lost his only son during the first Great War. My brother, De Villiers, reminds me that he was on active service with McGregor's son. The son was killed whilst on active service with the Black Watch in Flanders. McGregor wrote a somewhat touching tribute to his son, and he repeats in that book a remark by his son, who was a fine young fellow and one of the best of South Africans: "Father, I think you are too modest to be a judge and too honest for a lawyer." He was a man of great modesty of character. He was an exceedingly clever man, as those of you who read his judgments will see. He was a man of great learning, not only in the law. Sometimes his great learning caused him to have many doubts and difficulties. It caused him to have difficulty in coming to a conclusion, but he certainly was a man of very considerable learning and I do not hesitate to say that he was one of the cleverest of men. He did not achieve all he might have, but he was one of the cleverest sons of South Africa. He certainly was a man of great modesty, but it is not accurate that he was too honest to be a lawyer, because nobody is too honest to be a lawyer. He was a man of the most scrupulous exactitude in everything he did. His work was scrupulously done, and one of the things that worried him was what fees he should charge. I remember he was always afraid he might be charging too much. I remember on one occasion I was in a big trial case with him which lasted several days, and [that on] several occasions he discussed with me whether we should charge a refresher of six-and-four [guineas], or seven-and-five, and in the end decided on six-and-four.

He was scrupulously exact in the way he fought a case, and it was very interesting to hear how he conducted his cases. His charming sense of whimsical humour could not be denied. It is said that on one occasion he even caused Sir Henry de Villiers to smile.'

—Mr Justice G G Sutton, Judge President of the Cape Provincial Division, in his obituary address on 21 November 1946 ((1947) 64 *SALJ* 3 at 5–6).

The tolk

'A J McGregor, a most cultivated man, master of the aside, when he was at the bar was trying to establish the defence that the accused had not committed theft but only a delict: "My client, gentlemen of the jury, is in, as it were, a hybrid legal position." Die tolk: "Hij is een bastaard." (See Mr Justice F G Gardiner's reminiscences published in (1963) 80 *South African Law Journal* 415.)'

—Ellison Kahn 'The Seven Lamps of Legal Humour Part 1' 1984 *De Rebus* 156 at 159. (On the tolk, see also LANGENHOVEN; WAIFS AND STRAYS sv 'Tolk'; E B WATERMEYER; WESSELS; WYLDE.)

'The Eastern Districts Court used to sit on circuit at Cala, and in order to complete the roll, night sittings were usual. As there was no electric lighting the practice was to have a candle on each side of the judge, a candle on each side of the advocates' table, and a candle on each side of the dock. One evening a case commenced at 8 p.m. after the usual wining and dining. The learned Judge McGregor looked over the collection of candles and said to adv. F. B. van der Riet, who prosecuted, "Mr Van der Riet, are there two accused or is there only one?" The prosecutor rose and looked at the dock and said, "I can only see one, my Lord".'

—N E Wiehahn 'The Eastern Cape Division of the Supreme Court of South Africa' (1968) 9(2) *Codicillus* 24 at 29.

'Most cautious of Commentators, he is a master of parenthesis. . . . In his garden of legal flora he flits from flower to flower with the gay abandon of a butterfly, alighting on a hardy indigene here and poising with fluttering grace over the insidious fragrance of a delicate exotic there; while from the deeper recesses he culls for our delight the rarest gems from the dicta of the ages.'

—Fred B van der Riet [qv] 'Entre Nous' in *Index of the South African Law Journal Volumes XLV to LVIII* (1942) vii–viii.

SIR ROBERT MacILWAINE

1871–1943. Solicitor-General, Southern Rhodesia. KC (Ireland) 1923. Judge of the High Court of Southern Rhodesia 1930–7. President of the Water Court 1913–43. Knighted 1939.

The story of Ali Bi

'MacIlwaine, once Attorney-General [sic] of Southern Rhodesia, and later a judge, was a heavily built man, with a strong sense of humour. He was prosecuting Mahomet for arson. The defence was that at the time of the fire, before, during and after, and at all times material and relevant, the accused was sleeping at the house of Ali Hassan, six miles from the scene of the fire, and that therefore he could not have been a party to this fire. Ali Hassan went into the box to support the alibi. MacIlwaine knew the witness. They had met before in court. The Attorney-General grasped the arms of his chair and began to hoist himself to the perpendicular. With each jerk he spoke: "What—did—you—say—your name was?"

'"Ali Hassan, my Lord."

'Then, as he started on the downward journey, MacIlwaine added: "Are—you—sure—it is not ali—bi?"

'That was the end of the alibi and of Ali Hassan.'

—Eric Morris SC *Technique in Litigation* 3 ed (1985) 180. (Based on H H Morris KC *In and Out of Court* (1950) 27.)

ROBERT GORDON (ROBIN) McKERRON

1900–73. Professor of Law, University of the Witwatersrand, Johannesburg, 1926–46. Member of the Johannesburg Bar 1946–58. Subsequently Reader in Law at the University of Aberdeen and thereafter Professor of Law, Rhodes University until 1969. QC 1956. Author of legal works.

'Originally he intended to be a Romanist. But then he became interested in our law of delict, which was not served by an adequate textbook. His first draft, in handwriting, went up in flames in the fire that destroyed the University [of the Witwatersrand] library in 1931. Only some scattered notes were left.

'The situation was similar to that in which Thomas Carlyle found himself when John Stuart Mill told him that the maid had used almost all of his manuscript of *The French Revolution*, left with Mill for appraisal, to light the household fires. The reaction was the same. McKerron immediately set to work again. The first edition came out in 1933. The seventh had appeared before his death. It remained, as Professor A M Honoré has so aptly put it, as lean and muscular as its author.'

—Ellison Kahn 'In Memoriam: Professor R G McKerron' (1973) 90 *SALJ* 105 at 106.

'Robin McKerron was endowed with a splendid intellect and the gift of writing lucid and polished prose. He used to complain that putting his thoughts to paper did not come easily. That may have been because he was a perfectionist. I am reminded of what Abe Fortas remarked of Mr Justice Douglas of the United States Supreme Court, "his stern puritanical insistence upon individual excellence in himself and others" ((1964) 73 *Yale LJ* 917). This search for the ideal sometimes caused McKerron to wrestle with the expression of a thought, even the drafting of one sentence, for an hour or more. At times—it could be very late at night—a colleague of his would be called in, possibly by telephone, for aid. Or was it not rather as a vehicle to receive the oral communication of Robin McKerron's thoughts as they became formulated and started changing? Whenever I was the one chosen I reflected wryly on the saying that Molière tested his draft writings by trying them out on his cook.'

—Kahn op cit at 106.

'The swiftness of McKerron's mind could at times make it difficult for all but the best students to follow him with ease. Even his colleagues with whom he discussed legal problems could initially find that it required quite an effort to get the drift of what was troubling him; for he had the habit of starting to argue without setting out fully the underlying facts. These tended to emerge during the ensuing conversation, and one did one's best in the meantime not to appear too foolish.

'This is an illustration of what might be called the professorial aspect of McKerron's behaviour—professorial as the satirist or cartoonist would have it. It really was a manifestation of his absent-mindedness, caused by his intense concentration on the matter that was engaging the attention of his mind. It came out in other odd ways. The story is told at Wits how he once arranged by mistake two lectures on quite different subjects at the same time in adjoining rooms that had an interleading door. In order not to disappoint his students, he decided to lecture to both classes at the same time. This he did by talking for a few minutes in the one class, then leaving its members to take a note of what he had said while he did the same in the other class. Nearly an hour was spent by his darting from the one room to the other in this way. Then there was the occasion when he asked a colleague for a lift home from the University of the Witwatersrand, and became extremely concerned to find his motor car missing from his house. It took him some time to recollect that he had driven himself in it to the university that morning.'

—Kahn op cit at 106–7.

This story was told by Mr Joel Mervis, the distinguished journalist (he was awarded the degree of LLD honoris causa by Rhodes University), at the annual dinner of the Law Students' Council of the University of the Witwatersrand on 20 June 1977. Mr Mervis, who took his LLB degree at that university, was in the class at the time.

'Professor Robin McKerron was lecturing to the LLB students at the University of the Witwatersrand on Roman law. He dealt with the *dos*, the contribution made by the bride to the groom in regard to the marriage. To see whether he had made himself clear, he asked the class: "What did the bride give the man in Roman times?" To which Kathy Clarke (later Mrs Bresler) replied: "A dos"—pronouncing it with a long "o", as *dose*.'

—Ellison Kahn 'The Seven Lamps of Legal Humour Part 2' 1984 *De Rebus* 210 at 212.

HAROLD GRAHAM MACKEURTAN

1884–1942. Advocate and attorney, Durban, 1906–17. Founder of the Natal Bar and member of it 1917–42. KC 1919. MP 1922–4. Author of legal and other works.

The new Broome and the old sweeps

'In this company of lawyers, it is my sad privilege, which I regard with pride, to speak on behalf of the Bench, the Bar and the Side-Bar of Natal about the greatest, by far, of all the advocates who have ever practised in this court. And it is appropriate that I should be your spokesman, for he and I were close friends as well as contemporaries, and I was for some years his frequent opponent at the Bar, waging the unequal struggle of a mere man against a master. And all the time I watched, with unstinted admiration, the forensic exploits of this most gifted personality. I told him more than once that he should never have left London. If he had stayed there and politics had been kind, he might have been Lord Chancellor. He had all the attributes of that great office.

'His early promise as a boy at Durban High School blossomed at Trinity College, Cambridge, and the Inner Temple into a scholastic career of scintillating brilliance. He was the foremost student amongst his fellow undergraduates in the famous law school at Cambridge, and, in the wider sphere provided by the Inns of Court, he outstripped his fellows, thus proving himself, intellectually, to be the peer of the great lawyers of England. He returned to Natal to undergo the test of competition in the world of men. Once more he emerged with flying colours. As a young man, scarcely bearded, he reorganised the large practice of Shepstone and Wylie, helped—as he was helped throughout—by the gracious lady who later was to become his devoted wife, and, busy as he was, he found time to conduct cases in the Supreme Court. Soon his name was on the lips of every Natal lawyer. He had only to argue a case or two before that great court presided over by the eminent Lord De Villiers, with two giants—Sir James Rose Innes and Sir William Solomon—on either hand, for his reputation to spread far and wide. It was about this time that he decided to give up the dual practice and to become an advocate. Success was inevitable and instantaneous. It was not long before his table was littered with briefs from Natal and the other provinces—notably the Transvaal—and Southern Rhodesia. Thus he planted the seed from which grew the Natal Bar as we know it now. He saw that the dual practice of Natal could not compete, in the world of Bench and Bar, against the divided system of the other provinces. We would be left behind and the Natal Bench would be manned by judges from outside. So he set about obtaining recruits. My brother Carlisle and my brother Selke joined him. Later I did the same. We were the Natal Bar for some time and I like to think that the fellowship prevailing between four friends laid the foundation of that delightful relationship which existed during the whole of my time between the members of the Bar and exists, as I believe, today. Silk came as a matter of course and his practice grew in magnitude and importance. How he found time to write his work on sale and *The Cradle Days of Natal*, both classics in their way, is a mystery to me. He was a member of Parliament for a short time, but politics did not suit him and he wisely abandoned them. He appeared once before the Privy Council.

'But why this success, which appeared to be so easy and so inevitable? First, the high quality of a great intellect, added to that priceless instinct, given to few, of knowing from the very beginning which way a case should go. Second, a personality at once so human and so impressive that it made itself felt in any company. Third, a deep appreciation of the duty of the advocate and the way to perform it. You remember Judge Parry's "seven lamps of advocacy"—honesty, courage, industry, wit, eloquence (a little out of date and better described, perhaps, as precision of expression), judgment and fellowship. He kept them all burning brightly. Wherever he went he carried with him the lamps of wit and fellowship. Who could forget those spare half-hours spent with him in the robing room waiting for our cases to be called? It was laughter all the time. Who could forget those train journeys to Bloemfontein in his company when we went to argue cases before the Appellate Division? What would have been dull and tedious without him, became a sheer delight. He would be pleased, I think, if I told you of a remark of his, so priceless as to deserve a place here, even upon this sad occasion, especially as you, knowing the actors, will appreciate it as much as his audience did. The occasion was a dinner given by the Bar to one of their members who had been elevated to the Bench. His name was Broome. The other three judges—his recruits to the Bar—were invited. Who but Graham Mackeurtan could have created and given expression to the idea of "the new Broome among the old sweeps"? That is only one example among thousands of how he kept in trim the two lamps of wit and fellowship.

'We must learn a lesson from his life. Judge Parry said in his *Seven Lamps of Advocacy*: "The great advocate is like the great actor: he fills the stage for his span of life, succeeds, gains our applause, makes his last bow, and the curtain falls." This, alas, is all too true. What has Graham Mackeurtan left behind? A very precious memory, of course. But save for his work on the law of sale, so good as to be a *de facto* authority in his lifetime and now, by his death, an authority *de jure*, he has left us nothing authoritative. Would that circumstances had permitted him to take the seat on the Bench which came to me in 1931. It would have been a short apprenticeship for the Appellate Division. If that had happened, he would have given us judgments which would have been permanent additions to our jurisprudence and he would have found a resting-place in the select company of our great judges. But it was not to be. . . .'

—Mr Justice A A Roy Hathorn, Judge President of the Natal Provincial Division, at a special sitting of that division held on 22 December 1942 in memory of Mackeurtan, who had died four days earlier. See 1943 NPD vii; also (1943) 60 *SALJ* 4. ('Sweep: a disreputable person; a scamp, blackguard. *Slang and dialect*': *The Oxford English Dictionary*.) (See also FEETHAM.)

'Mackeurtan's sense of humour often employed an unexpected twist in the ending. For example, . . . Broome was appointed a judge of the Natal Supreme Court. A Bar dinner was held just afterwards, attended by the advocates and judges. Mackeurtan, as leader of the Bar, made a speech of welcome to the new judge. One rather expected him to say something about the new Broome sweeping clean. Instead, with characteristic humour and a jovial dig at the senior judges, what he said was, "Well, I hope the new Broome will get on all right with the old sweeps!"

'He wrote three books. The first was a collection of poems which he called, whimsically, *Slender Verses by a Stout Gentleman*. They have a delightful perception and a sensitivity of feeling. They include poems written when his children were born. Listen to the tender opening lines of what he wrote when his daughter Monica was born—

'Michaelmas daisies woke from their sleep when you came, dear,
Opened and shone like a foam-silvered sea,
Nodding and waving a wind-shaken welcome to you, dear,
In tremulous glee.'

'You see how tenderness and humility blended in the strength of mind of this remarkable man.

'The second book was a legal textbook, *The Law of Sale of Goods in South Africa*. It is a masterpiece. It is still the standard work on the subject. . . .

'The third book was an historical work called *The Cradle Days of Natal*. It traces the history of the colony up to 1845. A recent historian describes it as far and away the best secondary source of information on the subject.

'This story of Mackeurtan's life ends on a wistful note. This so-gifted man, this vivid expression of such varied talents, fell grievously ill. Because of his illness he was unable to accept the offer of an appointment as a judge of the Appellate Division of the Supreme Court. Would that our judicial literature had been enriched by some concise and lucid judgments from his pen! He was nursed devotedly by his wife Willis but, on 18th December, 1942, at the all-too-early age of 58 years, he died. He was a man greatly beloved.'

— Mr Justice G N Holmes 'Mackeurtan — Founder of the Natal Bar' (1969) 86 *SALJ* 496 at 498–9.

The odd point

'He could have had an appointment as a judge in the early 1920s but he refused it. He had a vast practice, he had an infinite capacity for work, he seldom stopped work before ten or eleven o'clock at night and he would get through his work at an enormous rate. I devilled for him for four years before I went off on active service during the war and it was a tremendous experience, a great training-ground, and any success which I may have had as a lawyer was due very largely to the influence of Graham Mackeurtan. "Look for the odd point, my boy", he would say to us. He used to say that solving a legal problem is like putting on a glove: you put it on your hand and you get all five fingers into the appropriate places, and all of a sudden another little one comes popping up in the palm of your hand. "That is the odd point, look for the odd point in the case, my boy."'

— The Hon D G Fannin, former judge of the Natal Provincial Division, in his dictated unpublished memoirs (1986) page 5.

'My experience of him was that he was scrupulously fair to his opponents and to the Court and he was always anxious that the Court should have the best materials available to decide a point of law. So much so that on one occasion, moved by this idea and by his innate kindness, he actually prepared another counsel's argument as well as his own. He and Carlisle had come to Maritzburg to prepare their respective arguments in a shipping case. They arrived one night and had arranged to do their work the next day. But Carlisle fell ill during the night and was not able to drag himself to the chambers they shared until the afternoon. As soon as he arrived, Mackeurtan persuaded him to go back to bed and provided him with the argument which he (Carlisle) delivered the next morning. The case was *In re "Gwydyr Castle"* (1920, N.P.D. 231).'

— Mr Justice A A Roy Hathorn 'Harold Graham Mackeurtan: An Appreciation' (1943) 60 *SALJ* 125 at 141.

'He had a very unusual mind. Most minds work in one direction at any given time. His mind worked, as it were, on a wide front. He seemed able to give adequate attention to several things at the same time without any apparent effort and his irrepressible sense of humour was always operating on this same wide front. It found expression in frequent and spontaneous flashes of wit. Here is an instance. During a dreary argument presented to a sleepy court by an opponent with an unusually monotonous voice, the audience was suddenly galvanised into attention by the speaker talking about the "crucical" point in the case. This ridiculous mispronunciation was too much for Mackeurtan. Without a moment's hesitation, he wrote these lines and passed them round the bar:

Our learned friend addressed the Court,
Made music more than musical,

But cut our languorous day-dreams short
By calling crucial crucical.'

—Op cit at 139–40.

Naked lights and Mrs Grundy

'Mackeurtan was consulted by some theatrical people in an affair which was urgent and very serious to them. The question was whether under an agreement they brought with them, they could stage a performance that very day. Mackeurtan went through the agreement, clause by clause, until he came to one which prohibited the use of naked lights. Mackeurtan's instantaneous comment was that he supposed that that was a concession to Mrs. Grundy! But the remark was lost on his clients. They had too much at stake to understand the joke and wondered whether they had come to the chambers of an advocate or to a mental hospital.'

—Op cit at 143–4.

'Tatham's departure [from the Bar on his appointment to the Bench] left the field open for Graham Mackeurtan, a very different type of man—a profound lawyer and intellectually far and away Tatham's superior. But as a forensic tactician Mackeurtan could teach Tatham nothing. Mackeurtan's success was due primarily to a personality which could only be described as colossal. This seemed to enable him to impose his will not only upon the Court but upon his adversary. Whenever I fought a case against him during his prime I seemed to find that in no time he and the judges were ganged up against me. Against him one seldom felt at one's best. Fighting cases against advocates of the class of Frank Shaw, Schreiner, Ramsbottom, Millin and Holmes I felt stimulated by the prowess of my adversary; against Mackeurtan I usually felt bewitched and bewildered.'

—F N Broome (former Judge President of the Natal Provincial Division) *Not the Whole Truth* (1962) 117–18.

'The smallish but growing band of advocates in Durban which I joined in that year [1935] was accommodated near the Law Courts in Temple Chambers, since demolished. The comradeship and *esprit de corps*, so traditional among advocates, owed much to the pervading influence and inspiration of Graham Mackeurtan, the pioneer of the Natal Bar. Quitting dual practice during the First World War, Graham rapidly established himself as the highest paid and leading advocate in the country. He was the guide, philosopher and friend of his colleagues, all of whom he regarded as his protégés. On occasion he would enlist myself, my associate Denis (now Mr. Justice) Fannin or some other underbriefed young junior to devil for him on a case. This gave us not only a welcome break from the tedium of waiting for briefs, but also instructive and fascinating glimpses into Graham's own personality and his manner of working.

'He was a tremendous man of massive build and weight, with a deceptively cherubic Pickwickian face. He possessed a devastating sense of humour, but was generous and kind-hearted to a fault. A *bon vivant* with a keen appreciation of good liquor, he lived hard and worked hard.

'He was doubtless too content as the benign colossus of the Bar to be lured into a judicial appointment. It was widely believed that, on his refusing an offer of the Judge Presidency in Natal, the Government was on the point of taking the then unprecedented step of appointing him from the Bar to the Appellate Bench, when he died.

'He was, however, lured briefly into politics. He stood first for Durban Point in 1921. Some weeks before polling day his wife gave birth to a son, to whom the candidate over-optimistically gave the name Justin—for when the votes were counted, Graham was just *not* in.

'A year later he was returned in a by-election to the House of Assembly, but it soon became apparent that he had neither the patience nor the temperament for politics. In the 1924 general election he declined re-nomination, returning to his practice and to writing in his spare time *The Cradle Days of Natal*, a book already prized as Africana.

'Of the many anecdotes told of Graham Mackeurtan, one concerns a witness who under cross-examination got so flustered that he suddenly broke wind with an unmistakable report. "Notice of motion, my lord," commented Counsel. The Judge, equal to the occasion, responded sweetly: "I think this should have been heard in Chambers, Mr. Mackeurtan."'

—Leif Egeland *Bridges of Understanding* (1977) 62–3. (The last anecdote may be a chestnut. In the *Sunday Tribune* 18 December 1988 the culprit was a leading London silk—in motion court.)

'When [Denis Fannin] was appointed to the Bench in the middle of 1959 I inherited one case from him as senior counsel to the trustee of the late Hajee Moosa Adam. . . . The testator had left a complicated will with a number of charitable bequests. The will gave rise to frequent litigation. In one of the early cases the great advocate Graham Mackeurtan appeared. Apart from being a brilliant advocate, he had a superb sense of humour. In announcing his appearance he said, "M'Lord, I appear for the estate of the late Hajee Moosa Adam—of blessed memory".'

—The Hon Ramon Nigel Leon *Truth in Action* (the reminiscences of the former judge of the Natal Provincial Division, not yet completed or published).

Some warts

'Of course he had his faults. He was the father of the Natal Bar and he expected to be so regarded. While he was always anxious to help younger men, he preferred that their success should be entirely due to his help and not to their own unaided efforts. He and Selke started as great friends, but when Selke began to show a preference for a more individual professional life the friendship ended. After Selke went on the Bench it is said that Mackeurtan was once walking along a corridor in the Supreme Court building when a young man came suddenly out of a doorway and bumped into him. "Who the devil are you?" asked Mackeurtan. "I am Judge Selke's clerk," was the reply. "Serves you damn well right," Mackeurtan retorted. Once, after they had ceased to be friends, they found themselves against one another in an appeal from a magistrate's court. The case related to the installation of machinery in a ship called the "Pickle". Selke's clients claimed that the machinery in the ship was defective; the defence was that Mackeurtan's clients had offered to put the machinery right but had never been given an opportunity of doing so. There had been a good deal of correspondence before the case started, and it was known that Selke had himself drafted the letters which his clients' attorneys had signed. In his argument Mackeurtan set out to ridicule Selke's clients and their attorneys, and so indirectly Selke himself. He dealt with the correspondence, so I was told for unfortunately I was not in Court, by giving its effect in narrative form something like this. "We offer to put the machinery right and ask when we may do so. We are told that the ship is at sea. We ask when it will be back and we are told on Monday. We call on the agents on Monday and they tell us the ship will not be here until Tuesday. We go on Tuesday and they tell us that it returned on Monday night but sailed again early on Tuesday on a week's voyage. We return after a week and we are told 'The ship has just sailed. Why did you not come yesterday?' And so the story goes on: jam tomorrow and jam yesterday—never jam today. So we write and ask them to fix a definite date on which the ship will be available without fail. They give us a date on which they undertake to have the ship ready. At last, we say, we are to have the opportunity we want. But what happens? We collect our fitters and welders and take them down to the Point only to see the wretched ship staggering down the channel out to sea again. How could we put the machinery right while the 'Pickle' kept popping in and out of port?"

'Owing to some glandular trouble Mackeurtan had the misfortune to be very much overweight, even as a child, yet in his younger days he played tennis with remarkable sprightliness. He often made jokes about this superabundant flesh—he even published a book of poetry called *Slender Verses by a Stout Gentleman*—but he disliked any reference to his figure by others. Once in his club a very senior member asked him: "How do you get your weight up?" His reply, in schoolboy language, is quite unprintable. The question was stupidly tactless; the answer was abominably rude.

'But I must leave Mackeurtan now. He was a great man who would have reached the very top of his profession in any country and against any competition. He was a great wit and he was universally popular. It is a pity that he has left so little behind him, apart from a tradition and a host of anecdotes. But his textbook on the *Law of the Sale of Goods* will bear his name through edition after edition so long as law continues, and his *Cradle Days of Natal* is a valuable historical work marred only by occasional outbreaks of facetiousness.'

—F N Broome (former Judge President of the Natal Provincial Division) *Not the Whole Truth* (1962) 119–20. (See also SELKE.)

ALFRED CHRISTO MALAN

1889–1963. Schoolteacher. Member of the Pretoria Bar 1919–39. KC 1937. Judge of the Transvaal Provincial Division 1939–57. Judge of Appeal 1957–9.

'The Butcher'

'Meantime, there had been another appointment out of the ordinary course, to fill the vacancy caused by the retirement of Centlivres on 31 January 1957 and make up the then complement of ten in the Appellate Division. The information was conveyed by Schreiner to his wife on 3 December 1956. "Well, today came the news that you will have received by now that your friend 'the Butcher' [A C Malan] is to take Albert's [Centlivres's] place. Curiously I had a note from 'the Butcher' this morning condoling with me but reminding me that others too had been passed over! He then spoke of looking forward to collaborating with me in the future. And yet it never struck me that he was coming here, so that when Albert came in a few minutes later and offered me 5/- if I could give the name of

the new man in three guesses I couldn't do it! Money chucked away! . . . I reckon
there will be some disharmony when the Butcher comes. He has ability but not
gentleness. Poor old Henry [Fagan] is very distressed. He did try to get Hal
[Ramsbottom] and I think he expected the Government to respond." A week
later Schreiner wrote to his wife: "It isn't quite clear why he [Malan] was
appointed. He is of course next puisne of the Transvaal after the unacceptable
Rammie. But as far as I know he is not *persona grata* with the Government." He
speculated on the possibility that some of Malan's colleagues had been anxious to
get rid of him. "He certainly has ability and if he is prepared to work he may be
a useful member as things go. Useful but hardly clubbable!" It was a fair
appraisal, for at the beginning of term the next year Malan was annoyed at being
given an inferior room, and some shuffling had to be done, Schreiner told his wife
on 25 February 1957. "'A.C.'", he continued, "will certainly liven up things. He
has his own way of disposing of problems—a quick way, and not necessarily a
mistaken way. But it remains to be seen whether he will do the solid sort of work
that is required here. He has merits, like all of us, even the humblest.'''

—Ellison Kahn in *Fiat Iustitia: Essays in Memory of Oliver Deneys Schreiner* (1983) 55–6.

His relations with his judicial brethren

'Shortly after Mr Justice Steyn came out of purdah [the twenty-one-day
boycott of him by the Johannesburg Bar] two things happened to me which
concerned him. I appeared before him in a civil appeal in which the presiding
judge was A C Malan. As usual the presiding judge took a strong line—so strong
that he attacked my argument from every corner and at his sarcastic worst,
causing me for the only time in my life in practice to seek solace in a whisky at
11.30 am. Worse than that, Mr Justice Malan ignored his colleague throughout
the proceedings, half turning his back on him, and proceeded to give judgment
without even consulting him. I have often wondered what would have happened
if L C Steyn had said "I do not agree".'

   —The Hon Ramon Nigel Leon *Truth in Action* (the reminiscences of the former judge
   of the Natal Provincial Division, not yet published, as the manuscript has still to be
   completed). (It is ironical that Mr Justice Steyn was appointed Chief Justice on 4 April
   1959, when Malan was still a judge of appeal. On Malan's retirement at the age of 70 on
   25 December that year he accepted an appointment as acting judge of appeal. Steyn CJ
   paid an affecting tribute to his memory: see below under *His relations with counsel*.)

'The story is told of Mr Justice Malan hearing appeals with Mr Justice L C
Steyn (later to become Chief Justice) shortly after the latter had been elevated to
the bench from the public service. Counsel had recently been an attorney, and
kept on addressing the bench as "your worships". Eventually Lucas Steyn turned
to Malan, who was presiding, and whispered to him: "Should you not show your
displeasure?" Malan whispered back, "I thought he was addressing you".'

   —Ellison Kahn 'The Seven Lamps of Legal Humour Part 1' 1984 *De Rebus* 156 at 158.
   (For the benefit of the laity, I should point out that a judge of the Supreme Court is
   referred to as 'my lord'; a magistrate, who is an officer of a lower court, is referred to
   as 'your worship'. An attorney has no right of appearance for a client before a judge; he
   may appear only before a magistrate.)

'I cannot resist adding a couple of further pieces of Malaniana. By the strangest
coincidence, at lunch today I seated myself next to two gentlemen, both of
whom, shortly after qualifying in law many years ago, had been clerks to Mr

Justice Leslie Blackwell. Neither had enjoyed the experience. Indeed, the second one, who had been recommended by the first to follow in his footsteps, asked the first at lunch, half jokingly, half plaintively, "What did you have against me?" The first recounted the tale of the only time Malan and Blackwell were on the provincial division bench together, hearing magistrates' courts appeals. Malan, I am told, disliked Blackwell heartily and resolutely refused to sit with him. The judge president, Gerry Maritz, had managed to see to this until one day it proved to be impossible. No other judge was available. Malan came across Blackwell's clerk in the corridor. "Are you Mr Justice Blackwell's clerk?" "Yes, sir" came the answer in trepidation. "Well, you can sell ringside seats for three guineas."'

—Ellison Kahn ibid.

'When Malan heard that—— , an advocate of no distinction whatever, had been appointed a judge, his disgust and fury were almost beyond description, but not even he could give public expression to his feelings. What he did was adjourn his court—not for the customary ten minutes as a mark of respect to the memory of a judge or advocate who has died, but for a whole hour.'

—Ellison Kahn's commonplace book.

His relations with counsel

'Most junior counsel and many silks were terrified of appearing before Malan, for not only would he refuse to tolerate papers out of order or ill-prepared or unsupportable contentions (no bad thing)—he was so often rude, sardonic, impatient, overbearing and a bully. But his characteristics were not of a piece, and he had his praiseworthy points. Some years later, in paying tribute to his memory in the Appellate Division, L C Steyn CJ said that Malan was one of the strongest and most colourful personalities he had known, with well-defined convictions, unafraid, dynamic and immovably independent. On Malan's death a moving letter appeared in the press by a man who had been his clerk in the Transvaal Court for seven years, in which he spoke of his inner kindness, his carefully hidden but keen sense of humour, his fortitude in the face of ill health, his dislike of publicity (unlike some of his colleagues, but exactly like Ramsbottom) and his very careful consideration of all factors before deciding on punishment of criminals ("the Butcher" was not fair), to which one should add his efforts to prevent his rebukes to counsel receiving publicity in the press. If a man can be a hero to his clerk, there must be good in him.'

—Ellison Kahn in *Fiat Iustitia: Essays in Memory of Oliver Deneys Schreiner* (1983) 53 (footnotes omitted).

'There is one story I should like to add that has, to my knowledge, never been put into writing: I heard it told by the victim in an after-dinner speech. The victim, who never made a claim to being an Adonis, was appearing in a running-down trial. He was attempting to show Malan J with the aid of models how the collision had occurred, and said: "If your lordship would now watch me." To which Malan J answered, with his famous stress on every word: "Mr ——, must I *look* at you as well as listen to you?" Later he said to Malan J: "I wish to change my argument. I am not happy with it." Turning his familiar purple and smiling his familiar freezing smile, Malan replied: "By all means Mr ——, by all means. Nothing is closer to my heart than your happiness."'

—Kahn op cit at 56.

'To score off Mr Justice Malan was something to be proud of. It happened occasionally. Counsel, appearing before Malan in Johannesburg in the Witwatersrand Local Division, was asking leave to effect service on a firm, with its headquarters in Prague in Czechoslovakia, not in Prague but on its branch in Rotterdam; in the circumstances, so he submitted, such service was preferable. Initially Malan was not impressed or sympathetic. "What difference can it make to your client?" he said. "After all, how far is Prague from Rotterdam?" The answer from counsel came pat: "As far as Johannesburg is from Bloemfontein." He got his order.'

—Ellison Kahn 'The Seven Lamps of Legal Humour Part 2' 1984 *De Rebus* 210 at 211, citing Isaac Goodman *Judges I have Known* (1969) 109. (For the benefit of any member of the laity who does not know the meaning of the reference to 'Bloemfontein', I point out that the word stands for the Appellate Division of the Supreme Court, which has its seat there.)

'Some years ago the Johannesburg Bar Council lodged an informal complaint with the Judge President against the judicial conduct of a newly appointed judge. It was claimed that, in a number of separate episodes, the judge had shown gross discourtesy and unreasonable impatience towards counsel. The Judge President declined to intervene. It seemed that it was no part of his duties to instruct individual judges in good manners or deportment. It must be recorded that the judge concerned mellowed, and that he came to be highly respected not only for his erudition and wisdom, but also for his compassion. His barbs, once aimed at counsel, became exquisite and finely-honed specimens of sarcasm, directed at litigants whose conduct was deserving of censure. A well-known example was his comment on the defence of a burly policeman, who was sued for damages for assault by an elderly and slightly built Black plaintiff. The plea was that the policeman had acted in self-defence and that he had had great difficulty in subduing the plaintiff. The judge said that the defendant's evidence "conjured up the epic of a titanic struggle between this emaciated policeman, only six feet in height and weighing barely 250 pounds, and a pocket Hercules, in his prime at 60 years of age". It may be that, after the passage of the years, a review of the complaints by the Bar would reveal that there was a good deal less incivility and a good deal more wit than was originally appreciated.'

—Mr Justice C S Margo 'Reflections on Some Aspects of the Judicial Function' in Ellison Kahn (ed) *Fiat Iustitia: Essays in Memory of Oliver Deneys Schreiner* (1983) 282 at 291–2.

'. . . [A] newly married young advocate . . . appeared before Malan in a certain *pro Deo* matter in which the accused was charged with the crime of rape. Counsel, as was only to be expected, was intensely proud of the role in which he was to appear, and invited not only some of his relations to be present in court for the trial, but also his wife.

'After the complainant explained how she had been outraged, the newly married young advocate rose to cross-examine her. The cross-examination had gone on for barely a few minutes, when Mr Justice Malan broke in with the comment:

'"Mr . . ., it is painfully clear to me that you do not have the slightest appreciation of the sexual process."'

—Isaac Goodman *Judges I Have Known* (1969) 113.

'In what must have been one of his last criminal cases in the TPD, the firm I was articled to briefed Joe Slovo to appear for the accused, and I sat in court

Preparing for his first case
Honoré Daumier (1808–79). Lithograph.

representing our firm. The prosecutor was introducing a number of exhibits into the case, and each time he handed one to the orderly to take over to the witness box Slovo got up, went to the front of the court, examined the exhibit and then went back to his seat. Eventually Malan lost his temper at all the jumpings up and down and said to counsel "Mr Slovo, this court is not a circus in which the clowns can jump in and out of the ring whenever they feel like it."'

—From a letter of 27 July 1989 by Mr Chris Niland to Ellison Kahn.

'Judge Malan's fine sense of humour was emphasised in a criminal case in which an Indian accused had pleaded guilty to a charge of receiving stolen property—a big quantity of stamps having been involved—well knowing the stamps to have been stolen.

'Defence counsel in that case—he is today one of the senior members of the Johannesburg Bar—who worked as a schoolmaster in his young days, made a plea to the court in mitigation of sentence. He indicated that the accused happened to be well known to him personally, adding:

'"He was a pupil at the Indian school where I was at the time a schoolmaster."

'Judge Malan asked counsel: "Do you think that that is a mitigating factor?"

'Counsel, in an effort to be humorous, replied that it might possibly be urged that the accused "had fallen under the wrong influence at the school when he was at an impressionable age."

'"I will consult the Criminal Code," instantly retorted Malan, "and I will see whether it is possible for you to serve part of the accused's sentence."'

—Isaac Goodman *Judges I have Known* (1969) 110–11. (Counsel must have been Fred Zwarenstein QC.)

'Malan, like many a judge, was impatient with long-winded counsel, of whom there are many. One is reminded of the celebrated interchange of remarks between the loquacious English barrister and the High Court judge. "My lord, I fear I am beginning to trespass on your lordship's patience." "Mr Jones, you have long since done so; you are now trespassing on eternity." Well, Malan was a little less polite on one occasion. The divorce roll was very long, and Malan was keen to see that undefended actions kept moving at the rate of about one every two minutes. Things went smoothly until counsel, for no good reason, started a protracted examination in chief of his client. It went on and on, Malan getting ever more purple in the face. Counsel then asked many details about the numerous children of the union. "And they are all minors?" "Yes, they are", replied the plaintiff. Malan J: "I suppose they were, Mr Robinson, before this case started."'

—Ellison Kahn 'The Seven Lamps of Legal Humour Part 1' 1984 *De Rebus* 156 at 158 (footnotes omitted).

'In later years a similar terror [to Greenberg J] on the bench was A C Malan, who could neither suffer fools gladly nor endure prolixity on the part of counsel. For David Gould, a brilliant advocate but unnecessarily repetitive and prolix, it was a nightmare to appear before Malan, whose patience was very brittle, and whose tongue was about the sharpest in the ranks of the judiciary.

'In a trial which was heard before Malan J and which was carrying on endlessly due to the fact that two rather slow batsmen in Dowling [qv] and Archie Shacksnovis [qv] were appearing on opposite sides, the judge eventually announced on the twentieth day that the court would resume at two in the afternoon, instead of the then customary 2 30 pm. At 2 10 pm that afternoon, when everybody had been assembled in the court for some time, Dowling eventually appeared and made his apologies for his late arrival, stating that it was due to the fact that his watch was slow, to which Malan J retorted that it seemed to him that even counsel's watches had been infected by the slowness of the proceedings.

'Malan himself had not been left unscathed by the bench when he was still at the bar. In a rape case he was appearing for the defence, and during cross-examination asked the complainant whether she had screamed, to which she replied that she tried to scream but was unable to do so as the accused was choking her. Malan then put his hands round his own neck, went through the motions of choking himself and emitting stifled screams. "There you are", said the triumphant Malan to the witness, "I've choked myself but still managed to scream." The judge, Greenberg J, replied: "Mr Malan, you have confirmed what I suspected, and that is, that even strangling won't silence you."'

—M Bliss QC 'Random Reminiscences' in *1877–1977 The Pretoria Bar/Die Pretoriase Balie* (1977) 57 at 58.

'The traditional bar dinner has on occasion been a riotous affair. The one given in honour of Malan on his appointment to the bench in 1939 ended in utter chaos. Malan had, like others at the bar, essayed into spare time farming operations with disastrous financial consequences, and to avoid more drastic proceedings against him, he had assigned his estate for the benefit of his creditors under the provisions of the then prevailing Insolvency Act. While replying to the toast in his honour at the dinner, Malan was much heckled and reminded of his farming operations. He tolerated this for a while and then lost his temper, announcing that if he encountered such disrespect when he was on the bench, he would deal with it ruthlessly. He then stalked out of the dining room of the Pretoria Country Club, leaving the whole party in utter disarray.'

—M Bliss op cit at 60.

His relations with the English language

'Malan, who had started working life as a schoolteacher, prided himself, with some justification, on his mastery of English. Shortly after the last war junior counsel appeared in a criminal trial before him. During the proceedings he received the customary tongue-lashing from Malan; but this time counsel was not prepared to accept it without protest—he had been an officer and then a prisoner of war who had escaped and led a hard life on the run thereafter; furthermore, he was about to leave the Bar. In the course of increasingly unpleasant exchanges, Malan said to the advocate: "Are you trying to be truculent, Mr—— ?", mispronouncing "truculent" as "true-sue-lent". "No, my lord", came the answer, "I am not trying to be truculent"—the word being pronounced correctly. For once Malan had no reply.'

—Ellison Kahn in *Fiat Iustitia: Essays in Memory of Oliver Deneys Schreiner* (1983) 56.

'Mr Justice Malan was one day quite innocently involved in an incident which I was specially asked not to report. It was obviously due to a misunderstanding of the pronunciation of the name of a certain English town. It happened during a divorce action at the Rand Supreme Court when an advocate—he is presently a prominent Silk—was examining a female plaintiff in the witness box. He put the usual preliminary question to her, that is, "Were you married at Holme, in England, on. . . ?"

'After the woman replied: "That is correct," Mr Justice Malan sarcastically asked counsel—in an obviously irritated mood—why people who came to South Africa from abroad, and who had lived here for many years, should persist in referring to England as "home".

'"I think that this practice should be stopped in our courts, and I think that counsel should do everything possible to stop the practice."

'When he concluded his little tirade, counsel advised the Judge that his client came from a place in England called "Holme", but which is normally pronounced in the accepted and correct English manner: "home".

'There was deep silence in court for a few seconds, and then counsel was given a hint from the Bench to continue his examination of the witness.

'A few minutes later—happily for the Judge—the court Registrar came towards the Press box and said to me:

'"Ike, the Judge has just asked me to tell you that he will be very pleased if you will kindly refrain from reporting the little misunderstanding."

'I decided to sacrifice a good little story in order to respect the Judge's wishes. I really had no option in the matter.'

—Isaac Goodman *Judges I Have Known* (1969) 112–13.

WILLIAM MORTIMER ROBERTSON (MORTIE) MALHERBE

1875–1964. Journalist. Public servant. Professor of Law, University of Stellenbosch, 1921–55.

'Wylie's counterpart at Stellenbosch—Professor W M R Malherbe—published extraordinarily little, although I do not think he quite equalled Socrates's distinction of publishing nothing. Nevertheless, one of the most moving tributes to Morty Malherbe which I ever heard—it came from that warm human being, the late Professor Swanepoel of Potchefstroom—was that he wrote his books in the hearts and minds of his students. Wylie had something of that quality.'

—Denis V Cowen 'Taught Law is Tough Law: The Evolution of a South African Law School' (1986) 51 *THRHR* 4 at 23. (On Professor Wylie, see WILLE.)

'Malherbe was a voracious reader with an enquiring intellect. As a prisoner of war in India following the Boer War, he claimed that his reading material consisted of the *Corpus Iuris.* . . . (Malherbe prided himself on having last driven on the day he acquired his driver's licence. He either walked or was driven. When he went on holiday from Stellenbosch to Natal, he sent his wife and daughter ahead by car, while he took the train.)'

—Jeremy Gauntlett 'J C de Wet at Seventy-five' 1987 *De Rebus* 581 at 583.

'Reeds op skool, tydens die behandeling van die Tweede Taalbeweging, het ek van hom gehoor—van W.M.R. Malherbe wat die eerste redakteur van "Die Brandwag" was. Toe was dit net nog 'n naam wat onthou moes word om matriek te slaag. Op Stellenbosch egter, sou dié naam onuitwisbaar op my gemoed ingebrand word.

'So tussen die doopverrigtinge deur moes ek, as voornemende regstudent, hoor van die grusame lot wat daar vanaf die derde jaar op my sou wag, d.w.s. as ek dosente soos De Wet en Yeats in die eerste twee jaar sou oorleef. In die derde jaar sou ek nie alleen kennis maak met Romeinse reg nie, maar met die drakoniese skrikfiguur, prof. W.M.R. Malherbe, Dekaan van die Regsfakulteit en ondergang van menige welmenende student. Nie net studente sou ril by die blote

MORTIE MALHERBE

'met helmet, koffertjie, reënjas (daar was geen teken van reën nie) en serp.'

(Hierdie foto van professor Mortie Malherbe is deur dr N J van der Merwe sonder die professor se wete in sy klas geneem. Sien (1982) 12 Nuntius 30 op 31.)

aanhoor van sy naam nie, maar ook die Raad en Senaat van die Universiteit sou glo baie versigtig met hom wees. Nader hy dan nie reeds tagtig, terwyl alle ander professore op vyf-en-sestig die tuig moet neerlê nie? Dit toon mos dat hierdie man nie gebonde is aan die norme wat vir die gewone mens geld nie, dat hy as 't ware princeps legibus solutus is.

'Dat hy geen gewone mens is nie, was dan ook dadelik duidelik by my eerste heimlike aanskoue, op 'n respekvolle distansie natuurlik, van die tengerige figuur en vaal reënjas (daar was geen teken van reën nie) en opvallende kakie helmet, daar waar hy sypaadjielangs onder die eike voortbeweeg het. . . .

'Lank voor agtuur op die oggend van die tweede dag (prof. Malherbe weier om sy lesings op enige ander tye as 8 vm en 4 nm 'n aanvang te laat neem) sit ons almal penregop in die klas en wag angstig op ons debuutlesing aan die voete van die legendariese leermeester. Met helmet, koffertjie, reënjas (daar was geen teken van reën nie) en serp is hy stiptelik daar. Die helmet word langs die kateder geplaas. Die jas en serp bly aan en die koffertjie onoopgemaak. Prof. Malherbe is gereed vir die lesing; ons vir die ergste.

'Skielik vlieg sy hand iewers uit 'n jassak en 'n vinger wys na Basil Wunsh.

'"Wie is jy?"

'"Ek is Wunsh, Professor."

'"Wat vir 'n ding?"

'"Ek is Wunsh, Professor."

'"Vyf?" (Ons begin senuweeagtig giggel.)

'"Nee, Professor. Wunsh!"

'"Kan julle hoor wat die man sê?"

'"Nee, Professor!!"

'"Man, ruk jou reg! Kan jy nie hoor ek vra wat jou naam is nie?"

'"W–U–N–S–H—Wunsh, Professor."

'" O ja, Bunsh, nè? Nou goed, Bunsh. . . ."

'En Bunsh het Basil gebly.

'Sas Strauss was volgende aan die beurt.

'"Wat's jou naam, man?"

'"Strauss, Professor." (Hardop.)

'"Sewe? Wat sê jy man? Kan jy nie sien ek is doof nie?"

'"Jammer, Professor. Strauss, Professor." (Nog harder.)

'"Nege? Kan julle hoor wat die man sê?"

'"Nee, Professor!!"

'"Aag wat, Professor, sê maar sommer net Struis." (In 'n moedelose half–fluister stem wat slegs vir die ore van sy bankmaat bedoel is.)

'"O ja, nou goed, Struis. . . ."

'En so het die eerste klas verloop en het Ewald Fichardt "Fiekart" geword en ek "Vannermerrel". . . .

'Wat was Mortie se geheim? Waarom het hy jou in die klas so geboei dat jy nooit konsentrasieprobleme gehad het nie? Ek dink sy onvoorspelbaarheid het baie daarmee te doen gehad. Jy het altyd die onverwagte by hom verwag, maar wanneer die verwagte dan gebeur, gebeur dit onverwags:

'Dit is in jou vierdejaar, dit is laatmiddag en hy gesels onderhoudend oor die teorie van die algemene persoonlikheidsreg. Alles gaan voor die wind. Daar is vanmiddag geen drama nie. Skielik haak die naald:

'"Op pagina 7 sê Molengraaff dit. . . ."

'Dis 'n nuwe naam. Van hierdie juris het ons nog nooit gehoor nie.

'"Op pagina 7 sê Molengraaff dit. . . ."

'Prof. Malherbe druk twee vingers teen sy hoof, bly 'n tydjie stil en dan kom dit weer:

'"Op pagina 7 sê Molengraaff dit . . ., begryp jy, Bunsh?"

'"Ja, Professor."

'Weer 'n rukkie stilte, en dan skielik:

'"Wat sê Molengraaff op pagina 7, Bunsh?"

'Tot vandag toe weet ek nie wat Molengraaff op pagina 7 te sê het nie, want vir die res van die periode is Mortie liries oor Bunsh se onkunde. . . .

'Dit is kort voor die finale mondeling oor al vyf jaar se werk in Privaatreg. Mortie vra vrae in die klas om ons in die regte gemoedstemming te bring vir die groot dag van afrekening wanneer jy vir 'n uur lank jou man sal moet staan voor die ganse doserende personeel van die Regsfakulteit. (Alle dosente moet dié mondeling bywoon, of hulle nou Privaatreg gee of nie, want die Dekaan beklemtoon dat die Privaatreg die basis van die hele regstudie is en geen juris durf dit verwaarloos nie.) Die spanning in die klas steek dié in enige Evkom-kragdraad ver die loef af.

'"Wat is die gevolge van 'n huwelik, Vannermerrel?"

'A, dis maklik. Dis eerstejaarswerk. Ek gaan die vraag goed beantwoord.

'"Wel, Professor, daar is die gevolge wat die partye se persone betref en die volge wat hulle vermoëns raak. . . ."

'"Fout! Jy sak soos 'n baksteen. Gaan koop vir jou 'n enkelkaartjie terug na Bloemfontein!"

'Die akademiese skavot open onder my voete.

'"Bunsh, wat is die gevolge van 'n huwelik?"

'"Soos mnr. Van der Merwe gesê het, Professor, moet ons onderskei. . . ."

'"Fout, man! Wat makeer jou?"

'"Antwoord die vraag, Fiekart!"

'"Ek het nie 'n 'clue' nie, Professor."

'"Ja juis!"

'"Volgende, wat is die gevolge van 'n huwelik?"

'Elkeen word gevra. Niemand weet nie. Die atmosfeer is dié by 'n Sondagskoolpiekniek wanneer dit begin reën. Eers word ons goed die kop gewas en daar word verduidelik waarom die Regsfakulteit van die Universiteit nooit kan oorweeg om ons op die weerlose publiek los te laat nie, en dan kom dit: '"Weet julle nie wat die gevolge van 'n huwelik is nie?" (Almal weet, maar niemand weet blykbaar nie.) "Die gevolge van 'n huwelik is dat die partye getroud is!"

'Mortie se neus krul so effens op en dan skatterlag hy. Onbeheersd doen ons mee. . . .

'Dit is jammer dat Mortie so 'n *horror publicationis* gehad het. "Vir wat sal ek publiseer?" het hy altyd gesê. "My studente is my monumente."

'Baie van die dinge wat sy oudstudente verkondig, is egter tweedehands. 'n Mens sou graag die *fons et origo* self aan die woord wou sien.

'Hoe groot die aansien was wat hy allerweë in regskringe geniet het, blyk o.a. daaruit dat daar na 'n ongepubliseerde klasdiktaat van hom verwys is in *Crookes, N.O. and Another v. Watson and Others*, 1956 (1) S.A. 277 (A), op bl. 297. In latere jare het appèlregter Toon van den Heever aan my persoonlik gesê hoe dit hom gespyt het om in vermelde uitspraak van Mortie te moet verskil. Hy het my ook vertel van 'n terloopse ontmoeting op die Bloemfonteinse stasie kort nadat daardie uitspraak gepubliseer is:

'"Kyk hier, Toon, wat is dit met jou?", sê iemand onverwags hier skuins agter hom op die platform.

'Regter Van den Heever groet beleefd, maar die enigste reaksie is:

'"Vir wat staan julle daar in die appèlhof en draai die trust *inter vivos* die nek om?!"

'Daaroor het Mortie altyd ontevrede gebly, want die trust, soos die persoonlikheidsreg, die wissel en estoppel, was een van die heilige koeie op sy regswetenskaplike akker.

'Elke mens ervaar van tyd tot tyd die onaangename sensasie wat "vrees" genoem word. As jy 'n regstudent op Stellenbosch is en mondelinge eksamen by Mortie is jou voorland, is vrees nie meer 'n sensasie nie, maar 'n lewenswyse.

'Die mondelinge eksamen word by Mortie aan huis afgelê. Dit is 'n groot ou spokerige groensinkdak-opstal. Waar die voordeurklokkie was, 'n klokkie wat seker vroeër jare die einde van menige akademiese loopbaan ingelui het, sit nou net 'n gat in die muur. Die res van die muur by die voordeur is oortrek van studentegraffiti en by die lees daarvan word jy een met 'n tydlose kosmos van vrees. In die sitkamer waar jou lot beklink gaan word, is wit lakens onheilspellend oor die meubels gedrapeer, want Mortie bly vir lange tye alleen op Stellenbosch. (Hy het glo ook 'n huis in Pretoria.) Net sy gemakstoel en die klavierstoeltjie wat vir jou bestem is, is ongelaken. . . .

'En dan was daar die ervaring van Basil Wunsh (spreek uit "Bunsh"). Die voltrekking van sy mondeling is vir die aand om sewe uur bepaal:

'Dis nie net donker op die stoep nie; die hele huis is in duisternis gehul. Hy klop met toenemende intensiteit aan die voordeur. Verder gebeur niks. In die lig van sy sigaretaansteker betree hy versigtig die huis. Met elke tree wat hy gee, roep hy gedemp:

'"Professor! Professor Malherbe! Dis ekke Basil Wunsh, hier. Ek kom vir my mondelinge eksamen in Romeinse reg."

'Of daar nog iets anders in die huis lewe, bly 'n digbewaarde geheim.

'Basil, roepende deur vertrekke waar slegs die lakens antwoord gee, kom by 'n slaapkamer. Dit lyk asof daar iets substansieels op die bed is. Altoos roepende, nader Basil bedeesd die bed. Daar lê prof. Malherbe, op die naat van sy rug, met reënjas en al (daar was geen teken van reën nie). Die besef kom: hy, Basil Wunsh, is die een wat prof. Malherbe dood aantref. Vlug?—Maak eers seker. Hoe bepaal 'n mens die intrede van dood? Hy besluit om 'n ooglid op te lig. Versigtig buk hy oor die bed. Skielik is daar 'n wysvinger voor sy neus en 'n stem vul die vertrek:

'"Vertel my alles wat jy weet van die *ius gentium!*" . . .

''n Gesindheid teenoor 'n leermeester word dikwels geprojekteer op die vak wat hy doseer. Mortie het egter by sy studente veel meer as 'n liefde vir die besondere vakke wat hy onderrig het, gewek. By hom het trouens die beoefening van die regswetenskap as passie, as bron van vreugde, as lewenstaak voorop gestaan. Deur sy sterk persoonlikheid, minsame geaardheid en puik, alhoewel onkonvensionele, onderrigmetodes is nie slegs kennis en kunde oorgedra nie, maar veral entoesiasme vir die studie van die reg. Talle van sy oud-studente het, begeestert, nie net van sy gedagtes nie, maar ook sy juridiese *Weltanschauung* op hulle beurt aan ander uitgedra. Vandaar die ongekende juridiese opbloei hier te lande.

'"My studente is my monumente, begryp jy?"

'"Nee, Professor, ek begryp nie, want hulle is slegs die bouaannemers. U monument is die Suid-Afrikaanse Regswetenskap."'

—N J van der Merwe 'Prof. Mortie Malherbe Soos Ek Hom Geken Het' (1982) 12 *Nuntius* 30 at 30–3, 54.

How a person dies

'Death has always been an important juristic fact, a *regsfeit*; it is an event to which the law attaches a variety of consequences. As jurists we are inclined to have regard to the consequences of death rather than to the concept of death itself. An

anecdote which is told of the late Professor Mortie Malherbe of Stellenbosch, a
very well-known legal luminary of yesteryear, illustrates this statement very
well. One day, it is said, he was conducting an oral examination on the law of
succession and he put the following question to the student: "How does a person
die?" The hapless student desperately searched his brains for the precious little
medical knowledge stored in them, and began by saying that the heart stops
beating, that the person stops breathing, that the body temperature starts falling,
etc. But Professor Malherbe, in his customary curt fashion, cut him short, saying:
"No man, you're on the wrong track; a person dies with or without a will!"'

—S A Strauss, *Doctor, Patient and the Law* 3 ed (1991) 361.

GERHARDUS JACOBUS MARITZ

1889–1964. Member of the Pretoria Bar 1913–26. KC 1926. President of the
Special Court for Hearing Income Tax Appeals 1926–30. Judge of the
Transvaal Provincial Division 1930–47. Judge President 1947–59.

Maritz goes to prison

'Towards the end of 1914 he was arrested on a farm near Warmbaths while
trying to join Jopie Fourie and the "rebels." This is how he describes his
experiences:

'"We all were irritated and frustrated . . . white feathers were being bandied
about and some newspapers were very pompous about how generous Britain had
been to the Afrikaners.

'"GERRIE."'
(Mr. Justice Maritz)
From *(1933) 2* South African Law Times *4*

'"I was a youngster—only 24—and I
decided that if it was a question of choosing
between common sense and blood, I would
stick to blood. I felt I couldn't sit back and
watch—I had to go out and fight.

'"I was arrested near Warmbaths and put
in the blockhouse there. Then I was taken
to the Nylstroom Jail and finally to prison
in Pretoria, where I spent about six weeks.
After that they let me out and I had only to
report to the police twice a week.

'"Some people cut me dead because of
this, but most of them said, 'You fool'
and soon forgave me."'

—*Sunday Times* 1 November 1959.

'Toe hy onlangs die gevangenis op
Nylstroom besoek het saam met sy
personeel, het hy na 'n sel gewys en gesê:
"Sien julle daardie sel—daar was julle
regter opgesluit gedurende die rebellie."
Die lede het hom verbaas aangekyk, dog
het hy gemeen wat hy gesê het, sonder 'n
sweem van hooghartigheid.'

—*Dagbreek* 1 November 1953.

'Hot on the heels of that disaster followed another near disaster. I was briefed for the respondent and drove up to Pretoria to argue an appeal. I entered the advocates' robing room at about 9.15 to robe, after which I would get out from the library the books which I needed for my argument. I unpacked my bag and then discovered to my horror that I had left my brief behind. In that brief were my notes of argument together with the list of cases which I needed. I was in a panic and decided that I would have to see the presiding judge, who was the Judge President, Mr Justice Maritz. He was one of the real characters on the Bench, who spent most of his time hearing criminal appeals and criminal trials: he did very little civil work. He was able to dispose of eleven criminal appeals in an hour by an interjection such as: "Mr Leon, I am with you on sentence, but if you persist in trying to argue the merits I am liable to change my mind." A nod was as good as a wink. Mr Justice Maritz also had an impish sense of humour but was a compassionate man. I entered his chambers with some trepidation, but thought that he would understand my human error. On the contrary, he was very brusque: "You must learn not to make these kind of mistakes, Leon", he said. "You will have to do the best you can." I left feeling very disconsolate and went into court in a state of absolute depression, not knowing how I would survive what was bound to be an ordeal. Moreover, I could not recall all the cases upon which I intended to rely, and there was no time in which to look them up. The appeal was called, and my opponent argued the case for the appellant. After his argument had been completed Gerrie Maritz said to me with an impish grin, "Mr Leon, it is not necessary to hear you". He could have given me that hint in chambers, but he wanted to make me sweat.'

—The Hon Ramon Nigel Leon *Truth in Action* (the reminiscences of the former judge of the Natal Provincial Division, not yet completed or published).

'Some time after Gerrie had retired, Louis le Grange (now Deputy Judge President) and I finished a case against each other in Pretoria. Louis suggested that we look up Gerrie. The latter questioned us closely about a case he had been told of—a criminal case of fraud that had been going on before Hill J for some eleven months. Gerrie found this very difficult to believe. In the end he summed it all up rather neatly by saying: "In three days he's either guilty or not guilty. Otherwise it's a civil case."

'On another occasion, I was waiting for my pro deo case to come on in his court. The client of the counsel immediately ahead of me had just been convicted. The SAP 69 form was handed in. It contained an impressive history of crime and punishment. Counsel then addressed Gerrie. He said that his client had been sent to a reformatory, had been whipped more than once, both with a light and a heavy cane, had been sent to gaol several times for various periods, and had also been sentenced to solitary and spare diet. None of this seemed to have helped. The only sentence that his client had never received was a suspended sentence. Perhaps that should be given a try! Gerrie agreed. So done.'

—From letters of 2 March and 12 April 1989 by Mr (now Mr Justice) W P Schutz SC to Ellison Kahn.

'MR. JUSTICE MARITZ ON THE BENCH—AND 15 MEN GO FREE
'*Justice with a big smile in Rand criminal court*

'The scales of justice shone shiny bright for 15 accused who appeared on serious

G J MARITZ
Caricature by Roy Sumner, from the Sunday
Times *1 November 1959*

charges at the Rand Criminal Sessions today. Their stories were told in quick time and in much less time the Judge President, Mr. Justice Maritz, had reached his decisions: the men were all set free.

'First to appear was Philip Shosi, a 23-year-old Native, on a charge of murder.

'"I plead guilty to culpable homicide," he told the Judge President.

'"Let us hear your story," said Mr. Justice Maritz.

'Shosi told how he was drinking with friends near Parktown on October 19.

'He told Cyprian Ngidi to move from where he was seated.

'Ngidi was in full view of any passer-by and if the police saw him they would all get into serious trouble.

'After an argument Shosi found himself backed against a fence with Ngidi menacing him with a sharp-pointed iron bar.

'"I pulled my knife and stabbed at him. He turned his head and I got him in the neck. He ran away. Later he was found dead."

'Mr. Justice Maritz found Shosi guilty of culpable homicide and asked Mr. A. Chaskalson (*pro deo* for Shosi) if he wished to address the Court on the question of sentence.

'Mr. Chaskalson: I don't think there is anything I can say, my Lord.

'Mr. Justice Maritz: Would five years meet the case?

'Mr. Chaskalson: I am in your Lordship's hands.

'Mr. Justice Maritz: This was as near to self-defence as anything could be. Shosi, you are cautioned and discharged.

'Next was a boy of 17 charged with raping a girl of 15 near Homelake, Randfontein, on October 4.

'The youth denied that he had raped the girl. She was his girl friend, he said.

'Mr. Justice Maritz: I don't like this case. Of course I don't like crime. I mean I don't like it from the Crown's point of view. Make the charge indecent assault.

'He called the complainant into the witness box.

'"She looks more than 15," said the Judge President.

'"She does look mature," said Mr. N. Barkhuizen, for the Crown.

'The Judge President: Ask him whether he pleads to indecent assault.

'The youth said he had never molested the girl. They had been lovers for six weeks before this complaint. They had been intimate once.

'Mr. Justice Maritz: I don't like it. Acquitted. Who's next?

'Next was Wilson Siboyana (23), a former police constable at Boksburg.

'Yesterday he was acquitted by Mr. Justice Maritz of a charge of murdering his wife.

'"Oh, my old friend," said the Judge President as Siboyana went into the dock, charged with robbery of two bicycles.

'Mr. Justice Maritz looked at defending counsel, Mr. H. H. Currie.

'"I was on the Bench yesterday and your client got off on a very serious charge. Do you want me to recuse myself?"—"No, my lord."

'The Judge President turned to Mr. Barkhuizen: "Do you want me to recuse myself?"—"No, my lord."

'Mr. Barkhuizen said he was prepared to reduce the charge to one of theft.

'The Judge President, who apparently did not hear, asked if assessors were necessary. He was told they were.

"Even when there will be no death sentence? I am certainly not going to impose the death sentence in this case."—"In all cases of robbery, my lord. But I am prepared to reduce the charge to theft."

'Mr. Justice Maritz: You have no objection, Mr. Currie?—No, my lord (laughter).

'The Crown had only one witness.

'"It is his word against that of the accused."

'After hearing the witness Mr. Justice Maritz looked at Siboyana: "You're acquitted."

'The proceedings had lasted 40 minutes. The remaining cases required assessors.

'Mr. Justice Maritz: It is 10.45. I didn't think we'd finish so soon. I only warned the assessors to be here at 11.20. The Court is adjourned.

'Soon after the adjournment, there were 12 more happy accused. Seven charged with rape were acquitted because of unsatisfactory Crown evidence.

'Then came five men charged with the murder of a man on Christmas Eve. The Crown led evidence of only one witness.

'Mr. Justice Maritz, facing the accused: "I have just heard a bad report about you. I don't mind your drinking. The police might object, but I don't. But when you have had a few drinks I object to your killing a man. What must I do with you?"

'No. 1 accused: I think it best that you should let us go, as we do not know anything about this.

'Mr. Justice Maritz: I think you are quite right. The prosecutor is not pressing for a conviction. Your defence has left it to me. There was only one witness and it is his word against yours. I don't know why I should believe him and not you.

'"You can all go home."'

—*The Star* 1 April 1959.

'I also have a report here of what I found in a newspaper about a court case and I would like to read it out as an example of the kind of case that I am referring to—

Charged with murdering a native by striking him on the head with a wooden pole, Palula pleaded guilty to culpable homicide before Mr Justice Maritz at the Rand Criminal Sessions. The plea was accepted. Palula's story was that another native had first hurt him by dropping a pipe on his foot and pleaded provocation. The Judge found that Palula had had provocation and sentenced him to a fine of £15 or seven months, ordering the fine to be paid at the rate of £2 per month.

I can well understand that Mr. Palula was just as surprised as any member of the public that he could kill another native and incur the amazing penalty of £15 and still have an opportunity of paying that off at £2 per month.'

—W H Rood MP *House of Assembly Debates* 21 February 1935 col 1939.

SIR ARTHUR WEIR MASON

1860–1924. Advocate and attorney in Natal 1881–96. Judge of the Natal Supreme Court 1896–1902. Judge of the Transvaal Supreme Court and Transvaal Provincial Division 1902–23. Judge President 1923–4. Knighted 1922.

'He did not spare himself in the discharge of his duties. Dr. Krause and I were engaged in a case which concerned the rejection of a large quantity (I think two thousand) of mining lamps of different sizes. They were heavy articles. The proceedings were interrupted by a public holiday. When we re-assembled it was found that his Lordship had sorted and classified the whole consignment into their different sizes. The energy expended on that work was prodigious. I don't think that any other Judge would have undertaken such a job.'

—H H Morris KC *The First Forty Years* (1948) 59. (See also CONNOR.)

HENRY JOHN MAY

1903–. Member of the Johannesburg Bar 1925–31. Attorney, Johannesburg, 1931–9. Member of the Natal Bar 1946–65. QC 1955. Journalist; author of legal and other works.

'My first case was a dock brief marked one guinea and it occupied me with consultations, preparation and court hearings for twenty-one days. An Indian was charged on numerous counts of fraud and he got off on all of them except one, and on that he was sent to jail for six months. From jail he wrote thanking me for my services and his letter ended with the words, "May Allah have mercy on your soul for the way you defended me." I hope it was a kindly interpretation he meant me to give to his words.'

—Henry John May *Red Wine of Youth* (1946) 6.

WILLIAM MENZIES

1795–1850. Judge of the Cape Supreme Court 1828–50.

'*Sir Walter Scott and Menzies J.* Dr C Graham Botha published a carefully researched biographical sketch of Mr Justice William Menzies (1795–1850) in the *Journal* in 1916 (vol 33 pp 385–404). He alluded to Menzies' knowing Sir Walter Scott. On 14 December 1813 Menzies, then a law student at the University of Edinburgh, was admitted to membership of the Speculative Society, a well-known debating society of the city. Scott was also a member. Botha continued: "William Menzies became acquainted with Sir Walter Scott in his student days, and Scott has left us an interesting note regarding their friendship." He then cited a passage from John Gibson Lockhart's famous biography of his father-in-law, the work commonly called (even by the *Encyclopaedia Britannica*) *Life of Sir Walter Scott*, though its correct title is *Memoirs of Sir Walter Scott* (first edition 1837–8; revised second edition 1839). Oddly enough, I came across this passage recently in looking at the biography, without remembering at the time that Botha had cited it. Unfortunately, Botha has it wrong. It is not Scott's note but Lockhart's note. Lockhart and Menzies were certainly friends, as Botha rightly pointed out. They were fellow members of the Faculty of Advocates, both having been admitted in 1816. In the biography Lockhart refers to a letter written by Scott in 1814, in which the novelist dwells on the time taken in the composition of the second and third volumes of his novel *Waverley*, which he published anonymously (for some whimsical reason) in July that year; Lockhart goes on to say (I cite from pages 331–2 of volume II of the biography as published in 1914 in London by Macmillan & Co) that it

"recalls to my memory a trifling anecdote, which, as connected with a dear friend of my youth, whom I have not seen for many years, and may very probably never see again in this world, I shall here set down, in the hope of affording him a momentary, though not an unmixed, pleasure, when he may chance to read this compilation on a distant shore—and also in the hope that my humble record may impart to some active mind in the rising generation a shadow of the influence which the reality certainly exerted upon his. Happening to pass through Edinburgh in June 1814, I dined one day with the gentleman in question (now the Honourable William Menzies, one of the Supreme Judges [*sic*] at the Cape of Good Hope), whose residence was then in George Street, situated very near to, and at right angles with, North Castle Street. It was a party of very young persons, most of them, like Menzies and myself, destined for the Bar of Scotland, all gay and thoughtless, enjoying the first flush of manhood, with little remembrance of the yesterday, or care of the morrow. When my companion's worthy father and uncle, after seeing two or three bottles go round, left the juveniles to themselves, the weather being hot, we adjourned to a library which had one large window looking northwards. After carousing here for an hour or more, I observed that a shade had come over the aspect of my friend, who happened to be placed immediately opposite to myself, and said something that intimated a fear of his being unwell. 'No,' said he, 'I shall be well enough presently, if you will only let me sit where you are, and take my chair; for there is a confounded hand in sight of me here, which has often bothered me before, and now it won't let me fill my glass with a good will.' I rose to change places with him accordingly, and he pointed out to me this hand which, like the writing on Belshazzar's wall, disturbed his hour of hilarity. 'Since we sat down,' he said, 'I have been watching it—it fascinates my eye—it never stops—page after page is finished and thrown on that heap of MS, and still it goes on unwearied—and so it will be till candles are brought in, and God knows how long after that. It is the same every night—I can't stand a sight of it when I am not at my books.'—'Some stupid, dogged, engrossing clerk, probably,' exclaimed myself, or some other giddy youth in our society. 'No boys,' said our host, 'I well know what hand it is—'tis Walter

Scott's.' This was the hand that, in the evenings of three summer weeks, wrote the last two volumes of *Waverley*. Would that all who that night watched it had profited by its example of diligence as largely as William Menzies!"

'Whether Lockhart and Menzies met again I cannot say.'

—Ellison Kahn in (1976) 93 *SALJ* 94–5.

'Certainly Menzies proved a very learned and a hard-working judge, though his irritability on the Bench led to numerous protests from his brethren, from legal practitioners and from editors of newspapers right up to his death in 1850. Even allowing for the robust language allowed in the mid-nineteenth century, it gives one a sense of shock to read that in May 1849 a Cape newspaper stated that

"the good folk of Grahamstown seem to be out of humour with Mr Justice Menzies' ill humour. Letters on the subject appear in the newspapers, and the *Frontier Times* takes occasion to reprove and compliment his lordship as follows: 'In a criminal case tried before the last Circuit Court, Mr Kift, of the firm of Birkenruth and Kift, of this town, was obliged, in self-defence, to address Mr Justice Menzies in the following terms: "My lord, no man is more anxious to pay all possible respect to the Court than I am; no man is more anxious to give the Court every possible satisfaction than I am; but, my lord, in my endeavours to do my duty, I submit that I am entitled to be treated by your lordship with common courtesy—and, my lord, if I am to be worried by your lordship's discourteous treatment, I shall be unable to give the Court that satisfaction which I am anxious to give." To this very proper and dignified rebuke the judge made no reply, excepting to remark that *he did not care what his anxieties were, and he could not help them.*" But he discharged no more of his ill-humour upon this witness, although he was under examination for more than four hours. We have reluctantly made these remarks, and we regret that they should have been so absolutely called for. We admire the discriminating acuteness and the great professional ability of Mr Justice Menzies. We have no reason to doubt or question his integrity and uprightness as a judge; and we are sure that it is a matter of real and sincere regret with the public, as well as with ourselves, that the able and talented first puisne judge of the Colony of the Cape of Good Hope should bring the administration of law and justice into disrepute, and his professional character into disrepute, by sullying the judicial ermine with habitual fits of unbearable ill-temper." (From Manfred Nathan "The Old Cape Bench and Bar" (1934) 3 *SA Law Times* 76.)'

—Ellison Kahn in (1976) 93 *SALJ* 95.

'There is perhaps only one reported South African case in which judges resorted to a passage at arms *inter se*. In 1849 the convict ship *Neptune* had been dispatched to the Cape by the Imperial Government to establish a penal settlement in the Colony. Leading citizens formed the Anti-convict Association, and *inter alia* sought to prevent all military and civil personnel from obtaining food and the necessaries of life. One Letterstedt disobeyed the boycott and was publicly denounced by members of the Association, against whom he then brought an action for £5,000 damages for loss of custom (*Letterstedt v Morgan* (1849) 5 Searle 373). The case was heard by Wylde C.J., Menzies J. and Musgrave J. The defendants excepted to the Court's competency inasmuch as the first two had given extra-judicial opinions favouring the Government and should therefore recuse themselves. The Court, Musgrave J. dissenting, rejected the exception in proceedings of incredible disorder (discussed in (1937) 54 *SALJ* 279 at 283ff):

'*Menzies J.*: I think the Chief Justice will agree with me that the discussion was not very irregular and such a waste of time.

'*Chief Justice*: I do not. I think it all utterly frivolous and irrelevant—

'*Menzies J.*: Because I think the Scotch authorities I have quoted show that declinatures are recognized—

'*Chief Justice*: Scotch law! The Court will adjourn.

On the following day:

'*Chief Justice*: . . . I move my brothers to hear nothing upon the subject of the recusation. The Anti-convict Association to the winds! I will hear nothing but the case before the Court. I will hear no more of knives and assassins and all the fallacious eloquence to which we were induced to listen yesterday—which could only mislead but, thank God, as far as this Court is concerned it merely enters one ear and comes out the other. Come then to business! Call the case!

'*Registrar*: The case has been called yesterday.

'*Chief Justice*: Then to business!

Shortly thereafter:

'*Chief Justice* (addressing a member of the public): Will you retire from that place, Mr. Powrie, and not be poring me with your eyes everlastingly?

'*Mr. Powrie*: There is no seat, my Lord.

'*Chief Justice*: Then, sir, you must retire from the Court. I am sorry there should be no seat for such a person!

'Wylde C.J. and Menzies J. then dismissed the exception and called on Porter, A.-G., for the plaintiff. He had hardly begun when the following exchanges took place:

'*Musgrave J.*: Do I understand you as proceeding to argument before the Court?

'*Porter, A.-G.*: Yes my Lord.

'*Musgrave J.*: Then I retire.

'*Chief Justice*: I thought you had waived all that!

'*Musgrave J.*: Oh no, no. [He then gave his reason why he felt compelled to withdraw, in the course of which he said:] Now I ask my learned brothers—

'*Chief Justice*: Don't ask us!

'*Musgrave J.*: Very well—I am sorry I addressed you.

'*Chief Justice*: You are wasting time.

'Thereafter Wylde C.J. gave his judgment, in the course of which he said: . . . The learned judge . . . has stated his views very fully.

'*Musgrave J.*: No!

'*Chief Justice*: I will not be interrupted! Do you wish to speak?

'*Musgrave J.*: I am off the Bench.

'*Chief Justice*: Do not interrupt me!

'Later Menzies J. delivered his judgment, in which the following occurred:

'*Menzies J.*: I am grieved to say that the responsibility which has been taken by the judge who has determined to retire, is a fearful responsibility. I warn him to consider well by Monday, whether he will persist in his determination—

'*Musgrave J.*: What!

'*Chief Justice*: You have no right to advise him.

'*Menzies J.*: I am not advising him.

'*Musgrave J.*: Very like it.

'*Menzies J.*: It is a fearful responsibility to say that because the Colony is in an excited state—

'*Musgrave J.*: Did I say that?

'*Menzies J.*: You may speak when I am done.

'*Musgrave J.*: But do not misrepresent me.

'*Menzies J.*: I will not look at the judge.

'On Menzies J.'s completing his judgment, Musgrave J. started speaking, whereupon—

'*Chief Justice*: Do you mean to speak sir?

'*Musgrave J.*: I mean to speak.

'*Chief Justice*: I am retiring.

'*Musgrave J.*: Do you mean to say I am not at liberty to speak?

'*Chief Justice*: I am retiring. The Court will proceed on Monday.

'But Menzies J. and Musgrave J. remained in their places and continued with the case, exchanging sundry pleasantries, accompanied by loud cheers from the spectators, until an irate Chief Justice re-entered the court and ordered them to their chambers.'

'On the Monday, the plaintiff withdrew his case; Musgrave J. became a popular hero. Of him Jones A.J.P. said in *Ex parte Kriger*, 1945 C.P.D. 252 at 254–5, that his "fame rests partly on his memorable dissent from the majority decision in *Letterstedt v Morgan*. . . . The judgments in that case are well worth perusing, as indeed all judgments should be, but specially because of its spirited protest against the attitude of his brethren, who were asked to recuse themselves in that case, which drew still more spirited and somewhat unjudicial observations from his brethren."'

—Ellison Kahn & Brian R Bamford 'Sugar and Salt: A Potpourri from Our Law Reports' (1965) 82 *SALJ* 53 at 55–7.

'The hearing commenced on Friday, 14th December, 1849, and but a brief report appeared in the press on the following day, which fortunately caused Menzies to open the case on the Saturday with "The report in the *Cape Town Mail* is utterly incorrect—it is the result of a person attempting to report what he is utterly incapable at the present of understanding." The result was that William Buchanan, the editor, who had personally taken a complete shorthand record of the proceedings, published in his paper thereafter a verbatim report of the whole case, thus preserving for all time the unseemly scenes. The following extracts from a contemporary leading article aptly describe the second day's hearing:—

"The Court was convened, the lawyers were met,
The judges all ranged, a terrible row,

when Mr. Brand [Christoffel Brand (q v) for the defendants], after a few brief explanations, quietly announced his clients' intention not 'to appear,' but to protest against the whole proceedings and appeal directly to the Queen. A bombshell falling into a powder magazine would hardly produce a greater effect. It broke upon the Bench—it broke down the case. . . . The Second Puisne Judge (Musgrave) refused to sit on the *ex parte* trial of a case which he had already been required in some degree to prejudge. This determination of a judge of unimpeachable honesty and learning—well-known moreover as a staunch upholder of the Royal prerogative and a strict legal formalist, was felt to be decisive of the contest. . . . The astonished and indignant citizens saw their Supreme Court made a theatre, in which the worst passions were openly exhibited. They saw the Hall of Justice converted into a forum, and the judges addressing harangues to the wondering public. They saw two of the three exalted functionaries overwhelming the third with covert sneers and open insults, browbeating their audience, rating their venerable Registrar like a lackey, by turns wheeling and defying the public and the Press, and making altogether a most deplorable scene, which has brought the whole judicial system of the Colony into complete discredit."'

—F St L S[earle] in (1937) 54 *SALJ* 283–4. (The lines of verse are a misquotation (possibly deliberate) of John Gay's *The Beggar's Opera* III xi air lvii: 'The charge is prepar'd; the lawyers are met;/The Judges all rang'd (a terrible show!').

Lucy Gray, a 27-year-old English woman who visited the Cape for two years from 1849 to 1851, conveyed in the journal she wrote that, as Alan F Hattersley *A Victorian Lady at the Cape 1849–51* (1951) 27 put it, 'most of the men of the law were notable bottle men, even in a community where it was said, the two principal diseases were billiards and brandy'. Again: 'All the judges, perhaps because official salaries were exiguous, lived beyond their means.' Lucy Gray wrote that of the judges and officials in the administration of the law, Mr Justice Musgrave was 'almost the only one who bears a good character'.)

LOUIS OSCAR MILLER

c 1896–1966. Member of the Johannesburg Bar 1922 until his death. A point-taker. A character.

He played the game according to the Rules—of Court

'He spoke with a staccato delivery in a deep, harsh voice in a unique mixture of a Yiddish accent, a Bronx accent and the broad South African accent that the books on English usage take such delight in describing (such as flat vowels, sharp and explosive consonants, and a rolling *r*). When I was a member of the Johannesburg Bar from 1945 to 1948 he was already one of the unforgettable characters: short, sallow, sturdy, with black hair beginning to recede, plastered down, assuredly not one of the (few) handsome advocates. His inside jacket sported the biggest array of pens and pencils ever known. On entering his chambers one had difficulty in seeing him at his desk, for piled in front of him was a high mound composed of a mixture of books and briefs. He never married, but of his private life there were many stories, for—to use a euphemism—"he loved the ladies"; but I call to mind what I heard John Murray J say to L O in the course of a trial, "Mr Miller, the less said about your client, the better". Indeed, that could be said of many of L O's clients, for his enormous junior practice (he did not take silk) was largely in the motion court and was concerned not with upmarket stuff but with provisional sentences, bills of exchange, insolvency, company matters and the like, often involving persons of standing far removed from that of a director of a mining house.

'L O was a tough opponent in court. Counsel on the other side whose papers were not in order had to be pitied, for L O never admitted anything and was a point-taker par excellence (he was reputed to have a standard remark to an instructing attorney, "Show me de bills and I'll show you de points"). He knew the Rules of Court intimately, he was an expert on bills of exchange, and he was a learned man in his way, not only in law. In the motion court L O sat in the front row on the end seat on the right-hand side to enable his instructing attorney to run in and out of court to fetch papers, for L O needed them constantly. Woe betide the junior who unwittingly sat in L O's seat.

'For all his lack of polish, L O had certain admirable qualities, notably kindness (which extended to the giving of financial assistance) and unselfishness.'

—Ellison Kahn's commonplace book, embellished with information gathered from much appreciated conversations with or letters from the Hon G A Coetzee, Mr (now Mr Justice) W P Schutz SC, Mr Basil Wunsh, Professor David Zeffertt and Mr (now Mr Justice) Ralph Zulman SC.

'In about 1960 I was in Miller's chambers as an articled clerk. We were going through a summons with a view to his drafting a plea. One of the early paragraphs in the summons contained some innocuous allegation and I made the remark that this would obviously be admitted. He sighed, put his pen down, and in that peculiar accent which you summed up so well, said "Niland, when the Judge walks into Court, looks at me and says 'Mr Miller do you appear for the defendant?' I get up and ask for an adjournment so that I can consider whether it is in my client's interest to make that admission." That remark has had an influence on my conduct of litigation ever since!'

—From a letter of 7 July 1989 by Mr Chris Niland to Ellison Kahn.

L O as a point-taker

L O used to say that he had two lists containing the names of his colleagues at the Bar: the one with the names of those to whom he would give advance notice of the points he was going to take, and the other with the names of those to whom he would not give notice. Sometimes the notice was only of five minutes' duration.

He also had two types of point (which he pronounced punt*), which have become part of the legends of the Johannesburg Bar, though ever fewer members know the source of their origin. The one type of point, which L O mentioned first, was of a preliminary nature; the other type went to the merits. Some judges did not appreciate—or pretended not to appreciate—the difference between the types, which will explain the opening story in the following communication by Mr (now Mr Justice) W P Schutz SC.*

'Vieyra J once told me that the legend had been re-enacted before him.

'*Miller*: Milord, I have five points and then anudder point.

'*Vieyra*: You mean you have six points, Mr Miller.

'*Miller*: No, Milord. I have five points and then anudder point.

'As to the points: The late Ernie Wentzel once told me that he had bought L O's TPD's and WLD's. They were heavily flagged. All the flags related to points taken either by or against Miller. One of his choicer points was taken in a provisional sentence action before an inexperienced acting judge from Pretoria. It related to the "true copy" of the promissory note annexed to the copy of the summons. On the original, Miller said, one could lift up the revenue stamp and see whether there was any writing under it. On the photostatic copy you could not do that. This proposition puzzled the acting judge greatly. Another of his points was taken a few weeks after South Africa had become a Republic. The summons on which default judgment had been granted was no good, he said. The printed form was issued in the name of Her Majesty the Queen. L O did not lack imagination.'

(Cf s 116 of the Republic of South Africa Constitution Act 32 of 1961, *S v Dwalath* 1963 (3) SA 763 (N), *S v Willie Breedt (Pty) Ltd* 1964 (2) SA 672 (T) and *S v Chan* 1964 (3) SA 624 (T).)

The redoubtable Mr Justice Greenberg meets his match

'The following tale was related by Mr Justice Greenberg himself.

'A tenacious Johannesburg advocate who passed away a couple of years ago, Mr L. O. Miller, had been engaged in arguing an involved civil appeal matter before his lordship at Pretoria. The argument went on for a whole day, and finally Mr Miller said:

'"I submit, my lord, that for these reasons the appeal should be allowed."

'Immediately came the sarcastic retort from the Bench: "For what reasons?"

'"Well, my lord," said Mr Miller, "it appears to me that your lordship has not been listening to what I have said, or that my argument has not been fully comprehended."

'Mr Miller then started to present his argument afresh, beginning with the remark that "the case I was endeavouring to put before your lordship is this".

'And the Judge sat unmoved, but seemingly disillusioned. Mr Miller actually spent another whole day arguing what he had already argued before.

'Mr Justice Greenberg is known to have commented afterwards that "it does not always pay for a Judge to be sarcastic to counsel".'

—Isaac Goodman *Judges I Have Known* (1969) 58. (See also GREENBERG.)

'Flattery, my lord, vill get you no-vair': the classic reply

'. . . Mr Miller once figured in an exchange of words with Mr Justice Bekker who, on that occasion, came off second best—just as did Mr Justice Greenberg.

'In the case in question, counsel had been appearing as junior to Mr N. E. Rosenberg, K.C., who was one of the most eminent of barristers in his time, in a complicated provisional sentence matter. At the conclusion of his argument, it was left to Mr Miller, in the absence of his senior, to argue an application for costs for two counsel in the case. Mr Miller, with unexpected modesty, intimated that he had no desire to argue on the application for costs in the absence of his senior, and applied for a postponement to enable his senior to attend court.

'"Why do you want a senior?" Mr Justice Bekker asked him. "A junior of your experience can surely argue on this application in the absence of your senior."

'"Flattery, my lord, will get you nowhere," replied Mr Miller.

'The matter was postponed to enable Mr Rosenberg to argue on costs.'

—Goodman op cit at 58–9. (The Hon G A Coetzee told me that on this famous occasion he was present in court, being then a member of the Johannesburg Bar, and that the presiding judge was Ludorf J. The reply of L O is better rendered as: 'Flattery, my lord, vill get you no-vair.')

The disappointed junior

This incident took place in the days when it was de rigueur for a junior to get two-thirds of the fee of his leader.

'Archie Shacksnovis KC [qv] got infuriated with his instructing attorney and, in the presence of his junior, L O Miller, told the attorney that he could now brief someone else. The attorney said, "What about your fee?" Shacksnovis: "I don't want a fee. Just remove yourself." Exit attorney. Miller to Shacksnovis: "Tell me, vat ish two-toids of nutting?"'

—Ellison Kahn's commonplace book, with thanks to Mr Basil Wunsh.

The disappointed would-be borrower

'A colleague saw the mound of books piled in front of L O's desk in his chambers, so high that L O's head was barely visible.

'Colleague: Louis why don't you get a bookcase?

'L O: It'sh difficult enough to boghroh [borrow] books. Who vill lend me a bookcase?'

—Ellison Kahn's commonplace book, with thanks to Mr (now Mr Justice) Ralph Zulman SC.

Some further Milleriana

'L O was briefed to appear for X, a financier who had had some unfortunate experiences with the criminal law. X was a very religious person. L O told the instructing attorney that he did not like the look of the case, and it was arranged that the attorney and X would see L O in his chambers. They arrived, and immediately X went to one of the walls and prayed long and earnestly. Then he sat down and uttered these words:

'"I have spoken to the Lord and he has said to me 'You cannot lose the case'."

'Miller, without a moment's pause: "Has He ghread [read] de affidavits?"'

—Ellison Kahn's commonplace book. The story was told to me by the late Hon G A Coetzee.

Coup de grâce

'In the late 1950s L O was appearing for an accused before Mr Wilson, a notoriously exacting magistrate. Wilson took a strong dislike to the demeanour of the accused. L O kept on making excuses, trying to damp the fire, but gradually became more and more exasperated. Then his client began picking his nose.

'Wilson: "Mr Miller, I have to speak to you about your client. He is picking his nose."

'Miller, responding immediately in his machine-gun-like voice: "Your vership, my client ish not picking *your* no-sh, he is not picking *my* no-sh, he is picking *his* no-sh."

'Wilson sat back in his chair, for once silent.'

—Ellison Kahn's commonplace book. The story was told to me by the late Hon G A Coetzee. (On Wilson, see also S MILLER.)

SOLOMON MILLER

1916–87. Member of the Orange Free State Bar 1938–62. KC 1950. Judge of the Natal Provincial Division 1962–76. Judge of Appeal 1976–85.

'In your portrait of L. O. Miller, you refer to his passage with the notorious Mr Wilson, magistrate. It reminded me of another story which I heard of the latter (it was told at the time of his appointment as Chief Magistrate of Durban, when he was causing havoc generally and in particular in his capacity as Chairman of the Liquor Licensing Board). The story also concerns the other Miller, the late Solly Miller, who in many respects was the complete antithesis of L. O. Miller. Softly spoken, cultured, humble and courteous, Solly Miller was one "import" to the Natal bench who was unhesitatingly welcomed and sadly missed when appointed to the Appellate Division.

'It seems that when still a junior counsel practising in Bloemfontein, Solly had been instructed in a magistrate's court matter in some place removed from Bloemfontein (the exact location of which I cannot now remember). Wilson was the presiding magistrate, and at the end of the day the case had, unexpectedly, not concluded. It could have been completed within not more than half an hour if the court had been prepared to carry on. Solly explained to Wilson that he was due to appear in an appeal before the Appellate Division the next morning and requested Wilson to carry on with the case until its conclusion that day or, alternatively, to adjourn it to a day convenient to him. Wilson refused and ordered that the matter should proceed upon the following morning.

'Solly Miller returned to Bloemfontein, made a number of urgent telephone calls that night and, having chartered an aircraft, appeared before Wilson as required. When Wilson remarked, sarcastically, that he was pleased to note that counsel had been able, after all, to be present, Solly explained that the appeal judges had agreed to allow the appeal to stand over until he returned, adding "But then you see, your worship, *they* are gentlemen". . . .

'May I conclude with another short reminiscence concerning Solly Miller. I apologise for its being a personal one, but it always epitomized for me his wonderously quiet humour.

'I was arguing an application before him and, for some contention, relied for my authority upon the case of *Estate Watkins-Pitchford & others v Commissioner for Inland Revenue* 1955 (2) SA 437 (A). After I had quoted the case he leaned forward, and, smiling innocently, asked: "What is the *ratio decidendi* in that case?"'

—From a letter of 19 September 1989 by Mr David Pistorius to Ellison Kahn. (In *Watkins-Pitchford* the court a quo held against the applicant on ground A. By a majority of three to two the Appellate Division dismissed the appeal. Of the three, two found on ground B and one on ground C. The two dissenting judges of appeal would have found for the appellant on ground D. What of a binding character emerges from these divergent judgments? That is the question posed in 1955 *Annual Survey of South African Law* 327.)

PHILIP MILLIN

1888–1952. Member of the Johannesburg Bar 1913–37. KC 1927. Judge of the Transvaal Provincial Division 1937–52. Co-author of *Wille and Millin's Mercantile Law of South Africa*.

Millin was married to the celebrated novelist, biographer and social historian, Sarah Gertrude Millin, a formidable woman with an abrasive personality.

'While Philip was softly spoken, calm, and reserved with the impeccable manners of the English gentleman on whom he modelled himself, Sarah Gertrude was vivid, loudly spoken, and impatient, with little regard for good behaviour. She liked to apply the word "aristocratic" to her husband and took particular pride because he had that quality despite a family background that was quite the reverse. While Philip had enormous admiration for his wife's intellect and ability, he was in a perpetual state of irritation at her unpleasant behaviour. He was forever remonstrating with her over her wilder statements and rudeness. . . .

'The few remaining extracts from the correspondence between the Millins show a remarkably warm affection, expressed explicitly and without reticence even in their middle years. Guests in their home were sometimes more than a little shocked to find Philip and Sarah Gertrude holding hands or sitting on one another's knees, a habit they were to continue until the end of Philip's life. People observing Philip's short-tempered admonitions to his wife were often prone to speak of the Millins' being "on bad terms". In fact, nothing could have been less true. What makes the relationship so remarkable is that its tensions did not disturb the essential closeness and happiness of the union.'

—Martin Rubin *Sarah Gertrude Millin: A South African Life* (1977) 46–7.

'Sarah Gertrude evidently felt as much satisfaction in the [bank] manager's recognition of her as an author as she did in making the profit [from a foreign exchange transaction permitted by the manager, arising out of South Africa's remaining on the gold standard]. This was the kind of incident which gave her enormous pleasure. She liked to be recognized as a celebrity and to be accorded privileged treatment. This trait of hers infuriated Philip, who disliked her habit of seeking what he termed cheap publicity, and who was scrupulously honest to the point of walking kilometres to discover the official rate of exchange in Italy rather than accept the inflated one offered by a shop.'

—Rubin op cit at 150–1.

' . . . In the six years since he had become a K.C., Philip's practice had grown immensely. He was now one of the leading barristers in the city [Johannesburg]. . . . His earnings were considerable during these years, far more than Sarah Gertrude's at any time in her career, and this, as much as the professional reputation he had acquired, contributed to his wife's feeling of satisfaction with his position. She was no longer worried that she had burdened Philip by being the more famous member of the family. Always sensitive to her husband's feelings, she was relieved that he need not fear being called "Mr Sarah Gertrude Millin", a prospect they both dreaded. The example of Olive Schreiner, whose husband had added his wife's name to his own and then been soured almost to the point of hatred by his subordinate position, loomed very large in the Millins' mind.'

—Rubin op cit at 157–8. (It is a fairly common fate — and why not? For instance, the undistinguished husband of the famous contralto Kathleen Ferrier, one Bert Wilson, resented being called Mr Kathleen Ferrier. See Hugh Canning in *The Listener* 28 April 1988 p 31.)

His appointment to the Bench

'Philip Millin (1888–1952) was scarcely more than two years older than Schreiner, but he had been in practice over seven years longer; for he had not joined the armed forces during the Great War, perhaps because his wife Sarah was then a pacifist and also felt that two men in the army from each family was enough. He was one of the men of whom Schreiner asked whether he was right in his intention to set up practice in Johannesburg; and he had said yes. Millin had taken silk in 1927, and had appeared in many important trials; his reputation as an advocate stood very high. Years later, on hearing of his death, Schreiner confided to his diary that "Philip was a very dear friend to me. There never was a more generous helper to the young advocate than he was to me and others."

'In February 1937 the Millins received a shock. John Murray (1888–1976) [qv] who had gone to the Bar in 1913 and taken silk in 1931, they learned was to become a judge on the 15th, and Oliver to be an acting judge from that day. Sarah Millin wrote to Oliver Schreiner on 31 January 1953, telling him that she proposed to deal with the matter in the autobiographical work she was writing and to let him know that she would express her gratitude for the attitude he took at the time. The book was published in 1955 as *The Measure of My Days*. In it Sarah Millin said that her husband had thus been passed over five times since 1929, when he ought to have had the offer of an acting judgeship. She had got her facts muddled, if by being passed over she meant that before 1937 those who had received their patents as silks in the Transvaal after Philip had been given preference over him. But now it had indeed happened. Piecing together the account in her letter and the subsequent autobiographical work (*The Measure of My Days* 162–9), according to Sarah Millin Oliver Schreiner came to the Millins' house one evening to tell Philip about the offers to Murray and himself. He knew that Philip desperately wanted an appointment, even though it meant his income would drop to one-third of what it had been. For years he had found Wessels CJ [qv] intolerable to appear before, regarding him as a bully; Wessels' behaviour in the appeal in the famous *Doornhoek* bribery prosecution (*R v Alexander & others* 1936 AD 445, where Millin had appeared for the Crown) had been such that Millin, who had a large practice before the Appellate Division, vowed that he would never appear before him again; and though Wessels had died in September of the previous year, the wound still hurt. Years before, Maritz, according to Sarah Millin, had told Philip that it was his negrophilism that was the cause of his claims being overlooked; but Philip believed it was because he was a Jew. Philip Millin had vehemently opposed his wife's writing the biography of Smuts, but she could not resist the great opportunity, though she promised not to let Philip see a word of it, so that there could be no embarrassment with Smuts. The all too flattering biography appeared in 1936. She now felt she had been a fool and let her husband down. "Negrophilism had nothing to do with it this time, for, if there was a passionate negrophilist, it was Oliver", she wrote in her autobiography in rather exaggerated terms (*The Measure of My Days* 162). Sarah Millin immediately concluded that the real reasons were anti-Semitism in the country, associated partly with the immigration of German Jewish refugees, which had led to the passing of the Aliens Act 1937 (aimed at restricting the entry of Jewish immigrants), and the fear of Smuts, the Minister of Justice, which Philip had expected, that he would be suspected of doing a favour to his biographer in return for her kind work. Oliver Schreiner told Philip Millin that evening that he could not accept a seat on the judiciary because it was Millin's due; but Millin would not hear of it, saying that Smuts would not appoint a Jew, and if Oliver refused the offer it would go to someone whom he would not be so glad to see on the Bench. Oliver, convinced, went home. The Millins did not approach Smuts, which Schreiner agreed was correct: "But I still expect to see Philip on the A.D. Bench, if I live so long", he told them. (This did not happen, which Schreiner regretted; on hearing of Millin's death he wrote in his diary that the Transvaal Bench on which he "worked so well and unselfishly . . . gave insufficient scope for his outstanding reasoning power, and strong sense of justice".) Later Smuts wrote to Millin confirming what he and his wife had believed were the reasons, and saying the promotion would come in happier times. Jan Hofmeyr, then in the Cabinet, sent a letter to Sarah Millin, saying that he knew nothing of judicial appointments until they had been made, and that he was most distressed at Smuts's weakness (see *The Measure of My Days* 166 and Alan Paton *Hofmeyr* (1964) 262). Smuts, who had received a diplomatic response from Philip and a devastating one from Sarah, then decided that the next vacancy would be filled by Millin; so he ascended the Bench on 4 September that year, barely a month after Schreiner's permanent appointment had come through.

'When Sarah Millin discussed her proposed autobiography with Schreiner in 1953, he asked her what Philip would have thought had she made him out to be a place-hunter. She replied that she would "try not to dishonour Phil", and in this she succeeded in large measure.'

—Ellison Kahn 'Oliver Deneys Schreiner: A South African' in *Fiat Iustitia: Essays in Memory of Oliver Deneys Schreiner* (1983) 1 at 25–7, some footnotes incorporated in the text, the rest omitted.

'I was delighted to get your wire reporting Philip's appointment. Really, Smuts has behaved excellently and the Bench will benefit greatly. I sent Philip a wire and got a fine reply inside 3/4 hour. Blakeway will be disappointed but I have no doubt that Philip's is the right appointment. It makes me feel much better myself that he has not had to wait very long.'

—Oliver Deneys Schreiner in a letter to his wife Edna, written on circuit from the railway coach housing judges on circuit, at Piet Retief, on 1 September 1937. Schreiner family papers. (Cyril Tennant Blakeway, member of the Johannesburg Bar, who took silk on 30 April 1935, four months after Schreiner and eight years after Millin, was appointed a judge in Southern Rhodesia in 1938.)

'There is a little joke which barristers tell of her [Sarah Gertrude Millin] and her husband after he was raised to the Bench to add distinction to an already distinguished judiciary: "Mrs. Millin's books are realistic because her husband writes them, and his judgments are lucid because she writes them." Both allegations, as lawyers would say, are wrong, for I have had experience of the quality of his opinions when he was Mr. Millin, K.C., and I have heard her give an extempore lecture on literature.'

—Henry John May (qv) *Red Wine of Youth* (1946) 12–13. (See also H H (HARRY) MORRIS; WESSELS; WILLE.)

"Mr F Zwarenstein, Q.C., noted among his colleagues at the Bar for his fine sense of humour and his great fund of jokes, rose to indicate to his lordship his objection to certain evidence being recorded on the grounds that it was, in his respectful opinion, quite inadmissible.

'Mr Justice Millin pointed out that he had already heard the evidence, and asked counsel what he was expected to do in the circumstances.

'"Do you expect me to divorce my mind from it?" he asked counsel.

'"Well, my lord," replied Mr Zwarenstein, "I am not asking your lordship for a divorce, but only for a judicial separation."'

—Isaac Goodman *Judges I Have Known* (1969) 136.

ALEXANDER MILNE

1899–1986. Member of the Natal Bar 1924–54. KC 1946. Judge of the Natal Provincial Division 1954–62. Judge President 1962–9. Judge of Appeal of the Courts of Appeal of Botswana, Lesotho and Swaziland 1969–79.

'Mr Justice Alexander Milne was the son of a seafaring Captain and was born at Aberdeen, Scotland, in 1899. His parents came to South Africa in 1907, and he went to school at Bethlehem. In the First World War he served in the East African campaign in Signals. He was under age but told the recruiting officer he would be nineteen years old on "27 November", omitting to add that it would be in a year three years later. . . .

' . . . He took endless trouble to get to the bottom of everything that came before him with the result that, in litigious matters, it was widely held by counsel that everyone left his court satisfied that justice had been done. He drove inventively and fast. From a standing start at a robot [traffic light] in Pietermaritzburg a left-hand turn from the right-turning lane, across two lanes of traffic, presented no problem. The writer was the admiring motorist on his left.'

—M D Southwood SC 'Fathers and their children on the Bench' *Consultus* vol 1(2) (October 1988) 21 at 23.

ERIC MORRIS

1916–89. Member of the Johannesburg Bar 1939–89. SC 1965. Son of H H (Harry) Morris (q v).

'VALEDICTION
BY A FRIEND

'Eric was an intensely private man, so few people knew the whole of him. His reserve hid an astonishing range of interests. Unusually distinguished in appearance, he was immaculate in his dress. He was a devoted family man, and in June would have been married for 49 years. He took great pleasure in the small things of life, which is the secret of happiness. His first job every morning was to feed the birds. He delighted in his pets. He loved flowers, and spent many hours in the garden. He was an outstanding amateur photographer. He played a formidable hand of bridge. He was an expert crossword puzzle solver. He was a regular theatre-goer. He enjoyed, and owned, beautiful paintings. He was knowledgeable about motor cars. He was handy about the house. He had read widely, and was at home with Shakespeare and the English poets. He could startle with the apt quotation. He had a mordant sense of humour. He was a champion swimmer, who in his day established and held the intervarsity 100-yard record, being awarded a full blue. He also concerned himself with others. It was he who ensured that the employees of the Johannesburg Bar were placed on a pension scheme. He worried about the garage attendant at Innes Chambers, who did not enjoy sufficient free time, and took steps to rectify what he considered an injustice. Above all, he was supremely a lawyer and a writer.

'Being Harry Morris's son, he had to be compared with Harry Morris. He adored his father, and had a fund of anecdotes about him. Harry Morris's cross-examinations were legendary, but Eric's were not inferior. His field was civil rather than criminal law. He had that insight into the character of a witness, that intuitive sixth sense about people, which is the hallmark of the great cross-examiner. But his success did not depend upon chance or flair. He worked. Attorneys did not wait for their opinions. He was methodical and tireless in preparation. To every case he gave every ounce. The judges of the Appellate Division said of his presentation of the *McAlpine* case that no matter had ever come before them so well prepared. He was known to have the hardest practice at the Bar. Attorneys brought him all the losing cases other counsel did not want to undertake. He took them and fought them. He never forgot a case or a point. He kept all his notes. Junior counsel once asked his advice on a point and was told "I argued that in the magistrate's court forty years ago". He went to his cabinet, extracted the argument he had presented forty years previously, and handed it to counsel, who was as flabbergasted as he was grateful. He was generous with his time, knowledge and experience. Hence his book.

'*Technique in Litigation* was written when Eric had just taken silk, and senior work was slow in coming. He wrote it in longhand, virtually in one stretch, so that the fingers holding the pen were rubbed raw. He wrapped sticking plaster around them and went on writing. That book is to be found in the libraries of the entire English-speaking world. It has been read (and favourably reviewed) in Hong Kong, Australia, Jamaica, Canada and the United Kingdom. He wanted it to be a guide to the perplexed young lawyer, degreed but inexperienced. It is that, but not only that. Every practitioner can and does find assistance in its pages. It is also very funny. Lawyers read it not only for information but also for pleasure. Of what other law book can that be said?

'Late in his career—too late—after almost fifty years of practice, he was translated to the Bench, in an acting capacity. Not every great advocate makes a great judge. Eric did. He brought to his task not only his experience, industry, knowledge and wisdom, but also a patience and a courtesy in addressing counsel which the Bar greatly appreciated. He loved his work, for all its attendant anxieties and responsibilities, and was grateful for the opportunity. He had hoped to continue in the office for some years. It was not to be.

'During the war Eric contracted hepatitis and was discharged from the army on that account. In the course of his recent and short illness, his liver failed. For the fortnight before his death he waged his last, his greatest and his most magnificent fight. Had he not suffered every complication, foreseeable and unforeseeable, probable and improbable, his will would have pulled him through. I have no doubt he went into death's dateless night unafraid.'

—(1989) 106 *SALJ* 534–6.

HENRY HARRIS (HARRY) MORRIS

1878–1954. Member of the Johannesburg Bar 1906–47. KC 1924. Noted defender of accused. Wit. Author of memoirs.

Roots

'William [van Reenen] married Dorothea Heibner in 1779. They had six children, one of whom was Daniel. Daniel married Johanna Elizabeth Grundlingh. They had four children, one of whom was Maria Louisa van Reenen. She married Doctor Philip Heinrich Kramer, a Cadet of the house of Hesse-Cassel. One of their daughters was my mother—Maria Kramer. On the

14th April, 1878, the entire van Reenen and Kramer family turned in their graves when they heard that one of their descendants had given birth to a child whose father was neither a van nor a von, nor even an Aryan. After this disclosure there will probably never again be a social gathering of the van Reenen clan, particularly as another female member has also transgressed. You never know who may turn up.

'My father, Hyman Morris, had been a teacher in the Jews' Free School, London. He migrated to the Cape and settled at Beaufort West, where he had to make two ends meet by being a bank manager during, and a reporter after, business hours. He arrived in Johannesburg in 1887. The services he rendered to the community and particularly the Jewish community were outstanding. . . .

'In the early days he was a member of the Johannesburg Sanitary Board.

'There is something to be said for a career which is not entirely concerned with Self.

'This apple fell far from the tree.'

—H H Morris KC *The First Forty Years* (1948) 16–17.

Appreciations and recollections

'I think . . . of his gaiety and his wit, his never-failing good humour. Those, however, were part of a very powerful personality. . . .

'But I think chiefly of his courage. An advocate who is engaged in great criminal trials requires much courage. . . . In such cases public feeling is often aroused and there is a pressure of public opinion of which defending counsel is very conscious and which he must have the strength to resist. As he stands between the accused and his accusers he is oppressed by a sense of isolation and loneliness. In such cases Morris's courage never failed. I have seen him during an adjournment, resting in his chambers, weary and dispirited; I have seen him return to court gay and debonair, his vigour unimpaired, showing to none the strain of the burden that rested on his shoulders. The strain was there, but so was the courage to bear it.

'I shall, I trust, be pardoned if I use the words that were spoken of him at his graveside and that so well describe him: "He was a gallant defender of men." No finer epitaph could be written.'

—Mr Justice Ramsbottom in a tribute to the memory of Morris in the Witwatersrand Local Division on 12 October 1954: see (1955) 72 *SALJ* 4–5.

'Like Falstaff, he was not only witty in himself, "but the cause that wit is in other men". The "other men" were mostly judges who used their dry wit on him.'

—*Rand Daily Mail* 7 October 1954. (The passage is in Shakespeare *2 Henry IV* I ii.)

'Harry Morris in his argument in Walker v. de Leeuw dragged in a yarn about an Englishman & a Scot who were standing at the roadside when a flock of sheep passed down the road. "That farmer has begun early," said the Englishman, "those sheep have been sheared already." "Yes," replied the cautious Scot, "on this side."'

—Oliver Deneys Schreiner in a letter to his wife Edna, 17 May 1922. Schreiner family papers.

'I have addressed over sixty judges and magistrates without number. I would like to say in passing that I have never met a discourteous magistrate. I have been

opposed by sixteen Attorneys-General and Crown Prosecutors and a great many
of their satellites. Of the scores of Public Prosecutors I have met, a very small
percentage was inclined to be suspicious and aloof. I can recall only one who was
discourteous.

'Something like twenty thousand witnesses have passed before me. Most of
them were fools. I have defended clients for every common law offence, except
treason. This is a crime usually committed by gentlemen, and gentlemen do not
come my way. I have defended professional men of every class, except architects.
These people appear to lack opportunity. Amongst the professional men for
whom I have appeared, doctors are an easy first—attorneys run second. I have
defended more doctors than all the other professional classes put together.

'Like an heirloom, I have been on a number of occasions handed down from
father to son. Once the reverse occurred. I had defended the son and twenty years
later the father, aged 82, arrived. He too was acquitted.'

—H H Morris KC *The First Forty Years* (1948) 43.

Telling the jury where it got off

'Here is a boast. I am the only man in the country who has ever told a jury,
after an adverse verdict, where it got off. My client, a storekeeper, was charged
under the Insolvency Law with contracting debts without any reasonable
expectation of being able to discharge them. He was found guilty. With that I had
no quarrel. The jury, steeped in commerce to a man, added to their verdict a
strong recommendation that the accused be severely dealt with "in the interests
of commercial morality". Before His Lordship could say anything I got up and
spoke to that jury. I told them about something of which they did not appear to
have heard, namely, the quality of mercy. I also reminded them of something
which they knew all about, namely, the foisting of unneeded stock on an
unwilling trader who feared that his credit would be stopped if he refused to buy.
Throughout these proceedings His Lordship remained silent. I think he agreed
with me. Instead of getting two years my client was sentenced to one month's
imprisonment, which was suspended.

'Some of my verdicts have been the subject of indignant letters to the Press.
Some of my sentences have been shockingly inadequate.

'Here is another boast. I have never been briefed by the Government Attorney,
which shows that the Government Attorney is also a good judge.

'So far as I can remember I did twenty-three murders. Two proved fatal. I
assisted in four others; one died.'

—Morris op cit at 45.

Harry Morris and Beauclerk Upington

'He had prepared his case [the defence of Sir Delves Broughton on a charge of
murdering the Earl of Erroll—see below] as usual with the infinite care and
foresight of a general planning an attack. A special airplane had flown him to
Nairobi, 2,000 miles from his home in Johannesburg, to appear in one of the most
remarkable murder trials of modern times.

'Once again he was in his renowned role of the great defender. Perhaps he was
the most famous in South African legal history. His contemporary, Beauclerk
Upington [q v], was another. But his star was beginning to wane while Morris's
was in the ascendancy.

'Both were South Africa's foremost advocates of their generation but there were as many dissimilarities as similarities in their character.

'Both practised for a lifetime over much the same period; each had a flair for handling witnesses of any temperament, instinctively detecting a liar and steering a case from near defeat to victory.

'Both were orators in their own field. But while Upington was unhurried, precise and sometimes lyrical in his silver-tongued eloquence, Morris was fluent and earthy, his voice high-pitched, often raspingly penetrating. (Sir William Solomon, Chief Justice of the Union, once called him "that man with the awful voice.")

'Each had the almost uncanny power of bending juries to his will.

'They were alike in another respect. They commanded large fees but regarded money only as a medium of exchange for more worthwhile things. Their generosity was boundless, their extravagance often foolish.

'The dissimilarities were more marked.

'Upington was an eccentric and alcoholic. In his later years he became unreliable, unpunctual, slothful, obnoxious.

'Morris, on the other hand, was abstemious, always dependable and fanatically punctual. He was an unremitting worker on behalf of his clients. Towards the end, when his practice dwindled to nothing, he became cantankerous and intolerant and, to some attorneys, intolerable.

'Behind Upington was an imposing and distinguished array of Irish forebears. His father was a famous barrister and Prime Minister of the Cape Colony and he inherited the parental talents and the name that went with them.

'Morris had no such personal advantages or influence. His father was a humble bank manager and tireless communal worker who did more for others than for himself. The son was a corporal in the South African War, an obscure attorney's clerk, then an unknown advocate matched against some of the most brilliant men to practise at the Johannesburg Bar.

'Morris and Upington were the greatest cross-examiners the South African courts have known. There are those who claim Upington was unrivalled in this art; others say the less suave Morris was as skilful but depended on perspiration more than inspiration, on bubbling good humour rather than on pungent wit and sarcasm.

'Morris loved applause and exulted in his great reputation, making up in exuberance and enthusiasm what he might have lacked in depth. He was quick to respond to calls from attorneys and clients throughout the country and appeared in more courts and before more judges and magistrates than any other advocate of his day.

'Upington was urbane, aloof and publicity shy and could rarely be tempted to leave the Cape though fame also awaited him elsewhere.

'In one respect Morris and Upington were very much alike. They were fearless and tireless in a fight for a client irrespective of his social position or financial standing. It did not matter if they had to retreat all along the line. They could, and often did, win the last battle with the jury.

'When they took the stage they dominated it. Their courts filled like a theatre on opening night. They died in the wings, ill and broken, away from the applause of their public.'

—Benjamin Bennett *Genius for the Defence: Life of Harry Morris, K.C.* (1959) 9–10.

'Then I shall sit down'

'[C G] Wiggett [KC, former Attorney-General of Natal] tells an amusing story of Morris's readiness, even anxiety, to avoid legal argument. He was appearing in a civil case before three judges in Pretoria. Presiding was a formidable and outspoken judge.

'"Civil law," Wiggett recalled, "was not Harry's strongest suit as he was the first to admit. Nor was a Bench of three judges the sort of forum in which he felt most at home."

'Morris stood up and began, but he had barely started on his first point when the presiding judge said: "There is no substance in that point, Mr. Morris."

'"Very well," Harry said cheerfully. "Then I shall proceed to my second point."

'"There is nothing in that point either," the judge said after a short while.

'"Very well," Harry said brightly. "Then I shall go on to my third point."

'But he fared no better this time. The presiding judge said: "Mr. Morris, that point takes the matter no further."

'"Very well, m'lords," Harry said with undiminished brightness. "Then I shall sit down." And he did.'

— Bennett op cit at 81–2.

'Ode to Archie'

'Morris's sense of fun sometimes expressed itself in rhyme and doggerel. When he sat in court awaiting the start of some minor matter or his junior was arguing a dull point of law, he would idly pen a word sketch of the judge or one of his colleagues.

'*Ode to Archie* was dedicated to Arthur ("Archie") Shacksnovis [q v], Morris's junior in the Bitterfontein case and brilliant colleague at the Johannesburg Bar in after years. He was short, thick-set, with enormous shoulders, an Oxford rugby Blue, writer, connoisseur and collector of old silver, gourmet and part-time broadcaster.

'Once he startled public and Bar alike by alleging legal men were too often too long-winded. Some lawyers saw this as a covert threat to their livelihood, some litigants as a welcome possibility of a reduction in legal costs.

'It was all very well for "Archie," Morris grumbled, "to abbreviate his daily court orations; he could supplement his income by broadcasting at so-much a minute." But what about others, like himself, who did not broadcast and had only the restricted courtroom air to exercise their vocal chords and talents?

'So he wrote:

Archie dear I understand
All the judges in the land
Held a meeting and agree
With what you told the 'Varsity
All addresses to the court
Should be, like you, sweet and short.
Greenberg J. and likewise P.
Have now sent out a new decree
Which bans and bars prolixity
And also stops verbosity. . .

'He went on dolefully:

And now Othello's occupation's gone
What have I to live upon?
You can broadcast and review
What is there for me to do?
It's not enough to talk by day
You needs must leave the beaten way
To spout by night
And land us in this awful plight.
Let all of us a lesson take
Do not talk for talking's sake.
I am annoyed and I condemn
But still I am, Yours H.H.M.'

—Bennett op cit at 184–5. (On the long-windedness of Shacksnovis, see MALAN.)

One of Harry Morris's greatest triumphs was his successful defence in Nairobi of Etonian Sir Delves Broughton, who was charged with the murder of a fellow Etonian, the Earl of Erroll, who had cuckolded him. The hearing of the trial ran for 27 days, from 26 May to 4 July 1941. Morris dealt with it in chapter XXVI ('Delves') in his memoirs The First Forty Years *(1948). The trial and its background were the subject of a fascinating book by James Fox,* White Mischief *(1982), on which the film by that name was based. The film, which met with a mixed reception, deviates from fact not only by (a necessary) simplification but also in several important happenings, particularly in making Broughton commit suicide immediately after his acquittal, and not seventeen months later. The portrayal by the Irish actor Ray McAnally of Harry Morris in court was an interesting cameo, but he was not Harry Morris—and most decidedly his voice was not Harry Morris's voice ('that man with the awful voice', as Sir William Solomon was said to have remarked—H H Morris* The First Forty Years *48). The trial caused a sensation in exposing a promiscuous and sybaritic mode of existence of a set of debauched and degenerate members of the British aristocracy and their hangers-on, all of whom had settled in Kenya. To call them hedonists would be to insult that word. The main male members, except one, were Etonians; the one was a Harrovian. Some of the female characters had South African connections. Morris in his memoirs makes out that in his view Broughton did not fire the pistol shot that killed Erroll in his motor car, which was found with his body in it two and a half miles from the Broughton house. He does not say that Broughton was innocent, but merely this: 'At least two persons must have taken part in this job' (p. 255). Fox (op cit 281–5), however, comes up with a pretty convincing account by Juanita Carbery, daughter (or apparently daughter) of a member of the set, of how Broughton confessed to her the day after the murder that he had done the deed. She was then 15, and kept mum until 1980, when for the first time she revealed Broughton's confession; and she revealed it to Fox. Harry Morris (loc cit) says of Broughton: 'He was a fine English gentleman.' When one reads Fox's book one can only wonder what an English gentleman who is not fine is like, for Broughton was a thief, a swindler and an embezzler, was a cruel, cowardly, charmless wastrel.*

'The transcript vividly records a great defence barrister at work. Harry Morris, later immortalised in a biography called *Genius for the Defence*, was described by a lawyer on the opposing team as "bluff, rough and impassioned, contemptuous

. . . prone to descend to burlesque, abuse, even insolence''. From a reading of this case, that description is unfairly pejorative. Morris would never insult a witness gratuitously, although he often managed to provoke one into angry retaliation. His style in court was aggressive, and sometimes abrasive. It relied upon a rich sense of humour, a sharp wit, and a degree of sarcasm. Morris also displayed an exceptional memory and a prodigious grasp of detail which he used to greatest effect in reducing expert witnesses for the prosecution, whenever possible, to the level of confused amateurs, tangling them up in petty contradictions.

'It was in his talent for manipulation and mystification that Morris truly shone as a barrister. He believed that expert witnesses, forensic scientists and the like, with their carefully prepared evidence and their professional sureness and self-esteem, were the easiest prey for a good defence counsel. Furthermore, Morris was a leading lay authority on ballistic science—the knowledge of guns and bullets, especially the microscopic markings found on spent bullets that could identify them with the barrel of a particular gun. On his arrival in Nairobi he told both Broughton and Kaplan [Broughton's solicitor] that he could defeat the Crown case on one simple point of ballistics alone.

'In fact Morris was perplexed that the Crown case had left him such a "simple answer" to give to the jury, namely to disprove the Crown's contention that the murder weapon was that same Colt .32 that Broughton had used for shooting practice at Nanyuki and which had subsequently been "stolen" from his house three days before the murder. But he gave no clue about his simple answer, even to his clients.'

—James Fox *White Mischief* (1982) 101–2.

'In the year 1941 at Nairobi, Sir John Delves Broughton was arrested and subsequently charged with the murder of the Earl of Erroll, Baron Kilmarnock. Hardly had Sir Delves found himself in the Nairobi prison when he received a cable from Lord Moyne, the Colonial Secretary (who was later shot in Cairo). Moyne was a school friend of Broughton's. The cable offered to do all Moyne could for his friend in his trouble. Sir Delves was much flattered by this attention and bore the offer in mind. Came the day when the defence required a postponement to meet the charge. The Attorney-General of Kenya refused to agree. The accused cabled to his friend, the Colonial Secretary, asking him to instruct the Attorney-General to agree. Hardly had the cable left when Sir Delves burst into laughter. A thought had passed through his mind. Twenty years before he had a transaction with Moyne which involved the transfer of some big insurance policies to his lordship and on which ever since Moyne had been paying heavy premiums. Was it likely in the circumstances that Moyne was going to help to save his friend's neck? Sir Delves thought it was highly unlikely. He was right. His friend refused to assist, but he was saved without his lordship's assistance.'

—H H Morris QC *In my Anecdotage* (1953) 20–1. (Corrections have been made to the date and certain surnames. Morris could have said that Moyne was living with Vera, Broughton's previous wife, though he refused to marry her.)

'Broughton had another great friend—-Lord Francis Scott. He was a man with a fine character and his word carried great weight in Kenya. One day, during the trial, Broughton said to his Counsel: "I would like you to call Lord Francis Scott." "Why?" said Counsel. "Well, we are great friends. We were at school together; he knows me very well and he knows that I am not the sort of man who would do a thing like this." After much discussion, Counsel vetoed the proposition. Three days later he heard the following story. On the morning on which Erroll's body was found in his car, Francis Scott and a number of others had appointments with Erroll, who was Military Secretary of Kenya. At half past nine there was no Erroll so someone rang up his house and was told that he had been shot. "Good God," said Scott. "Broughton must have done that because of Erroll's affair with Diana." (She was Broughton's wife.)'

—Morris op cit at 21–2.

'I Forgot.

'On my return from Nairobi after the Broughton trial the Rotarians did me the honour of asking me to lunch. As I entered the banqueting hall an official tried to catch me off my guard.

'"Who shot Erroll?"

'"My God," I replied, "I quite forgot to ask."'

— H H Morris KC *The First Forty Years* (1948) 172. (This oft-told story, which is usually better put with the question 'Did Broughton shoot Erroll?' and the answer 'I quite forgot to ask him', is sometimes related of the trial of Richard Louis Mallalieu in 1931 for murder. See the next entry.)

The trial in September 1931 of Richard Louis Mallalieu and Gwendolen Mary Tolputt before a jury for the murder of Arthur Victor Kimber, a Pietermaritzburg taxi-driver, was described by Morris as 'the most sensational trial that ever took place in South Africa' (The First Forty Years 200, in a chapter entitled 'Dicky'). 'Dicky' Mallalieu was the son of a former British MP. Tolputt had made a confession to a fellow inmate in the awaiting-trial cells, that Mallalieu had told Kimber to stop the taxi, then shot him in the left temple, pulled him out of the taxi, searched him for money, and then, as he was groaning, at the request of Tolputt shot him again in the head to finish him off. The confession was inadmissible against Mallalieu, and Matthews J rightly ordered a separation of trials. He was wrong, however, in acceding to the request of Morris, for the accused, that the trial of Tolputt be postponed until that of Mallalieu was disposed of; in holding that the trial judge had the power to determine the order of presentation of trials (Ex parte Mallalieu: In re R v Mallalieu and Tollputt 1932 NPD 80, overruled in R v Matsinya 1945 AD 802 by the Appellate Division, which held that the power vested in the Attorney-General). Mallalieu was acquitted. He was then prosecuted for fraud arising out of 'rubber cheques' he had signed, sentenced to a short term of imprisonment, and thereafter deported. The charge against Tolputt was withdrawn. She too was deported.

'Shortly after the trial my parents were with him [Morris] at the opera one night. At the interval my father asked him whether he thought Mallalieu was guilty. "You know, Jack", he replied, "I completely forgot to ask him!"'

—The Hon Ramon Nigel Leon *Truth in Action* (the reminiscences of the former judge of the Natal Provincial Division, not yet completed or published). Actually, Morris was convinced of the guilt of Mallalieu. He wrote to the well-known writer of books on South African criminal trials, Benjamin Bennett (see his *Some Don't Hang* (1973) 90; also Morris's letter reproduced opposite page 65): 'If you want to show enterprise, publish Gwen Tolputt's confession. . . . [E]very word is true.'

'She Remembered.

'The dear old lady beamed and then piped:

'"Mr. Morris, you don't remember me?"

'She was right.

'"I saw you at the Mallalieu trial. I can remember, as if it were yesterday, you getting up and saying to the jury, "Ladies and gentlemen."'

—H H Morris KC *The First Forty Years* (1948) 175. (Actually, Morris could only have said 'Gentlemen', as there were no women jurors in our history.)

The trial of Mrs Daisy de Melker (born Hancock-Smith, formerly Cowle, formerly Sproat), aged 46, on three charges of murder before Mr Justice Greenberg and two assessors aroused enormous public interest. She was accused of poisoning her first husband, William Cowle, by the administration of strychnine; of poisoning her second husband, Robert Sproat, in the same way; and of poisoning the sole survivor of her five children, Rhodes Cowle, by the administration of arsenic. The hearing of the trial ran for 30 days, from 17 October to 25 November 1932. Harry Morris led I A Maisels (later the eminent silk) for the defence. The accused was acquitted of the murder of her husbands but convicted of the murder of her son. She was sentenced to death and executed. Had she been acquitted on all charges she would have been arrested by the Southern Rhodesia police on three other charges of murder, including that of a fiancé, Bert Fuller. There is little doubt that she poisoned at least seven persons, including some other of her children. Morris in his memoirs, The First Forty Years *(1948) 217, 221, in a chapter entitled 'Daisy', pictures her as 'ruthless, remorseless and pitiless. . . . Her next victim [no doubt Mr De Melker] was to have gone about the time of her trial.'*

'DE MELKER EPISODE.

'During the de Melker trial Mr. Justice Greenberg developed a tremendous thirst for information. I have never known His Lordship to be so parched. He spent a whole day asking me questions, the answers to which he knew better than I did.

'H. H. MORRIS K.C.'

Sketch by 'Jacef' in (1932) 1 South African Law Times 238 in a series of sketches entitled 'Figures in the De Melker Murder Trial'

At precisely 4.29 he put another which I answered as best I could.

'"Mr. Morris", said His Lordship somewhat testily, "That is not an answer to my question."

'"I know that, my Lord. It is a means of escape, and (looking at the clock) it is time for escape."

'We "escaped".'

—H H Morris KC *The First Forty Years* (1948) 163. (For another 'De Melker episode', see GREENBERG.)

'She had a strong sense of humour. She complained one morning during the trial that she had had a bad night owing to neuralgia. In a moment of abstraction I advised her to take some arsenic, meaning aspirin. She, more than anyone, enjoyed the *faux pas*.'

—Morris op cit at 219.

The former Judge President of the Natal Provincial Division is recounting his experience as leader of the team appearing for Knight in his action for damages

'MRS D. L. DE MELKER'

Sketch by 'Jacef' in (1932) 1 South African Law Times 238 in a series of sketches entitled 'Figures in the De Melker Murder Trial'

for defamation against Findlay, a Durban attorney. The action arose out of a plea by Findlay to an action by Knight for his charges for an operation he had performed before his conviction and imprisonment on a charge of culpable homicide arising out of an abortion he had performed and on several charges of abortion, a conviction that led to his name being removed from the medical register. Findlay knew that there would be no evidence to support the defamatory allegations. The action succeeded: see Findlay v Knight *1935 AD 58, and also* L C STEYN *and* WESSELS.

'One amusing incident during the case comes to my mind. Our client had a somewhat flamboyant personality. On the morning of the trial he turned up dressed as though he were going to the races and sporting a colourful button-hole. This would not do at all. I had studied the proceedings in his criminal trial some years before and I had formed the impression that he had seriously prejudiced his case with the jury by his demeanour in Court and by his repeated attempts to score off the Attorney-General with smart replies in cross-examination. It was quite clear to me that Harry Morris would have had a much better chance of securing an acquittal if he had kept his client in order. I could not allow that sort of thing to happen again. So I said to him: "You are not going into Court to make an impression on the public, but to win your case. Now will you please go back to your hotel and put on a dark suit. And throw away that button-hole." I then gave him a short lecture on the danger of trying to be clever in the witness box. He was dumbfounded. But he went away and came back dressed, perhaps not quite as though he were going to a funeral, but certainly as though he had just left a vestry-meeting; and he gave his evidence like a lamb. After the case he said to me: "I wish Harry Morris had talked to me like that."'

—F N Broome *Not the Whole Truth* (1963) 146–7. (The Knight saga was of great public interest in Durban.)

Revenge

'Another prosecutor, however, had the last laugh over him, though he had to wait twenty years for it. Philip Millin, K.C., delegated by the Attorney-General to appear for the Crown at an important trial, was confronted by Morris with a ticklish point. If upheld, his case would have collapsed. Like the shrewd lawyer he was, he asked the judge for an adjournment to "consider the matter."

'Morris was both indignant and scornful. The Crown, represented by his learned friend, should be prepared to meet any point, at any time, any place. No adjournment should be permitted. The rights and convenience of the accused man must also be considered, and so on. The judge agreed. Millin had to do the best he could. The prisoner was acquitted.

'Twenty years passed. Millin was now a judge and Morris's son, Eric, appeared before him at a criminal trial. This time the Crown Prosecutor sprang a point and

Morris jnr. wanted an adjournment to consider the implications. Millin listened patiently to his arguments. Then he said in his silkiest voice:

'"Mr Morris, twenty years ago I appeared against your father in a criminal trial. He took a point for which I was not prepared. I asked for an adjournment to go into the matter. He objected and said counsel must be prepared to meet any point, at any time, any place. The court upheld his view and my application was refused. At that time I thought your father's objection a bad one. Now I think it a good one.

'"Your application for an adjournment is refused."

'The verdict this time was guilty.

'Morris recalled the story in his anecdotes but not what he actually said when he heard how Millin had the laugh over him. He contented himself with the written remark: "I once thought the objection was a good one. Now I know it isn't."'

— Benjamin Bennett *Genius for the Defence: Life of Harry Morris, K.C.* (1959) 183–4. (For a more detailed account, but with anonymous characters, see Eric Morris SC *Technique in Litigation* 3 ed (1985) 26–7.)

Recollections of Mr Justice Grindley-Ferris

'Some years ago, said Mr. Justice Grindley-Ferris, I was presiding at a jury trial in the Supreme Court, Johannesburg, of an Indian charged with making counterfeit coins. The Crown case was so extremely strong that defending counsel, Mr. H. H. Morris, K.C., who was for many years the leading criminal advocate practising in the Transvaal, must have realized that he had very little, if any, chance of success.

'At that moment one of the worst earth tremors I have ever experienced in Johannesburg shook the whole building. Without losing a moment, Morris said to the Crown witness: "Do you realize that even this Court building has to shake at the answer you have given?"'

— As reported in H H Morris QC *In My Anecdotage* (1953) 57.

'On one occasion Judge Barry and I were walking in the judges' corridor in the Supreme Court, Johannesburg, when we met Morris coming from the office of the Crown Prosecutor. Barry asked Morris whether he was appearing for the accused in the criminal case to be heard that morning. Morris replied in the affirmative, and Barry asked how long he thought the case would last. After looking thoughtfully at the ceiling for a moment, Morris replied that it would finish "as soon as I have finished my cross-examination of the complainant". That proved to be correct.'

— Mr Justice Grindley-Ferris in Morris loc cit.

'THE LAND OF EGYPT

'We were charged with keeping and/or frequenting a gaming house. The Magistrate looked at the names on the summons and then at the homogeneous collection before him. I read his mind.

'"Yes, your Worship, this is not the first time the Children of Israel have got into the House of Bondage through Faro."'

— H H Morris KC *The First Forty Years* (1948) 175. (Faro is a gambling game in which players bet against the dealer on what cards will turn up.)

'FICKLE

'She was an attractive girl. She was the complainant in a case in which the accused was charged with *crimen injuria*. She said that at ten to one she was standing at the door and a few yards away from her the accused was exposing himself.

'"Then," said she, "the factory siren blew and the accused went back to work."

'I observed that the accused had left one siren because of another. She rather appreciated this.'

—Morris op cit at 173.

Some responses

'On another occasion Morris did notice a junior, this time with more sympathy. The young man, excited but understandably nervous at appearing in his first case, staggered out of his chambers under the weight of a suitcase bulging with legal tomes. He had been admitted only a few days before and was determined not to be tripped up on any point of law that might arise.

'He rang for the lift. When it came he hauled his burden into it.

'Morris followed and surveyed the scene. Evidently thinking of his own early days, he said: "What the hell have you got in there? Bricks to drop in court?"

'Once he dropped a brick himself in the shape of an ill-timed joke he tossed into the jury box. The jurors did not see the joke but the accused man saw the inside of a jail for some years.

'He used to say: "You can tell the jury a joke or two. If you see ripples, so much the better. If you don't, be careful."

'There was an illustration of this once when his client was charged with attempted rape. The complainant was an over-scented woman with a high, proud bosom. She wore a tight-fitting, low-cut dress to accentuate it. In spite of her story of a fierce struggle until she was "rescued" by her husband, Morris suggested she had encouraged the accused man and had herself to blame for whatever happened.

'The woman indignantly denied it. The man was equally insistent that he had received a pressing invitation she seemed to regret only when her husband arrived unexpectedly.

'"Gentlemen of the jury," Morris said, "my learned friend, the prosecutor, says the complainant held out no inducement to the accused man."

'He glanced slowly round the court until his eye fell on the woman. The jury followed him, as he intended they should. He studied openly the plunging neckline.

'"Gentlemen," he said after a moment's pause, "I suggest you will not agree with the prosecutor but with me. I say the complainant must have held out two of the biggest and strongest inducements to my client."

'The verdict was not guilty.'

—Benjamin Bennett *Genius for the Defence: Life of Harry Morris, K.C.* (1959) 179–80.

'You go Bloemfontein; me go Bombay!'

'On one occasion, a well-known Rand K.C. defended an Indian before a Magistrate on a charge of unlawful possession of certain unwrought gold. This offence falls within the I.G.B. category, and the penalty is a heavy one.

'The case had been remitted to the Magistrate for trial. The latter convicted the

Indian and sentenced him. Thereupon the prisoner noted an appeal against the judgment and sentence of the Magistrate to the Supreme Court at Pretoria.

'On the appointed day, the Indian, who meantime had been released on bail, appeared and sat listening to his counsel arguing the appeal.

'In due course the finding and sentence of the Magistrate was upheld by the Judges, and the appeal dismissed.

'As the advocate was leaving the Court he felt a tug at his gown. His client stood beside him.

'"Well, Ramojee, what do you want?" the lawyer asked.

'"Oh, Mr. X, what me do now?" pleaded the Oriental.

'"You can either serve your sentence or apply for leave to appeal to the Appellate Court at Bloemfontein!" rejoined the advocate.

'The Indian looked into the face of the European as if to read advice therein, but, seeing none, he stood momentarily pensive. Then he said:

'"Oh, is that so. All right. You go Bloemfontein; me go Bombay!"'

—Napier Devitt *More Memories of a Magistrate* (1936) 126. (This famous story was told later differently by Morris in his memoirs, *The First Forty Years* (1948) 110–12. Sedat, an illegal immigrant, had been convicted of the forgery of promissory notes. Morris now takes up the account:

'As we walked out of Court Sedat said, "Where we go now?" I said, "Now we go Pretoria", meaning the Supreme Court.

' . . . The conviction was upheld. . . .

'As we walked out of Court Sedat said, "Where we go now?" I . . . said, "Now we go Bloemfontein", meaning the Appellate Division.

'He said, "No damn fear. You go Bloemfontein, me go Calcutta." He went.'

(According to Isaac Goodman *Judges I Have Known* (1969) 79, counsel was F E T Krause (q v). But Goodman must have made a mistake. There are several errors in his book.)

'D.S.O. AND BAR.

'We were in the Liquor Licensing Court. There were a large number of applicants who were returned soldiers—officers and men. Many of them had been decorated for their services. I was making an application for a common soldier who had been assigned to Q services, and therefore had no opportunity to distinguish himself in the field. I was making the point that the Court should not take into consideration the decoration an applicant may have been awarded. "It does not follow," said I, "that because a man has a D.S.O. and Bar that he should also have a bottle store."'

—H H Morris KC *The First Forty Years* (1948) 170–1. (Another, and possibly better, version of this renowned anecdote is that recounted by Leslie Blackwell, retired judge, in his memoirs, *Are Judges Human?* (1962) 146. After pointing out that it was suspected that many gallant ex-servicemen applying for a liquor licence were but fronts for moneyed men, he continues: 'Morris was appearing one day in the Licensing Court for a man who did not have the advantage of a war record. Referring to another applicant, who was resplendent in decorations, he said, "I am indeed gratified that this gentleman has returned from the war with a D.S.O., but need you grant him a bar as well?"')

'CRIME DOES PAY

'It happened in the High Court. One partner was giving evidence against another in a criminal case. I appeared for the accused and cross-examined the partner.

'"Have you ever had a fire, Mr Blank?"

'"Must I answer that question, My Lord?"

'"Yes."

'"Yes."

'"How many?"

'"Must I answer that question, My Lord?"

'"Yes."

'"Two."

'"Successful?"

'"Must I answer that question, My Lord?"

'"Yes."

'"Very."

'We were acquitted.'

—H H Morris KC *The First Forty Years* (1948) 162.

The joke that misfired

'If you can, throw a joke or two into the jury box. If you see ripples so much the better. Recently I tried one on a judge and assessors. My lunatic stood in the box. Felix du Toit, the psychiatrist, had said he was sane. I argued that you can never tell whether a man is sane or not. I told the story of Erskine. He was being badly beaten by a witness. A note came from the back of the Court, "Ask him if he knows the Saviour." Erskine asked the witness. The witness drew himself up and said, "Sir, I am the Saviour." That was the end of the witness. I saw ripples, but I got 12 years' hard instead of the Governor-General's pleasure.'

— Morris op cit at 151. (The verdict, then, was guilty, followed by a sentence of twelve years' imprisonment with hard labour, instead of detention in prison as mentally disordered until the Governor-General (in reality, the Government) decided what would happen to him ('the Governor-General's pleasure'): normally it would be detention in a mental hospital.)

'Ins and outs'

'Morris was at his most devastating when he cross-examined old lags who gave evidence against his clients, though even with them he used first the courteous approach if there was a chance of a favourable reply.

'One of these jailbirds had an arm-long list of previous convictions. Morris dealt with them piecemeal to show judge and jury the type of man they were asked to believe against the prisoner.

'"Tell my lord and the gentlemen of the jury," he said, displaying the formidable indictment of the man's misdeeds, "did you inform your employer of this collection of prison souvenirs?"

'The witness hesitated. "Well," he said grudgingly, "I told him about my ups and downs."

'Quick as a flash Morris said: "Yes, but did you tell him about your ins and outs?"'

— Benjamin Bennett *Genius for the Defence: Life of Harry Morris, K.C.* (1959) 174.

'WELL, WELL!

'We were in "A" Court of the Old Magistrate's Court building before Mr. van den Berg. It was raining cats and dogs. The water was pouring through the roof into the Court just behind me.

'Said the Beak: "There seems to be plenty of water in your part of the Court, Mr. Morris."

'"Yes, your Worship. That is why it is called the well of the Court."'

—H H Morris KC *The First Forty Years* (1948) 157. (On H H (Harry) Morris, see also CARTER; CURLEWIS; GREENBERG; GREGOROWSKI; INNES; KRAUSE; O D SCHREINER; SAUL SOLOMON; W H SOLOMON; WESSELS.)

GEORGE ANGUS MULLIGAN

1870–1960. Attorney, Johannesburg, 1897–1914. Member of the Johannesburg Bar 1915–60. KC 1942. Author of legal works.

'Born in Co. Armagh in 1870, Mulligan came from a lineage that in two steps went to the distant past; his father was born in 1807 (rumour hath it that he heard the newspaper-sellers shouting in the streets: "Victory at Waterloo!"); and his grandfather was a contemporary of Louis XVI, Marie Antoinette and George Washington. Seeking a new career, George Angus Mulligan came to Johannesburg at the age of 23, where he set about learning Nederlands to pass the Onderwijzers-Certifikaat 1ste Klas, prerequisite for entry to the Rechtsgeleerde Examen 2de Klas, set for admission as an attorney. Taught by a Hollander, he developed a good accent and found the task well within his compass. He took articles with Attorney J. J. de Villiers (admitted in 1888). Passing his law examinations in Dutch, the 27-year-old Mulligan went initially into partnership with Hedland A. Fry (who was admitted in the Transvaal in the same year) and then with W. H. T. Frost, in the firm of Frost, Mulligan and Routledge. Later the firm became Mulligan, Routledge and Pope, and finally Mulligan and Routledge. Only last year Johannesburg counsel had occasion to consider a deed prepared by Mulligan in 1898 in the days of the old South African Republic.

'The successful attorney, however, was attracted to the lure of the Bar in 1914. The quickest avenue to his objective was through eating dinners at King's Inns, Dublin, and passing the Bar examinations. The whole task took but a year and a half, and Mulligan then set up practice at the Johannesburg Bar which has lasted to the present day. He took silk in 1942. Until his retirement in May this year, he attended chambers regularly.

'Political affairs interested the young Mulligan. Even before leaving Ireland he claims to have been an odd character — an Irish Protestant born and bred in Ulster who was an ardent Home Ruler. When he came to the Rand he became a Reformer. During the South African War he fought on the British side with the Imperial Light Horse, and was wounded. It was then—so he says—that he persuaded the English of the virtues of Irish whiskey.

'For the first decade of the century he was a keen politician. His greatest pride lies in the part he played in the campaign that brought to an end the use of Chinese labour on the gold mines. Always a supporter of the Responsible Government Association, Mulligan stood as a candidate at Troyeville for that body under its adopted name of the National Party in the first Parliamentary election of 15th September, 1910. His opponent was J. W. Quinn, the well-known baker, who stood for the Unionist Party (the former Progressives), which was imperialistic and pro-big business and mining interests, while the Nationalists adopted a broad South Africanism that led to their speedy amalgamation with Botha's Het Volk Party under the name South African National Party. The fight at Troyeville was a forlorn cause for the Nationalists. Visitors to the Johannesburg Bar common-room will see the original of a cartoon of A. W. Lloyd (later for many years Parliamentary cartoonist of *Punch*) hanging on the south wall. Published in *The Star* (violently pro-Unionist) on 1st September, 1910, it is headed "Our Comic Candidates: No. 1", and depicts Mulligan clad in loin-cloth and armed with shield and spear tilting at a fortress shaped like a baker's hat and flourishing a flag with the insignia "J.W.Q." Beneath lies the inscription "Another Unsuccessful Raid by the Mad Mullah-gan". The protagonist of the drawing, looking considerably older than his then 40 years, is not quite bald and flourishes a magnificent Kaiser Bill moustache, but has the unmistakable Mulligan cranium. The result of the election (*The Star*, 16th September, 1910) was Quinn 1,172 votes; Mulligan: 785.

'Like William de Morgan, whose maiden novel *Joseph Vance* appeared when he was 65, Mulligan began writing only in later life. The *Continuous Digest of Union Statute Law* (written with H. J. (now Mr. Justice) Clayden) was published in 1930, and the supplement in 1933. Only in 1947 did he come forth with his first legal article ("Forfeiture Clauses in Contracts of Lease" (1947) 64 *S.A.L.J.* 506). Since then a spate of writings has issued, mainly concerned with contractual remedies. The great bulk have appeared in this journal. In 1953 was published his *Pothier's Treatise on the Contract of Letting and Hiring*, translated from the French, in which language Mulligan is an expert (he has the distinction of being an Officier de'Académie). All his publications are distinguished by a pellucid style, and seasoned with quotations, saws and sayings, always appropriate, witty and wise, culled from a wide reading in many languages.'

—Ellison Kahn 'George Angus Mulligan in His Ninety-first Year' (1960) 67 *SALJ* 235–6. (On Lloyd, see the Introduction, above.)

His father a drummer-boy at Waterloo?

'The late John Vorster's sister Mona handled my firm's work in Pretoria for many years and we became good friends. As a result, I holidayed a couple of times at "Oubos" after Vorster's retirement. Despite his political image, he was great company over sundowners. One evening we were talking about characters at the Jo'burg Bar whom we both knew. He told me the following story about Mulligan:

'One morning Vorster and a couple of other young advocates who had no work were sitting in the common-room having tea and passing the time. As this was in the mid-50's Mulligan was obviously a very old man. He came into the common-room, joined the youngsters and apropos of nothing at all remarked that his father had fought at the battle of Waterloo. The young barristers were openly disbelieving. This apparently incensed Mulligan, who stomped out, slamming the door. The next morning he again appeared in the common-room, went up to the same group of young advocates and hauled out a bunch of old documents which included his father's birth certificate, his father's military documents, and a certificate signed by the Duke of Wellington to the effect that the holder had been present at Waterloo.

'This latter document was apparently handed out to veterans some years after the actual battle. Evidently, Mulligan Senior had been a drummer-boy in Wellington's army and in those days drummer boys were apparently little more than children. Mulligan then demanded an apology for the slight that had been cast on his integrity the previous day and explained to Vorster that his father had been a very old man when he had married and produced a son.

'The point that John Vorster made was that he had known and spoken to a man whose father had fought at Waterloo!'

—From a letter of 27 July 1989 by Mr Chris Niland to Ellison Kahn. (My note of a conversation with Mulligan led to my writing that his father was born in 1807 (see the previous extract), too late to be a drummer boy at Waterloo. I may have misheard Mulligan, but he did not correct me. Perhaps his father was born in 1800. Still, once more, se non é vero, é molto ben trovato—if it is not true, it is very well invented (by John Vorster).)

The story calls for a reproduction of the following account by Mr Justice Felix Frankfurter of the United States Supreme Court of the descent of Professor Jeremiah Smith of Harvard Law School where Frankfurter had been a student of Smith's:

'He was born when his father was seventy, or seventy-one, and his father was born when his father was seventy odd. I think three generations of Smiths, four of them, almost spanned the history of this continent from the time that Columbus landed. He was the child of a second marriage. This really happened. One day he said in class, "Gentlemen, I hope you'll forgive me if I am somewhat"—what was his word, overwrought, or distraught, or forgetful?—"because this is a sad day for me. A hundred years ago today my little brother died."

'You have to figure that out.'

(*Felix Frankfurter Reminisces. An Intimate Portrait as Recorded in Talks with Dr. Harlan B. Phillips* (1960; Archer Books edition 1962) 38.)

'GEORGE ANGUS MULLIGAN
Q.C.'

Sketch in Sunday Express *9 March 1958*

'. . . The pen of George Angus Mulligan (31 January 1870–3 September 1960) was never still. Can anyone else in his eighties have approached his output? There were 22 full-scale articles and a number of notes. The majority of his compositions were on aspects of the law of contract. The last was produced in the year of his death. I remember George Angus with affection. He was a character of the Johannesburg Bar. In the Bar common-room hangs a cartoon by A W Lloyd, published in *The Star* in 1910, which shows Mulligan, who was then standing for election to the House of Assembly, depicted as the "Mad Mullah-gan". He looks old there. When I negotiated with him in the decade from 1950, he looked very old; and indeed he came from a distant era. His father was born in 1807, and was said to recall newspaper-sellers shouting "Victory at Waterloo!" (John Murray, the judge, most delightful of men, used to contend that it was not Mulligan's father who heard them—it was Mulligan himself.) George Angus, a very well-read man, was full of fun and wit. It bubbled forth whenever I went to see him in his old house, built in the early days of Johannesburg, in Parktown; it was demolished long ago, with so many other gracious homes, to make way for the College of Education. On several occasions I took him to my university to look up material; he used to sit in my room there and tear out unused sheets in examination scripts, on which he would later write his manuscripts in a very large and legible hand. To get him to agree to change anything he wrote was a major triumph that I seldom enjoyed. The title George Angus gave to an article of his in 1951 still amuses people: "No Orchids for Misrepresentation?"'

—Ellison Kahn 'The Birth and Life of the *South African Law Journal*' (1983) 100 *SALJ* 594 at 628–9.

'Mulligan when in his eighties was arguing an appeal in which he was dealing with a passage from Pomponius, the second-century Roman jurist, that was quoted in the Digest of Justinian. Mulligan was giving what he contended was the correct English translation of the Latin and stating what Pomponius really meant. One of the members of the court turned to another member and whispered "I wonder if he heard Pomponius say that."'

—Ellison Kahn's commonplace book.

SIR JOHN MURRAY MURRAY

1888–1976. Member of the Pretoria Bar 1913–37. KC 1932. Judge of the Transvaal Provincial Division 1937–55. Chief Justice of Southern Rhodesia 1955–61. Knighted 1958.

'John Murray is now on his blooming Asiatic Commission. He lunches with us at the [Pretoria] Club despite my protests that the table is reserved for judges and that mere commissioners have no place there.'

—Oliver Denys Schreiner (q v) in a letter to his wife Edna, 1 August 1938. Schreiner family papers. (The Commission was the Asiatic Land Laws Commission. Its report is UG 16 of 1939.)

CHOICE OF A CHIEF JUSTICE

' . . . My interview with him at his home was a short one. He was most courteous and after a short discussion said he would like to introduce me to his wife. This he did, and then made his exit. It seemed clear to me that his wife was the one who was to make the final decision. Anyway, in due course Mr. Justice Murray arrived in Rhodesia, where he became Chief Justice and was subsequently knighted. This was one of the most successful missions I carried out during my period of office as Minister of Justice and Internal Affairs with the Todd Government.

'Judge Murray was like a breath of fresh air. He completely changed the outlook which in the past had been handed down from a rather frozen and rigid judiciary. He knew men and affairs and was very human and understanding. Everybody liked him. The outlook and atmosphere which he introduced to the Rhodesian Bench still prevails today. He retired and went to live at Plettenberg Bay in South Africa, where he recently died.

'When he received his knighthood, he was acting Governor of Southern Rhodesia, as the then Governor was away on leave. A reception was held at Government House and I can well recall, as I am sure many other people can recall, that on being congratulated on the honour which had been conferred upon them by the Queen, Lady Murray, as she had now become, and who had a sense of humour all her own, remarked, "It took the Queen to make a lady out of me."'

—A R W Stumbles *Some Recollections of a Rhodesian Speaker* (1980) 60–1.

'"I don't think I feel disposed to follow your advice re inflicting myself on the bowling fraternity—possibly my 18 years on the TPD & 6 in Rhodesia gave me an aversion to any form of bias."'

—Ellison Kahn in *Fiat Iustitia: Essays in Memory of Oliver Deneys Schreiner* (1983) 39, quoting from a letter by Murray to Schreiner, dated 12 November 1972.

'A story is told of him [Murray] after a visit to the Court of Appeal in Bloemfontein some years ago. He was asked how he had fared before that august body. "Well," said he, "first of all I went to see my uncle Curly (Judge Curlewis [qv]), and he kept me for a long time telling me of the trouble he was having with his kidneys. Then I went to see Judge D., and he was complaining of his stomach ailments; and so it went on with the rest of the Bench. It wasn't an appeal at all; it was an organ recital!"'

—Leslie Blackwell (qv) *Farewell to Parliament* (1946) 198. (See also BLACKWELL; MULLIGAN.)

PATRICK FULLER O'HAGAN

1917–1966. Member of the Pretoria Bar 1942–55. Member of the Eastern Districts Bar 1955–8. KC 1952. Judge of the Eastern Cape Division 1958–66.

'When he was presiding over the criminal sessions at Umtata in 1963 there appeared before O'Hagan J. two native men charged with unlawfully entering, in broad daylight, that part of the post office where parcels and mail were sorted and bagged. It was alleged that the accused forced open sealed mailbags, and stole a quantity of registered letters and parcels before making their getaway. The thefts had perforce to be done in a hurry as at any moment post office officials might enter the sorting room and catch the thieves red-handed. The latter, however, effected their purpose with lightning speed and got away with the swag.

'Foolishly, seeking to make sure they would not be caught, the two men engaged the services of a woman witchdoctor, known to all and sundry by the name "Beauty". She prescribed certain medicines to make them invisible, or at least immune from prosecution. Her fee was payable by instalments, and when her clients failed to pay up, she took umbrage and told the whole story by reporting them to the police.

'The two accused denied all knowledge of the theft, and in their defence declared that to break the seals of mailbags was a difficult operation and they would have been caught long before they could have opened the bags. This allegation being denied by a postal official, the Judge, holding a stop-watch, ordered a demonstration to be given. The official, feverishly struggling with the seals, effected the opening in a trice.

'But that was not the end of the case. The witchdoctor, a vital witness for the prosecution, was not at hand to make her appearance when the trial was to be resumed after the demonstration. The Judge granted a short postponement for her to be found, but said that if she did not appear within half an hour the case would have to proceed without her.

'Time went by and there was no sign of the witness. I was prosecuting, and defending counsel, Adv. G. H. Titterton, said to me, "You'll be sunk if they can't find your lady." When only a few minutes remained, the Investigating Officer hurried into the court-room with the news: "She's here!" *Conticuere omnes intentique ora tenebant.* [Virgil *Aeneid* ii 1: "Every tongue was still, every face turned rapt upon her" (based on the translation in *The Oxford Dictionary of Quotations*).] In she came—a most incredible sight. The lady, bedecked with all the ornaments and paraphernalia of her craft, was so obese that she appeared to be wider than she was high. The court orderly, aided by a couple of sturdy constables, managed to wedge her into the witness-box. From this she protruded both fore and aft.

'The Judge was then summoned and I, as prosecuting counsel, gravely informed him. "This, m'Lord, is Beauty!" O'Hagan after gazing in astonishment at the witness-box, said: "Well, Mr Randell, if you say so."'

—George Randell *Bench and Bar of the Eastern Cape* (1985) 97–8. (Randell continues on page 99: 'Beauty gave her evidence very well, and the accused were found guilty.')

ALAN STEWART PATON

1903–88. Writer and politician (so he described himself in *Who's Who of Southern Africa*).

'As I grow older I am able to understand my father better. . . . I am sure that his autocracy at home was a compensation for his diffidence abroad. I do not know all the causes of this diffidence, but undoubtedly his lack of professional status was one of them. He moved in the world of the Supreme Court, a world of judges, registrars, advocates, attorneys. They talked a good deal, and his job was not to participate in their conversation but to take it down in shorthand and translate it into type. It is not the kind of job that a man of intelligence, and of gifts too, would wish to do all his life.

'He taught us to have a great respect for judges, especially for the Judge President. The one I remember best was Sir John Dove Wilson [qv]. He lived in a big house at Mountain Rise, and sometimes on our walks we would pass it. That was a long time ago, yet I remember that we did not pass it carelessly but with some kind of respect. I do not think my father would have carried on a Zulu conversation in front of the Judge President's house.

'We were also taught to raise our hats to Sir Michael Gallwey, who after his retirement [in 1901 as Chief Justice of Natal] spent much of his time sitting on the stoep of his little house in Church Street. We were very well-mannered, though I would think that was more my mother's teaching. We lifted hats, we walked on the outside of the pavements, we opened doors, we stood when ladies entered. There was only one thing I jibbed at, and that was calling a man "sir" unless he was a schoolmaster. How I could thus resist one of my father's wishes I cannot quite explain, but it may be that he being from the Scottish working class understood my unwillingness. Just why I was unwilling I can't quite explain either. But I agree that when I lifted my hat to Sir Michael Gallwey or Sir John Dove Wilson, I would say "sir."'

—Alan Paton *Towards the Mountain: An Autobiography* (1980) 18–19.

'The story of the Treason Trial I shall tell later, but I must record that on 6 December 1956, the day after the arrests, at a meeting in the Gandhi Hall, Durban, representatives of the Liberal Party and the Congresses launched a fund to assist treason trialists with their defence, and to provide maintenance and support for their dependants. The meeting was attended by four hundred people, of whom fifty were whites, one hundred and fifty Indians, and two hundred Africans. The proceedings were orderly, and Professor Leo Kuper and I spoke on behalf of the Liberal Party. There were six speakers, and all six were charged under Natal Provincial Notice No. 78 of 1933 with holding or attending or participating in (I am not sure which) a "meeting of Natives", without first obtaining the permission of the mayor of Durban. This ancient regulation was first promulgated to curb the activities of that charismatic black labour leader, Clements Kadalie, and his vigorous Industrial and Commercial Union, the I.C.U. . . .

'This was the first time in my life (and the last as far as I know at the time of writing) that I had ever sat as an accused person in the dock. . . .

'On the trial, which was twice adjourned, I remember only one thing, and that vividly. I said to Leo Kuper, my fellow member of the Liberal Party, that although this was the first time I had sat in the dock, I did not mind it at all. He said to me, with that gentle smile which was one of his great characteristics, "I don't like it at all."

'At the end of the trial we were all found guilty, the magistrate finding himself unable to upset the previous decision. The white and Indian accused were each fined five pounds, and the African accused three pounds. Our counsel announced that he would appeal. The verdict received much world publicity.

'On 1 August 1957 our appeal was heard in the Supreme Court in Pietermaritzburg. The presiding judge did not call on our counsel. Instead he asked the prosecutor whether a sack of oranges became, by the introduction of some lemons, a sack of lemons. Or whether a herd of Frieslands and Shorthorns was a herd of Frieslands. Or whether a meeting of members and non-members was a meeting of members. The prosecution replied that the answer to each of these shattering questions was Yes. The presiding judge finally asked whether there had on the occasion of 6 December 1956 been two meetings or only one, to which the prosecution replied that there had been only one. The judge then declared, after a decent interval and some discussion with his two fellow judges, intended no doubt to convey that the case put forward by the prosecution needed weighty consideration, that the appeal would succeed. I wrote a short account of this trial and signed it "One with No Convictions".'

—Alan Paton *Journey Continued: An Autobiography* (1988) 161–2. (Paton was quoting (not entirely accurately) from the judgment of Holmes J (Brokensha J and Fannin AJ concurring) in *R v Mall & others* 1958 (3) SA 872 (N). The magistrate found himself bound by the judgment of Caney J (Friedman AJ concurring) in *R v Seedat & another* 1957 (1) SA 27 (N), but the court in *Mall* held that if that aspect of the judgment in *Seedat* was part of the ratio decidendi (which it doubted), it was incorrect.)

PETRUS (PEET) CORNELIUS PELSER

1907–74. Attorney, Klerksdorp, 1943–74. Politician. Minister of Justice and Prisons 1966–74.

'*Wills and no wills*. Our judges have in the past caused problems with their wills.

'Sir John Wylde, first Chief Justice of the Cape Colony, made a will in 1856, a year after his retirement from judicial office. It was an underhand will with a reservatory clause. In 1857 he executed a signed but unwitnessed codicil under this clause. On his death in 1859 the Master asked the Supreme Court to pronounce on the validity of the codicil. The court said that the Master had acted very correctly in asking for its ruling. Nevertheless, the codicil was upheld. See *In re the late Sir John Wylde's Will* reported in 3 Buch 113.

'Ebden was another member of the judiciary who contributed to the Law Reports through his will. The question was whether he had complied with the formality prescribed by the Cape Wills Ordinance 1845 of a signature to each leaf. Again, the testament was upheld (*In re Ebden's Will* (1887) 4 SC 495). Unfortunately, the same good fortune did not attend the testamentary endeavours of Mr Justice Lansdown, for the requirement of a signature and two witnesses to each page had not been met. (See *Rand Daily Mail* 29 January 1957.)

'I have found one other reference to a judicial will. Mr Justice C L Botha, who had sat on the Orange Free State Bench from 1927 to 1939, found himself obliged in 1943 to request that court to order rectification of a will he had executed jointly with his late wife. This application was successful. (*Ex parte Botha* 1943 OPD 171.)

'The foregoing is by way of introduction to the failure of a former Minister of Justice to make a will at all. Mr P C Pelser, Minister of Justice from October 1966 to April 1974, died on 24 December last. He had been an attorney in Klerksdorp for many years prior to his parliamentary career, which began in April 1953. According to the preliminary inventory filed with the Master of the Supreme Court in Pretoria towards the end of January, his estate was worth R326 840. His widow, to whom the sympathy of all lawyers is extended, remarked that he "just didn't get round to making a will. A shoemaker never has a shoe. It would appear as if a lawyer never has a will." (See *Sunday Express* 26 January 1975.)'

—Ellison Kahn in (1975) 92 *SALJ* 109–10. Mr Justice Dowling (q v) also died intestate. See Isaac Goodman *Judges I Have Known* (1969) 37.)

SIR HENRY LUSHINGTON PHILLIPS

1825–96. Judge of the Natal Supreme Court 1858–80. Knighted 1880.

' . . . Phillips J revealed considerable talent and ability. His shrewdness and penetrating insight enabled him to grasp the essence of legal disputes and to discard irrelevant, obfuscating details. The expression of his judgments was characterised by clarity, forcefulness and fluency. . . .

'Yet, overall, Phillips J's contribution to the Natal Supreme Court was sadly deficient, and at times his impact was destructive. Phillips J came to Natal with no knowledge or understanding of Natal and its legal system, and he clearly indicated that he was unprepared to extend himself unduly in this direction. He expressed incredulity at the strength of local Dutch religious beliefs, and scorn for the Roman-Dutch laws "not clearly laid down in decisions, but raked up out of books published one or two hundred years ago". Throughout his legal career in Natal, his legal standards and concepts remained those he had formed in England. The legal sources upon which he normally relied were those established "at home": English practices, precedents and statutes. Even here, Phillips J's mode of reference could be casual and imprecise, as indicated by his recollection of "the case of James or Edwards, I am not sure which". And, at the conclusion of major civil trials, he increasingly came to spare himself all effort by simply concurring in one sentence.

'At least part of the reason why Phillips J was half-hearted in his efforts on the Bench was that much of his time and energy was channelled into commercial, sporting and social activities in Natal. Phillips J's commercial dealings repeatedly produced unseemly litigation, in which he was sued for unpaid debts and fines. His social ties made him especially susceptible to local prejudices and partialities. This was particularly evident in his treatment of Blacks, whose customs were dismissed with contempt, whose evidence was treated as less trustworthy than White evidence, and upon whom he imposed harsher sentences.

'Phillips J further undermined his worth as a judge by indulging in emotional outbursts. Judgments of brother judges were dismissed as "amateur" and "fallacious", arguments of advocates were condemned as "a waste of time", and litigants were branded as "vultures", displaying "meanness and tyranny". Phillips J's most unfortunate lapse came in November 1859, when he discovered in court that a prisoner whom he had sentenced to imprisonment had been granted remission of sentence by the Lieutenant-Governor. Phillips J resented the fact that the Lieutenant-Governor had omitted the usual courtesy of advising the judge, who had imposed the sentence, of the remission. Phillips J now launched a scathing attack on the "contemptuous" setting aside of his sentence and insinuated that the Lieutenant-Governor's remission was an act of weakness. The result of this was that, on 20 December 1859, Phillips J was suspended from office on the basis that he had made an unwarranted condemnation of the exercise of the royal prerogative and an offensive and disrespectful address calculated to discredit the local government. The matter was then sent to the British Secretary of State for his consideration, and he had no hesitation in condemning Phillips J as an "ill-advised and intemperate judge". However, "not without much hesitation", the Secretary of State decided to restore Phillips J to office, on account of "general expediency" and, in particular, to uphold the independence of the judiciary.

'By March 1874, Phillips J had clearly tired of Natal, and returned to England to attempt to secure promotion to another position. Until his official retirement nearly six years later, Phillips J spent little more than two years in the Colony. During this time, he conducted a range of missions in scattered parts of the British Empire, all the while retaining his office (and pension claims) in Natal. This caused much resentment amongst local colonists, who castigated the judge who had "humbugged the Colony completely and used it simply as a convenience" (*Natal Witness* 22 November 1879). He resigned from Natal in January 1880, ostensibly on account of grave medical disorders, though he died nearly seventeen years later in England.'

—Peter Spiller *A History of the District and Supreme Courts of Natal 1846–1910* (1986) 43–4. (Most of the omitted footnotes cite Natal newspapers.)

Arthur Walker, Dublin-born, was a cool, fluent and fearless Natal legal practitioner, and fairly competent despite his complete lack of legal training. That is the background to the following exchange of pleasantries.

'Once, when Phillips J abruptly interrupted an address of Walker with the comment, "We shall never have good law in the place until the Legislature gives us better lawyers", Walker's prompt reply was, "Does your Lordship mean at the Bar or at the Bench?" (*Natal Witness* 23/11/1869).'

—Peter Robert Spiller *The Natal Supreme Court: Its Origins (1846–1858) and Its Early Development (1858–1874)* (unpublished PhD thesis University of Natal 1982) 225.

'Significantly, only one publication in Natal reported his death in 1896, and this newspaper simply stated:

"London, Tuesday—Sir Henry Lushington Phillips, formerly a Judge of Natal, is dead."
(*Natal Witness* 12/12/1896.)'

—Spiller op cit at 185.

'That Mr Justice Siva [Phillips] is young in years, as well as junior in order, is, of course, not to be charged so much to his account as to that of those who caused his premature apotheosis. The consequence of this immaturity, however, is, that the fervour of youth, not being tempered by the snows of age, is too apt, by its incandescence (like the internal fires of the geologist), to occasion *faults* in the strata of his judgments, rather than symmetry in their "salient points"; for the impetuosity of his decisions causes them too often to break through, and dislocate, rather than to be insinuated into a conformity with the facts of the case. And again, being so dependent upon the passing impulse of the moment, there is a noticeable incongruity between his sentences, as delivered at different times, and the consideration of persons, rather than of principles, too frequently evinces the presence, in his godship, of the mortal passions of friendship and dislike.

'Another result, also, of youthful years and sanguine temperament, is to be found in his disregard of the lesson conveyed by the fact that, among the ancients, the symposium and the stadium were not usually to be found in close juxtaposition with the forum. However grateful may be the incense of popular applause, and the noisy cheers of a public banquet, these do not invariably tend to increase the respect of the adorers for the same object when seated on the tribunal; nor does an excellent judge of horses always make the best judge of men.

'Bland and polished in company, our deity is apt to be *brusque* and smutty on the bench; and while his views and ideas appear to result rather from unregulated feeling, than from any amount of scholarly knowledge of jurisprudence or abstract reasoning from data, a personal *animus* is often ill-concealed, and has sometimes been sufficiently conspicuous to be made a subject of open discussion. On the whole it may be said that this god appears to advantage in the parlour, still more so in the tavern, and least of all in the curule chair.'

—Thomas Phipson (under the pseudonym of 'Clio') in the *Natal Witness* 14 August 1863, reprinted in R N Currey *Letters and Other Writings of a Natal Sheriff: Thomas Phipson 1815–76* (1968) 96–7.

'About fifteen years ago, a Mr Krogh, a Dutch lawyer, who had been regularly educated at Universities in Holland and at Edinburgh, came here; and subsequently made a motion of an address to the Supreme Court, to much the same effect as your present remarks; proposing that a competent knowledge of Latin should form part of the examination on the admission of future candidates to either bar. . . .

'In reference to Mr Krogh's proposal, Mr Justice Phillips seemed to think that it was quite as easy for a Judge in Natal to get on without Latin as the Dutch Professor in the *Vicar of Wakefield* thought it was for him to do without Greek; and openly declared from the Bench that the only preparation he himself ever had for passing as a barrister in England was the "eating of a certain number of very bad dinners, and paying for them a very high price," and, as Mr Justice Connor was then (as he is still) the only competent Latin scholar on the Bench, it was no wonder that Mr Krogh's suggestion was very summarily and somewhat scornfully rejected.'

— Thomas Phipson in a letter published in the *Natal Witness* 17 March 1876, reprinted op cit 210–11.

OSWALD PIROW

1890–1959. Advocate and politician. Member of the Pretoria Bar 1914–29, 1939–59. KC 1924. MP 1924–9. Senator 1929. MP 1929–39. Minister of Justice 1929–33. Minister of Railways and Harbours and of Defence 1933–9. Leader of the National Socialist New Order 1940–5. Novelist and biographer.

'Mr. Pirow, the Minister of Railways with Harbours thrown in, once went buck shooting around Bloemfontein. When Pirow shoots, he shoots successfully. In due course, he arrived at the station with a buck, whereupon there was a rush of porters to secure this ministerial prize. The man who captured him was told that Mr. Pirow wanted the buck to travel by the same train as himself to Pretoria, so off they went to the department where these things are arranged. Here they found a moon-faced gentleman with large round spectacles filling in a form. The porter wasted no time. He said: "Mr. Pirow, the Minister of Railways, is here. He wants this buck to travel on the same train with him to Pretoria." Moonface went on writing. The porter repeated the observations but Moonface went on writing without paying any attention. The porter spoke for the third time and he spoke sternly. Moonface went on filling in the form and whilst doing so he said: "Mister . . . Pirow . . . the Minister . . . of Railways . . . must wait . . . like everyone . . . . else." Not until he had completely filled in that form and checked it did the buck receive attention. Pirow told me that he wanted to promote that clerk on the spot but the regulations did not allow of it.'

—H H Morris QC *In My Anecdotage* (1953) 19–20.

'Bloemfontein went off all right—judgment reserved. Rosenberg [qv] and I were persuaded to go for a walk with Pirow. He is, it seems, a notorious road devourer. At length we got back to the club after about an hour and a half, having covered, according to my estimate, twelve miles, according to Rosenberg's fifteen.'

—Oliver Deneys Schreiner (qv) in a letter to his wife Edna, 3 May 1922. Schreiner family papers.

'Toe Adv Oswald Pirow besluit het om af te tree het hy 'n junior nader geroep, hom meegedeel dat hy sy hele biblioteek aan hom skenk, op en af gestap in die kamer en uiteindelik die enkele boek wat daar was, aan hom oorhandig. Dit was 1918 JDR. In die boek het die letters AD verskyn en op navraag wat dit beteken het hy gesê dit staan vir Adolf Davis, "But don't let that worry you".

'Op 'n dag is Oswald Pirow deur 'n bekommerde junior wat nie gelukkig was met die stand van hul voorbereiding van die saak nie, in die hof gevra of hulle reg is vir die saak. Sy antwoord was: "Moet jou nie bekommer nie, sien jy daardie man daarbo (verwysende na die regter), ek het hom aangestel."

'Daar word vertel dat 'n prokureur Pirow na afloop van 'n verskyning gevra het wat sy fooi sal wees. Hy het meegedeel dat sy kliënte bekommerd is en graag wil weet. Pirow se antwoord was "My boy, you insert the digit, I will add the nought."'

—*1877–1977 The Pretoria Bar/Die Pretoriase Balie* (1977) 51. ('JDR' stands for Juta's Daily Reporter. Reports of the Cape Provincial Division. Published in 1916–25. Very seldom cited. Adolf Davis KC was also a member of the Pretoria Bar. On Pirow and the *Nafte* trial, see SAUL SOLOMON.)

'In my beginjaar aan die Pretoriase Balie was een van ons groot geeste wyle Oswald Pirow. Hy was 'n gedugte verhooradvokaat en 'n man met 'n baie deeglike mensekennis. In verband met 'n nuwe aanstelling op die regbank moes ons telkens hoor hoe die oubaas sê: "Never mind, chaps. Give him twelve months and he will be quite confident that he was appointed on his merits."'

—The Hon Mr Justice G G Hoexter at the National Bar Conference 7–8 April 1988. (See the record of the Conference page 199.) (See also ROOS.)

WILLIAM PITTMAN

1878–1964. Member of the Cape Bar 1904. Member of the Pretoria Bar 1905–25. KC 1924. Judge of the Eastern Districts Local Division 1925–44. Judge President 1944–8. Author of legal works.

In the following extract 'Van der Riet' is a reference to the unpublished autobiography of Mr Justice E F van der Riet.

'He was appointed to the Bench of the Eastern Districts Local Division in 1925, during the early stages of the first Nationalist Government, by Tielman Roos, then Minister of Justice. . . .

'Sadly he got off to an unfortunate start when he arrived in Grahamstown in 1925. Although a member of the Pretoria Bar, he had long been a lecturer at the university in Pretoria and the appointment as judge of one regarded as an academic and an outsider was received with resentment by the Grahamstown Bench and Bar. Their reception of his "importation" was anything but cordial.

'*VAN DER RIET: Soon after his arrival in Grahamstown Pittman drove his car one night up a steep street, Somerset Street, near St Andrew's College, and making a U-turn his car capsized. He broke his jaw and very nearly his neck. In consequence he acquired a pronounced lisp and a jaw not easily controlled. He found it difficult to pronounce the letter "s".*

'This disability made it easy for the wags to mimic him when he said such sentences as, "But the witness says she saw her sister on Thursday." Or, in reply to Counsel's "As your Lordship pleases", his angry retort, "It's not as I please!"

'On one occasion in East London he was presiding over a criminal trial in which a white man was charged with an assault on a black woman in Queen's Park. In his charge to the jury Pittman said, "Well, gentlemen, you have heard what the witnesses say they thought they saw, but I must point out to you that one day perhaps you might find yourself in similar circumstances." The accused was found not guilty.

'Not infrequently in criminal cases when reviewing the evidence to the jury, Pittman would make it very clear which version of the facts he considered they should accept. This he did, not in so many words, but by shaking his head slowly from side to side in disbelief when dealing with one version, or by nodding his head up and down in approval if he preferred the other. Those abundantly clear directions would not, of course, appear from a reading of the record.

'*VAN DER RIET: Pittman introduced to the Eastern Districts the growing cult of a lounge suit and felt hat in place of the morning coat with top hat, out of which a good story is told. In those days all the witnesses for all the cases due at a circuit town were subpoenaed for the first day of the sessions, and at Umtata in the Transkei the native witnesses all congregated in the courtyard behind the Court. At a certain session Gane was the judge, and to reach the robing room he had to walk through this courtyard. When he arrived, a tall and stately figure in a top hat, all the police and witnesses were called to attention. A witness in the case of Rex v A was duly impressed and asked his neighbour who the imposing man was, and he was told it was the judge. For some reason or other the case had to be postponed, so the witnesses were again present for the following circuit. Again they were called to attention as a little man in a lounge suit and felt hat walked through the courtyard. The same witness turned to his neighbour and asked "Who is that?" and he was told it was the judge. "But," he said, "you told me the big man in the tall hat was the judge." "Yes," said his neighbour, "but this is the Government's judge."*'

—George Randell *Bench and Bar of the Eastern Cape* (1985) 44–6.

'The story is told that Judge Percy Gane, shortly after his retirement, was called to give evidence before Judge Pittman in an important civil trial. Pittman sarcastically asked, presumably in retaliation for past hurts, "Well, Mr Gane, and what do *you* do?"'

—Randell op cit at 46.

'*Big Fred*' *refers to Frederick Barry van der Riet (qv), who practised at the Eastern Districts Bar from 1910 until his death in July 1955. He specialized in criminal trials before a jury. Most of his work was on circuit. A character.*

'Big Fred was his nickname and he was big in many ways. He had powerful shoulders and a strong neck and he towered above the average man. Kind hearted, generous, a bit blustery, but as straight as a die. He never pretended to be very learned in the law, but he was very definitely one of the great personalities of the Bar. . . .

'Tales are told of Fred's tussles with the Bench when Mr Justice Pittman was presiding—the two very different in temperament and physique. In a case during the last circuit before Pittman retired he is said to have interrupted van der Riet's flow of oratory to the jury. "No, no, Mr van der Riet. The witness did *not* say that." Fred was infuriated, gathered up his papers, making a great show, and roared, "For umpteen years your Lordship has been interfering with my addresses to the jury. I can't stand it any longer!" "For umpteen years, Mr van der

Riet, you have been misquoting the evidence and *I* can't stand it any longer!" No one knows quite what happened next but the Bar common-room has it that Billy and Fred were toasting each other with conviviality later that evening at the Judge's retiring party.'

— Randell op cit at 130, 133.

WALTER POLLAK

1903–71. Member of the Johannesburg Bar 1927–60. KC 1945. Member of the London Bar 1960–5.

'The following year [1928] Walter Pollak joined the part-time staff [of the Department of Law of the University of the Witwatersrand]. He was endowed with remarkable mental gifts. After gaining an MA with distinction in Classics from the University, he went up to Cambridge, where he took a first class in Parts I and II of the Law Tripos. From there he proceeded to Harvard, where he obtained the doctoral degree of SJD. A very modest person, he never allowed himself to be called "doctor". In 1928, aged 25, he commenced lecturing in constitutional law and the conflict of laws for our LLB, giving up these courses only in the mid-forties, after he had taken silk. The standards Walter Pollak set were exacting, and in the first year of his lecturing the mortality rate in his examinations was very heavy. Subsequent classes realized that the good old days had gone, and most students managed to cope. An impression of what he expected can be gathered from the story he told me of his examining constitutional law for the Public Service Higher Law Examination, a government examination. His co-examiner was Dr Manfred Nathan. A typical result was Nathan's giving a student 75 per cent, and Pollak 25 per cent, the average being 50 per cent—a pass.

'Pollak was a tall, heavy, deliberate-moving, slow-speaking and quick-thinking man. His even-paced and attractively pitched but somewhat monotonous voice was ideal in court, but not in the lecture room. In part of the course in the conflict of laws he simply read from his excellent book which was prescribed, *The South African Law of Jurisdiction*, and could not understand why the attendance of the class diminished, leaving only a handful left, including myself. He loved the Faculty of Law, on the board of which he served from 1932 until his ill-fated decision in 1960 to leave the country to go to the English Bar. It was a desperate hazard that he played—and he lost. . . .'

—Ellison Kahn *The Tablets of Memory* (1986) 7–8.

'Pollak's invariable last sentence in his last lecture for the year to conclude his courses in constitutional law and the conflict of laws was: "This course starts again in February next year."'

— Ellison Kahn's commonplace book.

'A retired judge of appeal recalls Pollak's clearness of thought, his sharpness of intellect, his carefully prepared arguments, analysed out in a simple set of propositions, not puffed out with padding, with nothing on the fringes, never wandering up side streets, always intellectually honest. His oral presentation was unhurried, unrepetitious, moving in logical sequence step by step to its conclusion. That same learned judge reflects with amusement on an occasion when the leader of the other side was one whose qualities were the very reverse, whose argument was so convoluted and confused that the court asked Pollak to explain what it really was, which Pollak for a while good-humouredly proceeded to do until, with grace, he submitted that this really was not his function.

'In his chamber work Pollak was renowned for the shortness of his opinions. Rarely did they run to more than three pages; and often they amounted to less than one page. Yet they were as thorough as the rest of his work. It was an experience to witness that agile brain in operation, to see the way in which it coped with the most complex problem, the contrast between the speed of that marvellous instrument and the slow, almost ponderous movements of Pollak consulting the law reports, statutes and textbooks housed in his magnificent library in that large room on the north-west corner of an upper floor in the advocates' chambers in His Majesty's Buildings.'

— Ellison Kahn 'In Memoriam: Walter Pollak QC' (1971) 88 *SALJ* 280 at 282.

'Let us pause to remember the essential humanity of the man behind the outward mask of impassivity. Those of us who were his students will cast our minds back with a fond smile to his odd conceits, such as his then affectation of a cloth cap, possibly because he could not buy a hat large enough for his head, and his few but firm dislikes, particularly of draughts, which we religiously created for his benefit in the old law library where he lectured by opening all the windows, causing a few minutes' delay while imperturbably he closed them. Many of his colleagues bear memories of closed car windows and sealed railway carriages. There will be those, like myself, who, when they doubt their abilities, will take courage from the reflection that there were times when they met up to the exacting standards of a man such as Walter Pollak. And there will be so many who will ever remember what he did for them, as I remember what he did for me.'

—Kahn op cit at 287.

'In a case involving the *contra fiscum* rule Walter Pollak KC was arguing that the rule applied. Schreiner JA made the observation that it could operate for and against the taxpayer, according to the circumstances; it was six of the one and half a dozen of the other, in fact a "toss-up". To which Pollak replied: "Whatever your lordships may do in the privacy of your chambers, in open court one has to give reasons!"'

—Ellison Kahn in *Fiat Iustitia: Essays in Memory of Oliver Deneys Schreiner* (1983) 34, referring to D Meyerowitz in (1971) 88 *SALJ* 532.

'Walter once told me that if he had his life over again he would not spend it once more advising wealthy men how to avoid paying the income tax they ought morally to pay.'

—From Ellison Kahn's commonplace book.

'Walter Pollak was lunching at the Middle Temple, five years after he had joined the London Bar. A man sat down beside him and started conversing with him. Pollak: "You are the first Englishman who has spoken to me for five years." "I am not an Englishman. I am a Scotsman."'

—Ellison Kahn's commonplace book 1 April 1988.

WILLIAM PORTER

1805–1880. Member of the Irish Bar 1831–8. Member of the Cape Bar 1839–66. Attorney-General (member of the Executive Council) of the Cape 1839–66. Member of the Cape House of Assembly 1869–73. CMG 1872.

'Of Mr. William Porter, in the later years, before he retired to England, I saw much. He lived at Rosebank, and every morning took the same train as I did, to Cape Town. He was a very tall man of impressive appearance; he had the same burning eyes as Bishop Grey, but a good deal wrinkled, and a full beard then turning white. He was generally accompanied by his *fidus Achates*, Mr Hugh Lynar, a stout, stumpy man, who usually carried the tiffin basket and followed in his grey alpaca coat, a long way behind the long-striding Attorney-General. Mr Lynar was an excitable man and often had high words with the stationmaster at Rosebank over some disputed railway charge. After he had loudly vowed he would never pay it, and retired in great dudgeon up the station platform, Mr Porter would come silently up to the ticket office and pay whatever there was to pay. William Porter has always been considered one of the greatest of South Africa's orators and lawyers. I think his delivery, his splendid presence, his fine figure— swaying slightly as he rolled out his telling periods—contributed to give his words an added eloquence. He spoke with great deliberation, and never, if I may use the expression, altered his pace, though he would give added volume to his voice to mark his emphasis, and fire to drive home his point. The last time I heard him speak was at a lecture by some noted traveller or missionary and the cheering when he had finished was a regular storm of applause. As a lawyer, Mr. Porter had a very high reputation, but it is not easy to judge from the Supreme Court reports how he would have compared with, say, Leonard or Lord de Villiers. Judge Cole told me that Porter believed in Leyser as de Villiers did in Voet.'

WILLIAM PORTER
From a photograph in the Cape Monthly Magazine
January–June 1859

—Victor Sampson *My Reminiscences* (1926) 35–6.

'Porter seems to have been an outstanding character. On a number of occasions he stood up to the Governor on controversial matters, and endeared himself to the people on one occasion when he stated "The Queen sent me here to prosecute and not to persecute".'

—R M MacSymon *Fairbridge Arderne & Lawton: A History of a Cape Law Firm* (1990) 48.

ROBERT JOSEPH POTHIER

1699–72. Professor of Law, University of Orleans. Great jurist. Often cited by writers on Roman-Dutch law.

'While the first volume of the Pandects was printing, Pothier fell dangerously ill; upon returning from a visit to one of his colleagues at Sologne, he came home on horseback with a fever. He had never before been ill; for although of a feeble temperament, he had preserved his health by regularity. The fever was to him a new and unknown visitation; he struggled against it for some days without knowing what it was; and then instead of sending for his physician he went out to consult him, and ask him what was the cause of the indisposition which he suffered.

'The physician immediately perceived what it was, and directed him to return home and go to bed. The illness became very serious, and his life was despaired of.

'Happily the disorder was overcome; but his recovery was not complete: he was deprived of the use of his limbs, and submitted with great composure to this privation which continued so long, that it was apprehended it would never be removed. He felicitated himself in having preserved the power of diligence and application. He appropriated a greater portion of his time to study, which the sedentary life that he was obliged to lead gave him a greater liberty of doing, and had given up the hopes of ever recovering the use of his limbs, after having tried several remedies without effect, when it was conceived that his power of walking might be prevented not so much by any absolute defect as by long disuse; he was advised to endeavour to walk by the assistance of two pullies, fixed in a groove attached to the beam of his chamber, which held him by the arms and allowed him to move his limbs, without their having to bear the weight of his body. He submitted to this attempt, and by degrees recovered the use of his legs which only retained a degree of stiffness. He had been a great walker before his illness. He afterwards walked sufficiently from necessity, for the further he advanced in age the more his occupations multiplied, so as to preclude any remission. When he was pressed to take exercise, he answered that he had sufficient in passing between his own house and the court. . . .

'Pothier had never any ground of complaint from the passions of himself or others. Nothing disturbed the tranquillity of his mind, no adventitious circumstances deranged the plan and uniformity of his life. Nothing occurred to give him pain except the loss of his friends, to whom he was attached with great sincerity.

'Perfectly free from all pecuniary anxiety, he consecrated the whole of his life to his functions, and the study of jurisprudence; he had no other duties to fulfil, nor any other inclination to gratify.

'He never had the smallest disposition to marry. He said that he had not sufficient courage for it, and that he admired those who had.

'Celibacy is doubtless the best and wisest course for a man frugal of his time, exclusively devoted to study, and peculiarly anxious for tranquillity. This condition separates him from the generality of mankind, it secures him from many evils, and, by limiting the objects of his attachment, relieves him from the principal sources of anxiety.

'No person ever availed himself of this advantage more than Pothier; he wished to enjoy it in its full extent, and thought himself excused from all attention to domestic affairs. His negligence in this respect would have been culpable in the head of a family. The fault in him became respectable from the motive which occasioned it. It originated from a sincere disregard for affluence, and a most disinterested character of mind. He, however, saw only the negligence that was produced by this sentiment, and reproached himself for it in the society of his friends. . . .

'No person was more assiduous in his attendance at the court; and he never omitted his lectures. Upon retiring to his study, he examined the procedures on which he was to report; received visits which are often made without any necessity, with a patience very uncommon in a person so much engaged; he gave advice and answered letters, the number of which increased as his reputation extended: how many contests has he prevented by the prudence of his counsel! how many family contests has he terminated by an amicable arrangement! the confidence of the public rendered him a voluntary tribunal.

'Although he devoted a large portion of the day to employment, it was often fully occupied without admitting any parts of it to be allotted to composition. He had a talent of leaving an employment and resuming it with equal facility. He always quitted it without fatigue; because his moderation extended even to his studies, which he never continued during the night. His supper, which he took at seven, closed the labours of the day. This plan was only deviated from on Wednesdays, when he deferred the hour of supper until eight; on account of a conference which he had with all the young magistrates, and with several advocates, whose pride it was to have been and to continue his pupils. These conferences were continued without interruption for more than forty years. . . .'

—'Eloge of M. Pothier, pronounced upon his decease, in the University of Orleans by M. Le Trosne, the King's Advocate, in the Presidial of Orleans' in *A Treatise on the Law of Obligations or Contracts by M. Pothier* translated by William David Evans (1802).

'R. J. Pothier (1699–1772), professor at the University of Orléans and counsellor to the Inferior Court of that town, was a true sage, a lay saint. His biographers show him to us as modest, disinterested, obliging, and charitable, fulfilling his double duties with a conscientiousness rarely seen, at work from four o'clock in the morning to nine at night, without any sort of recreation or social diversions. . . . His life is summed up in his works. These extensive writings . . . extraordinarily simplified the work to be done by the framers of the Civil Code; it has been said of them that they were an advance Commentary upon the Code. Still, Pothier had neither the originality nor the genius of Cujas and Dumoulin; it is as a popularizer that he has no equal.'

—*A General Survey of Events, Sources. Persons and Movements in Continental Legal History* (1912) Part III Ch II § 31 (by Jean Brissaud).

NORMAN CLEMENT BOLD PRICE

1887–1970. Attorney 1908–22. Member of the Pretoria Bar 1923–36. Member of the Johannesburg Bar 1936–45. KC 1938. Judge of the Transvaal Provincial Division 1945–55. Judge President of the Eastern Districts Local Division 1955–7.

'Counsel, pleading in mitigation of sentence for the accused found guilty on a charge of unlawful sexual intercourse across the colour line: "The accused did his best, but, alas, he gave way to temptation."

'Price J: "Considering what he had in his pocket, he anticipated if, indeed, he did not welcome it." '

—Ellison Kahn's commonplace book.

WILLIAM HENRY RAMSBOTTOM

1894–1960. Member of the Johannesburg Bar 1921–38. KC 1935. Judge of the Transvaal Provincial Division 1938–59. Judge of Appeal 1959–60.

'With complete integrity and independence of mind he devoted his energies, unstintingly and without regard for himself, to the unswerving pursuit of what is just and good, to the *ars aequi atque boni*, which all of us strive to serve. It is by reason of these qualities that his passing, more particularly in this Court, leaves a sense of enduring loss.

'As a man he was one of those who are accompanied by the respect and affection of their fellow-men wherever they go and whatever they do. The world is not so generous, and not so ready to forgive, as to render these things to those who do not deserve them. He did deserve them. He deserved them by the personal and judicial integrity, which was a constant and an open part, indeed almost a visible part, of the man himself; by the dedicated conscientious service so conspicuously demonstrated in every task he performed; by the attitude of sympathetic understanding so manifest in his regard for the convictions, sentiments and interests of others; by the instinctively high standards of conduct which made him a dependable guide for those who sought his advice in any personal problem; and by the modest and courteous friendliness so obviously characteristic of word and gesture. His personality proclaimed these things in a manner which left no room for misapprehension.

'In one of the works of Thomas Hardy I once found a very brief, a very simple, but a very expressive description of a man, in these words: "He was a good man and he did good things." When I think of William Ramsbottom, I shall think of those words, and I am sure, so will all of us.'

— From the address of the Chief Justice, Mr Justice L C Steyn, on 2 December 1960, in a tribute to the memory of the late Mr Justice Ramsbottom. The address is reproduced in (1961) 78 *SALJ* 4–6.

'Silk came in September, 1935, and three years later, on the sudden death of Mr Justice Ivan Curlewis, the offer of a seat on the Bench. Though he had had but little time to reap the rewards of a senior's practice following years of unremitting work, characteristically Ramsbottom K.C. answered what he felt was the call of public duty.

'Then followed those years of judicial service that have been such a source of pride and inspiration to his colleagues and the profession. Every inch a judge in looks and comportment, with what infinite patience he would explore all possible relevant facts; with what care he would address a jury in a criminal trial, summarizing the evidence and the various points made by counsel, guiding the members of the jury in language framed to help them understand such mysteries of law as the degree of proof required and the nature and value of direct and circumstantial evidence; with what courtesy he would treat witnesses and counsel. And withal there was that inner humility that comes from true nobility of spirit; that recognizes the infinitude of human problems and man's innate inability, no matter how well he be endowed with intellect and experience, to deal with them infallibly.'

— Ellison Kahn 'The Late Mr Justice W. H. Ramsbottom' (1961) 78 *SALJ* 1 at 2.

'This story reminds me of that very fine Judge, whose death nearly two years ago was so widely lamented—Hal Ramsbottom. He was slow, meticulous and sound. Often on Circuit he would sit to very late hours. At a Bar dinner in Pretoria, one of those occasions where the wits exercise their talents upon the Judges, a speaker was heard to say: "It is quite wrong to accuse dear Rammy of sitting for unduly long hours; he has frequently been known to adjourn his Court for breakfast!".'

— Leslie Blackwell (q v) *Are Judges Human?* (1962) 19–20.

'Towards the end of the war a possible opportunity of getting out of unexacting judicial work and into an entirely new field unexpectedly presented itself to me. The Principal of the Natal University College was due to retire shortly and a group of interested people approached me with the suggestion that I should allow my name to be put up for the appointment. In my restless state this suggestion appealed to me enormously. . . .

'I found the prospect of entering this new field most attractive. Here was work to be done which seemed infinitely more valuable and rewarding than hearing tiresome criminal appeals and matrimonial cases. Financially I would be very much worse off and I would have to retire long before I reached the judge's age limit. But what did that matter if I could devote my vigorous years to work that seemed so absorbing? I had almost decided to allow my name to go forward when I had a talk with Ramsbottom who was then a judge in the Transvaal. I had first met him as an opponent at the Bar, and during my period of service on the Transvaal Bench I had got to know him well and had fallen under the spell of his lovable personality. Notwithstanding his high ability promotion to the Appellate Division was denied him for years, and when at last it came the sands of his life were fast running out. When I told him about the change I had in mind he was aghast. When a man is appointed to the Bench, he said, he must regard himself as out of the running for appointment in any other field. In the case of a national emergency it might be different, but generally a judge must regard the Bench as the last phase of his career. The public must be given no reason to suppose that a judge is on the Bench only for the time being and until something better turns up. If I left the Bench, he said, I would be doing a thing which might to some extent undermine the independence and prestige of the Courts. I could not ignore the weight of these considerations, particularly when he quoted something that Innes had said on the subject, so I reluctantly withdrew my name.'

—F N Broome *Not the Whole Truth* (1962) 194–5. (Francis Napier (Frank) Broome (1891–1980) was a judge of the Natal Provincial Division from 1939 to 1950, and thereafter Judge President until his retirement in 1961.) (See also KRAUSE.)

TIELMAN JOHANNES DE VILLIERS ROOS

1879–1935. Member of the Pretoria Bar 1903–24. KC 1922. MP 1915–29. Minister of Justice 1924–9. Judge of Appeal 1929–32.

'*Mr. Tielman Roos meditating on G. K. Chesterton's statement that caricatures of celebrities may produce glorious beings so much better than themselves.*'

'*Mnr. Tielman Roos peins oor die gesegde van G. K. Chesterton dat spotprente van vermaardhede skitterende wesens kan voortbring so veel beter as hulleself.*'

Caricature by 'Quip' (Edgar Arnold Packer 1892–1932) from his Tielman (1925) 57

' . . . General Hertzog's Transvaal lieutenant Tielman Johannes de Villiers Roos . . . was born in the Cape and qualified there as an advocate but soon came to Pretoria where legal prospects were bright. He was easily the keenest intellect of his time and if his industry had been even normal he would have outstripped all opposition anywhere in the country. As it was he worked up a very substantial practice and is still remembered at the Bar for his outstanding legal strategy. In fact, I remember how one of his habitual opponents who knew twice as much law as Tielman, regularly got the jitters before going to Court because, as he confided to me once when I was his junior, "you never know what rabbit he is going to pull out of the hat". As a matter of fact his apprehensions were not unfounded. I remember one case in particular where he and Tielman were on opposite sides and where he left Court not quite sure whether he was on his head or his heels. Roos was for the Plaintiff in a malicious prosecution case.

'This type of action depends on proof that the Defendant set the law in motion and invariably the police, in the public interest, refuse to disclose the statement which led to the prosecution in question. In this instance, soon after opening his case Tielman presented an argument on onus of proof which was at best doubtful. The Court listened politely, because even his indifferent arguments were always interesting. Just as he got to the core of the question he told the Court the matter could stand over until his first witness had been called and put the police sergeant to whom the Defendant was supposed to have made the incriminating statement into the box. A straight request for the document would have met with an uncompromising refusal which the Court would have upheld, so Tielman started something else. He returned to the argument of onus and in the midst of it suddenly turned to the sergeant: "Just hand me that statement, will you. It will illustrate my point." Taken completely off his guard the policeman complied and the document was in the hands of the registrar before anybody except Tielman knew what had happened.

'The statement was in fact a series of unfounded and malicious accusations and the Plaintiff obtained heavy damages. I am not sure what would have happened if the case had gone on appeal, but in fact the Defendant paid up while the whole of the Pretoria Bar chuckled.

'In his political manoeuvres he was just as unpredictable as in Court, with this difference in his favour that the voters were much less critical than the Supreme Court Judges. . . .

'He was a man of magnetic personality with an unlimited gift for friendship.

Absolutely incorruptible and unselfish, he had the weird conviction that nothing could contaminate him. The result was a succession of friendships with people who were at best doubtful characters. In the end they were the cause of his downfall and a man who would most certainly have been a Prime Minister is to-day forgotten by all but a handful. His career was one of the most brilliant but also one of the most tragic of our political history. . . .

'Until I joined the Cabinet in June 1929 my primary loyalty had belonged to Tielman Roos. He was not only my best friend but also the political leader whom I had followed through thick and thin since 1913. When, therefore, General Hertzog told me Tielman had resigned by cable from Germany where he was undergoing bladder treatment, and offered me his portfolio I asked for leave to get into touch with him. I wired him as follows: "General Hertzog has invited me to join the Cabinet and take over Department of Justice. Will only do so if you approve and if you are financially provided for." By return I received the reply "I want you to accept".

'It is characteristic of General Hertzog that he allowed me to consult Tielman. He was offering a young man of thirty-eight years an outstanding honour and was asked to allow him to consult the former Minister—with whom . . . the Prime Minister was not on the best of terms—as to whether or not he should accept this offer. But General Hertzog could appreciate loyalty even when it was not directed to himself and my request, as I subsequently ascertained, did me more good than harm. In fact, it probably laid the foundation for our relationship which over the next thirteen and a half years became almost that of father and son. . . .

'When I cabled to Tielman after General Hertzog had offered me his portfolio, I had been concerned about his financial position. He had had a large and lucrative practice at the Bar but he was so good-natured that he was always helping some lame dog and more than one that just pretended to be incapacitated. While he was at Cape Town during the Parliamentary Session I had to make the rounds of the attorneys who had briefed him. In some cases I had to ask for his fees even before they were due. As his ministerial salary was about half of his earnings as a silk I did not expect him to have anything put by at the time of his resignation. Fortunately there was a vacancy on the Bench of the Appeal Court and immediately after his return I had the privilege of appointing him to the Appellate Division.

'It was a tribute to his unusual popularity that his elevation to our highest Bench met with universal approval although my action in appointing—only some months before—Mr. F. W. Beyers, the Minister of Mines, to an earlier vacancy in the Appeal Court had evoked a chorus of disapproval from the Bar. Resolutions were passed at the time demanding that in future no such appointments be made except from the ranks of the various Provincial Divisions of the Supreme Court.'

—Oswald Pirow *James Barry Munnik Hertzog* (1957) 75, 76, 77, 136, 139, 140. (Pirow went grievously wrong in stating that Beyers had been appointed to the Appellate Division before Roos. He was appointed three years after Roos. Furthermore, strictly speaking, Pirow as Minister of Justice could not appoint a judge—only the Cabinet could.)

TIELMAN ROOS
Caricature by D C Boonzaier
(1865–1950)

The barmaid

'Mr. Justice Tielman Roos was not on the Bench for long. I appeared before him once only. But I knew Tielman—that unforgettable character—a man of infinite charm—always smiling—ever ready to do a good turn—admired and loved by all who knew him. He was a fine lawyer. He never contradicted a judge, but he had his way in the end. The political imp. Inventor of "Secession" and the "Black Peril". His friendship paid dividends. He was a nepotist of the first order. He promoted his friends but did nothing for himself. He was the most unselfish of men. I have said that he was always ready to do a good turn.

'It was in 1928; the new Liquor Law was being debated. We were in the bar of the Queen's Hotel doing so. I was holding up the counter. Tielman was chatting to the lady on the other side.

'"How long have you been in the trade?" said he.

'"Only a year," said she.

'We had another and then Tielman went back to his room.

'A section of the Act protected the rights of barmaids who had been in the trade for two years or more. He promptly altered the draft to read one year.'

—H H Morris KC *The First Forty Years* (1948) 53–4.

' . . . [H]e was extremely sensitive; as Minister of Justice it was not easy for him . . . to recommend to the executive council that a sentence of death be confirmed.'

—W A Kleynhans in *Dictionary of South African Biography* I (1968) 681. (See also CARTER; WAIFS AND STRAYS sv 'Accused'.)

Vague and embarrassing

'The late Mr. Justice Stratford, Chief Justice of the Appellate Division, and the late Mr. Tielman Roos, also a Judge of the Appellate Division, when they were at the Bar frequently met in mortal combat. There came the time when Tielman was briefed by a Plaintiff to conduct certain proceedings in the Supreme Court, and so he set about drawing, what is called, a declaration. This is a document which is designed succinctly to give the other side an idea of the Plaintiff's case. The drawing of the document in this case was by no means an easy matter for reasons which we need not go into. The task of replying to this declaration was entrusted by the Defendant to Mr. James Stratford. He gave it one look—smote his head and said, "Good God, what is Tielman talking about?" Then he drew his reply. The burden of his song was that the declaration was vague and embarrassing—meaning that it was so badly drawn that no one could understand what it was about. At last the parties got into Court and here they argued for four hours as to whether it was a good declaration or an embarrassing one. Stratford maintained that this document could only be likened to a pool of mud and he never ceased emphasizing the point that it was the most embarrassing declaration he had ever seen. Tielman said it was a perfectly lucid and transparent document that would embarrass no one who had the slightest smattering of the English

language. At length the Court decided, perhaps wrongly, for Stratford was rarely at fault, that the declaration was a good one. As they walked into the robing room Stratford said: "But Tielman, why did you draw your declaration in that way?" "Oh, only to embarrass you, " said Tielman.'

—H H Morris QC *In My Anecdotage* (1953) 18–19. Eric Morris SC in his *Technique in Litigation* 3 ed (1985) 61n8 wrote that his father was 'referring, no doubt, with "poetic" licence, to *SA Railways & Harbours v Landau & Co* 1917 TPD 485'.

'I remember other clear instances of his irrepressibility. Once he arrived at Court to find his opponent, a great advocate well worthy of his steel, with a row of legal authorities lined up in front of him. Tielman, who had no books, quickly left for the Library, returning with about three legal books which he deposited with the cheerful remark, "Well, I must also have something." Whether they were necessary or relevant I was never told. The second remark was induced by the personnel of the particular Bench before which he was to appear. Due to preside was Stratford, a later Chief Justice, whose subtlety was such that many at the Bar referred to him somewhat reverently as "The Master". The other member of the Bench was to be Morice who had qualified in Scotland and who had spent some time in Holland in order to prepare himself for practice in this country. Morice was not without legal ability but was far from being a fluent speaker, indeed he was a very halting one. On entering Roos asked me what Bench he was due to have, whereupon I told him. Without a moment's hesitation he said, "But why these two? I can't follow the one and the other can't follow me".'

—The Hon C P Bresler *Tilt the Sack* (1965) 119–20.

'Mr Tielman Roos, not only on the platform, but in private, was always full of humour. I recall an occasion when I was with Mr Roos and a pompous individual was introduced to us. Roos was not greatly impressed, whereupon the individual drew himself up and said: "I am a Justice of the Peace, who are you?" To which Roos instantaneously replied: "I am the bloody fool who appointed you."'

—Morris Kentridge (qv) *I Recall: Memoirs of Morris Kentridge* (1959) 142. (Mr Kentridge was speaking of the

TIELMAN ROOS
Caricature by 'Quip' (Edgar Arnold Packer 1892–1932) from his Tielman *(1925) title-page, 50 and 56*

days when he was a front-bencher MP and Roos was the Minister of Justice.)

Another version

"'n Gebore Kapenaar uit Oranjezicht het hy vroeg na Transvaal getrek en vir daardie land en sy mense 'n hartstogtelike liefde ontwikkel. Die gesette figuur met die swart snor en helder blou oë was vanweë sy rondreise en vergaderings dwarsdeur Transvaal bekend. Sy geliefkoosde plek was altyd Pretoria en veral die ou Turkstrakoffiehuis wat 'n gemoedelike atmosfeer had. As mens hom soek en hy is nie in die hof of sy advokatekamer to vind nie, hoef mens selde verder as Turkstras te gegaan het. Daar was hy gewoonlik in 'n geselskap van ou vriende of aanhangers. Ook soms van politieke teenstanders; advokate, boere, besigheidsmanne, Afrikaanssprekend, Engelssprekend, Jode. . . . Tielman het die mens geneem soos hy hom vind en nie allerhande pale en perke gestel nie. Dikwels was die gesprek ernstig en die gesigte om hom bekommerd. Maar Tielman was steeds joviaal en skertsend; 'n soort robuuste Laggende Kavalier te midde van probleme en gevare. Trouens, vir diegene wat hom nie intiem geken het nie was hy meestal die hardslaande politikus of die spotvoël. Slegs 'n kleiner kring het geweet watter vrygewige en simpatieke hart onder die siniese dekmantel klop. Van hierdie voorgehoue sinisme kan baie staaltjies vertel word.

'Neem die dag toe hy, kort na sy ampsaanvaarding as Minister van Justisie, in 'n klein Oos-Transvaalse dorpie beland en die plaaslike hotel instap. 'n Groepie mans staan in die hotel en luister met die verskuldigde eerbied na 'n ietwat luidrugtige grootprater wat blykbaar baie met sy eie waardigheid behep is en besig is om die ander te imponeer. Hy sien die vreemdeling met die swart snor en helder blou oë die hotel instap en sê, meer gebiedend as uitnodigend:

"Kom, maak 'n drankie met ons."

"Nee dankie, ek verkies om op my eie te wees."

Die belangrike kêrel was dadelik geaffronteerd en sê vir die vreemdeling: "Meneer, weet u wie ek is?"

Die vreemdeling kyk hom effens aan en sê dat hy geen benul het nie en ook geen besonderbare belang stel nie.

Dit was vir die haan van die dorp te veel en hy stel homself in al sy gekrenktheid voor. "Ek, meneer, is die spesialse vrederegter van hierdie dorp. Wie is u?"

"Wie ek is? Ag, ek is maar net die Minister wat onnosel genoeg was om u tot hierdie amp te benoem," antwoord Tielman—en gaan sy gang.

'Hierdie siniese houding was Tielman eie en hy kon dit nooit afskud nie. Dit kon hom soms in moeilike situasies beland.'

—Dr J F van Rensburg 'Tielman Roos' in *So Onthou Ek (*'n *SAUK-Publikasie*) (1961) 76 at 76–7.

'One day I expressed my surprise to a senior at the Pretoria Bar regarding the appointment of So-and-So to the Bench. "Well," he said, "we all felt sorry for poor So-and-So. He is such a good chap, and for a long time he has had virtually no practice. So we made representations to the Minister of Justice [Roos], and got him put on the Bench."'

—Manfred Nathan *Not Heaven Itself: An Autobiography* (1944) 213. (The identity of the fortunate member of the Pretoria Bar is not difficult to ascertain. Suffice it to say that he was not appointed to the Transvaal Bench.)

'In 1927, eleven years after he [Saul Solomon] returned to the Johannesburg

'TIELMAN J. ROOS, Esq., K.C.'
From (1933) 2 South African Law Times *137*

Bar, at the age of 52 he was elevated to the Transvaal Bench. It was Mr Tielman Roos, the then Minister of Justice, who offered him the judgeship.

'That offer was made by Mr Roos in the most unorthodox manner imaginable. He was the most unconventional Minister of Justice that South Africa has ever had, and was accustomed to doing many things in an unconventional way. When making his offer to Mr Solomon, Mr Roos wrote the following on the back of a used crumpled envelope which had been addressed to him as Minister of Justice:

'"My dear Saul, are you prepared to accept an appointment to the Transvaal Bench? Tielman."

'Saul accepted the offer, and in due course his appointment was officially confirmed by the Cabinet, and gazetted in the usual way.'

—Isaac Goodman *Judges I Have Known* (1969) 156–7.

' . . . Tielman Roos, appointed a judge of appeal on 18 November 1929, . . . left the Bench on 22 December 1932 to return to politics and the Bar. . . .

' . . . The story is told of Tielman Roos, after he had descended from the Appellate Division, appearing before an additional magistrate in a village—let it be called Pampoenfontein—on behalf of an accused on an IDB charge. The judicial officer was overwhelmed. In his judgment he referred to the great honour paid to the court by the appearance before it of so eminent an advocate as the former judge of appeal, whose great reputation was known throughout the country—even in Pampoenfontein.'

—Ellison Kahn 'From Bench to Bar' (1977) 94 *SALJ* 362 at 364–6.

EDWIN RIDGILL ROPER

1885–1974. Member of the Cape Bar 1919–35. MP 1929–33. Member of the Johannesburg Bar 1935–45. KC 1937. Judge of the Transvaal Provincial Division 1945–55. Judge of Appeal of the Court of Appeal of the High Commission Territories 1956–68. President of the Court of Appeal of Botswana 1966–9, of Lesotho 1966–9, and of Swaziland 1968–9.

'At Sarah Gertrude Millin's party Roper told a story. (He is now 74, and acted on the Bench for ten months this year—four on the Transvaal Provincial Division and six in the High Commission Territories.) He said he had avoided a heart attack in an odd way. On the Bench he was listening to a doctor saying "The patient had constriction in the chest and complained of shortness of breath—it is clear that he had angina pectoris". "Good grief", said Roper to himself, "he is describing me." Off Roper went to a physician, who confirmed the diagnosis, ordered him to bed for a long period and placed him on a rigorous diet. Today there is no sign of any heart trouble. So the expert saved him—and, said Roper, he didn't ask for any free advice in return!'

> —Ellison Kahn's commonplace book 29 December 1960.

NORMAN E ROSENBERG

1889–1963. Member of the Johannesburg Bar 1915–63. KC 1935. (His second forename *was* 'E', just as President Harry S Truman's second forename *was* 'S'.)

'Irving Frankel QC and Harry Colman were appearing in a case, with Norman Rosenberg QC leading for the other side. The case was set down for a time just before Frankel was due to go abroad. After the first day Frankel went to Rosenberg and said "I feel I must apologize. I shall have to leave tomorrow in the middle of the case. My junior will carry on. I hope you will not be upset." "It's quite all right", answered Rosenberg, with his celebrated lisp. "I am not at all upset. But my client will be."'

> —Ellison Kahn's commonplace book 17 August 1963. (The late Harry Colman, a close friend of mine, was a very experienced and competent junior.)

'In every profession there is to be found at least one character who will never be forgotten by his contemporaries. —— was such a character. He was highly eccentric. When he was a junior he encountered Norman Rosenberg in the lift of the building where the advocates had their chambers. Rosenberg had then been at the Bar for nearly forty years and was the senior silk. His position at the Johannesburg Bar was still a dominant one. In his deep bass voice and curious accent —— addressed Norman Rosenberg as follows: "I say, Rosenberg, have you ever done an opinion?" Rosenberg, really taken aback for once, replied curtly: "Yes, one or two." ——: "Very tricky, aren't they?"'

> —The Hon Ramon Nigel Leon *Truth in Action* (the reminiscences of the former judge of the Natal Provincial Division, not yet completed or published). (For another story about —, see ETTLINGER.)

'Norman Rosenberg had had a very serious operation. ——, a charming and very concerned colleague, came to see him at the nursing home. He said in his kind and encouraging way, "You look so well, Norman". Rosenberg, with his famous lisp: "You bear my pain with remarkable fortitude."'

> —Ellison Kahn's commonplace book, with thanks to Professor David Zeffertt.

SIR (ALEXANDER) FRASER RUSSELL

1876–1952. Member of the Cape Bar 1901–15. Judge of the High Court of Southern Rhodesia 1915–31. Chief Justice 1931–42. Knighted 1931.

'Sir (Alexander) Fraser Russell . . . even tried to write a treatise on the law of sale in iambic pentameters, which are most suitable for heroic verse in English. Unfortunately, he did not get beyond the passing of ownership, but fortunately what he penned has been published in the *Rhodesian Law Journal* (1968, p 108). His manuscript was written on the back of some High Court indictments, from internal evidence almost certainly late in 1940 or in 1941. Here are a few lines.

' . . . Then there must be of course
Something to sell, existing at the time,
Or *in futuro* like my next year's crop,
Or even a right of action, like those stocks,
And shares, which agitate the minds of bulls
And bears upon the market on the Rand.
. . .

'The *pretium* must be definitely fixed,
Or else the parties must be quite agreed
Upon the method chosen for fixing it.
Thus you may sell me your old cricket bat
For such price as Bradman may declare;
If Bradman does not speak there is no sale.
. . .

' . . . [T]he risk falls on the purchaser
In spite of the old maxim *domino*
Res perit, for until delivery
The ownership remains in him who sold.
. . . It does seem
That it would be far simpler if the rule
With its exceptions could be quite repealed,
And if *res perit domino* could be
The law in future for this Colony.'

—Ellison Kahn 'The Seven Lamps of Legal Humour Part 3' 1984 *De Rebus* 251 at 252.

WILLEM SCHORER

1717–1800. Judge of the Hof van Flaandere and later President of the court.
Wrote important notes to Grotius's *Inleidinge*.

'What sort of a man was he, what could have possessed him, to give the widest
publicity, five years after it took place and when time's kindly shield was growing
stronger, to the nullity suit in which his wife established his impotence? Truly,
when manhood is challenged common sense sometimes flies out of the window;
and it matters not that the aggrieved male is a judge, as was Willem Schorer.

'The strange story is told in a folio size book of 106 pages, entitled *Process
tusschen Mr. W. Schorer, Raad ordinair in den Ed. Hove van Vlaanderen, en Juffrouw
Anna Elisabeth Eversdyck*, published in Leyden in 1755. The reader is warned that
there is something odd about the writer when, at the back of the title page, he
reads: "*Geene Exemplaaren werden voor echt erkent, als die den Uitgever eigenhandig
zal onderteekent hebben*", followed by a flourishing signature "W. Schorer". This
was Schorer's practice with his publications. Then follows a twenty-seven page
lament headed "*Voorberight aan den Lezer*", in which he confesses "*myn hartzeer
grooter is als myne onbeschaafde pen kan uitdrukken*" (p 3). The balance consists of
"*proces-stukken*". It starts off with a letter dated 22nd August, 1745, by Jan van
Bueren, maternal uncle of Anna, later to be appointed her *curator ad lites*, in which
he says, with a delightful formality, that the family had decided that since, five
years after the marriage (it took place on 30th June, 1740), Anna was still a virgin,
it was time that the union was dissolved. . . . They were determined to continue

PROCES

Ter eerſter Inſtantie gedecideert by het Ed. Agtbaare
GERECHTE
DER STADT
MIDDELBURG,
EN IN
A P P E L
BY DEN
HOOGEN RAADT
I N
HOLLAND.
TUSSCHEN
Mr. W. SCHORER,

Raadt ordinair in den Ed. Hove van Vlaandcren,

TER EENRE,
EN JUFFROUW
ANNA ELISABETH EVERSDYCK,
TER ANDERE ZYDE.

T E   L E Y D E N,

TER DRUKKERYE VAN ELIAS LUZAC, JUN.

En is te bekoomen te *Amſterdam* by Wor; *'s Hage*, O. en P. van Tholl; *Rotterdam*, Benan; *Dor*, van Braam; *Haariem*, Bosch; *Utrecht*, Spruit; *Middelburg*, Gillissen; *Leeuwaarden*, Mootln.

MDCCLV.

with the action, which, to their great sorrow, was necessary, hoping that their friendship with Schorer would nevertheless continue.

'Poor Schorer. He got in first with his action for annulment on the ground of his wife's incapacity for carnal intercourse; she counterclaimed for annulment on the ground of his impotence. She won before the Court of Middelburg in Zeeland and on appeal before the Hooge Raad, which on 31st July, 1749, confirmed the lower court's decision. Willem Pauw, member of the Hooge Raad, had no doubt that the bodily defect was his. (*Observationes Tumultuariae Novae* Obs 281, 284, 288. Note how long it could take for proceedings to reach a conclusion in the eighteenth-century Netherlands.)

'Schorer's case was that despite many and "*kragtdaadige*" attempts he had failed to have carnal intercourse with her because of her "*arctitude*" (p 34. *Oxford English Dictionary*: "Arctitude. [ad. med.L. *arctitudo*, f. *ar(c)tus*.] Tightness, straightness.") Indeed, at one stage he made efforts with such vigour that she was obliged to repulse him. There is much interesting testimony of midwives and medical practitioners, some on an order of the court *a quo* that both husband and wife be medically examined. A midwife, Janna Bals, found Mrs Schorer "*niet te naauw of te eng maar bekwaam, om met een man gemeenschap te hebben*" (p 40). She was supported by an affidavit of the Medical Faculty of Leyden. It was of no help to Schorer that three medical commissioners of the Court had found his external organs "*wel gesteld*" (p 63).

'It must have been a case of impotence *quoad hanc* only. Schorer married again, and his second wife was delivered of a daughter on 14th July, 1752. Anna, too, remarried and bore a child.'

—Ellison Kahn & Brian R Bamford 'Last Spoonful of Sugar and Pinch of Salt' (1967) 84 *SALJ* 452 at 459–60.

OLIVER DENEYS SCHREINER

1890–1980. Member of the Johannesburg Bar 1920–37. KC 1935. Judge of the Transvaal Provincial Division 1937–45. Judge of Appeal 1945–60. Judge of Appeal of the Court of Appeal of the High Commission Territories

1961–8, of Botswana 1966–9, of Lesotho 1966–9 and of Swaziland 1968. President of the Court of Appeal of Botswana 1969–73, of Lesotho 1969–73 and of Swaziland 1968–73.

'It has been said of R A Butler that he was the greatest Prime Minister Britain did not have. So it may be said of Oliver Deneys Schreiner that he was the greatest Chief Justice South Africa did not have.'

—Ellison Kahn 'Oliver Deneys Schreiner: A South African' in Ellison Kahn (ed) *Fiat Iustitia: Essays in Memory of Oliver Deneys Schreiner* (1983) 1.

In Collins v Minister of the Interior *1957 (1) SA 552 (A)—the* Senate *case—Schreiner JA, alone of the eleven members of the Appellate Division who heard the appeal, held invalid the legislative plan by which the Government, through packing the Senate in its favour by an Act passed by the ordinary bicameral procedure, secured the necessary two-thirds majority of both Houses of Parliament to enable it to remove the coloured voters from the common voters' roll.*

'It was a closely reasoned judgment, a classic dissent; to some South African lawyers it had a thrilling visionary quality, born of a mental power given to only a few judges, and not necessarily to everyone with a fine quality of mind. Opinions of commentators have differed on the result of the *Senate* case. . . . [I]t would not be unfair to say that those who have hitherto disagreed with the judgment of Schreiner JA remind one of what John Randolph, American statesman, once said of a judgment of the great Marshall CJ: "Wrong, all wrong, but no man in the United States can tell why or wherein."'

—Kahn op cit at 47.

His convictions

'The one real extravagance was the purchase during middle age—but not in later life—of fairly expensive motor cars, of which the best loved was a Packard, known affectionately as "Packie". Schreiner was inclined to drive rather fast, though in his letters he occasionally expressed amazement at the speed at which some of his friends drove. It may be that in England people tend to drive more slowly; at all events, when Sir Alfred Denning (subsequently Lord Denning) (1899–) visited my university in 1954, he returned from a trip to the Kruger National Park in a pensive mood, saying quietly to me that until his children were qualified in their careers he would prefer not to be driven by Oliver Schreiner again. Up to 4 March 1956 Schreiner was fined for exceeding speed limits three times; on that day he wrote to his wife "it is sweet of you to speak of my second conviction for speeding but actually it is my third—one opposite the Central Prison, Pretoria (£5), one just past Swartkops Aerodrome (£2) and now this one. Not bad though over a period of over 30 years' driving." The Pretoria conviction was probably the one recounted to me over forty years ago by a former clerk of his. Schreiner was driving from Johannesburg to the Palace of Justice in Pretoria. The car was stopped by a traffic officer, who wrote down the particulars in his "spot fine" book, and then asked the driver his name. The clerk interrupted, saying, "Mr Justice Schreiner"; the traffic officer was about to tear up the "ticket" when Schreiner said "Don't you do that". He would never pull rank; when he wrote to an official he did not use official or headed paper, but wrote on an ordinary lined pad and signed himself "O D Schreiner".'

—Kahn op cit at 22.

Boiling soap and cooking books

'The other anecdote was kindly related to me by Mr Eric Morris SC. It concerns what occurred during argument in the case of *Big Ben Soap Industries Ltd v CIR* 1949 (1) SA 740 (A). I take the liberty of quoting Mr Morris, with his inimitable style: "The company had, prior to the outbreak of war, and anticipating both the war and excess-profits duty, inflated its earnings as reflected in the balance sheet, the object being to establish a high 'pre-war standard' and so to reduce the excess profits. It was duly taxed on the inflated income. Later the secretary was ignominiously dismissed, and his wandering (minstrel's) feet led him to the Receiver of Revenue, where he sang his dreamy lullaby—or maybe it was a ballad, song or snatch. The chorus was 'treble tax'. Comes the appeal and Rosenberg KC (with him EM) is busy explaining very nicely to the court that if Big Ben wanted to pay more tax for 1939 (or 1940) than it should have, well that's all there is to it, and a pre-war standard, once determined, would make the Medes and the Persians look like a woman motorist who is hunting for a parking place. All is going very nicely until Schreiner JA leans forward and says 'Mr Rosenberg!' 'Yes, m'Lord?' 'I thought that the business of this company was boiling soap, not cooking the books.' 'As your lordship pleases.' Oliver sat back, almost as if embarrassed at his sarcasm, and uttered not another word during the appeal. His standards were such that he could not countenance or forgive anything which did not measure up to those standards."'

—Kahn op cit at 35. (See also MILLIN; POLLAK; E F WATERMEYER; WESSELS.)

Characteristics

'"It is a rather heavy [case] and I may not get the judgment done before we leave. But I'll do my best. Ludwig Mond, Alfred Mond's father, reckoned it was no excuse if he was told that a man who had messed something up had done his best. In fact he thought it made things worse, as there was then no prospect of improvement! A tough old bloke." (25 September 1960.) Of a certain medical practitioner he had met: "Apparently he has almost lost the gift of speech owing to the extreme loquacity of his wife who talks endlessly." (9 March 1958.) "My brethren . . . have left me as a dissenter on more than one occasion . . . so I must have misunderstood a couple of the cases." (21 March 1958.) "Henry [Fagan] . . . went to church this morning. I asked him to pray for me but I think he forgot. Pity." (23 March 1958.)'

– Kahn op cit at 63, quoting from letters by Oliver Schreiner to his wife Edna.

'[N]o bitterness or hatred entered his mind, or outright condemnation of failings or weaknesses of others, except where grave moral reprehensibility was clear. A vivid picture comes to my mind of him, in his eighties, rising from his chair at a gathering, and alone going up to meet and shake the hand of a man who had entered the room, a man of whom a judge had said harsh things in passing a few days before, remarks that had received considerable publicity in the media.'

—Kahn op cit at 92–3.

'Oliver Schreiner grieved at his losses, but he did not indulge in the egoism of self-pity or suffer the depression that so frequently stems from self-dislike. He regarded himself rightly as having a nature not particularly sensitive, which helped him sustain his burdens. Nor, until perhaps near the end of his life, did he lose that specially significant relationship which the advance of years makes it so difficult to sustain—the relationship with oneself.

'His outward demeanour can best be described by the cliché—a cliché for all its Shakespearean origin—that he did not wear his heart upon his sleeve. He would have shared William Plomer's belief that good manners demand a certain reticence. Sarah Gertrude Millin once said to me that someone close to Oliver had told her that there was a door in his soul through which no one had ever passed; to which I replied that Sigmund Freud had written that there are secret recesses of a man's soul that will not be revealed even to his psychoanalyst.'

—Kahn op cit at 92, referring to the death of Schreiner's wife in 1962, of his daughter in 1974 and of a grandson in 1978.

'His outlook was broadly optimistic. To all, his advice was to keep smiling, and he followed his own advice. I thought his attitude was that of Viscount (Sir Herbert) Samuel, the British statesman, who described himself as a "meliorist" (a term he borrowed from George Eliot), "meaning one who believes that the present is on the whole better than the past and that the future may be better still, but that effort is needed to make it so". There was one reservation, however, which he expressed in a letter to Centlivres: "the programme of apartheid is unjust and will come to a bad end, carrying us with it, unless there is an early change." In years closer to his death he found that encouraging changes were taking place.'

—Kahn op cit at 93.

'Frequently there is dissonance between a person's life and his work. W B Yeats wrote in a poem that "a man must choose perfection of the life or of the work". That may apply more to poets and novelists than to lawyers and judges; disorder and lack of magnanimity could follow from feeding one's work on one's instincts and emotions. It can, however, also happen in the law: a man may be charming and thoughtful in his personal life but not in his working life; or the reverse; or in both lives. Schreiner was in both.

'He had pride, pride not in the sense of an unduly high opinion of his qualities or arrogant bearing or conduct—far from it; but pride in the sense of what befits one's position, what prevents one doing anything unworthy. And he had the humility that clothes a person who is seeking for knowledge, not only in the natural sciences but also in the social sciences. He was not always self-assured, and when he was embarrassed a low whistle would escape his lips, though I could never catch the tune.

'Schreiner's life had its full measure of pain. His triumphs he waved aside like a gentleman; his disappointments and burdens he bore like a man. He met Dostoevsky's hope, that he would be worthy of his sufferings.

'What made him meet any situation were those crucial qualities in the make-up of a complete human being, a sense of humour and a well of fun. He would rarely allow them rein in his judicial work, for it might be at the expense of the litigants, the accused or counsel. But in private they would bubble forth.'

—Kahn op cit at 93.

'In his sixty years of connection with this university [the University of the Witwatersrand], Oliver Schreiner never deviated from his high democratic principles and belief that academic freedom is the hallmark of a true university. Racialism and racism were absolutely foreign to him. He had a lifelong concern with the interests of the black population and the needs of the poor and distressed. The colour bar was anathema to him. Privately he condemned the policy of apartheid. As far as he could, he washed his hands of it. There remains in my memory a simple striking statement he made to me in 1974 when we were discussing the removal of much petty apartheid by the Johannesburg City Council. At the time he was recovering from a stroke and suffering grievously from arthritis. He said that he could now sit at the bus stop and in a park. Never had he sat on a seat there marked "Whites only": "I always felt ashamed at the thought of sitting when some elderly African washerwoman had to stand."'

—Ellison Kahn *The Tablets of Memory* (1986) 4.

'Also linked to his essential courtesy, one felt, was his fierce independence. He would shrug aside offers of physical help. Any other offer of assistance was usually declined. It was with difficulty that I persuaded him to let the University type the manuscript of his Hamlyn lectures, which he had written in pencil in his legible hand. When one drove him home he would always ask, even if it were late at night, to be dropped at the corner so as not to take one out of one's way. The only method of combating the request was to say that one would be upset if he insisted on it. Last year after a Council meeting it was found to general consternation that the lifts were not working. On this occasion Schreiner had a driver and a car in the basement, fourteen storeys down. After talking to a colleague, I had a feeling that something was amiss. Where was the judge? He was in his eighty-ninth year, had had a stroke, and because of arthritis, despite operations on his hip walked with difficulty. I rushed down the stairs, to find him three floors down, steadily proceeding on his way. We walked down eleven more floors to his car.'

—Ellison Kahn 'Oliver Deneys Schreiner—The Man and His Judicial World' (1980) 97 *SALJ* 566 at 587.

'In the whole of his life he did not insure the contents of his house. Once he told me with a teasing smile: "I've never had a burglary; look at the money I've saved!" Nor did he have burglar bars on the windows, let alone a burglar alarm. A few years ago, late one evening, when I drove him home, he found that he had left his keys behind; he was locked out, and there was no one to let him in. I found it simple to open a window catch by inserting through an open fanlight a forked stick that I found in the garden. Again he had proved his point! My private opinion was that there was an understanding among the fraternity of thieves that he was a good man and he had to be left alone.'

—Kahn op cit at 588.

WILLIAM PHILIP SCHREINER

1857–1919. Member of the Cape Bar 1882–93, 1900–14. Attorney-General in Rhodes's Cabinets 1893 and 1894–6. Prime Minister of the Cape Colony 1898–1900. Senator 1910–14. High Commissioner in London 1914–19. CMG 1891. QC 1892. Privy Counsellor 1917. Father of Oliver Deneys Schreiner (qv).

'Intellectually he was very gifted, and he was a cultivated person. His letters contain occasional quotations, flowing naturally, not only from the English classics but also from the authors of ancient Greece and Rome and from writers in French. As far as an extremely busy professional and political life allowed, Schreiner read widely.

'A generally quiet and dignified demeanour normally hid a nervous, excitable, sentimental temperament; he was inclined to obstinacy, melancholy, depression and a feeling that he was isolated; and—save in legal matters—self-questioning. His temper was somewhat short, and when, as so often was the case, he was suffering from overwork, strain, worry or ill health, he was inclined to lose it. This tendency did not serve him well when he was conducting a case or arguing in court. The most celebrated outburst came relatively early in his career, in 1895, when he was Attorney-General. It was in the case of *Cook Brothers v The Colonial Government* (1895) 12 SC 86, in which, leading Juta QC, Schreiner succeeded in defending an action by the Cook brothers to have their rights sustained to certain concessions granted to them by Sigcau, the Paramount Chief, before the cession of East Pondoland to the Crown. Richard Solomon QC led for the plaintiffs. There was considerable interjection by members of the court, composed of De Villiers CJ and Buchanan and Upington JJ. The Chief Justice found for the Government on the law; but he expressed the court's sympathy for the moral claims of the plaintiffs, which, he said, the Government ought to bear in mind, the importance of the decision in law, and the considerable expense that could have been saved had the defendant excepted, as it should have, to the plaintiffs' declaration. In the circumstances, he said, each party should bear its own costs. Whereupon Schreiner burst out that he hoped the order as to costs was not associated with the personality of leading counsel for the Government. De Villiers CJ, stunned momentarily by this unprecedented reflection, turned pale, then said crisply that personalities did not colour his judgments, and strode out of court.

'But the episode was not typical of Schreiner in his court work.'

—Ellison Kahn 'Father and Son—W P Schreiner and Oliver' in *Fiat Iustitia: Essays in Memory of Oliver Deneys Schreiner* (1983) 100 at 107–8. (Seventeen years later Schreiner lost his temper in court in another untypical incident, this time with Juta QC. See JUTA.)

'Outside court Schreiner was normally sweet tempered, and was always considerate, with great charm of manner. Never did he refuse help to colleagues at the Bar who sought his advice; but not only to them—to anyone who came to him in distress. Young relatives were assisted by him financially, especially with their education. But he was a pretty easy mark for all. One letter will suffice. It was written by the unfortunate Melius de Villiers [qv] on 12 March 1914 from "Blanckenbergh" in Wynberg to "My dear Mr Schreiner"; it stated that previously he had made an arrangement with WP to look up authorities for him; that after the work of the University Commission was over, he (Melius) would have nothing to do, and did Mr Schreiner care to enter into such an arrangement again?'

—Kahn op cit at 109.

'MR W. P. SCHREINER'
*Caricature by D C Boonzaier (1865–1950) from
his* My Caricatures *(1912)*

'BETWIXT AND BETWEEN.'
*Caricature by D C Boonzaier (1865–
1950), from his* Owlographs *(1901) 50*

'W P Schreiner, MP. Willie pares his nails whilst reading the S.A. News at St James'
Sketch by Harry McCormick 1874–1917. Reproduced from 'From the Sketchbook of the late Harry
McCormick' *in Eric Rosenthal & Richard F Robinow* The South African Saturday Book *(nd:
?1948) 100 at 103*

EDMUND ADOLPHE SELKE

1890–1960. Member of the Natal Bar 1917–38. KC 1929. Judge of the Natal Provincial Division 1938–57.

'Selke was a man of deep culture, a scholar and a jurist, but his lack of some of the secondary and less academic qualifications for advocacy unfitted him for the rough and tumble of the Bar and deprived him of its highest prizes. This same deficiency unfitted him for the drudgery which comprises so much of the work of a puisne judge. Like Feetham, his right sphere was the Appellate Division and strictly on merit he ought to have been appointed to that Court. At the Bar and on the Bench he was apt to fall in love with some abstruse legal conundrum and would spend hours in discussing it without regard to the practical aspects of the case. Mackeurtan is reported to have said to him once when they were working together on a case: "That's enough of waiver and estoppel. Let us now get to the blood and guts." Like many scholars he was always quite unaware of the passage of time. Once in his early days at the Bar I was working with him in his chambers on a winter afternoon and we were continually interrupted by people telephoning him for appointments. His answer was the same each time: "I can't possibly see you this afternoon as I have arranged to play tennis." The last time he gave this reason I looked out of the window and noticed that the sun had set and the first stars were shining in the sky. Another more recent story is told of him. He was lunching with three acquaintances at a club when the conversation turned on the best age for retirement. He said that it was his fixed intention to retire when he reached the age of 65. Someone then asked him his age, and without batting an eyelid he gave it. It was 66. During my first eleven years on the Bench he was my senior, so that when we sat together he would preside. His unpunctuality and lack of all sense of time exasperated me. When it was time to go into court he would send for his secretary, start looking for papers, fill his fountain pen or put through a telephone call. It would usually be 10.05 a.m. before we took our seats. The mid-morning adjournment of fifteen minutes would usually be stretched to twenty-five. Often this would mean that some case would just not finish by 1 p.m. and would have to be resumed at 2.15 when I had been counting on a free afternoon for some other work. To one as fanatically punctual as I am this was quite infuriating. But there is an endearing sequel. As I shall tell later on, I became Judge President in 1950, and thereafter when we sat together it was of course I who presided. Never once did he keep me waiting. As 10 o'clock struck I would walk along to his room and he would immediately drop whatever he was doing and follow me into Court. With no prompting whatever from me he accommodated himself to my tiresome habits of punctuality. But there is much more in it than that. It would have been no more than human for him to feel resentment at my elevation over his head, but he never gave me an inkling that any such feelings had ever entered his mind. Throughout our remaining years on the Bench together he was an utterly loyal and always helpful colleague. When he retired before reaching the age limit the Bench lost something of dignity and culture that it could ill afford. He immediately became immersed in other activities but unfortunately his years of retirement were not many. During his lifetime I often applied to him the lines of Browning:

Others mistrust and say, 'But time escapes:
   Live now or never!'
He said, 'What's time? Leave Now for dogs and apes!
   Man has Forever.'
But now that he has gone I think his true epitaph will be found later in the same poem.

That low man seeks a little thing to do,
   Sees it and does it;
This high man, with a great thing to pursue,
   Dies ere he knows it.
   ★ ★ ★

Leave him—still loftier than the world suspects
   Living and dying.'
—F N Broome *Not the Whole Truth* (1962) 138–9. (See also MACKEURTAN.)

'On the Bench Carlisle served his country well. Unfortunately he and Selke often had to sit together and they seldom saw eye to eye on any case. Selke would regard him as quick and superficial while he would regard Selke as unendurably slow and meticulous. Judges may be classified into the quick and the slow, but it is not always the slow judges who are good or the quick judges who are bad, or vice versa. Classified on the basis of speed Carlisle and Selke were in different classes, but they were both good judges. Without Carlisle's speed the Court would have found it difficult to cope with the work to be done, and without Selke's thoroughness we would have been deprived of many learned investigations of the law's darker realms.'

—Broome op cit at 140.

Another version

'Carlisle never had any doubts, as he never saw any difficulties. Selke saw all the difficulties but was never able to settle his doubts.'

—A Natal Barfly, recorded in Ellison Kahn's commonplace book.

'Like many scholars he was unaware of the passage of time and very slow in giving judgment. But he had a great sense of humour, which he could use against himself. On one occasion Tony Croft-Lever, then a member of the Bar in Pietermaritzburg, was in his chambers. The phone rang. Selke answered, "No madam, this is not the cold storage", then turned to Tony and said "You know, for a moment I thought it was someone asking about a reserved judgment".

'He sat in the old Supreme Court building in Pietermaritzburg. The judges' parking area was in the process of being re-tarred. Selke walked on to a recently tarred area. A workman shouted "Hey you, get off my tar", to which Selke replied "That is a somewhat unconventional way of addressing one of her Majesty's judges". The workman then said "You a judge?" "Yes", replied Selke. "Then you ought to know better" said the workman.

'On another occasion when Selke was sitting upstairs in the court Paul Behrmann was on his feet addressing him. The registrar rushed in and informed Selke that the court had to be evacuated as a fire was expected. Selke: "Mr Behrmann, at long last one of your arguments has set the house on fire."'

—The Hon Ramon Nigel Leon *Truth in Action* (the reminiscences of the former judge of the Natal Provincial Division, not yet completed or published).

ARTHUR (ARCHIE) SHACKSNOVIS

1900–51. Member of the Cape Bar 1924–35. Member of the Johannesburg
Bar 1935–51. KC 1940.

The opinion in verse

'The opinion in verse printed below, which has become almost legendary in
legal circles in Johannesburg, was given by the late Arthur Shacksnovis, K.C., to
a Johannesburg firm of attorneys who appended at the end of their instructions
the statement that "an opinion in verse would be appreciated". They little
expected that their request would be complied with, but "Archie" Shacksnovis
was one who could not resist a challenge, even if it was not seriously made. The
result was this opinion, altered only so far as is necessary to avoid reference to
living persons and reproduced by kind consent of all parties concerned.

'It is only proper that a word be said about its author, whose lamented death
at the age of 51 occurred on 11th August, 1951. Born in Leeds, Arthur
Shacksnovis came to the Union as a child, and received his early education at
Marist Brothers College and King Edward VII School, Johannesburg, the
Transvaal University College, Pretoria, and the University of Cape Town, from
which he proceeded as a Rhodes Scholar to Oriel College, Oxford. There he was
awarded his Rugby Blue in his first term. Returning to the Cape in 1924, he
practised at the Bar at Cape Town until 1935, maintaining his interest in all forms
of sport, in particular rugby, a sport in which he represented Western Province
in many Currie Cup matches. He joined the Johannesburg Bar in 1935, where he
took silk in 1940, and practised until the end. For several years before his death
he was a member of the Transvaal Provincial Council.

'"Archie" Shacksnovis was a many-sided character. He had a brilliant mind
that could absorb the most complicated facts of an impending trial even though
instructed the night before the action. He had a resonant voice and a charm of
delivery that was effective not only in the law courts but also in broadcasting—
another of his many interests. He was a great collector of antiques, first editions,
bronzes and porcelains. He was famous as a gourmet. There was virtually
nothing that he touched that he did not excel at: in truth he was *vir capax omnium*.

'Ex Parte Three Suitors: Opinion
Said Lion the Suitor to Maiden the Lamb:
"You can take me for worse or just as I am;
And as for the Calendar, let's fix a date
As soon as may be ere your ardour abate."

"Yes, yes", said the lady, "But don't go so fast,
You needn't be nervous, my ardour will last.
Is yours to be ours as well as my own
Or that which you have to be all yours alone?"

"Oh no!", said the Lion, "Provided we wed,
On that there is *no* need to bother your head,
For Tommy and Walter and Bob we shall see,
And take the advice of those notaries three."

So they went hand in hand to visit a den,
Where, toiling and spinning, the three legal men

Evolved a nice contract all typed and green bound,
With wherefores and phrases of fine legal sound.

It recited the holy intent of the pair,
And the usual things antenuptially fair,
Excluding community, profit and loss
And power marital, lest either be boss.

And then they proceeded to add a clause 7 –
Materially gilding this match made in Heaven –
Whereunder the Lion said "I do agree
That I'll give, and shall cede, and shall make over free

To this fairest of maids as her property sole,
All furniture, goods, to £1,000 whole,
And two whole life policies, five hundred each,
Both payable when my life's span I shall reach".

And to seal this rare, goodly and generous pact,
Bob added what *he* thought the document lacked –
A further clause, 9, wherein fair Maiden said:
"I hereby declare to have accepted as read,

The gifts and donations and settlements all,
Although when you add them they seem rather small;
But I do by these presents accept the said gifts
Lest in the new lute there appear any rifts."

The couple then paid and awaited their day,
But the notarial three still had something to pay;
They bought some fine stamps and they stuck them all round
The blanks on that contract all typed and green bound.

They licked and they counted and counted and licked
Till fingers and tongues with the labour were ricked,
And when they had finished they put it away
In their bulky old protocols, ribboned and gay.

The couple got married and all had forgot
The legal and phraseological rot,
When a Revenue Pooh-Bah sent word to the three
That their protocols he would examine and see.

They sent him their protocols, having no qualms,
Nor excursions expected nor any alarms,
But they reckoned without the Commissioner's mind
Which was scrounging for stampage, whate'er it could find.

He scratched and he poked and he fiddled around
Till he came on the contract all typed and green bound,
When, like the tale's ogre, he roared, "Fee Fo Fum,
I smell here the blood of a penalty sum".

And he wrote a demand to the notaries three,
To say "I shall" means "I do", qua the fee;
And he told them to lick and to count o'er again,
For a cession's a cession whenever you gain.

And as for Act 30 of 1911,
As read with the Schedule, Item 19 *Sub* (7),
The question of stamping such cessions must be
In accordance with *Ford's* case, "18 T.P.D.".

So the notaries three went into a huddle,
And reckoned the Pooh-Bah was quite in a muddle.
For the case that he cited was right in its way,
But only as far as it purports to say

That in contracts like these, when a cession appears,
To the usual stampage just where it adheres
Must be added the stampage for cessions as well –
And that's all the judgment, page 50, can tell.

So they wrote to the Pooh-Bah and told him as much,
That his argument read to them like double Dutch,
That the point of the issue was like any nose plain,
A claim by the wife upon this would be vain,

Except to compel her said husband to make
A cession when called on, lest contract he break;
And why should the Pooh-Bah allow duty free
"Undertakings to cede", not "shall cede I agree".

The Pooh-Bah relentless returned to the fray
And insisted that penalties still they should pay.
He referred them to clauses both 7 and 9;
Said the latter effected a cession, in fine.

"No mere imposition of duty to cede"
Was created when wifey accepted the deed
Or the gift in such clear unequivocal terms
As clause 9 in its plain simple language affirms.

He even declared that whenever they should
Think it fit to ensure that the cession were good
By making two separate cessions beside,
The same stampage again they would have to provide.

With more anger than sorrow the notaries three
Proceeded to fork out the penalty fee;
With groans and with gnashing of oaths through their teeth
(To have read and understood not declaring beneath).

They went to a pundit, law-learned and fat,
And asked him to tell them just where they were at,
And whether pursuing the Pooh-Bah in court
Would regain them their money or make them more short.

He thought as he grunted and grunted and thought
That the quantum was *parvum* by law to be sought
But a principle major was therein involved,
If by favourable judgment it soon could be solved.

Imprimis, he told them the Pooh-Bah was wrong,
And was making submissions not legally strong;
With pen and with pencil and lexicon too,
He couldn't make "shall" ever equal to "do".

And in cases he sought, for like cessions to see,
Such as *Morkel* vee *Holm*, 2 S.C. 63,
The clause was in present and not future tense
With all proper wording to carry that sense.

Secundus, a test of the matter would be
The rights that would pass to a lawful trustee,
If the husband had been so poor and ill-fated
As just before marriage to be sequestrated.

In that event surely the trustee could say
Both the policies in the estate have to stay,
And the wife can but claim as a creditor too
As others concurrently would have to do.

And Thirdly, the Pooh-Bah himself must be loth
To back his opinion, when he expects both
A fee for the cession on the A.N.C.
And again some more stampage on cessions to be.

And Fourthly, the answer that wifey has said
She accepts by those presents *etcetera* as read,
Is bad, as the wording would be just the same,
For a promise to transfer a house in her name.

And Fifthly, the setting surrounding the deed,
The clear circumstances in which they agreed,
Have regard to futurity and no intent
To give out-and-out ere to marriage they went.

The wording conveys nothing more than just this,
That Maiden accepts, while she is still a miss,
Undertakings to give her when she is a wife
Some benefits meant for her married life.

Authority he was unable to find,
But lack of authority avails not to bind;
And interpreting English just as she is writ,
Appeared not to leave any doubt about it.

The notaries three ought therefore to win.
But lest by all this they be taken in;
The pundit advises on the law he doth see –
Not as puisne judges will opine it to be.

> Three notaries would a-suing go,
> "Heigho", said Counsel,
> Whether their client would let them or no;
>
> With a roly-poly gammon and spinach
> "Take cession from client", says Counsel.

A. SHACKSNOVIS.
Chambers,
29, VII.38.'

—Ellison Kahn 'The Opinion in Verse' (1956) 73 *SALJ* 94. (See also GREENBERG;
MALAN; L O MILLER; H H (HARRY) MORRIS.)

SIR SIDNEY GODOLPHIN ALEXANDER SHIPPARD

1837–1902. Member of the Cape Bar 1868–73. Attorney-General of
Griqualand West 1873–7. Acting Recorder of the High Court of Griqualand
1877. Member of the Eastern Districts Bar 1877–80. Judge of the Eastern
Districts Court 1880–5. Administrator and Chief Magistrate of the Colony
of British Bechuanaland and Deputy Commissioner for the protectorate of
Bechuanaland 1885–95. Knighted (KCMG) 1887.

Great expectations—unknown and foiled

'There was Sidney Shippard, the Attorney-General of Griqualand West,
destined to have power in a place and at a time when Rhodes needed someone to
do a bit of queer work for him. To this Sidney Shippard, in conjunction with the
British Colonial Secretary, Rhodes' first will assigns all his possessions that they
may use it to spread Britain over the world.'

—Sarah Gertrude Millin *Rhodes* (1933; Golden
Library edition 1936) 20, writing of Cecil John
Rhodes (1853–1902) in Kimberley in 1874–5.

'In Rhodes' second term at Oxford [1874]
his lungs, not yet strong enough to withstand the damp of England, were injured
afresh by a chill caught while rowing. It was
now a doctor wrote down in his case-book
(Rhodes himself later saw it) that he had not
six months to live.

'Rhodes gave up Oxford for two years,
returned to Kimberley, and there began to
work out a plan of life.

'In 1876 he returned to Oxford. . . .

'In the same year . . . he draws up the first
of those six wills in which, in one form or
another, he bequeaths his fortune to the
purpose of extending British rule throughout the world.

'The will itself is not more astounding than
the fact that Rhodes leaves the money which is
to alter the fate of all the world to two men: the
Secretary of State for the Colonies at the time
of his death; and Sidney Godolphin Alexander
Shippard, an Oriel man, until 1877 Attorney-
General of Griqualand West, later a judge,

'*The gentle* "SHIPPARD" *of Bechuanas
plains.*'

*Caricature by William Howard Schröder
(1852–92), from* The Schröder Art
Memento *(Pretoria 1894)*

then an administrator in a place and at a time very important to Rhodes, and, finally, a director of the Chartered Company. These are the actual legatees.

'It was what Rhodes was always doing in his wills: he bequeathed his money to one or two or more individuals, and left it to them to carry out his plans.'

—Millin op cit at 31–3. (Shippard, like Rhodes, went to Oriel College, Oxford. Shippard did not feature in any of the later wills.)

Judge versus administrator

'As a Judge of the Eastern Districts' Court, Sir Sidney earned a high character for profound learning, conscientious administration of Justice, as well as for absolute independence and strict integrity.'

—Almost certainly by H T Tamplin (q v), the editor of the *Cape Law Journal*. In (1897) 14 *Cape Law Journal* 120.

'His predilection for the Chartered Company sometimes caused him to adopt disingenuous methods and he did not always handle people and their disputes very capably.'

—A L Harington in *Dictionary of South African Biography* II (1972) 662 at 663. (And see the first extract—'when Rhodes needed someone to do a bit of queer work for him'.)

SIR WILLIAM JAMES SMITH

1853–1912. Member of the London Bar 1875–80, 1881–2; Judge of the Gold Coast Colony 1880–1. Judge of the Supreme Court of Cyprus 1882–92 and Chief Justice 1892–7. Chief Justice of British Guiana 1897–1902. Judge of the Transvaal High Court April–October 1902, of the Transvaal Supreme Court October 1902–May 1910 and of the Transvaal Provincial Division May 1910–12. Knighted 1896. President of the Special Treason Court, Natal 1900.

'In his bearing Sir William Smith was the perfect embodiment of justice. Some silly man one day said to me: "I think he looks like a butler." This man probably did not know the difference between a butler and a judge. I am reminded of a story Gerald Orpen, the well-known Cape Town accountant, tells against himself. He has long been one of my colleagues on the Income Tax Appeal Court. An appellant one day—this was before I became President of the Court—said: "Mr. President, I don't mind you hearing my case. But I object to that farmer (meaning Orpen) sitting there."

'Smith had a most disconcerting way with him. He never opened his mouth during the hearing of a case. I remember on one occasion I addressed him for three to four hours on end. He never batted an eyelid, but sat gazing at me like an owl, giving no indication of what he thought, or on which side he was. It was only when he came to deliver judgment that I realised he was in my favour.

'Smith now and then delivered himself of a witty observation—and it really was witty. He was a scholar, and loved the classics. It was he who introduced me to *A Shropshire Lad.* . . .'

—Manfred Nathan *Not Heaven Itself: An Autobiography* (1944) 208–9. (See also WESSELS last entry.)

'SIR WILLIAM SMITH.

'Sir William was an exotic. He had been Chief Justice of the Island of Cyprus.

If anyone could add lustre to the distinguished gathering which he joined he could do so. He had a very fine presence, and on the bench he was Dignity with a strong sense of humour. He was one of the few Judges I have seen who looked the part. Everyone who came into contact with him regarded him with mingled feelings of respect and affection.

'In the course of a trial he had repeatedly referred to the accused, who was charged with robbery, as Barabbas (the robber). After a while the coincidence became too much for His Lordship.

'"Mr. Interpreter, ask the accused what his name is."

'"Barnabas (the Good Man), My Lord."

'"Ah, then, I have been doing the gentleman an injustice."

'Counsel had quoted the headnote of a case and no more. Sir William was satisfied that Counsel had not looked at the judgment.

'"I suppose you want the order given in that case."

'"Yes, My Lord."

'"Very well, take your order without costs."

'I was not in Court, but I have no doubt that the kindly judge eventually gave the junior the order he wanted.'

'A Cypriot was the respondent in an application. He had an easy way of beating it. He went into the box and said, "No spik Engleesh."

'A voice from above addressed him in Romaic. The Cypriot gave one heavenward look and fell out of the box in a faint.

'The picture I have of this Judge on the bench will never fade from my memory.'

—H H Morris KC *The First Forty Years* (1948) 57. (Romaic is the modern Greek vernacular. Smith acquired a thorough knowledge of it when he was a judge in Cyprus. See (1911) 28 *SALJ* 467.)

'THE ORIENTAL MIND

'There never was, nor will there ever be, an Oriental who could say "Yes" or "No", or give a direct answer to a question. There is always a protracted discussion between the interpreter and the witness. In a murder trial before Sir William Smith, a Chinese witness said that there had been a dog near the scene of the murder.

'"What was the colour of the dog?" asked the Judge. Then there ensued a ten-minute discussion. His Lordship became impatient. "What does he say, Mr. Interpreter?" There were further lengthy negotiations.

'"He says, My Lord, it was a black dog."

'"Thank Heavens," said the Judge, "it wasn't a black and tan."'

—H H Morris KC *In and Out of Court* (1950) 61–2.

JAN CHRISTIAAN (CHRISTIAN) SMUTS

1870–1950. Member of the Cape Bar 1895–7. Member of the Johannesburg Bar 1897–8. State Attorney of the South African Republic (Transvaal) 1898–1901. Member of the Pretoria Bar 1902–7. Colonial Secretary and Minister of Education in Botha's Transvaal Cabinet 1907–10. MP 1910–50. Minister of the Interior, of Mines and of Defence 1910–12, Minister of Finance and of Defence 1912–15 and Minister of Defence 1915–19, in

Botha's Cabinet. Member of Lloyd George's British War Cabinet 1917–19. Privy Counsellor 1917. Prime Minister 1919–24, and Minister of Native Affairs and of Defence 1919–20, and Minister of Native Affairs 1920–4. Minister of Justice in Hertzog's Cabinet 1933–9. Prime Minister and Minister of External Affairs and of Defence 1939–48. KC OM CH FRS 1930. DTD. Statesman, soldier and philosopher.

Smuts, having won the Ebden scholarship, went up to Christ's College, University of Cambridge, in 1891. His academic achievements were outstanding.

'He had been the first man ever to take both parts of the Law Tripos in one year and had been placed not only first but "brilliantly first" in the examinations. He had won the George Long Prize in Roman Law and Jurisprudence, an unusual achievement, because the prize was never awarded except to candidates of the highest distinction and in most years was not awarded at all. On the recommendation of his examiners, Maitland and Bond, he was granted an extra year of the Ebden scholarship and an extra sum of money to make good its depreciated value. Six months later, in December 1894, he passed the Honours Examination of the Inns of Court, again first in his year and with two prizes, each of £50. At long last he had escaped the curse of poverty.'

—W K Hancock *Smuts: The Sanguine Years 1870–1919* (1962) 47.

A letter from Frederic W Maitland (1850–1906), Downing Professor of the Laws of England, University of Cambridge, renowned jurist and historian. Referring to this letter, Hancock (op cit at 46) says that it came 'from the greatest academic lawyer produced by the English universities within the past century and more'.

'The West Lodge
Downing College
Cambridge
15 June 1894

DEAR MR. SMUTS,

Will this do? I have seldom written a testimonial with a better will.

I think that I shall not be indiscreet in telling you that your place in Part II was due very largely to your exceptionally good essays.

I hope to hear of you again. At the Cape you have a most interesting state of things and I think that what you have learnt here will enable you to see the interest of it. I am always hoping that some day Cambridge will turn out a great Romanist—a Ihering who knows English law. Germans I fancy can never put themselves quite outside the system. An Englishman might do it—but then our own best lawyers are always immersed in practice. There is a great chance for you.

I am going to ask you to accept a copy of Bracton's Note Book which will come to you from the Press in memory of

Yours very truly
F. W. MAITLAND'

—*The Letters of Frederic William Maitland* edited by C H S Fifoot (1965) 121.

Jan "prefers to water his orange-trees and to study Kant's Critical Philosophy."

Caricature of Jan Smuts, then Colonial Secretary and Minister of Education in Botha's Transvaal Cabinet, by Arthur Wynell Lloyd (1883–1967) 'Holiday Hobbies' in "Sunday Times" Book of Cartoons (1907) 61

Another tribute

'When this South African farm lad went to Cambridge his object was to study law. We are told that his record of successes in the law examinations at Cambridge has never been equalled at the University.

'Incidentally, some years after the Boer War a retired Cambridge Professor of Law was entertained at a dinner in Johannesburg by some of his old students. He was asked whom, amongst all the many clever men who had attended his lectures over several decades, he considered the most brilliant. His reply was, "unhesitatingly I can say, J. C. Smuts".'

—'Smuts as Lawyer: An Intimate Study by One of His Pupils' (1950) 67 *SALJ* 339. (The 'pupil' was I Hayman, later a partner in the well-known Johannesburg firm of attorneys, Hayman, Godfrey and Sanderson.)

Smuts as a law teacher

'Smuts . . . went north to Johannesburg to practise as an advocate, with but scant success at first.

'He had few friends in Johannesburg and no influence at all. On the contrary, his anti-Rhodes attitude told against him. Johannesburg was still smarting from the collapse of the Reform Committee which had been formed to press the claims of the Uitlanders on the Republican Government. For the time being the Reform movement had been blown sky-high by the Jameson Raid.

'But Smuts' arrival in Johannesburg was an unqualified blessing to a group of articled clerks (of whom I was one) who were studying for the attorneys' law examinations in the Transvaal.

'The examination was a stiff one and the examiners were all practising barristers of the highest standing, among them Wessels, Curlewis, Esselen and Gregorowski [qqv]. It required a thorough knowledge of the subjects to satisfy them.

'The articled clerks were, of course, all fully occupied in their employers' offices during the daytime and consequently their studying had to be done after office hours.

'In those days there was no University and no law classes on the Rand. Imagine our delight when the word was passed round that a recent arrival from the Cape, Advocate Smuts, had started a law class for articled clerks. Some twelve to fifteen of us put down our names at once.

'Smuts was then a slender and slightly-built man, clean-shaven and with the pallor of a student. He had a small office in Marais Court, a building which stood beside the Rand Club in Commissioner Street. There we students went one night a week for over a year.

'Smuts' lectures to us were on Roman-Dutch law, the main examination subject. None of us had had any experience of law lectures and we found his discourse most illuminating. His love for his subject was evident. Always he took us back to the principles underlying the legal propositions which he stated. His expositions were clear and concise and it was a delight to listen to him. Small wonder that he inspired his class to great efforts, but of this more later. Suffice it to say that his pupils scarcely ever missed a lecture and that they became his life-long admirers and supporters. He could have been a brilliant professor of law.

'. . . Most of his pupils wrote their examination in October 1898, and were very successful. Another tribute to his ability as a lecturer!

'I append a letter from Smuts to one of his pupils. The letter was written by Smuts in his own handwriting from the Office of the State Attorney. It is typical of the unique quality of the man that whilst holding one of the great offices of State he could still find time to write to an insignificant youngster such a warm and inspiring, one could even say noble, letter. Small wonder that the letter is now a treasured heirloom. The letter is an exact copy save that the various names are replaced by initials.

'Pretoria, 30 Oct. 1898.

A.B., Esq., Johannesburg.

My dear B,

You don't know how sorry I am that I have so far been prevented from congratulating you on your brilliant success in the recent Procureurs Examen. Your marks were higher by many hundreds than those ever obtained before in this examination, and it is in my opinion not very probable that the record thus made will soon be lowered by somebody else. I feel proud to think that your beginnings in the law were watched by me with great interest and that in a certain minor way I may have contributed to your remarkable success. However, the honour is wholly yours and I therefore congratulate you most heartily.

This is however only the beginning. You are joining a profession which, among the Romans no less than among the Hebrews, was looked upon as a consecrated priesthood, working in a worthy manner for the attainment of the highest ideals of humanity. Ulpian says: 'Ut eleganter Celsus definit, jus est ars boni et aequi. Cuius merito quis nos sacerdotes appellet: justitiam namque colimus et boni et aequi notitiam profitemur, aequum ab iniquo separantes, licitum ab illicito discernentes, bonos non solum metu poenarum, verum etiam praemiorum quoque exhortatione efficere cupientes, veram nisi fallor philoso- phiam, non simulatam affectantes.'

These proud words of Ulpian's are true, for you will find in law not only a means of livelihood but also of moral and spiritual culture: and my wish for you is that you may press on till you enter that inner shrine where the legal right is seen to be but the symbol of that deeper Right which pervades the whole world.

Wishing you as much happiness and success as it is good for a wise man to have in this world.

I remain,

Yours very faithfully,

J. C. SMUTS'

—Op cit at 339–42. 'A.B.' clearly was Hayman. The celebrated passage in Latin is from Digest 1.1.1 pr, 1. The translation in Alan Watson (ed) *The Digest of Justinian* I (1985) by D N MacCormick reads: 'In terms of Celsus' elegant definition, the law is the art of goodness and fairness. Of that art we [jurists] are deservedly called the priests. For we cultivate the virtue of justice and claim awareness of what is good and fair, discriminating between fair and unfair, distinguishing lawful from unlawful, aiming to make men good not only through fear of penalties but also indeed under allurements of rewards, and affecting a philosophy which, if I am not deceived, is genuine, not a sham.' Peter Stein would translate *ars* not as 'art' but as 'craft' or 'systematic technique': see (1961) 77 *LQR* 247.

Smuts at the Bar

' . . . Let us pass on to the signing of the Treaty of Vereeniging in May 1902, which finished Smuts' work as a war leader and also, for the time being, as a politician. He returned to law. This time he opened an office in Pretoria and we saw him rarely in Johannesburg.

'He was now in excellent physical condition. His years in the field had hardened and broadened him, his former pale countenance was replaced by the bronzed face of a seasoned guerilla and he had grown a small beard.

'His return to the bar was a success from the very outset. Work poured in on him and he was soon one of the leading advocates in the country. He had worthy opponents in Leonard, Curlewis, Ward, Gregorowski and Esselen [q q v], but he held his own.

'As a practising lawyer Smuts showed most of the qualities of his lecturing. Whilst he may have lacked the eloquence of some of his adversaries he had an

excellent manner and presented his arguments in a clear, concise, logical and closely reasoned way which invariably won for him the ear of the Court. His presentation was always brief and he went to the heart of the issue at once; he never indulged in any flights of fancy or "purple patches" of eloquence. He was a competent cross-examiner and always knew his brief, but was at his best in an argument on pure legal principles; an intellectual performance. Also his written opinions in Chamber work were brief but models of clear thinking.

'The Law Reports of the Transvaal Supreme Court for the years 1903 to 1906 show how Smuts' practice grew and the ever-increasing number of important cases in which he appeared. His work was entirely on the civil side; criminal work did not appeal to him.

Caricatures of General J C Smuts, General J B M Hertzog and Colonel E H P Cresswell, Leader of the Labour Party, in 1924, prior to the formation of the National Party—Labour Party Government. By D C Boonzaier (1865–1950)

'So Smuts' course was set towards greater and greater distinction in law when once again he decided to abandon law and to re-enter politics and work directly for the land he so dearly loved.

'All the world knows his subsequent history.'

—Op cit at 340–1.

SAUL SOLOMON

1875–1960. Member of the Cape Bar 1900–2. Member of the Johannesburg Bar 1902–6. Anglican clergyman 1908–16. Member of the Johannesburg Bar 1916–27. KC 1919. Judge of the Transvaal Provincial Division 1927–55.

'"Died at his home in St. James, today, 11th December, 1960, at the age of 85, the Hon. Saul Solomon, formerly a judge of the Transvaal Provincial Division." What recollections are evoked by this laconic death notice! What a span of history; what memories of a distinguished family and one of its eminent sons!

'Saul Solomon was the first-born of Saul Solomon, M.L.A., the "Member for Cape Town", who, although never in the Ministry, was known as the Warwick of the Cape, the maker and unmaker of Ministries. Saul the elder married late in life Georgiana Margaret Thomson, who had shortly before arrived at the Cape from Scotland. His first child, Saul, was born when he was 57 years of age. Saul the younger came to bear a strong facial resemblance to his famous father.

'Among the many well-known cousins of Saul the judge were Sir William Solomon, former Chief Justice; Sir Richard Solomon, Attorney-General in the Crown Colony of the Transvaal, sometime Lieutenant-Governor of the Transvaal and first Union High Commissioner in London; and Sir Edward P. Solomon, Minister of Public Works in Botha's Transvaal Ministry. More distant relations included the Hon. Norman Price, formerly Judge President of the Eastern Districts Court; the late Mr Justice W. H. Ramsbottom; and Mrs Ramsbottom. (See the genealogical tree. . . .)

'Born a half-Jew, Saul Solomon was brought up in the Christian faith. Educated in England at Bedford Grammar School and Lincoln College, Oxford, he was called to the Bar at Lincoln's Inn in 1899. He practised in the Cape from 1900 to May, 1902, and thereafter in Johannesburg to May, 1906. Then he decided to enter the Anglican Church, and after reading for ordination in England, was ordained in 1908. After spending some time as Curate in the slum parish of Poplar, he returned to South Africa, becoming Curate of St. Mary's, Johannesburg, and then, in 1914, Rector of St. Saviour's, Claremont, in the Cape.

'At the beginning of 1916 Saul Solomon left the Anglican Church and became a Catholic. Returning to the Bar after nearly ten years' absence, he developed so large a practice that within three and a half years he took silk. Though he earned a reputation of charging high fees, so consummate an advocate was he, so conscientious, and so solicitous of his client's interests, that he enjoyed a very large share of the "big" work. His appointment to the Transvaal Bench in 1927 followed as a matter of course.

'As a judge Saul Solomon became known as a character. He was regarded, perhaps not unfairly, as being one of the less lenient in imposing criminal sentences. One of his habits was to nod his head as counsel made his points. The tyro thought that the judge was agreeing with him; the middle junior believed that the judge was following his points; but the silk knew that it might well mean that the judge had made up his mind against him. He was the one judge in South African history who could say that he divorced a couple whom he had married as a clergyman.'

—Ellison Kahn 'The Late Hon. Saul Solomon' (1961) 78 *SALJ* 7 at 7–8. (See also ROOS; WESSELS.)

'One day in our Court in Pretoria Saul was a few minutes late for some not particularly important appointment with the Judge President, Greenberg. "Forgive me, my dear fellow," he said in his usual bantering way, "you know that time is nothing to me". "Yes," said Greenberg, "that is what some of your prisoners have been saying."'

—Leslie Blackwell (qv) *Are Judges Human?* (1962) 69.

The Nafte murder trial

The trial of Nafte, a wealthy farmer, on a charge of murder before Saul Solomon J and a jury in the Bethal Circuit Local Division on 4 April 1929 was a cause célèbre. According to the report of R v Nafte 1929 AD 333, the jury found Nafte guilty of culpable homicide, adding a recommendation of mercy on the ground that they thought Nafte did not intend to kill the deceased, a black employee. The evidence showed that the only way Nafte could have caused the death of the deceased was by a severe flogging, by breaking his breastbone with a stone and by kicking in two of his ribs. The deceased died of shock caused by multiple injuries. Solomon J, finding Nafte guilty of cruelty, sentenced him to seven years' imprisonment and ten lashes. The Appellate Division refused to intervene, holding that neither the verdict of the jury nor its recommendation negatived any cruelty by Nafte; and that a judge was not bound by a recommendation of mercy, which was only advisory, and often anything but logical.

Dr Hjalmar Reitz was junior to Oswald Pirow for the defence. The following account by Reitz is marred by several obvious errors, but the third last paragraph is a gem which there is no reason to think is flawed.

Observe how Pirow anticipated the modern craze for jogging. (See also PIROW.)

The appeal was argued by Robin Stratford, not Bertha Solomon. Dr Reitz was thinking of the application by Mrs Bertha Solomon to Mr Justice Solomon (no relation by blood or marriage) to have the infliction of lashes postponed pending an appeal. Having obtained the agreement of the Attorney-General, she succeeded in obtaining the order. See Bertha Solomon Time Remembered *(1968) 61–2.*

'Robin [Stratford] is back from Bloemfontein where he appeared on behalf of the luckless Nafte who got his beating this morning. Robin has no complaints about the hearing accorded him. It was courteous but unyielding.'

—Oliver Deneys Schreiner (qv) in a letter to his wife Edna, 1 May 1929. Schreiner family papers.

'I was junior to Mr. Pirow when he defended Nafti [sic] on a charge of murdering a native.

'This Nafti was farming in the Bethal district on a fairly extensive scale so that he employed a large number of natives.

'One day he became annoyed with one of his natives for some quite trivial offence. I think the native had turned up late to work and had been sulky when spoken to.

'Nafti ordered him to be tied to a tree and this was done in such a way that the whole weight of his body was borne by his wrists. He was then severely beaten

SEGMENTS OF SOME BRANCHES OF THE SOLOMON GENEALOGICAL TREE[1]

JOSEPH S. — HANNAH MOSS
(1814)

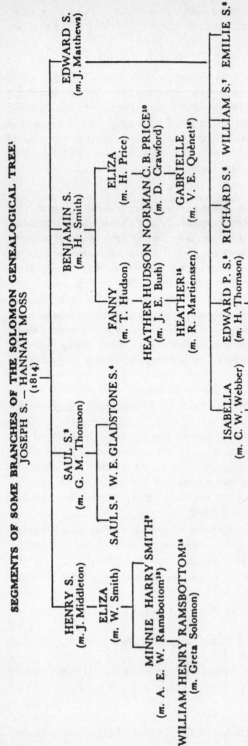

1 Information mainly from: W. E. Gladstone Solomon, *Saul Solomon* (London, Gollancz, 1930); and 'The Solomon Family (1735-1939)', a private document depicting the genealogical tree of the family, in the possession of its members, and kindly lent by W. A. Ramsbottom, Esq.

2 'The Member for Cape Town': famous Cape Parliamentarian of the last century.

3 Mr. Justice Saul Solomon, of the Transvaal Bench (ob. 1960).

4 Well-known artist.

5 Sir Edward P. Solomon, Minister of Public Works in Botha's Transvaal Ministry.

6 Sir Richard Solomon, Attorney-General in the Crown Colony of the Transvaal; Lieutenant-Governor of the Transvaal; First Union High Commissioner in London.

7 Sir William Solomon, former Chief Justice of the Union.

8 Distinguished in the fields of the temperance movement and social reform.

9 Former Deputy-Sheriff of the Witwatersrand.

10 The Hon. N. C. B. Price, former Judge-President of the Eastern Districts Local Division.

11 Prominent attorney in Johannesburg, member of the firm Webber, Wentzel, Solomon and Friel; M.P. for Troyeville, 1922-4.

12 For twenty-five years Chairman of the Johannesburg Hospital Board; member of the firm Webber, Wentzel, Solomon and Friel, attorneys.

13 Medical practitioner; Treasurer in Fischer's O.R.C. Ministry; first Administrator of the O.F.S.

14 Mr. Justice W. H. Ramsbottom (ob. 1960).

15 Heather Martienssen, Professor of Fine Arts in the University of the Witwatersrand, Johannesburg.

16 Mr. Justice V. E. Quénet, of the High Court of Southern Rhodesia.

— Ellison Kahn in (1961) 78 *S.A.L.J.* 9.

with a riem or a sjambok. And the beating continued intermittently for four or five hours; the native all the time being exposed to the blazing sun.

'Although it did not come out in the evidence, we were told that when the victim cried for water, this was given him by pouring boiling, or at least, very warm water, out of a kettle into his mouth. Unbelievable, and yet it was done. No wonder the native died that same night.

'During Mr. Pirow's address to the jury he said something to which the presiding Judge, Mr. Justice Solomon, took exception and a very heated argument ensued.

'During the judge's summing-up, or it may have been immediately after, Mr. Pirow told me that he was leaving and that I had to address the Court in mitigation. Everyone in court by this time knew that a conviction was bound to follow. Well, there I sat waiting for the jury to return and trying to think of something to say in mitigation, and there was not a thing that could be said, more especially as I knew many facts from our consultations which made the fiendish cruelty of the accused far worse than had emerged from the evidence, which was quite strong enough. And what a relief when just as the jury returned to the Court to pronounce their verdict, Mr. Pirow also slipped in and took his seat next to me.

'He had been for a run of several miles and had completely recovered his temper. He was, in fact, addicted to taking such strenuous exercise. It was his way of getting rid of his surplus energy.

'To the surprise of all and especially, no doubt, to that of Mr. Pirow, the jury brought in a verdict of guilty of culpable homicide instead of one of murder.

'He then addressed the Court in mitigation but I doubt very much whether the Judge paid much attention to his plea.

'In any case the sentence which was for several years' hard labour included the infliction of six lashes.

'Just after sentence was passed it was reported to the Judge that seven members of the jury had been in favour of a verdict of guilty of murder while two had obstinately stood out for culpable homicide.

'A deadlock had ensued and ultimately the seven had given in and agreed to make it culpable homicide.

'And this is the point and my reason for considering the case is worth recounting. The jury did not know that a verdict of seven to two was a valid one. Had they known this they would certainly, they are reported to have said, have brought in a verdict of murder and Nafti would as certainly have been hanged.

'I happened to defend the next case on the list, also a charge of murder, and Judge Solomon, in view of the miscarriage of justice in Nafti's case, went to great pains to explain clearly to the jury that seven could bring in a valid verdict.

'Lashes are considered the supreme indignity for a white man to undergo and immediately after the trial of Nafti an agitation was set on foot by his friends to try and save him from these lashes. An appeal was lodged to the Appellate Court and Mrs. Bertha Solomon, M.P., fought it to the best of her ability and I have been told that she did remarkably well seeing what a weak case she had. But the appeal was dismissed, and while very strong political and racial influence was being brought to get the Government to intervene and cancel the lashes, they were duly administered, and no man ever deserved lashes more.

'Evidently the friends of Nafti were very influential in the right quarters, for shortly after he commenced serving his sentence he was transferred to Baviaanspoort, where usually incurable inebriates and such like are confined in far more pleasant surroundings and under less stringent conditions than prevail in the ordinary gaols, and within a comparatively short period he was released.

'On the day of his release he came to my office, having been unable to contact Mr. Pirow as he told me. He was very excited and said that he was on his way to see Judge Solomon to tell him exactly what he thought of him.

'I explained to him that if he did anything like that he would certainly land in gaol again, and after considerable trouble I persuaded him to drop the idea.

'He died within two or three months of his release.'

—Hjalmar Reitz *The Conversion of a South African Nationalist* (1946) 104–7.

Another version

'THE OMISSION THAT WAS NOT FATAL

'A murder had been committed. Indeed, it was a brutal murder. An umfaan had been beaten to death by a farmer in circumstances most revolting. The countryside was ablaze and divided on political lines.

'One section—the Liberals—spoke of the deceased as "die arme naturel". The Nationalists called him "die kaffirtje". Counsel for the defence had but one view, and that was to get his client off. It was obvious, if the story told at the Preparatory Examination was true, that a Nationalist jury would be the Accused's best bet. Counsel set out to get a jury to suit the circumstances of the case. When the challenging was over, there appeared to be seven Nationalists and two United Party men on the jury. This was better than the most optimistic accused could ever hope for. There was an acquittal staring him in the face. After a protracted trial, His Lordship summed up. Counsel addressed the Court, and the jury retired to consider their verdict. They debated the matter at great length and with a considerable amount of heat. When the deadlock manifested itself, the division was seven to two. Seven Nationalists wanted to hang the Accused for killing "die kaffirtje", and two United Party men were all for letting him get away with "common assault". Eventually it was found that neither side could convert the other, and so they agreed upon a compromise. The verdict was "culpable homicide". His Lordship had omitted to advise the jury that seven to two was a competent verdict. The Accused should have been convicted of murder. He got lashes and a good stretch instead.'

—H H Morris *In and Out of Court* (1950) 76–7. (Is it our old friend Ben Trovato at work again? Se non è vero, è molto ben trovato—if it is not true, it is very well invented.)

The call to Rome

'Claremont today is probably the busiest shopping centre in the Cape Peninsula, outside of Cape Town itself. At its entrance stands the beautiful old Church of St. Saviour, which was founded by Bishop Gray more than 100 years ago.

'This is of interest to readers of this book because some 50 or 60 years ago it was the scene of an episode which rocked the Cape Peninsula and far beyond. Its incumbent, the Reverend Saul Solomon, announced from the pulpit that he was leaving the Church of England and going over to Rome. Who was this Saul Solomon? He bore a famous name. His father, also Saul, was a leading politician at the Cape in the eighties of the last century, and he was probably the shortest man who ever sat on the green benches of Parliament. He was founder of the great Argus company of today, and was a descendant of the famous Solomon family who were merchants at St. Helena in the days of Napoleon's captivity there. As they spread and multiplied after settling at the Cape, the Solomons drifted away from Judaism, and the first Saul was a pillar of the Congregational Church.

'The subject of this story went to Oxford on a scholarship, did brilliantly there, and came out to the Bar in Johannesburg early in the present century. He soon became what is known as a rising junior, and began to build up a large junior practice. Suddenly he startled everyone by throwing up his law practice and going back to Oxford to read for the Church of England. I met Saul originally when he was a curate, dog-collar and all, at St. Mary's Cathedral, Johannesburg. From there he went to St. Saviour's Church, then noted for its High Church practices, which became higher still under the Rev. Saul.

'Then, as we have seen, he startled the whole of South Africa by going over to Rome. There was no question of his remaining in the priesthood; he was married and had a family. So back to the Bar he went. This was shortly before the outbreak of World War I, when half the Johannesburg Bar was absent on active service. Partly because of this, but more because of his own exceptional ability, Saul had no difficulty in reinstating himself in the law, and eventually taking silk. As a senior he was notorious for the high fees charged, much higher than any other K.C. in South Africa.

'At last promotion came his way—if we can call it promotion to cut his income by two-thirds, and he became a judge. . . .'

—Leslie Blackwell (q v) *Blackwell Remembers* (1971) 122–3. (See also TAYLOR.)

Characteristics

'Saul and I were colleagues on the Bench for some years before his retirement. He was a whimsical fellow, full of oddities, and it looked as if his zest for hard work had been somewhat blunted as he approached retiring age. Whenever we sat together, and reserved judgment, I would suggest that I write the judgment for both of us, and usually, with a quaint smile, he would agree, saying that he could not stand between me and my appetite for the law, of which he had become conscious only since I had become his colleague.'

—Blackwell op cit at 123.

'He was sitting one day to pass sentence upon a man who had been found guilty of a serious offence. Counsel was addressing the court in mitigation of sentence. He unrolled the usual sob stuff, how his client was a young man with all his life before him (or was it an old man with nothing more to look forward to but the grave?), how he had a wife and two children (or was it that he was a lonely bachelor?), and so on. While counsel was proceeding two Jews walked into the court. They saw Saul smiling benignly as the address proceeded, almost seeming to pause to wipe away a judicial tear. One Jew nudged the other and said, "Vot a judge!" Then Solomon proceeded to sum up. "Your counsel," he said, "has stressed the various points in mitigation in your favour which I have carefully noted: that you are a young man, that you have a wife and two children. All this I will take into account." At this stage there was again a nudge, and again the remark, "Vot a judge!" Then Solomon concluded briskly, "but your offence, I must remember, is a serious one and I would not be doing my duty if I treated it lightly. The sentence is seven years' imprisonment with hard labour." The second Jew turned to his friend and said, "Vot a poker player!"'

—Blackwell op cit at 123–4.

Nodding again

'Everyone expected Saul Solomon to be a very great success on the bench. As an advocate—a forensic man—he was unbeatable. On the bench, however, he could not patiently endure the boredom of listening to cases badly presented by other people. His attention would lapse and he would appear to be asleep. Counsel would then take courage at the fact that he did not interrupt. Otto Beyers once remarked at a Bar dinner "You too readily assume he is accepting your arguments, but then, alas, you find there is *nodding* in it".'

—George S Findlay QC 'Looking Back' in *1877–1987 The Pretoria Bar/ Die Pretoriase Balie* (1977) 53 at 55.

Oliver Deneys Schreiner on Saul Solomon

'Saul is just leaving on circuit—he hates it more than heresy.'

'I went round to Saul's about half past five and chatted to him for an hour or so about circuit and the like. He really is keen on the administration of Justice. I think that he probably does a lot of good on circuit—he is so obviously in earnest on getting the wrong put right. He says he sleeps very badly on circuit.'

'I had a day in court in my running-down case. Saul gave the other side £300, I think £100 too much. Funny little chap, Saul. Extremely likeable. I really think the stage was his greatest chance. He would have enjoyed it so. Toby [Taylor; q v] also would have made a wonderful actor. I suppose the professions have a good deal in common.'

—Oliver Deneys Schreiner (q v) in letters to his wife Edna, 29 July 1928, 3 May 1929 and 8 May 1929. Schreiner family papers.

'CONSOLATION

'The Judge knew that the trial was going to be a protracted affair. The best thing to do was to prepare the jury for the worst. He reminded them of their duty as citizens. He said that it was a privilege to serve the State in the administration of justice. He said he knew what an immense sacrifice of valuable time they were about to make, and finally, in moving terms, he expressed his deepest sympathy for them on the coming ordeal.

'I asked His Lordship whether he would be good enough to extend some consolation to Counsel.

'"Mr. Morris," said Mr. Justice [Saul] Solomon, "your consolation is marked on your brief."'

—H H Morris KC *The First Forty Years* (1948) 173.

He married them and he divorced them

'I vividly recall one of the most interesting events of Solomon's career as Judge. It was in August, 1933, when I was engaged in reporting a long roll of unopposed matrimonial cases in the Rand Divorce Court. In one of these cases, Mr Morgan O. Evans, counsel for the plaintiff, handed to the court orderly a marriage certificate to be passed on by him to the presiding Judge. In doing so, counsel made a remark which he felt certain had instantly directed the attention of Mr Justice Solomon to the contents of the marriage certificate.

'Solomon looked at the certificate without betraying any emotion. He was about to put it down in an apparently unconcerned fashion when Mr Evans once again directed the Judge's attention to the contents of the certificate.

'"I respectfully assume, my lord, that you have noticed the signature which appears on the marriage certificate," he remarked.

'I was at the time of the opinion that the Judge must have noticed that the certificate clearly recorded the fact that he had himself married the litigants 17 years earlier, when he was a priest in Holy Orders at St. Mary's Church. His signature was clearly visible on the certificate.

'"Oh, yes," dryly commented the Judge as he shook his little head, and simultaneously glanced at the plaintiff in the witness box.

'"Thank you, my lord," said Mr Evans, who slyly winked at me in the Press box. He had told me earlier that morning that he had "a very good story" for me in a certain unopposed divorce case. I happened to be the only reporter in court at the time, and the appearance of my story of the unique marriage certificate incident in the following day's issue of the *Rand Daily Mail* created countrywide interest. The story also appeared in overseas newspapers, and has been referred to on innumerable occasions by writers of articles on Divorce Court happenings.'

—Isaac Goodman *Judges I Have Known* (1969) 159–60.

SIR WILLIAM HENRY SOLOMON

1852–1930. Member of the Cape Bar and then the Kimberley Bar 1878–83. Circuit Crown Prosecutor (later called Assistant Legal Adviser to the Crown) Griqualand West 1883–7. Judge of the High Court of Griqualand 1887–96. Judge of the Eastern Districts Court 1896–1902. Judge of the Transvaal High Court April–October 1902 and of the Transvaal Supreme Court October 1902–May 1910. Judge of Appeal May 1910–February 1927. Chief Justice March 1927–October 1929. Knighted (KB) 1907, KCMG 1913, KCSI 1914 (Knight Commander of the Order of the Star of India, following on the publication of the Report of the Indian Enquiry Commission (UG 16 of 1914), a commission of which Solomon was Chairman). Privy Counsellor 1928.

'Judge Solomon . . . came down to consult me about several matters connected with the Treason Court. . . . The little Judge is looking well but, as usual, painfully thin. He is a dear little man, and I shall greatly enjoy working with him in Pretoria, *when the time comes!*'

—Sir James Rose Innes (qv) to his wife 25 November 1901, prior to his assuming the position of Chief Justice of the Transvaal, Solomon having agreed to be first puisne judge. From Harrison M Wright (ed) *Sir James Rose Innes Selected Correspondence (1884–1902)* (1972) 321.

'William Solomon, of the Eastern Districts Court, and before that of the High Court of Griqualand, with fourteen years' judicial service, long-time friend and admirer of Innes, had gallantly agreed to serve as first puisne judge if Innes, who was hesitating, agreed to take the Chief Justiceship. "If you accept I will go with you." This was said to induce the acceptance of a post which, if refused, would almost certainly have gone to Solomon himself; which, if accepted, would result in Solomon's probably never attaining the highest position, for he was older than Innes by more than two years. (In fact Innes, by chivalrously retiring as Chief Justice of South Africa at the beginning of 1927 (the law governing his appointment did not impose the compulsory age of retirement at 70 that applied to all judges appointed after the passing of the Judges' Salaries and Pensions Act 16 of 1912), enabled Solomon to enjoy the sweetness of the office for two and a half years.)'

—Ellison Kahn 'James Rose Innes' in R M de Villiers (ed) *Better Than They Knew* II (1974) 57 at 72.

'Solomon was not only jurist but was also loved for his very human qualities. His colleagues and friends often referred to him as "the little judge" and "baby"—all indications of his popularity and the affection in which he was held. Apart from warm-hearted loyalty towards his friends, he was also endowed with a particularly fine sense of humour. He never missed the opportunity of making a joke but occasionally his sense of humour lost its delicacy and resulted in a sardonic expression and a sarcastic tongue.'

—M J (now Mr Justice) Strydom in *Dictionary of South African Biography* II (1972) 685. (See also INNES.)

'In my opinion, which I would hesitate to give were it not that all the members of the Bar who practised before him and whom I asked about it, agree, Sir William Solomon was the soundest lawyer we have had up to now on any of our Benches.

'He was so impartial, which of course is an attribute of all our judges; he was so patient, which has not always been the case with some others; he was so dignified and so sound. The strange fact emerges that he was not a success at the Bar. This recalls an anecdote that was told me. On the day after he was appointed a judge some friends met him in Adderley Street, Cape Town. One of them said, "Hullo, Bill, you seem to be looking for something?" to which he is said to have replied, "Yes, I am, I'm looking for some attorney with a large Supreme Court practice so that I can tell him to go to Hades." The same pleasant thought has often occurred to me, but so far I have been able to restrain myself.'

—Hjalmar Reitz *The Conversion of a South African Nationalist* (1946) 46–7.

'On one occasion he made a reply to the Chief Justice [Sir Henry de Villiers (q v)] which is well worth relating. He was arguing in an appeal case from the Kimberley Court on the question whether a mining company was the master of its contractor's servant, when de Villiers asked him, with a near approach to humour, whether a man could serve two masters. Solomon replied in his dry way that he knew there was high authority for the proposition that he could not, but he had looked into the books, and found that that authority did not hold in our Courts!'

—Victor Sampson *My Reminiscences* (1926) 56–7.

'I don't think Sir William Solomon liked me. Perhaps that was my fault. He is said to have referred to me as "that man with the awful voice". Perhaps that is what got on his nerves. I appeared before him in an arson case. The constable said that the distance between two points was X yards. I said he was wrong. I said I had measured it and it was Y yards. Later he admitted that I was right. A native

'Acting Chief Justice Solomon administering the oath to the members of the Cabinet, March 4, 1907.' *Sketch by Frank Holland* Political Cartoons Reprinted from the Star *(nd) 60.*

policeman also gave evidence. I asked him whether his memory had been refreshed since he gave evidence at the preparatory examination. He said "No". I asked him whether the policeman in charge of the case had not read his evidence over to him that very morning. He denied it. I told him that I had seen it done in the passage. He then admitted the fact. Sir William said curtly:

'"It seems to me, Mr. Morris, that you know too much about this case."

'"That is what I am here for, my lord."'

—H H Morris KC *The First Forty Years* (1948) 48.

'Sir William Solomon (later a Chief Justice of South Africa) was one of the rare persons who make good judges after having held civil service appointments. One reason for their comparative failure was that they had not gone through the rough-and-tumble experience of general practice at the Bar, had led cloistered lives in the seclusion of a government office, and had no knowledge of the world. Solomon was regarded as having the greatest ability of any judge on the Bench. He was cautious and logical, and had a rare power of disentangling and analysing complicated facts. Jim Leonard was very proud of the fact that when he was Attorney-General of the Cape (then a ministerial office) he had nominated Solomon, then a Law Adviser at Cape Town, to a judgeship at Kimberley, in the High Court of Griqualand. From Kimberley he went to Grahamstown, where he married a Miss Christian from Port Elizabeth. The story went that they took a large house at Grahamstown, and went through it. His wife said: "This will be the drawing room . . . this the dining room . . . this the morning room . . . this the sewing room—". "What about my library?" the judge ventured, timidly. "Oh—" she looked about, and then opened the door of a cupboard under the stairs—"this will do for your library, my dear."

'Solomon was sardonic in manner, and sarcastic in speech. He was seldom seen to smile, and then it was on the wrong side of his face. He looked sour, rather than stern.'

—Manfred Nathan *Not Heaven Itself: An Autobiography* (1944) 205. (Solomon had been a Law Adviser at Kimberley, not Cape Town.)

ALFRED LEONARD SPOOR

1877–1948. Patent agent.

'Spoor was trained as a marine engineer in the naval dockyards in Plymouth. He was destined for the Royal Navy, but he had defective vision, and in those days, that was that.

'Round about 1904 he was enlisted as a draftsman by the then firm of D M Kisch and Co, of which Charles Kisch, the son of the founder, D M Kisch, was the proprietor. Spoor had emigrated to South Africa and qualified as a patent agent by writing, in 1908, the examinations established (for the first time) by the 1902 Ordinance [the Patents Proclamation 22 of 1902 (Transvaal)]. When the 1916 Act [the Patents, Designs, Trade Marks and Copyright Act 9 of 1916] introduced examinations with a new syllabus, he sat them and passed. I have a hazy recollection that the papers were set and marked in London, as there was no one here fit to do so; but I am not sure about this.

'Spoor practised in partnership with Charles Kisch under the style of D M Kisch and Co. When the first World War broke out, Spoor was all for joining the Royal Navy, but he was forestalled by Charles Kisch, who joined the army and left Spoor to run the practice. This was to be one of the main bones of contention when the partnership was dissolved in 1920, and Spoor set up his own practice on 1 December of that year.

'In 1924 he opened a branch office in Pretoria, with Walter Chowles as the manager. Chowles was a colourful character. He had worked in London for W P Thompson and later for Cleveland, where he started at eight shillings a week. He had a fund of stories of the profession of patent agency in the early years of the century. He would tell of firms which are now universally known and highly respected that used to bribe Patent Office personnel to divert work their way. All this with great bursts of laughter. . . .

'Throughout their association he and Spoor carried on a running fight. I remember, when I took over the firm, finding copies of acrimonious correspondence in which Chowles refused to "take any more" and was going "to walk out". It would have been a pity from Spoor's point of view, because Chowles did all the agency work, which Spoor could not be bothered with, and all the trade mark work. Spoor regarded trade marks as a sort of subworld unworthy of the attention of a patent agent; but I don't remember him refusing any of the substantial profits brought in by the practice that Chowles had built up.

'Chowles was unqualified, but in those days anyone could be a trade marks agent, and Chowles was certainly well qualified, by experience at least, to be one. He had tried, unsuccessfully, to persuade the Court (Chowles vs The Registrar of Patents) that he was entitled to write the patent agents' examinations without surmounting the preliminary hurdle of matriculation. It didn't make any difference to him, as Spoor was not an attorney and could therefore run an office without a qualified man in attendance.

'Chowles was a chubby man, who bore a strong resemblance to Mr Punch. He had an infectious laugh and enjoyed a bawdy story. As I had leanings that way myself, I used to regale him with any that came my way. His fancy was that they were hatched at the YMCA, where I used to live at the time. Unfortunately, he was wrong. I still have happy memories of the gales of laughter that rewarded my efforts.

'He was a lovely man and I missed him enormously when he retired, and, not long after, died.

'Spoor was a character straight out of Dickens, in most ways the antithesis of Walter Chowles. He was a humourless, introspective man, tall, thin and dyspeptic. His standard garb was a brown suit, strictly Edwardian, with stovepipe trousers, a knitted black tie the same width all the way down, boots with hooks for the laces, and a brown felt hat perched on the top of his sandy head.

'He was a habitual pipe smoker. He used two types of tobacco, one that was called his "clients' tobacco", smoked when he was consulting, and harmless only when compared with the other, his normal tobacco. The latter had a high percentage of saltpetre, which sent sparks flying despite the little cap over the bowl. As a result, his suit became progressively more holey, until his secretary, Miss Stevenson, decided the time had come. She would then ring up Corner, the tailor, and say: "Please send Mr Spoor another suit, same as last." The same routine extended to his shirts and boots.

'He was an absent-minded man. Steve (Miss Stevenson) used to put reminder notes in his hatband. As likely as not, he used not to notice them, and he would stride down the street with bits of paper fluttering in his hat, like feathers on a Red Indian headdress.

'There is no doubt about his ability as a patent agent. At a time when the standard of specification writing in South Africa was deplorably low, he stood out as the master. I should think that he was the finest patent draftsman that this country has seen. But he was oddly naïve. Wesley John used to tell about the time Spoor advised him not to become a patent agent, because everything of any importance had already been invented. And this was probably before the first World War.

'His manner of working was individual. He wrote his specifications in a crabbed writing indecipherable to anyone except Steve, and then she would often have to type four or five alternatives for him to select the correct one, or reject them all. His writing tool was equally individual. Steve would buy him lead pencils, which she then cut up into one inch pieces and sharpened. He would hold them between finger and thumb and use them until blunted, when they would be junked in favour of the next fragment.

'I can't remember him ever going to the Patent Office. That sort of chore he left to Walter Chowles or to me. He was a perfectionist and a very hard taskmaster. . . .

'He was completely unsocial, or even antisocial. I never knew him take a client to lunch or go out to lunch himself. I never knew him use a Christian name: even one of his few intimates, if not his only intimate, Wesley John [qv], remained "John" to the last. I very much doubt if he knew what my Christian name was, even less that we shared one. I never knew him speak of going to a concert, a theatre or the pictures. His only hobby was cine photography, but as I never was given the opportunity of seeing the results, I don't know if they were any good.

'He was, I think, a lonely man. He lived apart from his wife, whom he used to visit for three weeks every year. Most of his evenings were devoted to work, with the aid of Miss Stevenson, who fulfilled the roles of secretary, bookkeeper, office manager, stand-by typist and general factotum. She had a flat in the same building in Joubert Park. Whether their relationship extended beyond work, was a constant source of speculation. The majority opinion was that it did. I don't know, but I hope it did for both their sakes.

'I don't know if he was stingy, or just oblivious. I never knew him give anyone in the office a raise in salary. Steve went from Kisch with him in 1920 at 35 pounds a month, and, when he died in 1948, she was still earning 35 pounds a month.

'I remained at my starting salary of one pound a day until I left to go to the wars.

'On my return from the wars, and with Spoor hovering close to death in hospital, Miss Stevenson was the only continuity link I had. She was, of course, non-technical, but she was able to bridge the gap on the admin side.

'After Spoor's death, she stayed on for a few months to see me through the tricky transition period, and then retired.

'Steve was a character in herself. She had been Spoor's secretary at Kisch, and had left with him, and was with him till his end.

'She was a large woman, who qualified for worst dressed woman of the decade. She was never without a cigarette dangling out of the corner of her mouth, surrounded by a yellow halo of tobacco stain. She never married, and appeared to have no interests beyond her job. She retired to live with her wealthy mother in Cape Town.

'I remember her with affection.

'In the late '60's on the occasion of one of my rare visits to Cape Town, I looked Steve up. To my amazement, the ragbag of earlier years was no more. She was an elegant, well-turned-out, soignée lady.'

—L J Fisher 'Some Memories of My Partner and Mentor, the Late A. L. Spoor' *The South African Institute of Patent Agents Newsletter* No. 32–6/88 p 10 at pp 10–12. (See also JOHN.)

CHARLES FRAMPTON STALLARD

1871–1971. Member of the London Bar 1895–1902. Member of the Johannesburg Bar 1902–36. KC 1910. MP 1929–38, 1939–48. Minister of Mines 1939–45.

'Leader of the Johannesburg Bar for many years, Stallard was a lesser lawyer than Mackeurtan [q v], but superior in forensic oratory. Tall and spare, this distinguished soldier was loved by all who served under him. His patrician features recalled those of the Iron Duke and were embellished by prominent John Bull sideburns. His bearing was erect and soldierly, and free even in his late nineties of any stoop. His views were ultra-conservative and die-hard, even by Victorian standards. He was not amused when I twitted him in Parliament as one "who in a previous reincarnation must surely have been the constitutional adviser to his prematurely deceased Majesty, King Charles the First". On non-white policy Stallard was closer to the Nationalists than to his own party. A confirmed bachelor, he deprecated almost to his dying day the participation of women in politics, and was wont to assert that most of our ills stemmed from the unwise extension of the franchise to women.'

—Leif Egeland *Bridges of Understanding* (1977) 98.

'In the general election in April 1938 Stallard was beaten. By now he had ceased to be in active legal practice. In 1936, when the Bar decided to move from Corporation Buildings to Empire Buildings, Arthur Suzman [q v], the honorary

'MR. C. F. STALLARD, K.C.'
Caricature by D C Boonzaier (1865–1950), from his
Rand Faces *(1915) 35*

secretary of the Bar Council, could not persuade him to go with the others. "Suzman," he said, "from where I come if we move once in a hundred years that is often."

'But political life still called. . . .

'Smuts took Stallard, as leader of the Dominion Party, into his Cabinet, just as he took in Walter Madeley, as leader of the Labour Party. From September 1939 onwards Stallard was Minister of Mines in Smuts's ministry. But the differences in political outlook caused the inevitable parting of the ways after the War. In December 1945 Stallard left the Cabinet, though until the general election of April 1948 he continued to represent Pieter-maritzburg (District) in the Assembly. . . .

'From the middle of 1948 Stallard retired to his farm Hope Woolith, 16 kilometres south-east of Johannesburg, where he had lived since the early years of the century, and little was heard of him save when the daily Press made mention of his ninetieth and ninety-ninth birthdays. On the last-mentioned event he said: "I propose to watch this distressful and disintegrating world for some time yet." The occasion of his turning 100 aroused much sentiment. By now he was becoming increasingly deaf and his eyes no longer permitted his reading fine print. Mentally, however, he was fully alert. He confessed to being an "unrepentant Victorian" and considered that almost everything decent and worth while had gone. What pride we had was in our past. There was little hope for the future. Mob rule had taken the place of law and order. The British Empire had gone and had yielded nothing in its place. Europe was nearing her end. (See *Sunday Times* 13 May 1971.)

'Merton College [of the University of Oxford] sent him a message: "From the oldest college to its oldest living member." The House of Assembly took the unprecedented step of resolving to extend its heartiest congratulations to him (*Debates* 4 June 1971 cols 8157–61). The Minister of Finance, Dr N Diederichs, spoke of him as a man "with self-control and with self-discipline that almost verged on the Spartan . . . who carried with him . . . the chivalry of a bygone age. He is a person who, through his own dignity, lent dignity to every occasion in which he took part. Col Stallard is a person who has remained mentally and physically strong. Perhaps it is because he rejects with so much contempt the decadence of the Western world which he sees today." The Minister said that Stallard had declined several offers of judgeships. That I am unable to verify. If Stallard had gone on the Bench he would have experienced difficulties, for he was unilingual. As the Hon J G N Strauss, a colleague of his in Smuts's Cabinet, said in a tribute paid to him on the radio, there were two things that Stallard had escaped in the course of his long life—matrimony and any knowledge of Afrikaans.

'Those who visited Stallard in his last few months noticed with dismay a sad deterioration in his physical condition. At his birthday celebrations at Hope Woolith in the presence of about five to seven hundred guests, clad in a lounge suit and wearing his medals he emerged from his study and walked slowly on the arm of Commandant C J Derby-Lewis, officer commanding the Witwatersrand Rifles, of which he had been honorary colonel for 34 years. An engraved scroll was presented to him on behalf of the Society of Advocates of South Africa (Witwatersrand Division) by Mr Herbert Rothschild SC, the Chairman of the Johannesburg Bar Council, and Mr John Coaker, one of the council members. . . .

'Then came a roll of drums and the skirling of 100 pipers drawn from various regiments, followed by a ceremonial march past of 100 men of the Witwatersrand Rifles. After Commandant C J Derby-Lewis had spoken in his praise, Stallard replied firmly and clearly for twenty minutes without a note and without a microphone—"Anyone who has not the voice to do it should not make a public speech", he used to say. "I am feeling very much as though I were in a dream in being here. I have been led from above undoubtedly and have been enabled to lead my life quietly. I have received many blessings from above, and of these I number friendship and admiration. Friends all, thank you for the game."

'Nine days later Stallard died. He was buried on 15 June on his farm in front of his private chapel of St Cuthbert's with full military honours from the Witwatersrand Rifles. The graveside service was conducted by the Rt Rev Leslie Stradling, Anglican Bishop of Johannesburg.

'A page of our history had come to an end.'

—Ellison Kahn 'In Memoriam: Colonel the Hon C F Stallard KC DSO MC 4 June 1871–13 June 1971' (1971) 88 *SALJ* 271 at 272–5.

His doctor remembers

'This afternoon I had a telephone call from Dr Henry Stein, whose rooms are in Southdale, in the southern part of Johannesburg. After introducing himself, Dr Stein said that Mr Mendelow had shown him what I had written about Stallard in the *South African Law Journal*, and he wanted to tell me more about Stallard. He had been Stallard's general medical practitioner—Southdale was not far from Stallard's farm.

'Stallard, he told me, used to walk around his farm, even in winter, right to the end, wearing a broad-brimmed hat and denim shorts. In the evening he always changed into his dinner suit. He would drink wine from his fine cellar. On his sideboard stood his splendid silver.

'Stallard's library was an enormous room. In winter a huge log would burn day and night in the fireplace, making it very hot. Owing to the heat, the size of the room, and Stallard's loss of hearing, Dr Stein would enter the house by the back door. Stallard used to tell him to come in by the front door; to which Stein would

'STALLARD: "OPEN, IN THE NAME OF THE LAW AND ORDER."'
Cartoon by John Michael ('Jock') Leyden (1908–) All the Best (1939) 45. From the Natal Daily News
19 April 1939

reply that if he knocked at the back door one of the servants would hear him, otherwise he would not gain entry.

'Once a week Stallard's driver would take him by car to the Rand Club, where Stallard would have a meal. En route Stallard would buy food supplies at a shop in Booysens.

'During Stallard's last illness Dr Stein called in the specialist physician, Dr Pericles Menof. Both wanted Stallard to go into a nursing home. He refused to do so, but did permit them to arrange the attendance of nurses day and night.

'Dr Stein asked Stallard, then 99, whether he had any relatives. "Yes," was the reply, "I have a younger brother who lives in Scotland. He is only 89."

'On the last day of his life Stallard insisted on getting up and going into his library. He sat in his large chair for five minutes, then said "I want to go to bed". After he had been in bed for a few minutes he slid gently from life.'

—Ellison Kahn's commonplace book 27 July 1990.

'Stallard is remembered more as an advocate, soldier and devout churchman than as a politician. He lived to celebrate his centenary on 5th June, 1971. This took the form of a moving and memorable function at his home, Hope Woolith, organized by the Witwatersrand Rifles, of which he had been Colonel-in-Chief for thirty-four years. Hundreds of his friends from all walks of life were present. After being accorded musical honours by a hundred pipers, he took the salute from a Guard of Honour and made the best of the many speeches I had heard from him in the thirty-eight years I had known him. He spoke without a note, but with deep feeling, and concluded by quoting from Tennyson: "I hope to see my Pilot face to face/When I have crost the bar." Within a fortnight Charles Frampton Stallard had crossed the bar.'

—Leif Egeland *Bridges of Understanding* (1977) 99.

'That grand old man, Charles Stallard, celebrated his hundredth birthday on June 5th, 1971, with a great party given by his friends and admirers. He and I were colleagues at the Bar from the day I entered in 1908 up to the day I left the Bar in 1943 to go on the Bench. We were also Parliamentary colleagues for many years. If I were asked to name the man who nearest approached to the beau ideal of an English gentleman, I could nominate no other than Stallard. What a fine character. A lifelong bachelor, and yet a patriarch among all and sundry who lived on his farm on the southern slopes of Johannesburg. A devout churchman, who built a church on his own farm for the benefit of his retainers. A connoisseur of wine. Ascetic-looking, yet no ascetic. He died peacefully seven days after his hundredth birthday. What a wonderful end to a wonderful career.'

—Leslie Blackwell (q v) *Blackwell Remembers* (1971) 205.

'Stallard invariably showed the greatest respect for the Bench and was reluctant, save in extreme cases, to express any adverse view on a judicial appointment; for the making of such appointments was a function of the executive alone. In the early nineteen-thirties such an extreme case seemed to arise, and Stallard presided over a Bar meeting at which there was a full discussion, in which he took part, of the Bar's right, or duty, to tell the Government that it disapproved of appointing active party politicians to the Bench. A resolution expressing disapproval was passed.

'Stallard firmly believed in the normal recruitment of the Bench from the Bar, a belief that was in line with a Bar resolution of 1919. But he rejected the notion that the Bench was the only proper end of a successful career at the Bar. Apart from politics, which, under a sense of duty, he chose for himself, there were various forms of public service in which the ageing advocate could usefully engage; and, in any event, an honourable and satisfactory finish was to remain in practice until one was forced by years or disability to retire to bed or bowling green.

'Stallard respected all juniors of the Bar as his brethren and sympathized with their difficulties. When a junior briefed with him was unhelpful Stallard suffered him, if not gladly, at least without obvious dismay. In keeping with this attitude was his rejection of the easy generalization that average ability, plus industry, would ensure success at the Bar. For he knew of many cases where poor health, diffidence, roughness of manner, or even sheer ill luck had kept above-average men from going as far as their intelligence and determination would otherwise have carried them.

'In court Stallard's stern, handsome face and fine choice of language could not fail to operate persuasively in support of his arguments, and in cross-examination he was a most effective exposer of the untruthful or evasive witness.'

—O D S[chreiner] (q v) 'Charles Frampton Stallard' (1971) 88 *SALJ* 275 at 276–7.

'He soon established a leading practice at the Johannesburg Bar, and rapidly rose to become one of its most eminent and sought-after members, and took silk within ten years of his call. He was the leader of the Johannesburg Bar and Chairman of the Johannesburg Bar Council from 1921 to 1924.

'In 1922 the Transvaal was convulsed by the "Rand Strike", followed by the declaration of martial law, a time in which violence was widespread. After public order was restored, a special criminal court was set up to try a very large number of serious cases in which 46 persons were charged with murder, 110 with high treason, five with sedition and 45 with other offences. Most of the accused were without adequate means to pay for their defence, and the burden of finding *pro Deo* counsel was cast upon the Transvaal Bar in numerous capital cases. It was quite unsuitable that such cases should be defended only by the most junior members of the Bar who were then taking cases *pro Deo*. At this time it was Stallard who, with his characteristic courage and sense of propriety, gave an impressive lead to the senior and established members of the Bar in appearing in these cases, and so overcame whatever reluctance there may have been to take on such arduous work without fees, or with only nominal fees, acting in a very unpopular cause.'

—N E Coaker 'Stallard: The Man and the Advocate' (1971) 88 *SALJ* 277 at 277–8.

GABRIEL STEYN

1885–1961. Public servant, prosecutor and magistrate 1906–19. Member of the Cape Bar 1919–46. KC 1944. Judge of the Cape Provincial Division 1946–55.

'The Judge's main claim to fame is, of course, his work on wills; *Steyn on Wills* is one of the best-known South African text-books. . . .

'In arguing in Court, as he sometimes found himself doing, against his book, he would have his attention drawn to that fact. Rising on one such occasion with aplomb, he remarked, "Ah, yes, m'lord, but that will be altered in the second edition".'

—M C G[racie] 'The Hon. Mr. Justice G. Steyn' (1947) 64 *SALJ* 1 at 2. (See also BUCKLE.)

LUCAS CORNELIUS STEYN

1903–76. Lecturer in Law, University of Stellenbosch, 1927–8. Professional assistant to the Attorney-General for South West Africa 1928–31. Attorney-General of South West Africa 1931. A Government Law Adviser 1933–44. KC 1943. Senior Government Law Adviser 1944–51. Judge of the Transvaal Provincial Division 1951–5. Judge of Appeal 1955–9. Chief Justice 1959–71.

'L C Steyn told me that he should never have gone into law. His real love was that of the soil. He came from a farming family from Viljoenskroon in the Orange Free State, a family with no legal connections whatever. As a child he went to school six miles away on horseback. He then let the horse loose until he had to go home, when he caught and saddled it and rode back. The reasons for his early retirement were his fatigue arising from his heavy work on the Appellate Division, and the call of the blood for the land. He settled on the farm "Eenkant" in the district of Viljoenskroon.'

'DR THE HON L C STEYN'

*Reproduced with kind permission of the Rand
Afrikaans University*

—Ellison Kahn's commonplace book 19 July 1971.

The former Judge President of the Natal Provincial Division is recounting his experience as leader of the team whose client was Knight, a former medical practitioner whose name had been removed from the medical register as a result of his conviction and imprisonment on a charge of culpable homicide arising out of an abortion he had performed and on several charges of abortion. The Knight saga was of great public interest in Durban. For other aspects of it, see H H (HARRY) MORRIS *and* WESSELS.

'Shaw and I were soon engaged upon what our client regarded as a much more important matter. He ardently desired to get back on the medical register, but there was little hope for him so long as his convictions of abortion and culpable homicide stood against him. He had obtained some further evidence which was not available to him at his trial, so we set about preparing a petition to the Governor-General for a free pardon. This involved many weeks of hard work. We had to familiarise ourselves with the whole technique of surgical abortion; for this purpose we were supplied with a complete set of gynaecological instruments and were instructed in their use. I hasten to explain, however, that we did not go so far as did the Attorney-General when he was preparing to conduct the prosecution of our client: he obtained the use of a female corpse. My knowledge on the subject of abortion is therefore strictly theoretical. Our aim was to include in the petition a full account of the trial, in readable narrative form. When we had completed the petition it was sent to the Minister for transmission to the Governor-General. The Minister however directed that Shaw and I should first appear before a Government law adviser and argue the whole case, after which the law adviser would submit a report to accompany the petition to the Governor-General. So in due course we spent some days in Pretoria arguing before a quiet, courteous young law adviser called Steyn. Naturally, we never knew the terms of his report, but it must have been adverse because the pardon was refused. The ex-doctor took further steps to secure the setting aside of his convictions but with no success, so he started to practise as a dietician, in which capacity I once consulted him and received some valuable advice which I have followed ever since: "Almost anyone can tolerate twenty cigarettes a day, but every one over that is poison." We remained on friendly terms until his death. He was a remarkable man with an unbounded capacity for making devoted friends and bitter enemies. Most but not all of his colleagues in the medical profession were in the latter category. It was said that his unpopularity with other doctors was due to his knack of curing people whom they had sentenced to death, but that of course is nonsense. Whether or not he was an abortionist, he was often guilty of conduct which was regarded as unethical. He was a born showman and kept no careful guard over his tongue. . . .

' . . . Shaw and I little knew that the young Government law adviser before whom we appeared in Pretoria was destined to jump straight from his office chair to the Bench of the Transvaal Supreme Court, thence to the Bench of the Appellate Division, thence to the seat once occupied by Lord de Villiers, Sir James Rose Innes and their illustrious successors as Chief Justice of South Africa, a feat without parallel in the history of our country.'

—F N Broome *Not the Whole Truth* (1962) 148–9.

MARTHINUS THEUNIS STEYN

1857–1916. Legal practitioner Orange Free State 1883–9. State Attorney 1889. Judge of the High Court of the Orange Free State 1889–96. President of the Orange Free State 1896–1902.

Early years in practice

'He had . . . begun to grow a beard, and he let it grow until it became one of the longest beards worn by a famous South African.'

—Johannes Meintjes *President Steyn: A Biography* (1969) 41.

His standing for election as President of the Orange Free State

'The only things that counted against M. T. Steyn were his youth and his lack of experience as a politician. "It is a weakness that will improve with the years," he commented wryly. On the other [hand] he was a well-known Judge, popular and sought-after. He was a born Free Stater, a descendant of distinguished South African families. He was learned and a patriot, a Republican to the core of his being.'

— Meintjes op cit 52–3. (Cf the celebrated reply of William Pitt the elder (1708–78) in the House of Commons on 27 January 1741: 'The atrocious crime of being a young man . . . I shall neither attempt to palliate nor deny.' 'If youth is a fault, it is one which is soon corrected': Goethe *Maxims and Aphorisms.*)

The reaction to his engagement to Tibbie Fraser

'Onder die lede van die Balie kon niks meer populêr gewees het nie, en op Philippolis het die verlowing 'n groot sensasie verwek.

'Mej. Fraser was die dogter van die alombekende ds. Fraser, wat toe alreeds vier-en-twintig jare in elke huisgesin van die omvangryke gemeente met vrou en al van harte bemind was.

'Dat die verlowing oral byval gevind het, kan nie beweer word nie. By vele was daar teleurstelling. Verskeie ou mense het gesê: "Wat! die dogter van onse Meneer met 'n advokaat gaan trou!"—dit was amper *sacrilegium.*

'In die oë van verskeie oues was 'n advokaat 'n ding wat wel nuttig kan wees om vir jou te pleit as jy voor die Hof beskuldig staan, maar verder moet 'n mens maar so min moontlik met hom te doen hê. Die ou spreekwoord: "Hy lieg soos 'n advokaat," gee presies weer wat die hart van ou pastorie-vriende met groot verontrusting vervul het.

'Een ou man het na ds. Fraser gekom en gesê: "Meneer, die advokatekoek is die enigste in die hemel wat nog nie aan gesny is nie. Jy kan 'n advokaat nie vertrou nie. Hy pleit net so hard vir 'n skuldige as vir 'n onskuldige—en dan nog daardie

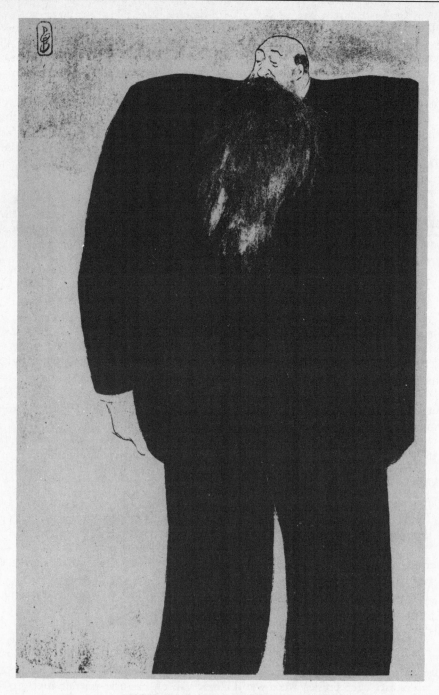

MARTHINUS THEUNIS STEYN
Caricature by D C Boonzaier (1865–1950), from his My Caricatures *(1912)*

Steyn! Ek het hom eendag verskriklik in die Hof hoor tekere gaan teenoor die beweringe van advokaat Krause. Toe die Hof verdaag, stap die twee soos boesemvriende daaruit—daar het jy dit: In die Hof wil hy Krause verskeur en ager die oë stap hy met hom gearmd. Aan so 'n man gee ek nie my dogter nie."

'Ds. en mevr. Fraser het maar geglimlag. Hulle het van die aanstaande skoonseun die beste verwagtings gehad.'

—N J van der Merwe *Marthinus Theunis Steyn, 'n Lewensbeskrywing* I (1921) 45–6.

JAMES STRATFORD

1869–1952. Member of the Cape Bar 1901–2. Member of the Johannesburg Bar 1902–21. KC 1912. Judge of the Transvaal Provincial Division 1921–7. Judge of Appeal 1927–38. Chief Justice 1938–9.

'One is inclined to recall the heroes of one's earlier days and say "there were giants in the earth in those days", but making due allowance for this weakness I think I can say with confidence that the South African Bar has in my time seen no one quite his equal. The qualities needed to make the perfect lawyer are such and so numerous that the perfect lawyer has probably never been and probably never will exist, nor did Stratford possess all those qualities. There have been many more learned men at the South African Bar and on the South African Bench. Indeed, he could not be described as learned. He knew "little Latin and less Greek"; he had but a nodding acquaintance with Afrikaans, Dutch and French. He knew no German or other modern language save his own and was therefore cut off from profound study of Roman and Roman-Dutch law. It is told of the great Lord Russell of Killowen that when he had come to the English Bar and there had risen like cream to the top, one of his colleagues, discussing him with another, said, "That fellow Russell doesn't really know much law", to which the other answered, "Yes, that may be so, but what he does know he knows well". Stratford, like Russell, had a profound grasp of legal principles and he had an almost uncanny power of analysis of complicated fact and a knowledge of which of conflicting principles must be applied. He was sometimes accused of over-subtlety, wholly wrongly, I think, for he was eminently practical and he had at his disposal a great fund of common sense. He never strained law against equity. If his juniors in a case laid before him an over-subtle argument he would say, "Your reasoning may be perfectly logical, but the facts of this case being as they are no court would act upon it". And this faculty of distinguishing the real from the unreal is plainly discernible in his judgments.

'There was no man at the Bar who prepared his cases more thoroughly. He worked rapidly and easily. He suffered from indifferent health, but, well or ill, he always worked vigorously. Clients could, if need be, have consultations with him when he was ill in bed. In Leeds he underwent a terrible operation, and when lying there in great pain and almost at death's door, curiosity would force him to ask his nurses why they did so-and-so to him. If their explanation was unsatisfactory, as it generally was, he would carefully and clearly point out its insufficiency.

'His cross-examination of witnesses was masterly. A favourite method of his was by argumentative questioning to drive the witness by logical process into making the desired admission. A noticeable feature of his advocacy was its extreme honesty. However attractive and favourable an argument might seem to be, if he thought it unsound he would decline to put it even when it was suggested to him by the court. He had legal convictions and he abided by those convictions. For him every legal problem had but one solution and it was almost incomprehensible to him that anyone should seek to solve the problem in any other manner. I remember his complaining to me of the advocacy of a very brilliant member of the Bar then in practice. "X", he said, "is prepared to argue a point either way. He has no legal convictions."

'Combined with Stratford's qualities already referred to must be mentioned his inherent sense of justice. He realized fully and never lost sight of the fact that the purpose of the courts was to do justice between man and man. Injustice was hateful to him.'

—G A Mulligan in (1952) 69 *SALJ* 1–2. (See also F W BEYERS; ROOS.)

'Stratford J: "Mr Jones, I fail to understand your argument."
'Jones (not his name, nor the name he was born with; a little man, not the brightest of counsel): "Yes, my lord, it is a difficult one to understand."'

—Ellison Kahn's commonplace book, based on the unpublished commonplace book of Fritz B Adler, of the Johannesburg Bar, kindly lent by Mr (now Mr Justice) W P Schutz SC. A well-known delicate story.

GEORGE GERHARD SUTTON

1880–1950. Member of the Cape Bar 1903–29. KC 1921. Judge of the Cape Provincial Division 1929–46. Judge President 1946–8.

The judge at the Show

'I had a cheery letter from Bill [Oliver Schreiner's brother]. . . . He says George Sutton [Oliver Schreiner's cousin, and at the time a judge of the Cape Provincial Division] tells a good story against himself. There was a big party at Govt. House about Show time, to which he & Agnes [Sutton's wife] were bidden. He found himself next to a titled dame from England who made kindly & condescending conversation, in the course of which she said to him "And what is your occupation?" George with becoming modesty, said "Oh, I am a Judge". "Just down for judging at the Show, I suppose?", said the Countess! I couldn't help wondering whether George as he conversed was potting a bit & dropping crumbs on his waistcoat—after all, the poor dame had some excuse!'

—Oliver Deneys Schreiner (q v) in a letter to his wife Edna, 13 March 1935. Schreiner family papers.

'Georgie', the terror to very junior counsel and articled clerks

'On 1 March 1939 I reported to Arthur Tancred on the 2nd Floor, Colonial Orphan Chamber Building, 41 Parliament Street, Cape Town, to start serving him as an articled clerk. . . .

'He was not in the least afraid to delegate matters, and did so in such a charming and friendly way, no matter whether it was a difficult case he was off-loading or a packet of cigarettes he needed. I learnt a great deal from this unique experience, and basked in his encouragement and appreciation of a job well done: whose knowledge and confidence wouldn't multiply in such a rich growing medium?

'How I enjoyed it all! I can still remember smiling happily to myself on Sunday evenings and looking forward eagerly to yet another week's work. In later years

I found the sheer delight in my work hard to believe, but it was a fact. I think the reasons for my attitude lay in the fact that I had very little real responsibility, that the work was all so interesting (and new) and that Arthur was so pleasant to work for. Where I did have full responsibility was in pauper matters, where I was on my own. They were enjoyable, too, with one nerve-racking exception: Georgie, alias the Honourable Mr Justice G G Sutton.

'Georgie deemed it his mission in life to keep newly admitted advocates and articled clerks up to scratch by searching out every slightest deviation from the Rules of Court and pouncing on the unlucky miscreants. The advocate was usually blameless unless perhaps he had not noticed the misdemeanour and drawn it to the Court's attention. It was more frequently the articled clerk who had to try to explain. At best there was a reprimand, with Georgie bouncing up and down in his chair with excitement and indignation. Rather worse was a postponement, worse still an "Order Refused". Worst of all was "Who is your principal? I want to see him. Go and ring him and tell him I want to see him here at once."

'We soon learnt never to set a matter down for hearing during a week in which Georgie was taking Third Division. So Georgie's stream of victims dried up—until the Court set it flowing again by slyly refusing to announce in advance who was taking Third Division. The secret then was to wait until a Tuesday before setting a matter down for hearing, by which time it was known which Judge was on Third Division. If it were Georgie, the matter would have to wait until the following week—but even this was not always possible. So every Tuesday the news would spread like wildfire among the articled clerks—"Don't worry, it's not Georgie" or "Oh Lord, its Georgie and I've got two matters on".

' . . . To us articled clerks, Georgie on the warpath was much more of a menace than Hitler on the move.'

—R M MacSymon *Fairbridge, Arderne & Lawton: A History of a Cape Law Firm* (1990) 180–2. (See also GREENBERG.)

ARTHUR SUZMAN

1905–85. Member of the Johannesburg Bar 1928, 1933–85. KC 1948.

'In March 1984 the University of the Witwatersrand conferred on Arthur Suzman the degree of LLD (honoris causa) "for his long distinguished service in so many fields of endeavour". His reply to my letter of congratulations included the following:

"I find it difficult to believe that this happy occasion is but a few days short of my call to the Transvaal Bar, 56 years ago.

"I readily confess to unusual industry and determination. I have learnt, however, that one never gets out of a case more than one puts into it and one seldom gets as much. In this context, I often tell my juniors of the occasion, many years ago, when my then junior (now on the Bench) remarked—

" 'But Arthur, this is our fifth draft!'

"To which I retorted, 'Yes, but you will readily concede that each is an improvement on the last!'

"Nowadays, in each major matter in which I appear, I begin to wonder whether it is to be my 'Swan Song'. Happily, however, I continue to sing, though perhaps not as lustily as heretofore."'

—Mr Justice H H Nestadt 'Arthur Suzman QC 31 October 1905–7 February 1985: A Tribute' (1985) 102 *SALJ* 320.

'It appears from his contribution to *Fiat Iustitia: Essays in Memory of Oliver Deneys Schreiner* (at 132) that he was the sole person admitted to the Transvaal Bar in 1928. He remained exceptional. He was relatively short of stature, but intellectually superior; courteous and softly spoken yet a powerful personality; kind and warm; on the other hand, an unyielding, formidable opponent in court; in many ways conservative and serious whilst at the same time having an engaging—indeed an impish—sense of humour. I understand from a colleague who spoke to him after the graduation ceremony that he said that the most difficult part of it was "to stand there and look modest". Perhaps he was a man of contrasts. On the other hand, he was consistent in his pursuit of excellence. This applied to whatever he undertook. And he achieved it in full measure.'

—Nestadt op cit at 320–1.

'He was meticulously thorough in his thoughtful preparation of a case. His industry and diligence were legendary. He worked long hours. His well-reasoned arguments were delivered with lucidity and a compelling conviction and persuasiveness. He had a skilful capacity to absorb and analyse complex facts. He delighted in using a mixed metaphor. In a recent patent matter his retort to a point made by his opponent was that "it was a red herring which backfired". He maintained his large and varied practice at the Johannesburg Bar to almost the end. He was devoted to the law. He had an enduring enthusiasm for it. His was a labour of love.'

—Nestadt op cit at 321.

'Arthur Suzman to a judge at a dinner party: "I have appeared in six cases in which the presiding judge died before delivering judgment."

'Judge: "You owe a duty to every judge before whom you appear to warn him of the risk he is running."'

—Ellison Kahn's commonplace book 11 September 1986.

Aphorisms of Arthur

'I'd rather have a wooden leg than fifty pairs of crutches.'

'Why don't I take it easy? Because if I stopped pedalling I'd fall off.'

'You ought to go on a trip abroad. The world doesn't end with Eloff Street.'

—Ellison Kahn's commonplace book, relating some of the aphorisms recounted at a memorial service to Arthur Suzman held on 11 March 1985.

'When these letters were sent, the respondent was, ex facie the letters, aware that Edwards, the purchaser, was dead. As Mr Suzman put it, . . . quite correctly: a dead man has no address.'

—Vermooten J in *Edwards v Tuckers Land and Development Corporation (Pty) Ltd* 1983 (1) SA 617 (W) at 624.

CHARLES ROBBERTS SWART

1894–1982. Member of the Orange Free State Bar 1918–48. MP 1923–59. Minister of Justice 1948–59. Minister of Education, Arts and Science 1949–50. Governor-General 1960–1. State President of the Republic of South Africa 1961–7.

'He retired in 1967 and led a quiet life on his farm De Aap (The Monkey) near Brandfort.

'With his usual light touch he told guests that he had never been able to decide whether the nameplate on his gate should read "C R Swart, De Aap" or "De Aap C R Swart".'

—Jaap Boekkooi in *The Star* 17 July 1982.

GEORGE MAURICE JEX SWEENEY

1900–81. Attorney, Durban 1924–6. Lecturer in Law, Natal University College, Durban, 1926–40. Senior Lecturer 1940–6. Associate Professor 1946–9. Professor of Law, University of Natal, Durban, 1949–60. Temporary Lecturer 1962–77.

PROFESSOR MAURICE SWEENEY
Caricature (1960) by John Michael ('Jock') Leyden (1908–).
From (1980–1) 2 Natal University Law Review preface

'Conscientious, hard-working and dedicated almost to a fault, Maurice made an excellent law lecturer, exuding warmth, humour and tolerance. It was he who created the School of Law at Durban. His long career in that city culminated in his elevation to a chair. . . . Maurice and his wife "Snib" had a splendid library; they were cultivated and charming people, who loved literature and music. . . . Allow me . . . to mention one incident, in a spirit of fond memory. As editor of the *South African Law Journal* I once asked him to review a book on a branch of the law I knew interested him. His answer was that he had never published a word on the law, and in his late sixties he had no intention of breaking his duck.'

—From Ellison Kahn's speech at the dinner on 19 October 1990 to celebrate the eightieth anniversary of the founding of the School of Law of the University of Natal, Pietermaritzburg.

HERBERT TRAVERS TAMPLIN

1853–1916. Member of the Eastern Districts Bar 1880–1902. QC 1898. Member of the Cape House of Assembly 1891–1902. Crown Prosecutor in the High Court of Griqualand 1903–9. Editor of the *Cape Law Journal* 1896–9.

'The lighter side of Circuit life was well represented in our midst. Tamplin was a host in himself, and around his name have gathered innumerable anecdotes. Tall, of enormous strength, impetuous, short-sighted, and addicted to practical joking, each of his qualities connected itself with anecdote.

'He stretches his arm over the top of a bathroom partition, seizes hold of the occupant within by the hair, and by sheer physical strength lifts him off his feet saying: "Blaine, you have been there long enough. Come out." It is not Blaine.

'Sir Godfrey Lagden, the British Resident at Basutoland, once met Tamplin in the passage of the Central Hotel at King Williamstown, at 6.30 a.m., walking up and down, in pyjamas, with a towel round his head, ringing the hotel dinner-bell. Sir Godfrey later on told me that there was a lunatic in the hotel, but that he had spoken soothingly to him, and managed to get him to put the bell down, but he thought the matter ought to be enquired into. I promised to take the necessary steps and after telling Tamplin the joke, introduced him to Lagden, who found that they had been at Charterhouse together.

'Tamplin was a general favourite throughout the Eastern Province, and to-day there are few persons who knew him, who have not a kind word for his memory, and a story to tell about his many and various doings. One of the best, to my mind, is his reply in Parliament to a wrathful Member who enquired of him, "Who is that braying like an ass?" "It is echo," said Tamplin, smiling at him. He made Sauer furious in the House once, when anxious to get his Estimates through, by insisting on reciting, on the question of the use of the Dutch language in schools, a long poem which Tamplin said was called "Die Springhans in die droogde." He brought the House down, especially by his pronunciation.'

—Victor Sampson *My Reminiscences* (1926) 67–70.

STANLEY SHELBOURNE (TOBY) TAYLOR

1875–1965. Member of the Johannesburg Bar 1904–30. KC 1919.

'A bombshell today. . . . Toby is leaving the Bar forthwith to join the Anglo-American. It will mean that he will be a rich man and will live for the most part in England. He only told me this afternoon. Naturally the tongues wagged. He will be a great loss to us as he set us all a high standard. . . . It is a strange end to Toby's South African venture isn't it? But apposite. He would not go on the Bench. Politics doesn't interest him. Had he stayed on at the Bar he would have begun to tire—to be overworked—to fall off. He now leaves at the top of his form, his reputation never higher. And he will have any amount of money. The Bar will be different without him.'

—Oliver Deneys Schreiner (q v) in a letter to his wife Edna, 16 January 1930. Schreiner family papers.

'In 1920 he was in his middle forties—vigorous, active, confident and tough—every inch the fighting advocate. He instinctively applied the maxim, so characteristic of good advocacy—*suaviter in modo, fortiter in re*. He was equally at home in submitting arguments based on documents and in handling witnesses in trial actions. Witnesses for the other side were less afraid, it seemed, of being shown by Toby to be untruthful, than of appearing to be unreasonable or slow in the uptake if they did not fall in with his suggestions.

'He was an exceptionally quick worker and thinker. On the quick working side he could page through a bundle of papers and extract what was important at a speed that astonished the man of normal capacity. Speed in his case was not a substitute for industry, but an addition to it, for he was a very hard worker. It was said that in one long appeal, in which Tilson Barry was junior to Saul Solomon and Toby, the first half of the night was given by Tilson to Toby, who worked late, and the second half, without noticeable break, to Saul, who worked early. Tilson had to seize opportunities for slumber in court.

'On the quick thinking, which must also be a clear thinking, side, it is said that there were occasions when Toby was arguing in the Witwatersrand Local Division before, and with, that other rapid reasoner, Ward J., when neither opposing counsel nor Toby's own junior was able to follow the course of the dialogue, so many were the steps omitted as being, to the protagonists, too obvious to require explicit statement. . . .

'Toby certainly had a persuasive way with him. It was difficult for a court when he was arguing to follow the old advice to listen courteously and patiently to counsel, but "heed not one damned word that he says". He would, of course, never commit what, under our practice, is the reprehensible solecism of giving the court his own opinion on questions of fact or law in the case. But as a good advocate he could subtly and inoffensively convey the impression that he had confidence in his client's case. He could present it as essentially reasonable, whether its basis was technically valid or not, and in that way he might overcome a proper measure of judicial sales resistance and so win a case that he should have lost. . . .

'Toby had a nice sense of humour and was a clever but not uncharitable mimic. One of the imitations that he most enjoyed was his quotation, in the broadest imaginable Scots, and with appropriate gesticulation, of the passage in the speech of Lord Shaw of Dunfermline in the *Cantiare San Rocco* case ([1924] A.C. 226 at 259), which reads, "No doubt the adjustment of rights after the occurrence of disturbances, interruptions, or calamities is in many cases a difficult task. But the law of Scotland does not throw up its hands in despair in consequence, and leave the task alone." Toby, like many other notable advocates, would certainly have made a great actor, had he gone on the stage. . . .'

—O D S[chreiner] 'Stanley Shelbourne Taylor, K.C., C.M.G., D.S.O., V.D., Croix de Guerre' (1965) 72 *SALJ* 421 at 422–3.

BENJAMIN ARTHUR TINDALL

1879–1963. Member of the Pretoria Bar 1903–22. KC 1919. Judge of the Transvaal Provincial Division 1922–37. Judge President 1937–8. Judge of Appeal 1938–49.

'So early in the morning?'

'. . . Tindall never encouraged humorous comments or laughter-provoking repartee on the part of counsel who appeared before him. When such attempts were occasionally made by counsel, he just ignored them. In fact, he had never at any time to my knowledge even given vent to a smile while he sat on the Bench of the Rand Supreme Court.

'And knowing him to be what he was, members of the Bar who appeared before him were ever careful to avoid making any comments of a humorous nature.

'One solitary mirth-provoking incident, however, does come to mind. At least, everyone in court seemed to regard it as being extremely funny—that is to say, everyone except Tindall himself. He certainly had no intention then to be deliberately funny. In fact, I feel convinced that he never even had a clue concerning the obviously humorous and human aspect of the remark which caused the laughter.

'It happened during the protracted hearing of a matrimonial action which was at the time popularly known as "the Castle on the Hill case". It was called by that name because the house in which the plaintiff lived, and in which certain alleged unsavoury happenings were stated to have occurred, had the appearance of a castle. It was situated on a high kopje in the Kensington suburb of Johannesburg.

'The plaintiff in this divorce action, the owner of a well-known and fashionable city hairdressing establishment, had sought a decree of divorce on the grounds of his wife's alleged adultery with a prominent member of the Johannesburg City Council who was cited as a co-defendant or co-respondent.

'Witnesses in this case related that men used to visit the plaintiff's home not only during various times of the evening, but also "early in the morning".

'And when one of the witnesses explained to the court the probable purpose of such visits, Mr Justice Tindall, with a rather wry face, said to the witness:

"Do you mean to say that they went there for that purpose so early in the morning?"

'Of course, the question created loud laughter.

'Many members of the Johannesburg Bar who remembered this incident, still recall Tindall's words: "So early in the morning?"

'It is the only funny incident which ever occurred in the utterly colourless career of this great Judge.'

—Isaac Goodman *Judges I Have Known* (1969) 170–1.

'. . . The late Judge Tindall was always a man of spare habit and young looking. At a social gathering his colleague, Chief Justice Watermeyer, remarked of him to a lady who was a fellow guest, "You wouldn't think, would you, to look at him that he was a sexagenarian?" "Oh, how terrible," she replied; "and he looks such a nice man too."'

—Leslie Blackwell (q v) *Blackwell Remembers* (1971) 127.

'In a case in which I prosecuted before Mr. Justice Tindall at Barberton the accused was found guilty and said to the judge through the interpreter, "We all know that your Lordship is very closely related to the Almighty, and for that reason I ask your Lordship to have mercy on me for what the evidence clearly shows that I have done!" I still like to believe that this eloquent plea had at least part of the desired effect.'

—Hjalmar Reitz *The Conversion of a South African Nationalist* (1946) 266.

'On the Appellate Division Tindall used to say nothing and to show nothing by way of facial expression. He simply flipped over the pages of the record, looking at the passages counsel referred to. At the very end of counsel's argument he would say: "Mr Jones, I wish to put a question to you." It was the killing question. According as you answered it satisfactorily or not, you won or lost your case.'

—Dr Percy Yutar SC in conversation with me in April 1988.

BEAUCLERK UPINGTON

1873–1938. Member of the Cape Bar 1898–1938. Member of the Cape House of Assembly 1908–10. KC 1912. MP 1915–19. Noted defender of accused. An eccentric. Son of Sir Thomas Upington (qv).

'Nothing pleased him more than to spar with a witness worthy of his steel, but woe betide such witness if he tried to score a personal point. Once when an able and experienced litigant was skilfully skating over thin ice in his evidence in chief Upington turned his penetrating stare upon him with an obvious pleasant anticipation of the cross-examination to follow. The witness turned in the box. "Stop glaring at me, Mr Upington. You will have your opportunity when I am finished," and then aptly added: "You look like a greyhound straining on the leash." "No, Mr. X, no," said Upington; "a terrier waiting for a rat!"'

—F St L S[earle] 'The Late Beauclerk Upington, K.C.' (1938) 55 *SALJ* 401 at 403–4.

BEAUCLERK UPINGTON
Caricature by D C Boonzaier (1865–1950), published in Die Huisgenoot

'Though at heart a kindly man who would never consciously injure anyone, he nevertheless at times fell into unapproachable moods, when those who understood him knew that he should be left alone. However, on one such occasion an innocent and friendly Junior, anxious to observe the ancient custom of lunching with his leader on the first day of trial, had the audacity to follow him as he slipped off during the lunch interval. The Junior's loquacious enthusiasm was soon damped with that well-known stare and a stern: "Young man, I have been compelled to have you next to me in Court all morning—is that not enough?"
. . .

'When he worked with Junior Counsel he was most kindly, instructive and encouraging and always ready to give praise where it was due. On the other hand if he considered his Junior too full of himself his stinging tongue would promptly relegate him to his proper place.

On one such occasion he announced to the Court "I appear, My Lords, in this matter with my learned friend . . . " a pause, while he bent down to his unfortunate Junior and said in an audible whisper "What did you say your name was?"'

—F St L S[earle] op cit at 404–5. (The last comment has also been attributed to Harry Morris. For a comparison of Beauclerk Upington with Harry Morris, see H H (HARRY) MORRIS.)

'The Cape Judge Louwrens and the famous advocate Upington had no great affection for each other. When Upington appeared before Louwrens there were always fireworks.

'One day . . . the two fought from 10 a.m. to 12.45 p.m. At this hour Louwrens glanced at the court's clock and said: "It is time for adjournment, Mr Upington. For the past few hours you have gone to great lengths to demonstrate your contempt for this court."

'Retorted Upington: "I am amazed, m'Lord. I thought I had gone to great lengths to conceal it."'

—From a talk by Mr Justice H H Nestadt, recounted in the *South African Jewish Times* 23 April 1976.

'When . . . he was offered a judgeship his comment was . . . explicit.

'"I would far rather stand on my feet all day and talk nonsense," he said, "than have to sit on my bottom all day and listen to it."'

—Benjamin Bennett *This Was a Man* (1958) 110.

The uncashed cheques

'Upington left scores of cheques uncashed. They ranged from a guinea or two to a hundred guineas and covered a period of nearly forty years. They were for drawing pleas, consultations, opinions, noting judgments and appearances in court. Even in his early days at the Bar, when most young advocates have to collect every outstanding guinea to pay their rent and scrape a living, he cared little about his fees.

'Throughout the years cheques lay unnoticed in drawers, forgotten bookmarks among the leaves of law tomes, or left to accumulate among heaps of unanswered letters and unpaid bills. One batch totalled £500 or £600; but they were probably only a small proportion of those that flowed in from attorneys in all parts of the Cape Province and vanished into oblivion in his chambers. It is more than likely his uncashed fees totalled several thousand pounds.

'Some attorneys, after Upington had ignored their polite, then exasperated, appeals to deposit their cheques, paid his fees direct into his banking account and sent him the deposit slips. Others felt that if he couldn't worry, neither could they.

'In the early 1900's the uncashed cheques were a trickle and for only a few guineas. By 1915 they had become a stream. One for twenty-five guineas was the reward for a hard-fought battle in an accident case. Another for forty-nine guineas was for appearance in a breach of contract dispute. A third was for nineteen guineas. Two years later the stale cheques were larger and amounted to nearly £300. One for a hundred guineas was left as a bookmark. Others were for twenty-nine and thirty guineas. Years afterwards another cheque for a hundred guineas was allowed to lapse.

'One cheque for three guineas was sent by an attorney of Richmond, Cape,

'Taking the field at Newlands to play the Navy: Upington (moustache, second from left at back) with some of his Bar colleagues. Leading them is Sir Henry Juta and on his left (with glasses) is J. T. 'Baby' Molteno. Behind him are (partly obscured) Howel Jones, R. Close (with straw hat, next to Upington) and T. L. Graham (hatless). Releasing a ball (rear) is Percy S. T. Jones who played cricket for South Africa.'

Caricatures by D C Boonzaier (1865–1950), from Benjamin Bennett This Was a Man *(1958) facing page 113 (the caption has been corrected)*

pinned to a letter asking for an opinion on the advisability of an appeal. Maybe Upington sent the opinion. Whether he did or not, he did not trouble to cash the fee.'

—Bennett op cit at 205–6.

SIR THOMAS UPINGTON

1844–98. Member of the Irish Bar 1868–74. Member of the Cape Bar 1874–92, 1896–8. QC 1880. Member of the Cape House of Assembly 1878–92, 1896–8. Attorney-General in Sprigg's Cabinet 1878–81. Prime Minister of the Cape Colony 1884–6. Attorney-General in Sprigg's Cabinet 1886–90. Knighted (KCMG) 1887. Judge of the Cape Supreme Court 1892–6. Attorney-General in Sprigg's Cabinet 1896–8.

As member and leader of the Bar

'On the elevation of de Villiers to the Bench, Simeon Jacobs, the Solicitor-General at Grahamstown, became the Attorney-General, a tall, lean, shadowy man, of whom many stories were told, but who was a lawyer of the narrow school of precedents, and nothing but precedents. At this time there began to come to the little station at Rosebank in the mornings, another barrister, who had bouts of illness at "Charlie's Hope," and who once or twice was reported to be dangerously ill—the Sir Thomas Upington of the future, who as a speaker, advocate, and Parliamentary debater, has never to my mind been surpassed in South Africa. He was always Merriman's master in the House, and only when he left it, did John X succeed to the first place. His rise at the Bar was phenomenal, though, in his modesty, he said that this was due in great measure to his having arrived when the profession was depleted of men; but that did not explain his ability, his quickness, and his comprehension of human nature, his fine voice, his rapier-like thrusts, and his oratorical play. J. W. Leonard may have been a greater lawyer, but no one that I have known was Upington's equal as an advocate. His readiness was never at fault. On one occasion, in addressing the Court at the close of a trial case, he submitted a point with great earnestness as his own to the Chief Justice. "Now, Mr. Upington," said de Villiers, leaning forward with his hands to his sides as was often his habit when impressive, "I suggested that point." "Yes, my Lord," said Upington at once, "and a most important point it was. I submit it settles the case." Even the Chief had to smile. But it was as a fighter to the last ditch in a losing case that Upington excelled. It was then that one saw him at his best, and recognized his resources of argument and courage. A winning case he was apt to treat with lack of interest. Leonard's weakness as a speaker lay in his exaggerated language; he exhausted his vocabulary on small affairs, and when big ones had to be dealt with, had nothing greater to give. But he was a great lawyer; and on his death Lord de Villiers said that he had never known any one strip a case and present its essential point as Leonard did.'

—Victor Sampson (q v) *My Reminiscences* (1926) 18–19.

'Sir THOMAS UPINGTON.
The Premier Q.C.'

Caricature by William Howard Schröder (1852–92), from The Schröder Art Memento *(Pretoria 1894)*

'The distinction between the two branches of the profession has always been maintained at the Cape. Without here discussing the pros and cons of that system, its chief merit is obvious; it trains a body of experts in whom zeal for a client is tempered by a sense of responsibility for the due administration of justice. Such training ensures a high professional level, and is an excellent preparation for judicial office. But if the system is to produce the best results there must prevail, among the members of the bar, not only a strong *esprit de corps*, but a careful observance of those rules of conduct and etiquette which experience has proved conducive to a high standard of honour and duty in the practice of advocacy. The extent to which the bar is permeated by the spirit of those rules must depend mainly on the seniors. By their precepts and example a body of professional opinion is formed, the steady pressure of which is a wholesome corrective to laxity. In this respect the Cape bar owes much to the man who in 1878 became its leader. (Sir Thomas) Upington arrived in South Africa, not as a junior but with considerable professional experience behind him. He was appointed Attorney-General just when the bar was in a plastic state of development, and he left his mark upon it. In Court he was a stickler for professional form. For instance, he impressed upon his juniors the impropriety of even the slightest sign of approval or dissent at remarks from the Bench. Such remarks should be dealt with by argument at the proper time, not by smile or gesture at the moment. Later experience has sometimes made me regret that that rule was not more generally observed. Manifestations of that nature are bad manners, and specially irritating because of the difficulty of suitably noticing them. Upington's forensic ability and his fidelity to the best traditions of the profession made him a good model for his younger brethren. An able and popular head of the bar.'

—James Rose Innes *Autobiography* (edited by B A Tindall) (1949) 32–3.

'In appearance Upington seemed to J. E. C. Bodley "like a circus ringmaster owing to his slim figure and drooping moustaches". Immaculately dressed, he was impressive in debate, his full-toned Irish voice commanding attention. His brilliant oratory and famed Irish wit placed him among the most outstanding speakers in the House of Assembly. . . . Without legal profundity, he was yet an eloquent and inspiring leader at the bar.'

—A F Hattersley in *Dictionary of South African Biography* II (1972) 758 at 759.

'Agin the Regulations'

'Judge [C T] Smith—who on circuit used to dress very much as I do when I go hunting for flowers—was met walking once by the Chief Constable of the district, in the days before motor cars, when Chief Constables used to ride out long distances to meet the Judge, and was asked whether the Judge was coming on, and what sort of a man the old Buster was; whereupon the old Buster, who was a gentle soul withal, replied, "Oh, he is not such a bad chap." The Chief Constable was told at the Judge's coach later that he had passed the Judge on the road, a little man in a snuff-coloured suit and smasher hat, and the Constable knew there was no mistake; he came on for the rest of the way behind the caravan. To Sir Thomas Upington, when Attorney-General, a similar experience happened. He used to tell the story against himself with that infectious laugh of his—the infectious laugh that used to cow Merriman in the House of Assembly. Upington, usually in his day accounted the best-dressed man in Cape Town, would don the most extraordinary costume on Circuit. On this occasion he had on a fearful suit of grey check, the checks some four inches square, with an old hat—how great men love old hats!—and he had come to hold an inspection of

Sketch of Sir Thomas Upington by Schröder
op cit

SIR THOMAS UPINGTON

'In appearance like a circus ringmaster owing to his slim figure and drooping moustaches' *Caricature from Benjamin Bennett* This Was a Man *(1958) facing page 16*

the works at the Zwartberg Pass, constructed by convict labour. He thought he would go and have a private inspection on his own account the afternoon before the official visit, and at the Pass he came upon the convict guard sitting smoking about a hundred yards from the convicts, his rifle against a rock yards away from him on one side, and his helmet yards away from him on the other. Upington said he would like to see the works. "It's agin the Regulations," said the Irish guard, without looking up. Upington thought, you are a fine fellow to talk about regulations, but meekly said he had come a long way and would like to see how the work was progressing. "It's agin the Regulations, I tell yer," repeated the guardian of order. Upington then began to use persuasion, whereupon the constable, looking up with animation, said, "Yer want to see the wurks?" "Yes," said Upington, "I am telling you I do." "Well," said the guard, "Yer see that farm down there; yer go there and steal a sheep, and yer shall see the wurks!" The next day at the official visit, Upington told us he looked at the guard out of the corner of his eye, and he saw the man's jaw drop and his rifle all but fall from his hands.'

—Sampson op cit 18–19.

Leaving the Bench

'. . . [H]is four years on the bench were not particularly distinguished. Although he excelled in handling witnesses, his legal learning was not profound. Lacking the temper of a great judge, he showed a distaste for inevitable social isolation and for what seemed to him "the boring dignity" of judicial life.'

—Hattersley op cit at 759.

'. . . [T]here is the Attorney-General, Sir Thomas Upington. He occupied a seat on the Bench of the Supreme Court for some . . . years, but he suddenly resigned that position in order to become, for the third or fourth time, Attorney-General of the Colony. I fancy that the somewhat placid monotony of judicial life jarred upon him, for, as Byron says, "quiet to quick bosoms is a hell" and if ever a man possessed a quick bosom, it is my friend Sir Thomas Upington.'

—The Hon Mr Justice Cole *Reminiscences of My Life and of the Cape Bench and Bar* (1896) 131.

'Rhodes's resignation was accepted before Sir Hercules Robinson returned to Cape Town, and Sprigg, not for the first time in his career, was called to fill a vacancy he had done nothing to create. Upington resigned his judgeship to become Attorney-General; though a return from the Bench to politics is, under no circumstances, ideal, there had in this instance been none of the "negotiations with party politicians" which the Chief Justice deprecated. The tie between the two men, so dissimilar in character, so divergent in outlook, was singularly close; and Upington came to the help of his old colleague on a sudden emergency. Neither the motive, nor the result of his action, however, can affect the wholesome rule that a man who accepts judicial office should, in schoolboy phrase, "take it for keeps".'

—Innes op cit at 129–30.

'Reference to the proposal that the Chief Justice, Sir J. H. de Villiers, K.C.M.G., should become Prime Minister of the Cape Colony, has been made on another page. Where the Chief Justice refused or hesitated to tread, however, a colleague on the Supreme Court Bench, who, it is understood, during the four or five years of his Judgeship, never once differed from the rest of the Court upon any question of law, stepped in. It may be noted that upon the retirement from office of the Right Hon. C. J. Rhodes, Sir Gordon Sprigg, Treasurer-General in Mr. Rhodes's Cabinet, became Prime Minister, and forthwith cast about for an Attorney-General. The Hon. W. P. Schreiner, C.M.G., the Attorney-General of the ex-Cabinet, declined. The Hon. J. Rose-Innes, an effective opponent of the late Cabinet, also declined. The new Premier turned to the Supreme Court Bench, doubtless remembering the "brave days of old" in which he and Mr. Justice Upington had "faced the music". It would appear that the strictures upon the petty intrigues of party politics expressed by the Chief Justice had awakened no responsive chord in the breast of his distinguished Puisne. For Mr. Justice Upington forthwith resigned his judicial office, and cheerfully became the Attorney-General of the new Cabinet, as well as, presumably, once more, the leader of the Bar.

'The return of Mr. Justice Upington to the Bar forms a precedent upon which we have no desire to comment at any length. The proceeding is certainly unusual outside the neighbouring Republics where, in the past, it has been somewhat too common, but we would express the hope that the precedent now set will not be followed in the future by Judges of the Supreme Court.'

—Anon 'Recent Events in Legal Circles' (1896) 13 *Cape Law Journal* 18. The writer was almost certainly the editor, H T Tamplin (qv).

FRANÇOIS PETRUS (TOON) VAN DEN HEEVER

1894–1956. Member of the South West Africa Bar 1921–6. Senior Government
Law Adviser 1926–8. Law Adviser to the Department of External Affairs
1928–33. Secretary for Justice 1931–3. State Attorney 1931–3. Judge of the
High Court of South West Africa 1933–8. Judge of the Orange Free State
Provincial Division 1938–48. Judge President 1948. Judge of Appeal 1948–56.
Author of legal works. Afrikaans poet and short-story writer.

Early years; subsequent career; character

'Toon and I arrived on the same day in 1914 at the Transvaal University
College, Pretoria. He was a freckle-faced red-haired young man who had come
all the way from the Highveld under his own power, and when I first saw him
he was leaning on his bicycle engaged in a lively humorous conversation with a
small group. I became a very close friend of his during the years 1914–1915 and
1916, and it soon became evident to me that he was blessed with a subtle, original
and enquiring turn of mind which probed everything without showing
over-much respect for most orthodoxies. It would, for example, have come as a
great surprise to the people in the Highveld had they been informed that he had
begun to study various religions and that on numerous occasions he crossed the
road from College House (which I had so christened in a burst of barren
imagination) to attend a Hillcrest Monastery in order to study its doctrines and
observe its ritual.

'Down the years, it seemed to me, he had decided to hitch his wagon to the
maxim or doctrine *"homo sum, humani nihil a me alienum puto"*. All manner of
books came his way and all manner of discussion took place in his room. These
occasions were marked by much subtlety and wide, if sometimes unexpected,
excursions which the ordinary University student would have been inclined to
regard as somewhat heretical. That he became one of the best and most arresting
debaters was foreordained. As an example of his roving interest he soon acquired
a quotable knowledge of Greek literature, philosophy and art, through English,
German and Dutch sources because it was one of his sorrows that he had never
acquired any Greek . . . .

'Perhaps this is an appropriate stage at which to indicate the origin of "Toon".
Even on the rugby field his sense of humour pursued him, and he took great
pleasure in calling scrum-half Le Roux "Duimpie" until the latter in desperation
called out "Ag man, jou groot toon". More humorous insinuations followed, but
both "Duimpie" and "Toon" stuck. Toon never made the first team but
thoroughly enjoyed the lustiness of the game and it must be explained that he was
a man true of his hands. He must have been the first Judge to pilot his own
aircraft; he could handle a rifle; and on a proper occasion had been known to take
off his judicial coat.

'Toon left the T.U.C. at the end of 1916 to join the civil service, where his
advancement was expectedly rapid. In 1926, after having been appointed senior
Law Adviser to the newly established Department of External Affairs, he
accompanied General Hertzog to the Imperial Conference and thereafter he
attended more conferences before becoming Secretary for Justice.

'I have often wondered whether a remark I made to Pirow one day exerted any
influence on Toon's future. Pirow came to speak about him, saying that however

able he was no one could remain in his, Toon's, position while the latter persisted in differing from his chief, General Hertzog. My reply was that in any event Toon would never be happy until he was placed where he could grapple with legal problems because he had already exhibited a bent for research. Some time later he was appointed a Judge in South West Africa. There may of course have been no connection between this conversation and the subsequent appointment. Of course these two distinguished men remained good friends. On one occasion when they met on Bloemfontein station Toon quite instinctively took the General's suitcase and started along carrying it but after a short distance had been covered Hertzog relieved him of it, saying that it was not fit and proper for a Judge to carry a politician's bag. It was while he was there in South West Africa in comparative leisure that he was able to devote himself to legal research with the result that he became known as "The Watchdog of Roman Dutch Law". . . .'

—The Hon C P Bresler *Tilt the Sack* (1965) 167–9.

The motorbike and the judge of appeal

'Hoewel sy waardevolle bydrae tot ons reg sy grootste prestasie is, kan nie nagelaat word om op sy veelvuldige belangstellings en prestasies buite die regte te wys nie. Sy talente het hy op 'n wye gebied aangewend—die verskeidenheid van bedrywighede wat hy beoefen en bemeester het, bied 'n insig in die wese van hierdie begaafde en rustelose mens. Hy het in die Bondelswarts-opstand in Suidwes geveg; hy was 'n vaardige vioolspeler en musikus; hy het met sy eie vliegtuig in lugvaartkringe bekendheid verwerf en was 'n ere-kolonel in die Suid-Afrikaanse Lugmag; hy was 'n suksesvolle boogskutter en rolbalspeler. Hy was 'n geniale spreker en het hom as vriend, geestige raconteur en imposante redevoerder ewe tuis gevoel onder prokureursklerke, advokate, regters, akademici, hoogwaardigheidsbekleërs en die nederigste burgers.

'Toe hy reeds lid van die Appèlhof was, het hy 'n motorfiets aangeskaf en, ongeag die gemeenskap se opvattinge oor die gepastheid van appèlregters op motorfietse, op dié manier probeer sorg vir sy vervoer na die hoogste hof in die land. Soos die meeste motorfietse, het ook syne nie aan die hoë verwagtings van die eienaar voldoen nie en begin moeilikheid gee. Na baie gesukkel het hy eindelik die volgende brief aan die betrokke handelaar geskryf:

'"To forestall the possible conclusion that my difficulties are due to inexperience, let me assure you that I have owned and driven many motorcycles, high-powered as well as low-powered.

'"About two months ago I bought a . . . motorcycle from you. For 130 miles it ran smoothly but had no power whatsoever. . . . Then it began unaccountably to stall and refuse thereafter to come to life again. If I succeeded in getting it to go, the engine revolutions would increase proportionately to the throttle opening up to the point where one would normally change from first gear into second. Thereafter the engine would give no response to further throttle until about full throttle was reached, whereupon there would be violent acceleration which is disconcerting and dangerous in traffic. (Om nie eers van waardigheid te praat nie!)

'"I suspected carburettor trouble. . . . I handed it over to one of the most highly skilled and qualified Aircraft Engineers in the country. . . . He and his staff worked on it a whole working day. He could not remedy the fault. . . .

'"Thereafter I handed the machine over to a person who . . . is an expert with motorcycles and is usually asked to 'hot-up' and tune machines for motor-cyclists. . . . Today he gave up in despair.

'"As I intimated to you when I bought the machine, I required it as a means of transport between the Appeal Court and my home. As you know this is the Appeal Court for the whole of South Africa, South-West Africa and Southern Rhodesia. Counsel come from far and I simply cannot afford ever to be late. Reliability is therefore a very essential requisite in my means of transport. . . . I have found the bicycle purchased from you thoroughly unreliable and unsatisfactory."

'Hy sluit die brief af met 'n versoek dat òf die motorfiets herstel word òf die koop gekanselleer word. Vermoedelik is dit gekanselleer aangesien die Appèlregter en sy hortende motorfiets nie baie lank deel van die Bloemfonteinse straattoneel uitgemaak het nie.'

—M L B[enade] 'Toon van den Heever' (1964) 10 *Codicillus* 31 at 32.

'The halicon days'

'In 1934 I took silk. Well, not so much took it, but found the patent in the post, addressed to me by registered-post letter. I had not applied for it, as is usually the case, but Toon, with the connivance of the Secretary for Justice, had got the Minister to confer the honour upon me.

'The following year, while he was away on a Government commission, I acted as judge of the High Court (again Van den Heever's work). I was aware that it was part of the duties of the judge to inspect the prisons. I went to the local prison and was approached by one of the inmates, whom I had, as acting Attorney-General, successfully prosecuted, with the complaint that there was no suitable literature in the gaol, only religious and semi-religious books. I sympathized with him and promised to have the matter attended to.

'When I got back to my chambers I looked among Van den Heever's books and spotted his volume of Afrikaans poems. It struck me that I might have the volume delivered to the gaol, but I thought better of it, as I explained to Van den Heever on his return, because I felt that the prisoner had been sufficiently punished by his five years' sentence.

'We had an orchestra in Windhoek made up mostly of Germans engaged in an assortment of occupations—an attorney, a taxi-driver, an accountant, an insurance agent, an estate agent, a shop assistant and others. They played classical music. Toon was one of them. He played second violin and could safely have played third or fourth violin.

'He also took up golf in a mild way. A match, President (Grindley-Ferris AJ) versus Vice-President, had long finished. Toon was drawn with the Government Attorney. We waited a long time. Ultimately the two errant figures emerged out of the darkness.

'It transpired that Toon was interested in mineralogy and had spent a lot of time picking up and examining specimens of the many stones that disfigured our fairways (there were no grass fairways). In the process the game had been completely forgotten.

'Life in those days was easy, friendly, and unconventional. We all knew one another—farmers, members of the police force, railway employees, civil servants, professional men and traders. "Them's were the halicon days", as Sam Weller might have put it. No gross national products, no balance-of-payment deficits (the Union Government attended to that) and, Heaven be praised, no income tax (until 1945).

'I had two horses. Toon and I used to go riding out of town. On our way back we would dismount and enjoy refreshments at his home, which was about a mile from mine. On one occasion, when we were about to resume our homeward journey to my house at which the horses were stabled, we decided to race each other back. We galloped joyfully through the streets of Windhoek and in the process passed the police headquarters. As we dismounted a mounted policeman, who appeared to have followed us, rode up, made inquiries, and took our names and addresses.

'We did not know what would happen and what offences we would be charged with. We knew the legal maxim that the public is presumed to know the law, but did not think it applied to advocates. After a few weeks of anxious waiting we received a letter from Captain Prinsloo from the police, whom we knew personally, telling us that our conduct had caused the police authorities grave concern. The original intention had been to charge us with riding recklessly through the streets of Windhoek to the great danger of the public, but after prolonged consideration they had decided that from the way in which we had been riding we were a greater danger to ourselves than to the public, and so they were dropping the charge.'

—I Goldblatt 'Early South West Africa—Bench and Bar' (1978) 95 *SALJ* 120 at 128–9.

A surveying error

'The late Mr Justice van den Heever . . . piloted his own aeroplane and at one stage in his career as Judge of Appeal rode a motor-cycle to and from court. His interest in mechanical means of conveyance unfortunately once led him to assume a knowledge of matters of surveying that was erroneous. In a case (*R v Pretoria Timber Co (Pty) Ltd* 1950 (2) SA 163 (AD)) concerning the meaning of the phrase "The area bounded by the following points, which are themselves included, namely Bank, Pienaars River, Largo [etc.]", after stating that an area is normally defined by lines and not points, he went on to discuss the nature of these lines on the assumption they were straight: "If they are literally straight they would be partially underground. If—as one would on that supposition naturally assume—they are to be rhumb-lines, I fail to see how within a reasonable time the ordinary mortal is to locate them on the earth's surface" (at 183). A professor of land surveying (G B Lauf in (1955) 72 *SALJ* 423) gently chided the learned judge, stating that he could not accept "the contention that one assumes such lines to be loxodromes or rhumb-lines. . . . [S]uch a choice may come naturally to a navigator at sea or in the air, but to a surveyor it is not only unnatural but wholly unacceptable." He also regretted Van den Heever J.A.'s mentioning Bonne's projection: "Bonne's projection is such that neither a loxodrome nor a geodesic is a straight line." The narrow scope of the doctrine of judicial notice thus received lay support—lawyer, stick to your law!'

—Ellison Kahn & Brian R Bamford 'Another Spoonful of Sugar and Pinch of Salt' (1965) 82 *SALJ* 375 at 379–80. (Some footnotes included in text, others omitted.)

Tributes

'The death of "Toon" van den Heever came as a great shock to me because it is only a few months ago that he told me the intricacies of making a catapult from an old tyre to shoot mouse-birds and miaowing cats. That indeed sums up this great man.'

—'An Afrikaner's Diary' *The Star* 31 January 1956.

'On 29 January 1956 Toon van den Heever died, at the tragically early age of 61. It was out of term, and Schreiner was in Johannesburg; but he went to Bloemfontein to attend the funeral. Van den Heever's daughter Leonora (now Miss Justice Van den Heever) thanked him for his telegram, letter and wreath, "and even more for the fact that you came down for Toon's funeral. He was the hub of our universe, not only husband and favourite father, but guide, philosopher and friend, jester, handyman—everything."'

—Ellison Kahn in *Fiat Iustitia: Essays in Memory of Oliver Deneys Schreiner* (1983) 41, quoting from a letter of 7 February 1956.

'Toon' the writer

'Regter Van den Heever se grootste prestasie buite die regsgebied om is sy bydrae tot die Afrikaanse letterkunde. Ook hier kan hy in sekere sin as baanbreker gesien word. In 1919 verskyn sy bundel *Gedigte*, wat hy later verwerk en met toevoegings in 1931 onder die titel *Eugene en ander Gedigte* laat verskyn. In 1951 word die Hertzogprys op grond van hierdie bundel aan hom toegeken. Die besondere betekenis van sy letterkundige bydrae bestaan daarin dat hy 'n oorgangsfiguur is tussen die tydperk toe ons digters nasionale temas, die oorlogsmart en die natuur besing het, en die latere tydperk wat gekenmerk word deur 'n soeke na lewens- en geesteswaardes in die meer moderne styl. In sy gedigte raak hy onderwerpe aan en worstel hy met gedagtes wat in daardie tydvak van ons letterkunde nuut en selfs as te gewaagd beskou is: die godsdiens en geloof, die fisiese en sinnelike bekoring en skoonheid van die vrou, die genot van die oomblik liewer as die onbekende ewigheid, soos blyk uit reëls soos die volgende:

As die dag nie sterflik was nie kon hy westergloor nie win,
As die dood nie erflik was nie het ons nooit mekaar bemin;
En as rantsoen vir jou liefde sou'k die god'likheid verbeur
Vir die wellus van jou lippe bly die ewigheid verbeur.

'Toon van den Heever se tweede bundel, *Die Speelman van Dorestad*, verskyn in 1949 en word gevolg deur 'n bundel kortverhale, *Gerwe uit die Erfpag van Skoppensboer*. Daarna het sy Muse geswyg.'

—M L B[enade] 'Toon van den Heever' (1964) 10 *Codicillus* 31 at 32.

'As a poet and author he had to wait a considerable time before a cold and pioneering generation of his own people began to appreciate his gifts. For example *Eugene en ander Gedigte* published in 1919 only received recognition together with other works when he received the Hertzog Prize for literature in 1951, the same fate of course befalling other works such as *Die Speelman van Dorestad* and *Uit die Erfpag van Skoppensboer* and so on. He had moments of cynicism as *In die Park*, where he appears as "an angry young man" somewhat bitter and frustrated, and even in later works he sometimes loses poetic rapture, but some selection or rejection cannot affect the work of an artist whose voice was among the first of his generation to introduce some intellectual and philosophic strain into his writing.'

—The Hon C P Bresler *Tilt the Sack* (1965) 169.

'F. P. van den Heever the judge was known to the literary world as Toon van den Heever. As an Afrikaans poet he broke away from the traditional themes of nature, *volk* and *vaderland*. His fine fresh verse dwelt largely on the problems of the soul. He also published a much appreciated volume of short stories, *Uit die Erfpag van Skoppensboer*. As a judge, though he gave several notable judgments in Afrikaans, he wrote as a rule in English. His dicta are unmistakable. They have his imprint on them as much as the first Lord Macnaghten's and Lord Mackay's dicta have theirs. He could coin as striking a phrase as Macnaghten, and while his English syntax was not as convoluted as Mackay's he was as capable as that Scottish judge of using arresting sentence construction or digging into his phenomenal vocabulary to hammer home his point.'

— Ellison Kahn & Brian R Bamford 'A Penultimate Spoonful of Sugar and Pinch of Salt' (1966) 83 *SALJ* 208 at 213–14.

'Soos 'n frisse wind oor die veld trek en die hele natuur in beweging bring, so werk hy deur sy dicta in die vonnisse, speels, meeslepend, opwekkend, prikkelend tot teenspraak, verrassend deur sy vondste. Byna altyd skerp is sy analise, meesterlik soms sy sintese. 'n Juris met 'n wonderlike verbeelding begaaf met die beskikking oor 'n woordeskat om daaraan vaak op gelukkige, selfs digterlike wyse uitdrukking te gee.'

— Professor Daniel Pont in (1956) 19 *Tydskrif vir Hedendaagse Romeins-Hollandse Reg* 89.

FREDERICK BARRY VAN DER RIET

1881–1955. Member of the Eastern Districts Bar 1910–55. A character.

'Fred van der Riet (nephew of F J W and cousin of E F (Bobby) van der Riet) was a great personality of the Grahamstown Bar. He was a big, heavily built man, and of ever-expanding girth as the years went by. His work at the Bar was mainly concerned with criminal matters, particularly during the colourful days of the Transkei circuit, when many a jury was induced (persuaded) to grant an acquittal by Fred's powerful oratory, his deep voice and his substantial presence.

'In Grahamstown Van der Riet frequently appeared in the criminal appeal court, on brief from Transkeian attorneys, pleading most earnestly with the judges even though the proven facts were very much against his client. On one occasion, so the story is told, when the court was clearly "not with him" he implored their lordships "Please, m'lords, I ask your lordships to allow just this one appeal, though I am not suggesting that it should be regarded as a precedent".'

— From a letter of 18 February 1976 by Dr George Randell, formerly member of the Eastern Districts Bar, to Ellison Kahn. (See also PITTMAN.) (Fred van der Riet was not a mere Rumpole type. See his delightful description of the literary graces of Mr Justice McGregor under the heading McGREGOR, and the next extract.)

In the following extract 'Back' is a reference to the unpublished memoirs of A W Back of the Eastern Districts Bar.

'F.B., a nephew of Judge F.J.W. van der Riet, was a unique figure.

'*BACK: He approached more nearly to the type illustrated by Montagu Williams of the Old Bailey Bar than any other I have met. He was very good at special kinds of jury trials, and could say things to the Court that no one else could, or would, dare to say. I have heard him say on more than one occasion, "Do you know what I would do in this case M'Lord, if I was the judge trying it?" While the Bench waited with mild expectancy, he would state his solution. Of course it would always be in favour of his client and sad to say the court was generally reluctant to adopt it. He was a vigorous fighter and had a good sense of humour, often laughing at himself and his methods.*

. . .

'Most of Fred's income came from the Transkei Circuits—Umtata, Butterworth, Kokstad in particular. The attorneys all knew that he would throw his full weight into any case entrusted to him. And that was not only figuratively speaking. His commanding physical presence certainly impressed the jury, who were directed that they could not possibly convict his client. It was almost as if he simply was not going to let them. At home in Grahamstown, between circuits, briefs to argue appeals would come in for him from attorneys who well knew that Fred would put every ounce into his argument—nothing would remain unsaid on behalf of the appellant. If perchance briefs on circuit were few and far between for Fred and he was short of money for his train fare, nothing loath, he would set out on foot with his impecunious friend and gentlemanly colleague Arthur Upington. . . .

'When he was taken to hospital on the occasion of his last illness his devoted daughter, Mavis Arnot, found at the bedside some of his favourite books: *Selected Works of Ovid, The Odyssey of Homer* (William Cowper), *Selected Epigrams and Martial Essays* (William Hazlitt), Ruskin's *The Eagle's Nest, Talks of Spirit Friends of Bench and Bar,* and Dryden's *Plutarch.* Mrs Arnot wrote: "Cicero not there at his bedside? Nor any of his beloved Shakespeare. Not even the tiny leatherbound volume of Omar Khayyam?" These, she says, were his favourites, which he always had with him on circuit, and she concluded that they must have been taken with him to the hospital. On the fly-leaf of his volume of the *Corpus Juris Civilis* she found he had written some doggerel:

'"If you rewrote the Digest,
And I revised the Code,
We'd frolic with opinions
That never were Justinian's,
And dance with quip and high jest
Down learning's royal road;
If you rewrote the Digest
And I revised the Code!"

. . .

'His strong personality and engaging wit during his years of practice gave rise to a mass of folklore in local legal circles. The story goes that during a particular circuit, on the morning after a rather festive night, he mistakenly put a witness in the box to lead his evidence—quite forgetting that the witness had completed his evidence the day before. When the judge said "But didn't we have this witness yesterday?" van der Riet, realising his mistake, tried to cover it up by saying, "My Lord, the witness was so good in his evidence yesterday, that I thought your Lordship would like to hear him again this morning!"

'Fred van der Riet was a grand fellow. The attorneys enjoyed his visits to East London. He would take up his stance at the end of the counter at the Beach Hotel and regale whoever came in with stories of the courts. He had written two index volumes of the *South African Law Journal,* and encouraged me to write a third volume. He kindly consented to write a foreword which he described as a *prooemium* to my *opusculum*. Unfortunately the printer's error had it as "*opusculem*". Fred was appalled at this, and wrote, "Oh Randell! Why, oh why, did you let them disgrace me like that?"'

—George Randell *Bench and Bar of the Eastern Cape* (1985) 130–4. (On Arthur Upington, see LAURENCE. Arthur Upington was the brother of Beauclerk (qv), and was as eccentric as he. A fine classical scholar, Arthur had a distaste for the law, though he was an advocate of distinction and a wit. As a schoolboy Randell saw Arthur on circuit: 'his clothes were crumpled, and large holes in both his socks showed white patches of skin above the heels of his shoes' (op cit at 124).)

'In one circuit town Fred was the prosecutor and he was pleased to find that about twenty cases were on the roll. To his dismay, one accused after another pleaded guilty. (In those days many comparatively minor cases were tried in the circuit courts.) When the last man tendered a plea of guilty too, this was too much for Fred, who said "No! Surely you can't plead guilty on this indictment!" (Worthy of a Bateman cartoon.)'

—From a letter of 21 November 1982 by Dr George Randell to Ellison Kahn.

BAREND VAN DYK VAN NIEKERK

1939–81. Senior Lecturer in Law, University of Zululand, 1966–7. Senior Lecturer in Law, University of the Witwatersrand, Johannesburg, 1967–71. Professor of Law, University of Natal, Durban, 1971–81. 'Rebel with causes.'

In June 1970 he was charged before the senior judge of the Transvaal Provincial Division, Mr Justice C J Claassen, sitting with two assessors, the late Mr Herbert Rothschild SC and Dr C P Joubert SC (now Joubert JA), with contempt of court. The charge arose out of his article 'Hanged by the Neck Until You Are Dead', which was published in (1969) 86 South African Law Journal 457. It was alleged that it had impugned the impartiality of the judiciary in the imposition of the death sentence. After a three-day trial he was acquitted, the court finding an absence of mens rea (dolus) on his part: S v Van Niekerk 1970 (3) SA 655 (T).

'While Barend never minded being in the public eye—to be sure, he enjoyed it—the trial was a great strain on him; he was then only 31 years of age, and in the operation of the law a bit of an innocent abroad. Even then, his irreverent sense of fun would out. At the time he was suffering from a very severe cold and cough. When he went into the dock he brought with him a large bottle of cough mixture. One of his interests at the time was the manufacture of *mampoer*—home-distilled spirit, commonly called peach brandy. The cough mixture had, as the old *Punch* cartoon put it, a "little bit of something in it".'

—Ellison Kahn 'In Memoriam: Barend van Niekerk' (1981) 98 *SALJ* 402 at 406.

In the course of his judgment Claassen J said of Barend van Niekerk that 'we think he is talkative, inclined to be pompous and somewhat foolish' (at 659).

'I have just read your very moving tribute to Barend van Niekerk published in volume 98 of the *South African Law Journal*.

'I was privileged to be one of Professor Van Niekerk's students at the University of the Witwatersrand in 1970 and 1971. Your reference in your tribute to the prosecution of Professor Van Niekerk arising out of the article "Hanged by the Neck Until You Are Dead" brought to mind an incident which took place immediately after Professor Van Niekerk's acquittal. If my memory serves me correctly, and I am sure that it does, in delivering his judgment Mr Justice C J Claassen described the accused as being talkative, pompous and inclined to be foolish.

'Immediately prior to Professor Van Niekerk's resuming lectures after his acquittal, one of the students in my class wrote in large letters on the blackboard in the lecture room: "WELCOME BACK DR VAN NIEKERK". Beneath this he wrote in brackets: "beware, he is talkative."

'Professor Van Niekerk entered the lecture room to much cheering and applause and very soon saw what was written on the blackboard. He turned to the class and with a huge (and very typical) smile he announced: "Yes, and the judge also said that I was pompous and inclined to be foolish. But, never mind, I consoled myself, I was in good company."

'A remark of that nature reinforces your assessment that he had not learned his lesson and was indicative of the man you have so accurately described and paid tribute to in the *Law Journal*. We are certainly the poorer for his passing. . . .'

—From a letter of 21 September 1981 by Mr Mitchell Ramsay to Ellison Kahn.

Alan Paton's funeral tribute

'This country is ruled by an authoritarian government. It does not really care for freedom of speech or communication. It believes that literature, especially the novel, should be controlled. It is highly suspicious of the press. It treats harshly those who are militant in opposition to the policies of racial separation, even while—and this is a great paradox—it itself is telling the world that it is moving away from discrimination. It administers security laws that are not to be found elsewhere in the Western World, to which world it desperately wants to belong. It has the power to frighten people, to make them keep silent, to make them say "I don't discuss politics", to make a white man afraid to show a black woman a courtesy, to make us afraid to protest against any injustice, to make us afraid to go into a police station to make some perfectly legitimate inquiry about some detained person, to make us shadows of ourselves. Yet it is this same country that throws up a Barend van Niekerk, who refused to go down on his belly before the state, who espoused something far greater than the cause of law, namely the cause of justice. And I could mention many others, but I shall not do so. When people call this the greatest tyranny in the world, they are talking nonsense. Barend van Niekerk would have soon been dead under Hitler or Stalin or Amin or the Ayatollah Khomeini. There are many injustices in this country, but we can thank God that we have so many people who condemn them, and who use their lives to try to remove them from the life of our society. That is why we are here today to give thanks for the life of Barend van Niekerk. [The speaker then gave the words of a blessing.]

'I have one last word to say about this blessing. It asks God to give Barend peace, now and for ever. Well, I am not sure that Barend would want peace for ever. Rather let us ask that he should rest for a week or two before he starts campaigning for improvements in heaven.'

PROFESSOR BAREND VAN NIEKERK

Caricature by John Michael ('Jock') Leyden (1908–). From (1980–1) 2 Natal University Law Review *preface: 'Saving the old Durban Station'—one of Barend van Niekerk's successful crusades*

—Alan S Paton in his funeral oration on 6 July 1981 (see (1981) 98 *SALJ* 411 at 413–14). (It is reprinted in Barend van Niekerk's book, published posthumously in New York in 1987, *The Cloistered Virtue* xix.)

'Rebel with causes'

'"Rebel with a cause" is how a newspaper referred to him on his death. With many causes, I should say. Critic of the Government, of the judiciary, of the legal profession, of environmental pollution, of the death sentence, of racialism, of racism, of the treatment meted out to prisoners, of suppression of freedom of speech, convener of the Save our Station campaign in Durban, champion of the salvation of our historic and cultural heritage, campaigner of justice for all. Unlike the typical white South African of liberal sentiments and humanitarian ideals, he did not handle reality delicately with a pair of tongs. A torrent of words flowed from his lips and his pen, frequently leaving the listener and the reader breathless—and the editor busy with his blue pencil. His oratory moved audiences; to me when he delivered a public speech he sounded like an eloquent politician: only he was not a political animal in any sense, and was pleading for justice or reform.

'He was a flamboyant character, a wily opponent, a cutter of bureaucratic red tape; but he was no Felix Krull. For authority he had a splendid lack of regard. How he loved—there is no other way of putting it—taking the mickey out of people. Everyone who knew him well will have treasured memories of his trampling on cant, pomposity, self-righteousness and smugness; his pricking of the bubble of self-importance enveloping those "drest in a little brief authority". I remember him at an official function coming up to a judge who had participated in one of his trials, introducing himself, and saying "How do you feel about meeting one of the criminals you sentenced?" A newspaper reporter in a touching tribute to his memory recollected the occasion when, after watching in growing disbelief a Commissioner finish sentencing pass-law offenders at a spanking pace, he sauntered to the Commissioner's room and casually said to him: "I have seen your sausage machine in operation. Does it always work like this?" (Arthur Konigkramer in *The Daily News* 26 June 1981).

'Barend's search for justice often took him into neighbouring states. For an ordinary man these would have been dangerous situations. But Barend could worm and talk his way out of almost anything. Diplomatic niceties, official channels, passport problems—all were nonsense and there to evade. If necessary, he said, the bottle of good brandy he always kept in his back pocket on his travels would change hands and work wonders.'

—Ellison Kahn 'In Memoriam: Barend van Niekerk' (1981) 98 *SALJ* 402 at 409.

'During the late night of Saturday 20 June 1981 or the early morning of the next day, in a room in a small hotel in the remote village of Copacabana on the shores of Lake Titicaca in Bolivia, Barend van Dyk van Niekerk died, alone, not known to anyone in the area. It took some time for the local authorities to identify him. . . .

'I felt an infinite sadness. It was almost as though a beloved nephew had left this life. How ironic, in a way, that this vibrant, colourful man should suddenly be removed from us in the silence of the night far from home in an obscure hotel room in a faraway land. And yet his death, in a sense, went with his personality; he was a citizen of the world, at ease and self-confident anywhere, on the move whenever he felt that his obligations to his family and university allowed. Wanderlust would seize him. Sometimes I, as one of his oldest friends, on hearing of Barend's darting into strange parts of the globe, would recall W J Turner's lines:

"The houses, people, traffic seemed
    Thin fading dreams by day;
Chimborazo, Cotopaxi,
    They had stolen my soul away!"

'. . . Barend was only 42 years old. . . .

'He was buried in Durban at noon on a balmy mid-winter day, in the soft rolling green hills of Stellawood cemetery.

'He was so vital; he lived his life so intensely; he tried so hard to contribute to the attainment of justice, peace and decency; and I shall never see him again.'

—Kahn op cit at 402–3, 411.

'As for courtesy, well, some writers use a rapier and some use a battleaxe. My dear departed friend Barend van Niekerk used a battleaxe. He was thrice tried as a result. The first trial was for contempt of court arising out of an article on the death penalty from his pen that I published in the *Journal* in 1969 and 1970. I felt partly responsible for what happened, though I had toned down the original version. I was not prosecuted, probably because the authorities realized that I am one of nature's innocents, ignorant of the law and incapable of mens rea; nor were the publishers, Juta's, prosecuted, though poor James Duncan had to travel to Pretoria and go into the witness-box. To quote the words of R E G Rosenow (later Mr Justice Rosenow) published in the *Journal* in 1944 (61 *SALJ* 14 at 16), referring to the decision of Van den Heever J in *Engelbrecht v Engelbrecht* 1942 OPD 191 that a marriage of a minor without parental consent is void—words often savoured by me: "The wrestler who has suffered an aeroplane spin and a body slam to the mat has very little say in the proceedings immediately thereafter, but when the mists have disappeared from his mind, he will endeavour to analyse the cunning grips that led to his ultimate undoing." In other words, he will emerge from his ordeal a wiser and more astute man. Barend really thought me a bit of a coward when I subjected his many later manuscripts to rigorous scrutiny, and sometimes rejected them. To some extent I probably was and am a coward, but I also wanted and want to look after the interests of my publishers and printers. All I can say is that despite my being careful, I am not a censor, and am prepared to publish the sort of material that appeared in articles in the last couple of years, when it would have been so easy to say "I am not looking for trouble or criticism". But I admit that sometimes I feel like I felt some thirty years ago, when I was standing quietly at a bus stop, waiting for the vehicle and minding my own business, and up came a very large dog, which looked at me quizzically and then, raising his left hind leg, gave evidence that it had decided I was a lamppost.'

—Ellison Kahn 'The Birth and Life of the South African Law Journal' (1983) 100 *SALJ* 594 at 625–6. (Some footnotes included in text, others omitted.)

JAN HENDRIK FREDERIK EDUARD RUDOLF CLAUDIUS GEY VAN PITTIUS

1879–1931. Member of the Pretoria Bar 1907–25. KC 1924. Judge of the Transvaal Provincial Division 1926–31.

'Gey van Pittius, who did not remain on the Supreme Court Bench very long owing to his sudden and unexpected death, presided many years ago in Johannesburg in a cause célèbre known as the "Tothill Case". "Gey", as he was known, had been a member of the delegation which, as the result of Tielman's [Tielman Roos's (qv)] impish note to the twenty-nine powers assembled at Versailles in 1919, went to Paris in order to put the case there for the re-establishment of the two old republics. While Gey was at the Bar his income had been supplemented by the salary he was paid as a lecturer in Roman and Roman-Dutch law at the Transvaal University College. The result was of course that while at the Bar his appearances in Court were none too frequent. Once on the Bench, however, he made it quite clear that he would not be trifled with. His ruling passion was a game of bridge, and it was this passion which sometimes led to judgments remaining in arrear long enough to cause great embarrassment to all concerned.

'Well, one morning while Pirow, Oom Klaas de Wet (later a Chief Justice) and I were having coffee, Oom Klaas broached this delicate matter to Pirow, who was then Minister of Justice, and who was known to be most jealous of the reputation of his Judges, of all his Courts and of course of the whole Department of Justice. Pirow had just returned from one of his big-game hunting expeditions and after listening to Oom Klaas for a while he remarked with a typically Pirowian grunt, "Well, it seems to me that the period of gestation of a Gey judgment is something like that of the cow elephant in the jungle—just under two years." I have a shrewd idea of what the outcome of this coffee party was.'

—The Hon C P Bresler *Tilt the Sack* (1965) 149.

HENDRIK STEPHANUS VAN ZYL

1876–1955. Member of the Cape Bar 1903–20. KC 1919. Member of the Cape House of Assembly 1905–10. Judge of the Cape Provincial Division 1920–35. Judge President 1935–46.

'[He] was by far the youngest of a very large family. His father P. H. S. van Zyl had been married twice before and his mother three times, so that there were twenty-two half-brothers and -sisters and twenty step-brothers and -sisters.

'Until the age of eight he had no education. He was nine years old before he discovered, as he once said, "to his everlasting regret that there were other books in the world besides the big family Bible".'

—M A Diemont in *Dictionary of South African Biography* V (1987) 837.

'In 1898 is hy na Cambridge waar hy as student te St. John's College ingeteken het as regstudent. Kort na sy aankoms daar was die wolke wat Suid-Afrika betref maar donker en dreigend. Maar Hendrik van Zyl selfs as student was altyd 'n man wat sy man kon staan en nooit het hy gehuiwer om sy standpunt duidelik te kenne te gee en sodoende het hy die bewondering en die respek van Britte op Cambridge uitgelok—tot so 'n mate dat 'n jong Boer-student—'n onwrikbare teenstander van die Britse beleid wat die Boere-oorlog betref—deur die studente te midde van die oorlog gekies was as President van die Cambridge Union—'n keuse wat eer en hulde aan albei verstrek het. Ek kan nie beter doen as om die woorde van *Granta*, die tydskrif van die Universiteit van Cambridge, aan te haal nie:

'"For more than eighteen months this country has been in conflict with the two South African Republics. During the whole of that period Mr. H. S. van Zyl, a Boer, inspired by all the intense patriotism of his people, has advocated persistently and unflinchingly, in countless speeches and in innumerable conversations, on public platforms, or wherever he found two or three seriously-minded men gathered together, the cause which he has at heart. And Mr. H. S. van Zyl is now President of the Union. That we should imagine is a unique record. . . .

'"The Union has done itself honour. In electing Mr. van Zyl to preside over its debates it has not only paid a compliment to the 'high seriousness' of his oratory, but has also acknowledged the tact and courtesy with which he has advocated opinions which must necessarily be unacceptable to a great majority of its members. . . ."'

—Mr Justice J E de Villiers, Judge President of the Cape Provincial Division, 'In Memoriam: The Hon. H. S. van Zyl' (1956) 73 *SALJ* 1 at 2. (See also HOEXTER.)

CARL FRIED(E)RICH PETER JACOB VON BRANDIS

1827–1903. Soldier. Public servant. Special Landdrost of the Witwatersrand 1886–1900. A character.

'My recollection of Captain von Brandis is of a well-built man of medium height, always dressed in a neat grey beard with grey topper and grey morning coat to match. His limp was compensated by a walking stick. I never saw him on horseback.

'He did both administrative and judicial work. Part of the former was the pacification of the angry mob. He had a way of his own. "Look what you have done to my flower garden." The crowd had broken down his fences and trampled on his garden in a demonstration against his guest, the old President. Incidentally, they tore down the Republican flag which was hoisted in the garden. This was at the corner of Smal and Kerk Streets. Never was a mob more ashamed of itself.

'When he was not pouring oil on troubled waters he would be attending marriage ceremonies. He was a hero. He would make amends to the bride for what he had done to her. He kissed everyone, no matter how plain. He kissed some more heartily than others. The extra heartiness was by way of compliment to the groom.

'The last time I saw him was just before the outbreak of the Boer War. Two of my friends had thoughtlessly anticipated events. There was but one thing to do and that was to get the Captain to regularise the affair and give them his blessing. I was the witness and the fellow who threw the wedding breakfast for three.

'She was very beautiful. In a second, without a word having been said, the Old Man knew that she was under age and that he was to be the Man of the Hour. He started a lengthy examination. He wanted to know a lot of things. He wanted to know why she looked so young. He said she did not look twenty-one but more like eighteen. He wanted to know where her parents were. He wanted to know why her skirts were so short. I do not remember all the questions, nor any of the answers, but the latter were worthy of the occasion. This dreadful ordeal lasted for half an hour. It was the most gruelling experience I had ever had. Every now and again he turned to Mr. U. P. Fischer, his clerk, and asked him whether he thought that he should marry them. Mr. Fischer gave the appropriate answer. He then started to sign the marriage certificate and stopped periodically to ask Mr. Fischer whether he should sign the certificate. The Old Man got the answer he wanted. He did this three times over the short distance covered by "C. von Brandis". At last he said, "Very well, my dear," and stuck on the final "is". He knew he had done wrong but he knew it was in a good cause.

'He knew no law, but he was strong on equity.'

—H H Morris KC *The First Forty Years* (1948) 62–3. (See also WAIFS AND STRAYS sv 'Lawyers in general'.)

'The situation became tense and a climax was reached when, in March, 1890, President Kruger paid a visit to Johannesburg. . . .

'His speech was greeted with shouts of "God Save the Queen" and the singing of "Rule Britannia", and his own Republican flag was torn down from its mast over the public buildings in the market square. Kruger meantime had retired to the house of Capt. von Brandis, the local *landdrost*—chief magistrate—where he proposed to spend the night.

'But he was not left long in peace. By nightfall, a huge and angry crowd had assembled outside the house and the air echoed to their jeers and catcalls. Kruger heard the rumpus and wanted to go out and speak to the accursed *rooineks*—for all his faults he never lacked courage—but his host restrained him. Capt. von Brandis knew his own people—he had been first magistrate on the Rand since the beginning and had built up an enormous personal popularity because of his genial manner and his habit of seeing that everyone got fair play.

'He went out on to the *stoep* himself. The crowd was already out of hand and the advance guard had surged over the garden to the veranda, intent on getting inside and confronting the President. Nor were they daunted by the presence of some of Kruger's armed bodyguard who barred the way with their fingers on the triggers of their guns.

'Capt. von Brandis faced them calmly and sternly.

'"You are Englishmen," he said, "and I always understood that an Englishman's home is his castle. This is my home and the President is my honoured guest!"

'The crowd hesitated. Von Brandis was their friend and they would not willingly cause him offence. But the sense of injustice still flamed in their hearts and they shifted restlessly, while angry murmurings ran through their ranks.

'Von Brandis came a few steps nearer to where the ringleaders stood and made a gesture towards the trampled garden.

'"What are you boys up to?" he demanded. "You've ruined all my wife's flowers and she won't half take it out of me when she finds out!"

'His words were greeted by a shout of sympathetic laughter and the ringleader apologised and called for three cheers for the magistrate. Then, ordering the others to disperse, he and his followers set about cleaning up the garden and repairing the broken fence, while the President's bodyguard, laying their guns aside, joined in. And perhaps only von Brandis knew that, by his own superb tact and good humour, he had averted a tragedy.

'Von Brandis was one of the outstanding figures on the Rand in those days. Despite the fact that he had once been a Prussian officer of the old school, he had endeared himself to everyone and was regarded more as a father than a law-giver. As a magistrate, he was noted for his unconventional handling of the cases brought before him and it was whispered that many of the fines he was compelled to impose were secretly paid out of his own pocket, while he had a soft spot in his heart for feminine offenders and could never bring himself to record a conviction against them. In the years to come, his name was to be remembered always with loyalty and affection, and commemorated in practical form when it was given to one of the city's most important public squares.'

—F Addington Symonds *The Johannesburg Story* (1953) 104–6.

BALTHAZAR JOHANNES (JOHN) VORSTER

1915–83. Member of the Johannesburg Bar 1955–8. Minister of Justice 1961–6. Prime Minister 1966–78. State President 1978–9.

'Mr. B. J. Vorster, the Minister of Justice, at a dinner given in his honour on Friday by the Johannesburg Bar, said that he believed in a free and independent judiciary. . . .

'During his introductory speech, the chairman of the Bar Council, Mr. G. Colman Q.C., said that Mr. Vorster had been a good colleague and a loyal member of the Bar.

'At this stage, Mr. Vorster interjected: "Tell that to the SUNDAY TIMES".'

—*Sunday Times* (Johannesburg) 12 November 1961; not reported elsewhere. (See also MULLIGAN.)

WAIFS AND STRAYS

Accused

The dog and birth control

'Humour is occasionally encountered in legal treatises and articles. An excellent example is the note in the *Yale Law Journal* in 1961 (volume 70 page 1205) headed

"Man, his Dog and Birth Control: A Study in Comparative Rights". It is shot through with irony and sarcasm. The name of the author is not revealed. Arthur John Keeffe, who wrote an appreciation of the note in the *American Bar Association Journal* ((1961) 47 *ABAJ* 1015), attributed it to one George Spelvin. Later he explained that in the world of the American theatre "George Spelvin" is the name used for a mere walk-on role or for an actor who plays two parts in one play or a part in each of two plays performed in one evening, say *Cox and Box*. One gets the message: the author surely was the Yale professor who appeared for the parties who sought the order in the then leading case on the constitutionality of anti-contraception statutes, *Poe v Ullman* 367 US 497 (1961). Keeffe went on to make his customary joke: "Because that Yale article is such a brilliant job and this Yale George Spelvin is such an unusual and talented fellow, I shall violate my usual rule and disclose that he is ——." The note dealt with a Connecticut statute then in operation for some seventy-five years, which made it a criminal offence for any person to use any drug, article or instrument to prevent conception, or to assist, cause or counsel anyone to do so. The question whether this law was invalid because it conflicted with the Bill of Rights was raised before the United States Supreme Court in *Poe*, a suit for a declaratory judgment. By a majority of five judges to four the court held that there was no justiciable controversy. Four of the majority judges based their conclusion on the facts that the statute had yielded only one prosecution (in 1940) and that contraceptives were openly sold throughout the state of Connecticut. The fifth judge (Brennan J) simply found that the issue was not ripe for adjudication. During the course of argument Mr Justice Frankfurter interjected, it is said with a straight face: "A person might not buy them for use. Some people might just want to collect them. People collect all sorts of queer things. Some people collect matchboxes. I know a man who collects sausage containers."

'The author of the note asked whether a recent development of an oral contraceptive for bitches would attract the application of the Connecticut birth-control law. The drug reduced the bitch's desire for sexual intercourse; but if nevertheless intercourse took place, it prevented conception, and that would apparently fall within the reach of the statute. Not that the bitch could be prosecuted, because, though she was privy to the forbidden act, she did not administer the drug herself, and it could be argued that it was administered against her will. Nor could it be contended that a dog was a person, unless—"of course"—it were incorporated. Furthermore, a bitch was incapable of understanding the nature and quality of

'You are acquitted! You deserved gaol—you brazen rascal! Yet it's always sweet to save one's fellow man.' (Overcome with gratitude, the thief pilfers the purse of his defender as a memento of loving esteem.)

Honoré Daumier (1808–79). Lithograph.

the proscribed act. Therefore it would be unlikely that the animal could be successfully prosecuted. (The learned George in a footnote referred to "the paucity of dog psychiatrists" to test the mental defect of the animal. He then stated: "True, it is said that in 1594 a dog was found guilty in a court of law in Leyden, Holland, executed by hanging before a cheering populace and then drawn and quartered. But Holland is a civil-law jurisdiction." It is a pity that George did not give references. See, for example, . . . "A Dog's Trial for Homicide" (1907) 24 *South African Law Journal* 233, on a court order of 1595 that a dog be hanged and his corpse remain on the gallows as a deterrent to other dogs and to all, and in addition "all his goods, should he have any, to be confiscated and forfeited for the benefit of the countship". I suspect that it is the case referred to by George, who gives the wrong date of 1594.) It was also arguable that the statute was intended to regulate only human sexual activity. If it did apply to dog owners, would it be unconstitutional as a deprivation of property without due process of law? On the other hand, why should bitches be deprived of what have been called "the most intimate and sacred experiences in life"?'

—Ellison Kahn 'The Seven Lamps of Legal Humour Part 4' 1984 *De Rebus* 306 at 307, 309. (See also BURGERS; CHASSENAEUS.)

'I.G.B. and H.R.H.

'He had been an honest youth. He was always a religious man and a devout Catholic.

'In his youth he got a raw deal in Kimberley. He was falsely trapped for I.D.B. and went to the breakwater. That was the end of him as a good citizen, but he was proud of the fact that he still remained an honest man. Everyone who sold him gold got a square deal. If you threw a parcel into his yard and called, no matter how long after, there would be no question about the receipt of the parcel or its weight, and you would be paid out the market price which prevailed at the time. In this way he built up a big connection and ultimately became the biggest dealer on the Rand.

'He was at all times a very serious man without any sense of humour. When he was making his will his attorney, who did have a sense of humour, suggested that he should leave something to the Chamber of Mines.

'"Why should I leave anything to the Chamber of Mines?"

'The attorney saw that he was on to a good thing and suggested leaving £50 to the police.

'"The police, the police," he shouted, "the police—why should I leave anything to the police? What the hell have the police ever done for me? I am not going to leave anything to the police."

'As an attack of apoplexy was threatening, the attorney explained that he was only joking. The testator became even more furious when he was told this. He could not understand how an attorney could joke while a client was engaged in the serious business of making his will, and it was only an abject apology that saved the attorney from losing a client.

'It took the police years of hard work to get him, but as they say, "The pitcher goes to the well until it breaks."

'One day an Indian boy of about ten years of age arrived. He explained that his uncle in Delagoa Bay had sent him to enquire about the price of gold. That innocent little Oriental came away with a calculation in the dealer's handwriting. A few weeks later the youngster returned with a thousand pounds in notes and his big brother. He explained that he was not strong enough to carry the gold and therefore he had brought assistance. As the two traps walked out of the house, Stephen Brink, the head of the Gold and Diamond Department, walked in. He said to the I.G.B., "You have a thousand pounds in notes in your safe and here is a record of their numbers. Kindly open the safe."

'Dr. Krause and I were briefed for the defence. About three days before the trial the accused's nerve failed him and he disappeared, estreating his bail of a thousand pounds.

'For ten years he wandered through the Continent of Europe, suffering acutely from homesickness. He visited this country at least twice on false passports, but eventually he decided that he would rather go to gaol than live in the South of France.

'The surrender was negotiated and bail was fixed at a thousand pounds. At the appointed hour I introduced Major Trigger to my man at Marshall Square. The Major said, "Well, X, I am very pleased to meet you." Mr. X felt flattered. He did not see the joke.

'Now that he was arrested it was difficult to know what to do with him. Ten years had elapsed and both the witnesses were in India. I put up a proposition to the Attorney-General. I told him I knew the witnesses were in India and that if

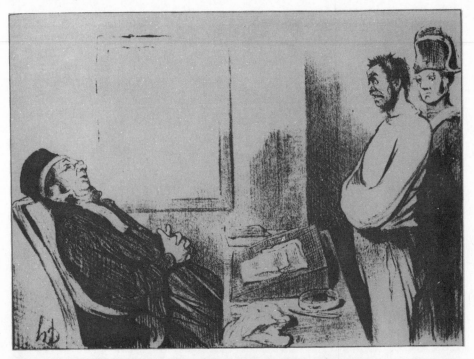

MEN OF THE LAW

'So you were hungry, you were hungry. I'm also hungry almost every day, but I don't therefore steal.'

Honoré Daumier (1808–79). Lithograph.

'The advocate has rendered full tribute to the rare talent exhibited by the public prosecutor in his indictment; the Attorney-General made a point of paying a well-deserved tribute to the admirable eloquence of defending counsel; the President of the court congratulates both orators; in short, everyone is extremely satisfied, except the accused.'

Honoré Daumier (1808–79). Lithograph.

'Counsel for the defence'
[The theatricality of the advocate and the sly, false demureness of the accused woman.]
Honoré Daumier (1808–79)

he did get them it would be with great difficulty. I suggested that the matter be remitted to the Magistrate and if that were done the accused would plead guilty.

'He said, "How do I know that if I remit the matter he will plead guilty?"

'I replied, "X says so. He is a man of his word."

'He said, "Very well."

'This is where H.R.H. comes into the picture.

'There was a rumour abroad that on the arrival of the Prince of Wales an amnesty would be granted to certain long-term convicts.

'In Cape Town Tielman Roos [qv] told me to go back to Johannesburg as soon as possible and get my man convicted, because very shortly the date would be fixed which would determine who should come within the terms of the amnesty. We got the case on just in time. My man pleaded guilty and was sentenced to twelve months' imprisonment with hard labour, of which he served, as a result of the amnesty and good conduct, a comparatively short period.

'After he came out he gave up the gold business. He went in for diamonds.'

—H H Morris KC *The First Forty Years* (1948) 105–7.

Rape in the river

'There was the classic reply of the accused in a trial in Rhodesia, when the prosecutor put it to him that he had raped the complainant in a river. The accused retorted angrily: "What do you think I am—a duck?"'

—Ellison Kahn 'The Seven Lamps of Legal Humour Part 2' 1984 *De Rebus* 210 at 211.

Advocate

'THE REFEREE

'It happened on Circuit. The Accused was being tried for attempted rape. The husband, a policeman, was giving evidence. He said that on the night in question he and his wife retired to rest about ten o'clock. At about midnight he was awakened by the uneasy stirring of the sleeping lady. He then saw the Accused, who was a complete stranger to him, lying on the other side of his wife, attempting to have intercourse with her. The witness said he jumped up and blew his police whistle.

'"Why did you blow your whistle?" His Lordship asked.

'"Offside," came in a loud whisper from a Junior Member of the Bar.'

—H H Morris KC *In and Out of Court* (1950) 28–9. The author says in his preface: 'It is the classic creation of ex-Senator Hartog.' (Gus Hartog was a member of the Johannesburg Bar and in later life a senator in the Parliament of the Union of South Africa. I heard him recount this anecdote at a Bar dinner some time in the period 1945–8.)

A rogue advocate

'Arthur Sime Knox had been a member of the Natal Bar for many years. He was an urbane, charming man and a brilliant cross-examiner. I once took over an adultery case which he had started and where evidence was heard in Durban on commission. He had cross-examined the private detective and I read the cross-examination in the record. It was superb. There was nothing unfair about it, but it was cleverly planned and executed. And he never delivered the coup de grâce until every escape route had been completely blocked and the witness could not escape. He was cultured and talented too. A good painter, a connoisseur of

'The widow under the protection of her legal adviser's honesty . . . and understanding.'
Honoré Daumier (1808–79). Watercolour.

good food and wine and a scratch golfer at one time. But there was an ugly side
to him, too. He was the perfect confidence trickster, because he had such smooth,
such impeccable manners.

'D H Lawrence wrote:

"How beastly the bourgeois is
especially the male of the species—

Presentable, eminently presentable—
shall I make you a present of him?"

'Arthur Sime Knox was presentable, eminently presentable. He was also a
crook. In 1952 he had been found guilty in a magistrate's court (while a member
of the Bar) of being in unlawful possession of firearms and housebreaking
implements. He and others were apprehended by the police while driving down
the North Coast at night. The magistrate sentenced Knox to two months'
imprisonment without the option of a fine. Knox's appeals to the Natal
Provincial Division and the Appellate Division both failed. He was struck off the
roll of advocates in 1953 (*Society of Advocates of Natal & another v Knox & others*
1954 (2) SA 246 (N)). About ten years later he applied for his readmission as an
advocate. The Society of Advocates of Natal opposed the application, and I was
briefed to appear for the Society, with Brian Hardman as my junior. Rex Welsh
and Len Hurt appeared for Knox. I met Knox for the first time about an hour
before the hearing: suave, polished and charming. Rex Welsh told me that he was

quite prepared to put Knox in the witness-box so that I could cross-examine him. I declined the invitation for tactical reasons, saying that I was quite content to argue the case on the papers. I did this because Arthur Williamson was on the Bench, new to Natal, and I thought that Knox might pull the wool over his eyes. I made the right decision. We argued that Knox had demonstrated by his conduct that he was unfit ever to practise at the Bar again. The court agreed. Knox was down but by no means out. He continued until the end of his life to be involved in all sorts of schemes: he was a great stayer. My friend Cecil Nathan told me a few years ago that on one occasion his doorbell rang at 2 am. It was Knox. "Have you got a million rand? I have a scheme" he said. Nathan sent him off very rudely, but Knox was not offended. Like many rogues he had a thick skin.'

—The Hon Ramon Nigel Leon *Truth in Action* (the reminiscences of the former judge of the Natal Provincial Division, not yet completed or published). I have taken the liberty of adding a few details to his account. Knox was not a member of the Society of Advocates, a voluntary association to which almost all practising advocates belong. But he could practise as an advocate without being a member.

To elaborate a little on the sentence of imprisonment. The firearms (pistols) and implements (a helmet, fawn-coloured raincoats, a pair of handcuffs and a jemmy-bar) were found after midnight in the car in which Knox was in charge.

'I say, colleague, you are for the defendant today against me in exactly the same type of case in which I was for the defendant three weeks ago. I say, that's comical!'
'I shall reply with the very words you used then. It's amusing: when we have to, we strike at each other with each other's words!'

Honoré Daumier (1808–79). Lithograph.

'Watching brief'

Jock Leyden (1908–) in Henry Field Raquel Welch and Me *(1985)*

The Appellate Division found that Knox and his companions had been engaged in a joint nefarious enterprise, Knox, the leader, intending to impersonate a policeman and the pistols to enable the party, at the very least, to make a show of force.

Slip of the tongue

'Paddy Lloyd, dramatically: "I call the deceased, my lord."

'Deathly hush, while everyone's hair stands slowly on end.

'" . . . I mean the accused, my lord."'

—1963 *Rhodesia and Nyasaland Law Quarterly* 311.

A misconception leading to a miscarriage of justice

'Turning now to the advocates whom I knew, my earliest recollection was of Mr Janion. Mr Janion practised as an advocate in Pietermaritzburg. I think he was the only man who practised exclusively as an advocate. He had a signboard outside his office: Mr Janion, Advocate. He was a notable man, with a great sense of humour and a biting tongue. He had a splendid criminal practice, and stories about him are legion. It is said that on one occasion he was arguing a criminal appeal from the judgment of a Mr de Villiers St Pol, a magistrate who was notorious for lengthy judgments. He was quoting from a passage in the judgment, when Sir John Dove Wilson said: "Mr Janion, what passage are you referring to?", whereupon he said "the fifteenth line of the fourth page of epistle according to St Pol, my Lord!" It was also said that on another occasion the same magistrate had referred to the statement of a witness as being pregnant with possibilities. In the appeal Janion said: "My Lord, I can only say that that it was a misconception on the part of the magistrate which has led to a miscarriage of justice!" Mr Janion was also notable for his alcoholic consumption, which was remarkable

SKETCH OF COUNSEL BY MR JUSTICE M A DIEMONT IN HIS NOTEBOOK

Reproduced from The Star *12 June 1975*

in many ways. It was said that in his last days he was kept alive on an unbroken diet of champagne.'

— The Hon D G Fannin, former judge of the Natal Provincial Division, in his dictated unpublished memoirs (1986) page 4. (On a wall in the School of Law building of the University of Natal, Pietermaritzburg, hangs a framed photograph bearing the title: 'N.U.C. Pietermaritzburg 1910–1911.' ('N.U.C.' stands for the then Natal University College, predecessor of the University of Natal.) In the front row, on the right, sits 'J. d'H. de V. St. Pol', looking very dapper, sporting a moustache, the very essence of the beau garçon.)

'EKSEPSIONABEL

'Wyle regter Eddie de Beer (vroeër van die Vrystaatse regbank en later appèlregter) het altyd met groot genot die volgende staaltjie van wyle regter Chris Botha (voormalige regter-president in die Vrystaat) vertel, wat gedateer het uit die dae toe die twee here in Bloemfontein jong advokate was in aangrensende kamers.

'Chris Botha het 'n lywige opinie gehad om af te handel. Dit het heelwat naslaanwerk in die ou bronne geverg. Hy het Eddie genader om hom by te staan

Counsel and Client
Honoré Daumier (1808–79). Lithograph.

met die navorsingswerk. Eddie het egter so pas 'n opdrag ontvang om 'n deklarasie op te stel. "Goed," sê hy toe aan Chris, "Ek sal jou help, maar dan moet jy die deklarasie vir my doen." Hiertoe was Chris bereid.

'So gesê, so gedaan. Chris se opinie is voltooi en Eddie se deklarasie is ingedien.

''n Week of wat later stap Chris by Eddie in.

'"Jammer, Eddie", sê hy met 'n vonkeling in die oog, "ek het nou opdrag ontvang om namens die verweerder op te tree in die saak waarin ek die deklarasie vir jou opgestel het. Ek het die deklarasie nagegaan. Dit is nie in orde nie en ek sal eksepsie moet aanteken."

'Chris het dit gedoen. En die eksepsie is gehandhaaf.'

—(1962) 6 *Codicillus* 45.

'Mr I A Maisels QC, one of the most gifted advocates of his generation, has turned 80.

'And at a party thrown in his honour by the Johannesburg Bar, another venerable silk—Mr Iggy Isaacs QC, aged 92—made a telling observation on the times.

'When Mr Maisels was admitted to the Bar, he said, "ANC" still stood for antenuptial contract.'

—*Sunday Times* 1 December 1985.

'An Amsterdam advocate consulting his authorities'

Reproduced from A Catalogue of Early Law Books in the University of the Witwatersrand Law Library *(1987) compiled by Jean Cowley and edited by J E Scholtens opposite page 108*

'A WELL-KNOWN ADVOCATE ON HIS STEED OUTSIDE THE OLD SUPREME COURT
'Charles Davidson Bell, *circa* 1860. *Published copyright by permission the William Fehr Collection.*
Reproduced from (1967) 84 South African Law Journal *opposite page 209. Possibly the advocate was Petrus Johannes Denyssen (1811–83), who was elevated to the Bench in 1865.*

Aptonyms and ineptonyms

Surnames that are aptonyms or ineptonyms are scattered through the reports of legal cases. How fitting that the secretary of the plaintiff grain co-operative should be one Snodgrass (*Suid-Afrikaans Sentrale Koöperatiewe Graanmaatskappy Bpk v Thanasaris* 1953 (2) SA 314 (W)); that the executor of the estate of a deceased testator whose will caused problems of interpretation was one Will (*Will v The Master & others* 1991 (1) SA 206 (C)); that H M Scrivenor should have been a notary public (*Thomson, Watson & Co v Spiller* (1857) Watermeyer 17); that the owner of a lorry should be called Tanque (*Vlok v Ocean Accident & Guarantee Corporation Ltd* 1962 (4) SA 25 (W)); that one of the traps in an IDB transaction bore the name Danger (*R v Majoni* 1969 (2) SA 595 (RA)); that an expert witness should have the patronymic Onions (*Gifford v Table Dock & Breakwater Management Commission* (1874) 4 Buch 96); that the life insurance representative who brought an action was one Hawker (*Hawker v Life Offices Association of South Africa & another* 1987 (3) SA 777 (C)); that in a certain matter the judge, the two parties and counsel bore the same surname (*Van Zyl v Van Zyl* 1936 CPD 463); that the celestial corporate style of the plaintiff in *Divine Gates and Company v African Clothing Factory* 1930 CPD 238 should prove of no assistance; that the prosecutor of two youths for crimen injuria was Mrs M M Mann, the accused being successfully represented by the prosecutor's husband, Mr Colin B Mann (for the Mann-to-Mann contest, see *Rand Daily Mail* 22 June 1973); that the plaintiff who had signed a document without reading it in *Wiley v African Realty*

Trust Ltd 1908 TH 104 was an attorney; that it was Challinger who sued Speedy
Motors (1951 (1) SA 340 (C)); that the applicant who failed in his attempt to have
his race classification as a Chinese changed to a classification as a white should
have the surname Pinkey (*Pinkey v Race Classification Board & another* 1972 (3) SA
631 (A)); that the Trade Discount Company, having lost against Steele, should
win against Gold (*Trade Discount Company v Steele* 1949 (4) SA 121 (O); *Gold v
Trade Discount Co (Pty) Ltd* 1951 (3) SA 123 (T)); that it was Mr Zambia who was
charged with entering South Africa unlawfully (*S v Zambia* 1966 (4) SA 12 (GW));
that Mr Innocent should be found guilty (*R v Innocent* 1966 (2) SA 362 (R)); that
K O Bang should be involved in a case of total loss (*K O Bang v Natal Lloyds*
(1907) 28 NLR 344); that the holder of a hotel liquor licence in Kuruman should
be Nasopie (Edms) Bpk, 'nasopie' meaning 'one for the road' (see *Nasopie (Edms)
Bpk en andere v Minister van Justisie en andere* 1979 (3) SA 1228 (NC) and 1979 (4)
SA 438 (NC); *Cowburn v Nasopie (Edms) Bpk en andere* 1980 (2) SA 547 (NC);
Nasopie (Edms) Bpk en andere v Minister van Justisie en andere 1982 (1) SA 134 (A)).

On the other hand, why should Mr America have sued Mrs America (born
Africa) for divorce? Hall AJ remarked that this was the first occasion on which he
had heard that America had lost interest in Africa. After the order had been
granted, counsel said: 'There is no longer a United States.' (CPD 4 February 1965
The Star 4 February 1965.) Just as strange a concatenation of nations occurred in
a successful claim in a South African court by a Dutch passenger who had been
bitten by a Russian wolfhound on board a British vessel called the *German*.
(Unreported, cited by Benjamin Bennett *This Was a Man* (1958) 47–8.)

It was sad that Mr Old should have been found guilty of driving when drunk
(*R v Old* 1969 (3) SA 333 (R)).

Mrs Bass bore an appropriate name (*R v Bass* 1959 (3) SA 63 (C)). She had been
prosecuted for requiring her tenant to pay rent in excess of that determined by the
rent board. She pleaded that she was supplying a meal and so was not hit by the
legislation, inasmuch as in terms of the lease the tenant was entitled to be supplied
twice or thrice weekly with—fried fish. The defence failed, as this was held to be
a service.

One might think that Fakir (*R v Fakir* 1952 (1) SA 421 (A)), Pundit (*Devchand
v Pundit* 1952 (1) SA 164 (N)) and Prophet (*Prophet v Prophet* 1948 (4) SA 325 (O))
would have been canny enough not to get enmeshed in a law suit. But the
surnames Goliath (*Marine and Trade Insurance Co Ltd v Goliath* 1968 (4) SA 329
(A)) and Caesar (*Caesar v Caesar* 1973 (2) SA 760 (R)) could justifiably have given
the holders of them confidence in court.

He who bore the name Wise bore an ineptonym, for he was convicted of
robbery (*S v Wise* 1975 (1) SA 597 (RA)). One Meek was bold enough to sue for
damages for personal injuries arising out of a motor-vehicle collision, but he was
held to be 70 per cent at fault (*Meek v South African Mutual Fire and General
Insurance Co Ltd* 1975 (2) SA 223 (N)). The surname Love did not suit a defendant
who was sued for payment of a sum lent to him on overdraft and who tried
unsuccessfully to raise a preliminary technical point (*Barclays National Bank Ltd v
Love* 1975 (2) SA 514 (D)). A striking ineptonym was Dry, the married name of
a woman who had fatally shot her husband after they had been drinking and
become argumentative; she was found guilty of culpable homicide and sentenced
to four years' imprisonment, two suspended for three years. (See *The Star*

3 September 1986.) In a case concerning maintenance for a divorcée, a man with the same inappropriate surname had been living in concubinage with her, she being an alcoholic, while, according to her, 'Mr Dry is a man who likes his liquor' (*Schlesinger v Schlesinger* 1968 (1) SA 699 (W) at 700). On the other hand, the alias Sam Booza sported by one Lesson, found drunk, dressed in women's clothing, in a gutter was an aptonynm (*R v Lesson* 1906 EDC 185).

The protagonists of criminal prosecutions and civil proceedings have sported surnames reflecting every month except June and December. Rex, Regina or the State has prosecuted a January ((1893) 7 EDC 154; 1903 ORC 15); a Januarie (1958 (3) SA 74 (E)); a February ((1883) 3 EDC 226); a Februarie and Mei ((1841)—see 10 SC 382); an April ((1895) 5 EDC 177; 1920 CPD 235; 1960 (4) SA 615 (N); 1985 (1) SA 639 (NC)); a May ((1904) 18 EDC 63; 1912 EDL 1; 1961 (3) SA 548 (O)); a Mei (1935 CPD 1); a July ((1886) 4 HCG 238; 1925 TPD 878; 1928 EDL 318); an August ((1887) 5 SC 216); a September ((1894) 8 EDC 104; 1920 CPD 617); an October ((1906) EDC 61; 1916 CPD 57); an Oktober (1950 (2) SA 50 (C)); and a November ((1901) 18 EDC 38; (1907) 24 SC 612). March was involved in a civil case (*Nasson v March* (1901) 9 HCG 37); so was April (*Cape Town Municipality v April* 1982 (1) SA 259 (C)); so was October (*October v Rowe* (1898) 15 SC 110).

A zoo can be created from the names of those involved in legal cases. At the one extreme is Adam Muis, cause of the disturbance in *In re Kok and Balie* (1879) 9 Buch 45—see at 48. At the other extreme are the accused Oliphants ((1886) 5 EDC 330, 331; 1950 (1) SA 48 (O); 1989 (4) SA 169 (O)) and Olifants (1950 (2) SA 514 (O); 1951 (1) SA 48 (O); 1977 (4) SA 954 (T)). There emerge in the reports of criminal cases a Piet Buffel (1916 OPD 197), a Buffel Dikgat (1928 GWL 11), a Jakhals ((1883) 3 EDC 118, 224), a Bull (1941 OPD 114), a Duiker (1958 (3) SA 853 (T)), a Sprinkaan (1918 TPD 270), a Vogelstruis (1909 EDC 234; 1911 EDL 402), a Lynx (*R v Lynx Charley* (1904) 18 EDC 136), a Wurm (1951 (1) SA 366 (SWA)), a Seekoei (1982 (3) SA 97 (A)), a Mamba (1957 (2) SA 420 (A)), a Mule (1990 (1) SACR 517 (SWA)), and Seals (1990 (1) SACR 38 (C)). A Tiger makes his appearance in *Johnson v Tiger* 1979 (1) SA 920 (NC).

Meals, food, drink and drugs can be found among the characters in the law reports to satisfy any taste. In the criminal cases among the names of those accused Breakfast is offered (1937 EDC 97; 1970 (2) SA 611 (E); 1984 (3) SA 302 (E)), with a Tafel (1921 CPD 437) supplied with Tomato ((1896) 13 SC 77) and Koffie (Koffee) ((1909) 10 HCG 373; 1911 EDL 138). Those feeling low are offered both Whisky (Scotch) (1963 (1) PH H136 (SR)) and Whiskey (Irish) (*R v Whiskey Kamonema* 1931 SWA 1). Consolation can be found with Snuif ((1895) 2 Off Rep 294; (1896) 3 Off Rep 1) followed by a Sneezum (1943 EDL 295); and euphoria with Dagga ((1904) 18 EDC 250.)

One finds among the surnames of those prosecuted a Baby (1924 TPD 426; 1985 (2) SA 61 (Ck)—Swartjong Baby, convicted of robbery, and who had a string of convictions, was sentenced to a year's imprisonment by a magistrate; on review the Supreme Court considered that strokes should also have been imposed); also a Mama, furnished with assorted and bilingual Tities ((1907) 24 SC 437), Titties (1918 CPD 357) and Tieties (1943 GWL 52; 1990 (2) SA 461 (A)). (The word, labelled as vulgar by *The Concise Oxford Dictionary*, passed the

Registrar of Companies: cf *Titty's Bar and Bottle Store (Pty) Ltd v ABC Garage (Pty) Ltd* 1974 (4) SA 362 (T).) There follows a Mtumtum (1946 EDL 327) for Tiny Tim (1914 TPD 505).

Humble and poverty-stricken must have been some whose names appear among the accused in the pages of the law reports: Armoed (1936 EDL 214), Rondganger (1913 EDL 168), Vlenterbaatje (1925 GWL 48) and Pickup (1932 NPD 216). But contrast Gentleman John (1908 EDC 129) and Alli Baba (1923 SR 7). Appearance, personal or by a forbear, apparently was the origin of the surnames Witbooi (1944 SWA 31; 1982 (1) SA 30 (A) etc), Witbors (1975 (4) SA 641 (NC)), Swartbooi (1960 (4) SA 178 (SWA)) and Geelbooi (1925 TPD 97). What of Stephen Jood (1949 (1) SA 298 (GW))?

The origins of some of the names of those prosecuted go to the outer bounds of speculation. Whence Dumdum (1952 (3) SA 584 (T))—from the Anglo-Boer War?; Mauser Shugoola (1920 TPD J/C 314, cited in (1964) 9 *Codicillus* 16); Ryperd Boesman (1942 (1) PH H63 (SWA)); and, above all, Jy (1963 (4) SA 966 (O))?

When one leaves the law reports and considers those concerned with the administration of the law, one occasionally finds a fitting name. How appropriate was that of the late Mr Justice Law of the Natal Provincial Division, whose death at the age of 56 on 28 November 1990 was mourned by all who knew him. The civil commissioner in Kimberley around 1882 was a Mr Judge (Hans Sauer *Ex Africa . . .* (1937) 41).

—Based largely on Ellison Kahn & Brian R Bamford 'Another Spoonful of Sugar and Pinch of Salt' (1965) 82 *SALJ* 507.

Attorney

'TAKING THE COW BY THE HORNS

'An attorney, who was acting for the defendant in a seduction and affiliation case, found that he could not go on with the trial on the morning of the hearing. He ran round to a brother attorney with the cover and explained that he had to leave town on urgent business, and asked his colleague to appear for him. He said that it was a very simple case and that he did not think that his client had a hope. The case was called and, to the horror of the deputy, there stepped into the box a lady with whom he had himself been intimate a few years before. When his turn came to cross-examine, he did so with great apprehension. He determined to forestall her.

'Said he: "So you say the defendant was intimate with you?"

'"Yes."

'"I suppose you'll next say that I was intimate with you?"

'"Of course you were."

'The Magistrate turned to the plaintiff's attorney: "Mr. Jones, for heaven's sake take your client out of the box. I can't believe a word she says."

'That was the end of the case.'

—H H Morris KC *In and Out of Court* (1950) 45.

George Williams, son of the Dean of Grahamstown

'Another character in that office was George Williams. I shall deal with him at some length as I regard him as the most remarkable person I have ever met and

'Seventeenth-century Dutch jurists in
consultation'

Reproduced from A Catalogue of Early Law Books
in the University of the Witwatersrand Law
Library *(1987) compiled by Jean Cowley and edited
by J E Scholtens opposite page 72*

even more remarkable after his death. He was a small man with a full shaggy beard, tousled hair always needing a haircut, and wearing the most untidy assortment of baggy clothing imaginable. He had on a cardigan waistcoat, although it was the hot month of February, and round his waist was a home-made string girdle from which dangled an assortment of pencils and a rubber eraser. He spoke with a high-toned drawling voice which had a surprising carrying power so that I often tracked him in quite a big building by his piping voice. He had a Gilbertian sense of humour, and he also possessed an extraordinary accurate memory for authoritative judicial judgments on a vast variety of subjects.

'As an example of his curious sense of humour, he once said in a serious voice, "The tramway company make the most impossible demands of their customers. In my tram there is a notice, 'Don't Spit on the Floor'—but Mr. Hermans, I cannot possibly reach the ceiling no matter how hard I try." Throughout our long association he always called me "Mr. Hermans", which in its way was something of a compliment, as he called several others about him, "You blithering idiot". He was peppery and irascible at times, because, as he often pointed out, he could not carry out the Bible injunction, "Suffer fools gladly".

'On one occasion I overheard him speaking to someone in the Land Bank—after getting very excited about some delay in their office, he said, "Now put me through to your General Manager". There was a pause while this was done, and he then continued. "Is that the General Manager?—what is your telegraphic address?" He was no doubt told, whereupon he retorted, "Please change it to SOMNOLENT".

'He had an interesting and forensically useful theory about fools. He regarded all persons with whom he had to have dealings for the first time as careless fools. He would say, "If the fellow in the Post Office who will have to transmit this telegram can possibly make a mistake, he will do so—so do not give him unnecessary help by writing indistinctly or misspelling a word—leave that to him to do. Also never use the word 'not' in a telegram—it can easily become 'now' in the hands of a professional fool."

'He was such a caricature of a man naturally with his unkempt beard and baggy clothes that he became the favourite subject for many amateur caricaturists and some of these caricatures were very good and amusing. He seemed to like this, no matter how grotesque he looked in the picture.

'Before I speak of his strange death, I feel that I should say that he was regarded as the best conveyancer in South Africa and also a wonderful draftsman of wills, deeds and legal documents. His honesty was absolute, sometimes even absurd. For example, he found an extra £5 note in his pay packet one day. It was meant to be an increase in salary. He took it back at once and said he did not deserve an increase in pay. He was also consulted by Government Departments on contemplated new Acts of Parliament. He was particularly good on taxing Acts, which was remarkable as he had no money sense in his own affairs.

'To understand the strange happening at his death, I must give some detail of his private life. He was the son of the famous Anglican Dean of Grahamstown who had the guts to bar his own bishop from preaching in the Grahamstown Cathedral because he differed from him on some important matter of policy. Dean Williams was tried in some ecclesiastic court and defrocked and he subsequently died of poverty and starvation which his son could not prevent.

'It must have been about that time in his life that George Williams embraced the Roman Catholic faith, and during the many years that I knew him he walked down every day from his home in St. Quentins Road in the Gardens to the Roman Catholic Cathedral to attend Mass. His wife had been an invalid and she died in my presence some years before the old man. They had a faithful Malay cook-housekeeper called Minna, with one eye, and she devotedly looked after all the old chap's needs. More and more, in his later years, he relied on me for those things which an aged father could expect from a son.

'Because of this, I sat at his bedside on the last day of his life. When I left him at about 6 p.m. he was very near his end. I told Minna when I left that she should ring me at my home at any time during the night if she needed me. She rang about 10 p.m. to tell me that he had passed away and I suggested that I would meet the undertakers at his house at 9 a.m. the following morning.

'When I walked into his home at the time fixed, I got the surprise of my life. His bedroom was immediately on my right so I went straight into it. I had left that old man in torn, not too clean pyjamas, with a long tangled white beard stained and discoloured. There was no sign of him in his bedroom, which was in a dreadful state of disorder. I knew that Minna could not carry him, so something else had supervened since the night before. Minna came in showing signs of great distress and exhaustion. She did not speak but took me by the hand into the dining room, and there I saw something truly amazing. The scruffy old gentleman had been completely transformed. He lay in state on the table clothed from head to foot in a brown monk's habit. His snow-white beard had been carefully cleaned and combed and covered his breast, on which was also a huge Crucifix which his hands seemed to be holding. On his feet, which just protruded from his habit, were monk's sandals, and his face seemed more peaceful and happy than I had ever seen it in my life. For the first time, in the years I had known him, he was "properly" dressed for parade.

'I discovered that the old fellow had, for some years, been a lay brother in some religious order. Minna had been told to ring another number as well as mine, and about midnight the brotherhood appeared at his death bed, bathed him, and went through the full induction ceremony over his body. Although I would possibly not have recognised him, St. Peter no doubt did.'

—Harry H Hermans *The Law—My Master: Reminiscences of an Attorney* (1970) 12–14. (George Frederick Charles Williams was the son of Frederick Henry Williams (1829–85), Dean of Grahamstown from 1865. The account by Hermans is not accurate. The Cape Supreme Court and the Privy Council found in favour of the Dean and against the Bishop, Nathaniel James Merriman. See *Merriman v Williams* (1880) Foord 135, 196 (PC). The quarrel was over the status of the Church of the Province of South Africa.)

The conveyancer

'Another odd character was old Mr. Peters. He must have been even older than George Williams, and right up to the end of his long life in the middle of the twentieth century he was practising the system of conveyancing in vogue before 1891. Acts of Parliament could come and go, Peters ignored them. He could reminisce happily at times. It was a deeds office regulation that deeds went through their full examination in a week. A deed lodged on, say, a Monday would be fully examined and if in order would come up for registration on the following Monday. This was the only modern innovation that old man Peters fully approved of: it made conveyancing much cheaper for the conveyancer, he said. Prior to 1891, there was no such rule. The few conveyancers in practice put their deeds in a special cupboard in the deeds office and the examining staff would, when they felt like work, go and collect a deed or two to while away the time. Sometimes deeds remained unexamined in the cupboard for months at a time. Mr. Peters said, "If a deed was at all urgent, all you did was to pin a £1 note so that one inch, no more, was visibly sticking out of it, when you put it into the cupboard. Then your deed would be examined the very next day. But you never got your £1 note back, sad to say."'

—Hermans op cit at 147–8.

'The clerk's office of Messrs. Dodson and Fogg was a dark, mouldy, earthy-smelling room, with a high wainscotted partition to screen the clerks from the vulgar gaze . . .':

Charles Dickens The Pickwick Papers *(1837) chapter XX.*
Illustration by 'Phiz' (Hablôt Knight Browne) 1815–82)

The popular funeral

'An attorney had an appointment with a silk, who insisted on punctuality. The attorney failed to keep the appointment; time passed; the silk became ever more annoyed. Eventually the attorney appeared, with profuse apologies. "Why are you so late?" asked the silk. "Well, I felt I had to attend a funeral I heard about at the last moment, too late to get into touch with you." "Whose funeral was it?" "The funeral of —." "But this colleague of yours was hardly a reputable person", responded the silk. "No, he was not", answered the attorney. "But I simply had to go to the funeral. In fact several hundred attorneys were present." "For heaven's sake, why did you all feel you had to be there?" "Well, we wanted to make dead sure that he was put six feet under ground."'

—Ellison Kahn's commonplace book. (This story, though slightly embellished, is essentially true.)

False teeth only for regional magistrates

'Years ago there was an attorney in Johannesburg who had a thriving criminal practice. Don't misunderstand me; I mean defending criminals. Let me call him Mr Jonah. He was a character. One day he appeared before a magistrate, defending his client. He said something that sounded a little like English, but was really incomprehensible; something like "Yappear fr yaccused." The magistrate asked him to repeat himself, which Jonah did, equally unintelligibly. The magistrate, vexed, asked Jonah why he could not speak properly. "Havn't got false teeth in" was the construction the magistrate finally and correctly gave to the answer. "Why haven't you got your false teeth in?" "I put m' false teeth in only for regional magistrates."'

—Ellison Kahn 'The Seven Lamps of Legal Humour Part 2' 1984 *De Rebus* 210 at 211. The story comes from Professor David Zeffertt, who vouches for its accuracy.

£65 724 12s 6d in cash

'Old Frederick Beecher Steer could have stepped right out of a book by Dickens or Thackeray. He was always immaculately dressed, wore a flower in his button-hole and a bowler hat—in a city in which bowler hats were almost unknown. He was a stickler for doing things correctly and he had a good strong voice—you always knew when he was about. Of a morning, he would stride up to the huge desk behind which the Registrar of Deeds sat, in an office big enough to hold fifty or sixty conveyancers, all signing their deeds "in the presence" of the Registrar of Deeds, and he would take off his bowler hat with a flourish; he would then place his deeds before the Registrar and announce in a loud clear voice, like a High Priest at a sacred ceremony, "Those deeds bear My signature, Mr. Registrar". There was no doubt that his signature carried his full stature as a man of business.

'He used to say that in his home he was as soft as butter but in his office he was made of granite, yet to me as a very young man he was a model of courtesy. When you looked at him over his desk you saw a slogan on the wall above his head reading, "The customer is always right," and he made you feel that you were the "customer". This was different from another old Cape Town character, Conrad Heinrich Hablutzel, a venerable auctioneer, who died within a few years after I was qualified to do business with him—I wish I could have seen more of him. His slogan on the wall as you approached him read, "Man is dust—dust settles—are you a man?"

'When I first started to practise conveyancing, there was a very high code of etiquette and personal prestige among conveyancers and very few defalcations in payment. A senior conveyancer's word was his bond, and his cheque handed over to the seller's conveyancer was normally regarded as being as good as payment by the Bank of England—it took a very brave man to query it. Some conveyancer once had the temerity to suggest to Mr. F. B. Steer that as the transaction involved a great sum of money, he wanted either a bank guarantee that his cheque was good or payment in cash. Mr. Steer took him at his word. He presented himself at the Deeds Office on the morning of registration of the deed with two coloured porters each pushing a loaded wheelbarrow. Payment could still be made in gold in those days and the bags in the two wheelbarrows contained £65,724 12s. 6d. made up of the coins of lowest denomination, in copper, silver and gold that had to be accepted as legal tender. Mr. Steer also demanded a receipt for the cash payment. I do not know when he got it but no one ever again asked Steer for a payment in cash, his cheque was accepted until he died. That was the granite in the man.

'The butter in his nature also came to my notice. He had seen military service in South West Africa at some time in his life and he kept his old military greatcoat as a souvenir of which he was very proud. Quite late in life, he bought a farm on the Cape Flats, to which he hoped to retire. By this time he had long ceased to practise conveyancing, so it is excusable that he did not notice that the farm consisted of several portions of land. He insisted on a servitude condition being inserted in the deed that he was to be buried on the farm in his military greatcoat. By some accident the condition was repeated in each paragraph of the deed, which therefore suggested that Frederick Beecher Steer would be buried in four different places. He was actually buried many miles away.'

—Harry H Hermans *The Law—My Master: Reminiscences of an Attorney* (1970) 148–9.

Corporation

A corporation (company) has 'neither body to be kicked nor soul to be damned'. Judges and lawyers are fond of writing or speaking these or similar words. (Thus Centlivres CJ, delivering the judgment of the majority of the court in *Commissioner for Inland Revenue v Richmond Estates (Pty) Ltd* 1956 (1) SA 602 (A) at 606: 'A company is an artifical person with no body to kick and no soul to damn. . . .'; and Lord Denning MR in *British Steel Corporation v Granada Television Ltd* [1981] 1 All ER 417 (CA) at 439: '[A] corporation . . . has no body to be kicked or soul to be damned.') They are aware of the fact that the sentiments were expressed by someone at some time, but I wonder how many have tried to find the actual source.

According to the revised reprint of the second edition (1970) of *The Oxford Dictionary of Quotations* (the various impressions of the first edition and the first impression of the second edition had gone grievously wrong in their attribution and sources), the first Baron Thurlow (1731–1806), the Lord Chancellor, said: 'Did you ever expect a corporation to have a conscience, when it has no soul to be damned, and no body to be kicked?' Then follows: '*John Poynder in* Literary Extracts from English and Other Works, *1844, vol i, gives this version*: Lord Chancellor Thurlow said that corporations have neither bodies to be kicked, nor souls to be condemned, and therefore do as they like.' To which the third edition (1977) adds: 'Usually quoted as "Did you ever expect a corporation to have a conscience, when it has no soul to be damned, and no body to be kicked?"'

A similar thought escaped the lips of Sydney Smith (1771–1845), the renowned English wit. It is to be found in volume I of *A Memoir of the Reverend Sydney*

Smith. By his daughter, Lady Holland, in the first edition (1855) on page 376, and in the second edition (also 1855) on page 379. The exact words (alas, ungrammatical) are: 'You remember Thurlow's answer to some one complaining of the injustice of a company. "Why, you never expected justice from a company, did you? they have neither a soul to lose, nor a body to kick."'

The conclusion to be reached is that the popular version of the 'body and soul' of a corporation (company), while it has rhythm, the foot being an anapaest (two unaccented syllables, followed by one unaccented syllable), is inaccurate. It is as inaccurate as the belief that the sentiment 'man proposes, but God disposes' comes from the Bible; though there are expressions in the Bible to that effect, the wording comes from *Imitatio Christi* (chap 1 § 19) by Thomas à Kempis: *Nam homo proponit, sed Deus disponit.* It is as inaccurate as the attribution to Sherlock Holmes of the words 'Elementary, my dear Watson': what was said can be found in the short story 'The Crooked Man' in the collection *The Memoirs of Sherlock Holmes*:

'"Excellent!" I [Dr Watson] cried.
'"Elementary", said he [Sherlock Holmes].'

Probably the first jurist to comment on the absence of the soul of the corporation was Sir Roger Manwood (1525–92), Chief Baron of the Exchequer, who, according to the entry under his name in the *Dictionary of National Biography* (*DNB*) (vol XXXVI (1893) 108), expressed the opinion in a case decided in 1592, and stated to be found in 'Bulstrode, "Reports", pt. ii. p. 233', that 'as touching corporations, that they were invisible, immortal, and that they had no soul, and therefore no subpoena lieth against them, because they have no conscience nor soul'. (The same extract, with minor variations, appears on page 319 no 6 of *Stevenson's Book of Quotations* (1934), which acknowledges the *DNB* as the source.) If one turns to page 233 of Bulstrode's Reports (80 ER 1085), one finds the case of *Tipling v Pexall*, decided in 1614, where Coke CJ is reported to have said something very similar in a case concerning the misnomer of a corporation (I preserve the quaint punctuation and spelling of the time): '. . . the opinion of Manwood Chief Baron, was this, as touching corporations, that they were invisible, immortall, and that they had no soule; and therefore no subpoena lieth against them, because they have no conscience nor soule; a corporation, is a body aggregate, none can create soules but God, but the King creates them, and therefore they have no soules; they cannot speak, nor appear in person, but by attorney, and this was the opinion of Manwood Chief Baron, touching corporations.'

The most celebrated of all such expression of views is that of Sir Edward Coke (1552–1634), who sat on the Bench from 1606 to 1617, and is one of the greatest of English judges and jurists. It was in *The Case of Sutton's Hospital* (1612) 10 Co Rep 1a and 23a (77 ER 937 and 960). Coke CJ said (at 326): '. . . the corporation itself is only *in abstracto*, and rests only in intendment and consideration of the law; for a corporation aggregate of many is invisible, immortal, and rests only in intendment and consideration of the law. . . . They cannot commit treason, nor be outlawed, nor excommunicate, for they have no souls. . . . A corporation aggregate of many cannot do fealty, for an invisible body can neither be in person, nor swear . . ., it is not subject to imbecilities, death of the natural body, and divers other cases.'

Stevenson (p 319 no 2) makes out that Grotius in *De Jure Belli ac Pacis* book 2 chapter 9 made mention of this judgment, in the following striking way (in translation): 'Lord Coke gravely informs us that corporations cannot be excommunicated, because they have no souls, and they appear to be as destitute of every feeling as if they had also no bowels. . . . There is no truth but one point through which they are vulnerable, and that is through the keyhole of the cash box.' (Unfortunately, I cannot find the passage in Grotius's great work. It was published in 1625, so it is possible that the passage *is* there; but I should be surprised if it were.)

Stevenson (p 319 no 9) gives one other relevant quotation, which he says is from a speech at the Tralee assizes by Howel Walsh, to be found in 'William Hone *Table Book*'. (On William Hone (1780–1842), see *DNB* vol XXVII (1891) 243. *Table Book* must be *The Table Book, of Daily Recreation and Information* (London 1878), originally published as volume 3 of *The Every-day Book and Table Book* (London 1831). Neither work is accessible to me. I can find no information about Howel Walsh.) Walsh's words were: 'A corporation cannot blush. It is a body, it is true; has certainly a head—a new one for every year; arms it has and very long ones, for it can reach at anything; . . . a throat to swallow the rights of the community, and a stomach to digest them! But who ever discovered, in the anatomy of any corporation, either bowels or a heart?'

The first sentence was quoted by H L Mencken (1880–1956), the renowned American philologist and satirist, in his *A New Dictionary of Quotations on Historical Principles from Ancient and Modern Sources* (New York 1946) on page 223. He says '*c.* 1820', and of Howel Walsh 'an English lawyer'; and he adds the following gloss, of which he says: 'Ascribed to an unnamed Western judge in ERNST and LINDLEY: *Hold Your Tongue*, 1932.' (This must be a reference to Morris L Ernst and Alexander Lindley *Hold Your Tongue! Adventures in Libel and Slander*, which was published also in London, by Methuen in 1936; it is not accessible to me.) 'A corporation is just like any natural person, except that it has no pants to kick or soul to damn, and, by God, it ought to have both!'

Finally, I may mention one variant—the dictum of Buckley LJ that a corporation has 'neither body, parts or passions' (*Continental Tyre and Rubber Company (Great Britain) Ltd v Daimler Co Ltd* [1915] 1 KB 893 (CA) at 916).

The absence in a corporation of a real body and mind has caused much difficulty, as we all know from our readings about the 'piercing (or lifting) of the veil', analogies with sentient beings, and the strong tendency to attribute to a corporation the mental states and actions of the natural persons who control it. Lord Lindley once remarked: 'To talk about imputing malice to corporations appears to the Lordships to introduce metaphysical subtleties which are needless and fallacious' (*Citizens' Life Assurance Co Ltd v Brown* [1904] AC 423 (PC) at 426). 'A human being has a body and a mind and the mind always accompanies the body; the mind therefore resides (if a mind can be said to reside) where the body resides. A corporation has no body but it has what by analogy can be called a directing mind. . . . In the case of *De Beers Consolidated Mines v Howe* [1906] AC 455 at page 458, Lord Loreburn stated the law as follows: "In applying the concept of residence to a company, we ought, I think, to proceed as nearly as we can upon the analogy of an individual. A company cannot eat or sleep, but it can keep house and do business. We ought, therefore, to see where it really keeps house and does business"': thus Watermeyer JA in *Estate Kootcher v CIR* 1941 AD

256 at 260. 'A company', said Lord Parker of Waddington in the great case of *Daimler Co Ltd v Continental Tyre and Rubber Co (Great Britain) Ltd* [1916] 2 AC 307 (HL) at 344–5, '. . . is a legal entity, a creation of law. . . . It is not a natural person with mind or conscience. To use the language of Buckley LJ, "it can be neither loyal nor disloyal. It can be neither friend nor enemy."' Still, there were strong obiter dicta in that case that a company can assume the character of the enemy if those in control of it have this character. In the words of Goldin J in *R P Crees (Pvt) Ltd v Woodpecker Industries (Pvt) Ltd* 1975 (2) SA 485 (R) at 487, the 'lifting of the corporate veil is possible and may be necessary in order to prove who determines or who is responsible for the activities, decisions and control of a company. Thus, a company can be under complete control of and its activities entirely dictated by another person but that does not deprive it of its distinct legal personality. A person in captivity may be entirely subject to and his conduct completely dictated by his captor. Nevertheless he still retains an existence and is a separate entity from the person who has complete power over and direction of him.'

The absence of actual body, heart and mind of a corporation makes it immune to the frailties of human flesh. It can live for ever; it cannot suffer pain; it cannot be imprisoned. But it cannot have all the consolations of ordinary existence. Thus it cannot be the guardian of a minor: 'The relationship between guardian and ward is a personal one, necessitating personal contact and a human relationship which cannot be rendered by a corporation' (per De Villiers J in *Ex parte Donaldson* 1947 (3) SA 170 (T) at 173). However, as Lord Loreburn LC pointed out in *De Beers Consolidated Mines Ltd v Howe* supra, a 'company cannot eat or sleep, but it can keep house and do business'.

For all its want of actual human attributes, however, the corporation has evoked some cynical comments by South African judges, who have been unable to resist indulging in anthropomorphism. Innes CJ said in *CIR v Lunnon* 1924 AD 94 at 96: 'Companies, no doubt, are not conspicuous for generosity. Corporations, however early they assimilate the more predatory human qualities, do not as early acquire the higher attributes; and gratitude is not a feeling which we generally associate with joint stock activity.' And Carlisle J remarked in *Bothma v Bucknall* 1951 (1) SA 697 (N) at 700–1 that 'the Companies Act . . . may not be a very suitable garb with which to clothe a Church—indeed in this case it has proved unseemly . . .'.

—Based on a note by Ellison Kahn in (1982) 99 *SALJ* 307.

Judge

'HE FIXED HIM

'The Learned Judge had read the papers for the forthcoming Motion Day. There was one application that caught his attention in particular. It was the complaint of a man who had applied to the Town Council for leave to erect a kerbside petrol pump. The Municipality refused to grant leave and was now vigorously opposing the application. The Learned Judge could not make out why. There was something about the matter that made him suspicious.

'On the Sunday morning before the hearing of the application the Learned Judge drove down the street referred to in the petition and there he found a petrol station. The Learned Judge was a fine conversationalist. While his tank was being filled he had a talk with the proprietor.

'"Isn't there another filling station in this street?"

'"Well," said the proprietor, "there was a bloke who thought that there was going to be one, but I fixed him."

'The Petrol Pump Merchant liked the topic, so he spread himself. He told his agreeable customer how he had done it and what it cost. The agreeable customer was a good listener, but occasionally he chipped in with a question just to clear up the position. The customer complimented the merchant on his astuteness and left. Now there are two petrol pumps in that street, and the merchant does not know what went wrong.'

—H H Morris KC *In and Out of Court* (1950) 13.

'DEFEATING THE ENDS OF JUSTICE

'The Plaintiff was suing for damages, which he alleged were caused by his foot catching in the brass nosing of a stairway down which he was walking. During the first morning of the hearing Counsel suggested an inspection in loco at 2.30.

'At one o'clock the Judge visited the building. There he found a brawny man with a heavy hammer hammering down the brass nosing.

'"Well, my man," said His Lordship, "and what are you doing?"

'"Well," said the carpenter, "a bloke fell down these stairs the other day and broke his leg, and now he is suing my boss for damages. The old Judge is coming to see the place, so I am tidying it up a bit for him."'

—Morris op cit at 86–7.

'Yes, they want to convict this orphan, whom I don't consider young, as he is 57. But, none the less, he is still an orphan. I always comfort myself, gentlemen, that the court always looks with open eyes upon the wrongful conduct.'

Honoré Daumier (1808–79). Lithograph.

Horace Flather, editor of The Star *newspaper, Johannesburg, is discussing the case of* Pienaar & another v Argus Printing and Publishing Co Ltd *1956 (4) SA 310 (W), in which two members of the South African Senate sued the company that owned the newspaper for damages for defamation. The action arose out of a leading article in* The Star *in which certain senators were censured for accepting seats in the Senate, which had been enlarged by the ordinary bicameral process to give the Government an artificial two-thirds majority in Parliament, enabling it to disenfranchise coloured voters. Bram Fischer QC appeared for the defendant.*

'We saw him [Fischer] . . . almost every other day before the date set down for the hearing and I remember asking him if he knew who the judge was likely to be. He had no idea, he said. I suggested offering up a prayer for someone with an English background like Ramsbottom or Williamson and Fischer said drily: "On the contrary, if your prayers mean anything, ask for an Afrikaner judge. The English judge will lean backwards to be fair to the plaintiffs, the Afrikaner judge will do the opposite. Pray for the Afrikaner".

'How right he was. The case was heard before Mr Justice Ludorf and no one could have been fairer or kinder than he. Two or three times he intervened during my severe cross-examination to say that he thought the question had been pressed far enough and he was sufficiently impressed by one thing I said to make a point of it in his judgment.

'I had pleaded that there was a distinction between criticism of a politician and criticism of a private individual.

'Politics in South Africa is a robust thing. It is not for the squeamish. It is only for the strong and the impure in heart. It is very much like all-in wrestling, but not so entertaining. Few holds are barred. It is the only game played in this country without a set of rules and without a referee.

'That is what I feel—and felt when I was giving evidence—and I conveyed to the court a toned-down version of it.

'In his reserved judgment Mr Justice Ludorf, as predicted, found against *The Star*, but instead of the £10 000 damages claimed he awarded only £100, in, as he pawkily pointed out, "devalued currency". . . .

'One thing only remains to be added, and it is not without its amusing aspect. The case ended on Friday afternoon. Judgment was reserved.

'I had been the last witness and having stood in the box for some hours I was feeling jaded and anxious. The Supreme Court is half a mile from *The Star* office and I knew that at 4.30 a car would call and pick me up.

'I was standing on the steps of the Supreme Court waiting when I heard footsteps behind me and someone say "Good afternoon". I responded to the greeting and glanced quickly at the back of the man who had made it. It was Mr Justice Ludorf.

'Then I saw him getting into a diminutive car and I went cold with horror for I knew that at any moment the car from the office would arrive for me, that it would be a big car, and that it would be driven by a chauffeur in uniform. In my mind, the contrast was appalling: the sight of me climbing regally into the luxurious Mercedes Benz while the judge tootled home in his Mini could cause him to increase the damages by thousands! It was almost *lèse majesté*.

'Just at that very moment my car arrived at the entrance to the Supreme Court grounds, effectively blocking it for any other vehicle wanting to come in or go out. I waved frantically to the driver to continue round the block while I disappeared from view into the court corridor.

'When I emerged again I made an anxious survey—Mr Justice Ludorf had gone and my own car had not yet circumvoluted the block.

'Never was I so pleased with the Johannesburg traffic congestion!'

—Horace Flather *The Way of an Editor* (1977) 160–2. (Ludorf J said at page 318 of the report of *Pienaar's* case: '. . . the courts must not avoid the reality that in South Africa political matters are usually discussed in forthright terms. Strong epithets are used and accusations come readily to the tongue. . . . How soon the audiences of political speakers would dwindle if the speakers were to use the tones, terms and expressions that one would expect from a lecturer at a meeting of the ladies' agricultural union on the subject of pruning roses!')

Today a judge would drive a state-owned luxury Mercedes-Benz or BMW motor car; every judge is supplied with one for his private use.

The riposte

'In the early days of Natal, during the period of Responsible Government, long before the Union of the Provinces, a certain Judge of high repute, who was duly knighted, happened to take a stroll up Longmarket Street, Pietermaritzburg. He was met by a police constable. The dignitary of the law took it amiss because the constable did not stand to attention and did not proffer the salute.

'Judge: "Why don't you salute? Don't you know who I am?"

'Constable: "Who are you?"

'Judge: "I am the Judge of the Supreme Court."

'Constable: "Good job, stick to it."'

—F W Ahrens *From Bench to Bench* (1948) 52.

Mr Justice Ronald (Ronnie) Wordscrambler

I give this fictitious name to a former judge who, though his real name has often been stated in the press, must have his identity protected in these pages, which should not embarrass the living. It is tempting to term him Mr Justice Malaprop, but it is a temptation that is to be resisted. True, as will be seen, a number of the sayings attributed to him belong to the realm of malapropism: the unintentional misuse of a word through confusion with a word of similar sound, resulting in a ludicrous result, such as *under the affluence of incohol*. Other sayings, however, are the result of the confusion of two English idioms or expressions; or of English and Afrikaans words, idioms or expressions; or of a delicate and subtle thought that cannot be conveyed by conventional language.

Several valued friends and correspondents vouch for the accuracy of a large number of these remarks, and indeed often give me the name of the particular recipient or auditor (which I shall refrain from revealing). But I have a shrewd idea that a few are apocryphal; and that a number of the genuine ones were said by Mr Justice Wordscrambler out of a sense of fun. (An Australian university principal once wrote that anyone in his position who did not have a sense of fun was guaranteed to go mad—and I can appreciate the accuracy of this remark. Perhaps it also holds good for a judicial officer.) The late Mr Justice G A Coetzee, however, assured me that by and large the clangers (perhaps this is rather a harsh word) were actually dropped by Mr Justice Wordscrambler unwitting of his error.

Probably in many instances unnecessarily, I shall from time to time try to give my understanding of what Mr Justice Wordscrambler intended to say.

To start with malapropisms:

To a friend: 'When you go on the Bench, life becomes circumcized [circumscribed]'.

Friend: 'You mean a bit cut off?'

As counsel: 'My lord, I now come to my carnal [cardinal] point.'

As counsel: 'The answer has now doomed [dawned] on me.'

Colleague: 'Where are you going, Ronnie?' Ronnie: 'To buy a book.' Colleague: 'Van Schaik's is a good bookshop.' Ronnie: 'I always go to the ANC.' [CNA—Central News Agency.]

As counsel: 'Let me illuminate [enlighten] your lordship.'

As counsel: 'My submission is neatly pinpricked [pinpointed] in paragraph 6.'

A variant: As counsel: 'Just to sum up, my lord. I want to pinprick my point.'

As a judge, when asked whether his previous acting appointment on the Bench counted for pension purposes: 'Yes—it was a retrogressive [retrospective] appointment.'

As a judge to a colleague: 'I went down to my farm and walked to the vlei. It was beautiful. The walruses [bulrushes] were ten feet high.'

To a judicial colleague, on the work of the so-called Erasmus Commission on alleged irregularities in the former Department of Information: 'This is a very contagious [contentious] matter.'

To a judicial colleague: 'Bowels takes about two hours.'

As counsel, to a colleague: 'He was talking a lot of thrash [trash].'

As counsel, to a colleague: 'They managed to coil [crawl] out of it.'

Of a colleague at the Bar: 'He's such a plastic [placid] chap.'

To a colleague: 'I'm crazing [craving] for a cigarette.'

To a colleague at the Bar: 'We'll get her under the canine [canon] law.' Colleague: 'That'll serve the bitch right.'

From the Bench: 'Don't let that deturb [? deter or disturb] you.'

To a newcomer at the Bar: 'A young advocate can get to the top by devious [various] means.'

From the Bench: 'That would not be clear to an outstander [? outsider].'

To a judicial colleague, who arrived late at a party Wordscrambler was hosting: 'Solly, here's the bar—humiliate [? help] yourself.'

From the Bench, to witness: 'Jy moenie getuienis uit jou mou [*sleeve*—should be *duim*] suig.' (Witness looks puzzled. 'Jy weet wat ek bedoel?' Witness: 'Er—er, ja—dit is om gevolgtrekkings te. . . .' 'Nee—dit is om getuienis op te maak.' (Case 8–9 May 1968.)

Next, the wrong word:

At the Bar, to a colleague: 'Solly, I've got a sitter.'
Solly: 'Yes—I thought you had a pretty good case, Ronnie.' Ronnie: 'Solly, you misunderstand me. I mean I've got to sit down and work like hell to puzzle it out.'

To a judicial colleague: 'You take a piece here and a piece there, and then everything falls into place like a crossword [jigsaw] puzzle.'

To a judicial colleague: 'So during the war you flew in Europe, America, Africa and the East! You must have gone halfway round the bulb.'

To a colleague at the Bar: 'I want my bone [pound] of flesh.'

To a colleague at the Bar: 'That suits me down to the teeth.'

To a judicial colleague's attractive wife, whom he had not met for years: '*I* may not have a pretty face, but I have the brains [memory] of an elephant.'

Of opposing counsel: 'He's barking around [beating about] the bush.'

To a judicial colleague: 'The case was easy fry [meat].'

About his summer holiday: 'I didn't wear my frock once.' [*Frok* is Afrikaans for vest, singlet.]

To a friend: 'Don't go honeybrushing me.' (From the Afrikaans *iemand heuning om die mond smeer*; flatter someone, butter someone up, soft-soap someone.)

Of a witness who was involved in a lot of matters: 'He had a finger in every tart.' (I heard the same remark fall from the lips of a professor of French at an important meeting.)

In an art gallery, looking at a *stillewe* by Frans Oerder: 'I love a quiet [still] life.'

Next, the confused or conflated idiom or expression:

To a colleague: 'The arrangement was as safe as a house on fire.'

As counsel: 'My lord, I haven't studied the odds and evens [ins and outs] of the matter.'

As counsel: 'The plaintiff is now skating on the thin edge of the wedge.'

As counsel: 'What my learned friend says flows down my back like a duck's water.'

To a friend: 'Since then we have all passed a lot of water under the bridge.'

As a newcomer to the Bar, after hearing Oswald Pirow arguing a case: 'It was wonderful. He spoke with his tongue up his sleeve.'

A variant—as counsel: 'What has the witness up his cheek?'

From the Bench: 'Counsel must speak up more as I'm sitting at an angle here and he's facing me with his back.'

To his instructing attorney: 'We're both in a dark boat.' (? in the same boat—in the dark.)

To a colleague: 'We're feathers of the same flock.'

To a friend: 'I prefer to be a small fish in my own backyard.'

From the Bench: 'Is this a prim [fit] and proper case for relief?'

On the South West Africa Delimitation Commission: Chairman: 'Look at these lovely dunes.' Ronald: 'But this is not the desert prim and proper [pure and simple].'

—Based in part on Ellison Kahn 'The Seven Lamps of Legal Humour Part 2' 1984 *De Rebus* 210.

'CONVERSATION AT A MOTEL

'Clerk: Name, please.

'Traveller: Mr Justice and Mrs Clayden.

'Clerk: I'm sorry, Mr Justice, this is a respectable motel.'

—1967 *Rhodesian Law Journal* 23.

Optimistic counsel

'Improper opening remarks of inexperienced counsel in an appeal to the Transvaal Provincial Division (Nicholas and Moll JJ) from a conviction in the magistrate's court: "My lords, when I first read the papers I felt very pessimistic about the prospects of success on appeal. When I read them a second time I felt far less pessimistic. When I read them a third time I felt quite optimistic."

'Moll J: "We have read them only once."'

—Ellison Kahn's commonplace book 10 March 1975.

Orr Street

'Female witness: "I live in Orr Street." Judge: "How do you spell it?"'

—Ellison Kahn 'The Seven Lamps of Legal Humour Part 1' 1984 *De Rebus* 159; adapted from 1969 *Rhodesian Law Journal* 106.

'From the many occasions I have sat in a courtroom—mainly as a reporter, I hasten to add—I have found very little to laugh about in those sombre and somewhat drab surroundings. The judges and the magistrates who preside at the court sessions are, with rare exceptions, not given to outbursts of humour. They much prefer to finish the whole unpleasant business and get home to their scotch and sodas as soon as decently possible.

'Of course, there are always the exceptions. When the witness complained to the judge at a celebrated murder trial that she was hard of hearing, he growled at her: "Madam, judging by the rubbish being spoken here, you aren't missing much." Or when the plaintiff screamed at the defendant: "God will punish you for your lies!" the judge remarked caustically: "In this court I am the sole authority."'

—Joe Podbrey in *Rand Daily Mail* 27 January 1983.

Juror

'This morning I spent in Court watching the Criminal Sessions in progress. One of the jurymen whose names were called out for duty was Percy Sherwell; but he was "challenged". Challenging jurors is meant to be a protection against possible bias or interest; in this instance, and I understand more frequently than not, it is a device to avoid duty. You get one of the counsel who happens to be a friend to challenge you and off you go to your office or your golf!'

—Oliver Deneys Schreiner (qv) in a letter to his wife Edna, 12 October 1920. Schreiner family papers. (Percy William Sherwell (1880–1948) was a great cricketer, who captained South Africa in thirteen test matches between 1905 and 1911.)

ADDRESSING THE JURY
Sketch by Professor Marinus Wiechers
Reproduced from 1990 31(2) Codicillus 38, with kind
permission of the University of South Africa

Lawyers in general

'*Lawyers and the names of Johannesburg streets, squares and parks.* As one who has spent decades at the University of the Witwatersrand, Johannesburg, I have heard the names of judges and other legal officers, and of legal practitioners, of the old South African

Republic and the Edwardian Transvaal slip on countless occasions from the lips of persons who did not know of whom they were speaking. The southern front of the university is on Jorissen Street. Ameshoff Street would carry one through the main eastern gates were it to continue beyond Jan Smuts Avenue. Immediately nearer town than Jorissen Street is De Korte Street. Eastwards, up the hill past the Civic Centre, in the centre of bustling Hillbrow—the Soho of Johannesburg—lies Kotze Street. Hillbrow also sports Esselen Street. Juta Street runs through Braamfontein and Wanderers View. In Pageview and Triomf, Krause Street can be found. The appellation Von Brandis is attached to a supposed square in the centre of town. For sixty-six years it has ceased to be a public place, however, except on the lips of cynics, for around Union the authorities took what was then the only piece of open ground in the middle of the shopping area for the construction of the Supreme Court. This led to a public outcry, which was fruitless. Today an enormous tower block [stands] behind the existing Supreme Court building to add to its facilities. But perhaps it is not inappropriate that the gallant Captain Von Brandis, of whom more later, should sacrifice his park for the enforcement of the law. His name is also attached to the street running through town past the west side of the fictional square, and to streets in Marshalltown, in Albertville, in Paarlshoop and in Turffontein. Morice Street is in Denver, Wessels Street in Johannesburg central. In The Hill Extension is (or was) to be found Frank Lucas Park. Manfred Nathan Park is situate in Crosby. Through Kenilworth and Towerby runs Van Hulsteyn Street.

'All of the surnames mentioned can be found in Dr Anna Smith's *Johannesburg Street Names* (1971), that meticulous work of love by the former City Librarian of Johannesburg. The names of judges of the South African Republic are placed in the index under the heading "Z.A.R. Government and Other Officials and Volksraad Members". What are so many judicial officers doing in such close association with members of the executive and the legislature? Wessels, Krause and Morice are listed under "S.A. Historic Personages". Frank Lucas and Manfred Nathan are to be found among the "Johannesburg Worthies", where also appears Hollard of Hollard Street in Marshalltown. William Emil Hollard [qv] a "worthy"! Dr Smith gives a biographical sketch of this remarkable legal practitioner on pages 217–18. . . .

'Jorissen Street was named after S G Jorissen (1857–1889). (See Smith op cit 253.) He was elevated to the Hoog Gerechtshof on 12 October 1886. The person chosen to fill his post was his father, Eduard Johan Pieter Jorissen (1829–1912 [qv]. This probably unique event hardly proved a success, for Jorissen *père* was not only without formal legal training but also temperamental and devoid of many of the ideal judicial qualities. The sittings of his court were characterized by constant brushes with counsel. The Hon C P Bresler, formerly of the Transvaal Bench, gives a delightful pen sketch of Jorissen in *Tilt the Sack* (1965) 141–3. When he was appointed a judge "his conduct became a welter of eccentricities". . . . Nothing appears to have been written of the short life of Jorissen *fils*.

'Herman Arnold Ameshoff (1860–1905) sat on the Bench of the South African Republic from 1889 to the outbreak of the Anglo-Boer War. His seems to have been a reasonably good appointment. The same cannot be said of the appointment of Benedictus de Korte (1859–1922) [qv], after whom, according to Dr Smith, it is generally believed De Korte Street was named. . . .

'Esselen Street must have been named after Ewald Auguste Esselen

(1859–1918) [qv], who sat on the Transvaal Bench from 1886–1890 and was State Attorney from May 1894 to September 1895. Thereafter he resumed practice and became one of our greatest advocates.

'Of the eminent judge John Gilbert Kotzé (1849–1940) [qv], whose name is enshrined in Kotze Street (the acute accent has been lost), so much has been written that it suffices to say that he was the only judge of real distinction appointed in the old South African Republic, on the Bench of which he sat from 1877 until his controversial dismissal by President Kruger in 1898. From 1881 he had been Chief Justice.

'Juta Street was possibly named after Jan Carel Juta, one time Registrar of the Supreme Court and subsequently a landdrost (Smith p 259).

'That brilliant and astute advocate, who subsequently became a sound trial judge, Friedrich Eduard Traugott Krause [qv], according to Anna Smith (p 281) was probably the person after whom the street bearing his surname was called some time in the nineteen-hundreds. I should say it was almost certainly so, for he was a member of the Johannesburg Town Council and of the Transvaal Legislative Assembly at the relevant time. . . .

'Anna Smith (p 346) thinks "it is possible" that Morice Street in the suburb of Denver was named after George Thomas Morice (1858–1930), the Scotsman who sat on the Transvaal Bench from 1890 until the Anglo-Boer War. This surname (of French origin) is so uncommon in South Africa that it seems very likely indeed. Denver had been established before the outbreak of that war.

'Captain Carl von Brandis (1827–1903) [qv], Special Landdrost of the Witwatersrand from 1886 to 1900, surely was the person intended to be honoured by the square and various streets of that name in the city. He was a highly respected, very competent and much-liked man.

'Only one of the judges of the old South African Republic has not been accounted for in what I have written: Antoine François Kock [qv], who was elevated to the Bench on 8 June 1898. As he held office only until the outbreak of the Anglo-Boer War, there was probably no newly created township in which a street could be called after him. . . .

'Wessels Street, according to Dr Smith, was probably so called after J W Wessels [qv], who had come from the Cape Bar in 1887, and had immediately acquired a large practice. The street name is to be found on a map of Johannesburg of 1890. Wessels was later to become the learned judge and subsequently Chief Justice.

'While Anna Smith deals fully with the career of Dr Manfred Nathan [1875–1945; member of the Johannesburg Bar from 1897–9, 1901–31; President of the Special Court for Hearing Income Tax Appeals 1931–45] in her notes on the square that bears his name, she is, for someone of her erudition, disappointingly brief on Frank Lucas Park—"presumably named after F. A. W. Lucas who was a councillor from 25 October 1911 to 10 November 1915 . . . " (p 168). Surely he was the Frank Lucas who was so honoured. Dr Anna Smith for once has not done full justice to a figure of historical note. . . . Frank Lucas [1881–1959], of whom many, I among them, have fond memories, attended the National Convention in 1908; was a member of the Transvaal Provincial Council from 1914 to 1917, where he led the Labour Party and promoted rating legislation that gave partial expression to his life-long belief in the doctrines of Henry

George; was one of the applicants who in 1914 obtained an interdict—too late—to stop Smuts's illegal deportation of nine strike leaders aboard the SS *Umgeni* and who chartered a coaster in a vain attempt to intercept the ship; was appointed the first chairman of the Wage Board in 1924, a position he held until 1936; was perhaps the main force behind the creation of the General Council of the Bar of South Africa; and at the advanced age of 68 ascended the Transvaal Bench.

'Nowadays streets are not named after incumbents of judicial posts. Perhaps it would be considered to be bad form or even improper for a township developer to seize on the surname of a judge or a retired judge still alive. Nor are all the streets, parks and squares bearing judicial names places of which the person sought to be honoured, were he alive, would be proud to be associated with. Nevertheless it is pleasant to think that the legal profession sometimes pays suitable tribute to the memory of the eminent departed, if not in the name of a street, in the name of a building, Innes Chambers, the home of the Johannesburg Bar, is a case in point. [To which may be added Schreiner Chambers, a virtually adjoining building, an addition to the advocates' home.]

'That leaves Van Hulsteyn Street, so called after Sir Willem van Hulsteyn (1865–1939), who was a partner in the leading Johannesburg firm of attorneys of Van Hulsteyn, Feltham and Ford. . . . It would appear that the controversial Sir Willem (knighted in the coronation list of Edward VII for services to the Crown) himself played a part in the naming of the street—no shrinking violet he. (See Smith p 552.) Van Hulsteyn, a Hollander by birth, was a member of the Reform Committee of 1896. He subsequently became a member of the Transvaal Legislative Assembly and from 1915 to 1920 was a member of the House of Assembly. It is perhaps not generally known that Van Hulsteyn was the father of the actress Marda Vanne, who was the first wife of J G Strijdom, Prime Minister from 1954 to 1958; it was a union that soon ended in a divorce.'

—Ellison Kahn in (1977) 94 *SALJ* 98.

Legislator

The Cape Times *of 5 August 1966 contains a photograph showing Mr Justice Van Wyk; the Minister of Justice, Mr Vorster; Mr Justice Beyers, Judge President; Mr Klopper, the Speaker of the House of Assembly; Mr Justice Van Zyl; and Mr Justice Watermeyer. They are seated on the bench of the new civil court of the Supreme Court, Cape Town, and are convulsed with laughter at the remark made on behalf of the Bar and the attorneys'profession by Mr Gerald Gordon QC, Chairman of the Cape Bar Council, at the ceremony when the new court was opened.*

Gerald Gordon QC (looking at the Minister of Justice and the Speaker): 'There is a great deal of litigation arising out of the interpretation of statutes whose meaning is not always clear. Never in the history of judicial conflict have so many' (gesturing to the crowd of advocates and attorneys in the well of the court) 'owed so much' (pointing to the briefs on the desks) 'to so few' (looking back up at the bench).

GERARDI A WASSENAER J Cᵘ

PRAXIS IVDICIARIA

In twee onderscheyde deelen versat

T'UTRECHT.
By LACOB van POOLSUM,
A. MDCCXLVI.

SEVENTEENTH-CENTURY DUTCH COURT SCENE

Described as inaccurate by Professor J E Scholtens in A Catalogue of Early Law Books of the University of the Witwatersrand Law Library *(1987). Facing page 64.*

Litigant

'A MAN IN A MILLION

'He was a schoolmaster. Schoolmasters are rarely opulent; he certainly was not. The only real asset he had was a sense of honour; that paid no dividends.

'He had a second cousin, a man of means. This second cousin drew a will, in which he appointed the schoolmaster his executor and left him a legacy of a thousand pounds. The rest of the estate was left to the testator's relatives in England. This will was drawn by the testator's attorney. Shortly after the death of the testator another will came to light. The new will was accepted by the Master as a genuine document. On the face of it it appeared to be in order. In it the housekeeper and a third person, a business acquaintance of the testator, were made beneficiaries for substantial amounts. The schoolmaster was appointed executor and his legacy was raised to five thousand pounds. The rest of the estate was left to relatives in England. All that this executor had to do was to accept the appointment, wind up the estate and collect five thousand pounds; but five thousand pounds or no five thousand pounds, he felt that there was something wrong about this will and he was determined to upset it on one ground or another. Moreover, he had to do so at his own expense and if he succeeded he would be the clear loser of four thousand pounds. The ground upon which he succeeded is immaterial, but it is sufficient to say that when I came into the matter I found the will was being attacked on the wrong ground. We ended by attacking it on the right ground and succeeded. He lost four thousand pounds and a good deal of his time.

'"Take him for all in all, I shall not look upon his like again."'

—H H Morris KC *The First Forty Years* (1948) 112–13.

'THE LAW AND LOVE

'The Young Attorney sat on top of the world and surveyed the landscape beneath. Everything in the garden was lovely. He had money in the bank, his practice was growing, and he had just become engaged to a beautiful and accomplished young lady. What more could a man want?

'To him there entered a colleague—a stranger.

'"My name is Levy. I am your senior in the profession, but, in the

'True, you have lost your case, but at least you must have enjoyed the eloquence of my pleading'

Honoré Daumier (1808–79). Lithograph.

LAWYERS AND LITIGANTS

'At last! We have obtained the division of the spouses' property.'

'It's about time, the case has ruined both of them.'

Honoré Daumier (1808–79). Lithograph.

circumstances of this case, I thought it would be better to call on you than to write to you. My client, Mr. Lewis, intends suing his wife for a divorce on the ground of adultery. You are named as the co-respondent."

'"It's a lie—it's a damned lie. I don't know the woman."

'"My client does not want to expose his wife if a settlement can be arrived at. He is prepared to sue her for a divorce on the ground of desertion."

'"Tell your client that I am not going to be blackmailed by him or anyone else. I don't know the woman."

'"I think it would be as well if you saw my client. You see, we have the evidence. On the night of the 7th May you booked a room at an hotel in the name of Mr. and Mrs. Smith. You may disguise your name, but you can't disguise your handwriting. Moreover, the night porter, who knows you, saw you and the lady go upstairs together. I might as well tell you that we know that Mrs. Lewis is wearing a gold wristlet watch which you gave her to celebrate the occasion, and it bears the date the 7th May. It will be in the interests of all parties if you meet my client."

'"Your client is a liar and a blackmailer, and if he calls on me I shall tell him where he gets off."

'Three days later Mr. Lewis called. Said he to the young attorney: "It is immaterial to me on what ground I sue my wife. The option is yours."

'"I suppose my option is to pay blackmail. I don't know your wife and I am not paying."

'"Unfortunately for you, my wife admits the affair. Every co-respondent calls it blackmail. The law calls it damages."

'"And what are the damages you claim?"

'"I don't really want anything for myself. My wife will have to leave the country. You will have to pay her first-class fare, rail and boat, to London. She will have to be provided with a complete outfit. She must have enough money to keep up appearances on the boat. She will require portmanteaux and suitcases. You will have to give her £50 per month for three months while she is looking for something to do. That will only be a matter of £400. If it is more I shall make up the difference. You can think it over."

'Mr. Lewis left.

'The Young Attorney rang up the wife.

'"Your blackmailing husband has been here. He wants £400. What am I to do?"

'"Don't worry, it will be all right."

'"What do you mean, don't worry? I am worrying. I have not slept for three nights."

'"Anyway, don't worry."

'"Dammit," he shrieked, "don't keep telling me not to worry. I am worrying. You should see me—I am all skin and bone."

'"Oh, well, if you are worried, come up to my room."

'"Your room!" he shouted, "Your room! Haven't I had enough trouble without being caught in your room? If I meet you it will be in a wide-open space with a witness."

'"All right, I will meet you in the park at 4 o'clock this afternoon—but don't worry."

'Here he slammed down the receiver.

'They met. She was wearing the wristlet watch.

'"Now I will tell you a story. My husband and I lived together for years as Mr. and Mrs. Lewis. Everyone thought we were married. We were not. We had a daughter. She is now eight. Eventually we decided to get married in order to legitimise her. You see this watch? Well, you gave me that watch a week before we got married."

'Once again Romeo was on the top of the world. He gazed at the pleasant prospect beneath, and in the distance he saw Mr. Levy's office. His whole being was shot with joy. He seized the telephone.

'"Mr. Levy, have you seen your client's marriage certificate?"

'"No."

'"Well, you had better have a look at it."

'"I shall when I prepare Counsel's brief."

'"You had better look at it before that."

'He put down the receiver and turned to the contemplation of a Land Flowing with Milk and Honey, and a wife—his own.'

—H H Morris KC *In and Out of Court* (1950) 38–40.

Magistrate

'Sam' Ellman, who died at Simonstown in 1932, was a legendary, beloved figure, who started working life as a public prosecutor and then became an assistant magistrate.

'No one who knew the late Mr. Ellman, for a number of years Assistant

'THE WEIGHTED SCALES OF JUSTICE'
Sketch by H E Winder (1897–1982) Sunday Times
29 July 1979
Reproduced with kind permission

Sketch by E (Liz) Warder (1940–)
The Star *9 February 1979. Reproduced with kind permission*

Magistrate at Cape Town, could fail to have been captivated by his genial personality. Possessed of a fund of general knowledge, and gifted, moreover, with the keenest sense of humour, "Sam" (as he was affectionately known to his many friends) was the most entertaining of company. . . .

'But it was on the Bench that Ellman shone; a shrewd judge of human nature, and endowed with a distinct flair for the law, he made an ideal magistrate. He believed in interlarding the dullness of court proceedings with spices of humour, and this fact alone made it indeed a pleasant task to appear in cases before him. He was quick to spot the prevaricating witness, and had a habit of indulging in a little cross-examination of his own, often to the complete discomfiture of the witness.

'A master of repartee, Ellman could, when occasion arose, tinge his remarks with sarcasm, which completely "floored" counsel, attorney or witness who crossed swords with him.

'A good example of this is to be found in his reply to an attorney who had been particularly lengthy in cross-examination, and who persisted in plying witnesses with questions which had already been dealt with. Ellman, becoming impatient, requested the attorney not to take up the time of the Court by irrelevant questions and repetition. "Surely," protested the attorney, "your worship will allow some latitude?" "I don't mind giving you latitude," said Ellman, "it is your longitude that I object to!". . .

'On another occasion he squashed an impudent witness in a neat way. At the conclusion of the examination Ellman addressed the witness. "And now, Mr. Jackson, will you tell the Court whether your wife . . . " "You mean Mrs. Jackson, I presume," interrupted the witness, in a rather offensive manner. "I'm sorry," politely rejoined Ellman, "I was under the impression that Mrs. Jackson was your wife!"

'In a recent criminal case counsel commenced his examination of the accused in

this way: "You are the son of the Reverend ——?" Ellman interrupted: "Mr. X,"
said he, addressing counsel, "I presume your client is aware that he is not
compelled to answer any questions which may incriminate him!"

'One day Ellman, feeling the cold, requested the Court constable to turn on the
heating apparatus. The constable, being unable to get the heating appliances to
function, informed the Court that it apparently was not operating. "Why, of
course," said Ellman, "I overlooked the fact that this is a court of 'summary'
jurisdiction."

'Ellman was once transferred to Germiston, and on the day of his arrival he was
called upon to try a case of theft. The defending attorney commenced his opening
remarks in somewhat the following fashion: "Your worship, the first question I
am constrained to ask in this case is, where is the *mens rea*? I say, where is the *mens
rea*?" "I am sorry to interrupt you," said Ellman, "but to tell you the truth, I only
arrived this morning, and am a total stranger.". . .

'Ellman was once transferred from the Reef to a small country dorp where he
was quite out of his element. He was unable to accustom himself to his new
surroundings, and in the course of a few months became a recluse, and was
generally voted as being unpopular with the residents of the dorp. Matters
became so bad that eventually a petition was set on foot asking the authorities at
Pretoria to transfer him. The local M.P.C., on hearing of this petition,
approached Ellman, pointed out what was happening, and offered to do anything
he could to assist him. "You can do me one great favour," said Ellman to the
gentleman who had so kindly intervened. "Please let me be the first signatory to
the petition.". . .

'One day, on the race-course, Ellman was greeted by a stranger saying "Good
morning, Mr. Ellman, how are you?" Ellman looked at the man and said: "I am
sorry, I can't place you." "Oh, surely you can," was the reply. "Don't you
remember you placed me for six months!". . .

'A precocious young attorney once invited the following rebuke. It was at the
end of the Crown case and Ellman enquired of the prosecutor whether he
proposed to proceed with the matter. A discussion ensued between Ellman and
the prosecutor, which was interrupted by the young attorney jumping to his feet
and claiming the right to address the Court on his client's behalf. "Certainly,"
said Ellman. "You have a perfect right to address the Court but, in the interests
of your client, I intend to acquit him first."

'Ellman was once offered a big sum of money to secure the granting of a
bottle-store licence. The incident occurred in a flourishing mining town in the
Transvaal, where Ellman, in his capacity as Resident Magistrate, was chairman of
the Liquor Licensing Board. There were two applications before the Court for
two new bottle-store licences, evidently assets of considerable value. Before the
sitting of the Licensing Court Ellman was "approached" on behalf of one of the
applicants and offered a very substantial payment if he could secure the granting
of the licence. The net outcome of this intervention was that the application of the
"offeror" was refused, whereas the other applicant was successful. In recounting
the story afterwards, Ellman, referring to the bribe, said: "What a fool that man
was! He should have made the offer in the name of the other man!"

'It had been suggested to Ellman that on his retirement he should write a book
of reminiscences. He said that if he did so he would like to name it "Grains of

Chaff—Picked up by the Beak.'' What an interesting, humane and humorous record this would have proved to have been!'

—Fritz Sonnenberg (attorney of Cape Town) 'A Human Magistrate' (1933) 2 *South African Law Times* 32–4.

'Sam' Ellman: other versions and stories

'The wittiest and most versatile of all the junior magistrates was the late Sam Ellman. He was equally at home on the Bench, on the turf, on the golf course and at the round table.

'We were dealing with a gambling joint. Things were not going too well for my 54 clients. I looked ahead and sent a note to the Beak.

'"Please don't order the confiscation of the chips. The school is short."

'That night Sam presented the school with a nice new set of chips.

'I went to Benoni one day to appear before him. I went into his office to pay my respects to the Magistrate—that is to say, to ask Sam how he got on last night. He said, "What do you fancy for the Manchester Cup?" I said I did not know anything about the race. He named some horse as a good thing. I told him I had no time to go round Benoni looking for bookmakers. He said, "Give me the money." I gave him £2 and followed him out to the pavement. There stood Dan Isaacs. Sam whispered to Dan and I saw my money pass. Ten minutes later the Court sat. First case called was Dan Isaacs, charged with keeping a bucket shop.

'"Guilty, your Worship."

'"£50 or a month."

'"Thank you, your Worship."

'He was playing a round of golf with a lady. Said she, "Do you think I am attracting much attention?"

'"Yes," Sam said, "even the golf ball is looking round."

'Sam followed the horses with zeal. When he was in Johannesburg and then Germiston, and later at Benoni, he was satisfied. There were plenty of racecourses available. Sam was then sent to Witbank, which he said was no place for a white man. He became disagreeable to everyone and within a month he had reached his ambition. He became the most unpopular man in the district.

'Sam started his campaign of annoyance by irritating the local Attorney the very first day he was there. He deliberately misunderstood that Attorney. It was a theft case. The Attorney had worked himself up to a pitch. "Where, your Worship", he enquired, "is the mens rea?"

'"I don't know", said Sam. "You had better ask the Sergeant. I have only been here half an hour."

'The local M.P.C. called on him. "Mr. Ellman, we don't want to do anything behind your back. We are getting up a petition for your removal. Is there anything I can do in the matter?"

'"Yes", said Sam, "bring me the bloody thing, I want to sign it."'

—H H Morris KC *The First Forty Years* (1948) 69–70.

'THE CHILDREN OF ISRAEL

'The editors of two Jewish papers were locked in litigation. The action was to be tried by Mr. Harry Jordan.

'The parties, witnesses, Counsel and Attorneys, and even the Yiddish interpreter, were Jews.

'As the Magistrate ascended the Bench the crowd rose, and a wit was heard to say: "For now the Children of Israel are gathered before the Jordan."'

—H H Morris KC *In and Out of Court* (1950) 88.

All music is sacred

'Many quaint stories are told of the old-time Judges and Landdrosts, the latter of whom, though not men of much education, possessed great common sense and wide experience.

'The late Mr. van den Berg (whose son is a well-known K.C. in London practice to-day), First Criminal Landdrost of Johannesburg, on one occasion tried some musical folk on a charge of breaking the Sunday law by holding a secular concert on the Sabbath. He acquitted them on the ground that all music was sacred. . . .'

—Napier Devitt *Memories of a Magistrate* (1934) 1935 edition 32–3.

Riding in a 'decanter'

'Another fine old official was Mr. Kenne van Breda, magistrate of the Paarl, but he was like "necessity"—he knew no law. He knew High Dutch very well, but English imperfectly, and owned a large vineyard at the Paarl. Once, when he came to Cape Town on horseback to spend a week's leave, a swarm of locusts visited the Paarl and destroyed the grape crop. Mr. van Breda, when he heard of the disaster, galloped back and afterwards said to a friend, "I rode my horse back all the way in a decanter, when I heard that the jumping-cocks [sprinkane] had eaten all my cock-legs [hanepoot]." Mr. van Breda was a sportsman and owned a racehorse named "Blackstone." On one occasion he was trying a very intricate case when the clever solicitor, Andries van Reenen, in his address to the court, quoted from Blackstone's *Commentaries* and said, "I refer your worship to Blackstone, page ——" Mr. van Breda tore off his spectacles and said, "Look here, Mr. van Reenen, Blackstone was a good horse and won me many races, and now he lies in an honoured grave, and if you drag his name into this dirty case again I will order you to sit down."

'But I can come nearer than those old fogies and recall the fact that a great friend of mine once said to me, "George, what do you do when the plaintiff's and defendant's witnesses swear diametrically opposite to one another?" "Well," I replied, "I try to sift out which is the more likely story, but it is often very difficult." "That's just it," replied my friend, "and in such a case, I chuck up a coin underneath the bench, heads for plaintiff, tails for defendant; you can only be right or wrong, and more often than not the toss is correct. In one such case I had, the party who lost appealed to the Supreme Court in Cape Town and the judge confirmed my verdict, so that I almost began to have faith in the toss!"'

—*Memoirs of Senator the Hon. G. G. Munnik* (1934) 128. On Munnik, see page 336 below. (See also BUCHANAN; CARTER; JORISSEN.)

Registrar

Summoning Voet

'The following occurred at the Circuit Court in Durban many years ago. The learned Judge called for authorities on Roman Dutch Law and he requested the Registrar to send for Voet, van der Linden and Maasdorp. The Registrar whispered to the Court Orderly, repeating the names of the authorities just mentioned. In due course the Orderly shouted out the names of these three, three times outside the Court, viz.: Voet, van der Linden, Maasdorp. None of these three responding to his shouting, he returned to the Court, saying: "In default, my Lord," much to the amusement of Bench and Bar.'

—F W Ahrens *From Bench to Bench* (1948) 52.

Signing his own death warrant

'The Registrar of the [Supreme] Court was Mr Thomas Henry Bowles, an English barrister, a man of excellent family and a polished gentleman, though somewhat eccentric. It is said that a wicked lawyer's clerk once induced him when he was very busy at other Court work to sign his own death-warrant, commanding the sheriff to hang Thomas Henry Bowles by the neck till he was dead.'

—A W Cole (qv) *Reminiscences of My Life and of the Cape Bench and Bar* (1896) 8.

Testator

Bequest to dogs' home

'The [will] . . . dug up by Fenton Bresler in his *Second-Best Bed: A Diversion on Wills* (1983) 13 . . . illustrates the testament made in a fit of spleen. Apparently one "Skit" Fielding, wealthy and eccentric, had threatened that on his death he would leave "the lot to the bloody dogs' home". In 1965, when he died at the age of 75, it was found that he had left R1 500 000 to the SPCA, including a 50-acre estate in Kloof, which—I hope all this is correct—the organization used as an animal hospital and home. The resultant noise, so it is said by Bresler, gave point to Fielding's complaint and boast: "These snobs around here only put up with me because I gave them a golf course and a cricket ground. But when I die they will have to put up with me for eternity."'

—Ellison Kahn in (1984) 101 *SALJ* 383.

Bequest to a company

'Leaving money to the state is one thing; leaving money to a company is another. Yet we have the authority of Voet 28.5.2 for the proposition that a juristic person can take a benefit from a will. The classic case in South Africa is the will of John Campbell Bitcon, who died in December 1976 at the age of 94. He was born in Ireland in 1882. In 1903 he came to this country, where he did very well in business, particularly in the building industry. At one stage he was chairman of the Southern Building Society and Village Main General Mining Company. He married twice, but he had no children, and he survived both his wives. During his lifetime he created the Bitcon Foundation for educational and charitable purposes. A few days after his death the press reported the contents of his will. He left R2 000 to each of his two domestic servants and R50 000 to the Bitcon Foundation. The residuary heir was Bitcon Holdings and Trust Co Ltd, of which he had been chairman, and the shares of which were quoted on the Johannesburg Stock Exchange. The company got about R2 000 000 baksheesh. It

'Reading the will'
Honoré Daumier (1808–79). Lithograph.

had 553 000 shares, of which the family was said to hold over 300 000. Bitcon left a brother and two sisters in America, and a number of nieces and nephews in South Africa and abroad. The press said that "thousands of shareholders stood to benefit". Indeed they did, as after the announcement of the contents of the will the quotation on the Stock Exchange of Bitcon shares rose from 275 cents to 600 cents. But the old man did not have the welfare of the outside shareholders primarily at heart. I remember the attorney who drew up the will telling me that there were certain financial advantages to be gained by the family.'

—Ellison Kahn in (1983) 100 *SALJ* 538.

A gramophone record entitled 'You Don't Have to be Jewish' goes like this: 'To my brother-in-law Louis, who lived with us all of his life, who never had to do a day's work, who knew how to handicap the ponies better than anybody, who only smoked the finest cigars—mine; to my brother-in-law, Louis, who all his life said I would never remember him in my will—Hullo, Louis!'

'*Ex parte St Clair Lynn* 1980 (3) SA 163 (W) concerned the validity of the will of Edgar August Smorenburg, a clause of which read: "To my son-in-law Major A J ——, who has never been to see me, of his own accord, during my illness—Hullo Aubrey." Coetzee J said (at 165E–F): "This undoubtedly indicates that the testator was not, to put it at its lowest, in favour of his son-in-law. Perhaps it also demonstrates his sense of humour. It is not a case of simply omitting to leave anything to his son-in-law. He mentions him by name and, following the punch line of the well-known joke, he concludes by leaving to him just the greeting 'Hullo Aubrey'."'

—Ellison Kahn in (1983) 100 *SALJ* 746.

Tolk

'DEMONSTRATIEWE GETUIENIS

'Uit die Departement van Justisie se Opleidingsafdeling kom die volgende staaltjie: By kruisondervraging van 'n Bantoe-klaer in 'n aanrandingsaak wou die prokureur weet presies hoe hard die beskuldigde die klaer sou geklap het. Die klaer het omslagtig aan die tolk probeer verduidelik, maar kon skynbaar nie na dié se bevrediging vordering maak nie. In 'n poging om finaal aan die tolk se verstand te bring hoeveel geweld daar gebruik is, haak die klaer toe onverwags af en gee die tolk—wat binne sy bereik gestaan het—'n taai klap en sê aan laasgenoemde: "So het hy my geklap." Vir 'n oomblik was die tolk uit die veld geslaan, maar was nie links nie en klap op sy beurt die klaer dat hy behoorlik uit die getuiebank steier, met die woorde (aan die landdros): "Edelagbare, die getuie sê só het die beskuldigde hom geklap."'

—(1963) 8 *Codicillus* 34.

'The weariness of long cases in Court is also an admirable setting for a *jeu d'esprit*. Burton tells a good story of a Judge at the Burghersdorp Circuit Court, who often indulg[ed] in learned quotations to bucolic juries, [and] once described a prisoner to the jury as a Machiavellian sort of person. The Dutch interpreter, who did not know what the Judge was referring to, but was not to be outdone, translated that the Judge said he was a "maak-zooals-u-wil zoort van kerel"! It was of this Judge that an interpreter once told a jury, when his lordship was wandering into literary regions, that the Judge was now quite off the point, but that when he returned to it, he would again interpret.'

—Victor Sampson *My Reminiscences* (1926) 72.

Horns of a dilemma

'Illustrative of amusing situations which arose in the law courts in the old days, on one occasion a well-known judge who, though bilingual himself, employed an interpreter to interpret in Afrikaans, was the unwilling hero of the incident. During the hearing a difficult point had arisen.

'Judge: "Tell the witness the court is on the horns of a dilemma".

'Interpreter to witness: "The Judge says he is now on the horns of an animal of which I myself have never before heard. . . ."'

—Napier Devitt *Memories of a Magistrate* (1934) 1935 edition 32–3. (On the tolk, see also LANGENHOVEN; McGREGOR; E B WATERMEYER; WESSELS; WYLDE.)

'I walked and I walked and I walked . . . '

'One of our judges, who was not over-patient, was trying a case in which a native witness was giving evidence. This witness would make long statements and the interpreter kept on interrupting him. The judge told the latter not to interrupt the witness but to let him say what he wanted to say.

'The witness was describing how he had followed the accused and come upon him just as he was crossing a river. He spoke for quite a long time and, when he paused for breath, the interpreter translated "I walked a very long distance and came to a river."

'Said the judge,"Mr. Interpreter, I told you just now not to interrupt the witness, but you must also translate everything he says, you must not simply give me what you consider to be the effect of his evidence. That is for me and the jury to judge, not for you. So please interpret everything he says."

"'Yes, My Lord," and the witness goes at it again for about a minute and the interpreter translates—

"'I took the left turning out of the main road and I walked, and I walked and I walked, and I walked, and I walked and I walked—" The interpreter repeated these words "and I walked" about twenty times. Everyone in the Court was smiling and even the impatient judge ultimately saw the point. He stopped the interpreter and said, "That is enough Mr. Interpreter, I see that I was wrong in reprimanding you, let the witness continue his evidence and let us hope that he gets to the river before the accused is out of sight."'

—Hjalmar Reitz *The Conversion of a South African Nationalist* (1946) 263.

"'Mr Interpreter, what *did* the witness say?"
"'Bugger all", your worship.
"'Funny, I could have sworn I saw his lips move."'

—(1974) 14 *Rhodesian Law Journal* 6.

Witness

"'The court takes a very serious view of your case," said the magistrate. "This is the fifth pedestrian you have knocked down in seven months." "Pardon me," said the woman motorist with dignity. "Four. One of them was the same person twice."'

—*Rand Daily Mail* 13 July 1948.

'Accused: I swore at him, your worship but I cannot repeat the things I said in court. Basically I said: "What do you think you are doing?"'

—*The Star* 4 September 1981.

'RES GESTAE

'Die Kleurling met die perdewaentjie was betrokke in 'n ernstige botsing met 'n vragmotor. Toe hy uit die hospitaal ontslaan is, het hy pylreguit na sy

SKETCHES OF WITNESSES BY MR JUSTICE M A DIEMONT IN HIS NOTEBOOKS
Reproduced from Rapport *4 May 1975*

prokureur gegaan en 'n groot eis teen die versekeraar van die vragmotor ingestel vir persoonlike skade gely, en teen die eienaar vir die skade aan die waentjie en sy verlies aan die twee perde wat weens ernstige beserings doodgeskiet moes word. In die hof was die eiser 'n eersteklas getuie. Tydens kruisondervraging deur die verweerder se advokaat het dit egter begin lyk asof die eiser moeilikheid gaan ondervind. "Jy beweer nou dat jy gruwelike pyn en leed gely het ten gevolge van die botsing," stel die advokaat dit aan hom, "maar ek sal getuienis aanvoer dat jy onmiddellik na die botsing aan 'n konstabel gesê het dat jy niks makeer nie." "Dja maaster, dit is so, maar ek sal explain", antwoord die eiser. "Maaster, sien, toe ek nou daar lê langs my waentjie, kom die constable aangestap. Die een kant van my lê my een perdjie en skop, die ander kant lê die anner een. Die constable kyk die perdjies so, toe vat hy sy revolver en skiet eers die een perdjie dood en toe die anner. Toe kom die constable na my en hy sê: 'En jy, Gammat, is jy ook besig om dood te gaan?' Your Worship, toe reply ek hom gou: 'Nei Sarge, ek het nog nooit beter gevoel in my hele lewe nie!'"

'Vertel deur adv. A. Mendelow, S.C.'

—(1965) 6(1) *Codicillus* 26.

'AN EMERGENCY OPERATION

'The C.I.D.—Gold and Diamond Department—had been looking for him. He had been missing for some time, but he was now back in circulation. Rumour had it that he had been recuperating in South-West Africa, and, what is more, he had taken his girl friend with him. That did not seem to be the place to take a girl friend, but there it was.

'The C.I.D. picked him up in the street and boldly accused him of I.D.B. He had no change of clothing, so perforce he had to take them to his flat, the

SKETCHES OF WITNESSES BY MR JUSTICE M A DIEMONT IN HIS NOTEBOOKS

Reproduced from The Star *12 June 1975*

whereabouts of which they did not know. Here they found the inamorata. An intensive search of the person of the accused and of his flat revealed nothing. One lad had a bright idea; they picked up the doll as well. At the Charge Office she was asked whether she would submit to an intimate search by a wardress. "Certainly not." Would she mind the District Surgeon? She would not allow any surgeon—District or otherwise—to lay his hands on her, but she had no objection to her own doctor.

'The Police rang up her doctor. The situation was explained to him.

'"Mrs. Howard says she is a patient of yours."

'When the doctor heard the name he knew just where he stood. This was the time for histrionics.

'He said he did not remember the lady. He saw so many people. He said in any case he did not fancy the job. Could they not take her elsewhere? The Police said it was in the interests of Justice that the search should be made and he was the only one who could make it. They added that it might exonerate her. The doctor agreed—but with great reluctance—so he said.

'The lady was shown into the consulting-room. The door was locked. They shook hands. They talked about her present and future. He knew her past. Then the doctor unlocked the safe door, opened a drawer, dropped something in, closed it and relocked the door.

'He showed the lady out and called the escort in.

'Let's see, witness. It is important for you to give exact and complete details of your day's activities on 12 April last.'
'But, Mr President of the Court, it was nine months ago.'
'That doesn't matter. Tell us anyway.'

                        Honoré Daumier (1808–79). Lithograph.

'"There are indications that there had once been some obstruction, but it is no longer there."

'The doctor went to the Club for a drink. It had been a good day's work.

'The Accused were released and the docket was closed.'

—H H Morris KC *In and Out of Court* (1950) 59–60. For another version, see H H Morris QC *In My Anecdotage* (1953) 10–11, where the author starts the story as follows: 'I knew a doctor who had a large practice but I never found out whether it was a side or main line. He dealt in gold and diamonds with great success. He was never caught. He once travelled from Johannesburg to Paris with a skull that was stuffed with diamonds. Every official who handled that skull on its journey did so with respect and reverence.'

The 'old fools' on the Bench

'But there is no need to go out of the borders of our own country for an opinion on the competency of our lawyers. The Native is a shrewd observer of their qualities; and occasionally we get a glimpse of his reactions. A typical case was that of the prisoner who was being tried by three learned judges of the Native High Court on a serious charge. The prosecution had closed its case and the prisoner was asked to say if he had any evidence to lead for his defence. This resulted in a long exchange in Zulu between the interpreter and the accused, which appeared to have no relevancy to the simple question asked. The end of it was that the interpreter said the prisoner had no evidence; whereupon he was convicted and sentenced.

'But when the Court arose, and one of the judges was passing along the corridor to his room, he happened to meet the interpreter and stopped him. "What was that long conversation about, between you and the prisoner," he enquired, "when he was asked if he had any evidence to lead in his defence?"

'The interpeter was diffident. "Oh, I could not give that up," he said. "It had no relation to the question." Which only stimulated His Lordship's curiosity. "But the case is finished; it can do no harm for me to know, and that conversation very much intrigued me."

'"Well," said the interpreter, "if I give you a free interpretation of the gist of what he said, it amounted to this: 'If those three old fools up there cannot convict me on the evidence they have heard they are not fit for their jobs'."'

—'Luctor' *Tales of a Grandfather in the Law* (1949) 291.

Scene of the crime

'The following exchanges took place in Rhodesia: "After you had been raped, did you show the police the scene of the crime?" "No, but I showed the doctor." Again: "You have given his lordship your version of the facts, but I must put it to you . . . " "You can put it where you like, Mr Treacy." In a Johannesburg newspaper some . . . years ago appeared a report of a crimen injuria case in that city: Complainant: "He put his hand up my dress, your worship." Prosecutor: "And did he impair your dignity?" Complainant: "No, your worship, he never came near it."'

—Ellison Kahn 'The Seven Lamps of Legal Humour Part 2' 1988 *De Rebus* 210 at 212, citing (1974) 14 *Rhodesian Law Journal* 86; op cit at 176; *Rand Daily Mail* 7 September 1974.

'Testimony behind closed doors'
Honoré Daumier (1808–79). Lithograph.

'THE CONNOISSEUR

'The interpreter read the indictment to the accused, a native, and told him to plead. Then there followed a long discussion between the two. His Lordship became impatient.

'"What does he say, Mr. Interpreter?"

'"What he says, My Lord, is not relevant, and I am telling him so."

'"It is for me to say, Mr. Interpreter, what is relevant and what is not relevant. What does he say?"

'"He wants to know, My Lord, what Your Lordship paid for the red blanket you are wearing."'

—H H Morris KC *In and Out of Court* (1950) 58.

'THE DOLL

'The Judge in his scarlet robe sat motionless on the Bench. A native woman was ushered into the box. After she had been led by the Prosecutor, His Lordship turned his face slowly towards her to ask a question. With a loud shriek the witness fell to the floor of the witness-box. When she came round the Interpreter asked her what was the matter. "It is alive, but when I came into Court I thought it was a doll."'

—Morris op cit at 10.

CHARLES GEORGE WARD

1864–1923. Member of the Kimberley Bar 1891–8. Member of the Southern Rhodesia Bar 1898–1902. Member of the Johannesburg Bar 1903–10. KC 1905. Judge of the Transvaal Provincial Division 1910–23.

'Ward was short and concise in his address to the Court, and was often caustic in manner.

'He had a thorough knowledge of English case law, which he had thoroughly read and digested. Though he had a large practice, he sometimes spoke gloomily to me about future prospects. Now and then he went on a little "binge." One afternoon he was due to open a defamation action for the plaintiff. Esselen [q v] was on the other side. They had been lunching at their club, and sat over it a long time, and both forgot that the case was coming on. Their juniors rushed in, and dragged them off to the Court. Ward had forgotten what the case was about, and when the case was called before Mason [q v], Ward rose, and solemnly began to read out the summons: "Edward the Seventh, by the grace of God," etc. Mason adjourned the proceedings. An incident of this kind, however, did not affect Ward's practice, and when Union came in 1910 he was the first new judge to be appointed, mainly for the Witwatersrand. This was at the same time as Japie de Villiers (who later became Chief Justice) was appointed to head the Pretoria Bench. Ward sat at Pretoria very seldom. He practically made the Witwatersrand Court his own. He died prematurely, when on a visit to England, in 1923.'

—Manfred Nathan *Not Heaven Itself: An Autobiography* (1944) 218–19. (See also TAYLOR.)

EGIDIUS BENEDICTUS WATERMEYER

1824–67. Judge of the Cape Supreme Court 1857–67.

Only the decent epigrams of Martial

' . . . Mr. Justice Watermeyer [reminded me] of a prosperous English farmer or grazier. . . .

'The ablest and most learned judge who has occupied the Cape Bench in my time was, I think, Mr. Justice Watermeyer. He was not only a deeply read lawyer but an excellent classic, and had much literary taste. When I was editor, conjointly with the late Professor Roderic Noble, of the "Cape Monthly Magazine," he used to send as translations in English verse the epigrams of Martial, admirably done. I remember that when he sent in the last one he wrote: "I think I have now sent you a translation of every *decent* epigram that Martial ever wrote; the rest, of course, I cannot touch.". . .

'I have said that he was a good classic, and his brother, Mr. Fred Watermeyer, afterwards a member and an ornament of the Cape Bar, was equally so. The brothers used to correspond with one another in Greek for the sake of practice. . . .

'Judge Watermeyer was a great admirer of Mr. Porter [q v], and the admiration was mutual. Mr. Porter once wrote of him: "Of so vast ability that he could have succeeded without industry, and of so great an industry that he could almost have succeeded without ability."'

—A W Cole *Reminiscences of My Life and of the Cape Bench and Bar* (1896) 7, 34–5, 37.

The interpreter (tolk)

'John Emmett, the father of Mrs. (General) Louis Botha, was for years an interpreter at Swellendam. His translations were full of humour. On one occasion, when Judge Watermeyer was sentencing a prisoner to death, he said, "Prisoner at the bar, you have sent this unfortunate man to that country from whose bourn no traveller returns." Which Emmett translated by saying, "Die Regter sê, jy het die kêrel op tog gestuur." The judge was so annoyed at this free translation that he said, "Sit down, Mr. Interpreter, sit down, I will deliver my charge first in English and then in Dutch." (There was no Afrikaans in those days.) When the judge had finished his eloquent and solemn address to the prisoner and sentenced him to death, he said, "Stand up, Mr. Interpreter. Will you kindly tell the gentlemen of the jury that what I have just done was your duty, but that you were incompetent to perform it." Emmett was determined to turn the laugh against the judge and said, "Here van die jurie, die Regter sê ek moet vir julle sê dat wat hy net nou gedoen het was my plig, maar dat ek te vrot was om dit te doen!" Upon which there was a roar of laughter in the court.'

—*Memoirs of Senator the Hon. G. G. Munnik* (1934) 52. (Senator George Glaeser Munnik (1846–1935) was a civil commissioner in the Cape Colony and later mining commissioner and thereafter landdros for Zoutpansberg. During the Anglo-Boer War he was for a period acting State Attorney of the Transvaal. He was a talented writer. One of his grandsons is Mr Justice George Glaeser Anderson Munnik, former Judge President of the Cape Provincial Division.)

The same story has been told of Sir John Wylde. See WYLDE. (On the tolk, see also LANGENHOVEN; McGREGOR; WAIFS AND STRAYS sv 'Tolk'; WESSELS; WYLDE.)

ERNEST FREDERICK WATERMEYER

1880–1958. Member of the Cape Bar 1905–22. KC 1921. Judge of the Cape Provincial Division 1922–37. Judge of Appeal 1937–43. Chief Justice 1943–50.

'We jog along here very pleasantly. The work is markedly more thoroughly done than when one sits in a Provincial Division—at least where the "one" is I. Matters are heard—some of them—that one would be ready to dispose of in a rough and ready fashion without much delay, but we go over them with the utmost care and choose the words, as far as possible, that leave no room for mistake. Each judgment is gone over with a fine comb. It is certainly instructive to me—I work at it and pick up the ropes. The team is a delightful one to work with—each full of ideas and each with his own methods. But they function as one very satisfactorily. The Chief, Billy [Watermeyer—his nickname was 'Billy'], is a very wise judge with a big and well-stored brain. He guides our discussions with the artistry of a company chairman.'

—Oliver Deneys Schreiner (qv) in a letter to his wife Edna, 11 March 1945. Schreiner family papers.

SIR JOHANNES (JOHN) WILHELMUS WESSELS

1862–1936. Member of the Cape Bar 1886. Member of the Pretoria Bar 1887–99. Judge of the Transvaal Supreme Court 1902–20. Judge President 1920–3. Judge of Appeal 1923–32. Chief Justice 1932–6. Knighted 1909.

Unjudicial manner

'Wessels had made a great name at the Bar, and was expected to make a good judge. But he turned out a disappointment. He usually decided a case before it was called on the roll, and as frequently changed his mind about it. He used to give a ferocious glare through his glasses, while his light-brown moustache literally bristled. He was very rough on juniors, and one at least retired from practice because of remarks made by Wessels. After hearing the evidence in a case he would call upon the counsel against whom he had made up his mind to open his argument—this being taken as an indication that he did not wish to hear the opposing counsel. Then, in the middle of the first counsel's argument, he would stop him, turn to the counsel who was fondly expecting judgment in his favour, and say: "What do you say about that?" Frequently this counsel would be taken aback by the sudden question, would flounder about, and finally sit down, whereupon Wessels would gaze out of the window, or at the wall, would fling the papers to the other side of his desk, and say: "Application refused." I can claim, however, that I soon learned to "size him up." One day I was briefed, in an application to wind up a company, to apply for the appointment of a certain person as liquidator. I got up and made my application. Wessels threw the papers to one side, and scribbled something in his note-book—he always scribbled, and seemed to love scratching pens (I believe that, as an affectation, he used the old-fashioned quill pens). I guessed that he had written down the name of the nominee of the other side. "I protest, my lord, against your deciding that matter without hearing what I have to say." "What! you protest! What right have you to say such a thing?" "My lord, I am here to present my client's case to you, and you cannot possibly do justice unless he is given a hearing. He is the principal creditor, etc." Wessels drew his pen through what he had written in his book, wrote something else, and pulled the papers back towards him. Then it was "all up" with the other side.

'This sort of thing spoiled Wessels' reputation. He was erudite, and could give a sound judgment if he liked. But his unjudicial manner prejudiced the entire profession against him. Nevertheless, by rotation, he became Chief Justice of South Africa. Off the Bench, he was always genial and kindly.'

—Manfred Nathan *Not Heaven Itself: An Autobiography* (1944) 205–6.

'Today has been a tiring one. It is hard work wrestling with witnesses whom one believes to be lying but who twist and wriggle with the assistance of at least one of the Bench. Old Wessels is a most trying old bird and the sooner he packs off to the Appellate Bench where he can be kept in order the better.

'Wessels has been cantankerous as usual—he really is a poisonous chap on a trial bench. His judgment in the previous case where the man was found guilty was a miserable piece of argument, nothing more.'

'I had a long day of it in court with a fair number of brushes with Wessels, an ill-mannered old pig if ever there was one. . . . Wessels constantly interposed

'THE RIGHT HON. SIR J. W. WESSELS, CHIEF
JUSTICE OF SOUTH AFRICA.'

Caricature by 'Imp' in (1934) 3 South African Law Times
99

between the Crown witness & my
questions—answering for them and so
giving them the clue to my reasoning.
It is annoying. My man is at present in
the box and so far has told his story
well; but tomorrow I expect Wessels
will bellow at him and shout him
down. . . . I really don't think they
should convict on the Crown's evidence; but Wessels is not a man one can
trust and I think de Waal always takes
a pessimistic view of an accused's
character.'

'My man got off this afternoon.
Wessels, after strongly favouring the
Crown for over two days, turned a
complete volte face after the local
inspection and was sweetness itself to
my remaining witness—not too
strong a one—and fairly beat Welsh
[A S Welsh for the Crown—Welsh
was then Crown Prosecutor in Johannesburg; as a KC he was Attorney-
General of the Transvaal from 1927 to
1941]—about the head as soon as he
began to argue. In the end they never
even called on me. That is Wessels all
over, most unjudicial.'

—Oliver Deneys Schreiner (q v) in letters
to his wife Edna, 13, noon 14, evening 14
and 15 February 1923. (The trial was
before a special criminal court that could
be empanelled to hear charges of murder
and treason. In this instance it was
composed of two judges. The prosecution arose out of the 'Rand Revolt' of 1922.) (See
also MILLIN.)

'Barbarian who had read books'

'Sir John Wessels was one of our great judges. We have never had anyone like
him, and it will be a long time before we do. He was a man of strong character,
forceful, blunt and pugnacious. In his court there was but one Man, one Mind
and one Voice. To him a spade was a spade, and not an agricultural instrument.
And yet, with all this, he was an exceedingly kind-hearted man. His judicial
career was full of incidents in which the other party usually came off second best.
He feared neither Prince nor Pauper. There are more stories told about him than
all his contemporaries put together.

'He was a versatile man who had read everything worth reading and who knew
everything worth knowing. One of his intimate friends referred to him as "a
barbarian who had read books".

'Before the Boer War he practised at the Pretoria Bar. He appeared for the Reformers in the "Reform Trial"—a trial which was of no forensic interest but of some historic importance.

'After that war he joined the Bench of the Transvaal Provincial Division and became its Judge-President. Later he rose to the position of Chief Justice of the Union.

'Wherever he may be now, he is likely to be making it lively for everyone, including Providence.'

—H H Morris KC *In and Out of Court* (1950) 3.

The deserter

'Although I do not claim to have had much of a practice at any time during my two periods of fifteen years in all at the Bar, I find on looking back that I actually appeared before every single one of our Chief Justices, although not necessarily in the appeal court, except Lord de Villiers. . . .

'The one for whom I had the greatest affection and for whom I still have the greatest respect is Judge Curlewis. Not that he was the greatest lawyer but because I knew him more intimately. My respect for him is based on the fact that when the Anglo Boer War broke out he immediately went to the front although not in a combatant unit, and did what he could for his adopted country. In this he differed greatly from another of his colleagues at the Pretoria Bar, who later became a Chief Justice. This gentleman, although of Dutch descent and although he had done remarkably well as an advocate in the Republic, abandoned it to its fate when trouble came. He must have left Pretoria in a great hurry for I helped to smoke some of his excellent cigars which he had left in the desk of his office.'

—Hjalmar Reitz *The Conversion of a South African Nationalist* (1946) 43.

The great scientist, Sir William Crookes, a 'liar'

'The old generation of Randites chiefly recalled Wessels by his conduct of the Cyanide Case, an action brought to test the validity of the McArthur-Forrest claim to a patent for their method of gold extraction by means of cyanide. The Chamber of Mines contested the patent, the action being brought in the name of James Hay, the chairman of the Chamber. Wessels led for them. Wessels cross-examined Professor P. D. Hahn, a celebrated chemist and analyst, who had taught him chemistry at the South African College. Wessels: "I want you to answer two or three questions." He took down the answers carefully. "Now, on account of your answers, I have to put one more question. Has the science of chemistry changed?" Hahn: "The science of chemistry can't change." Wessels: "Then I must draw your attention to the fact that the answers you have given me are diametrically opposite to what you taught me in the South African College."

'It was during the same case that Judge Jorissen said: "Mr. Wessels, don't ask him (meaning Sir William Crookes, the great scientist, who was giving expert evidence for the other side) another question. He is lying, the Court knows he is lying, and he knows he is a liar." Thereupon Sir William Crookes left the witness box. The next witness to be called was Professor Tatlock. He absolutely refused to go into the box.

'Once Judge Lange, of Kimberley, was acting on the Pretoria Bench, Wessels presiding. A barrister named H. was arguing. The time came for him to reply to the speech of opposing counsel. Wessels was overheard to say to Lange: "Shall we hear him again?" "No. He'll only mess up his case." And judgment was given for H.'

—Manfred Nathan *Not Heaven Itself: An Autobiography* (1944) 207.

'Mr Wessels, the persuasiveness of your arguments is in inverse proportion to the vehemence with which they are expressed.'

—Sir Henry de Villiers, then Chief Justice of the Cape Colony. Source not traced. From Ellison Kahn's commonplace book.

'HE CONCURRED

'MacPherson was charged before Sir John Wessels with I.G.B. It was an iron-clad, cast-iron cinch for the Crown. The detectives had sewn and tied up Mr. MacPherson good and plenty. There was little he could say in his defence and that little was unintelligible.

'After Sir John Wessels had driven a few large-sized nails into the coffin of the Accused, he invited the jury to consider the situation.

'The jury rose in their places and, without any hesitation, found the Accused "Not guilty".

'Sir John glared at them and then turned to the Accused, smiled, and said: "I suppose, MacPherson, you are the most astonished man in this Court?"

'"I am, My Lord; I am."

'MacPherson bowed to His Lordship and took his departure.'

—H H Morris KC *In and Out of Court* (1950) 7–8.

'I am addressing the other members of the Court'

'The big trials at that time [1897] went to Pretoria, where were the leaders of the Bar, Esselen and Wessels, while Curlewis had the leading junior practice. Wessels was by far the busiest man at the Pretoria Bar. He then wore a beard, and had a Boanerges voice. Nothing daunted him. Once he was addressing three judges in the High Court. Jorissen presided. Wessels must have made him impatient, for he said: "Sit down, Mr. Wessels." Wessels sat down, but immediately jumped up again, and continued his address. "I have just told you to sit down, Mr. Wessels." "Yes, your Honour; but I am now addressing the other members of the Court." (I use the words "your Honour," because "my Lord," the real equivalent, would be inappropriate to a republican Court.)'

—Manfred Nathan *Not Heaven Itself: An Autobiography* (1944) 133–4.

'We gave Wessels J a very patient hearing'

'The strongest character I ever met was Sir John Wessels. He was dynamite. To appear before him was a liberal education. Motion day in his court was motion day and not slow-motion day. Juniors, dying and bleeding, lay strewn all over the place. Stentor with an Oxford accent: he roared his way through every court in which he sat. He fought all and sundry. If he was short of material he turned on his brother judges. If you got a word in you were lucky. As Frank Shaw said going out of the Appellate Division: "Well, we gave Wessels a very patient hearing." He was deeply read and very well informed. He knew a good deal about most things. An intimate friend described him as "A barbarian who had read books".

'He had an exceedingly strong sense of justice. On a proper occasion he spared neither prince nor pauper and yet he was very human. I have heard the break in his voice as he comforted a distressed woman in the witness box. He was forthright and had no time for bunk. "Don't speak to me," he roared, "about this man and woman living together in sin. They are to all intents and purposes husband and wife."'

—H H Morris KC *The First Forty Years* (1948) 48–9. (See also F W BEYERS.)

'Sir John Wessels had been appointed a Judge as far back as the 29th March 1902, that is even before the signing of the Treaty of Vereeniging. A little more than thirty years later he became Chief Justice of the Union. We were all impressed by his brilliance and industry, as well as by his cheerful, challenging personality. From the very outset, as an advocate, he showed that his clients could rely on an extremely high degree of ability fortified by a combative approach. He certainly demonstrated these qualities effectively when he appeared on behalf of the Reformers at their preparatory examination as well as at the trial in the course of which Sir James Rose-Innes Q.C. appeared with him, although the latter did not have audience of the Court owing to some requirement of a Rule of Court prescribing a registration with which Sir James had not complied. Wessels was not in the least overawed by the fact that he had to cross-examine Judge Ameshoff who was a witness in the case, and Dr. Coster for the State found him a caustic and vigilant opponent. Indeed Wessels was the last person to be overcome by anybody and he used to be particularly challenging when the great James Leonard appeared before him. Of course his great irrepressibility tended to lead him into more than one pitfall or impasse, but he never bore grudges and he emerged from the thrust and parry with uniform good humour. . . . He was on very good terms with his colleague, John Stephen Curlewis, whom he sometimes found to be too slow and meticulous to his liking. One day he walked into the Judge's passage, asking "Where is Curly? Opposing the unopposed work?" Although Sir John was a monument of learning and erudition, and enjoyed the command of half a dozen languages, he never allowed his achievements to stifle his warm and friendly approach. He was known on Circuit to see personally to the comfort of his Registrar, on many occasions leaving fruit at his bedside.'

—The Hon C P Bresler *Tilt the Sack* (1965) 74–5.

'Fetch the Registrar—dead or alive'

'We were all in our places one motion day. His Lordship was on the bench. After a few moments of silence he noticed the absence of the Registrar:

'"Mr. Morris, fetch me the Registrar."

'"Dead or alive, my Lord?"

'"As you please."

'I found the Registrar in the corridor at the back of the bench, having his last puff.

'"The Old Man's in court. He is going to break your bloody neck for you." We came in.

'"Mr. Morris, I shall do nothing so drastic."'

—H H Morris KC *The First Forty Years* (1948) 49.

Impatient, intolerant, unkind

'Sergeant Ballantine, one of the leaders of the English Bar in the days of Queen Victoria, wrote a volume of reminiscences which has retained its popularity for lawyers right up to the present day. Writing of one of the greatest of the English Chancellors he said:

'"He had no compassion for weakness, and he crushed where he ought to have striven to raise. It is of no value to a sufferer to be told, even if it be the fact, that under an offensive demeanour there exists a kind heart and amiable disposition: such knowledge affords no comfort to a young barrister who has been snubbed before his first client and the entire Court."

'As I read this criticism of a Judge of a hundred years ago, I could not help thinking of a South African Judge of fifty years ago. When I came to the Bar in Johannesburg in 1908, at the age of 23, I was just about as callow and unfledged as any youngster could be. I had not been to a law school because there was none. I had not served as clerk to a Judge because I did not have the opportunity. I had spent three years in an office as an articled clerk but had hardly ever seen the inside of a Court. I had my law degree and nothing else. The Judge I have been referring to was Sir John Wessels, quick, learned, impatient and most unkind to struggling juniors. He was of the same type as Lord Chancellor Campbell, who was criticised by Sergeant Ballantine. Juniors would enter his court with a species of lively dread, and I always felt that he went too far.

'One of my most painful recollections, after a year or two at the Bar, was a Pro Deo defence before Wessels. My client was a native who, in a quarrel, had killed a compatriot. We tendered a plea of guilty of culpable homicide, which the Crown agreed to accept. After a consultation with my client I decided to put him into the box to tell his story, and I informed the Judge that I proposed to do so. Looking at me sharply Wessels said, "Is this really necessary Mr. Blackwell?" I replied "I have talked to my client, my Lord, and he is anxious to tell his story to the Court." "Very well," said Wessels impatiently, "call your witness." The accused then went into the box and, at one point of his story, said that he was not under the influence of liquor when he struck the fatal blow. At once Wessels looked up and said to the interpreter, "Tell him, Mr. Interpreter, that if he was drunk when he committed this crime he will receive a light sentence; if he was sober when he committed it he will receive a heavy sentence. Now ask him the question again—was he drunk or sober?" I rose to my feet to protest, because I thought this was a grossly unfair proceeding. "Sit down, Mr. Blackwell, sit down" thundered Wessels. The question was put by the interpreter, and my native client gave an answer which has remained with me to this day as perhaps the finest reply ever given by a witness, white or black, to a question from the Bench. "Tell his lordship," said he, "that if I am to be punished for telling the truth, then I am ready to be punished; I was sober, not drunk, when I struck the blow." Wessels then proceeded to pass sentence. Addressing the accused he said: "Your counsel has seen fit to call you to give evidence in mitigation of sentence. He is not to be congratulated on the result. If he had not done so I might perhaps have passed a sentence upon you of two years, but in view of your statement to me that you were not drunk when you struck the fatal blow, the sentence cannot be less than five years." I left the Court virtually in tears, feeling that I was responsible for the extra years my client would have to serve, and with the thought that I would then and there have to retire from practice at the Bar. At that time I was barely 25, and I got over it; but the memory of that day has always remained with me as an example of judicial impatience and intolerance, and I always hoped that if in the years to come, I ever rose myself to the Bench, I would remember this case.'

—Leslie Blackwell (qv) *Are Judges Human?* (1962) 16–18. *Did* he remember it?

'*A very patient hearing*'

'The Indian community had refused to pay the Transvaal Poll Tax when first it was levied. They thought it was time they got the franchise. An Indian was convicted in the Magistrate's Court, Pretoria, for refusing to pay. It was a test case. The matter went to appeal. The Court was crowded with Indians. The matter was of the greatest importance to them. The appeal was hopeless. Sir John was on the Bench.

'"My Lord, my first point is that there can be no taxation without representation. I make that point in order to pass to my second."

'"Mr. Morris, what reasons have you for making that point?"

'"My Lord, I have two hundred reasons sitting at the back of the Court."

'"Oh, very well."

'He gave me a very patient hearing. In his judgment he dealt with every point seriously and exhaustively. The appeal was dismissed. Every Indian in the community was satisfied. They had had a good hearing. The Supreme Court had decided. They paid and nothing more was heard of the matter.'

—H H Morris KC *The First Forty Years* (1948) 51.

'THE INTERPRETER

'My old friend, the late Horace Kent, was a master of the English language. Every expression was "a cameo of felicitous diction". He was the Prosecutor on Circuit before Sir John Wessels in a case which arose out of a faction fight. He said to a native witness: "And so you quitted the scene of the fray, repaired to your domicile and there armed yourself with the accoutrements of war."

'Sir John: "Jy het jou kierie gaan haal." (You went to fetch your stick.)'

—H H Morris KC *In and Out of Court* (1950) 7. (On Kent, see (1968) 85 *SALJ* 99; on the tolk, see also LANGENHOVEN; McGREGOR; WAIFS AND STRAYS sv 'Tolk'; E B WATERMEYER; WYLDE.)

The former Judge President of the Natal Provincial Division continues his discussion of the case of Findlay v Knight *1935 AD 58: see H H (HARRY) MORRIS.*

'After the trial there was the inevitable appeal. The appellant had retained Philip Millin (later a distinguished judge until his untimely death) and Rosenberg, both then of the Johannesburg Bar. The case started on a Thursday before Chief Justice Wessels and Curlewis, J. E. R. de Villiers and Beyers. Wessels was never a silent member of the Court; he usually made up his mind quickly and expressed his views with vehemence. (Once when Shaw was asked how he had fared on an appeal in Bloemfontein he replied: "I gave Wessels a very patient hearing".) On this occasion he soon showed himself to be violently in favour of our side, and for the whole of Thursday and most of Friday he gave Millin hell. He decided to sit on Saturday to finish the case, I suspect because there was a public function in Bloemfontein which he wanted to avoid. When I started to reply on Friday afternoon it was obvious that he did not want to hear me, and he tried hard to get me to sit down. But I was not happy about the other members of the Court, and I did not want to be left with a minority judgment in my favour by Wessels, with the other three against me. To make it worse, de Villiers soon showed himself to be strongly against me, so strongly that I decided that nothing could be done about him. So I concentrated on the remaining two. Curlewis, as he often was, was plaintive and querulous—as though he was anxious to understand what the case was all about but just couldn't. (I should explain that this querulous façade concealed the magnificent brain of a great judge.) . . . [W]ith one judge (Wessels) apparently in my client's favour and one (de Villiers) apparently against him, my task was to obtain from the other two such a complete acceptance of the propositions upon which my case depended that they could be trusted not to change their minds later. Thus, much of my argument consisted of putting questions to them—a course, however, which I do not recommend. But it worked this time and I was soon satisfied that I had at least three members of the Court with me, so I sat down. Millin then stood up to some more heavy punishment from Wessels and the argument ended at 4.30 p.m. on Saturday with judgment reserved. By 5 p.m. we were on the road home, travelling through most of the night. When judgment was eventually given I was surprised to find that de Villiers had come round to the majority view, so we secured a unanimous judgment dismissing the appeal, the report of which will be found in 1935 A.D. 58.'

—F N Broome *Not the Whole Truth* (1963) 147–8.

More on his rudeness on the bench

'For years he [Philip Millin] had found Wessels CJ intolerable to appear before, regarding him as a bully; Wessels' behaviour in the appeal in the famous *Doornhoek* bribery prosecution (*R v Alexander and others* 1936 AD 445, where Millin had appeared for the Crown) had been such that Millin, who had a large practice before the Appellate Division, vowed that he would never appear before him again. . . .'

—Ellison Kahn in *Fiat Iustitia: Essays in Memory of Oliver Deneys Schreiner* (1983) 25–6. (Millin, when he sat on the Bench, was often intolerant and rude himself.)

'From his own account he must have been a tough proposition at the Bar.

'Saul Solomon, in an argument before Wessels, showed his strong disapproval of his Lordship's view of the matter by banging the desk, causing the inkpots to jump up and the pens to roll down.

'Later he called on the Judge.

'"Sorry, Judge, heat of the moment."

'Before Counsel could proceed Wessels said, "That's all right, Solomon, you be rude to the Bench—I used to be."

'It is said that Hollard once went into the High Court in Pretoria, placed a sjambok on the desk before him and explained to the astonished Court that this was no gesture of disrespect, but a prophylactic against further aggravation from his learned friend.

'A massive backvelder had been listening to Wessels for the greater part of the day. It was now his turn to be cross-examined. Goliath looked down on David and said in Afrikaans, "See here, little man, you can sit on the Judge—you can sit on the witnesses, but God help you if you sit on me."

'He could be brevity itself. An umfaan, a diminutive weakling, was charged with raping the colossus of the kraal. After the accused had pleaded not guilty, Sir John turned to the jury and said, "Gentlemen, the charge is rape. There stands the accused and there stands the complainant. Consider your verdict."

'"And to think," said he to one of his Registrars, "that his father was such a nice respectable old gentleman." He was referring to me.'

—H H Morris KC *The First Forty Years* (1948) 52–3.

'My very first appearance in the Appellate Division was in 1933 in a case which, from the annotations noted against it, seems to have been referred to on many occasions: *Rex v Manasewitz* 1933 AD 165. Sir Etienne [de Villiers] was the junior member of the Bench presided over by Wessels CJ, the other members of which were Curlewis JA, Stratford JA and Beyers JA. Anyone who reads the facts of this case will realise that I was hardly likely to meet with a friendly reception from the Court of Appeal. . . .

'It was necessary to make an application for leave to appeal before the Court, not as may now be done by a written application for leave to appeal. My matter was not heard until the afternoon of 3 March 1933. Consequently I spent the morning listening to argument in the case of *Roodepoort-Maraisburg Town Council v Eastern Properties (Prop) Ltd* 1933 AD 87. Brink KC, at that time one of the leaders at the Johannesburg Bar, was having what one would call a rough time. Those who appeared before Wessels CJ very often had what is commonly known as a "rough time", and speaking from personal experience I can only say that nobody before whom I ever appeared could give counsel a rougher passage than Wessels CJ did if he was apparently against you.

'This is what I heard, *inter alia*—
Wessels CJ: "*Oh! is that your point, Mr Brink?*"
Brink: "*Yes, m'Lord, that is the point that I have been trying to make for two days and haven't been allowed to.*"
There was an immediate explosion.
Wessels CJ: "*How dare you say such a thing! There has been far too much talking in this case already.*" (*As far as I could see, most of the talking had been done by Wessels CJ.*)

'After Wessels had let himself go as it were, Curlewis JA, in his ever courteous manner, said in a quiet voice: "No, Mr Brink, I don't think you should say things like that. This Court always listens to counsel and merely puts its difficulties to him."

'Stratford JA also added a few words of disapproval of Brink's statement.

'*Manasewitz's* case came on shortly after Rosenberg KC had replied and one can imagine what I felt like having regard to the "merits" of my matter and what I expected was going to happen to me. My worst fears were realised when I got up to say that this was an application for leave to appeal. Wessels CJ interrupted me saying: "Leave, leave to appeal—you don't oppose this, Mr Hoal?" Hoal KC was the Attorney-General of the Free State and I have no doubt that he intended opposing leave to appeal, but the manner in which Wessels had spoken probably led him to believe that Wessels in any event was going to throw the matter out.

To say that I had a rough time is an understatement, and when I sat down Wessels
CJ turned to Curlewis JA who was sitting on his right and in a whisper, which
I am sure could have been heard at the back of the Court, said "You don't want
to hear Hoal, do you?" Curlewis JA agreed as did Stratford JA and Beyers JA
when the same question was put to them. When it was put to Sir Etienne, the
junior member of the Court, I witnessed what I would imagine was a most
unusual, if not unique, occurrence. De Villiers JA got up, walked to the centre of
the Court where Wessels was sitting and had an argument with him. I could not
hear what was said but eventually Wessels turned around and said "Oh, all
right—Yes, Mr Hoal?" Hoal then argued. I attempted to reply and judgment was
reserved. There were five judgments given in the matter. It should be appreciated
that the full record of the case was not before the Court as the matter had come
before it as an application for leave to appeal and Wessels CJ decided that the full
record had to be obtained before he could pronounce upon the matter. The same
view was expressed by Beyers JA. Curlewis JA dissented. He agreed with the
judgment of the TPD and that the appeal should be dismissed. Stratford JA
agreed with the main judgment, which really gave the *ratio decidendi* of the case,
given by De Villiers JA. When the matter came before the Court of Appeal again
after the record was received by it, the appeal was allowed (1934 AD 95), the
judgment of the Court being given by De Villiers JA.

'I am told that this case is still regarded as the leading case on *autrefois acquit* and
consequently it is still referred to by law students today. The judgment given by
De Villiers JA speaks for itself as an example of lucidity, brevity and logic. This
was a characteristic of all judgments of his, whether given in the OPD or in the
AD, which I have had the privilege of reading.

'I would just like to add a few words about Wessels CJ. Although he could give
counsel a rough time, he could also take it. That he was a great judge is beyond
question. His contribution to the law, not merely as a judge but as a writer, is
well known. If he was wrong, he would rightly admit it and handsomely on
occasion apologise to counsel or to a witness if he felt that he had treated him
roughly or unfairly.'

—I A Maisels QC 'Sir Etienne de Villiers' (1989) 2(1) *Consultus* 61 at 61–2.

Wessels gets his comeuppance

'I was present once in the Supreme Court in Pretoria when there was quite a
scene between Wessels and Gregorowski [q v]. Greg, as we used to call him, had
been a Judge in the Republican days, and it was he who had presided in 1896 over
the trial of the Reformers, passing the death sentence on the ringleaders, and
Wessels had been one of the counsel who appeared before him for the defence.
After the Anglo-Boer War Greg returned to the Bar in Pretoria and soon built up
a fairly wide practice. On the occasion of which I am speaking, Wessels, who was
presiding, was in one of his most trying moods, and kept on interrupting Greg
in no friendly fashion. At last counsel could stand it no more. Throwing his brief
down on the desk, he said, as I now remember his words, "I can no longer
continue my argument before this Court if your Lordship persists in interrupting
me in this fashion; your Lordship's impatience is notorious at the Bar, and it
prevents counsel from doing justice to their clients." This, coming from counsel
of Wessels' own age and standing, soon himself again to be a Judge, not from a

trembling junior, made the Court sit up. The other Judge hastily intervened to restore peace, and Wessels added, "I will listen to you Mr. Gregorowski, as long as you please, if you do not persist in repeating your argument." The breeze blew over and calm was restored.'

—Leslie Blackwell [qv] *Are Judges Human?* (1962) 18.

'HIS LORDSHIP MEETS THE ARMY

'It was during the 1922 revolution. We were under arms and Martial Law. His Lordship arrived one morning at the Law Courts on Von Brandis Square in a state of mild excitement. The first person he saw was his registrar.

'"Do you know, Cloete," he said in a voice which has to be heard to be appreciated, "I had a most extraordinary adventure last night. Most extraordinary. I had been writing letters and I walked down to the pillar-box at the corner. Suddenly I heard someone shout: 'Halt! Who goes there?'"

'The historian will now carry on.

'A soldier came out of the darkness. He was fully equipped and looked tough. He appeared to be looking for an enemy to practise on.

'"Where are you going, my little man?" said he. (Sir John was indeed a little man.)

'"I am only going to the pillar-box to post these letters."

'"Very well," said the soldier, "go to the pillar-box, post your letters"—and here the soldier, who came neither from Oxford nor Cambridge, selected the lowest phrase he could find to express the simple idea that the Judge-President of the Transvaal Provincial Division should clear off home.

'"And what did you do, Judge?" said the dismayed registrar.

'"Me? I went to the pillar-box, posted my letters and did as directed."

'And so authority bowed to authority.'

—H H Morris KC *In and Out of Court* (1950) 6–7.

'You can tell them, what few juries seem to know, that they are the sole judges of the facts. I once saw Sir John Wessels run into a stiff breeze through not minding his own business. He expressed his surprise at and his disapproval of a verdict of "Not Guilty", and wanted to know how the jury came by it. The foreman, a man of strong character, told his Lordship that the responsibility for the verdict was theirs and that the reasons for the decision were no concern of his. His Lordship dropped the matter.'

—H H Morris KC *The First Forty Years* (1948) 151.

'*A letter from W J Smith J to J W Wessels J.* In 1969 I published in the journal a little piece entitled "The Romance of a Law Library" ((1969) 86 *SALJ* 107), in which I traced the various successive owners of certain books in the library of the University of the Witwatersrand Law School. One of the most interesting finds was J L Beck's five-volume edition of the *Corpus iuris civilis* (Leipzig 1825–36). It bears the bookplate of Baron Pollock, Chief Baron of the Exchequer from 1844 to 1866, with the motto "*Audacter et Strenue*". Apart from his excellence as judge and his founding a distinguished line of English jurists, including Sir Charles Pollock (1823–97), Baron of Exchequer and Judge of the High Court, Sir Frederick Pollock, the eminent jurist, and Sir Ernest Pollock (later Lord Hanworth), Master of the Rolls, Pollock CB is noteworthy for his having fathered twenty-four children, eleven by his first wife and thirteen by his second (see Lord Hanworth's *Lord Chief Baron Pollock* (1929) 89–90).

'After Pollock's bookplate follows the signature of W J Smith—Sir William Smith [qv], who was appointed to the Transvaal Bench on 12 April 1902, after having served as Chief Justice of British Guiana since 1897. Next comes the stamp of J W Wessels, who had been elevated to the same court the previous month, and was to become Chief Justice. I am indebted to Professor J E Scholtens, Emeritus Professor of Roman Law in the University of the Witwatersrand, Johannesburg, for drawing my attention to the following letter by Smith to Wessels attached to one of the volumes of Beck:

> "[Printed] Judge's [*sic*] Chambers
> Supreme Court
> Pretoria
> 10 Oct. 1912

"My dear Wessels

I think that you once admired my edition of the Code. It looks somewhat bulky but it is in fact a very small acknowledgement of many acts of unvarying kindness & of much assistance sorely needed alas—which I always experienced at your hands. Will you accept it as such and let it find a resting place on your shelves?

> Yours truly
> W. J. Smith"

'It surely was a parting gift, for Sir William Smith died at the age of 59 in London on 15 November that year.'

—Ellison Kahn in (1976) 93 *SALJ* 220–1.

GEORGE WILLE

1880–1966. Member of the Johannesburg Bar 1905–20. Professor of Law, University of Cape Town, 1920–46. KC 1924. A character.

'The poetical flourishes'

'George Wille was born in Graaff Reinet in 1880. He died at Hermanus in 1966, in his eighty-seventh year. His father came to South Africa from Germany. His mother was a Baumann, a distinguished South African Jewish family. George was baptised as a member of the Anglican communion, though in later years he gave the impression of being agnostic. He was a tallish, well-built man with an erect and impressive bearing. He was proud of his Jewish blood and often said in class during the years of Hitler's madness:

"I am half Jewish and, although Hitler would hate to hear me say so, I know which is the better half."

'However, those were grim days, and he also honoured the German strain in him. He went to school in Hastings, England, and studied law at Cambridge University (Christ's College) where he obtained the degrees of BA LLB. A barrister of the Middle Temple (he was called in 1903), he was admitted to the Johannesburg bar in that interesting but difficult period of so-called "reconstruction,'' under Milner, between the Anglo–Boer War and Union. He practised as an advocate in Johannesburg for well over a decade.

'The demand for his services as an advocate seems to have been of the kind which saved him, on the one hand, from the purgatory of over-worked success, and, on the other, from the limbo of briefless frustration. . . . His practice certainly left him sufficient time to devote his considerable talents to legal writing.

'A comprehensive book on *Landlord and Tenant in South Africa* came from Wille's pen in 1910. . . .

'His next publication was a work of co-authorship. That classical text, *Mercantile Law of South Africa*, now in its 19th edition and still going strong, first appeared in 1917 as the joint work of George Wille and Philip Millin (later Mr Justice Millin). Sarah Gertrude Millin (the judge's wife and a well-known writer) used to say that it was her husband who made the major contribution, a view which was not shared by Professor Wille and which angered him considerably. One of his favourite classroom exercises was to ask us to guess who wrote which chapters, giving as a clue the following acid guideline:

"The solid and accurate law is mine, the poetical flourishes are Judge Millin's."

Fortunately, by then the book had become a fused integral whole, rightly known simply as "Wille and Millin."'

—Denis V Cowen 'Taught Law is Tough Law: The Evolution of a South African Law School' (1988) 51 *THRHR* 4 at 9–10. (See also MILLIN.)

'Oxford men: Too many poets'

'Wille loved Cambridge and gave her more than a normal share of loyalty. It was almost a fierce loyalty, involving disdain for Oxford. He used to growl about Oxford men: "They are too smooth for my liking. Too many poets. You have to watch your daughters with them." One wonders what Wordsworth and Rupert Brooke (to mention two who spring to mind) might have said about the dig that Oxford rather than Cambridge produced poets.

'When Adrian Roberts's *South African Legal Bibliography* was published I lent my copy to Wille. His eye fell immediately on the brief biographies of South African judges which appear at the back of the book. He counted how many had been to Cambridge, how many to Oxford, and returned the book to me with a handwritten annotation recording that 36 had been educated at Cambridge, only 25 at Oxford, making a total of 61 out of 144.'

—Denis V Cowen op cit at 17.

John Kerr Wylie (1884–1948) was appointed as the W P Schreiner Professor of Roman Law and Jurisprudence at the University of Cape Town in 1924, holding the chair until the time of his death. The story is told that on first seeing him Wille took an instinctive dislike to him and refused to have anything to do with him. Certainly he voiced his dislike of Wylie. (Further on Wylie, see MALHERBE.)

'Professor Wille was a man of extreme likes and dislikes. He was what Doctor Johnson admired—a good hater. He had a low opinion of Professor Wylie, a sentiment which was reciprocated; and both men expressed their views of each other quite openly and with little regard for the subtleties of innuendo. Wille would quite literally froth when told that Wylie disagreed with him on whether a lessee under a short lease, who was in occupation, enjoyed a real right; or on whether one could be said to have a "real," in the sense of an "absolute," right in one's reputation—topics on which Wille was not disposed to brook opposition. I have forgotten now who used to call whom "that learned baboon"; maybe they both used that expression of contempt. No matter.

'Although it is a pity that they did not communicate more—for they might have learned much from each other—the opposition between the two men was, on the whole, good for the faculty. It produced a creative tension, not a destructive one. It also compelled independent research. Wille and Wylie often seemed both to be right, though in apparent disagreement, and it was instructive to try to find an explanation and, if possible, a method of reconciliation. It often transpired that they would be talking about quite different things under the same name.'

—Denis V Cowen op cit at 17–18.

'Poets' again

'Fortunately, Wille had a robust disposition and a sense of humour. He could enjoy a joke against himself. Here is a memorable example. While lecturing on defamation, he was saying brutal things about someone one day. He paused and said to the class: "I have been saying that publicly for years. Why doesn't the damned scoundrel sue me for defamation?" He was expecting the answer: "Because what you say, sir, is true and it is in the public interest to be told that particular truth." Instead, he got from that gallant and sparkling soul, Percy Burton (one of Churchill's "few" in the Battle of Britain) the quiet reply: "If I were acting for you I would argue that your language is not defamatory." "How so, Mr. Burton? I am trying my best to expose the shameless rogue for what he is, though I am well aware that I may be damaging him." "Well, sir," said Burton, "there is a difference between defamatory words, which are likely to lower the reputation of a person in the mind of a reasonable man, and mere vulgar abuse which leaves the hearer cold; and your intemperate language belongs to the latter category." Wille, to his credit, joined in the laughter and Percy in due course got his first class. Wille's bark was much worse than his bite.

'Poets and poetry were anathema to George Wille. His ultimate disparagement of a person was to call him a poet. He had, for example, a poor opinion of the writings of Maasdorp, Lee and McKerron; and they were all labelled poets. One of them—I think it was Maasdorp—was the major poet, while Lee and McKerron were dismissed as minor poets; though I must say that it was never clear to me whether it was worse, in Wille's idiom, to be a major or a minor poet.'

—Denis V Cowen op cit at 18.

'Concrete from the neck upward.'

—Reputed remark about a colleague on the staff of the Faculty of Law of the University of Cape Town, made by Wille to one of his classes. From Ellison Kahn's commonplace book.

'Professor Wille wrote few articles—I cannot recall more than two or three. His books are of a didactic nature rather than works of extensive research. His lectures were of a similar nature. The emphasis was always on logic, clear thinking and exactness of language and of legal concepts. In bringing out these qualities of the Roman-Dutch legal system George Wille excelled, and he has left his stamp on several generations of lawyers. His lucid lectures, interspersed with touches of eccentricity, remarkable outspokenness and recurrent mention of a few pet aversions, which to the present writer's regret included Roman law and some eminent professors (whom he branded as poets rather than lawyers), were always a stimulating experience. No colleague or court, however exalted, escaped his critical comments nor students his witty barbs, but few of the recipients have ever resented these—grand testimony to the respect in which he was held.

'His clarity of language and thought was carried over into his books.'

—B Beinart 'Professor George Wille' (1966) 83 *SALJ* 389 at 390.

'Wylie used to scoff at Wille's obsession with the distinction between real and personal rights, and once said that he could imagine Wille's recounting it in a wedding toast.'

—From a letter of 30 June 1988 by Mr Gerald Gordon QC to Ellison Kahn.

FREDERIC CONDÉ WILLIAMS

1844–1917. Judge of the Natal Supreme Court 1881–3.

Williams, a Cambridge BA and barrister of the Inner Temple, was originally on the editorial staff of a Birmingham newspaper. Then he joined the English Bar. After four years' practice he was appointed a district judge in Jamaica. From there he was promoted to the Natal Bench. Then he was promoted to the Bench of Mauritius. In his autobiography, From Journalist to Judge, *Williams complained bitterly of the lack of proper respect paid in England to a colonial judge; and even more bitterly of his small salary, a salary that got smaller in real terms every time he was moved to another colony on promotion. '. . . [T]here is no judicial income of any supreme court in the colonial service which admits of material saving to any one but an anchorite. . . . For my own part, "promotion," as a colonial judge, meant to me, throughout my career, a steady diminution in income . . .' (p 235).*

The Attorney-General (a Minister of the Crown in those days) referred to in the subjoined extract was Michael Henry Gallway (1826–1912), who was born in County Cork, Ireland. From 1890 to 1901 he was Chief Justice of Natal. Could he have been an 'old' Irish gentleman in 1881?

'We arrived in Natal on the 23rd of April 1881. On the afternoon following, there entered to us, in our hotel at Durban, a lachrymose old Irish gentleman who wanted to know what on earth we had come to Natal for. "Ye can't live on yer pay," he said; "ye'll only get into debt like yer brotherr judges." A whisky and soda was unavailing wholly to assuage this good Hibernian's despondency; and he departed almost in tears. He proved to be the Attorney-General of the colony!'

—Frederic Condé Williams *From Journalist to Judge* (1903) 234. (See also PHILLIPS.)

SIR WALTER THOMAS WRAGG

1842–1913. Judge of the Natal Supreme Court 1883–98. Knighted 1891.

'Sir Walter Wragg had a strong individuality, the peculiarities of which no one who had personal or official relations with him could venture to ignore. Possessed of considerable ability and charm of manner and conversation, eminently conscientious, painstaking and fair as a judge, an excellent host, bringing round him the best society in our small capital, it may yet be doubted whether he ever had a really intimate friend, or whether anyone could be quite at ease with him. For beneath his perfectly sincere geniality, there always lay the risk of stumbling into a cause of offence or disagreement; and those whose duties brought them into closest contact with him best knew how warily they must approach any matter of difference, unless they felt able to face the consequences. Before coming to Natal, Sir Walter had lived in Ceylon, where as a district judge he had probably grown accustomed to receive in fullest measure the deference due to judicial authority. Notions of divine right may thus have been impressed on his mind; but, whatever their origin, they had developed into a ruling instinct, affecting not only his official views but his attitude in private life. . . .

'While the peculiar cast of Sir Walter's mind came less into prominence in court than when he was off the bench, his exacting demands upon the court staff sometimes made matters difficult. In the office, he was dictatorial, insisting upon all sorts of privileges, even if his fellow judges disagreed or shrugged their shoulders. The dignity of office left no room for a sense of humour, and yet he was not pompous, and there was no affectation about him. He insisted upon the number of natives attached to the court as messengers being increased, so that each judge might have one at his own disposal. When it was granted, none of the judges except Sir Walter made any use of the messengers. Sir Walter thereupon appropriated two of them to his own personal service, keeping one at the house for errands of every sort, and stationing the other at the gate of Government House, in case the Governor should require to send for Sir Walter, a puisne judge. Whether he was ever sent for and how long the thing continued, I do not know; but everyone knew that Mpondo, one of these men, and the usher himself, were at his constant call and dared not object. Their souls were not their own.

'One morning Mpondo came to me in a terrible state of fear. He had been employed by Sir Walter to deliver a large number of invitations to a dance, wherever the addresses might be; and one of them lived at Richmond, 25 miles away. Even poor Mpondo felt that this was too much, so he bought a shilling stamp (to make sikker) and posted the letter. But he got afraid, and was terribly anxious about what might happen. And it did chance that the recipient wrote and told Sir Walter that he had found a shilling stamp on the letter. I was not there to see what happened afterwards.'

—Christopher Bird 'Some Recollections of Natal Judges' in *Later Annals of Natal* (1938) compiled and edited by Alan F Hattersley 205–7. (Also in (1936) 5 *South African Law Times* 213.) Bird (1855–1922), a prominent Natal public servant, wrote from personal acquaintance.

'Many other stories are told of Sir Walter Wragg. On the first day of term, and at criminal sessions in Maritzburg, the judges wore their soberly-coloured "full dress" robes. But Sir Walter brought with him a magnificent bright-red silk gown. And when on circuit, against the usual practice, he wore the silk gown even when making his visit to the gaol and to each prisoner. On one occasion, at the close of a circuit at Estcourt, his stately robes seemed to have deeply impressed an imaginative Irish convict, who regarded him with immense awe, addressing him repeatedly as "Your Eminence." After showing the judge out, the magistrate stepped back for a moment, and asked the Irishman why he called the judge by that title. "And was that just the judge?" cried the astonished prisoner. "Be all the saints, then, and me believing all the time it was a Cardinal."'

—Bird op cit at 208.

'The personality of Wragg comes out in his judgment in *In re R v Camrooden* (1894) 15 NLR 335, reproduced in (1975) 92 *SALJ* 335. He deals in a very serious tone, full of the consciousness of the dignity of his high office, with the important question whether Indians should enter court with uncovered head and with bare feet, or else be in contempt of court. The Supreme Court held that this state of dress (undress?) was not required. Wragg said: "Hindus mostly go barefoot and cover the head, while Mohammedans and Parsees cover both head and feet. Mohammedans take off their sandals on entering a church, and in Ceylon usually left their sandals outside the court. The difficulty in Natal is that, the climate being a cooler one, they wear heavy boots with socks, and, as I did not consider that it was desirable for them to take off their boots, I thought that the court might agree to a compromise and be satisfied with a respectful salute by lifting the hand to the forehead and saying 'Salaam!' Although I had been accustomed in Ceylon to a different state of things, where the highest respect is shown by the natives to the court, yet I was satisfied with this compromise. . . ."'

—From Ellison Kahn's commonplace book, with thanks to Mr Justice J M Didcott.

SIR JOHN WYLDE

1781–1859. Chief Justice of the Cape Supreme Court 1827–55. Knighted 1827.

He was the brother of Thomas Wilde (1782–1855), who, under the title of Lord Truro, was Lord Chancellor from 1850 to 1852. John Wilde signed his marriage certificate (1805) as Wylde and assumed that name. (It appears that his name had been accidentally entered as 'Wylde' in the books of Trinity College, University of Cambridge, to which he was admitted in 1799 as a sizar (a member receiving an allowance from the College to enable him to study) and that he kept to the change throughout his life (Stephen Darryl Girvin The Influence of British Legal Education and Practice at the Bar on the Judges Appointed to the Supreme Courts of Southern Africa 1827–1910 (unpublished PhD thesis University of Aberdeen 1990) 111).) His wife had borne him nine children by 1825, when he left the post of Judge-Advocate of New South Wales to return to England without his wife but with six children, to take the degree of LLB at the University of Cambridge for the next two years and then to await a new post, which turned out to be that of Chief Justice at the Cape.

'. . . [W]hen I joined the Cape Bar . . . Sir John Wylde . . . had already been struck by paralysis, and was unable to take his seat on the Bench. I made his acquaintance, nevertheless, and found him an exceedingly pleasant and genial old gentleman, with the manner and style of speech of a bygone generation. He was a brother of the celebrated Sergeant Wylde [sic], afterwards Sir Thomas Wylde [sic], and eventually Lord Truro and Lord Chancellor of England. Apparently the brothers were no great admirers of each other. Sir John used to say "That brother Tom of mine owes all his success to his loud voice and boisterous manner." Sir Thomas said "Poor John mistook his vocation: he ought to have gone on the stage." There was a little truth in both opinions. Sir Thomas was a very noisy advocate, but a man of vast ability. Sir John had not a tenth part of his brother's legal knowledge, and certainly was apt to be theatrical in his manner and language. One or two stories will indicate his propensity in that direction. A woman had been convicted of the murder of her husband, and Sir John, who had to pass sentence of death on her, thus addressed her—"Woman! woman! where is thy husband?" which the interpreter rendered by "Vrouw, vrouw, waar's uw man?" Sir John continued—"Alas! he has gone to that country from whose bourn no traveller returns!" The interpreter said: "Hij is op tocht gegaan."

'Fortunately Sir John knew no Dutch, or he might hardly have appreciated the interpreter's ingenious translation of his Shakespearian sentence. On another occasion he addressed a convicted thief as "You miserable man," and the same interpreter rendered it "Gij verdoemd schelm!" Even Sir John's ignorance of Dutch could not hide from him the fact that the interpreter had rendered him as using profane language on the Bench, and his reproof to that gentleman is said to have been eloquently indignant.'

> —The Hon Mr Justice A W Cole 'Reminiscences of the Cape Bar and Cape Bench' (1888) 5 *Cape Law Journal* 1 at 2–3. A 'Sergeant' (usually spelt 'Serjeant') was at one time a member of the highest order of counsel at the English Bar, the Order of the Coif. The order was dissolved in 1877. (For the same story, see WATERMEYER. On the tolk, see also LANGENHOVEN; McGREGOR; WAIFS AND STRAYS sv 'Tolk'; E B WATERMEYER; WESSELS. On Wylde's shortness of temper, see MENZIES.)

Accused of incest with his then pregnant daughter

'Wylde CJ became embroiled in controversy at an early stage of his work as Chief Justice and member of the Cape Council of Advice. On taking the oaths as a member of the Council, he objected to having to take the oath of secrecy and, when then forced to do so, took his revenge by filling twenty-seven pages of the Council's minute book with his remonstrances. (See R Kilpin *The Romance of a Colonial Parliament* (1930) 45.) The Governor took up the matter with the Colonial Office and by July of 1828 Wylde had been informed that his services as member of the Council were no longer required. R W Hay [the Permanent Under-Secretary at the Colonial Office], who corresponded with the Governor on the matter, left little doubt as to how he viewed Wylde's conduct:

> "It is impossible for one to have shown more gross ignorance than Sir John Wylde has done of some points upon which he ought to have been better informed, as well as of his own situation as the head of law in the colony, and I cannot but feel extreme regret and disappointment that he is, to all appearance, so little calculated to execute judiciously the important duties which are assigned him. I am not without hope that a timely reproof will bring the Chief Justice to reason and that you will be able, by judicious management, to keep him within the proper bounds of his station and remain on good terms with him." (Letter dated 19 July 1828. See H B Fine *The History of the Cape Supreme Court and its Role in the Development of Judicial Precedent for the Period 1827–1910* (unpublished LLM dissertation University of Cape Town 1986) 74.)

This was not the first occasion in which there were difficulties with the attitude and behaviour of Wylde. The most serious incident occurred during the period from 1831 to 1833, when Wylde was accused of incest with his daughter and an official investigation was ordered by the Colonial Office. The reports had arisen

when Wylde had mysteriously retired to Halfway House (located between Cape
Town and Simonstown) with his pregnant daughter, supposedly to conceal her
condition. When there was official correspondence with him over the allegations,
it was reported that "Sir John was, or appeared to be, much shocked. . .". (Letter
from the Governor from Cape Town 24 June 1833. Colonial Office, Cape of
Good Hope (Original Correspondence) 45 (153).) Records held by the Colonial
Office reveal that there are more than twenty letters which passed between the
Colonial Office and Wylde on the matter. There was considerable press
speculation but there was much support for Wylde, including an address from the
advocates practising in Cape Town, who referred to the reports "with abhorrence
and disgust", considering them as "the offspring of the most malignant and base
depravity" and looked "forward to a continuance of your services for the public
interest as the only reparation your wounded feelings can possibly receive and the
best atonement for the outrage so wickedly committed on the moral state of our
society". (Letter published at the request of the advocates in the *South African
Commercial Advertiser* of 17 April 1833 and signed by Hendrik Cloete, Denyssen,
Faure, Neethling, Brand, De Wet and Hofmeyr.) Wylde replied in full measure
to this expression of confidence, saying that "unhappily for me, this pestilential
hydra-enemy of our public and private peace has been scotched indeed, but not
destroyed. I have to writhe under its incubus and have resolved as to myself,
believe me, to expire its victim or to exterminate it for ever." (Reply dated
10 April 1833 and published in the *South African Commercial Advertiser* of 17 April
1833.) There were also addresses from the attorneys and notaries of Cape Town,
and these too elicited long replies from Wylde. (*De Zuid Afrikaan* of 26 April
1833.) Reports continued to appear in the local newspapers until July 1833, but
Wylde was officially exonerated.'

—Girvin op cit at 206–8. Some of the footnotes have been incorporated in the text.

His divorce action

'He was not popular with everyone and his rather flamboyant way of life gave
rise to a good deal of gossip. In 1831 such unsavoury rumours about his private
life began going the rounds that the Colonial Office instructed Sir Lowry Cole to
ask W. for an explanation. If he could not clear his character he would have to
resign. The subsequent investigation showed that, if the rumours were not
unfounded, they were certainly much exaggerated. It appears that he enjoyed the
pleasures of the table beyond, it was said, the limits of temperance, and he
certainly lived beyond his means. The matter ended officially with the
Governor's report to the Colonial Office, but, feeling that W. should have the
opportunity of publicly vindicating his character, members of the bar presented
him with an address on 10.3.1833 in which they expressed their confidence in his
innocence. Similar addresses were presented to him by the attorneys and notaries
and all were later published. His public image was not improved by the
unannounced arrival of his wife in the *Ledda* on 27.5.1835, and with her a
daughter born three years after W.'s departure from Australia. He promptly sued
for divorce on grounds of adultery. The case came up before Judge Menzies, who
refused to grant the divorce. It was obtained from a New South Wales court,
however, in 1836.'

—A F Hattersley in *Dictionary of South African Biography* II (1972) 861 at 862. (Professor Hattersley, distinguished historian, has made some grievous errors. He should have consulted the case of *Wylde v Wylde* (1835–6) 1 Menzies 209. Then he would have seen that Wylde's action for divorce came initially before Menzies and Kekewich JJ. The declaration of the plaintiff stated that he had left New South Wales in February 1825, his wife remaining behind; that he had not seen her since until after her arrival at the Cape on 27 May 1835, accompanied by a daughter born on or about 30 April 1829. The defendant admitted the truth of the allegations. But the court, delivering judgment on 1 August 1835, was not satisfied with the proof of adultery; it wanted some direct evidence of the birth of the child on the date alleged. Evidence was then taken on commission in New South Wales, in which the wife's brother confirmed what Wylde had alleged, and a doctor stated that the wife had given birth to a daughter in April 1829. With this further testimony the court gave Wylde his divorce order on 23 February 1836.)

This is not the only reported legal decision bearing Wylde's name. In *In re the late Sir John Wylde's Will*, decided by Hodges CJ, Cloete J and Watermeyer J on 22 December 1859, and reported in (1873) 3 Buch 113, the Master of the Supreme Court had his doubts about the validity of a codicil made under a reservatory clause in the ordinary 'underhand' will by Wylde, who had signed the codicil but not had it witnessed. The court said that the Master had 'acted with great propriety in asking the opinion of the Court upon a matter which is attended with such weighty consequences' (per Hodges CJ at 114); but it had no doubt about the validity of the codicil. The Wills Act 7 of 1953 put an end to such codicils.

YVES (YVO, IVO, ERVOAN, HÉLOURY, IVES, EVONA), ST

1253–1303. Ordained priest 1285. Canonized 1347. Lawyer. Ecclesiastical judge at Rennes. Patron saint of lawyers.

As a lawyer he defended the oppressed. In Brittany, where his festival is kept on, 19 May, he is known as 'the poor man's advocate'. The Hymn to St Yves runs:

Illustration from the cover of the Northwestern Law Review. It is the seal of the School of Law of Northwestern University, Chicago. John Henry Wigmore was a professor in and Dean of the Law School. St Ives—'Sanctus Ivo Patronus Advocatorum'—is in the middle, with a poor man on the one side and a rich man on the other.

> *'Advocatus, sed non latro,*
> *Res miranda populo.'*

(Advocate, but not rascal, an astonishing thing to the people.)

The cathedral in the town of Tréguier, in Brittany, has a monument to St Yves. In the cathedral is a tablet bearing the arms of the St Yves family, and expressing the homage of the United States of America, with the date '21 Aout [August] 1932'. John Henry Wigmore, of Evidence fame, presented the tablet. (See William R Roalfe John Henry Wigmore: Scholar and Reformer *(1977) 265.) See also John H Wigmore 'St. Ives, Patron Saint of Lawyers' (1932) 18 American Bar Association 157 and 'A visit to the Shrine of St. Ives, Patron of our Profession' op cit 794.)*

A superb statue of St Yves stands in the foyer of the Law School of Northwestern University.

The Honor Society of the University of Denver is named after St Yves.

Oddly enough, St Yves is not mentioned in The Oxford Dictionary of Saints. *In* The Times *in March 1989 correspondents debated the question: who is the patron saint of lawyers? There was some backing for St Hilarius (Hilary) of Poitiers (c 300–67), after whom the Hilary Term of legal administration of England and Wales is named; he is described in* The Oxford Dictionary of Saints *as 'gentle, courteous and friendly'.*

'The traditional account of the way in which lawyers acquired their patron saint was given nearly three centuries ago by William Carr. He recounted "a story I mett with when I lived in *Rome*, goeing with a Romane to see some *Antiquityes*, he shewed me a Chapell dedicated to one St. *Evona* a Lawyer of *Brittanie* who he said came to *Rome* to Entreat the *Pope* to give the *Lawyers* of *Brittanie* a *Patron*, to which the Pope replyed that he knew of no *Saint* but what was disposed of to other Professions, at which *Evona* was very sad and earnestly begd of the *Pope* to think of one for them: At the last the *Pope* proposed to St. *Evona* that he should goe round the Church of St. *John* de *Latera* blind fould, and after he had said so many Ave *Marias*, that the first *Saint* he layd hold of, should be his *Patron*, which the good old *Lawyer* willingly undertook, and at the end of his Ave Maryes, he stopt at St. *Michels* Altar, where he layd hold of the *Divell*, under St. Michels feet, and cryd out, this is our Saint, let him be our *Patron*, so beeing unblindfolded and seeing what a *Patron* he had chosen, he went to his Lodgings so dejected, that in a few moneths after he die'd and coming to *heavens* Gates knockt hard, whereupon St. *Peoter* asked who it was that knockt so bouldly, he replyed, that he was St. *Evona* the *Advocate*, Away, away said St. *Peter* here is but one *Advocate* in *heaven*, here is no roome for you *Lawyers*, O but said St. *Evona*, I am that honest lawyer who never tooke fees on both sides, or ever pleaded in a bad Cause, nor did I ever set my Naibours together by the Eares, or lived by the sins of the people; well then said St. *Peter*, come in. This newes comeing downe to *Rome* a witty Poet writ upon St. *Evonas* Tomb these words: St. *Evona* un *Briton, Advocat non Larron, Haleluiah."'

—Sir Robert Megarry *A Second Miscellany-at-Law* (1973) 41–2, quoting from William Carr *Remarks of the Government of Several Parts of Germanie, Denmark, Sweedland, Hamburg, Lubeck, and Hansiatique Townes, but more particularly of the United Provinces, with some few directions how to Travell in the States Dominions* (1688) 80.

'In the Middle Ages the following verse was sung about this lawyer for the poor:

St. Yves was of Brittany
A lawyer not a thief
To the wonder of the people.

That he did not enrich himself from those who looked for justice and moreover knew how to give creative content to his feeling for social justice is clear from the following anecdote. As a judge he was confronted by a rich man who asked for compensation from a beggar because he was always lingering around his kitchen to get a sniff of the odors of food. He [St Yves] just clinked a coin and finished the affair with the sentence that the odor of food was amply compensated by the sound of money.'

—Ties Brakken *Legal Services and Lawyers' Activism: A Comparative Study of Some Recent Developments in the Use of Law* back cover.

TREGUIER, France—Jean Le Mapillan, a lawyer from Nantes, trod solemnly through the cobbled streets of this medieval town, helping to carry a gilded reliquary that holds the skull of St. Yves, the patron saint of lawyers.

'Although St. Yves has as much in common with modern corporate lawyers as the Virgin Mary has with Madonna, lawyers from around the world flock each year to Tréguier, perched on Brittany's rugged hills, to remember this town's saintly favorite son.

'On the third Sunday in May, lawyers from France, Spain, Belgium, Britain and elsewhere, along with thousands of Bretons, file out of St. Tugdual Cathedral, squeeze past the timbered houses on Rue St. Yves and head over the hill toward the chapel on the site where St. Yves was born in 1253.

'As the procession inches through town, black-robed lawyers are usually on hand to help white-frocked priests bear the reliquary.

'The Bretons often say there never was a man more just or saintly than Yves Hélory of Kermartin. . . . As the diocese's judge seven centuries ago, he often ruled in favor of the poor, ignoring the bribes that rich litigants would offer him.

'Lawyer, judge and priest, he slept on a bed of straw and wood shavings and turned his family manor into a hospice. When a beggar came to him complaining of the cold, Yves, son of a noble family, took off his cloak and gave it to the poor man.

'When not serving on the bench, Yves often worked for no fee as a lawyer representing the poor—"Pro Deo," he would say—and is credited with having inspired legal aid for the poor.

'"Lawyers worship him, but we don't try to imitate him so much," Mr. Le Mapillan said during the feast that followed the mile long procession to the Saint's birthplace. "You would have to be a real hero to live like him. Can you imagine a judge nowadays giving his robes to a poor man, and showing up in court in jeans?"'

—Steven Greenhouse 'Honoring a Saintly Lawyer: Pilgrimage to the Past' *New York Times* 6 June 1991.

Index of Names Mentioned

Only names specifically mentioned and not mentioned merely in passing are mentioned in this index; **bold** *figures indicate entries and other main items*

Index of Topics